LINEAGES OF BRAHMAN POWER

Suny Series in Hindu Studies

Wendy Doniger and Brian Collins, editors

ROSALIND O'HANLON

Lineages of Brahman Power

Caste, Family, and the State in Western India 1600–1900

SUNY
PRESS

First published by Permanent Black D-28 Oxford Apts, 11 IP Extension, Delhi 110092 INDIA, for the territory of SOUTH ASIA.
First SUNY Press edition 2025.
Not for sale in South Asia.

Cover credit: Front: James Prinsep's engraving from the 1830s, showing a Brahman pandit teaching in a part of the Banaras temple. Back: Left to right, the guide depicts Kamalakarabhatta in discussion with fellow pandits, followed by images of the four principal classes of Hinduism's varna order.

Cover design by Anuradha Roy.

Published by State University of New York Press, Albany

Printed in the United States of America

EU GPSR Authorised Representative:
Logos Europe, 9 rue Nicolas Poussin, 17000, La Rochelle, France
contact@logoseurope.eu

For information, contact State University of New York Press, Albany, NY
www.sunypress.edu

Library of COngress Cataloging-in-Publication Data
Names: O'Hanlon, Rosalind, author.
Title: Lineages of Brahman power: Caste, family, and the state in western India / Rosalind O'Hanlon
Description: [Albany] : [State University of New York Press], [2025] |
Series: SUNY series in Hindu Studies | Includes bibliographical references.
Identifiers: ISBN 9798855803228 (hardcover) | ISBN 9798855803235 (ebook)
More information available at https://lccn.loc.gov/2024000343.

Contents

Preface vii

Acknowledgements ix

Introduction: Between Brahman and Sudra in Colonial Western India 1

BRAHMIN FAMILIES IN MOTION

1 Speaking from Shiva's Temple: Banaras Scholar Households and the Brahman "Ecumene" of Mughal India 66

2 Entrepreneurs in Diplomacy: Maratha Expansion in the Age of the Vakil 108

FAMILY, GENDER, AND THE STATE

3 Disciplining the Brahman Household: The Moral Mission of Empire in the Eighteenth-Century Maratha State 150

4 Brahman Lineages Beyond the Mughal Court 175

5 Gotmai's Suit: A Brahman Woman of Property in Seventeenth-Century Western India 203

CASTE AND THE "EARLY MODERN"

6 What Makes People Who They Are? Pandit Networks and the Problem of Livelihoods in Early Modern Western India (*with Christopher Minkowski*) 221

7 The Social Worth of Scribes: Brahmans, Kayasthas, and the Social Order in Early Modern India 267

8 Discourses of Caste Over the Longue Durée: Gopinatha and Social Classification in India, *c.* 1400–1900 (*with Gergely Hidas and Csaba Kiss*) 311

ORAL TRADITIONS AND DOCUMENTARY CULTURES

9 Performance in a World of Paper: Puranic Histories and Social Communication in Early Modern India 349

10 In the Presence of Witnesses: Petitioning and Judicial "Publics" in Western India, *c.* 1600–1820 392

Index 435

Preface

THE TEN ESSAYS presented here were written during my time at the Faculty of Oriental Studies (now the Faculty of Asian and Middle Eastern Studies) in Oxford, between 2007 and 2020. The Introduction to the essays, written specifically for this book, picks up their theme – the social history of early modern Maharashtra's Brahman communities – and traces some aspects of it through the colonial nineteenth century to the 1920s. The ways in which the different Maratha Brahman communities engaged with remaking the region's politics and society under colonialism is a story that has yet to be explored in any depth. Yet it is a particularly important one, because it did so much to shape the terms on which the wide range of reformist and progressive critics of colonial caste were able to assemble their own political and social constituencies. The Introduction was also an opportunity for me to return to the themes of low-caste, Dalit, and gender history during the colonial era with which I began my research career – to see how these looked when placed in the context of longer-term histories of caste, and above all to engage with the exciting new scholarship in this field.

Taking up themes in Maharashtra's early modern history was very much a new departure for me. It was made possible in large part through the generosity of colleagues in Oxford, particularly of Chris Minkowski, David Washbrook, Imre Bangha, Shailendra Bhandare, and the many friends who shared their expertise at the meetings of the Oxford Early Modern Project which ran through my time there.

As will be clear from many of the essays here, I found the broader perspective of the "early modern", and the debates that swirled around it, to be as transformative for me as were the Subaltern Studies perspectives from which I benefitted at an earlier stage in my research career. Very many scholars working on histories across the world have, of course, contributed to these debates. I owe most, though, to the work of Sanjay Subrahmanyam, Muzaffar Alam, and Sheldon Pollock. It was through their scholarship that an erstwhile colonial historian like myself first, and rather belatedly, appreciated how differently the world could look when viewed through the lens of the early modern. Without that broader lens, the explorations here into the history of Maratha scribal elites would have been much the poorer.

I owe an equally unrepayable obligation to Permanent Black's Rukun Advani, editor and advisor nonpareil in all matters of literary sense and style, for encouraging me in this project and for his patience in helping me see it to a conclusion.

Grateful thanks are also due to the librarians and staff of the Bhandarkar Oriental Research Institute, Pune; the Bharat Itihas Samshodhak Mandal, Pune; the Asiatic Society of Mumbai; and the Mumbai Marathi Grantha Sangrahalaya. Their rich Marathi collections, and the experience of the library staff that maintain them with such dedication, were invaluable in preparation of the essays presented here.

On a practical note, I should explain that I have endeavoured to bring the use of diacritical marks, as well as spelling and other stylistic conventions, into some sort of uniformity across the essays presented here. I apologise in advance for those inconsistencies that remain.

CAMBRIDGE 2025

Acknowledgements

SOURCES OF FIRST publication of the essays republished in this book are given below. I acknowledge the kind consent of their copyright holders. I am particularly grateful to Christopher Minkowski, Gergely Hidas, and Csaba Kiss for their permission to include our jointly authored essays.

1. "Speaking from Siva's Temple: Banaras Scholar Households and the Brahman 'Ecumene' of Mughal India", *South Asian History and Culture*, vol. 2, no. 2, 2011, pp. 253–77.
2. "Entrepreneurs in Diplomacy: Maratha Expansion in the Age of the Vakil", *Indian Economic and Social History Review*, vol. 57, no. 4, 2020, pp. 1–32.
3. "Disciplining the Brahman Household: The Moral Mission of Empire in the Eighteenth Century Maratha State", in Kumkum Roy, ed., *Looking Within, Looking Without: Exploring Households in the Subcontinent Through Time* (Delhi: Primus Books, 2015), pp. 67–389.
4. "Brahman Lineages Beyond the Mughal Court", in Richard Eaton and Ramya Sreenivasan, eds, *The Oxford Handbook of the Mughal World*, online publication, pp. 1–9.
5. "Gotmai's Suit: A Brahman Woman of Property in Seventeenth Century Western India", in Toke Knudsen, *et al.*, eds, *Festschrift to Christopher Minkowski* (Leiden: Brill, 2023), pp. 449–65.
6. "What Makes People Who They Are? Pandit Networks and the Problem of Livelihoods in Early Modern Western India" (with Christopher Minkowski), *Indian Economic and Social History Review*, vol. 45, no. 3, 2008, pp. 381–416.
7. "The Social Worth of Scribes: Brahmans, Kayasthas, and the Social Order in Early Modern India", *Indian Economic and Social History Review*, vol. 47, no. 4, 2010, pp. 563–95.

8. "Discourses of Caste over the Longue Durée: Gopinatha and Social Classification in India, *c.* 1400–1900" (with Gergely Hidas and Csaba Kiss), *South Asian History and Culture*, vol. 6, no. 1, 2015, pp. 102–29.
9. "Performance in a World of Paper: Puranic Histories and Social Communication in Early Modern India", *Past and Present*, vol. 219, 2013, pp. 1–40.
10. "In the Presence of Witnesses: Petitioning and Judicial 'Publics' in Western India, *circa* 1600–1820", *Modern Asian Studies*, vol. 53, no. 1, 2019, pp. 52–88.

Introduction

Between Brahman and Sudra in Colonial Western India

Caste, Merit, and Mobility in Modern India

A YOUNG COLLEAGUE once asked me why it was that in recent years my research interests had shifted from movements of lower-caste protest to Brahman social history. In the discussion that followed, I explained that I was by no means alone in making this shift. The history of caste-based forms of exclusion and their deeply oppressive consequences had long, and rightly, occupied centre-ground for studies of caste of every kind. Brahman communities had attracted rather less scholarly attention, the figure of the Brahman appearing in our studies as a kind of timeless "other", the apex of the caste system, invested with all that is elitist and hierarchical.[1] Further research into their sociology might contribute, I thought, to our understanding of the resilience of caste in the colonial era and beyond.

Since then, scholarly understanding of Brahman social histories has developed at pace. Much recent work explores the interplay between caste and class, with the further impetus that new digital technologies have given to existing Brahman educational advantages.

I have benefitted from conversations with many friends and colleagues over the years in which I have been working on the themes in this essay. I would particularly like to thank Alok Oak, Chris Minkowski, Shailendra Bhandare, the late David Washbrook, and the participants in the workshops of the Oxford Early Modern Project. Unless otherwise specified, all translations from the Marathi are my own. All errors are, of course, also my own.

[1] For this point, see in particular Bairy, *Being Brahmin*, pp. 1–2.

As Fuller and Narasimhan have described it, Tamil Brahmans' accumulated privilege during the colonial period, and above all their willingness to leave their land, has enabled many to make the journey from caste to class – evident from the movement of traditional scholars, priests, colonial bureaucrats, modern IT workers, and now the globe-trotting professionals of the high-tech industries.[2] India's elite IITs have been a key step in this trajectory, described in Ajantha Subramanian's study as remarkable for their ability to present merit as somehow casteless, emerging out of individual achievement rather than shaped partly by family cultural capital.[3] Satish Deshpande has observed a similar process in India's system of caste-based reservations. Those who apply for reserved quotas do so as casted subjects. The Brahmans who come in through the "open" category appear to succeed rather through their own individual merit.[4]

Bairy observes the same phenomenon from the perspective of Brahman communities themselves, for whom the best strategy has been to emphasise that caste is now only an aspect of family "culture". Thus we see caste as operative primarily in the electoral sphere, and in education and employment, where lower castes seek protection in the reservations system.[5] Hence, as Balmurli Natrajan and others have suggested, it is not Sanskritisation through which caste and casteism are sustained. It is rather through "culturalisation", the transmutation of caste from a socially pervasive structure of privilege into something that is apparently a dimension of private life.[6] Caste in a political field subject to such an elision produces a powerful logic of exclusion. As Pandian points out, this associates the language of caste with backward-looking and particularistic interests, and a distraction from the "casteless" project of nation building.[7]

Present-day ideas of a national "casteless" modernity may seem very far removed from the essays in this volume. With a focus on the Marathi-speaking regions of early modern India, the essays explore the

[2] Fuller and Narasimhan, *Tamil Brahmans*.
[3] Subramanian, *The Caste of Merit*.
[4] Deshpande, "Caste and Castelessness".
[5] Bairy, *Being Brahman*, pp. 259–62.
[6] Natrajan, "From Jati to Samaj".
[7] Pandian, "One Step Outside Modernity".

social organisation and increasingly all-India roles of Maratha Brahman and other Maratha scribal elites in Mughal India. Some of the themes addressed do seem to have marked parallels with early twenty-first century histories. The states and societies of early modern India had their own new "knowledge economy", evident from the expansion of paper use and the development of new bureaucratic techniques to support the recording of property rights and collection of revenues. Mobile elites with the right scribal skills were well placed to exploit these opportunities. Family and household were the settings in which such skills were passed down, and cultural capital accumulated.

In other ways, the differences could hardly be more marked. Brahman caste in the early modern centuries was not elided or minimised. Rather, it was a public guarantee of ritual acceptability which opened access to privileged spaces and relationships of many kinds. It was clearly advertised with religious and sectarian bodily marking, styling of the hair, appropriate dress, personal comportment, and language use. However, this ready visibility was no guarantee that Brahman identity would be stable. Fierce contests sometimes surrounded the question of what made a Brahman and who could be accepted as one. Such contests seldom revolved around the dignified criteria of the dharmasastra alone. They were also shaped by local and often rancorous struggles for advantage in which wealth, reputation, and the support of powerful neighbours played a part, and the conduits of argument lay as much in popular performance as in Sanskrit textual exchanges.

Given these unexpected parallels and striking differences, it is hoped that the essays here will be of interest to scholars of caste and the making of Brahman identity both in the early modern centuries and eras closer to our own times. India's Marathi-speaking regions offer particularly rich material for study of these many historical lives of caste. With their vernacular critique of the empty formalism of caste hierarchy, the region's bhakti poets attracted a social following that crossed caste boundaries.[8] As Christian Novetzke has described in his discussion of the phenomenon of "the Brahman double", some of the most trenchant poetic critics of caste were themselves Brahmans. These counterposed features of Maharashtra's religious culture

[8] Novetzke, *The Quotidian Revolution*; Keune, *Shared Devotion.*

shaped its distinctive "Bhagavat dharma", an acceptance of the order of varna and caste, but moderated by the egalitarian social ethic of bhakti.[9]

It was in the Maratha regions too that the great warrior leader Chhatrapati Shivaji Bhosle (1630–1680) carved out a new kingdom in the face of Mughal invasion.[10] In the eighteenth century, the Chitpavan Brahman ministers of the Bhosles took on the mantle of rulership directly. Marathas carried their flag to the banks of the Indus and led the subcontinent's most stubborn resistance to the East India Company. The Pune court also entrenched Brahman values at the heart of the state. It enforced dharmic social norms on all Brahmans, periodically drove down the ritual dignities of other castes, and imposed rigid social disabilities on Dalit communities.[11] It was also from Maharashtra – the region that Christophe Jaffrelot has called the "crucible of Indian nationalism" – that many of India's most important colonial political leaders emerged: Vishnusastri Chiplunkar (1850–1882), Lokamanya Tilak (1856–1920), M.G. Ranade (1842–1901), G.K. Gokhale (1866–1915), and India's prominent Hindu nationalist Vinayak Damodar Savarkar (1883–1966). Brahman predominance within this leadership also helped to spark the region's vibrant non-Brahman movements as well as India's pathbreaking Dalit struggle under the historic leadership of Dr Babasaheb Ambedkar (1891–1956).[12]

In the rest of this Introduction, I explore the colonial aftermath of these early modern Brahman histories. Many aspects of western India's colonial experience are already well known. The Christian missionary challenge, Anglophone educational institutions and their social effects, and the new arenas of vernacular print and public associational culture have long attracted scholarly attention.[13] My purpose in this very broad field is to focus down on two much more limited nineteenth-century issues: the troubled history of relationships between

[9] Novetzke, "The Brahmin Double"; Vaudeville, "The Shaiva-Vaishnava Synthesis".

[10] Gordon, *The Marathas*, pp. 59–90.

[11] Kotani, *Western India*, pp. 115–35.

[12] Cashman, *The Myth of the Lokamanya*; Jaffrelot, *Hindu Nationalism*; Rao, *The Caste Question*; Bakhle, *Savarkar*.

[13] Naregal, *Language Politics*; Deshpande, *Creative Pasts*; Masselos, *Towards Nationalism*; Kidambi, *The Making of an Indian Metropolis*.

Brahman subcastes, and the arguments of many Maratha Brahmans that – in the fallen era of the Kaliyuga – only Brahmans and Sudras in the varna order could be said to have survived.[14]

Although these questions had a long pre-colonial history, they continued to matter in the colonial era. For many Brahman intellectuals, a cohesive Brahman leadership offered the best promise of building new kinds of Hindu solidarity. Brahman perceptions of the varna order were critical to the longer-term development of non-Brahman politics in western India. Whatever the pre-colonial social associations of the term "Sudra", there is evidence from the 1840s that not only non-Brahman elites but also many among the region's popular classes found the designation increasingly at odds with their sense of self-worth. The orthodox insistence that all were Sudras, elaborated and publicised in print, aggravated the sense of grievance that non-Brahman communities of many kinds experienced as they reflected on the social changes around them.

Maratha Brahman Communities in the Early Modern Centuries: An Overview

The early modern centuries saw a range of remarkable transformations across the subcontinent, many driven by the emergence of regional states under the Mughal imperial umbrella. Patrons in royal courts, lordly households, sectarian centres, and shrine towns sought Brahman servants to serve as wise counsellors to kings, secretaries proficient in the arts of letter-writing, accomplished ritualists, scholars learned in religious law, poets able to praise their employers, conscientious record keepers, and eloquent emissaries with a knowledge of languages and law.[15] In the Deccan's relatively dry and famine-prone environment, Brahmans from western India often travelled to pursue such opportunities. As well as serving regional courts, they founded leading

[14] I do not address here the older literature on the relationship between kings and Brahmans. See Raheja, "India: Caste, Kingship and Dominance Reconsidered".

[15] Kinra, *Writing Self, Writing Empire*; O'Hanlon and Washbrook, "Munshis, Pandits and Record-Keepers"; Wink, *Land and Sovereignty*, pp. 67–84; Bayly, *Caste, Society and Politics*, pp. 64–96; Narayana Rao, Shulman, and Subrahmanyam, *Textures of Time*, pp. 19–22, 93–139, 239–48.

scholarly dynasties in the vibrant intellectual centre of Banaras. From this vantage point, they also developed an India-wide classification – of five great gauḍa and five great drāviḍa groupings – within which every regional Brahman community could find its place. The framework effectively offered a recognisable and hence portable supra-regional identity.[16]

One key to their professional success lay in the household and extended family, where professional skills were passed down to sons, often educated within the household alongside other families' sons, in extended networks of educational exchange. Sons frequently took up complementary professions, some travelling to take up new opportunities, while others looked after the household's needs at home. Such strategies added to families' skills, extended their social networks, and diversified their activities to spread risk. Manuscript collections, which were essential professional tools, were also held within the household. Like households in many social settings, those of Brahmans often worked as corporate structures, braiding together different forms of expertise towards their common survival. More so than those of many other communities, Brahman households often represented significant concentrations of skill and cultural capital.[17]

Like Brahman communities everywhere in early modern India, Maratha Brahmans acted as arbiters of social conflicts. They did so through the Brahman judicial assemblies that flourished across the shrine towns of the Maratha country and formed part of the religious and judicial infrastructure of the Marathi-speaking regions.[18] They also concerned themselves very closely with the essential qualities of Brahmanhood. In broad terms, the answers might have seemed obvious. The things that made a Brahman were family descent, observation of the order of varnas and ashramas, and full acceptance of the revealed texts of the Vedic tradition classified as śruti ("heard") and the prin-

[16] Deshpande, "Pañca Gauḍa und Pañca Drāviḍa"; Venkatkrishnan, "Ritual, Reflection and Religion".

[17] For the early modern household, see Guha, *Beyond Caste*, pp. 117–41; Guha, "The Family Feud"; O'Hanlon, "Speaking from Siva's Temple", and idem, "Brahman Lineages".

[18] Eaton, *A Social History*, pp. 145–50; Gune, *The Judicial System*; O'Hanlon, "Gotmai's Suit", and idem, "In the Presence of Witnesses".

cipal smṛiti ("remembered") literature. Also important were a set of approved social practices, including conformity to caste boundaries, observance of the norms of purity and pollution, and maintenance of gender-related rules such as hypergamous marriage, child marriage, and proscription of widow remarriage.[19]

But such questions were never straightforward. Their complexity opened the way for the first of the two preoccupations explored here: the difficult relationships between Brahman subcastes. The textual corpus of the dharmasastra offered examples of movement across varna boundaries, special rules applicable in the fallen era of the Kaliyuga, and latitude given to communities to follow their own traditions.[20] Moreover, judgements about a community were commonly made both in the light of the dharmasastra and its long-established practices.[21] Brahman communities themselves varied very widely in their material circumstances, livelihoods, sectarian affiliations, branches of Vedic learning, language usages, and relationship to local states.[22] The religious professions alone spanned an enormous range, from the prestige of learned lineages such as the Maratha Bhatta family of Banaras, to itinerant mendicants who depended on alms and cash earned in return for petty ritual services.[23]

Maratha Brahman identity was also mediated by local subcaste. Subcastes would often, but not always, share sectarian affiliations and association with local settlements. However, subcastes did not always share branches of Vedic learning. Such differences could present barriers to intermarriage, such that the same Brahman subcaste might share relations of commensality but not of marriage. A further key area of complexity lay in internal hierarchies within the subcaste, created by differences of wealth, family connections, and professional

[19] See Kane, *History of Dharmaśāstra*, vol. 2, pt 1, pp. 107–54. For a medieval discussion of how categories of caste could be known, see Gurevitch, "The Epistemology of Difference".

[20] For movement across varna boundaries, see Sathaye, *Crossing the Lines of Caste*.

[21] O'Hanlon and Minkowski, "What Makes People Who They Are?", pp. 384–5.

[22] Deshpande, "Vedas and Their Śākhās".

[23] For the Bhatta lineage, see Benson, "Saṃkārabhaṭṭa's Family Chronicle".

reputation. Such hierarchies were marked by asymmetries in the exchange of marriage partners, since the rules of hypergamy meant that wife-giving was associated with a lower status than wife-taking.[24]

Such internal diversity certainly marked Maratha Brahman communities.[25] Some – Chitpavans, Karhades, Deshasthas – were relatively numerous and successful. Others – Devrukhes, Govardhanas, Javals, Kramavants, Palshes, Tirguls, Savashes – were sometimes recent migrants into the Deccan, smaller in number and their populations local. Such subcastes periodically suffered challenges to their status as respectable Brahmans. The subcaste of Shenvi Saraswats presented particular difficulties of classification since their diet included fish and because they tended to work as scribes and teachers rather than religious scholars or priests. To accommodate the anomaly, some scholar assemblies determined that they were not "ṣaṭkarmī" Brahmans, entitled to all six of the capabilities that marked a Brahman, but "trikarmī" Brahmans, with access to the lesser three that were the prerogatives of every member of the twice-born.[26]

But there were also powerful pressures towards consensus. Open inter-Brahman rivalries risked damaging the idea of Brahman spiritual authority itself as an eternal essence standing above mundane local quarrels. Early modern Brahman communities everywhere lived with this inherent tension – between the reality of what was often a very competitive social world and the abstract ideal of Brahmanhood. Maratha Brahman scholars in Banaras had a distinctive social role in this regard, the consequence of their geographical distance from the Maratha country and their India-wide reputation as the dignified arbiters of the conflicts of others. They tended to suggest more flexible norms for the recognition of Brahman status, and to urge conciliation upon contending parties.[27]

[24] Tambiah, "From Varna to Caste", pp. 218–23.

[25] Patil, "Conflict, Identity and Narratives", pp. 15–22.

[26] The six capabilities were commissioning a sacrifice and performing a sacrifice; studying and teaching the Veda; and making and accepting gifts. Of these six, the more prestigious three – performing a sacrifice, teaching the Veda to others, and accepting gifts – were reserved for Brahmans alone. Kane, *History of Dharmaśāstra*, vol. 2, pt 1, p. 105.

[27] O'Hanlon, "Speaking from Siva's Temple", pp. 266–7.

While the broad parameters of Brahman identity were stable, the rapid social change of the early modern centuries shifted the balance of advantage between different subcastes. A well-known development lay in the rise to political prominence of the Chitpavan subcaste of the Konkan littoral. As successive peshwa ministers peopled the state administration with their own caste-fellows from the Konkan, they generated tensions with other Brahman communities, some of whom deprecated the lower level of learning among the newcomers, and declined to eat with them.[28] With their court connections, many Chitpavan families developed greater assertiveness in their local rivalries with other Brahman subcastes for control over temple resources, land, and village office.[29]

On the second broad question explored here, most Maratha Brahman scholars adhered to the orthodox view that only Brahmans and Sudras still survived in the Kali age.[30] The god Parashuram, sixth incarnation of Vishnu, was said to have wiped Kshatriya kings from the face of the earth after the warrior sons of King Kartavirya slew his own father, Jamadagni. In western India's rendering of this episode, Parashuram retired thereafter to his favoured lands in the hills and valleys of the Sahyadri mountain range, which he populated with pious Brahmans. As Bayly has suggested, the Parashuram tradition flourished when mainly warrior-based forms of caste society were giving way to those in which Brahmanical norms held sway.[31] This raised a broader issue which, as Pollock has suggested, shaped a new genre of early modern commentary on rājadharma (the duties of kings). What basis of authority did Mughal India's many new regional states possess? Was it the exercise of power itself that constituted kingship, or could legitimate rulership only be exercised by a king properly consecrated by priests willing to recognise him as a Kshatriya?[32]

These arguments emerged most commonly in Brahman relation-

[28] Deshmukh, *Aitihāsik Goṣṭī*, pt 1, pp. 76–7.

[29] For examples of such conflicts, see Oak, *Bālājī Viśvanāth Peśve*, pp. 171–2; Divekar, *Govardhan Brāhmaṇāncha Itihās*, pp. 98–110.

[30] Deshpande, "Kṣatriyas in the Kali Age?"

[31] Bayly, *Caste, Society and Politics*, p. 77; O'Hanlon, "Performance in a World of Paper", pp. 102 6.

[32] Pollock, *The Ends of Man*, pp. 69–76.

ships with the Maratha warrior lineages who were their principal patrons, and with the Kayastha communities who were their most significant scribal rivals. If classified as Kshatriyas, males of both communities would be entitled to the transformative upanayana ritual of the twice-born, in which investment with a sacred thread marked a boy's transition from childhood to the beginnings of adult responsibilities and relationships. Conducted with Vedic mantras, the whole sequence of saṃskāra rites of passage designated for the twice-born represented the stages through which individuals might ascend to higher stages of consciousness and demonstrate their fitness for corporate life. Many authorities prescribed twelve saṃskāras for Sudras of approved descent, not including the upanayana, and a meagre five for those classed as "mixed jatis" whose descent was tainted by disapproved marriages or other forms of violation. At best, saṃskāras for Sudras were accompanied by simple mantras from puranic texts.[33]

Such differences were not simply procedural matters. Often occasions for great social celebration, the saṃskāras of the twice-born conferred political advantages of many kinds, to aspiring rulers as well as to those hoping to serve as prestigious scribes. The well-known episode of Chhatrapati Shivaji's consecration in 1674 as a royal Kshatriya not by local Brahmans, but by the Maratha master of ritual from Banaras, Gagabhatta (*fl.* 1660–1680), is suggestive of these tensions. During the eighteenth century, however, conventions shifted towards lesser forms of ritual for the Bhosle family, which suggested that they were indeed entitled to the upanayana ceremony, but not necessarily with Vedic rites. During a contested discussion of the question at Satara in 1749, one Brahman sastri offered a remark, repeated by conservatives well into the twentieth century, that the subsequent extinction of Gagabhatta's lineage was penalty for his error.[34] The upanayana of Chhatrapati Shahu II of Satara (1763–1808) in May 1778 was said to have been done with puranic rather than Vedic rites.[35]

Leading Maratha scholars in Banaras in this period also wrote new manuals offering a limited form of dignified ritual for "clean"

[33] Kane, *History of Dharmaśāstra*, vol. 2, pt 1, pp. 191–3, 198–9, 268–74; Flood, "Hinduism".

[34] See the Satara Brahman assembly discussion in 1749 of this issue, in Bendrey, *Mahārāṣṭretihāsāchī Sādhane*, vol. 2, p. 494.

[35] Dongare, *Śrīsiddāntavijayagrantha,* Appendices, p. 106.

Sudras. With its prescriptions for Sudras, the *Śūdrakamalākaraḥ* of Kamalakarabhatta (*fl.* 1620–1640) – the author being uncle to Gagabhatta – became one of the Maratha country's most widely influential works of religious law.[36] In keeping with the greater flexibility often to be found in the judgments of Banaras scholars, Kamalakara also took a slightly more accommodating view of the Kshatriya question. In an aside in this work, he suggested that amongst these Sudra communities might still be found some Kshatriyas, but in a lapsed form, requiring expiation before any could regain their right to a full upanayana.[37]

Both of these questions – rivalries between Brahman subcastes, and the insistence of many Brahman scholars that none but Brahmans and Sudras survived in the Kaliyuga – were fought out in a range of literary genres. Stories of Maratha Brahman origins featured prominently in western Maharashtra's pre-eminent purana of place, the *Sahyādrikhaṇḍa*. It was in the "Parashuram kṣetra" of the Sahyadri mountain range that the god was said to have settled his Brahman communities, who turned out to be none other than the Chitpavans. The story thus helped associate Chitpavans in particular with the story of Parashuram's extirpation of the Kshatriyas, and with entitlement to lands and offices in the region. Collins has described the added significance that Parashuram took on for the Chitpavan peshwas of the eighteenth-century Pune court. Not only did the story reaffirm their preeminence in the "Parashuram kṣetra", but, as Brahmans who had become warriors themselves, they also shared in the god's mixed nature.[38] Caste histories also included hybrid narratives, such as the *Śatapraśnakalpalatā* (Wishing Creeper of One Hundred Questions) of Madhava, which retailed many of the *Sahyādrikhaṇḍa* histories, but with further scandalous additions of its own.[39]

With accompanying vernacular commentaries, these puranic histories also enjoyed a life in popular performance. Narrated by puranika

[36] Benke, "The Śūdrācāraśiromaṇi of Kṛṣṇa Śeṣa"; Kamalakarabhatta, *Śūdrakamalākaraḥ*, pp. 14–15. For the text's influence, see O'Hanlon, "Disciplining the Brahman Household".

[37] Kamalakarabhatta, *Śūdrakamalākaraḥ*, pp. 93–4; Deshpande, "Kṣatriyas in the Kali Age?", pp. 19–20.

[38] Collins, *The Other Rāma*, pp. 208–14. See also Janaki, "Paraśurāma".

[39] Madhava, *Śatapraśnakalpalatā*; Patil, "Conflict, Identity and Narratives", pp. 33–205.

priests, itinerant balladeers, and professional storytellers, and adapted to the particular setting of the Maratha country, the powerful themes of these stories were of deep interest to local communities. Some were amused by tales of scandals hidden in their Brahman neighbours' pasts. Others, such as Kayastha scribal elites, were infuriated by the implication that, since they were not Brahmans, they could claim only the social worth and ritual dignities of Sudras. Within just a year of the passing of power from the Pune court to the East India Company, these latter concerns were to emerge in a series of heated conflicts that drew in some of Bombay's key caste elites as they sought to adjust to their changing political environment.

Sitting with the Record Keepers: A Secretary and His Lineage in Satara

A memorable scene in the work of the great historian A.R. Kulkarni takes place in the airy rooms of a colonial bungalow in Satara in 1819. Newly built, the bungalow was home to James Grant (1798–1858), Resident at the Satara court of the young Maratha Raja Pratapsinh (1793–1847). The scene Kulkarni describes is one of technical discussion. Grant, his agent, and a small group of secretaries and record keepers are in attendance. Documents of many kinds are brought in and subjected to detailed examination. Sometimes fresh records and different officers are called for. Members of the group come and go, breaking for meals, and leaving Grant's bungalow at the end of the day. The scene, of course, shows Grant gathering materials for his landmark *History of the Mahrattas*, published in 1826. In his magisterial account of Grant as a historian, Kulkarni describes the daily meetings as nothing less than a "history workshop".[40]

We know about these conversations because Pratapsinh himself recorded many of them in his daily diaries. The group of officers was small but diverse. Aside from Pratapsinh himself, it included the prolific and now aged author of bakhar chronicles, Malhar Ramrao Chitnis (d. 1823), along with his son, Balwantrao Malhar (d. 1843). Also present was the court's accomplished Persian scribe and Sanskrit

[40] Kulkarni, *James Cuninghame Grant Duff*, p. 152.

scholar, Aba Parasnis; and Vitthalpant Phadnis, whom Grant had appointed as dewan to the Raja. Grant's confidential agent, Balajipant Natu, who had earlier been in the service of the powerful Raste family of Pune bankers, also joined the discussions.[41]

The Chitnises were one of those long-serving Kayastha families able to embed themselves in the administration of India's early modern states. Malhar Ramrao's great-great grandfather, Balaji Avaji (d. 1681), had served as a trusted secretary at Shivaji's court. His great-uncle, Govindrao (d. 1785), had played a major role at the court of Shahu I (1682–1749) at Satara.[42] As Shahu lay dying late in 1749, Govindrao had prepared the documents which invested his peshwa minister, Balaji Bajirao (r. 1740–1761) with responsibility for governing on behalf of his young heir. Both Balaji Avaji at the time of Shivaji's consecration in 1674, and Govindrao at the Satara court in 1749, had clashed bitterly with Brahman court sastris over the entitlements of Kayasthas to Vedic ritual.[43] As Prachi Deshpande has suggested, Malhar Ramrao's bakhar chronicle of Shivaji, commissioned in 1808 by Chhatrapati Shahu II (1763–1808), conspicuously attributed the success of the Maratha state not to its later peshwa ministers but to Shivaji's own ruling family and their trusted Kayastha servants.[44]

Not surprisingly, given the complex relations of power and dependency running between different members of the group, clear emotional undercurrents tinged the discussion. Grant often appeared high-handed in his treatment of the officers. As the officers arrived in the morning to begin their work, he seems to have reproached them: "Why have you come so late? I told you to be quick."[45] Despite their

[41] Sardesai, *Papers Referring to Pratapsinh*, pp. 1, 18–30; Grant Duff, *History of the Mahrattas*, p. 449; Deshpande, *Creative Pasts*, pp. 78–9. See in particular Vendell's insightful study, "Scribes and the Vocation of Politics", pp. 334–40.

[42] For Govindrao Chitnis, see Vendell, "The Scribal Household in Flux", pp. 550–3.

[43] O'Hanlon, "The Social Worth of Scribes", pp. 584–8; Bendrey, *Mahārāṣṭretihāsāchī Sādhane*, vol. 2, pp. 491–5; Deshpande, "Kṣatriyas in the Kali Age?", pp. 6–7.

[44] Deshpande, *Creative Pasts*, pp. 78–9. For an extended analysis of this work and a very helpful family tree, see Vendell, "Scribes and the Vocation of Politics", pp. 309–21, 384.

[45] Sardesai, *Papers Referring to Pratapsinh*, p. 22.

explanation that most archives from the Shivaji period had been lost when the fort at Raigad fell to Aurangzeb's forces, he pressed them to renew their searches, sometimes brusquely querying the veracity of what he was given. Anxious about losing the documents, Pratapsinh and his officers attempted discreetly to prevent Grant from keeping them at his bungalow rather than returning them to the palace archives at the end of the day.[46]

Balajipant himself intervened frequently and officiously, calling into question Balwantrao's understanding of Maratha administration and the dating system for its documents. To Balwantrao's evident annoyance, he also echoed Grant's demand for additional papers. Pratapsinh's diary reported: "Then Balajipant asked Balwantrao Chitnis, haven't you got anything more in your daftar? Balwantrao replied, I already showed you the papers we have in Pune. You made a copy of them. We have also given you copies today. We have even given you a copy of the bakhar. Beyond these, we do not have any other records." In his desire to please Grant, Balajipant actively threatened Balwantrao. "If more papers are found some time later, it won't be good for you."[47] Under the pressure of Grant's questioning, Balwantrao defended his father's bakhar as an unimpeachable source of authority: "I regard what my father wrote to be true. Beyond that, what do we know? If he wrote that something did not happen, he knew the difference between the true and the false."[48]

These remarkable exchanges take us into the room where Balwantrao and his father, as author of the bakhar, are questioned by an intellectually curious but suspicious and fact-driven colonial historian, and by his combative agent Balajipant Natu. Their conversations suggest the undercurrents of pride, defensiveness, exasperation, and resentment at the questioning of the status of Malhar Ramrao's bakhar. His own presence for some of the discussion clearly lent an additional edge to the situation. It may also be possible to see here an undercurrent of Pratapsinh's well-known dislike for Balajipant, whom he regarded as another Chitpavan Brahman seeking to deprive the Bhosle lineage of its power, and whose services as a dewan he had

[46] Ibid., pp. 20–1.

[47] Ibid., p. 25.

[48] Ibid., p. 28.

recently declined. Shortly afterwards, Balajipant resigned in agitation from Grant's service when he discovered that Pratapsinh had been putting it about that he was being investigated for corruption.[49]

But the discussions were not confined to Grant's bungalow. In 1820, perhaps sensing the rewards to be gained at the Satara court from a song critical of the historical record of the peshwas, a Satara balladeer named Anand wrote his "Light on the Rise to Good Fortune of the Chitpavans".[50] He opened with plenty of scurrilous detail about the gruesome origins of the Chitpavans according to the *Sahyādrikhaṇḍa*, represented in the purana as having been created by the god Parashuram taking humble fishermen and purifying them through the fire of a burning ground on the sea shore.[51] His song described how it had been with the mid-century ascent of the Peshwa Balaji Bajirao that Chitpavans had come to dominate the Maratha state: "The Diwan, the Phadnis, the Daftardar, the officers of the subhas, they were appointed in every place, their importance increased, clerks were attached for every duty, with appointments in every province, they gave the kingdom away."[52]

It is more than possible that Anand had heard local gossip about the tensions at the Satara court and referred to them to give topicality to his material. His song lamented that it had actually been the Kayasthas who first taught the Chitpavans their skills of writing, only to see their protégés grasp all the administrative jobs for themselves.[53] The devoted service to Shahu I of Malhar Ramrao's great-uncle Govindrao at Satara also featured in Anand's song. It had been Govindrao that the Peshwa Balaji Bajirao had approached to discover Shahu's wishes for the succession, and Govindrao the good servant, "who brought clear thinking into the affairs of the state", who had carried out those wishes in handing over the seals and emblems of the kingdom.[54] Anand concluded his song with a further reference to the pe-

[49] Ballhatchet, *Social Policy*, pp. 21, 94–5, 235–6.

[50] Anand, *Chitpāvan Bhāgyodya Dīpikā*, pp. 306–7.

[51] Ibid., pp. 278–92.

[52] Ibid., p. 329.

[53] Idem.

[54] Ibid., pp. 320–3. I am indebted to Ashwini Mokashi for assistance with translation of these passages.

jorative story of Chitpavan origins and their alleged repudiation as pure Brahmans by other Brahman communities in the city.[55]

We cannot know whether Anand's praise for the Chitnis lineage ever reached the ears of Balwantrao and his father. However, his strictures on the Chitpavan community might well have been welcome to them. Shortly after their bruising experience at the hands of Balajipant Natu, Natu and a small group of Chitpavan conservatives launched an all-out assault on the ritual entitlements of Kayastha and other non-Brahman elites like themselves. The issue was their public entitlement to the upanayana ceremony for their sons, and to the full range of saṃskāra life-cycle rituals conducted with Vedic mantras, affirming them as members of the twice-born. Given his family's history, it was not surprising that Balwantrao went on to lead the Kayastha disputants. Pratapsinh himself led the elite Maratha campaign, which continued on into the 1830s through a lengthy series of public debates with the orthodox.

Historians are familiar with many aspects of these campaigns of the 1820s, and particularly with their character as a response to the Company's declared unwillingness to enforce precolonial caste norms.[56] Less well appreciated, however, is these elite communities' intense concern with the damage to their "honour" (abrū) that would occur if their access to these life-cycle rituals was withdrawn, such that they were publicly deemed to be Sudras. Balwantrao's Kayastha campaign drew the community together in a display of remarkable solidarity across much of the Deccan. Violence broke out in Pune as orthodox Brahmans and their supporters confronted those of the elite non-Brahman communities in the streets, temples, and public meeting places of the city. In June 1827, Balwantrao's Kayastha community issued an angry public declaration. Despite the community's clear record of rights to Vedic ritual, the declaration stated,

> The Brahmans have again started a dispute with us. They have been holding meetings in Pune in places like Tulsibag, making licentious speeches, ridiculing us and maligning us. They do not care about our honour (abrū) while engaging in such activities. They do not think about

[55] Ibid., pp. 334–7.

[56] Wagle, "A Dispute"; Wagle, "Ritual and Change"; Kulkarni, *The Satara Raj*, pp. 187–93.

> peoples' innermost urge to preserve honour. In thousands they gather and create commotions.

Moreover, the letter continued, Brahmans themselves no longer served in their own appropriate professions. They worked as bankers, merchants, shopkeepers, soldiers, and servants for money, they spent time teaching songs to the lowest dancing women, even as they punished others for wishing to chant Vedic mantras with their rituals. Instead of pleading for their services, the Kayasthas should kindle their own sacred fire and perform their own Vedic rituals if the Brahmans refused to do these for them. The letter emphasised that such actions were provisional and not a declaration of hostility directed at all Brahmans: "Brahman castes are respected by all, and are a refuge to all. Keeping all satisfied, they should maintain proper order in society. But they act quite to the contrary."[57]

Remarkably tenacious in his pursuit of an issue that had mattered over some seven generations of his family, Balwantrao's campaign also demonstrated the elements of conservatism of these "Vedokta" demonstrations of the 1820s. Their critique of Brahmans was perhaps more reminiscent of the censure of secular Brahmans that forms a theme in some bhakti poetry than it was of non-Brahman activists' later fierce denunciation.[58] Like the later activists, Kayasthas and others proposed performing their own rituals, but largely because their Brahman contemporaries declined to perform them in the way that the Kayasthas expected. While these demonstrations cannot be seen as direct forerunners of the non-Brahman movements that were to emerge from mid-century, they were important in other ways. To explore this question, let us look more closely at the conservative Brahman leadership that emerged to pursue these campaigns.

Agents of Orthodoxy in the Company State

Faced with the Bombay government's reluctance to intervene in caste disputes, a distinctive group of four orthodox Brahmans with

[57] Dongare, *Śrīsiddāntavijayagrantha*, Appendices, pp. 110–12; Wagle, "Ritual and Change", pp. 157–61, 178. I have here used Wagle's translation.

[58] Eaton, *A Social History*, p. 134.

close links to the old Pune court emerged to impose controls of their own.[59] Nilakanthasastri Thatthe (1750–1834) had been a senior pandit at the Pune court, his teachers including sastris from a scholarly lineage famous for its hostility to the twice-born aspirations of all but Brahmans.[60] Chintamanrao Patwardhan (1776–1851) came from a leading military family at the court. In his negotiations with Elphinstone over his large estate at Sangli, he pressed for restoration of the peshwa's office, prohibition of cow slaughter, and an end to the use of Brahmans as labourers for the Company. In 1823, Elphinstone described Chintamanrao as a "professed malcontent" who was "desirous of being considered as the last representative of Hindoo independence."[61] A third member of the group was Balajipant Natu. He was closely connected to Nilakantha, since his daughter Tai had married Nilakantha's adopted son Narayanasastri in 1818, bringing an enormous dowry with her.[62] The fourth member of the group was Malhar Shrotri, a scholar in the last peshwa's service subsequently employed as an official sastri to the Company's court. In 1819, both Nilakantha and Malhar Shrotri were amongst those learned sastris to whom Elphinstone's government gave substantial pensions in recognition of their learning.[63]

In setting out to frustrate the Vedic aspirations of the elite non-Brahmans, these unusual allies sought to preserve the Pune court's old role in the maintenance of caste discipline. In the precolonial setting, however, such decisions had emerged out of a process of extended deliberation, almost always involving the court's shifting factional politics. Local pandit assemblies took part, as did the more conciliatory scholar communities of Banaras. Decisions over ritual entitlements were periodically renegotiated and often reversed.[64] But the efforts of Nilakantha's group took place in the absence of any of these constraining circumstances. Their objective therefore emerged as the abrupt public dismissal of elite non-Brahmans as menial Sudras, without the possibility of negotiation or appeal. Its impact was conse-

[59] Wagle, "Ritual and Change", p. 149.

[60] Deshpande, "Kṣatriyas in the Kali Age?", pp. 110–13.

[61] Ballhatchet, *Social Policy*, pp. 66–9, 205.

[62] Thatthe, *Thaṭṭhe Kulavṛttānta*, p. 123.

[63] Ballhatchet, *Social Policy*, p. 87.

[64] For an example, see Wagle, "The Chāndrasenīya Kāyastha Prabhus".

quently much the greater. This was both for the parties immediately caught up in the dispute, and for later non-Brahman intellectuals seeking to understand the meaning of such decisions, and of the social implications of the category of Sudra itself.

Nilakantha and Malhar Shrotri took the lead in April 1823 against the Devajna Sonars, first to test the Bombay government's withdrawal from matters of caste discipline. Nilakantha and Malhar demonstrated considerable skill, and some sharp practice, in managing the Brahman assembly called to consider the question. The pair gathered a large crowd of Chitpavans then in the city to receive their "dakṣiṇā" pensions.[65] In his later complaint, the Sonar champion Trivengadacharya described how the crowd pelted him with mud and tore his clothes as he struggled home after the meeting. When it reconvened, he alleged that Nilakantha manipulated the outcome by attaching his own new text to the long paper roll of pandit signatures collected in favour of the Sonars' case.[66] Clearly, the move met with some partial success. In 1826, Jagannath Shankarsheth (1803–1865), a wealthy Sonar philanthropist from Bombay, complained publicly that priests in the shrine towns of Wai and Nasik had refused to let him bathe in the river because he was a Sudra.[67]

Nilakantha and his supporters then turned their attention to the Kayasthas, summoning the assembly in the Tulsibag temple about which Balwantrao Chitnis had complained so angrily. Again, Nilakantha's party seem to have employed some heavy-handed tactics. They persuaded the assembly to support them by assuring the pandits present that the Shankaracharya of Shankeshwar had used the great authority of his office to rule against the Kayasthas. In separate letters, Chintamanrao and Nilakantha circulated his edict to the Brahman communities of the southern Maratha country. Chintamanrao's letter asserted in the bluntest terms that the Kayasthas were the offspring of a mixed caste, even lower than Sudras.[68] Nilakantha listed the leading sastris who had been present at the Tulsibag assembly, and the many

[65] The Pune court had rewarded Sanskrit scholarship in this way, and the Company continued the practice during the 1820s: Deshpande, "Pune: An Emerging Center", pp. 61–4.

[66] Wagle, "A Dispute", pp. 144–5, 153–9.

[67] Thakare, *Grāmaṇyāñchā Sādyant Itihās*, pp. 195–6.

[68] Dongare, *Śrīsiddāntavijayagrantha*, p. 107.

Sanskrit authorities supporting its position. He pointed specifically to the role of Parashuram: how could the Kayasthas say they were Kshatriyas entitled to Vedic rituals when it was known that the god had extirpated Kshatriyas from the earth? Rather than chasing Vedic rites reserved for others, "each should look each to their own dharma for protection."[69]

However, the attempts of Nilakantha and his group to exploit the authority of the Shankaracharya proved difficult to sustain. In November 1830, the Shankaracharya retracted his edict. He explained that Balajipant and Chintamanrao had threatened to implicate him in a conspiracy against the British unless he co-operated, which would result in the Company's confiscation of his estates.[70] He included Pratapsinh and the elite Marathas as well as the Kayasthas in this new statement: "The Chhatrapati Sarkar has always been addressed with the title 'Kṣatriya Kulāvataṃsa' by the Brahman pandits, sastris, and other Brahmans of religious centres. But it was Chintamanrao who wanted to prove that the Kshatriyas became extinct. But, according to the sastras, the Kshatriyas do exist."[71]

How had the group been able to push their views so far? Nilakantha undoubtedly provided their intellectual firepower. But, as Madhav Deshpande has suggested, his "Kāyastha Prabhū Dharma Darśa", written at the height of the campaign against the Kayasthas, looks very much like "a work of convenience", much less erudite than his work as a grammarian, and perhaps produced because of his family connection with Chintamanrao.[72] We know that the text was circulated: Sakhopant Limaye, financial minister to another branch of the Patwardhan family, recorded that he had made a copy of Nilakantha's work "for my own and for others' benefit", dating his copy to 1827.[73]

There is another textual puzzle which may offer insights into the tactics of the conservative group. They were almost certainly involved

[69] Ibid., p. 109.

[70] Wagle, "Ritual and Change", pp. 149–53, 167.

[71] Dongare, *Śrīsiddāntavijayagrantha*, 114–15; Wagle, "Ritual and Change", p. 167. I have here used Wagle's translation.

[72] Deshpande, "Kṣatriyas in the Kali Age?", pp. 11–15; Thatthe, *Kāyastha Prabhū Dharma Darśa*; Gode, "The Date".

[73] Thatthe, "Kāyastha Prabhū Dharma Darśa", f. 7r. For Sakhopant's library, see Gode, "The Date", pp. 136–7.

in the production of another work on the Kayasthas, the *Parabhūjātinirṇaya* (Determination of the Caste of the Prabhus). This text bears no date. Its author signed himself only as "a certain learned sage".[74] It has attracted scholarly interest because it contains thirty-three hitherto unknown verses said to include the direct orders of Shivaji's son Sambhaji (1657–1689).[75] The work tells the story of Govindrao Chitnis, grandson of Shivaji's scribe Balaji Avaji Chitnis, great-uncle to Malhar Ramrao and, as described above, would-be defender of Kayastha rights to the Satara Brahman assembly of 1749. In dramatic and colourful terms, the *Parabhūjātinirṇaya* describes Govindrao's defeat and disgrace at that assembly.

As the *Parabhūjātinirṇaya* narrated it, the assembly had reviewed many sastric authorities pronouncing the Kayasthas lower even than Sudras in status.[76] But they were most persuaded by verses laid before them said to have been written by Shivaji's son Sambhaji. The verses described Sambhaji's brutal refusal to allow Shivaji's secretary Balaji Avaji Chitnis to hold an upanayana for his son, his crushing description of Kayasthas as impure meat-eaters from whose hands even Sudras would not accept water, and a shattered Balaji Avaji "who returned home, with his head bowed down", to send away the guests assembled to celebrate his son's thread ceremony.[77] After its deliberations, and "having consulted the *Jātiviveka*, the *Sahyādri*, Gagabhaṭta's *Paddhati* and what has been said by Sambhuraja and Nilakantha", the assembly of 1749 gave its decision against the Kayasthas, and the disgraced Govindrao had to leave the court.[78]

Writing in the 1940s, the historian V.S. Bendrey, a leading scholar of Shivaji's court, but himself also a Kayastha, suggested that the work was a production of Nilakantha's own party in the 1820s. He pointed out that the wording in Sambhaji's "order" was identical to the Shankaracharaya's verdict given against Kayasthas before he confessed that he had been coerced. Bendrey also drew attention to the fact that other authorities quoted in the text were almost identical to those in other

[74] *Parabhūjātinirṇaya*, f. 1r.

[75] Bendrey, *Keśava Paṇḍita's Daṇḍanītiprakaraṇam*, 38–47; Gode, "The Date".

[76] *Parabhūjātinirṇaya*, ff. 7r–8r.

[77] Ibid., ff. 8v–11r.

[78] Ibid., f. 12r.

readings of standard authorities prepared by Nilakantha's party in the 1820s. Also, Bendrey pointed out, there is no contemporary record of Sambhaji ever having had this kind of judicial role, and the Sanskrit said to have been spoken by him was very corrupt and ungrammatical.[79] The deliberate reference to "Nilakantha" as a trusted authority, although a chronological misplacement, also lends weight to Bendrey's thesis.

Other later supporters of the Kayasthas believed that Nilakantha's party was not above fabricating documents. K.T. Gupte, secretary in 1919 of the Chandraseniya Kayastha Prabhu History Mandal, alleged that Chintamanrao Patwardhan's friends had "set up a factory in Sangli for the production of fake religious books."[80] It is impossible, of course, to be certain of the history of these documents. It is also important to remember that Bendrey was writing in the years after the long-running late colonial debate between the Kayasthas and some Brahman historians. By then, the issue was not simply one of community ritual prestige so much as the emergence of a many-stranded new nationalist discourse offering conflicting interpretations of the relative "contributions" of Brahmans and Kayasthas to Maharashtra's history.[81]

Many of Nilakantha's students went on to scholarly prominence in the next generation. Identified in the Thatthe family history as his pupils were Kruppa Dravid and Govindacharya Ashtaputre. Their signatures appear on a letter of April 1827 to the Brahman community of Mahuli, urging it to fall in behind the decision of the Tulsibag assembly.[82] Some intellectual connections ran alongside close family ties. Morsastri Sathe was cousin to Nilakantha and the natural father of Narayansastri, given in adoption to Nilakantha and married to Balajipant Natu's daughter Tai.[83] In the 1840s, Morsastri and Narayansastri, together with Tryambaksastri Shaligram and Govindacharya Ashtaputre, were teachers in Poona Hindoo College and oversaw the distribution of dakṣiṇā grants.[84] By mid-century, Tryambaksastri was the leader of orthodox opinion in Pune city. Another of Nilakantha's

[79] Bendrey, *Keśava Paṇḍita's Daṇḍanītiprakaraṇam*, pp. 40–1.

[80] Gupte, *Rājavāḍyānchi Gāgābhaṭṭī*, p. 1.

[81] Deshpande, *Creative Pasts*, pp. 104–9.

[82] Wagle, "Ritual and Change", p. 157.

[83] Thatthe, *Thaṭṭhe Kulavṛttānta*, p. 123.

[84] Jambhekar, *Memoirs and Writings*, vol. 3, pp. 498–9.

intellectual heirs, Bhaskarasastri Abhyankar, emerged in Satara as the leading grammarian of his generation, and his accomplished son, Vasudevsastri, later authored a very conservative work on social reform issues, the *Dharmatatvanirṇaya*.[85]

Of course, intellectual affiliation with Nilakantha as a grammarian did not necessarily mean sharing his views on social issues. Nonetheless, this was a formidable assemblage of scholars sharing a broad commitment to many of the values of a traditional Sanskrit education. They came to dominate colonial educational institutions through into the middle of the nineteenth century. Their manuscript libraries too were important. A decade after his death in 1834, Nilakantha's own manuscript library was still available for consultation in Pune.[86] As we will see, it was from this same library that an important social conservative of the next generation, Ganesh Bapuji Malvankar, drew his copy of the *Śūdrakamalākaraḥ*, in order to launch the first printed edition of the text in 1861.

Before the coming of the Company, decisions about the varna status of the elite communities examined here had involved a complex and often reversible deliberation between many parties. Nilakantha's group sought to uphold a very narrow version of the Pune court's historic range of preferred caste norms, and to drive the unceremonious public dismissal of elite non-Brahmans as Sudras. Whatever the truth of the contemporary and later allegations about forgery and force majeure, there was no mistaking the group's emphasis on Sudra status as a menial one. It was not surprising, therefore, that Balwantrao Chitnis and other elite non-Brahman leaders responded with such acute dismay. Equally important for the future, as we will see, was the way in which these social developments came to shape the views of the first generation of aspirant non-Brahman intellectuals.

Family and Mobility in the Colonial State

These successful conservative scholars and their Brahman allies were very much the beneficiaries of the Company government's initial support for Sanskrit education. For other well-placed Brahman families

[85] Deshpande, "Kṣatriyas in the Kali Age?", p. 12.

[86] Kulkarni, "Charles D'Ochoa", p. 139.

adjusting to the new regime in the 1820s and 1830s, an Anglophone education for their sons offered the most promising future. The new forms of education and employment did not, of course, develop in a vacuum. As is well known, these decades saw the emergence of the Company's new liberal vision for the relationship between family, law, and the state. There were deep contradictions here. The Company state's anxiety to preserve the stability of the traditional social order pulled against its desire to reward the labour of individual families, to replace preparation conducted within the household with professional education, and to commute the rights of hereditary village officers in favour of paid clerical employees of the state.[87]

As Rachel Sturman has suggested, these moves entailed particular consequences for families able to exchange older forms of advantage for new avenues towards professional mobility. With this "mobility of social capital", such families now placed a greater premium on the immediate family's talents and its useful social connections.[88] Bhau Mahajan (1815–1890), of the Chitpavan Kunte family of wealthy salt-pan supervisors in the Konkan, offers a useful example. His brother-in-law, Bhau Chatre (1788–1830), had already moved to Bombay as secretary of the recently established Bombay Native Education Society. In the early 1820s, the young Bhau Mahajan was brought to the Chatre household in Bombay to continue his education. Accompanying him was the young Balsastri Jambhekar (1812–1846) from a Karhade family of modest means that had served occasionally as reciters of puranas at the Pune court. First Jambhekar and then Bhau Mahajan moved to the Bombay Native Education Society's English School. By the end of the 1830s, Bhau Mahajan was a scholarship holder at the Elphinstone Institution and Jambhekar an Assistant Professor. Both emerged as leading intellectuals in Bombay's public life, Bhau Mahajan as founder editor in 1841 of the first exclusively Marathi newspaper, *Prabhākar*, and Jambhekar as a prominent social reformer and eminent educationist before his premature death in 1846.[89]

[87] Sturman, *The Government of Social Life*, pp. 70–106; Metcalf, *Ideologies of the Raj*, pp. 28–65.

[88] Sturman, *The Government of Social Life*, pp. 101–3.

[89] Naik, "Bhau Mahajan", pp. 64–5; Jambhekar, *Memoirs and Writings*, vol. 1, pp. 33–89.

For the Maratha Brahman population lacking such skills and connections, the experience was often very different. As Richard Tucker has suggested, the early decades of the Company's government saw, rather, the erosion of their older livelihoods and a struggle to find alternatives.[90] The largesse of the Pune court itself, expressed in flows of gifts and feasting throughout the ritual year, was in no way matched by the Company's decision to continue support for Sanskrit teaching and learning within its own "Hindoo College" established in 1821.[91] Elsewhere, the displacement of older elite families meant a reduction in employment for teachers offering a traditional Sanskrit education, and for priests, astrologers, and local sastris serving the religious needs of more prosperous households.

Further challenges to this traditionalist educational and religious establishment came from mid-century. Early generations of graduates like Bhau Mahajan and Jambhekar, often college-educated teachers and assertively reformist in outlook, were establishing a real presence in the mofussil towns.[92] They developed new local audiences for the presidency's burgeoning Marathi vernacular press and challenged the authority of the old class of local Brahman teachers, scholars, and priests. In revenue administration, as the Company's government sought to make revenue collection more uniform and transparent, Brahman Kulkarni families found themselves from mid-century increasingly bound into new documentary routines and systems of appointment by examination. This was the start of a longer term weakening of the legal claims of Brahman village office holders.[93]

The decline in older livelihoods for some Maratha Brahman communities thus took place alongside a considerable expansion of opportunity for a relatively small group of others, experienced and perhaps perceived as the consequence of individual and family merit. Patterns of migration also changed, with a shift towards movement over relatively short distances in place of the transregional journeyings that had earlier been a key source of upward mobility for Maratha Brahman

[90] Tucker, "Hindu Traditionalism", pp. 333–5.

[91] Deshpande, "Pune: An Emerging Centre", pp. 74–80.

[92] Naregal, *Language Politics*, p. 90; Masselos, *Towards Nationalism*, p. 87.

[93] Deshpande, *Scripts of Power*, pp. 234 43; Sturman, *The Government of Social Life*, pp. 99–105; Kotani, *Western India*, pp. 161–83.

families.[94] In this, their experience may have been part of the wider contraction in long-distance mobility that many historians have observed to be the result of Company policy from the 1820s.[95]

The fragmentation of the Maratha empire also meant the loss of opportunities for Brahmans to serve as revenue collectors, diplomats, and news writers.[96] The Brahman bankers, moneylenders, and traders who serviced its war economy disappeared with its demise.[97] The larger Maratha princely states – Indore, Gwalior, Kolhapur, Baroda, Nagpur – still remained as sources of employment. But in Nagpur, as Vendell describes it, Kayastha scribal elites rather than Brahmans were dominant in the management of state affairs.[98] In Baroda, the Company's government sought to reduce its dependence on Maratha Brahmans in the state administration, turning instead to Nagar Brahmans from Gujarat.[99] In Satara, as we have seen above, the young Raja's accession in 1822 triggered a direct challenge to the power of Brahman administrators at his court.

Banaras itself, long the mainstay of Maratha Brahmans looking far afield for opportunity, saw the disappearance of the Pune court's pious largesse to visiting Maratha scholars, pilgrims, and mendicants.[100] However, the city's religious and artistic culture was now shifting away from the scholastic and ritualist heritage long associated with Maratha Brahmans, and towards the Vaishnavite bhakti vision of Bharatendu Harischandra (1850–1885) as the basis for a "national" Hindu faith.[101] Perhaps significantly, Bharatendu's play *Premajoginī*, written in 1874–5, offered a deeply unfavourable depiction of the city's remaining Maratha Brahman families. He portrayed them as still absorbed in the niceties of judicial procedure, wrangling over fine points of

[94] O'Hanlon, "Speaking from Siva's Temple", pp. 255–7.

[95] For these themes, see in particular Bayly, *Indian Society*, pp. 136–68; Singha, "Settle, Mobilise, Verify"; Washbrook, "India 1818–1860"; Ramusack, *The Indian Princes*, pp. 76–84.

[96] O'Hanlon, "Entrepreneurs in Diplomacy"

[97] Divekar, "The Emergence", pp. 436, 442.

[98] Vendell, "Scribes and the Vocation of Politics", pp. 201–17.

[99] Roberts, "The Movement of Elites", pp. 249–50.

[100] Desai, *Banaras Reconstructed*, p. 87.

[101] Dalmia, *The Nationalization of Hindu Traditions*, pp. 79, 98–106, 390–429.

dharmasastra, and wrapped up in anticipation of the rich feasting and alms they hoped to secure from their patrons. For Bharatendu, at least, these characteristics belonged to the past and were entirely at variance with his own future vision of an all-inclusive Hindu dharma.[102]

The experience of Vishnu Bhatt Godse (1827–1904), from an insecure priestly family of Chitpavans in the Konkan littoral, offers a tangible example of these contrasting fortunes. Hoping to pursue a life of prayer and sacrifice, his father had in 1838 retired from his job serving a Brahman grandee who had been attached to the Pune court. Back in their ancestral village, where they had a small patch of land, the brothers of the family brought in some money through their rudimentary skills in accounting, astrology, and Sanskrit grammar. They were just able to stay afloat, until marriage expenses drove them into unsustainable debt. Vishnu Bhatt then heard that Baiza Bai, widow of the late Maratha ruler of Gwalior in Central India, was planning a lavish sacrifice. He wrote to the Maratha priests in her service, who replied with an invitation to join them and earn a share in the promised fees. Fatefully, the year was 1857.

As Vishnu Bhatt journeyed across the North Indian countryside, he kept a journal which offers an extraordinary eyewitness account of the violence of the Mutiny Rebellion, the North Indian courts affected by it, and the trials of travellers at the hands of predatory militias and Company troops. Vishnu Bhatt was fortunate in the periodic fees he was able to earn at the Maratha courts of Gwalior and Jhansi, the hospitality he received from Maratha Brahman families still scattered across North India, and the opportunities he found to learn from their scholarly discourses. He also saw close at hand the terrible consequences for Nana Saheb (b. 1824), adopted son of the exiled Maratha Peshwa Bajirao II, of his decision to lead the rebel force against the British at Kanpur.

After an absence of almost three years, Vishnu Bhatt did return home safely, welcomed back to his village amidst touching scenes of tears, joy, and prayers of thanks at the village temple. But he bore just a few small gifts for his brothers and sisters, and a carefully carried jar of holy water from the Ganges and Godavari rivers to pour over the heads

[102] Harischandra, *Premajoginī*, pp. 222–30. I am very grateful to Shailendra Bhandare for help in translation of this text.

of his parents to cleanse them of their sins. Reflecting later, in 1883, he said: "We undertook a journey to a far-off land to earn some money for paying off family debts. After undergoing many happy and unhappy experiences, we could not earn much. Perhaps this was ordained for us."[103]

Vishnu Bhatt's memoir thus reveals much about the way in which the coming of the Company affected a village-level priestly family. It shows the consequences of the disappearance of the Pune court for the family, and their struggle to find work for the next generation of priests. Their response to privation was to follow older paths of Brahman family migration to the royal courts of Central and North India, where they found shelter in family and community networks amidst the violence. The expansion of Anglophone education in Bombay and Pune meant that opportunities of a more promising kind actually lay closer at hand. Exploiting them, however, meant abandoning the family's ancestral livelihood in a way that neither Vishnu Bhatt nor his family were willing, or able, to contemplate.

Measures of Social Worth: Brahman Communities in the 1840s

These emerging divides in culture, opportunity, and eventually degrees of professional success, were naturally difficult to manage. Missionary challenges, disputes over the value of the different knowledge traditions, the Company state's changing position on support for traditional Sanskrit scholarship, and the emergence of new educational opportunities for urban elites had the effect of polarising opinion amongst Brahman communities. In this setting, Anglophone reformers in particular began to assign varying measures of worth to different Brahman livelihoods and professional skills.

In 1849, heated arguments took place over the system of dakṣiṇā funds that were used to support Sanskrit learning. The young Chitpavan journalist and outspoken reformer Gopal Hari Deshmukh ("Lokahitawadi", 1832–1892) was particularly associated with this dispute. Having studied at the Government English School in Pune, he worked during the 1840s as a clerk in the Pune office of the Agent for Sardars in the Deccan. He was at that point deeply engaged in writing his very well-

[103] Pande, *Vishnu Bhatt*, pp. 208–9.

known "Hundred Letters". They attacked every aspect of Brahman social leadership and religious culture, contrasting the backward-looking rote learning of old-fashioned pantojis, and the contribution to national progress and the common good that might be offered by properly trained Anglophone schoolteachers.[104]

In 1849, he came to learn through his work in the Sardars' office that there were unspent balances in the dakṣiṇā fund. He drew this to the attention of a group of Anglophone reformers and students who gathered to read newspapers and exchange gossip at the Pune Native General Library. The library had been established a year earlier with government support, and by a group that included Lokahitawadi himself. The information prompted the group to draw up a petition to the Bombay government, pressing for the unspent funds to be put towards supporting useful vernacular composition and translation. The petition, said to be "from the English students of Poona", was submitted to the Bombay government in October 1849.[105]

One of this group, Keshav Shivram Bhavalkar (1831–1902), left a detailed account of this event. A small group of Anglophone reformers had actually prepared the petition. Apart from Lokahitawadi and Bhavalkar, they included Brahmans associated with the girls' schools recently started by the leading non-Brahman intellectual and activist Jotirao Phule (1827–1890).[106] Among them were the wealthy philanthropist Annasaheb Chiplunkar (1842–1896), Bapu Raoji Mande (a clerk in the office of the Pune City Commissioner), and Vishnu Moreshwar Bhide (a senior teacher in the Poona College).[107] Armed with their text, the reformers visited the two schools in the city offering English classes, where Annasaheb Chiplunkar read out a summary of the petition. A number of the students signed – until a senior teacher read the

[104] Athalye, *Lokahitavādī*, pp. 9–10, 31–3. As an example, see Deshmukh, *Lokahitavādīnchī Śatapatre*, letter no. 97, no date, p. 110.

[105] "Memorial of the English Students at Poona", *Bombay Times and Journal of Commerce*, 24 October 1849. See also the excellent discussion in Naregal, *Language Politics*, pp. 83–9, and for the library, Joshi, *Puṇe Varṇan*, pp. 116–18.

[106] For the non-Brahman movement, see Rao, *The Caste Question*, pp. 39–80; Vendell, "Phule's Satyashodh"; Sarwate, "Reimagining the Modern Hindu Self", pp. 14–68; O'Hanlon, *Caste, Conflict and Ideology*; Keer, *Mahatma Jotirao Phooley*.

[107] Keer, *Jotirao Phooley*, p. 30; Bhavalkar, *Ātmavṛtta*, p. 105. I am very grateful to Suraj Thube for sharing this material with me.

whole petition and announced it to be an affront to Hindu dharma. Many of the students then took fright, demanding that Chiplunkar return their signatures. This left the petition with just thirty-nine names, including those of the organisers.[108]

This account enables us to make better sense of the petition itself. Sharing in many of the themes of Lokahitawadi's "Hundred Letters", the petition reads very much as though its Anglophone reformer-authors were aware of the arguments that would best sway the liberal and utilitarian decision-makers in the Bombay government. The petition condemned the system of life-time dakṣiṇā stipends for traditional Brahman scholars as a misuse of "public" funds because it incentivised idleness amongst its intellectually lazy recipients, who would rather travel many miles to pick up their tiny pensions than exert themselves to find a productive livelihood:

> Your petitioners beg to observe that the Duxna fund as it is now distributed contributes only to the increase of idleness and indolent habits, and its consequent miseries among the Brahman recipients, who travel a great distance of many miles to receive their pittances, which in most cases little exceeds Rs 20, and in many falls as low as eight. The Duxna fund, therefore, is far from doing good to the country generally, or to the persons who receive individually. Many recipient Bhuts are not learned, and have forgotten all they knew when they were admitted to the share. The Duxna fund is not then applied to the end for which it was established. It has been lamentably degenerated, and may be called a waste public fund full of abuses.

The reformers emphasised instead the importance of rewarding individual labour and initiative. They represented themselves as clear-minded Anglophone professionals whose ambition would not be weakened by the prospect of support from public funds:

> On the other hand, the annual salary of the lowest English clerk, engaged in a public office, who has but a smattering knowledge of the English language, seldom falls below the amount of the highest prize here proposed for the English students. Add to this the great demand for them, and the frequent opportunities they have of rising higher and bettering their condition, and the prizes for English candidates shall immediately be found to be less tempting and less liberally fixed than those of the Pundits.

[108] Bhavalkar, *Ātmavṛtta*, p. 106.

The reformers followed this up with an appeal to social utility. Even if the present dakṣiṇā pensioners were still learned men, "of what use can they be to the nation at large? The cultivator, the gardener, the carpenter, the blacksmith, who are the most useful members of society, and from whom the Duxna fund is wrung, could not, under the old system, share in its benefits, nor can they be civilised by it."

"The nation" thus featured largely in the reformers' arguments. The old system, they said,

> was founded on the old, illiberal, and barbarous prejudice of confining learning to the Brahman caste, and locking up its stores from the people generally. On the contrary, the present plan is calculated to civilise the nation in general, and to lay open for its benefit those stores of learning and wisdom which, being locked up in a language not generally known, have been wholly inaccessible to the nation at large.[109]

As news of the reformers' petition spread across the city, it met with a severe backlash. Bhavalkar described a huge crowd of gurus, vaidikas, sastris, and mendicants – many of them having come in to the city from other towns – that assembled in the Rama temple at Tulsibag to denounce the petitioners. Morsastri Sathe, cousin to Nilakanthasastri Thatthe, and his adopted son Narayansastri, were also present, demanding that the petition be handed over to them. The petitioners were only able to get through the hostile crowd to the post office with an escort of police constables, and Jotirao Phule's Dalit supporters, who turned out to protect them. But this was not, Bhavalkar affirmed, a matter of Brahmans against non-Brahmans. Rather, reflecting the enormous groundswell of popular support for the traditional recipients of dakṣiṇā stipends, the protests were as if "all the Hindus had joined together as one."[110]

The reformers' petition posted, the existing Brahman beneficiaries of the fund quickly followed with their own, asking for a continuance of their grants on the grounds that their studies of the dharmasastra supported the moral order of Hindu society.[111] But their appeal brought little result. The new Dakshina Prize Committee was set up in 1851 along the lines the reformers had envisaged. In the same year, the Poona Hindoo

[109] "Memorial of the English Students", p. 736.

[110] Bhavalkar, *Ātmavṛtta*, pp. 107–8.

[111] Naregal, *Language Politics*, p. 85; Kumar, *Western India*, pp. 39–40.

College and the city's two English schools were amalgamated into the Anglophone Poona College. In 1857, all but one of the traditional sastris were transferred to the government's Marathi translation department, on reduced stipends. The new college's Sanskrit Department itself was brought under the supervision of European scholars and directed towards philological modes of Sanskrit learning.[112]

In embryonic form, the petition, and the letters of Lokahitawadi whose themes it developed, were expressed in the language of an emerging professional class. They applauded the ambitions of rising clerical professionals and talented literati keen to succeed through their own merits, who nonetheless shared an ethical sensibility and sense of service that qualified them to speak on behalf of "the nation". The language recalls Sturman's description above of the mid-century colonial state's drive to encourage individual industry and professional education, and its consequences in fostering new kinds of mobility and accumulated social advantage within smaller family groups. There were, of course, deep contradictions. As is well known, the great majority of leading reformers, like Lokahitawadi himself, struggled to move away from older caste and gender norms in their personal lives.[113] Nonetheless, the language itself of liberal Brahman modernity, and its transmutation into educated scribal merit, was constructed out of rhetorical rejection of traditional Brahman learning, just at the moment when the latter seemed to be weakening in its claims to official support.[114]

Brahman Histories in the Vernacular Sphere

As is well known, the arrival in India of the theory of an "Aryan invasion" marked a very significant shift in debates about caste. Most intellectuals, nationalists, and social reformers across the subcontinent accepted the case for an ancient Indo-Aryan family of languages, but diverged significantly in what they saw as the implications of the theory itself. They also differed in their vision of the social order that

[112] Deshpande, "Pune: An Emerging Center", pp. 74–8; Naregal, *Language Politics*, pp. 80–91.

[113] Apte, "Lokahitavadi", p. 206; Keer, *Mahatma Jotirao Phooley*, pp. 126–8.

[114] For the growth of a middle class in colonial India, see Joshi, *The Middle Class*, and idem, *Fractured Modernity*.

might emerge with a revival of this golden age: what shape Hindu religious culture and communal relations might take in such an order, its implications for caste and gender norms, and whether Brahmans would have a distinctive leadership role within it.[115]

As Madhav Deshpande has shown, contemporary attitudes and values shaped arguments in Maharashtra about an ancient Aryan migration and the possibility of a restored Vedic society. The ideas were flexible enough to appeal to a social reformer like Vishnusastri Pandit (1827–1876), the great advocate of widow remarriage, for whom the gender equality he perceived in "Aryan" culture represented a powerful argument for the rights of women in his own day.[116] But it could also appeal to social conservatives like the Pune schoolteacher M.M. Kunte (1835–1888), who viewed the Aryan presence as a superior civilisation established over that of the non-Aryan indigenes.[117]

For other intellectuals, what mattered was what they saw as Maharashtra's distinctive blending of Aryan and Dravidian influences. The distinguished philologist R.G. Bhandarkar (1837–1925), and historian and judge M.G. Ranade, had very different scholarly interests, but both laid great emphasis on this blending. For both, therefore, the boundaries between "Aryans" and "Sudras" had actually long been permeable, making the modern order of caste itself essentially a social construct. They were also early members of the theistic and bhakti-oriented Prarthana Samaj. Both drew their personal religious orientation from the Samaj's "Hindu Protestantism", as Ranade termed it, seeing in it a modern rendering of the shared culture of bhakti which had also given the region its distinctive social cohesion.[118]

Much more consciously egalitarian in his social thinking, the scholar Rajaramsastri Bhagwat (1851–1908) was connected with the Samaj through his brother, Bhaskar Hari, though not himself a member. His linguistic and sociological researches suggested that there were actually few traces of any "Aryan" past in Maharashtra, its language and

[115] Deshpande, "Aryan Origins"; Thapar, "The Theory of Aryan Race".

[116] Pise, "Viṣṇu Paraśurām Śāstrī Paṇḍit, ch. 5, pp. 12–13.

[117] Deshpande, "Aryan Origins", pp. 414–19.

[118] Bhandarkar, *Vaiṣṇavism*, pp. 87–99, and idem, "Social History of India", pp. 4–15; Dandekar, "Ramakrishna Gopal Bhandarkar"; Naik, "Social Composition", pp. 502–3; Ranade, *Religious and Social Reform*, pp. 197–228; Devare, "M.G. Ranade and Bhakti".

religious culture owing far more to the Dravidian influences of the South. He too saw Maharashtra's social unity as derived from the culture of its bhakti saints, but believed this culture to embody older spiritual principles embodied in the Vedas and the Upanishads, from which he drew his own faith. This led him to make a fundamental distinction between two kinds of religiosity. These were what he called brāhmaya or brāhmaṇi dharma, the widely shared non-dualist philosophy which was Maharashtra's most precious inheritance from the bhakti saints, and the religious culture of what he described as the karmaṭh or orthodox Brahman, hidebound by ritual and obsessed by differences of caste.[119]

Early non-Brahman intellectuals were particularly quick off the mark to see the Aryan theory's potential for their own political purposes. Under the pen-name "A Hindu", the merchant Tukaram Tatya Padwal (1836–1898), Phule's friend and business colleague, brought out his *Jātibhed Vivekasār* (Reflections on Caste Divisions) in Bombay. A revised and expanded version was published in 1865, naming Phule as the publisher.[120] Padwal's work made the critical connections that were to become such a familiar part of non-Brahman ideology: that an ancient "Aryan people" had imposed their rule on India, oppressed and exploited its indigenous inhabitants, and termed them "Sudras", meaning "menial", as a permanent marker of their inferiority.[121]

Within this framework, Padwal's book offered a wide-ranging critique of Brahman privilege. He repeated the *Sahyādrikhaṇḍa*'s stories of the tainted origins of many Brahman communities. He deprecated the illusions of prestige that caste encouraged amongst the many other communities aiming to raise their status. "The Rajputs say, we are Kshatriyas, the Marathas say, we are Kshatriyas, thc Prabhus say, we are Kshatriyas, the Panchakalshes, the Vadavals, the Sutars all say, we are Somavanshi Kshatriyas, the Khatris say, we are Kshatriyas." Others insisted that they belonged to the Vaishya varna, putting on the

[119] Bhagwat, *Rājārāmaśāstrī Bhāgavat*, pp. 14–15; Bhagwat, "Brāhmaṇ va Brāhmaṇi Dharma", pp. 160–1. See also the discussion in Keune, "Eknāth Remembered and Reformed", pp. 225–33.

[120] Padwal, *Jātibhed Vivekasār*, pp. 1–2. For Padwal's work, see in particular Jaywant, "Reshaping the Figure of the Shudra", and idem, "Secularizing Caste" for Satyashodhak politics in the age of vernacular print.

[121] Padwal, *Jātibhed Vivekasār*, pp. 24–5.

sacred thread and taking it off as they liked. The practice had even spread as far as simple Kunbi farmers "who call themselves Kshatriya Marathas, and put on a great big thick cotton thread like the Brahmans, so long that it reaches right down their legs."[122]

The real position, Padwal concluded, was that over time all castes had intermingled. Caste and varna were not immutable but represented, rather, the slow fossilisation of what had once been a simple division of labour. Driving home his argument with liberal quotations from a remarkably wide range of Sanskrit authorities, including the *Sahyādrikhaṇḍa* and Kamalakarabhatta's *Śūdrakamalākaraḥ*, he suggested that all of India's inhabitants, even Brahmans, were now of mixed parentage.[123] As Ketaki Jaywant has put it, Padwal's analysis made a critical shift. Sudra identity was not a consequence of ancient karmic sin. It was rather the original term that Aryan Brahmans had applied to their oppressed victims, designating them as essentially menial, and concealing their own heterogeneous descent.[124]

An important question for us to ask here is how far the elite non-Brahman disputes of the 1820s, and particularly their strong objection to the status of Sudra, may have shaped these perspectives of the 1860s. Padwal's intense aversion to pride in caste meant that his starting points clearly differed from those of elite non-Brahmans in the 1820s. But what he did share in common with them, and the wide range of caste communities that he observed seeking to move their varna classification upwards, was a particular sensitivity to the associations attached to being classified as a Sudra. He laid a marked emphasis on the degrading character of this classification: "So these days, there are many jatis who are counted as Sudras. Their origin is probably to do with the mixing up of varnas. Amongst them are many jatis who came originally from Kshatriyas, Vaishyas and Brahmans. When their miserable condition forced them into very menial occupations, then they were made into Sudras."[125]

For the elite non-Brahmans of the 1820s, the aversion to the term arose out of their existing high social status, and the manner in which their defeat at the hands of Nilakantha and his group had come about.

[122] Ibid., pp. 34–5.
[123] Ibid., pp. 136–58.
[124] Jaywant, "Re-shaping the Figure of the Shudra", pp. 401–3.
[125] Ibid., p. 58.

For non-Brahmans mid-century, a range of colonial developments further intensified the sense that a single global meaning of degraded status attached to the category of Sudra. As Chakravorty has argued, the early decades of the nineteenth century saw selected and convenient Brahman-Sanskrit texts elevated into canonical status. Such texts were often those, such as the Manusmṛti, which offered a schematic understanding of Hindu society as composed of a rigid caste order, with Sudras as a despised stratum at the bottom. Missionary interventions sometimes made the same argument, particularly in the context of the Aryan Invasion theory. The Scottish missionary and educator John Wilson, whom Phule quoted in his own work, referred to Sudras as "the enslaved and servile classes of the country conquered by the Aryas." As Rao has suggested, the education policy of the Bombay government, with its exclusion of Dalit and "low-caste" children from government schools until later in the century, reinforced the same sense.[126]

It is clear that Brahman conservatives were also sharply aware of these very negative connotations and sought to ameliorate them. In 1861, the year in which Padwal brought out the first edition of his book, two Bombay sastris, the Chitpavans Ganesh Bapuji Malvankar and Vishnu Bapuji Bapat brought out the first lithograph edition of the *Śūdrākamalākaraḥ* in Bombay. Padwal himself had cited this text several times. The sastris' preface to the work, and its colophon, described their purpose: "For some time now, some of the dharmasastras have been printed and published as books. But those books do not treat the saṃskāras and other rituals of Sudras separately in the way they do for Brahmans. So no-one has paid them any particular attention." But it was important that people should know about these ritual entitlements, the editors suggested, because they were much more generous than people seemed to think.

> Knowing that people believe mistakenly that Sudras are not eligible for these rituals, Kamalakarabhatta prepared his book the *Śūdrakamalākaraḥ*. He prepared another great work of dharmasastra, the *Nirṇayasindhuḥ*, which is famous everywhere and very useful to people. It has been

[126] Chakravorthy, *The Truth About Us*, ch. 4; Wilson, *India Three Thousand Years Ago*, p. 56; Phule, *Sārvajanik Satya Dharma Pustak*, p. 486; Rao, "Colonial State as 'New Manu'".

> printed. Similarly, the *Śūdrakamalākaraḥ* can be a very useful book for people, and with its support, Sudras can have all of their proper rituals, but it has not yet been published.

Readers, they said, would find in the book information about all of the ceremonies appropriate to each of the four varnas, so "it would be very proper if everyone acquired this book." They added, "We have set the trade price of this book at one and a half rupees, so everyone will be able to get it."[127]

Remarkably, and in a testament to the enduring conservative legacy of Nilakanthasastri Thatthe, it had been to his family library that the sastris had turned for their manuscript copy of the *Śūdrakamālakaraḥ*. They described their great labours in preparing the lithograph: "So that this book would be a good and accurate copy, we took great pains and brought very old and accurate copies from the houses of the late Nilakanthasastri Thatthe and Tryambaksastri Baba Shaligram, and scrutinised them carefully."

As noted above, Tryambaksastri was himself also a member of Nilakantha's intellectual lineage, and went on to employment in the Poona Hindoo College. Maratha scholar families were extremely protective of their manuscript libraries during the later nineteenth century, granting access only rarely and reluctantly to visitors from outside their immediate circles.[128] That Malvankar and Bapat were granted such permission suggests their close relationship with the Thatthe family.

In bringing out the book, therefore, the sastris hoped to counter the particularly negative associations the category of Sudra had acquired. They sought to reassure those so designated that it carried entitlements to the dignified rituals, including twelve saṃskāras for Sudras of respectable descent, described in their purchased copy of the *Śūdrākamalākaraḥ*.[129] It may also be that Malvankar hoped with this gesture to present himself as an impeccably orthodox Chitpavan in the tradition of Nilakantha himself. Bringing out a commercially attractive printed edition with manuscripts from the library of the great scholar

[127] Kamalakarabhatta, *Śūdrākamalākaraḥ*, pp. 2–3.

[128] Minkowski, *Sanskrit Scientific Libraries*, pp. 87–93.

[129] Kamalakarabhatta, *Śūdrakamalākaraḥ*, pp. 14–15.

might enable him to appeal to a conservative Hindu audience that did not question their Sudra status but welcomed the more generous view of their rights correctly put forward by Kamalakarabhatta. But for the emerging community of non-Brahman intellectuals and activists like Padwal, the status of Sudra was now irredeemably menial. What Malvankar's work may really reveal is just how out of touch he was with this developing sentiment.

"Enterprising Men, and Gifted with Intelligence": Shenvi Saraswats in the Age of Vernacular Print

Malvankar's role here, and that of the remarkable group of Chitpavan intellectuals, journalists, jurists, and publicists who were to inspire a new nationalist vision from the early 1870s, raises the wider question as to whether we can speak of a distinctive Chitpavan political-cultural leadership. The long history of colonial stereotypes about Chitpavans makes this a difficult question.[130] Malvankar's own identity as a Chitpavan came to the fore again in 1868, when Bombay's Chitpavan orthodox came into conflict with the city's Shenvi Saraswat reformers. The conflict followed local-level clashes during the 1850s between Chitpavan and Shenvi Saraswat families over the latter's alleged status as lesser, "trikarmī", Brahmans.[131]

At issue in 1868 was the campaign launched by Vishnusastri Pandit and M.G. Ranade in support of the rights of Hindu widows, particularly Brahman widows, to remarry. In response, the Bombay orthodox formed the Society for the Protection of Hindu Dharma. Vithoba Anna Daftardar, scholar of Vedantic poetry whose family had been officials at the Pune court, took the lead, but Malvankar was also a prominent member. In June 1868, Bal Mangesh Wagle, an accomplished Shenvi

[130] For Chitpavan communities, see Chapekar, *Chitpāvan*; Johnson, "Chitpavan Brahmins"; Patterson, "Changing Patterns"; Gokhale, *The Chitpavans*. For colonial stereotypes, see Cashman, *The Myth of the Lokamanya*, pp. 17–44.

[131] Padwal, *Jātibhed Vivekasār*, p. 144; Kanavinde, *Sārasvat Brāhmaṇ*, pp. 102–10; Gunjikar, *Sarasvatīmaṇḍal*, p. 47. For broader studies of the community, see Wagle, "History and Social Organisation"; Conlon, *A Caste in a Changing World*.

Saraswat lawyer and member of the reformist Prarthana Samaj, attempted to gain entry to the Society's meeting. Malvankar refused him entrance on the grounds that the meeting was for Brahmans only. A scuffle ensued and Malvankar made a formal complaint for criminal assault.[132]

The lengthy trial that followed rehearsed all the arguments about Shenvi Saraswats' Brahmanhood. This included the distinction, which Malvankar set out in his deposition, between "ṣaṭkarmī" and "trikarmī" Brahmans. At the end of the hearing, the British magistrate ruled that, as a Shenvi Saraswat, Wagle was in common sense a Brahman, and so no offence had been committed. The case sparked off heated arguments in the press. To defend the Shenvi Saraswat position, and demonstrate the community's continued harassment by Chitpavan Brahmans, the Shenvi Saraswat journalist Bhavani Vishvanath Kanavinde collected and published the correspondence.[133]

Urmila Patil suggests that we might see Malvankar's defence of orthodoxy as a "Chitpavan" initiative, but without falling into essentialisation. She argues that the debate shows Chitpavan intellectuals like Malvankar pushing a definition of Brahmanhood itself as the essence of religious orthodoxy, and its particular characteristic a highly developed Sanskrit intellectualism. On this view, authentic Hindu tradition itself was founded in the Sanskrit discourse of the sastras. Chitpavans were simply, as its foremost defenders, carrying forward the beacon of true dharma as their forefathers had done before them.[134] As we have seen, some Chitpavans saw other ways, particularly in the culture of bhakti, of thinking about their identity as Brahmans and its connection with Hindu religious norms. But for the majority, Patil suggests, the orthodox definition did more to affirm their sense of the community's worth.

Patil's perspective certainly helps makes sense of the clash between Chitpavans and Shenvi Saraswats, and the latter's strategy in

[132] Nadkarni, *A Short History*, p. 147; Tucker, "Hindu Traditionalism", pp. 340–1.

[133] Kanavinde, *Sārasvat Brāhmaṇ*, pp. 7–11. Kanavinde was an Anglophone scholar and student of German literature: Ranade, *Miscellaneous Writings*, p. 14. For the dispute, see Kolhatkar, "Widow Re-marriage".

[134] Patil, "Conflict, Identity and Narratives", pp. 225–7, 356–8.

fighting off the challenge to their Brahman identity. Whilst they emphasised their capability in questions about dharmasastra, they emphasised more strongly their competence in the arena of vernacular print, their understanding of the proper etiquette in public debate, the dignity of the professions through which they preferred to earn their living, and their moral superiority over those who pursued backward-looking caste quarrels. This represented, of course, a deep contradiction, albeit of a different kind from that noted above in the case of Anglophone social reformers. For all that Kanavinde and other Shenvi Saraswats were defending their position as prestigious "ṣaṭ-karmī" Brahmans, they were doing so essentially in the "uncasted" language of modern professional competence.[135]

Many of the issues discussed continued the older arguments about Shenvi Saraswats. Where, Kanavinde asked in the first of an exchange of letters with Malvankar, was the textual evidence that Chitpavans were the gurus of his Saraswat community, or that the Saraswats' fish-eating made the Chitpavans superior to them? How could it be argued that Saraswats' exclusion from relations of marriage and commensality made them inferior, when many Chitpavan and Deshastha families likewise excluded each other?[136] Some part of this friction clearly emerged from the proposal to establish a school in Bombay where Shenvi Saraswat boys would be trained as priests, able to minister to their own communities in the manner that Chitpavan priests had refused to do. Writing to the *Vartamān Dīpika* of 20 November 1869, "Vishvanath" even suggested that the new Shenvi Saraswat priests could minister to the Chitpavan community.[137]

The older networks of Brahman assemblies worked effectively in this newspaper setting. Some editors adapted consciously to the "modern" conventions of periodical print: that letters should be signed and dated, their arguments clear, the correspondence not indefinite or vexatious, and proof offered of the authenticity of any documents referred to. A "Gauda Brahman" sent in to the *Indu Prakash* of 9 August 1870 what was said to be a copy of a sammatipatra issued by Banaras

[135] For Saraswat middle-class identity in colonial Bombay, see Kidambi, "Consumption, Domestic Economy and the Idea of the 'Middle Class'".

[136] Kanavinde, *Sārasvat Brāhmaṇ*, p. 31.

[137] Ibid., p. 83.

pandits in 1851, declaring Shenvi Saraswats to be impeccable "ṣaṭ-karmī" Brahmans. The newspaper published it, along with an assurance that Kanavinde would publish the original in full in his forthcoming book.[138] The attachment of names to letters became a sign of modern practice. Vireshwar Chatre, editor of the Baroda-based *Sudnyān Bodhak*, reproached a correspondent who had simply signed himself "Ksh". "This is the city of Bombay. Rather than going in for such antics, the letter writer should publish his name openly."[139]

What particularly inflamed the controversy was the entry into it of Padwal's *Jātibhed Vivekasār*, with its Marathi translations of passages from the *Sahyādrikhaṇḍa* about tainted Brahman origins. Remarkably, in a letter of 1 August 1869 to the *Mitrodaya*, Kanavinde protested that Malvankar had ignored his private letters in defence of the Shenvi Saraswat case. Instead, Malvankar had merely sent him a copy of Padwal's book, with the disparaging passages about Shenvi Saraswats marked with slips of paper.[140] Kanavinde took Malvankar to task for this breach of decorum: "You are a leading orator at the Hindu Dharma Sabha. It follows that you must be a very learned man. But it is a dharma of the learned that they should offer proper proof of what they are saying."[141]

Madhava's *Śatapraśnakalpalatā* also reappeared in these furious exchanges. Clearly impressed by the impact of Padwal's printing of Marathi translations of passages from the *Sahyādrihaṇḍa*, Kanavinde went a step further. He incorporated into his book some of the most scurrilous passages about Chitpavans, Karhades, and Devrukhes from the manuscript of Madhava's work, with Marathi translations arranged alongside the Sanskrit. Lest readers from these communities take offence, he pointed out: "This is the book that the Chitpavan Bhats and other Brahmans greeted with such excitement as an authority on the Saraswat community. But what can we say – when they brought this book to public attention, they can't have looked at what it said about themselves."[142]

[138] Ibid., pp. 25–7.
[139] Ibid., p. 35.
[140] Ibid., pp. 16–18, 25.
[141] Ibid., p. 24.
[142] Ibid., pp. 162, 163–79.

Alongside these extracts, Kanavinde published some well-known anti-Chitpavan passages from colonial sources. From Hamilton's *Description of Hindostan*, published in 1820, he took the account of the last Peshwa Bajirao II: "Although his family is Brahminical, yet not being of the *highest order* the purer classes of Brahmins *refuse to eat with them*, and at Nassick, a place of pilgrimage near the source of the Godavery, he was not allowed to descend by the same flight of steps used by the holy priests."[143]

Kanavinde and his colleagues challenged their Chitpavan adversaries in other ways. He explained that few of his community historically had chosen priesthood, from their dislike of what they regarded as demeaning religious beggary: "Most of the Shenvi Brahmans, being enterprising men and gifted with intelligence, have from a long time, thought it proper to maintain themselves by actions preferable to mere preaching and begging."[144] An exchange between "a Ratnagiri Konkanastha" and "a Ratnagiri Saraswat", published in Kanavinde's own *Vartamān Dīpika* of 9 October 1689, disputed what constituted true Brahman scholarship. The former disparaged the work of Shenvi Saraswats as mere derivative commentary. But in fact, the "Ratnagiri Saraswat" pointed out, the scholars most commonly acknowledged as leading authorities – pandits such as Banaras' Kamalakarabhatta – were in truth writers of commentaries.[145] Kanavinde thus defined a modern Brahman as a man of public affairs, at home with the modern world of print but also knowledgeable about the sastras, with the full dignity of Brahman ritual personally available to him but very much above seeking to earn his living through it.

Other Shenvi Saraswats sought to associate themselves with this image of modern professional expertise in slightly different ways. In 1877 the prominent Orientalist scholar J. Gerson da Cunha (1844–1901) brought out what he presented as a work of modern scholarship, a full critical edition of the *Sahyādrikhaṇḍa*, based on the collation of fourteen different versions of the manuscript collected from across India.[146] The journalist Ramchandra Bhikaji Gunjikar (1843–1901),

[143] Ibid., pp. 120–1.
[144] Ibid., pp. 121–2.
[145] Ibid., pp. 151–3.
[146] da Cunha, *The Sahyādri-Khaṇḍa*, pp. 1–3.

founder in 1867 of the *Vividh Dnyān Vistār* newspaper, and author of Marathi's first historical novel *Mochangaḍ*, published a quasi-sociological survey of all Maratha Brahman communities.[147] His *Sarasvatīmaṇḍaḷ*, published in 1884, strove for the appearance of a modern approach, including practical information about trades and professions, distinctive marks of language, food habits, religious practice, and places of settlement. Like Kanavinde's, however, his account of Shenvi Saraswats consisted in the main of a defence against their critics.[148]

Not surprisingly, this deeply contradictory position attracted criticism from contemporary Brahman reformers hostile to all forms of Brahman pride in caste. Rajaramsastri Bhagwat, whose aversion to ideas of a superior Aryan culture we have seen above, took issue with Gunjikar on this point. His *Jaśās Tase* (Tit for Tat), published in 1885, reproached Gunjikar for his obsession with caste and for the Saraswat fixation on the *Sahyādrikhaṇḍa*, "as if it was the Veda itself."[149] His approach to the vexed question of the modern varna order also reflected his sensitivity to its intensely divisive nature. In his *Marhāṭhyāsambandhāne Chār Udgār* (A few remarks about the Marathas), published in 1887, he urged his fellow Brahmans to accord Vedic ritual entitlements to the region's elite Maratha families: "If Brahmans wish to remain the religious leaders, then they should first of all stop belittling the Kshatriyas of Maharashtra."[150]

This reformist Brahman rejection of rivalries among Brahman subcastes also emerged in the work of the campaigner for widow remarriage, Vishnusastri Pandit. Leaders from the Devarukhe community had approached him in the early 1870s. They asked for his help in showing that other Brahmans' disdainful treatment of them had no basis. In making his case that Devrukhes were Brahmans of good repute, Vishnusastri also gave most weight to the very long list of successful professionals who could be named in the community: men in

[147] Bhate, *History*, p. 121.

[148] Gunjikar, *Sarasvatīmaṇḍaḷ*. For an alternative, essentially sastric riposte to the Chitpavan challenge, see Patil, "Conflict, Identity and Narratives", pp. 308–61.

[149] Bhagwat, *Jśās Tase*, p. 16.

[150] Bhagwat, *Marhāṭhyāsambandhāne Chār Udgār*, pp. 181–2.

government service, court vakils, men working in collectors' offices, registrars, revenue surveyors, mamledars, chief constables of police, railway clerks, schoolteachers, accountants, clerks in the government press, staff members in the Public Works and Revenue and Customs departments. It was these professional and clerical workers, "many men in service, of weight and authority", that he adduced most strongly in support of the Devarukhes' standing as respectable Brahmans.[151]

The real problem for the Devarukhes, he explained, lay in Brahman caste feuding: "Every small Brahman community considers itself more excellent than others, looks down on its neighbours, and so spreads malice towards each other, in a manner which simply does not happen among castes in other varnas."[152] He finished his book with an appeal to Hindus' common Aryan identity, and the special place of Brahmans within it. He urged all Brahmans who were in the habit of disparaging the Devarukhes: "So take your Aryan body which is the soul of the four varnas, which your thoughtlessness has wounded to the quick, and work together to restore its limbs to strength. This is the absolute duty of all Aryan sons."[153] Vishnusastri was prescient here. As we will see, this theme of Brahman solidarity was to become increasingly important from the last decade of the century.

The arguments of Kanavinde and his Shenvi Saraswat supporters, as well as those that Vishnusastri put forward in defence of the Devarukhes, reveal the complex interplay between caste and class noted above in the language of the Anglophone reformers. They sought to counter the Chitpavan-led challenge to their standing as Brahmans by identifying themselves as modern professionals, at home equally in the worlds of vernacular print, contemporary sociological scholarship, and salaried administration in the colonial state. In doing so, what was effectively a language of class enabled them to denigrate the Chitpavan critique by associating it with regressive forms of casteist feuding. For Chitpavans like Malvankar – editor of an authoritative printed edition of the *Śūdrākamalākaraḥ*, vehement defender of the chastity of Hindu widows, and protagonist of a narrow scriptural defini-

[151] Pandit, *Devarūkhyāviṣayī Śāstrasamat Vichār*, pp. 9–17.
[152] Ibid., p. 1.
[153] Ibid., pp. 58–9.

tion of what made a Brahman – the thing that mattered was the defining of Brahmanhood itself in terms of Sanskrit scriptural orthodoxy, and of Chitpavans as the foremost defenders of that orthodoxy.

"The Fearless Speech of the Critic": Chiplunkar and the Satyashodhaks

These arguments about what made a Brahman took place in a very rapidly changing social and political milieu. Drought, famine, agrarian riots, and the political crisis of 1879–80 seemed to point up many of the inadequacies of M.G. Ranade's moderate style of nationalist campaigning associated with the Sarvajanik Sabha, founded in 1870.[154] The critique came from Tilak, Chiplunkar, and their new generation of largely Chitpavan and much more uncompromising nationalist leaders. For them, Indian subjection to colonial control took intellectual and psychological forms that were as important to break as the political and law-enforcement institutions of rule. From the early 1880s, assaults on the Sabha also came from non-Brahman critics who saw its largely Brahman members as ignorant of the poverty, dirt, and misery in which most poor farming households actually lived.[155]

This was the setting in which the well-known rupture between Maharashtra's political "moderates" and "extremists" first began to appear.[156] However, the real signal of change came in the 1870s rather than in the last decade of the century. Vishnusastri Chiplunkar started to publish his journal *Nibandhamālā* early in 1874. With its extraordinary literary and intellectual range, its scathing critique of the colonial state, its ferocious defence of many Hindu social institutions, and its hostility to non-Brahman political assertion, Chiplunkar's Marathi journalism transformed the region's political landscape.[157] Interestingly, there were pedagogical connections, through Vishnusastri's father, with Nilakanthasastri Thatthe. The distinguished scholar

[154] Tucker, "The Proper Limits of Agitation".

[155] For Ranade and Phule on this question, see Sturman, *The Government of Social Life*, pp. 85–92.

[156] For a recent account, see Oak, "Political Ideas of B.G. Tilak", pp. 145–69.

[157] For an overview, see Deshpande, *Creative Pasts*, pp. 100–4; Naregal, *Language Politics*, pp. 250–62.

and journalist Krishnasastri Chiplunkar, later to become head of Pune's Teacher Training College, was tutored at the Pune Sanskrit College by Morsastri Sathe, whom we saw above as cousin to Nilakantha and father of his adopted son. The young Krishnasastri so impressed Morsastri with his ability in Sanskrit that Morsastri nicknamed him "Brihaspati" – teacher to the gods and master of all wisdom.[158]

In proposing a new kind of Brahman nationalist leadership grounded in deep appreciation of past Brahman achievements in politics and culture, but cut free from outmoded beliefs and practices, Chiplunkar found his principal readership amongst lower-middle-class consumers of Marathi periodical print.[159] Many were Brahmans working in petty service roles in administration or small private commercial ventures. Their clerical livelihoods often held out limited prospects. They were often sharply aware of the indignity of working within a colonial establishment that privileged Anglophone expertise over their own vernacular experience. Many were also stung by non-Brahman attacks. These, of course, were the audiences that Lokamanya Tilak was to mobilise with such spectacular success from the 1880s and after.

Chiplunkar found many targets of attack in Marathi political culture. But he reserved his most savage ridicule for the writing of Jotirao Phule and others associated with the non-Brahman movement. His antagonism to lower-caste political aspiration and disdain for the literary efforts of "Sudras" emerged most sharply in his reviews of their work, published in *Nibandhamālā* in 1877.[160] Phule's *Gulāmgirī* ("Slavery"), published in 1873, drew his particular scorn. As Vendell has suggested, Phule aimed to present an imagined history for Maharashtra's popular classes that would serve as the basis for political solidarity in the present.[161] For Chiplunkar, however, Phule's literary effort was a preposterous attempt to run through millennia of history in a single work which mixed up chronologies in an absurd way and imputed nonsensical new meanings to well-known vernacular words.

[158] Deshpande, "Pune: An Emerging Center", p. 82.

[159] Deshpande, *Creative Pasts*, pp. 112–13.

[160] For Chiplunkar's attack on Phule, see also Naregal, *Language Politics*, pp. 255–8.

[161] Vendell, "Phule's Satyashodh".

Much of his review was laden with sarcasm. He ridiculed Phule's attempt at a broad historical sweep: "In his book *Gulāmgirī*, this great pandit has been able to throw together everything from heaven to hell! Wherever we look, our eyes are absolutely dazzled by the light of this flame 'Jyoti'."[162] His attempt to find new meanings for old words was also nonsensical:

> Looking at his knowledge of etymology, we would have to say that we have had Panini, Bhattoji and other grammarians, and in Europe Max Müller and others send their grammatical works to us, but he outdoes them all! In his *Gulāmgirī*, Jotiba gives derivations for words like "dvija", "Brahman", "vipra", "Sanskrt", "Martanḍ", and so on, that even Paṇini's great-grandfather would never have dreamed of![163]

But the most striking theme in Chiplunkar's critique lay in his derision of Phule's learning as the work of a Sudra, intended for other Sudras. He described the great weight of supporting research which had gone into Gibbon's writing, and compared it with Phule's brief composition: "Look at our Sudra historian! He has written such an elegant history that there is no evidence to support it at all!"[164] As for Phule's aim to free his Sudra countrymen from manipulation by Brahman-authored books, "No-one has ever heard of a Sudra sastri knowledgeable enough to understand such books. So, how on earth is someone who can't tell the beginning from the end of these so-called 'fraudulent' books, to teach anything about them to the so-called pandits Tukoba, Sadoba, Mankoba of the 'wise Sudra circle' in his hare-brained society?"[165]

Towards the end of 1877, Chiplunkar broadened his attack to the new *Dīn Bandhu* of Phule's colleague Krishnarao Bhalekar, and to Padwal's *Jātibhed Vivekasār*. He emphasised that his quarrel was not with "our poor Sudra brothers, who are still ignorant and easily deceived", but rather with the self-styled teachers who were leading them astray.[166] He mocked the way in which Phule, Padwal and others had tried to turn puranic works back against the Brahmans whose history they narrated:

[162] Ibid., p. 444.
[163] Ibid., pp. 444–5.
[164] Ibid., p. 448.
[165] Ibid., p. 452.
[166] Chiplunkar, *Nibandhamālā*, Year 4, no. 48, 1877, in vol. 2, p. 1019.

> Our Sudra protagonist has undergone much labour churning through such great books as the *Sahyādrikhaṇḍa* and the *Jotibā Khaṇḍa*, and made a great show of his learning, and sits fussing away about whether these Brahmaṇas are of a higher rank, and these of a lower rank. This is all pointless. Leaving aside this stupid pursuit, our Sudra hero should always remember that whether the Chitpāvanas were raised up out of a funeral pyre, or came from Iran, still any number of *Gulāmgirīs* or *Jātibhedasāras* won't equal the qualities they showed then, and still do today.[167]

The fact was, Chiplunkar asserted, Chitpavan force of arms had conquered the whole of Hindustan in the last century, and the community still possessed their extraordinary abilities. He concluded with a message to "our young Sudra brothers":

> Our suggestion to Mr Phule is that if he thinks it is his duty to improve the lot of his caste brothers, it will never happen by him writing books like *Gulāmgirī* and cursing those who are in every respect better than him. However much the Brāhmaṇas may be liars, and however bad, yet one thing is undeniable: tied to their waists, they carry the keys to the treasure-house of knowledge. There is no way for other castes to improve without their help.[168]

There was undoubtedly a personal context to these angry exchanges. In *Gulāmgirī*, Phule had attacked Vishnusastri's father Krishnasastri in his role as secretary of the Dakshina Prize Committee. He had suggested that the Committee's work lacked any real educational seriousness, given that the whole Education Department was dominated by Brahmans. Indeed, echoing Morsastri Sathe's epithet "Brihaspati" for his favourite student, Phule mocked Krishnasastri as "the great Brihaspati".[169]

It is unlikely that Phule and his colleagues were particularly surprised by Chiplunkar's attack, given their own willingness to trade blows with the orthodox. Even given this history, Chiplunkar's derisive dismissal of Phule's work as that of a Sudra stands out as an example of casteist bravado that was very much an exception in the *Nibandhamālā*. It also conflicted with his own professed belief that what

[167] Ibid., p. 1023.
[168] Ibid., p. 1024.
[169] Phule, *Gulāmgirī*, p. 180.

made a good literary critic was a fearless engagement with the text, but also a peaceable disposition and sympathetic approach.[170]

As we have seen above, the categorisation of "Sudra" had by mid-century come to suggest not just public inferiority but active stigmatisation. When used, as Chiplunkar did, with the very obvious intention to demean, the term became additionally objectionable. Unsurprisingly, resentment at the term and the history it carried continued to attract non-Brahman hostility in the 1880s and after. This hostility was to find further expression in the Kolhapur Vedokta controversy of 1899–1903. In 1899, it came to light that Narayanrao Rajopadhye, hereditary family priest to the Kolhapur Raja Shahu (1874–1922), was using puranic mantras for his personal rituals, on the grounds that he was not a Kshatriya but a Sudra.[171] The dispute that followed bore many parallels with Pratapsinh's contest with Nilakantha's orthodox group back in the 1820s.

The context, of course, was very different. Shahu had considerable latitude to act against his Brahman opponents, dismissing Narayanrao Rajopadhye for his insistence that Sudra ritual was appropriate, and threatening to confiscate the estates that came with his royal office. His co-operation with the colonial suppression of "extremist" political organising in the state made Kolhapur, and the Vedokta issue, a focus for conservative nationalist campaigning. Dismissal of non-Brahman concerns was therefore commonplace in the conservative press. In August 1900, in his newspaper *Samartha*, Vishnu Govind Vijapurkar wrote slightingly about Shahu's insistence on Vedic rituals for his family, and in his journal *Granthamālā* repeated the story about the misfortunes that befell Gagabhatta after his consecration of Chhatrapati Shivaji.[172]

In October 1901, Tilak's *Kesarī* also deprecated the Maratha concerns as a passing conceit, and the Maratha families who cherished them as much diminished in courage and patriotism compared to

[170] Chiplunkar, *Nibandhamālā*, Year 3, no. 15, 1877, in vol. 1, pp. 352–72.

[171] For this controversy, see Keer, *Shahu Chhatrapati*, pp. 77–98; Copland, "The Maharaja of Kolhapur".

[172] Keer, *Shahu Chhatrapati*, pp. 84–5; Kanade, *Gurūvarya Pro. Viṣṇu Govind Vijāpūrkar*, pp. 35–6; Sarwate, "Reimagining the Modern Hindu Self", pp. 85–95.

their great ancestor Shivaji. "Famous and universally respected authorities" had concluded that Kshatriyas and Vaishyas had disappeared from the world in the modern age.[173] Writing in the *Viśvavṛitta*, the conservative historian V.K. Rajwade also regretted the non-Brahman resurrection of this ancient dispute at a time when all India was focused on the Swadeshi movement.[174] Although the political context was so different, it seems remarkable how little these core conservative beliefs about the varna order had changed since the 1820s.

Conclusion: Coming Home to the Family

As Sarwate has argued, the Kolhapur Vedokta dispute marked a turning point in the history of Maharashtra's caste politics. The 1920s saw a renewed wave of polemical attacks on Brahmans as the Marathi press reached broader audiences, and non-Brahman polemicists turned to provocative images of the body and sexuality in their mockery of Brahmans. At the same time, the Kolhapur focus on Vedic ritual laid the foundation for non-Brahman articulations of a unified Hinduism which came close to the Hindutva visions of Savarkar. Gandhi's capture of the Congress and the fracturing of other parties in the Bombay Presidency also prompted new questions about Brahman political leadership.[175] Neither the model of Brahman orthodoxy associated with Tilakite politics, nor the bhakti-tempered reformism of Ranade, Bhandarkar, and Bhagwat, nor the Saraswat emphasis on the Brahman as a modern man of public affairs seemed an adequate response to a newly energised Hindu nationalism with emerging counterparts in many regions of India.

The search for a strategy took many forms over the interwar decades. Some intellectuals, such as Mahadevsastri Divekar and Laxmansastri Joshi – associated with the Pradnya Pathshala in the shrine town of Wai near Pune – explored ways in which traditional concepts

[173] Tilak, "Marāṭhe āni Vedokta Karma".

[174] *Viśvavṛitta*, May 1906, cited in Sangave and Khane, *Rajarshi Shahu Chhatrapati Papers*, vol. 3, pp. 352–6.

[175] Sarwate, "Reimagining the Modern Hindu Self", pp. 14–84. For a recent analysis of Tilak's last years in politics, see Oak, "Political Ideas of B.G. Tilak", pp. 208–247.

of Hindu dharma could be reshaped to promote Hindu and Indian national unity.[176] Others, like Keshav Baliram Hedgewar, founder in 1925 of the Rashtriya Swayamsevak Sangh, looked to develop a distinctive Maharashtrian approach to Hindu self-strengthening and personal discipline. As Jaffrelot has observed, the Sangh's first generation of "sadhu" volunteers were almost all middle-class Maratha Brahmans, attracted by its combination of traditional Brahmanical and martial values.[177] Others again, like the Gandhian Vinoba Bhave, another graduate of the Pradnya Pathshala, looked actively to discard their formal Brahman identities by immersing themselves in the practical work of Gandhi's ashram at Ahmedabad and in volunteering as satyagrahis.[178]

In the course of these engagements, Brahman intellectuals and literati found new ways to address the two very longstanding issues explored here. Echoing the prescient initiative of Vishnusastri Pandit in the 1870s, an early preoccupation of the Pathshala lay in promoting the idea of a single broad Maratha Brahman community. Notably, Mahadevsastri Divekar included vegetarian Shenvi Saraswats in his 1927 work, "Bringing Brahman subcastes into unity".[179] In the teeth of continuing orthodox opposition, he and others began to make the case that the Hindu social order had always consisted of four varnas rather than merely of Brahmans and Sudras. Many elite non-Brahmans could therefore be accepted as Kshatriyas and Vaishyas.[180] Given the political storms of the 1920s and 1930s, however, it may have seemed doubtful to many contemporaries whether such long-delayed concessions would gain real political traction.

[176] These debates are examined in full in Sarvate, "Reiminaging the Modern Hindu Self". See also Khandkar and Khandkar, *Swimmming Upstream*, pp. 12–32, 38–50; Deshpande, *Creative Pasts*, pp. 179–202.

[177] Jaffrelot, *Hindu Nationalism*, p. 45; Ganneri, "The Hindu Mahasabha in Bombay".

[178] Khandkar and Khandkar, *Swimming Upstream*, pp. 16–19; Ostergaard, "Indian Anarchism".

[179] Divekar, *Brāhmaṇātīl Poṭ-Jātīnche Ekīkaraṇ*, pp. 55–62. For later-nineteenth-century writing on this theme, see Wagle, "Three Letters", and Tilak's *Kesarī* editorials: "Konkaṇastha, Deśastha va Karhāḍe". I am grateful to Alok Oak for sharing this material with me.

[180] Sarwate, "Reimagining the Modern Hindu Self", pp. 74–7.

Other Brahman concerns were coming to the fore too. Sarwate points out that the decline of Brahman influence in Maharashtra's political life coincided with the literary resurgence associated with the progressivist fiction of Narayan Sitaram Phadke (1894–1978). This new literature offered an idealised vision of private life, romance, and heterosexual love in the modern urban Brahman family, and provided a means of escape from the difficult political realities of the late colonial decades.[181] Relatedly, Botre sees the late colonial proliferation of Brahman writing about the "science" of sexuality within the family as a way to address the loss of Brahman control over social reformist movements.[182]

Well-to-do urban Brahman families began to invest the home and family life with new significance in other ways too. Starting as a predominantly Chitpavan phenomen, the new genre of the Kulavṛttānta family history emerged and began to flourish. Patterson estimated that some sixty-four such histories were published between 1914 and 1963, with many more in preparation, covering hundreds of lineage branches and hundreds of thousands of individual family members.[183] The product of exhaustive research and enquiry – the later publications profusely illustrated with studio-posed black and white photographs – each volume described individual and family success in education, the professions and government service, achievement in cultural and artistic activities, acts of charity and religious piety, and pleasure in the enjoyments of home and private life.[184]

These histories offer a new way of seeing the family itself. The densely packed pages tell stories of unfolding family achievement, of the striving of individual fathers and mothers, husbands and wives, sons and daughters. The photographs begin with the sombre individual patriarchs of the late nineteenth century, and move forward to the smartly dressed and smiling family groups of the 1940s, '50s and '60s. With their carefully staged group photographs and profuse information about each individual, the families seem to embody successful passages

[181] Ibid, pp. 167–219. See also Sequeira, "The Sciences of Love".

[182] Botre, "The Body Language of Caste".

[183] Patterson, "Chitpavan Brahman Family Histories", p. 397.

[184] For helpful contextual analysis, see Chickerur, "Brahman Women as Cultured Homemakers"; Haynes, "Masculinity"; Karve, *The New Brahmans*.

from tradition to modernity. The caste of the family seems simply incidental: what makes it all possible is the hard work, talent, and amiable qualities of individuals.[185] Yet they were also produced within a framework that emphasised their significance for public and national life. As Krishnaji Vinayak Pendse – founder of the Kulavṛttānta Sangh in 1938 and author of a guide for aspiring family genealogists – insisted, all such family histories were nothing less than the building blocks of the nation's history itself. He published the guide in 1949, immediately after the wave of attacks on Maharashtrian Brahman families that followed the murder of Gandhi in January 1948 by Nathuram Godse.[186]

We can perhaps see here a further stage in the development of nineteenth-century arguments about true Brahmanhood, with their distinctive interplay between caste and class. Building on the remarkably resilient legacy of Nilakanthasastri Thatthe, conservatives like Malvankar associated it with the purest Sanskrit scriptural orthodoxy. By contrast, and often in deeply contradictory ways, Anglophone reformers sought to speak publicly as uncasted subjects. Some defined their value to the nation in terms of their skills as mobile professionals, their individual labour and enterprise, and their willingness to embrace new ideas. Others defined themselves more in terms of the obligation they felt to weave a fresh synthesis between old and new in Maharashtra's uniquely valuable communitarian spiritual traditions. In the interwar years, however, none of these approaches seemed likely to contribute to Brahman social cohesion, or to offer a viable model for Brahman social leadership in the future.

It was in this setting that the family and its affectionate embrace took on significant new prominence. As evidenced in the realm of literature – as in the Kulavṛttānta family histories – it was in the "private" sphere of the family that well-worn cultural practices affirmed a sense of identity, and that its accumulated educational experience was made available to support the striving of its individual members. Again, this prefigures the modern moment of "culturalisation", of caste's transmutation into an aspect of private life. Yet viewed over the much

[185] As an example, see Pathak, *Gokhale Kulavṛttānta*, in its second edition by 1978, and amounting to over a thousand pages.

[186] Pendse, *Kulavṛttānta Mārga Darśana*, p. 1; Patterson, "Shifting Fortunes".

longer-term perspective offered in the essays that now follow, this reduced role in the front line of politics does not seem altogether new. Rather, the focus on strategically placed cultural institutions, and above all on the formidable vehicle of the family as a key instrument of mobility, has echoes of an older era of Brahman power and influence.

References

Anand, "Chitpāvan Bhāgyodya Dīpikā", in Vaijnath Sastri Vyasa, ed., *Sadbodhacintāmaṇī* (Bombay: Arya Prakash Press, 1875).

Apte, Mahadev L., "Lokahitavadi and V.K. Chiplunkar: Spokesmen of Change in Nineteenth Century Maharashtra", *Modern Asian Studies*, vol. 7, no. 2, 1973, pp. 193–208.

Athalye, Krishnaji Narayan, *Lokahitavādī Hyānche Charitra* (Pune: Chitrashala Press, 1926).

Bairy, R., *Being Brahmin, Being Modern: Exploring the Lives of Caste Today* (London: Routledge, 2010)

Bakhle, Janaki, *Savarkar and the Making of Hindutva* (Princeton: Princeton University Press, 2024).

Ballhatchet, Kenneth, *Social Policy and Social Change in Western India, 1817–1830* (London: Oxford University Press, 1957).

Bayly, C.A., *Indian Society and the Making of the British Empire* (Cambridge: Cambridge University Press, 1988).

Bayly, Susan, *Caste, Society and Politics in India from the Eighteenth Century to the Modern Age* (Cambridge: Cambridge University Press, 1999).

Bendrey, V.S., ed., *Keśava Paṇḍita's Daṇḍanītiprakaraṇam* (Pune: Aryabhushan Press, 1943).

———, *Mahārāṣṭretihāsāchī Sādhane*, 2 vols (Mumbai: Mumbai Marathi Grantha Sangrahalaya, 1966).

Benke, Theodore, "The Śūdrācāraśiromaṇi of Kṛṣṇa Śeṣa: A 16th Century Manual of Dharma for Sudras", University of Pennsylvania PhD thesis, 2010.

Benson, James, "Saṃkārabhaṭṭa's Family Chronicle", in Axel Michaels, ed., *The Pandit: Traditional Scholarship in India* (Delhi: Manohar, 2001), pp. 105–18.

Bhagwat, Durga, *Rājārāmaśāstrī Bhāgavat* (Mumbai: Swastik Publishing House, 1947).

Bhagwat, Rajaramshastri, *Jśās Tase-Puravṇī* (Bombay: Family Printing Press, 1885).

———, *Marhāṭhyāsambandhāne Chār Udgār* (1885), in Durga Bhagwat, ed., *Rājārāmaśāstrī Bhāgavat Yānche Nivadak Sāhitya*, 5 vols (Pune: Varda Books, 1979), vol. 1.

———, "Brāhmaṇ va Brāhmaṇī Dharma", in Durga Bhagwat, ed., *Rājārāmsāstrī Bhāgavat Yānche Nivadak Sāhitya*, 5 vols (Pune: Varda Books, 1979), vol. 2, pp. 107–72.

Bhandarkar, R.G., "Social History of India", in C.Y. Chintamani, ed., *Indian Social Reform* (Madras: Thomson and Co., 1901), pp. 1–26.

———, *Vaiṣṇavism, Śaivism and Minor Religious Systems* (Varanasi: Indological Book House, 1965).

Bhate, G.C., *History of Modern Marathi Literature 1800–1938* (Pune: Arya Bhushan Press, 1939).

Bhavalkar, Keshav Shivram, *Ātmavṛtta* (Nagpur: Vidarbha Samshodhan Mandal, 1961).

Botre, S., "The Body Language of Caste: Marathi Sexual Modernity", University of Warwick PhD thesis, 2017.

Cashman, Richard I., *The Myth of the Lokamanya: Tilak and Mass Politics in Maharashtra* (Berkeley and Los Angeles: University of California Press, 1975).

Chakravorthy, Sanjoy, *The Truth About Us: The Politics of Information from Manu to Modi* (Gurgaon: Hachette India, 2019).

Chapekar, Narayan Govind, *Chitpāvan* (Badlapur: L.N. Chapekar, 1966).

Chickerur, Shraddha, "Brahman Women as Cultured Homemakers: Unpacking Caste, Gender Roles and Cultural Capital Across Three Generations", *Journal of Gender Studies*, vol. 30, no. 4, 2021, pp. 417–28.

Chiplunkar, Vishnusastri, *Nibandhamālā*, 2 vols (Pune: Varda Books, 1993).

Collins, Brian, *The Other Rāma: Matricide and Genocide in the Mythology of Paraśurāma* (New York: SUNY Press, 2020).

Conlon, Frank F., *A Caste in a Changing World: The Chitrapur Saraswat Brahmans* (Berkeley: University of California Press, 1977).

Copland, Ian, "The Maharaja of Kolhapur and the Non-Brahman Movement, 1902–10)", *Modern Asian Studies*, vol. 7, no. 2, 1973, pp. 209–25.

da Cunha, J. Gerson, *The Sahyâdri-Khaṇḍa of the Skaṇḍa Purâṇa* (Bombay: Thacker, Vining and Co., 1877).

Dalmia, Vasudha, *The Nationalization of Hindu Traditions: Bhāratendu Hariśchandra and Nineteenth Century Banaras* (Delhi: Oxford University Press, 1997).

Dandekar, R.N., *Sanskrit and Maharashtra* (Poona: University of Poona, 1972).

———, "Ramakrishna Gopal Bhandarkar and the Academic Renaissance in Maharashtra", *Annals of the Bhandarkar Oriental Research Institute*, vol. 69, no. 1, 1988, pp. 283–94.

Desai, Madhuri, *Banaras Reconstructed: Architecture and Sacred Space in a Hindu Holy City* (Seattle: University of Washington Press, 2017).

Deshmukh, Gopal Hari, *Aitihāsik Goṣṭī* (Bombay: Nirnayasagar Press, 1892).

———, *Lokahitavādīnchī Śatapatre*, ed. P.G. Sahasrabuddhe (Pune: Continental Press, 1977).

Deshpande, Madhav M., "Pañca Gauḍa und Pañca Drāviḍa. Umstrittene Grenzen einer traditionellen Klassifikation", in M. Bergunder and R.P. Das, eds, *"Arier" und "Draviden", Konstruktionen der Vergangenheit als Grundlage fur Selbst-und Fremdwahrnehmungen Sudasiens* (Halle: Verlag der Franckeschen Stiftungen zu Halle, 2002), pp. 57–78.

———, "Aryan Origins: Arguments from the Nineteenth Century Maharashtra", in Edwin Bryant and Laurie Patton, eds, *The Indo-Aryan Controversy: Evidence and Inference in Indian History* (London: Routledge, 2005).

———, "Kṣatriyas in the Kali Age? Gāgābhaṭṭa & His Opponents", *Indo-Iranian Journal*, vol. 53, 2010, pp. 95–120.

———, "Vedas and Their Śākhās: Contested Relationships", in Francois Voegeli, *et al.*, eds, *Devadattīyam. Johannes Bronkhorst Felicitation Volume* (Bern: Peter Lang, 2012), pp. 341–62.

———, "Pune: An Emerging Center of Education in Early Modern Maharashtra", *International Journal of Hindu Studies*, vol. 19, nos 1–2, 2015, pp. 59–96.

Deshpande, Prachi, *Creative Pasts: Historical Memory and Identity in Western India, 1700–1960* (New York: Columbia University Press, 2007).

———, *Scripts of Power: Writing, Language Practices, and Cultural History in Western India* (Ranikhet: Permanent Black, 2023).

Deshpande, Satish, "Caste and Castelessness: Towards a Biography of the 'General Category'", *Economic and Political Weekly*, vol. 48, no. 15, 13 April 2013, pp. 32–9.

Devare, Aparna, "M.G. Ranade and Bhakti as a New Grammar for Indian Political Life", in Vinay Lal, ed., *India and Civilisational Futures* (New Delhi: Oxford University Press, 2019), pp. 215–39.

Divekar, Mahadevsastri, *Brāhmaṇātīl Poṭ-Jātīnche Ekīkaraṇ* (Pune: Samartha Bharat Press, 1927).

———, *Govardhan Brāhmaṇānchā Itihās* (Pune: V.G. Ketkar, 1937).

Divekar, V.D., "The Emergence of an Indigenous Business Class in Maharashtra in the Eighteenth Century", *Modern Asian Studies*, vol. 16, no. 3, 1982, pp. 427–43.

Dongare, Mahadev Ganesh, *Śrīsiddāntavijayagrantha* (Kolhapur: Missions Press, 1907).

Eaton, Richard M., *A Social History of the Deccan, 1300–1761: Eight Indian Lives* (Cambridge: Cambridge University Press, 2005).

Flood, Gavin, "Hinduism", in Jean Holm and John Bowker, eds, *Rites of Passage* (London: St Martin's Press, 1994), pp. 66–89.

Fuller, C.J., and H. Narasimhan, *Tamil Brahmans: The Making of a Middle Class Caste* (Chicago: University of Chicago Press, 2014).

Ganneri, Namrata R., "The Hindu Mahasabha in Bombay (1923–47)", *Proceedings of the Indian History Congress*, vol. 75, 2004, pp. 771–82.

Gode, P.K., "The Date of the Kāyastha Parabhū-dharmādarś'a of Nīlakaṇṭha Sūri", in P.K. Gode, ed., *Studies in Indian Cultural History*, vol. 3 (Poona: Bhandarkar Oriental Research Institute, 1969), pp. 1–36.

Gokhale, Sandhya, *The Chitpavans: Social Ascendancy of a Creative Minority in Maharashtra 1818–1918* (Gurgaon: Shubhi Publications, 2008).

Gordon, Stewart, *The Marathas 1600–1818* (Cambridge: Cambridge University Press, 1993).

Grant Duff, James, *History of the Mahrattas*, 2 vols (London: Longmans, Rees, Orme, Browne and Green, 1826).

Guha, Sumit, "The Family Feud as a Political Resource in Eighteenth-century India", in Indrani Chatterjee, ed., *Unfamiliar Relations: Family and History in South Asia* (New Brunswick: Rutgers University Press, 2004), pp. 73–94.

———, *Beyond Caste: Identity and Power in South Asia, Past and Present* (Leiden: Brill, 2013).

Gune, V.T., *The Judicial System of the Marathas* (Poona: Deccan College Post-Graduate and Research Institute, 1953).

Gunjikar, Ramchandra Bhikaji, *Sarasvatīmanḍal* (Bombay: Nirnayasagar Press, 1884).

Gupte, K.T., *Rājavāḍyānchī Gāgābhaṭṭī* (Bombay: Indu Prakash Press, 1919).

Gurevitch, Eric, "The Epistemology of Difference: Caste and the Question of Natural Kinds in the Courts of Medieval India", *Journal of South Asian Intellectual History*, vol. 5, no. 2, 2023, pp. 217–51.

Harischandra, Bharatendu, "*Premajoginī*", in Shivprasad Mishra, ed., *Bharā-*

tendu Granthāvalī, pt 1 (Varanasi: Nagarini Pracharini Sabha, 1975), pp. 164–230.

Haynes, Douglas E., "Masculinity, Advertising and the Reproduction of the Middle-Class Family in Western India, 1918–1940", in Henrike Donner, ed., *Being Middle-Class in India: A Way of Life* (New York: Routledge, 2012), pp. 23–46.

Jaffrelot, Christophe, ed., *Hindu Nationalism: A Reader* (Princeton, N.J.: Princeton University Press, 2007).

Jambhekar, G.G., ed., *Memoirs and Writings of Acharaya Bal Shastri Jambhekar* (1812–1846), 3 vols (Pune: G.G. Jambhekar, 1950).

Janaki, Kumari S.S., "Paraśurāma", *Purāṇa*, vol. 8, no. 1, January 1966, pp. 52–82.

Jaywant, Ketaki, "Secularizing Caste: Mapping Nineteenth Century Anti-Caste Politics in Western India", University of Minnesota PhD thesis, 2012.

———, "Reshaping the Figure of the Shudra: Tukaram Padwal's Jatibhed Viveksar (Reflections on the Institution of Caste)", *Modern Asian Studies*, vol. 57, no. 2, 2023, pp. 380–408.

Johnson, Gordon, "Chitpavan Brahmins and Politics in Western India in the Late Nineteenth and Early Twentieth Centuries", in Edmund Leach and S.N. Mukherjee, eds, *Elites in South Asia* (Cambridge: Cambridge University Press, 1970).

Joshi, N.V., *Puṇe Varṇan* (Bombay: Oriental Press, 1868).

Joshi, Sanjay, *Fractured Modernity: The Making of a Middle Class in Colonial North India* (New Delhi: Oxford University Press, 2001).

———, *The Middle Class in Colonial India* (Delhi: Oxford University Press, 2010).

Kamalakarabhatta, *Śūdrakamalākaraḥ*, ed. Ganesh Bapuji Malvankar and Vishnu Shastri Bapat (Bombay: Lithographed Text, 1861).

Kanade, Ramchandra Govind, *Gurūvarya Pro. Viṣṇu Govind Vijāpūrkar* (Pune: Chitnis Literary Press, 1928).

Kanavinde, Bhavani Vishvanath, *Sārasvat Brāhmaṇ* (Bombay: National Press, 1870).

Kane, P.V., *History of Dharmaśāstra*, 5 vols (Poona: Bhandarkar Oriental Research Institute, 1941).

Karve, D.D., *The New Brahmans: Five Maharashtrian Families* (Cambridge: Cambridge University Press, 1963).

Keer, Dhananjay, *Mahatma Jotirao Phooley, Father of the Indian Social Revolution* (Mumbai: Popular Prakashan, 1974).

———, *Shahu Chhatrapati: A Royal Revolutionary* (Bombay: Popular Prakashan, 1976).

Keune, Jon, *Shared Devotion, Shared Food: Equality and the Bhakti-Caste Question in Western India* (New York: Oxford University Press, 2021).

Khandkar, Arundhati C., and Ashok C. Khandkar, *Swimming Upstream: Laxmanshastri Joshi and the Evolution of Modern India* (New Delhi: Oxford University Press, 2019).

Kidambi, Prashant, *The Making of an Indian Metropolis: Colonial Governance and Public Culture in Bombay, 1890–1920* (Aldershot: Ashgate Press, 2007).

———, "Consumption, Domestic Economy and the Idea of the 'Middle Class' in Late Colonial Bombay", in Sanjay Joshi, ed., *The Middle Class in Colonial India* (New Delhi: Oxford University Press, 2010), pp. 132–53.

Kinra, Rajeev, *Writing Self, Writing Empire: Chandar Bhan Brahman and the Cultural World of the Indo-Persian State Secretary* (Oakland: University of California Press, 2015).

Kolhatkar, Wamanrao M., "Widow Re-marriage", in C. Yajnesvara Chintamani, *Indian Social Reform* (Madras: Minerva Press, 1901), pp. 282–311.

Kotani, Hiroyuki, *Western India in Historical Transition: Seventeenth to Early Twentieth Centuries* (New Delhi: Manohar, 2002).

Kulkarni, A.R., *James Cuninghame Grant Duff: Administrator-Historian of the Marathas* (Kolkata: K.P. Bagchi and Company, 2006).

———, "Charles D'Ochoa – A French Orientalist of the Mid-Nineteenth Century", in A.R. Kulkarni, ed., *Studies in Maratha History* (Pune: Diamond Publications, 2008), pp. 130–48.

Kulkarni, Sumitra, *The Satara Raj, 1818–1848: A Study in History, Administration and Culture* (New Delhi: Mittal Publications, 1995).

Kumar, Ravinder, *Western India in the Nineteenth Century* (London: Routledge and Kegan Paul, 1968).

———, "The New Brahmans of Maharashtra", in D.A. Low, ed., *Soundings in Modern South Asian History* (London: Weidenfeld and Nicolson, 1968), pp. 95–126.

Madhava, *Śatapraśnakalpalatā*, Sanskrit Ms. no 19, P.M. Joshi Collection, Bhandarkar Oriental Research Institute.

Masselos, J.C., *Towards Nationalism: Group Affiliations and the Politics of Public Associations in Nineteenth Century Western India* (Bombay: Popular Prakashan, 1974).

"Memorial of the English Students at Poona", *Bombay Times and Journal of Commerce*, 24 October 1849.

Metcalf, Thomas R., *Ideologies of the Raj* (Cambridge: Cambridge University Press, 1995).

Minkowski, Christopher, "Sanskrit Scientific Libraries and Their Uses: Examples and Problems of the Early Modern Period", in Florence Bretelle-Establet, ed., *Looking at It from Asia: The Processes that Shaped the Sources of History of Science* (Springer: Paris 2010), pp. 81–114.

Nadkarni, M.K., *A Short History of Marathi Literature* (Baroda: Steam Press, 1921).

Naik, J.V., "Social Composition of the Prarthana Samaj", *Proceedings of the Indian History Congress*, vol. 48, 1987, pp. 502–11.

———, "Bhau Mahajan and His Prabhakar, Dhumketu and Dnyan Darshan: A Study in Maharashtrian Response to British Rule", in N.K. Wagle, ed., *Writers, Editors and Reformers: Social and Political Transformations of Maharashtra, 1830–1930* (New Delhi: Manohar, 1999), pp. 64–81.

Nanda, B.R., *Gokhale: The Indian Moderates and the British Raj* (New Delhi: Oxford University Press, 1977).

Narayana Rao, Velcheru, David Shulman, and Sanjay Subrahmanyam, *Textures of Time: Writing History in South India, 1600–1800* (Delhi: Permanent Black, 2001).

Naregal, Veena, *Language Politics, Elites and the Public Sphere: Western India Under Colonialism* (Delhi: Permanent Black, 2001).

Natrajan, Balmurli, "From Jati to Samaj", in "Caste Matters: A Symposium on Inequalities, Identities and Disintegrating Hierarchies", India-Seminar 633 (April 2012): 58–62, available at https://www.india–seminar.com/2012/633.htm, accessed 27.11.2023.

Novetzke, Christian, "The Brahmin Double: The Brahminical Construction of Anti-Brahminism and Anti-Caste Sentiment in the Religious Cultures of Precolonial Maharashtra", *South Asian History and Culture*, vol. 2, no. 2, April 2011, pp. 232–52.

———, *The Quotidian Revolution: Vernacularization, Religion and the Premodern Public Sphere in India* (New York: Columbia University Press, 2016).

Oak, Alok, "Political Ideas of B.G. Tilak: Colonialism, Self and Hindu Nationalism", University of Leiden PhD thesis, 2022.

Oak, Pramod, *Bālājī Viśvanāth Peśve* (Pune: Continental Press, 2005).

O'Hanlon, Rosalind, *Caste, Conflict and Ideology: Mahatma Jotirao Phule and Low Caste Protest in Nineteenth Century Western India* (2nd Edition: New Delhi: Permanent Black, 2010).

———, "The Social Worth of Scribes: Brahmans, Kayasthas and the Social Order in Early Modern India", *Indian Economic and Social History Review*, vol. 47, no. 4, 2010, pp. 563–95.

———, "Speaking from Siva's Temple: Banaras Scholar Households and the Brahman 'Ecumene' of Mughal India", *South Asian History and Culture*, vol. 2, no. 2, April 2011, pp. 253–77.

———, "Performance in a World of Paper: Puranic Histories and Social Communication in Early Modern India", *Past and Present*, vol. 219, May 2013, pp. 87–126.

———, "Disciplining the Brahman Household: The Moral Mission of Empire in the Eighteenth-Century Maratha State", in Kumkum Roy, ed., *Looking Within, Looking Without: Exploring Households in the Subcontinent through Time* (Delhi: Primus Books, 2015), pp. 367–89.

———, "Entrepreneurs in Diplomacy: Maratha Expansion in the Age of the Vakil", *Indian Economic and Social History Review*, vol. 57, no. 4, 2020, pp. 1–32.

———, "Brahman Lineages Beyond the Mughal Court", in Richard Eaton and Ramya Sreenivasan, eds, *The Oxford Handbook of the Mughal World*, online publication, pp. 1–9.

———, "Gotmai's Suit: A Brahman Woman of Property in Seventeenth Century Western India", in Toke Knudsen, *et al.*, eds, *Festschrift to Christopher Minkowski* (Leiden: Brill, 2023), pp. 449–65.

———, and Christopher Minkowski, "What Makes People Who They Are? Pandit Networks and the Problem of Livelihoods in Early Modern Western India, *Indian Economic and Social History Review*, vol. 45, no. 3, 2008, pp. 381–416.

O'Hanlon, Rosalind, and David Washbrook, eds, "Munshis, Pandits and Record-Keepers: Scribal Communities and Historical Change in India", *Indian Economic and Social History Review*, Special Issue, vol. 47, no. 4, 2010.

Ostergaard, Geoffrey, "Indian Anarchism: The Curious Case of Vinoba Bhave, Anarchist 'Saint of Government'", in David Goodway, ed., *For Anarchism: History, Theory, Practice* (London: Routledge, 2013), pp. 201–16.

Padwal, Tukaram Tatya, *Jātibhed Vivekasār* (Mumbai: Ganpat Krishnaji's Press, 1865).

Pande, Mrinal, ed. and trans., *Vishnu Bhatt Godshe Versaikar, 1857: The Real Story of the Great Uprising* (New Delhi: Harper, 2011).

Pandian, M.S.S., "One Step Outside Modernity: Caste, Identity Politics and the Public Sphere", *Economic and Political Weekly*, vol. 37, no. 18, 4 May 2002, pp. 1735–41.

Pandit, Vishnusastri, *Devarūkhyāviṣayī Śāstrasamat Vichār* (Mumbai: Indu Prakash Press, 1874).

Parabhūjātinirṇaya, Bhandarkar Oriental Research Institute, no. 567 of 1883–4.

Pathak, G.R., *Gokhale Kulavṛttānta* (Pune: S.S. Gokhale, 1978).

Patil, Urmila Rajshekhar, "Conflict, Identity and Narratives: The Brahman Communities of Western India from the Seventeenth Through the Nineteenth Centuries", University of Texas PhD thesis, 2010.

Patterson, Maureen, "Chitpavan Brahman Family Histories: Sources for a Study of Social Structure and Social Change in Maharashtra", in Milton Singer and Bernard S. Cohn, eds, *Structure and Change in Indian Society* (Chigaco: Aldine Publishing Company, 1968).

———, "Changing Patterns of Occupation Among Chitpavan Brahmans", *Indian Economic and Social History Review*, vol. 7, no. 3, 1970, pp. 375–96.

———, "The Shifting Fortunes of Chitpavan Brahmans: Focus on 1848", in D. Attwood, ed., *City, Countryside and Society in Maharashtra* (Toronto: University of Toronto, 1988), pp. 35–58.

Pendse, Krishna Vinayak, *Kulavṛttānta Mārga Darśana* (Pune: K.V. Pendse, 1949).

Phule, Jotirao, *Gulāmgirī*, in Y.D. Phadke, ed., *Mahātma Phule Samagra Vāngmay* (Mumbai: Maharashtra State Board of Literature and Culture, 1991), pp. 109–92.

———, *Sārvajanik Satya Dharma Pustak*, in Y.D. Phadke, ed., *Mahātma Phule Samagra Vāngmay* (Mumbai: Maharashtra State Board of Literature and Culture, 1991), pp. 429–528.

Pise, Pravin Balasaheb, "Viṣṇu Paraśurām Śāstrī Paṇḍit Yānche Ekonisāvyā Śatakātīl Sāmājik Kāryātīl Yogadān", Pune University PhD thesis, 2017.

Pollock, Sheldon, *The Ends of Man at the End of Premodernity* (Amsterdam: Royal Netherlands Academy of Arts and Sciences, 2005).

Raheja, Gloria Goodwin, "India: Caste, Kingship and Dominance Reconsidered", *Annual Reviews in Anthropology*, vol. 17, 1988, pp. 497–522.

Ramusack, Barbara N., *The Indian Princes and Their States* (Cambridge: Cambridge University Press, 2003).

Ranade, M.G., *Religious and Social Reform* (Bombay, Claridge and Co., 1902).

Ranade, Ramabai, *Miscellaneous Writings of the Late Hon'ble Mr Justice M.G. Ranade* (Bombay: The Manoranjan Press, 1915).

Rao, Anupama, *The Caste Question: Dalits and the Politics of Modern India* (Berkeley and Los Angeles: University of California Press, 2009).

Rao, Parimala V., "Colonial State as 'New Manu': Explorations in Educational Policies in Relation to Dalit and Low Caste Education in Nineteenth Century India", *Contemporary Education Dialogue*, vol. 16, no. 1, 2019, pp. 84–107.

Roberts, J., "The Movement of Elites in Western India under Early British Rule", *The Historical Journal*, vol. 14, no. 2, 1971, pp. 241–62.

Sangave, Vilas, and B.D. Khane, *Rajarshi Shahu Chhatrapati Papers, Volume III* (Kolhapur: Shahu Research Institute, 1985).

Sardesai, G.S., ed., *Papers Referring to Pratapsinh, Raja of Satara* (Bombay: Government Central Press, 1934).

Sarwate, Rahul, "Reimagining the Modern Hindu Self: Caste, Untouchability and Hindu Theology in Colonial South Asia, 1899–1948", Columbia University PhD thesis, 2020.

Sastri, Lalji Vaijanath, *Sadbodhachintāmaṇī* (Bombay: Arya Prakash Press, 1875).

Sathaye, Adheesh, *Crossing the Lines of Caste: Viśvāmitra and the Construction of Brahmin Power in Hindu Mythology* (New York: Oxford University Press, 2015).

Sequeira, Rovel, "The Sciences of Love: Intimate 'Democracy' and the Eugenic Development of the Marathi Couple in Colonial India", *History of the Human Sciences*, vol. 36, no. 5, 2023, pp. 68–93.

Singha, Radhika, "Settle, Mobilise, Verify: Identification Practices in Colonial India", *Studies in History*, vol. 16, no. 2, 2000, pp. 151–98.

Sturman, Rachel, *The Government of Social Life in Colonial India* (Cambridge: Cambridge University Press, 2012).

Subramanian, A., *The Caste of Merit: Engineering Education in India* (Cambridge, M.A: Harvard University Press, 2019).

Tambiah, S.J., "From Varna to Caste Through Mixed Unions", in Jack Goody, ed., *The Character of Kinship* (Cambridge: Cambridge University Press, 1973), pp. 191–229.

Thakare, K.S., *Grāmaṇyānchā Sādyant Itihās* (Mumbai: Tatvavivek Press, 1919).

Thapar, Romila, "The Theory of Aryan Race and India: History and Politics", *Social Scientist*, vol. 24, nos 1/3, 1996, pp. 3–29.

Thatthe, Nilakanthasastri, "Kāyastha Prabhū Dharma Dharśa", Limaye Collection, Bhandarkar Oriental Research Institute, Pune.

Thatthe, Parasuram Vinayak, *Thaṭṭhe Kulavṛttānta* (Pune: Dnyanvilas Press, 1935).

Tilak, Lokamanya, "Konkaṇastha, Deśastha va Karhāḍe", in *Kesarī,* 11 January 1881 and 13 November 1990.

———, "Marāṭhe āni Vedokta Karma", in *Kesarī*, 22 and 29 October 1901.

Tucker, Richard P., "The Proper Limits of Agitation: The Crisis of 1879–80 in Bombay Presidency", *Journal of Asian Studies*, vol. 28, no. 2, February 1969, pp. 339–55.

———, "Hindu Traditionalism and Nationalist Ideologies in Nineteenth-Century Maharashtra", *Modern Asian Studies*, vol. 10, no. 3, 1976, pp. 321–48.

Vaudeville, Charlotte, "The Shaiva-Vaishnava Synthesis in Maharashtrian Santism", in Karine Schomer and W.H. McLeod, eds, *The Sants: Studies in a Devotional Tradition of India* (Delhi: Motilal Banarsidass, 1987), pp. 215–28.

Vendell, Dominic, "Phule's Satyashodh and Subaltern Consciousness", *Comparative Studies of South Asia, Africa and the Middle East*, vol. 34, no. 1, 2014, pp. 52–66.

———, "Scribes and the Vocation of Politics in the Maratha Empire, 1707–1818", Columbia University PhD thesis, 2018.

———, "The Scribal Household in Flux: Pathways of Kayastha Service in Eighteenth-century Western India", *Indian Economic and Social History Review*, vol. 57, no. 4, October–December 2020, pp. 535–66.

Venkatkrishnan, Anand, "Ritual, Reflection and Religion: The Devas of Banaras", *South Asian History and Culture*, vol. 6, no. 1, 2015, pp. 141–71.

Wagle, Narendra K., "The History and Social Organization of the Gauḍa Sāraswata Brāhmaṇas of the West Coast of India", *Journal of Indian History*, vol. XLVIII, nos 1–2, 1970, pp. 7–25 and 295–333.

———, "A Dispute Regarding the Pancal Devajna Sonars and the Brahmanas of Pune Regarding Social Rank and Ritual Privileges: A Caste Study of the British Administration of *Jati* Laws in Maharashtra, 1822–1825", in N.K. Wagle, ed., *Images of Maharashtra: A Regional Profile of India* (London: Curzon Press, 1980), pp. 129–59.

———, "The Chāndrasenīya Kāyastha Prabhus and the Brahmans: Ritual, Law and Politics in Pune, 1789–90", in G.D. Sontheimer and P.K. Aithal, eds, *Indology and Law: Studies in Honour of Prof. J. Duncan M. Derrett* (Wiesbaden: Franz Steiner Verlag, 1982), pp. 303–28.

———, "Ritual and Change in Early Nineteenth Century Society in Maharashtra: Vedokta Disputes in Baroda, Pune and Satara, 1824–1838", in Milton Israel and N.K. Wagle, eds, *Religion and Society in Maharashtra* (Toronto: University of Toronto, 1987), pp. 145–81.

———, "Readmission of Sripat Sesadri: Dharmasastra vs Public Consensus, Bombay 1943–45", in A.R. Kulkarni and N.K. Wagle, eds, *Region, Nation and Religion* (Bombay: Popular Prakashan, 1999), pp. 136–56.

———, "Three Letters of Govind Babaji Joshi on Inter-*jati* Marriage in Nineteenth-Century Maharashtra", in N.K. Wagle, ed., *Writers, Editors and Reformers: Social and Political Transformations of Maharashtra, 1830–1930* (New Delhi: Manohar, 1999), pp. 201–17.

Washbrook, D.A., "India 1818–1860: The Two Faces of Colonialism", in Andrew Porter and Wm Roger Lewis, eds, *The Oxford History of the British Empire, Vol. III: The Nineteenth Century* (Oxford: Oxford University Press, 1999), pp. 395–421.

Wilson, John, *India Three Thousand Years Ago* (Bombay: Smith, Taylor and Co., 1958).

Wink, Andre, *Land and Sovereignty in India: Agrarian Society and Politics Under the Eighteenth Century Maratha Svarājya* (Cambridge: Cambridge University Press, 1986).

1

Speaking from Shiva's Temple

Banaras Scholar Households and the Brahman "Ecumene" of Mughal India

Introduction

A CONSISTENT THEME IN recent social histories of early modern India has been the opportunities, as well as the challenges, that scribal specialists encountered during this era.[1] From the perspective of intellectual history too, the early modern centuries have been a particular focus of interest. The Sanskrit intellectual cultures of this period are now the subject of an impressive body of scholarship.[2] In particular, attention has focused on contemporary intellectuals' engagement in self-consciously new and often more deliberately historical modes of thinking about their disciplines, frequently characterised by contemporaries as "navya", although within a broader intellectual

[1] Alam and Subrahmanyam, "Making of a Munshi"; Narayana Rao, *et al.*, *Textures of Time*, pp. 93–139; Subrahmanyam, "Aspects of State Formation"; Alam, "Culture and Politics"; Chatterjee, "History as Self-representation"; Guha, "Speaking Historically"; Bayly, *Caste, Society and Politics*, pp. 64–96; O'Hanlon and Washbrook, "Munshis, Pandits and Record Keepers".

[2] Particularly, of course, in the project "Sanskrit Knowledge Systems on the Eve of Colonialism". See http://www.columbia.edu/itc/mealac/pollock/sks/papers/index.html, and Pollock, *Language of the Gods*. For a review of the project, see Kaviraj, "The Sudden Death of Sanskrit Knowledge", pp. 119–42. For more recent discussions, see Pollock, "Is There an Indian Intellectual History?", pp. 533–42.

culture still deeply committed to ideas of continuity and stability.[3] This concern with "newness" has provoked much disagreement.[4]

In terms of social history, there is still much that we do not yet know about these Brahman intellectuals, and the nature of their social authority and ritual entitlements. What did Brahman privilege in its various different forms really mean in contemporary social terms, and what shifts and negotiations were necessary to maintain it? Being able to act and be treated as a Brahman was not only a matter of securing due recognition from those who were not Brahmans. Just as important, Brahman social authority rested on the ideals of unity and community among Brahmans themselves. How did Brahmans of this period articulate these ideals in early modern India?[5]

These are important questions. The early modern centuries, and the framework of the Mughal empire in particular, brought significant opportunities for Brahmans. The Mughal demand for cash revenues created substantial new advantages for Brahman office holders in the revenue systems of regional states, while the expansion of settled agriculture benefitted those, often Brahmans, with access to capital to undertake its development. Brahman families willing to combine scribal skills, religious prestige, and access to cash were able to accumulate substantial property rights in this setting.[6] The expansive cultural strategy developed at Akbar's court as well as at many regional courts drew in ambitious and talented Brahmans seeking patronage, and promoted exchange between them.[7] Improved communications implied benefits

[3] See in particular Pollock, "New Intellectuals".

[4] See Pollock, "Pretextures of Time", pp. 366–83, and Narayana Rao, Shulman, and Subrahmanyam, "A Pragmatic Response", pp. 409–27.

[5] I thank Sheldon Pollock for a very helpful discussion of Brahman privilege. See also Houben, "The Brahmin Intellectual", pp. 463–79; Parry, "The Brahmanical Tradition", pp. 200–25; O'Hanlon and Minkowski, "What Makes People Who They Are?", pp. 384–6; Gurevitch, "The Epistemology of Difference". For the importance of historicisation, see van der Veer, "Concept of the Ideal Brahman", pp. 67–80, and Smith, "The Sacred Center".

[6] For western India, see, for example, Preston, *The Devs of Cincvad*; Perlin, "Of White Whale and Countrymen"; and Fukazawa, *The Medieval Deccan*, pp. 1–48 and 73–87.

[7] For a survey of these themes, see Asher and Talbot, *India Before Europe*, pp. 126–85.

for many different Brahman communities, from lowly priests who serviced North India's pilgrim trades, to intellectuals who sought wider audiences for their work, to sectarian leaders looking for recruits among new devotees.[8]

These same processes contributed to the emergence of Banaras, city of Shiva, as a destination for hopeful Brahman migrants. This was an unrivalled centre for Sanskrit education, a place where the learned could make their reputations with well-connected sponsors, and the pious meet wealthy patrons. Banaras also benefitted from its Mughal setting at another level. Particularly in matters of ritual entitlement and Hindu religious law, its pandit communities supplied the moral and judicial authority that some Muslim state officials of the period felt themselves unable to do. The latter sometimes referred difficult questions of religious law to the city, since its "pandits" were the appropriate experts to decide matters pertaining to "Hindus".[9] For leading scholar families in Banaras, this meant an opportunity to develop expertises in the practical context of disputes brought to them from outside the city. Derrett has rightly observed that Banaras' leading pandit family, the Bhattas, were influential because they were willing to apply their deep knowledge of religious law to the resolution of practical socio-political disputes within the Maratha regions and beyond.[10] Connections of this kind were one of the many different ways in which Banaras stood at the centre of what, following Christopher Bayly, we might call Mughal India's Brahman "ecumene".[11]

But the Mughal milieu also imposed significant strains. Regional economic development and new forms of commercialisation enabled some Brahmans to accumulate wealth and lucrative offices, but others had to cling on to petty local priestly roles or continue as poor farmers. These changes deepened class divides between different Brahman communities, often resulting in fission and the creation of new subcastes, of new hierarchies of worth amongst Brahmans themselves. This posed an acute challenge for Brahman religious authority. One way in which

[8] Bayly, "From Ritual to Ceremony", p. 163.

[9] See O'Hanlon, "Letters Home", p. 228, and O'Hanlon, "The Social Worth of Scribes".

[10] Derrett, "Kamalakara on Illegitimates", p. 231.

[11] Bayly, *Empire and Information*, pp. 180–211.

dharma, or right action in the world, could be known for Brahmans was through the example of the śiṣṭa – the community of the learned and well-conducted.[12] At the same time, a person could be known as a member of the śiṣṭa only by the fact that his actions were according to dharma. As Madhav Deshpande has pointed out, this involved a circularity. Sometimes this could be avoided, by maintaining that the śiṣṭa were in fact the pious and learned of the ancient world, such that their behaviour could be known outside the mutable world of the present.[13] But, as we shall see, the pandit families of Banaras thought of themselves very much as the śiṣṭa in the present. This made acrimonious divisions between Brahman subcastes particularly damaging.

Brahman communities from the Maratha regions felt these challenges acutely.[14] The old religious centres of the Konkan littoral, and the shrine towns that clustered along the Godavari, Bhima, and Krishna rivers, clearly offered an environment in which the learned and the pious could flourish. Outside these centres, the relatively poor and famine-prone agrarian economy of the Deccan plateau impelled Brahman families to diversify – spread their risks beyond the precarious livelihoods to be earned as petty teachers, village priests, astrologers, or small farmers. In some cases, this meant one or more members of the family migrating to Banaras; in others, it meant deploying their literate skills in state service and revenue administration. These opportunities expanded under the Bahmani kings and their successors in the states of the Deccan Sultanate, and then, of course, within the Maratha state of the warrior king Shivaji. It became almost a cliché for seventeenth-century observers, including bhakti critics, that what Maratha Brahmans prized above all were secure positions in state service.[15] These changes were to result in deepening divisions of status, wealth, and

[12] Davis, "Dharma in Practice", pp. 813–30. I am also grateful to Sheldon Pollock for assistance with this point.

[13] Deshpande, "The Changing Notion of *Śiṣṭa*", pp. 75–116.

[14] For general histories of society and state in western India in this period, see Fukazawa, *The Medieval Deccan*; Gordon, *The Marathas*; Wink, *Land and Sovereignty*; Eaton, *A Social History of the Deccan*; Kotani, *Western India*.

[15] See, for example, the satire of the South Indian poet Venkatadhvari, writing during the 1630s in his *Viśvaguṇādarśacampū*, vss. 133–8, 111–17; and *Tukārām Gāthā*, vol. 2, nos 6163–6.

opportunity amongst the region's Brahman communities, and unseemly factional struggles that reached their climax under the Brahman governments of the eighteenth-century Maratha state.

As a consequence, in part, of these regional pressures, a substantial community of Maratha Brahman scholar families had emerged in Banaras by the middle of the sixteenth century. The scholar households of the city were able to mobilise substantial cultural and practical resources to address these problems of "early modernity". Within the household or pandit gharāṇa, skills were passed to new generations. Locating their assemblies in the city's temple to Visvesvara – Shiva in his guise as Lord of All – reconstructed probably with patronage from leading lights at Akbar's court, Maratha pandit families were able to advertise an arena where disputes could be resolved and Brahman unity restored. The expanding conduits of news, discussion, and social communication associated with the Mughal court and its regional client states facilitated these families' efforts. Drawing on older universalising geographies of Brahman identity in this new Mughal context, they addressed their letters of judgment to Brahman communities across the "gauḍa" and "drāviḍa" regions of northern and southern India, and appealed explicitly to a "we" of the pious and discerning, the "good people" of the Brahman śiṣṭa.

This remarkable position of social and intellectual leadership exercised from Banaras thus emerged very much within the context of the Mughal imperial framework. This also meant, however, that the gradual decay and disintegration of that framework and the passing of political power to India's regions from the end of the seventeenth century spelled the waning of this remarkable social formation within thc city.

Families in Motion: Maratha Brahman Migrations to Banaras

The growth of Maratha Brahman dominance in Banaras had some of its beginnings in the city's own changing religious culture. Bakker and Isaacson suggest that Qutb al-Din Aibak's destruction of many of the city's older temples and shrines in 1194 prepared the ground for the rise of Banaras as the uniquely favoured city of maraṇamukti, where Shiva's teachings, whispered into the ear of the dying, brought certain liberation to the soul.[16] The *Kāśīkhaṇḍa* described the ancient king Divodas' relinquishing of Kasi so that Shiva could make his home in his beloved city. The purana marks a point in the consolidation of this "new" Banaras as the subcontinent's supreme centre of spiritual power and stronghold of Shaivite Brahman prestige. It described in detail the awe-inspiring temple to Visvesvara in the centre of the city, with its four mandapams (pavilions): the Aisvarya to the north, the Jnana to the east, the Mukti pavilion – beloved home of Shiva himself – to the south, and the Srngara pavilion in front of it.[17] The dating both of the *Kāśīkhaṇḍa* and the Visvesvara temple it celebrates remains controversial, although there is clear evidence for the destruction of a Visvesvara temple in the first half of the fifteenth century, when materials from it appear in nearby Jaunpur.[18]

The *Kāśīkhaṇḍa* gained particular depth and resonance from the relationships that it described between Kasi and pious people and places elsewhere in the subcontinent. The Vedic sage Agastya, with his southern associations, occupies a prominent place in the narrative. The "southern" direction (dakṣiṇā āśā) was represented in a particularly alluring way, the sensuousness of its spice-filled airs, luscious fruits, swelling mountains, and charming languages causing the gods themselves to linger there.[19] This quickly opened the door to regional translations

[16] Bakker and Isaacson, *Skandapurāṇa. The Vārāṇasī Cycle*, pp. 66–82. See also Eck, *Banaras*; Altekar, *History of Banaras*; Parry, *Death in Banaras*; Minkowski, "Nīlakaṇṭha Caturdhara's Mantrakāśikhaṇḍa".

[17] *Kāśikhaṇḍa*, Purvārdha, adhyāya 79, vss. 70–5.

[18] Bakker, "Construction and Reconstruction", p. 43. Bakker and Isaacson argue for the late thirteenth or early fourteenth century, and a link with Hindu responses to the challenge of Islam. Smith suggests that both *Kāśīkhaṇḍa* and the temple pre-date the Muslim invasions and express the imperial ambitions of the eleventh-century Kalacuri kings and the Shaiva Siddhanta cults with which they were associated. Bakker, "Construction and Reconstruction"; Smith, "The Sacred Center"; idem, "Renewing the Ancient". See also *Kṛtyakalpataru* of Bhaṭṭa Lakṣmīdhara, introduction by Aiyangar, pp. lxxxv–lxxxvi, for a twelfth-century description of Banaras which does not mention the *Kāśīkhaṇḍa* or a great Visvesvara temple. Smith suggests a deliberate omission by its author, minister to the Gahadavalas who had displaced the Kalacuris and patronised different Shaiva institutions.

[19] Tagare's English translation of the *Kāśīkhaṇḍa* suggests that the author may himself have been a southerner: Tagare, *Kāśī Khaṇḍa*, Pūrvārdha, pp. 10–11, n. 1.

of the *Kāśīkhaṇḍa*, which promoted the consoling attractions of the "South", with its own holy spots from which the pious soul could long for Kasi but without experiencing the pains and disappointments that encounters with the real city sometimes brought.[20]

Also adding to the prestige of Banaras was its expanding population of scholars, amongst which learned families from the Maratha regions came to predominate. External events may have precipitated particular waves of migration: the fall of Yadava Devagiri in 1294, the decline of nearby Paithan as a centre of Brahman learning, the catastrophic Deccan famines of the fourteenth and early fifteenth centuries, and the affluence of Banaras itself during the fifteenth century brought about by its close proximity to Jaunpur under the Sharqi dynasty.[21] We know quite a lot about the most prominent of the Maratha pandit families – Bhattas, Devas, Sesas, Puntambkars, Caturdharas, Bharadvajas – who migrated in this way, but less about the practicalities of their migrations.[22] These often took place as a series of smaller and local moves. Once established in Banaras, there were commonly comings and goings over several generations before a distinctive "Kasi" branch of the family emerged. In addition, Banaras was commonly only one destination for migrant families, who might despatch further members to establish themselves at other courtly or religious centres flourishing within the Mughal imperial framework.

The Sesa family provide a good example.[23] The most detailed family history that we have traces their origins back to a thirteenth-century ancestor, Ramakrishna, who held lands in Nanded, an important centre

---

Smith's suggestion of a Kalacuri imperial association for the *Kāśīkhaṇḍa* would certainly help explain its "southern" themes, since the Kalacuris themselves had impotant links with central and southern India. I thank Travis Smith for helpful exchanges on these themes.

[20] Shulman, "Ambivalence and Longing", pp. 192–214.

[21] For Paithan, see Morwanchikar, *The City of the Saints*. For Jaunpur, see Asher and Talbot, *India Before Europe*, p. 97.

[22] See O'Hanlon, "Letters Home".

[23] For the Sesa family and their links with Nanded, Bijapur, and Banaras, see Benke, "The Śūdrācāraśiromaṇi of Kṛṣṇa Śeṣa", pp. 17–55. Older sources are Kanole, "Nāṅḍeḍache Śeṣa Gharāṇe", pp. 56–73, and Aryavaraguru, "On the Sheshas of Benaras", pp. 245–53.

of learning and pilgrimage on the eastern Godavari.[24] He had three sons, Ganesapant, Vitthalapant, and Bopajipant. Ganesapant and his descendants remained in Nanded. The descendants of Vitthalapant left for Bijapur, and in the 1560s we find one of them, Vamana, son of Anant Sesa, working as royal librarian to Ali Adil Shah I (r. 1558–1579).[25] Vamana's grandson was the Marathi poet Waman Pandit (1608–1695), who spent his youth in Bijapur but went to Banaras for his education in Sanskrit.[26] Another notable descendant of the Nanded family was Narasimha Sesa, who moved to the Bijapur court probably in the first half of the sixteenth century. His expertise led the pandits at the court to confer on the family the title of Bhaṭṭa-bhaṭṭāraka (revered among scholars).[27] His son was the grammarian Krishna Sesa, who emerged, as we shall see, as a prominent leader of the Banaras pandit community by the 1580s.

But by this time other Sesas, probably descendants of Vitthalapant, were already well established in Banaras. One Vishnu Sesa moved there from Nanded, according to the family history, in the later fifteenth century. A family story conveys something of the individual ways in which such decisions might have been taken, and the relationship with broader family strategies. Vishnu Sesa moved to Banaras for his Sanskrit studies after developing a settled dislike of his elder brother's wife – for her scoldings about his study habits. In Banaras, he quickly excelled as a grammarian, early winning the title of sabhāpati (lord of the assembly) for his outstanding performances in debate.[28] It is not clear exactly what the relationship was between this branch of the family and the father and son Narasimha Sesa and Krishna Sesa mentioned above. If, as seems likely, there was a connection, it meant that when Krishna Sesa moved to Banaras he was going not to a city where he would be a stranger but to a place where there was an established network of Sesa households, with a reputation as grammarians already developed. Moreover, the links between Banaras and Nanded continued. In a

[24] Kanole, "Nāṅḍeḍache Śeṣa Gharāṇe ", pp. 56–73.

[25] Joshi, "'Ālī Ādil Shāh I of Bījāpūr".

[26] Kanhere, "Waman Pandit", pp. 305–14.

[27] Aryavaraguru, "On the Sheshas of Benaras", p. 247. I thank Sheldon Pollock for suggesting the appropriate translation of this title.

[28] Ibid., pp. 60–1.

family document confirming a division of lands in Nanded, dated to 1629, one Vasudevapant Sesa, "resident of Kasi", is a party to the document.[29]

Such continuing connections are evident in the lives of less-well-known pandits too. Ramachandra, a member of the Jade family of Karhade Brahmans from Narwe in the southern Konkan, moved to Banaras in the first or second decade of the seventeenth century, following a visit of the distinguished philosopher saint of Banaras, Bhaskarananda, to the family's home. By the 1630s, the Jade family was appearing in the city's pandit assemblies. Annotations to the catalogue of the extensive library that the family built up reveal their continuing interest in the work of scholars back in the Konkan.[30] Members of the Arade family of Karhades, also from the southern Konkan, migrated south to Karnataka, and east to the town of Saugor (modern Sagar) in modern Madhya Pradesh, as well as to Banaras. The family were well settled in the city by the 1630s, when the scholar Narayanabhatta Arade flourished as a logician and learned commentator on dharmasastra and kāvya, and the family sufficiently well established to take part in the pandit assemblies. However, Narayanabhatta maintained his links with the South, recording that he completed works at Hyderabad in 1640 and at Pune in 1651.[31]

The Scholar Household and the Brahman "Ecumene" in Banaras

Following the work of Bayly and others, we now have some understanding of the place of Banaras and its scholar-intellectuals within the Indian "ccumene".[32] Pandits such as Narayanabhatta of the Bhatta family during Akbar's time, and Kavindracaraya during the time of Shah Jahan, negotiated with the Mughal court on behalf of wider constituencies of the Hindu pious. They maintained good connections with the

[29] Ibid., p. 61.

[30] Sarma, "Manuscripts Collection of the Jade Family".

[31] Gode, "Some Authors of the Ārḍe Family", pp. 17–24, and Katre, "Nārāyaṇabhaṭṭa Ārḍe", pp. 74–86.

[32] Bayly, *Empire and Information*, pp. 180–211; Bronkhorst, "Bhaṭṭoji Dīkṣita on Sphoṭa", pp. 3–41; Pollock, "New Intellectuals"; Minkowski, "Sanskrit Scientific Libraries"; O'Hanlon, "Letters Home".

Mughal court, Kavindracarya particularly through the relationship he enjoyed with Shah Jahan's son Dara Shukoh.[33] They received addresses of thanks for their services from grateful Brahmans in other parts of India.[34] Rulers and sometimes pandit communities themselves conferred titles in public recognition of conspicuous learning.[35] Honours and rewards were also bestowed for success in the public disputations that great men as well as rulers staged as a form of prestige entertainment and elite cultural patronage.[36] In terms of religious culture, Advaitin views were beginning to come to dominate the literate institutions and public arenas of the city.[37]

However, what remains less well explored is the role of the scholar household in this quasi "public sphere".[38] Well represented in Banaras, the great sectarian maṭhas were themselves powerful centres of teaching, learning, and scholarly communication.[39] Many sanyasis appear as the teachers of scholar-pandits in particular disciplines. In the sanyasi Kavindracarya the city found one of its most brilliant scholars, teachers, and conduits of patronage to the learned and pious.[40] By the middle of the seventeenth century, as Bernier recorded, Rajput patronage founded schools for pupils of the elites in the city.[41]

For most Banaras scholars, however, the household provided the vital mainstay of their working lives. It is difficult to find direct accounts of the pedagogy of the scholar household. Vedic tradition prescribed that a Brahman boy undergo his initiation before joining the household of his instructor. This relationship was understood very

[33] Raghavan, "Kavīndrakalpalatikā".

[34] Sharma and Patkar, *Kavīndracandrodaya*. For a less well-known address, see *Nṛsiṁha–sarvasva Kavyām*, in Shastri, *Descriptive Catalogue*, vol. 4, pp. 81–5. I thank Chris Minkowski for assistance with translation of this text.

[35] For the award of titles, see Shastri, "Dakshini Pandits".

[36] For these traditions of debate, see Vidyabhushan, *Indian Logic*, pp. 1–21, 55–114.

[37] Minkowski, "Advaita Vedānta in Early Modern History". For other recent discussions of an early modern "public" in India, see Fisher, *Hindu Pluralism and the Public Sphere*, and Novetzke, *The Quotidian Revolution*.

[38] For a penetrating discussion of the neglected sphere of the household, see Chatterjee, *Unfamiliar Relations*, pp. 1–45.

[39] Scharfe, *Education in Ancient India*.

[40] Raghavan, "Kavīndrācārya Sarasvatī", pp. 159–65.

[41] See Bernier, *Travels in the Mogul Empire*, pp. 334–5.

much in filial terms, some texts representing the student quite literally as an "embryo" within the teacher's body.[42] Most students seem to have been educated partly within their own households, as we saw happening in the Sesa family. Many contemporaries prefaced their writings with elaborate tributes to their fathers as teachers: Narayanabhatta himself recorded that he had learned all of the sastras at the feet of his own father.[43] Fathers sometimes wrote texts for the instruction of their sons, as Kamalakarabhatta did when he composed a work on mantras for his son Anantabhatta.[44] We can think of many lineages where particular disciplines were a speciality: the Bhattas and Devas for mīmāṃsā, the Sesas for grammar, the Puntambkars for logic. As sons matured, they might write alongside their fathers, and in some cases complete their works. Gagabhatta completed his father's digest, the *Dinakaroddyota*.[45] Samkarabhatta edited and added to the work of his father Nilakanthabhatta, who was the cousin of Kamalakarabhatta and author of major works on religious law.[46] As Benke has shown, Krishna Sesa very likely completed the *Govindārṇava* of his father Narasimha.[47] The intensive ritual work of the householder is likely also to have offered opportunities for the education of sons.[48] Considerable investment thus went into the training of sons, for they represented in effect the family's future intellectual capital.

Marriage strategies were consequently important for pandit households in building up their resources and reputations. When Mahadeva Bharadavaja came to Banaras, he married the daughter of the Nilakanthabhatta just mentioned, and established the Bharadvajas thereafter as a leading scholarly family in the city.[49] Sometimes marriage relationships with families back in the Maratha regions could be equally effective.

[42] Scharfe, *Education in Ancient India*, p. 98.

[43] Kane, *Vyavharāmayūkha of Bhaṭṭa Nīlakaṇṭha*, p. vii.

[44] Kane, *History of Dharmaśāstra*, vol. 2, pt 1, p. 929.

[45] Kane, *Vyavahāramayūkha of Nīlakaṇṭha Bhaṭṭa*, p. xi.

[46] Ibid., p. xxiii.

[47] Benke, "The Śūdrācāraśiromaṇi of Kṛṣṇa Śeṣa", p. 30.

[48] Davis makes the point that the household was the foremost institutional locale for ritual observance as required in the laws of dharmasastra. Davis, *The Spirit of Hindu Law*, p. 39.

[49] Shastri, "Dakshini Pandits", p. 13.

The Arade family in Banaras, whose migrations we followed above, had long established ties with the eminent Padhye family of scholars from the Konkan and Pandharpur, the Padhyes sending sons to study with Arade teachers in Banaras, and the Arades marrying their daughters to Padhye sons.[50]

But, of course, students learned in other scholar households beside their own. Banaras in this period offered an extraordinary wealth of teacherly talent: long-settled scholars and recent arrivals, local householders and sanyasis from the city's monastic institutions, polymaths and single-discipline specialists. Bhattoji Diksita had Krishna Sesa as his teacher in grammar, and the prominent scholar-sanyasi of Banaras, Narsimhasram, as his teacher in Vedanta.[51] The poet Nilakantha Sukla had Bhattoji Diksita as his teacher in grammar, and Bhatta Srimanda in alaṃkāraśāstra.[52] Some contemporaries had teachers in many different individual disciplines: Nilakantha Caturdhara recorded the names of six, in the Vedas, Vedanta, sacrificing, logic, yoga, and śrauta.[53]

Bernier's well-known description of the "private houses" in which most Sanskrit teaching took place in Banaras of the 1660s may reflect these accommodative arrangements. The masters were "dispersed over different parts of the town in private houses, and principally in the gardens of the suburbs, which the rich merchants permit them to occupy. Some of these masters have four disciples, others six or seven, but this is the largest number."[54] Thus, in the Sesa household the great grammarian Bhattoji Diksita was a pupil of Krishna Sesa, being educated in the same household as Krishna Sesa's son Viresvara. Viresvara's student, the great poet Panditaraja Jagannatha, would thus have received his education alongside Viresvara's own son, Cakrapani.[55]

[50] Katre, "Nārāyaṇabhaṭṭa Ārḍe", p. 74, and Pangarkar, *Moropant*, p. 113. My thanks to Janaki Bakhle for this text.

[51] Gode, "The Identification of Gosvāmi Nṛsiṁhāśrama", pp. 447–51.

[52] Gode, "Nīlakaṇṭha Śukla", p. 471.

[53] Gode, "Date of the Bhāṭṭabhāṣāprakāśikā", p. 69.

[54] Bernier, *Travels in the Mogul Empire*, pp. 334–5.

[55] This combustible mix of filial and quasi-filial relationships could also fuel animosities: see Bronkhorst, "Bhaṭṭoji Dīkṣita on Sphoṭa", pp. 12–15; Minkowski, "I'll Wash Out Your Mouth With My Boot", pp. 113–36, and Bali, *Bhaṭṭoji Dīkṣita*, pp. 6–7.

The scholar household thus included the networks of quasi-filial relationships established by teachers and their students. In terms of household strategy, this made excellent sense. It widened the pool of intellectual talent on which a family could draw for the education of its sons. It was an essential component of a scholar's reputation, which depended not only on the works of learning that he wrote but on the numbers of famous students trained by him, and who went on to spread his traditions of learning further afield.[56] It guarded against the possibility that there might be no sons, or sons who lacked aptitude for the profession of their fathers.

The creation and maintenance of manuscript libraries were other ways in which scholar households operated as joint intellectual and pedagogical concerns. Great libraries were naturally associated with royal households and with the maṭhs of the ascetic orders.[57] But Maratha scholar-intellectuals in Banaras were able to accumulate significant manuscript libraries. In March 1651 in Pune, the mobile scholar Narayanabhatta Arade composed his *Pūjāsāgara*, a compendium of correct ritual practices. But he apologised for some parts of the work because, he explained, he was away from Banaras and did not have access to all of the materials he needed to consult while he was out of town.[58] The Jade family noticed above amassed a very substantial library, particularly in works of Advaita Vedanta. The early-nineteenth-century catalogue to the library suggests that it was cross-referenced according to discipline, making it an effective intellectual tool for a working scholar.[59]

Such libraries were part of the family's capital, intellectual as well as material, and a key basis for their livelihood.[60] The work of sons and pupils was important, adding to the household's stock of manuscripts by the copying of new ones or the replacement of texts worn out through use, or damaged by careless handling, spillages, the ravages

[56] See the discussion in Kelkar, "Mahārāṣṭrātīl Kāhī Paṇḍit Gharāṇe", pp. 29–34.

[57] Minkowski, "Sanskrit Scientific Libraries".

[58] Katre, "Nārāyaṇabhaṭṭa Ārḍe", p. 86.

[59] Sarma, "Manuscripts Collection of the Jade Family",

[60] For libraries as tools of livelihood, see Minkowski, "Sanskrit Scientific Libraries", pp. 97–105. See also Sastry, *Kavindracharya List*, for the catalogue to Kavindracarya's library.

of insects, damp, and other such enemies of paper documents.[61] Borrowing and lending texts, often a few manuscript pages at a time, was another way of augmenting the household's collection.[62] Such lending was sometimes a source of anxiety and exasperation, of the kind that the peshwa Bajirao I (r. 1720–1740) expressed when he found that the copy of the *Vedabhāṣya* he had lent was difficult to trace, as it had been passed from hand to hand.[63]

Something of this personal relationship between the text, the copyist, the needs of the household, and the household's reputation with others emerges in the discourse of the seventeenth-century poet-saint Ramdas on the study of writing. This discourse included detailed guidance on the preparation of good ink and even strokes of the pen in forming each Devanagari character, "so that a person looking at it will think that the whole book, from the first letter right to the end, has been written by the same pen."[64] The young were reminded that while their eyes could take in small print, the eyes of the old could not, and they should therefore make their letters big enough to accommodate the deficiences of their elders. The margins needed to be sufficiently generous so that wear on the edges of the pages would not damage the inscribed area. If a manuscript was written with this degree of skill and care, "people will imagine all sorts of things about who could have written it, and they will say, 'We must see this man'."[65]

The unity of the scholar family and its intellectual production also came together in matters of law. A very important question for such families was that of vidyādhana (gains of learning). Were the earnings of learning and teaching the property of the individual scholar, or did such wealth belong to the whole household? Nilakanthabhatta explored this point in his *Vyavahāramayūkha*, written between the second and fourth decade of the seventeenth century. The work affirmed

[61] Gough, *Papers*, p. 22.

[62] A brisk movement of manuscripts between elite Maratha households is described in Sardesai, *Selections from the Peshwa Daftar* (hereafter *SPD*), vol. 18, nos 78–84.

[63] Sardesai, *SPD*, vol. 9, no. 68 (undated).

[64] Ramdas, *Dāsabodha*, daśak 19, samās 1, "Lekhankriyānirūpan", pp. 433–4. For these aspects of scribal practice, see also Deshpande, *Scripts of Power*, pp. 112–26.

[65] Ibid., p. 434. See also Gode, "Saint Rāmadāsa's Discourse", pp. 127–8.

the rights of the individual in wealth obtained by teaching, by the exhibition of learning or ability in disputation, or by "means of eminent study". However, reflecting the influence in southern India of the scholar-jurist Mitaksara, Nilakantha affirmed the jointness of the scholar household's property. Wealth acquired by brothers from learning gained within the family, or as the result of the father's teaching, or acquired by one scholar brother whilst he was being supported by another, constituted the joint property of the whole family, on which members had a claim if the property were to be divided.[66]

These were not just abstract discussions. In the Sesa family, it is striking that of the two brothers Viresvara and Narayana, the former is not known to have left any works, whereas the latter found time to write. Aryavaraguru speculates that Viresvara's engagements as a teacher took up all his time, and we have noted some of those engagements above.[67] Would his earnings have gone to support the whole household, including the family of his scholarly brother? Family and property rights affected relationships in other ways too. In the well-known rivalry between Nilakantha and his cousin Kamalakarabhatta, one issue they differed about was the degree of ownership that fathers had in their sons. Although Nilakantha had emphasised the jointness of the scholar household, he stopped short of arguing that this gave rise to any actual right of property in sons or in wives. Kamalakarabhatta took a more assertive view of the internal dependencies of the extended family. In his great compendium the *Nirnayasindhuḥ*, he asserted that only a fool could think that a man had no rights of ownership in his own son.[68]

It was also as part of successful extended families that Maratha scholar-intellectuals presented themselves in their writings. At the start or end of their works, authors described the accomplishments of their lineage, acknowledged their debts, and advertised their own talents. Raghavabhatta, the late-fifteenth-century author of a commentary on the Śākuntala, described his grandfather Ramesvarabhatta,

[66] Kane, *Vyavahāramayūkha of Nīlakaṇṭha Bhaṭṭa*, pp. 136–8. See also Kane, *History of Dharmaśāstra*, vol. 3, pp. 581–5. This aspect of Hindu family law generated continuous litigation in the colonial law courts, until the passing of the Hindu Gains of Learning Act in 1930. Newbigin, *The Hindu Family*.

[67] Aryavaraguru, "On the Sheshas of Banaras", p. 250.

[68] Kane, *History of Dharmaśāstra*, vol. 1, pt 2, p. 941.

an expert in dialectics residing in Nasik on the banks of the Godavari, and his father, Prthvidharabhatta, well versed in mīmāṃsā and Vedanta. Prthvidharabhatta migrated from Nasik to Banaras, where Raghavabhatta was born. Raghavabhatta evidently considered himself a worthy scion of the house, for he described himself as an expert in vedānta, logic, mīmāṃsā, mathematics, medicine, erotics, music, and other arts.[69] The colophons of pupils were equally effective in advertising the merits of the scholar-intellectual, as the Maratha scholar Raghunatha Navahastha made clear in the eulogies to his teacher Anantadeva that appear in many of his works.[70]

Families displayed themselves together in person too. As we shall see, fathers and sons, teachers and their students appeared together in the "public" forum of pandit assemblies. Scholar-brothers might attend competitive public debates together. Bhattoji Diksita and his brother Rangojibhatta went to the Ikkeri court of Venkatappa Nayaka I (1595–1629), where they defeated a Madhva ascetic in debate and received many honours.[71] The award of titles to individuals sometimes had a public afterlife for their families. Vishnu Sesa's title of "sabhāpati" and Narasimha Sesa's title of "bhaṭṭa-bhaṭṭārākar" continued to be enjoyed in person by the Sesas after his death.[72]

We can gain only fragmentary glimpses into other aspects of the life of the Brahman scholar household. Deshpande suggests that these families may have spoken Marathi at home, with a Hindi dialect for communicating with neighbours, and Sanskrit as the language of learning.[73] We do not know how far they shared the same hearth. Krishna Sesa had a brother, Chintamani, and his two sons, Viresvara and Narayana, noted above. They, their parents, their wives and children, would very likely have occupied the same family home, perhaps in a wada, the old-style mansion built around a courtyard that was a typical form of domestic architecture in Maharashtra of the period.[74] But would the four sons of Samkarabhatta, grandson of the first Bhatta to move to

[69] Gode, "Date of Rāghavabhaṭṭa".

[70] Sarma, "Raghunātha Navahastha", pp. 69–82.

[71] Gode, "The Contact of Bhaṭṭoji Dīkṣita with the Rulers of Ikkeri", p. 205.

[72] Aryavaraguru, "On the Sheshas of Benaras", p. 247.

[73] Deshpande, "On Vernacular Sanskrit", pp. 32–51.

[74] For the wada as a family home, see Bhagwat, "Home and the March of Times".

Banaras, have continued to live in the same household? At some point, of course, such households would need to have divided, with implications for division of family property and many other formerly joint arrangements.

The family history written by this Samkarabhatta demonstrates many strategies of the migrant scholar household.[75] In the first decade of the sixteenth century, his grandfather Ramesvarabhatta moved from Paithan some eighty miles west to Sangamner, where he set up as a teacher. Failing to have a son, he and his wife went to Kolhapur to worship the family deity, taking his students with him. The visit was successful and, with the couple convinced that she was carrying a son who would be a great scholar, the family went on to Krishnadevaraya's Vijayanagar to see its wealth of learning. Their son, Narayanabhatta, was born in 1513, but he developed consumption. So the family, again along with Ramesvara's students, went to Dwarka for a cure. Here, Ramesvara spent some time training a local student to carry on his own intellectual traditions in that city. From there Ramesvara returned to Paithan. After some three or four years in the city, he and his household left for Banaras, where they settled. Here, the remarkable Bhatta dynasty emerged. Outstanding scholars in many disciplines appeared from the next four generations of sons and cousins, whose working lives spanned the middle of the sixteenth century to the end of the seventeenth.[76]

However, Samkarabhatta made it clear that the quasi-filial connections between leading members of the Bhatta family and their pupils were equally important as a measure of his family's success. He describes how famous scholars came from Dravida, Gurjara, Kanyakubja, Malwa, Braja, Mithila, the Himalayan regions, Karnata, Utkala, the Konkan, Gauda, Andhra, Mathura, Kamarupa, and other parts of India to learn with his father and grandfather.[77]

The scholar household was thus a mainstay in the lives of Banaras' Maratha intellectuals. What made possible the brilliant achievements of so many of their members during the sixteenth and seventeenth centuries was precisely the corporate and familial dimension of their

[75] Benson, "Saṃkārabhaṭṭa"s Family Chronicle", pp. 105–17.

[76] For the Bhatta family tree, see Kane, *Vyavahāramayūkha of Nīlakaṇṭha Bhaṭṭa*, p. xvi.

[77] Shastri, "Dakshini Pandits", p. 12.

lives which we, perhaps, do not often associate with individual intellectual distinction. The household provided an exceptionally high degree of specialised training and accumulation of expertise, very much as heritable craft specialisations produced outstanding levels of skill in other areas of the early modern Indian economy.[78] In Mughal Banaras, there was a unique concentration of such households, linked by ties of family, migration, and pedagogy to Brahman communities elsewhere in India, creating a critical mass which multiplied in its effects.

The scholar household in this setting was not a "private" sphere in any simple sense, contrasted with the "public" of the city and its political and intellectual life.[79] It was part of a wider network of pedagogy which itself constituted an important dimension of the Brahman "ecumene". In many ways, it was an ideal milieu for students to acquire the deep disciplinary expertises and intellectual confidence that the training of the household could provide, but in a setting of considerable intellectual and cultural heterogeneity. Here, shifting populations of mobile scholars, seekers of enlightenment, ritual specialists, travelling ascetics, and pilgrims could open up wider horizons for students and prompt them to ask new questions about established bodies of knowledge, their intellectual underpinnings, and their relation to one another as well as to the pressures and dilemmas of the present. Such might have been the context, at least, in which the scholar-intellectuals of early modern Banaras and their compeers at centres elsewhere in India wielded their remarkable disciplinary skills – but, in some cases, for the purposes of reappraisal and critique of the foundations of those disciplines themselves.

Geographies of Brahman Identity

From their vantage point in Banaras, how did these scholar families view Brahman communities in other parts of India?[80] Around the end of the first millennium, there seems to have begun a gradual move

[78] For a recent discussion, see Washbrook, "India in the Early Modern World Economy", pp. 87–111.

[79] For a discussion of this "public" dimension of the household, see Guha, "The Family Feud", pp. 73 94.

[80] For geo-political space in the Sanskrit "cosmopolis", see Pollock, *Language of the Gods*, pp. 189–222, and Inden, *Imagining India*, pp. 244–62.

to develop a classification of regions as markers of Brahman origins and affiliation, in addition to the older identifiers of family śākhā (branch of Vedic study) and gotra (exogamous lineage unit).[81] Certain geographical concepts emerged with especial significance. Dakṣiṇātya (southerner) seems to have been an important and perhaps prestigious identifier for many Maratha pandits. It was associated with the old centres of Brahman learning on the Godavari and other rivers of central-southern India, perhaps seen from the perspective of Mughal Banaras as the pristine remains of older traditions of small-town scholarship and piety that had remained untouched by the sometimes uncomfortable compromises of the present.[82] Many scholars described themselves as "southerners" in this way.[83] Some part of Narayanabhatta's reputation depended on his consistent advocacy of the intellectual traditions of "the south".[84] An important part of these lay in the distinctive Mitākṣarā approach to family law, as we have seen in the compendium of family law, the *Vyavahāramayūkha*, compiled by Narayanabhatta's son Nilakantha.

Dakṣiṇātya scholars in Banaras were numerous enough to attract hostile comment. The Kanyakubja Brahman Dhiresvara Misra was teacher in logic to Nilakantha Caturdhara. In his compendium, the *Dvijarājodaya* (rise of the kingdom of the twice-born), composed about 1630, he made a series of sarcastic attacks on what he called the navīna-

[81] Vaidya, *History of Medieval Hindu India*, vol. 3, pp. 375–81. For a discussion of Brahmin migrations, see Datta, *Migrant Brāhmaṇas*, and a review of the work in Witzel, "Towards a History of the Brahmins", pp. 264–8. See also Kane, "Gotras and Pravaras"; Kosambi, "On the Origin of Brahmin Gotras", pp. 21–80; Witzel, "On the Localisation of Vedic Texts and Schools", pp. 173–213, and Witzel, "Regionale und überregionale Faktoren", pp. 37–76.

[82] Memories of Vijayanagar as exemplary "Hindu" kingdom clearly played some role here: see Hawley, "The Four Sampradāys". I thank Jack Hawley for many insightful discussions of this theme. Samkarabhatta's family history represents Vijayanagar as a place of learning, but an unhappy place, whose ruler offended Ramesvara by attempting to give him an elephant. Benson, "Saṃkārabhaṭṭa's Family Chronicle", p. 110. See also Guha, "Frontiers of Memory", pp. 269–88.

[83] See, for example, Krishna Sesa's description of his father: Kanole, "Nāṅḍeḍache Śeṣa Gharāṇe", p. 62. The term could also include Gujarat: Gode, "Harikavi alias Bhānubhaṭṭa", p. 113.

[84] Benson, "Saṃkārabhaṭṭa's Family Chronicle", pp. 12–13.

dakṣiṇātyāḥ – the "new southerner" or "southerners". Sometimes he referred to these, perhaps with some irony, as the dakṣiṇātyaśiṣṭammanyāḥ (southerners who fancy themselves learned).[85] It may be possible to see here the resentment of a Kanyakubja Brahman for the collective esprit de corps of the city's dakṣiṇātya Brahmans, who seemed to think of themselves very much as the learned śiṣṭa of the contemporary world.

As we shall see, however, Brahmans in the city as well as those in the regions who looked to the learned in Banaras for the resolution of disputes, sought to develop a more comprehensive classification of the mobile Brahman communities of the subcontinent, and one without particular regional partialities. By the end of the first millennium, we begin to see evidence of such a classification based on the notion that there were pañca gauḍa (five northern) and pañca drāviḍa (five southern) communities of Brahmans.

How did this classification arise? "Gauḍa" we know variously as the name of the ancient kingdom of Gauḍa in west Bengal; the country in which Bengali is spoken; and as a collective name for the eastern regions of India.[86] Generic territorial names were often a combination of cultural and linguistic regions together with elaborate classifications on the basis of numbers: the "fifty-six countries" of India, the "seven Koṅkaṇas" of the Konkan region, the "five drāviḍas" said to be part of the realm ruled by the Colas, the "three Kaliṅgas" of the old Kalinga empire in central-eastern India.[87]

As Whitney Cox has suggested, however, these territorial names could be recruited to new uses, to describe peoples rather than territories, and in a more deliberately systematising way.[88] Perhaps significantly, given their location between North and South, the earliest

[85] Katre, "Dvijarāodaya", pp. 144–55. I thank Sheldon Pollock for suggesting this translation.

[86] Sircar, "Gauḍa", pp. 123–34.

[87] In an inscription of 1024–5 CE, for example, the western Chalukya king Jayasimha III described his triumphs: "the eradication of the Cola, the mighty overlord of the five drāviḍas, the requisition of the treasure of the lords of the seven Koṅkaṇas." Hultzsch, "Inscriptions of the Kailāsanātha Temple at Kānchīpuran", p. 113. I thank Whitney Cox for a discussion of these points, and translation of this Tamil inscription. For these geographies, see Sircar, *Studies in the Geography of Ancient and Medieval India*, pp. 68–109.

[88] Whitney Cox, personal communication.

uses of the pañca gauḍa and pañca drāviḍa classification together seem to be from the Maratha regions. A Rastrakuta grant of 926 CE from the town of Samyana in the northern Konkan describes the gifting of revenues for the feeding of nine persons belonging to the pañca gauḍīya maha parisad (great assembly of the five gauḍas) settled in the town.[89]

The most widely circulated early reference to the pañca gauḍa/pañca drāviḍa formulation together is in western Maharashtra's "purana of place", the *Sahyādrikhaṇḍa*.[90] This purana describes the god Parashuram's settlement of the region with its many different Brahman communities. In the context of a discussion about the origins of Chitpavan Brahmans, Skanda asks Mahadev to explain the tenfold division of Brahmans. Mahadev's reply is interesting because it indicates that while the classification itself was recognised, which Brahmans actually belonged to each grouping was still indeterminate:

> The Dravidas, Telangas, Karnatas, Madhyadesas and Gurjaras are the pañca drāviḍas. The Saraswatas, Kanyakubjas, Utkalas, Maithilas and Gauda are the pañca gauḍas. These are the ten kinds of Brahmans. Similarly, some say that the pañca gauḍas consist of the Trihotras, Agnivaisyas, Kanyakubjas, Kanojyas and Maitrayanas. All these divisions of Brahmans were made by the rishis. Throughout this wide land, each of them follows the practices of their own countries.[91]

Mahadev hastened to add that nonetheless all shared the distinguishing marks that united all Brahmans. "All of these Brahmans have the gayatri mantra, and they have their rituals said with Vedic mantras. They all have the same six karmas."[92]

[89] Sircar, "Rashtrakuta Charters from Chinchani", pp. 46–7.

[90] The only standard edition is da Cunha, *The Sahyâdri-Khaṇḍa of the Skanda Purāṇa*, published in 1877. The purana was probably in existence by the twelfth century, since fragments are quoted in the *Chaturvargacintāmaṇi* of Hemadri, minister of the Yadava king Mahadeva: Hemadri, *Chaturvargacintāmaṇi*, vol. 1, pp. 718–9 and vol. 3, p. 306. We do not know, however, when these particular verses of the purana were written. See Levitt, "The Sahyādrikhaṇḍa: Some Problems". The quotations below are from da Cunha's edition.

[91] *Sahyādrikhaṇḍa*, Uttarārdha, Adhyāya 1, "Origins of the Chitpavans", vss. 1–2.

[92] Ibid., vss. 5–6. A Brahman's six karmas or ritual privileges and duties were adhyāyana and adhyāpana, studying and teaching the Veda; yajana and yājana,

An inscription of 1425 CE, in the Virinchipuram temple in the northern Arcot district, records the proceedings of an assembly of Brahmans. While it does not allude to the "five drāviḍas", it does show the way in which affiliations of gotra and śākhā persisted alongside this emerging vocabulary of regional affiliations for Brahmans. The Brahmans who signed the document committed themselves neither to give, nor to take, money at the marriage of a daughter. "According to this, if the Brahmans of this kingdom of Paḍaivīḍu, Kaṇṇaḍigas, Tamiṛas, Teluṅgas, Ilāḷas, of all gotras, sūtras and śākhās conclude a marriage, they shall, from this day forward, do it by kanyādāna."[93] Regional identifications of this kind for Brahmans were commonplace by this period.

But what "work" did the more specific classification of "five gauḍa" and "five drāviḍa" communities of Brahmans do, over the long period of its development? Madhav Deshpande suggests a link with earlier phases of Brahman migration south of the Vindhyas. It provided a framework for what were often fierce political battles that continued into the early modern period, to explain the cultural differences between Brahman communities of different regions, to include some within the ambit of approved Brahman identities and exclude others.[94] Further research is needed into the uses of this classification in other regions of India. However, it is possible too that it emerged earliest and most clearly among Brahmans of the Maratha regions precisely because these regions lay between "North" and "South", making it particularly important for these Brahmans to establish a clear geography of Brahman identity within which their own communities could be located.

The Maratha scholar intellectuals of sixteenth- and seventeenth-century Banaras and their constituencies in the regions were active players in the development of the classification. As we shall see, for Brahmans back in the Maratha country who took their disputes to Banaras the clear grid of regional affiliations represented in the pañca

---

conducting and procuring a sacrifice; and dāna and pratigraha, giving and accepting gifts. Apte, *Social and Religious Life*, p. 8.

[93] Hultzsch, "Inscriptions At and Near Virinchipuram", p. 84. Padaividu was a kingdom in North Arcot.

[94] Deshpande, "Pañca Gauḍa".

gauḍa/pañca drāviḍa conception was attractive because it offered the chance to anchor local and perhaps precarious identities within a framework that aspired, at least, to be recognised across the subcontinent. For the pandit assemblies themselves, the classification provided an authoritative grid onto which they could map the place of every local Brahman community. It offered an extremely useful tool in determining what and who a Brahman was, and in bringing cohesion to the fractious communities who claimed that status for themselves.

The pañca gauḍa/pañca drāviḍa conception also came to fulfil an important judicial role. It suggested both comprehensiveness of representation among the assemblies of Brahmans brought together to consider questions of ritual authority and religious law, and the broad Brahman audiences to which they addressed their findings. In this sense, one might almost see this conception, articulated from Shiva's own city, as a Brahman version of the tour d'horizon contained in the royal digvijaya, enumerating all of the different regional Brahman communities of the subcontinent claimed as a part of its unifying sociological framework. Brought to bear in the new communicative spaces of Mughal India, this older universalising geography of the Sanskrit cosmopolitan sphere enabled the assemblies to present themselves as something like an all-India deliberative Brahman "public".

The Banaras assemblies and their appeals gave a powerful forward impulse to the wider currency of the pañca gauḍa and pañca drāviḍa conception. By 1749, for example, we find the concept invoked at the Satara court as a means of demarcating the ritual entitlements of Brahmans from those of their Kayastha rivals.[95] We saw above the ties of teaching and marriage that linked the Arade family of Banaras with the Padhyes of the Konkan. In 1756, the Padhye brothers were locked in bitter dispute at the peshwa's court in Pune over their rights to priestly office in the Konkan. The brothers demanded: "Let us you and we sit down together in front of the five draviḍas, and talk of the justice in this case."[96] The classification also entered popular traditions of narrative poetry, appearing in the kathā of one Anand, whose poem about the rise of Chitpavan Brahmans was performed at the Satara

[95] Bendrey, *Mahārāṣṭretihāsachī Sādhane*, vol. 2, no. 457 of 8 June 1749, pp. 491–5.

[96] Pangarkar, *Moropant*, p. 108.

court in 1820.[97] By the start of the nineteenth century, in colonial and Indian commentaries alike, the categories of pañca gauḍa and pañca drāviḍa had become the standard way of classifying the subcontinent's Brahman communities.[98]

Speaking from Shiva's Temple: The Locale of the Assemblies

Let us turn now to the Visvesvara temple in Banaras, which the pandit assemblies advertised as the location for their meetings. The temple was rebuilt during Akbar's time, probably during the 1570s or 1580s, under the leadership of Narayanabhatta of the Bhatta family.[99] I have argued elsewhere that the temple followed the earlier cruciform layout described in the *Kāśīkhaṇḍa*.[100] The traveller Jean-Baptiste Tavernier, touring India between 1638 and 1643, described "the pagoda of Benares, which, after that of Jagannath, is the most famous in all India, and of equal sanctity." It was built in the form of a cross, with four equal arms, in the middle of which "a lofty dome rises like a kind of tower with many sides terminating in a point, and at the end of each arm of the cross another tower rises, which can be ascended from outside. Before reaching the top there are many niches and several balconies, which project to intercept the fresh air; and all over the tower there are rudely executed figures in relief of various kinds of animals."[101] As Michell has suggested, the temple so constructed illustrates the way in which Mughal building techniques could be brought into the service of Hindu ritual requirements.[102]

[97] The poem is printed in Lalji Vaijanath Sastri, *Sadbodhacintamani*, p. 182.

[98] Raja Radha Kanta Deva, *Śabda-Kalpadruma*, vol. 2, p. 370, first published in 1820; Gunjikar, *Saraswatīmanḍal* pp. 4–5; Bhattacharya, *Hindu Castes and Sects*, p. 24; Russell and Hiralal, *Tribes and Castes*, vol. 2, p. 357.

[99] See O'Hanlon, "Letters Home", p. 218.

[100] Ibid., p. 219. See also the discussion and photographs of the present-day remains of Narayanabhatta's temple in Michell, "Temple Styles", p. 80, and Gutschow, *Benaras*, p. 34. Michell questions the link with the *Kāśikhaṇḍa*'s structure. However, this may be a misreading of Prinsep's 1827 reconstructed ground plan of the temple, which shows a cruciform construction of four mandapams, as described in the *Kāśikhaṇḍa*. Prinsep's plan is reproduced in Altekar, *Benaras*, p. 50.

[101] Tavernier, *Travels in India*, vol. 2, p. 180.

[102] Michell, "Temple Styles", p. 82.

Visiting the city in September 1632, the traveller and commercial prospector Peter Mundy went inside the temple

> where, in the middle, on a place elevated, is a stone in forme like a Hatters blocke plaine and unwrought, as per the figure; on which they that resort powre water of the River, flowres, rice, Butter, which here (by reason of the heat) is most comonly liquid, whilest the Bramane reads or sayes something which the Vulgar understands not. Over it hanges a Canopie of Silke and about it severall Lampes lighted.[103]

Tavernier also ventured inside, where he saw many other deities, their presence suggesting a broad and inclusive religious culture for the temple: "Bainmadou", Vishnu in his guise as Veni Madhava, lord of the junction of the three sacred rivers, Ganges, Jamna, and Sarasvati, which meet together at Prayag; the massive gold figure of Vishnu's mount, Garuda; and Murlidhara, Krishna playing the flute.[104]

The Central Asian traveller Mahmud Balkhi, who toured North India between 1624 and 1631, noted the bustle and crowds of pilgrims visiting what he called "the temple of Lala Bir Singh":

> This temple is situated in the heart of Banaras, and is made of stone and brick. Its height is 130 zira (yards) and the interior circumference is one hundred zira (yards), consisting of wonderful aspects and high verandahs. Outside this grand and matchless building are a school, a worship house, an inn, about 80 houses in all, fully occupied and engaged. Although the worship was coming to an end, the men and women were dispersing, nearly thirty thousand women and men together and close (to each other) were present on that unique place. Orators, reciters of holy books, dominis, and all the administrators of affairs and others were present. Everyone stayed with their respective guides. Due to the large crowd and the ecstasy due to religious songs, it was difficult to keep one's bearing there.[105]

The charismatic deities of the temple were beginning to attract the attention of Rajput rulers anxious to associate themselves with its power. At some point in the decades after the rebuilding of the 1580s, the Visvesvara temple may have benefitted from the beneficence of Vir Singh Bundela, ruler of Orccha between 1605 and 1627, for

[103] Mundy, *Travels*, vol. 2, p. 123.
[104] Tavernier, *Travels in India*, vol. 2, pp. 181–2.
[105] Quoted in Habib, *Medieval India*, p. 147.

here we see Mahmud Balkhi describing it as the temple of "Lala Bir Singh".[106] Raja Jaisingh of Amber also established close links with the temple. He built a school attached to it for the education of children of noble families.[107] He also constructed a shrine to house Parvati, consort of Shiva, in her form of Annapurna, goddess of nourishment and food, and a presiding deity of Banaras. This deity, Tavernier tells us, had formerly been in the Visvesvara temple itself, but "the Raja desiring to have this idol in the pagoda of his house and to remove it from the great pagoda, has expended in gifts to the Brahmans and in alms to the poor more than 500,000 rupees, which make 750,000 livres of our money." Newly adorned with jewels and pearls, the goddess stood in a specially constructed shrine attached to the Raja's house.[108]

What do we know about the Mukti mandapam itself, where the pandit assemblies described themselves as meeting? Its name suggests a peculiarly sacred quality: in the very city of mukti (liberation), this is liberation's own pavilion. Let us go back to the *Kāśīkhaṇḍa*, because for his late-sixteenth-century guide to Kasi, the *Tristhalīsetuḥ*, Narayanabhatta reproduced much of the *Kāśīkhaṇḍa*'s fourteenth-century description.[109] Having described the whole temple as the place of his greatest happiness and beautiful abode of his sports, Shiva goes on to the Mukti mandapam itself. "To the south thereof is the abode of the glory of salvation, my pavilion. I stay there always. That is my hall of assembly, sadomaṇḍapa."[110]

After reproducing Shiva's description of the extraordinary merits that pilgrims would gain by actions performed in the pavilion, Narayanabhatta departed from the text of the *Kāśīkhaṇḍa* and inserted his

[106] In the early eighteenth century, the Kayastha scribe Bhimsen also attributed the temple to the generosity of Vir Singh: *Tarikh-i Dilkasha*, p. 3.

[107] Tavernier, *Travels in India*, vol. 2, pp. 182–3. See also Gode, "Bernier and Kavīndrācārya Sarasvatī", and Gode, "Some Evidence".

[108] Tavernier, *Travels in India*, vol. 2, p., 184.

[109] It is likely that he composed this work after the temple rebuilding, since he implies that visiting pilgrims would see a new *liṅga*: "though here the liṅga of Visvesvara is removed and another is brought in its place by human beings, owing to the times, the pilgrims must worship whatever liṅga is in this place." Narayanabhatta, *Tristhalīsetuḥ*, p. 208. I thank Vincenzo Vergiani and Jim Benson for assistance with translation here.

[110] *Kāśīkhaṇḍa*, Pūrvārdha, Adhyāya 79, vs. 54; Narayanabhatta, *Tristhalīsetuḥ*, p. 188.

own lines, perhaps to re-emphasise the associations of the pavilion with discussions in matters of religious law: "Because one can worship in the pavilion of liberation, and converse on matters of dharma there, as well as listen to the puranas, a man who is a receptacle of dharma should live in Kasi."[111] Narayanabhatta's text then returned to the *Kāśīkhaṇḍa* for his description of the other three pavilions. But it was the Mukti mandapam, the "southern" pavilion, whose prestige and spiritual potency shine out most in these passages that he reproduced. The suggestion of "southern" authorship for the *Kāśīkhaṇḍa* can only be speculative. What is certain, however, is that by the time of Narayanabhatta the "southern" pavilion was acquiring associations with a new kind of "southern" prestige, in the southern (dakṣiṇātya) origins of many of the learned scholars who were coming to dominate the assemblies held there.

Perhaps most interestingly, the Mukti mandapam seems to have been familiar to Brahman audiences outside the city. The *Vāḍeśvarodaya-kāvya*, by one Vishvanatha of the Pitre family of Karhade Brahmans from the Konkan, was completed in the third or fourth decade of the seventeenth century.[112] The work celebrated the temple to Vadesvara, family deity of many Chitpavan Brahmans, at Guhagar in the Ratnagiri District of the Konkan. Amongst the many stories he told, Vishvanatha described how pandits in the sacred Mukti mandapam at Banaras had held investigations to determine whether the presence of the gods in the great peaks of the Sahyadri range transformed those peaks into gold, as a Suta (teller of puranic histories) had told them. Was śabdaprāmāṇya (the authority of the puranic scriptures) greater than pratyakṣaprāmāṇya (the authority of evidence that could be seen through practical observation)? A messenger was despatched to find out. The mountains, when he got there, were made of ordinary earth. But the lump of soil he carried back with him to show his masters in Banaras was transformed into gold as soon as it came within the boundaries of the city. After seeing it, the doubters in the Mukti mandapam found their confidence in the truths of the eternal Vedas restored – and happily, perhaps, the authority of the sastras and the truths of visual evidence to be at one.

[111] Narayanabhatta, *Tristhalīsetuḥ*, p. 189.

[112] Pusalkar, *Vāḍeśvarodaya-Kāvya of Viśvanātha*, p. 66. Pitre is a Karhade name: Gode, "Origin and Antiquity", p. 25.

Speaking from Shiva's Temple: The Assemblies and Their Judgments

It was thus very much in the setting of Mughal Banaras, with its links with the Mughal court, and with its elite culture of Rajput patronage and pious public building, that the Maratha scholar-intellectuals were able to find a place of such grandeur for their meetings. The form of their assemblies was straightforward: it was the standard dharma-sabhā or pariṣad of learned Brahmans called to settle disputes or prescribe penances in matters of religious law.[113] The disputes brought to them were very much the local consequences of the wider pressures of "early modernity" discussed at the start of this essay.

Devarukhe or Devarsi Brahmans and their relations with the Chitpavan community in the Konkan were the subject of an ongoing struggle. Devarsis who had migrated to Banaras were successful, indeed prestigious ritual specialists. However, their caste-fellows who had remained behind in the Konkan were locked in a dispute with their Chitpavan Brahman neighbours, which seems to have had its origins in the Devarukhes' refusal to work as labourers for their wealthier Chitpavan neighbours.[114] A Marathi letter of 1583 sent from Banaras back to the Konkan reported that the pandit assembly held in the Mukti mandapam to discuss the matter had urged reconciliation: "All this community of Brahmanas (he samasta brāhmana), the Chiplunas, Devarsis and Maharastras, have the same vedic karmas (samāna vaidika karmi) and there is authority for sharing of food together. It was also agreed that Brahmans should not conduct hostilities with each other. This much was agreed by common consent." The judgment concluded with a reminder of the solemn prestige of the assembly's meeting place: "Let he who says there should be no exchange of food be brought to the place of Sri Visvesvara."[115]

Shenvis or Saraswat Brahmans, communities of successful trading people, farmers, as well as administrative servants of the Portuguese, the East India Company, and the local states of the Konkan littoral were

[113] See Kane, *History of Dharmaśāstra*, vol. 2, pt 2, pp. 965–73.

[114] For this dispute, see O'Hanlon and Minkowski, "What Makes People Who They Are?"

[115] Pimputkar, *Chitaḷebhaṭṭa Prakaraṇa*, pp. 76–7. For the provenance of these letters, see O'Hanlon, "Letters Home", pp. 239–40.

the subject of repeated attack, particularly from Karhade Brahmans, for their livelihoods as traders and farmers, and for the fact that they ate fish. Hence, the Karhades argued, Saraswats were not eligible for all of the six karmas or ritual duties and entitlements that distinguished a Brahman.

Again, the Banaras pandit assemblies urged unity, describing themselves in remarkably authoritative and expansive terms. In Visvesvara's own city, "the whole community of the excellent pañca drāviḍas, that is to say, Dravidas, Andras, Karnatakas, Maharastras and Gurjaras" had met "in the Mukti mandapam of Srisvami's temple." They sent their greetings to "the pañca drāviḍas and pañca gauḍas who live in the region of the Sahyadri mountains of the dakṣiṇa deśa." The judgment that they had come to was that the Shenvis or Saraswats of the region were in fact "eastern Brahmans of the pañca gauḍa community." In eating fish, they were simply following the prescriptions of Parashuram, who allowed all those who came to settle in the Konkan to follow their long-established customs. The assembly concluded with a reminder of their status: "This is the opinion of the śiṣṭa."[116]

In 1657, the scholar families of Banaras again found the question of the Devarukhes before them. The stakes in the very large assembly that met to consider it were particularly high because some Brahman families in the city had themselves contracted marriage relationships with the Devarukhes, or "Devarsis" as they were known in the city. Hence the assembly was vehement in its defence of the community: "They are of the nature that they can perform Vedic sacrifices on their own behalf and on behalf of others, they purify the line in which they dine, thcy arc worthy people as family relations, and are of the nature of being absolutely excellent Brahmins. And it is decided that the śiṣṭa do have family relations with them." Dire consequences would follow any disagreement: "Anyone who speaks against this decision, reached by the wise, is a desecrator of the god Vishvanatha and a murderer of Brahmins."[117]

We do not know whether this dispute came from outside Banaras, perhaps from critics back in the Maratha regions, or from local

[116] Gunjikar, *Sarasvatīmaṇḍal,* Appendix 2, pp. 22–4.
[117] Pimputkar, *Chitaḷebhaṭṭa Prakaraṇa*, pp. 78–81.

malcontents like the Kanyakubja Brahman Dhiresvara. But the suggestion that Devarsis were less than excellent Brahmans struck at the heart of the scholar household as a social as well as an intellectual enterprise. If, as the judgment above suggests, some leading families had contracted marriages with Devarsis, any taint would spread to all of their social relationships. Nor could this have remained merely a "social" matter. Any question over the pandit household's social reputation would have been likely to affect the networks of teaching and co-residence so central to its livelihood and reputation. Even more important, such questions about the social standing of the household might well have spread to affect perceptions of the intellectual work carried on within it.

This helps us to make sense of the remarkable assembly of pandits who met to consider the question.[118] Maratha pandit families therefore made up the core of those attending, twenty-three of the seventy-seven signatories to its judgment identifiable as Maratha Brahmans. In these signatures, it is also the extended scholar family that stands out. Members of the Bhatta, Sesa, Deva, and other Maratha pandit families were present, alongside an extraordinary array of other scholars and intellectuals, householders, and ascetics from the Maratha country, from Bengal, and from southern India.

Conclusions

Within a few years of this meeting, however, the world of these scholar-intellectuals began to undergo profound changes. With the execution in 1659 of Dara Shukoh, a key link between the Banaras pandit communities and the Mughal court disappeared. A decade later, in 1669–70, for reasons that are not clearly understood, Aurangzeb ordered the Visvesvara temple to be pulled down, along with the Vaishnava temple at Mathura, and important parts of the temple at Vrandavan.[119] With the emperor embarked on a protracted struggle with his Maratha adversaries in the Deccan, and their prestigious meeting place reduced to rubble beneath a mosque placed conspicuously

[118] For further discussion of these assemblies, see O'Hanlon, "Letters Home".

[119] For these episodes, see Horstmann, "The Temple of Govindadevajī", and Pauwels, "A Tale of Two Temples". See also the discussion in Asher, *Architecture of Mughal India*, pp. 254–5.

atop its visible remnants, the political climate of Banaras turned increasingly adverse for the city's Maratha pandit families.[120] Scholars from the Bhatta and Deva families, in particular, moved to associate themselves with Shivaji's court at Raigad in the Maratha regions. As is well known, pandits from these families played a central role in his consecration as a royal dharmic king in 1674.[121]

This was a prescient move. If the Mughal imperial framework had helped bring into being the remarkable Brahman social formation studied here, the fragmentation and decay of that framework, and the shifting of political as well as judicial power to Maharashtra's regions, were also to mean the gradual passing of many of this formation's judicial and intellectual functions from Banaras to the regions too. Within the Mughal context, Maratha scholar pandits had benefitted from the disjunction between the royal authority of Muslim courts in North India, and authority in matters of Hindu religious law. The city's intellectuals were to some extent able to step into this gap, and to provide mediation and judicial expertise in a wide range of disputes without the benefit of close support from Hindu royal authority. Their vantage point in Shiva's own city may have had a special aptness in this particular context. As noted above, one of the central narrative themes of the *Kāśīkhaṇḍa* described the evacuation of royal power from the city so that Shiva could make his abode there. However, the rise of the Maratha empire created in effect conditions for a re-attachment of Brahman authority to the royal power of "Hindu" states in the new courts of western India, whose ministers early evinced a determination to build up their own textual resources and local expertise in matters of religious law.[122] This development was to erode the position of Banaras and its scholar-intellectuals, and to shift many of their functions to Pune, Satara, Kolhapur, Tanjore, and Baroda – and, in the eighteenth century, to a new generation of expansive Rajput rulers with their own ritual ambitions.[123] It was the Pune court that now

[120] Michell suggests that this positioning was deliberate, a lesson to the city's Maratha Brahmans for having sheltered Shivaji during his flight from Agra three years earlier: Michell, "Temple Styles", p. 80.

[121] See Bendrey, *Coronation of Sivaji the Great*.

[122] See Bhave, *Peśvekālīn Mahārāṣtra*, pp. 97–8, 375–96.

[123] See Horstmann, "Theology and Statecraft"; Horstmann, *Der Zusammenhalt der Welt*; Peabody, *Hindu Kingship*. Maratha Brahmans at these courts are

inherited the task of mediating conflicts between Maharashtra's Brahman communities, and of pressing and persuading all of them to adhere to common norms of conduct appropriate to the śiṣṭa.[124]

However, these eighteenth-century changes should not allow us to overlook the strategic effectiveness with which the scholar households capitalised on the opportunities that the Mughal imperial framework brought them in Banaras. The intellectuals of these households carried older regional geographies through into the "ecumene" of early modern India, to construct a new kind of arena within which the strains of "early modernity" could be mediated and deflected. They contributed substantially to the systematisation of the Brahman community identities examined here, in ways which set the terms for colonial classifications. Their close familiarity with Deccan society meant that their writings in the field of dharmasastra – Kamakalarabhatta's *Nirṇayasindhuḥ* and his cousin Nilakanthabhatta's *Vyavahāramayūkha* – remained definitive texts throughout the colonial period, enshrining their conceptions of ritual entitlement, family relationships, and property rights. Carried into the Maratha country and beyond, their ritual expertise helped to secure the authority of a new generation of regional states in the eighteenth century, and to ensure that the morals and law of the dharmasastras found a central place within them. As Minkowski has shown, these pandit communities of the sixteenth and seventeenth centuries were equally influential in the realm of theology. They laid the intellectual foundations of the modernised "big-tent" Advaitic Hinduism that later came to be something like the "establishment position" in India's religious culture during the colonial period and after.[125]

Whatever the complexity of their intellectual approaches to innovation in their own disciplines, these scholars were highly inventive in their practical engagements with the novel opportunities and pressures of their own times. They were adept at finding ways to protect the principles of Brahman unity and Brahman privilege, and to give these principles new force and social relevance. If, as some historians

---

discussed in Gode, "Viśvanātha Mahādeva Rānaḍe", and Gode, "Some New Evidence Regarding Devabhaṭṭa Mahāśabdc".

[124] O'Hanlon and Minkowski, "What Makes People Who They Are?"

[125] Minkowski, "Advaita Vedānta in Early Modern History".

suggest, the eighteenth century was to see the emergence of a "Brahman Raj" in India that lasted through the colonial period, some of its most important foundations were laid in the scholar households of Banaras in the preceding two centuries.[126]

References

Alam, Muzaffar, "The Culture and Politics of Persian in Precolonial Hindustan", in Sheldon Pollock, ed., *Literary Cultures in History: Reconstructions from South Asia* (Berkeley and Los Angeles: University of California Press, 2003), pp. 159–71.

———, and Sanjay Subrahmanyam, "The Making of a Munshi", *Comparative Studies of South Asia, Africa and the Middle East*, vol. 24, no. 2, 2004, pp. 61–72.

Altekar, A.S., *History of Banaras* (Banaras: Culture Publication House, 1937).

Apte, V.M., *Social and Religious Life in the Grhya Sutra* (Bombay: Popular Book Depot, 1931).

Aryavaraguru, Ranganathasvami, "On the Sheshas of Benaras", *Indian Antiquary*, vol. 51, November 1912, pp. 245–53.

Asher, Catherine B., *Architecture of Mughal India* (Cambridge: Cambridge University Press, 1995).

———, and Cynthia Talbot, *India Before Europe* (Cambridge: Cambridge University Press, 2006).

Bakker, Hans T., "Construction and Reconstruction of Sacred Space in Vārāṇasī", *Numen*, vol. 43, no. 1, January 1996, pp. 32–55.

Bali, Suryakant, *Bhaṭṭoji Dīkṣita: His Contribution to Sanskrit Grammar* (Delhi: Munshiram Manoharlal, 1976).

Bayly, C.A., "From Ritual to Ceremony: Death Ritual and Society in Hindu North India since 1600", in Joachim Whaley, ed., *Mirrors of Mortality: Studies in the Social History of Death* (London: Europa Publications, 1981), pp. 154–86.

———, *Empire and Information: Intelligence Gathering and Social Communication in India, 1780–1870* (Cambridge: Cambridge University Press, 1996).

Bayly, Susan, *Caste, Society and Politics in India from the Eighteenth Century to the Modern Age* (Cambridge: Cambridge University Press, 1999).

[126] Bayly, *Caste, Society and Politics*, pp. 64–96.

Bendrey, V.S., *Coronation of Shivaji the Great* (Bombay, P.P.H. Bookstall, 1960).

Bendrey, V.S., *Mahārāṣṭretihāsachī* Sādhane, 2 vols (Mumbai: Mumbai Marathi Grantha Sangrahalaya, 1966).

Benke, Theodore, "The Śūdrācāraśiromaṇi of Kṛṣṇa Śeṣa: A Sixteenth Century Manual of Dharma for Śūdras", University of Pennsylvania PhD thesis, 2010.

Benson, James, "Saṃkārabhaṭṭa's Family Chronicle", in Axel Michaels, ed., *The Pandit: Traditional Scholarship in India* (Delhi: Manohar, 2001), pp. 105–18.

Bernier, François, *Travels in the Mogul Empire, AD 1565–1668* (London: Oxford University Press, 1914).

Bhagwat, Vidyut, "Home and the March of Times in Wada Chirebandi", in Irina Glushkova and Rajendra Vora, eds, *Home, Family and Kinship in Maharashtra* (New Delhi: Oxford University Press, 1999), pp. 113–27.

Bhatta Laksmidhara, *Kṛtyakalpataru*, ed. K.V. Rangaswami Aiyangar (Baroda: Oriental Institute, 1943).

Bhattacharya, Jogendra Nath, *Hindu Castes and Sects* (Calcutta: Editions Indian, 1896).

Bhave, V.K., *Peśvekālīn Mahārāṣṭra* (New Delhi: Indian Council for Historical Research, 1973).

Bhimsen, *Tarikh-i Dilkasha*, ed. V.G. Khobrekar (Bombay: Government of Maharashtra, 1972).

Bronkhorst, Johannes, "Bhaṭṭoji Dīkṣita on Sphoṭa", *Journal of Indian Philosophy*, vol. 33, no. 1, 2005, pp. 3–41.

Chatterjee, Indrani, ed., *Unfamiliar Relations: Family and History in South Asia* (Delhi: Permanent Black, 2004).

Chatterjee, Kum Kum, "History as Self-Representation: The Recasting of a Political Tradition in Late Eighteenth Century Eastern India", *Modern Asian Studies*, vol. 32, no. 4, 1998, pp. 913–48.

da Cunha, J. Gerson, ed., *The Sahyâdri-Khaṇḍa of the Skaṇḍa Purâṇa* (Bombay: Nirnayasagar Press, 1877).

Datta, Swati, *Migrant Brāhmānas in Northern India. Their Settlement and General Impact c. AD 475–1030* (Delhi: Motilal Banarsidass, 1989).

Davis, Donald R., "Dharma in Practice: Ācāra and Authority in Medieval Dharmaśāstra", *Journal of Indian Philosophy*, vol. 32, no. 5, 2004, pp. 813–30.

———, *The Spirit of Hindu Law* (Cambridge: Cambridge University Press, 2010).

Derrett, J. Duncan M., "Kamalakara on Illegitimates", in idem, *Essays in Classical and Modern Hindu Law*, vol. 3 (Leiden: E.J. Brill, 1977), pp. 230–40.

Deshpande, Madhav M., "The Changing Notion of Śiṣṭa from Patanjali to Bharatṛhari", in Saroja Bhate and Johannes Bronkhorst, eds, *Bharatṛhari, Philosopher and Grammarian* (Delhi: Motilal Banarasidass, 1993), pp. 75–116.

———, "On Vernacular Sanskrit: The Gīrvāṇavāṅmañjarī of Dhuṇḍirāja Kavi", in idem, *Sanskrit and Prakrit: Sociolinguistic Issues* (Delhi: Motilal Banarsidass, 1993), pp. 33–51.

———, "Pañca-Gauḍa und pañca-Drāviḍa. Umstrittene Grenzen einer traditionellen Klassifikation", in M. Bergunder and R.P. Das, eds, *"Arier" und "Draviden", Konstruktionen der Vergangenheit als Grundlage fur Selbst-und Fremdwahrnehmungen Sudasiens* (Halle: Verlag der Franckeschen Stiftungen zu Halle, 2002), pp. 57–78.

Deva, Raja Radha Kanta, Śabda-Kalpadruma (Varanasi: Vidyavilas Press, 1961).

Eaton, Richard M., *A Social History of the Deccan, 1300–1761: Eight Indian Lives* (Cambridge: Cambridge University Press, 2005).

Eck, Diana L., *Banaras, City of Light* (London: Routledge and Kegan Paul, 1983).

Fisher, Elaine M., *Hindu Pluralism and the Public Sphere in Early Modern South India* (Berkeley: University of California Press, 2017).

Fukazawa, Hiroshi, *The Medieval Deccan: Peasants, Social Systems and States* (Delhi: Oxford University Press, 1991).

Glushkova, Irina, and Rajendra Vora, eds, *Home, Family and Kinship in Maharashtra* (New Delhi: Oxford University Press, 1999).

Gode, P.K., "The Date of Rāghavabhaṭṭa, the Commentator of Kālidāsa's Abhijñānaśākuntalam and Other Works", *Calcutta Oriental Journal*, vol. 3, 1936, pp. 177–84.

———, "Date of the Bhāṭṭabhāṣāprakāśikā and Identification of its Author with the Guru of Nilakaṇṭha Caturdhara", *The Mīmāṁsā-Prakāśa*, vol. 3, no. 6, 1 June 1938, pp. 65–71.

———, "Some New Evidence Regarding Devabhaṭṭa Mahāśabde, the father of Ratnākarabhaṭṭa, the Guru of Sevai Jaising of Amber (AD 1699–1743)", in *Poona Orientalist*, vol. 8, nos 3–4, 1943–4, p. 132.

———, "Saint Rāmadāsa's Discourse on the Writing and Preservation of Manuscripts and Its Importance for the History of Indian Palaeography", *New Indian Antiquary*, October–November 1944, pp. 126–8.

———, "Bernier and Kavīndrācārya Sarasvatī at the Mughal Court", in P.K. Gode, ed., *Studies in Indian Literary History*, vol. 2 (Bombay: Singhi Jain Sastra Sikshapith, 1954), pp. 364–79.

———, "The Identification of Gosvāmi Nṛsiṁhāśrama of Dara Shukoh's Sanskrit Letter with Brahmendra Sarasvatī of the Kavīndra-Candrodaya – Between AD 1628 and 1658", in P.K. Gode, ed., *Studies in Indian Literary History*, vol. 2 (Bombay: Singhi Jain Sastra Sikshapith, 1954), pp. 447–51.

———, "Nīlakaṇṭha Śukla, a Romantic and Pugnacious Pupil of Bhaṭṭoji Dīkṣita and His Works: Between AD 1610 and 1670", in P.K. Gode, ed., *Studies in Indian Literary History*, vol. 2 (Bombay: Singhi Jain Sastra Sikshapith, 1954), pp. 468–75.

———, "Viśvanātha Mahādeva Rānaḍe, a Cittapāvan Court-poet of Raja Ramsing I of Jaipur and His Works, Between AD 1650 and 1700", in P.K. Gode, ed., *Studies in Indian Literary History*, vol. 2 (Bombay: Singhi Jain Sastra Sikshapith, 1954), pp. 259–73.

———, "Some Authors of the Ārḍe Family and Their Chronology – Between AD 1600 and 1825", in P.K. Gode, ed., *Studies in Indian Literary History*, vol. 3 (Poona: Prof. P.K. Gode Collected Works Publication Committee, 1956), pp. 17–24.

———, "The Contact of Bhaṭṭoji Dīkṣita with the Rulers of Ikkeri", in P.K. Gode, ed., *Studies in Indian Literary History*, vol. 3 (Poona: Prof. P.K. Gode Collected Works Publication Committee, 1957), pp. 203–6.

———, "Harikavi alias Bhānubhaṭṭa, a Court Poet of King Sambhāji and His Works", in P.K. Gode, ed., *Studies in Indian Literary History*, vol. 3 (Poona: Prof. P.K. Gode Collected Works Publication Committee, 1957), pp. 100–27.

———, "The Origin and Antiquity of the Caste-Name of the Karahāṭaka or Karhāḍa Brahmins", in P.K. Gode, ed., *Studies in Indian Cultural History*, vol. 3 (Poona: Bhandarkar Oriental Research Institute, 1969), pp. 1–36.

———, "Some Evidence about the Location of the Manuscript Library of Kavīndrācārya Sarasvatī at Benares in AD 1665", in P.K. Gode, ed., *Studies in Indian Cultural History*, vol. 3 (Poona: Bhandarkar Oriental Research Institute, 1969), pp. 71–6.

Gordon, Stewart, *The Marathas 1600–1818* (Cambridge: Cambridge University Press, 1993).

Gough, A.E., *Papers Relating to the Collection and Preservation of the*

Records of Ancient Sanscrit Literature in India (Calcutta: Office of Superintendent of Government Printing, 1878).

Guha, Sumit, "The Family Feud as a Political Resource in Eighteenth Century India", in Indrani Chatterjee, ed., *Unfamiliar Relations: Family and History in South Asia* (Delhi: Permanent Black, 2004), pp. 73–94.

———, "Speaking Historically: The Changing Voices of Historical Narration in Western India, 1400–1900", *American Historical Review*, vol. 109, no. 4, 2004, pp. 1084–1103.

———, "The Frontiers of Memory: What the Marathas Remembered of Vijayanagar", *Modern Asian Studies*, vol. 43, no.1, 2009, pp. 269–88.

Gune, V.T., *The Judicial System of the Marathas* (Pune: Sangam Press, 1953).

Gunjikar, R.B., *Sarasvatīmaṇḍal* (Bombay: Nirnayasagar Press, 1884).

Gurevitch, Eric Moses, "The Epistemology of Difference: Caste and the Question of Natural Kinds in the Courts of Medieval India", *Journal of South Asian Intellectual History*, vol. 5, no. 2, 2023, pp. 217–51.

Gutschow, Niels, *Banaras: The Sacred Landscape of Vārāṇasī* (Stuttgart/London: Edition Axel Menges, 2006).

Habib, Irfan, *Medieval India. Researches in the History of India 1200–1750* (Delhi: Oxford University Press, 1999).

Hawley, John Stratton, "The Four Sampradāys: Ordering the Religious Past in Mughal North India", *South Asian History and Culture*, vol. 2, no. 2, April 2011, pp. 160–83.

Hemadri, *Chaturvargachintāmaṇi*, 6 vols (Calcutta: Biblioteca Indica, 1873–1911).

Horstmann, Monika, "The Temple of Govindadevajī: A Symbol of Hindu Kingship?", in N.K. Singhi and Rajendra Joshi, eds, *Religion, Ritual and Royalty* (Jaipur: Rawat Publications, 1999), pp. 118–31.

———, *Der Zusammenhalt der Welt: Religiöse Herrschaftslegitimation und Religionspolitik Maharaja Savai Jaisinghs (1700–1743)* (Wiesbaden: Harrassowitz, 2009).

———, "Theology and Statecraft", *South Asian History and Culture*, vol. 2, no. 2, April 2011, pp. 184–204.

Houben, Jan E.M., "The Brahmin Intellectual: History, Ritual and 'Time out of Time'", *Journal of Indian Philosophy*, vol. 30, no. 5, 2002, pp. 463–79.

Hultzsch, E., "Inscriptions At and Near Virinchipuram", *South Indian Inscriptions*, vol. 1, 1890, pp. 82–4.

———, "Inscriptions of the Kailāsanātha Temple at Kānchīpuran", *South Indian Inscriptions*, vol. 1, 1890, p. 113.

Inden, Ronald, *Imagining India* (Oxford: Basil Blackwell, 1990).

Joshi, P.M., "'Ālī Ādil Shāh I of Bījāpūr (1558–1580) and His Royal Librarian: Two Ruqa's", *Journal of the Bombay Branch of the Royal Asiatic Society*, vols 31, no. 2, 1956–7, pp. 97–107.

Kane, P.V., *History of Dharmaśāstra*, 5 vols (Poona: Bhandarkar Oriental Research Institute, 1968–77).

———, "Gotras and Pravaras", *Journal of the Bombay Branch of the Royal Asiatic Society*, vol. 11, nos 1 and 2, 1935, pp. 1–18.

———, *Vyavhāramayūkha of Bhaṭṭa Nīlakaṇṭha* (Poona: Bhandarkar Oriental Research Institute, 1926).

Kanhere, S.G., "Waman Pandit: Scholar and Marathi Poet", *Bulletin of the School of Oriental and African Studies*, vol. 4, no. 2, 1926, pp. 305–14.

Kanole, V.A., "Nāṅḍeḍache Śeṣa Gharāṇe", in Surendranath Sen, ed., *Mahamahopadhyaya Prof. D.V. Potdar Sixty First Birthday Commemoration Volume* (Poona: Samartha Bharat Press, 1950), pp. 53–76.

Kāśikhaṇḍa (Baroda, 1908).

Kāśī-Khaṇḍa, ed. and trans. G.V. Tagare: *Skanda-Purāṇa*, Part 10, 2 vols (Delhi: Motilal Banarsidass, 1996).

Katre, S.L., "Nārāyaṇabhaṭṭa Ārḍe, His Works and Date", *Bharatiya Vidya*, March–April 1945, pp. 74–86.

———, "Dvijārajodaya: A Forgotten Dharma Nibandha: Identification of Its Author with a Guru of Nīlakaṇṭha Caturdhara", *New Indian Antiquary*, vol. 6, October 1943, pp. 145–55.

Kaviraj, Sudipta, "The Sudden Death of Sanskrit Knowledge", *Journal of Indian Philosophy*, vol. 33, no. 1, February 2005, pp. 119–42.

Kelkar, N.C., "Mahārāṣṭrātīl Kāhī Paṅḍit Gharāṇe", in *Kelkarakṛt Lekh Saṅgraha*, vol. 4 (Pune: Chitrasala Press, 1915), pp. 29–34.

Kosambi, D.D., "On the Origin of Brahmin Gotras", *Journal of the Bombay Branch of the Royal Asiatic Society*, vol. 26, no. 1, 1950, pp. 21–80.

Kotani, H., *Western India in Historical Transition: Seventeenth to Early Twentieth Centuries* (New Delhi: Manohar, 2002).

Levitt, Stephen, "The Sahyādrikhaṇḍa: Some Problems Concerning a Text-Critical Edition of a Purāṇic Text", *Purana*, vol. 9, no. 1, 1977, pp. 8–40.

Michell, George, "Temple Styles", in George Michell and Rana P.B. Singh, eds, *Banaras: The City Revealed* (Mumbai: Marg Publications, 2005), pp. 79–87.

Minkowski, Christopher, "Nīlakaṇṭha Caturdhara's Mantrakāśikhaṇḍa", *Journal of the American Oriental Society*, vol. 122, no. 2, 2002, pp. 329–44.

———, "I'll Wash Out Your Mouth With My Boot: A Guide to Philological Argument in Mughal-era Banaras", in Sheldon Pollock, ed., *Epic and Argument in Sanskrit Literary History: Essays in Honor of Robert P. Goldman* (Delhi: Manohar, 2010), pp. 113–35.

———, "Sanskrit Scientific Libraries and Their Uses: Examples and Problems of the Early Modern Period", in Florence Bretelle-Establet, ed., *Looking at It from Asia: The Processes that Shaped the Sources of History of Science* (Springer: Paris 2010), pp. 81–114.

———, "Advaita Vedānta in Early Modern History", *South Asian History and Culture*, vol. 2, no. 2, April 2011, pp. 205–31.

Morwanchikar, R.S., *The City of the Saints: Paithan Through the Ages* (Delhi: Ajanta Publications, 1985).

Mundy, Peter, *The Travels of Peter Mundy in Europe and Asia 1608–1667*, 4 vols (London: Hakluyt Society, 1907–25).

Narayanabhatta, *Tristhalīsetuh*, ed. R. Gokhale and H.N. Apte (Pune: Anandashram, 1915).

Narayana Rao, Velcheru, David Shulman, and Sanjay Subrahmanyam, *Textures of Time: Writing History in South India, 1600–1800* (New Delhi: Permanent Black, 2003).

———, "A Pragmatic Response", *History and Theory*, vol. 46, no. 3, October 2007, pp. 409–27.

Newbigin, Eleanor, *The Hindu Family and the Emergence of Modern India* (Cambridge: Cambridge University Press, 2013).

Nilakantha Bhatta, *Vyavahāramayūkha*, ed. and trans. P.V. Kane and S.G. Patwardhan (Poona: Aryasamsrkti Press, 1933).

Novetzke, Christian Lee, *The Quotidian Revolution: Vernacularization, Religion and the Premodern Public Sphere in India* (New York: Columbia University Press, 2016).

O'Hanlon, Rosalind, "Narratives of Penance and Purification in Western India, *c.* 1650–1850", *The Journal of Hindu Studies*, vol. 2, no. 1, 2009, pp. 48–75.

———, "Letters Home: Banaras Pandits and the Maratha Regions in Early Modern India", *Modern Asian Studies*, vol. 44, no. 2, March 2010, pp. 201–40.

———, "The Social Worth of Scribes: Brahmins, Kayasthas and the Social Order in Early Modern India", *Indian Economic and Social History Review*, vol. 47, no. 4, 2010, pp. 563–95.

Pangarkar, L.R., *Moropant: Charitra aṇi Kāvyavivechana* (Mumbai: Hindu Agency Booksellers and Publishers, 1908).

Parry, Jonathan, "The Brahmanical Tradition and the Technology of the Intellect", in Joanna Overing, ed., *Reason and Morality* (London: Tavistock, 1985), pp. 200–25.

——, *Death in Banaras* (Cambridge: Cambridge University Press, 1994).

Pauwels, Heidi, "A Tale of Two Temples: Mathurā's Keshavadeva and Orcchā's Caturbhujadeva", *South Asian History and Culture*, vol. 2, no. 2, April 2011, pp. 278–99.

Peabody, Norbert, *Hindu Kingship and Polity in Precolonial India* (Cambridge: Cambridge University Press, 2003).

Perlin, Frank, "Of White Whale and Countrymen in the Eighteenth Century Maratha Deccan", *Journal of Peasant Studies*, vol. 5, no. 2, 1979, pp. 172–237.

Pimputkar, R.S., *Chitaḷebhaṭṭa Prakaraṇa* (Mumbai: G.S. Joshi, 1926).

Pollock, Sheldon, "New Intellectuals in Seventeenth Century India", *Indian Economic and Social History Review*, vol. 38, no. 1, 2001, pp. 3–31.

———, *The Language of the Gods in the World of Men. Sanskrit, Culture and Power in Premodern India* (Berkeley and Los Angeles: University of California Press, 2006).

———, "Pretextures of Time", *History and Theory*, vol. 46, no. 3, October 2007, pp. 366–83.

———, "Is There an Indian Intellectual History? Introduction to Theory and Method in Indian Intellectual History, *Journal of Indian Philosophy*, vol. 36, nos 5–6, 2008, pp. 533–42.

Preston, Frank, *The Devs of Cincvad* (Cambridge: Cambridge University Press, 1989).

Pusalkar, A.D., *Vāḍeśvarodaya-Kāvya* of Viśvanātha, *Journal of the Bombay Branch of the Royal Asiatic Society*, New Series, vol. 27, no. 1, 1951, pp. 66–78.

Raghavan, V., "Kavīndrācārya Sarasvatī", in Bimala Churn Law, ed., *D.R. Bhandarkar Felicitation Volume* (Calcutta: Indian Research Institute, 1940), pp. 159–65.

———, "The Kavīndrakalpalatikā of Kavīndrācārya Sarasvatī", in *Indica: The Indian Historical Research Institute Silver Jubilee Commemoration Volume* (Bombay: St Xavier's College, 1953), pp. 335–41.

Ramdas, *Dāsabodha* (Poona: Bhat and Co., 1915).

Russell, R.V., and Rai Bahadur Hira Lal, *Tribes and Castes of the Central Provinces* (London: Macmillan, 1916).

Salomon, Richard, *The Bridge to the Three Holy Cities. The Sāmānya-praghaṭṭaka of Nārāyaṇa Bhaṭṭa's Tristhalīsetu* (Delhi: Motilal Banarsidas, 1985).

Sardesai, G.S., *Selections from the Peshwa Daftar*, 45 vols (Bombay: Government Central Press, 1930–4).

Sarma, K.V., "Raghunātha Navahastha and His Contribution to Sanskrit and Marathi Literature", *Vishveshvaranand Indological Journal*, vol. 7, no. 1, 1969, pp. 69–82.

———, "The Manuscripts Collection of the Jade Family of Varanasi and the Literary Output of the Jade Authors", *Vishveshvaranand Indological Journal*, vol. 9, no. 2, 1971, pp. 347–57.

Sastri, Lalji Vaijanath, *Sadbodhachintamani* (Bombay: Arya Prakash Press, 1875).

Sastry, R. Ananta Krishna, *Kavindracharya List* (Baroda: Gaikwad's Oriental Series, 1921).

Scharfe, Harmut, *Education in Ancient India* (Leiden: Brill, 2002).

Sharma, Har Dutt, and M.M. Patkar, *Kavīndracandrodaya* (Pune: Oriental Book Agency, 1939).

Shastri, Haraprasad, *Descriptive Catalogue of Sanskrit Manuscripts in the Government Collection Under the Care of the Asiatic Society of Bombay*, 12 vols (Calcutta: Asiatic Society, 1917–66).

Shastri, M.H., "Dakshini Pandits at Benaras", *Indian Antiquary*, vol. 41, January 1912, pp. 7–13.

Shulman, David, "Ambivalence and Longing: Vyāsa's Curse on Kāśī", in Benjamin Z. Kedar and R.J. Zwi Werblowsky, eds, *In Sacred Space: Shrine, City, Land* (London: Macmillan 1998), pp. 192–214.

Sircar, Dineschandra, "Gauḍa", *Indian Historical Quarterly,* vol. 28, March 1952, pp. 123–34.

———, *Studies in the Geography of Ancient and Medieval India* (Delhi: Motilal Banarsidass, 1960).

Sirkar, D.C., "Rashtrakuta Charters from Chinchani", *Epigraphia Indica*, vol. 32, 1957–8, pp. 45–60.

Skandapurāṇa: The Vārāṇasī Cycle, ed. Hans T. Bakker and Harunaga Isaacson (Groningen: Egbert Forsten, 2004).

Smith, Travis LaMar, "Renewing the Ancient: The *Kāśikhaṇḍa*. and Śaiva Vārāṇasī", *Acta Orientalia Vilnensia*, vol. 8, no. 1, 2007, pp. 83–108.

———, "The Sacred Center and Its Peripheries: Śaivism and the Vārāṇasī Sthala-Purāṇas", Columbia University PhD thesis, 2007.

Subrahmanyam, Sanjay, "Aspects of State Formation in South India and Southeast Asia", *Indian Economic and Social History Review*, vol. 23, no. 4 , 1986, pp. 357–77.

Tavernier, Jean-Baptiste, *Travels in India* (London: Oxford University Press, 1925).

Tukaram, *Samagra Tukārām Gāthā*, ed. Tukaram Tatya Padaval (Pune: Varada, 1996).

Vaidya, C.V., *History of Medieval India* (New Delhi: Cosmo Publications, 1979).

van der Veer, Peter, "The Concept of the Ideal Brahman as an Indological Construct", in Gunther D. Sontheimer and Herman Kulke, eds, *Hinduism Reconsidered* (Delhi: Manohar 1991), pp. 67–80.

Vidyabhushan, Satis Chandra, *A History of Indian Logic* (Delhi: Motilal Banarsidass, 1971).

Washbrook, D.A., "India in the Early Modern World Economy: Modes of Production, Reproduction and Exchange", *Journal of Global History*, vol. 2, no. 1, 2007, pp. 87–111.

Wink, Andre, *Land and Sovereignty in India: Agrarian Society and Politics Under the Eighteenth Century Maratha Svarājya* (Cambridge: Cambridge University Press, 1986).

Witzel, Michael, "Towards a History of the Brahmins", *Journal of the American Oriental Society*, vol. 113, no. 2, 1993, pp. 264–8.

———, "Regionale und überregionale Faktoren in der Entwicklung vedischer Brahmanengruppen in Mittelalter" in H. Kulke and D. Rothermund, eds, *Regionale Tradition in Südasien* (Wiesbaden: Steiner, 1986), pp. 37–76.

———, "On the Localisation of Vedic Texts and Schools", in G. Pollett, ed., *India and the Ancient World: History, Trade and Culture before* AD *650* (Leuven: Departement Oriëntalistiek, 1987), pp. 173–213.

Wright, Samuel, "History in the Abstract: 'Brahman-ness' and the Discipline of Nyāya in Seventeenth Century Vārānasī", *Journal of Indian Philosophy*, vol. 44, no. 5, November 2016, pp. 1041–69.

2

Entrepreneurs in Diplomacy

Maratha Expansion in the Age of the Vakil

Introduction

WRITING IN 1784, the Hyderabad chief secretary Lala Mansaram recalled the arrangements of Nizam ul Mulk (1671–1748) for the vakils or agents of other chiefs as they arrived at the Hyderabad court to represent the interests of their masters:

> The Nizam ordered: "The vakils of many notable chiefs arrive at the camp individually. Many of them are put to great distress. It is better if all these remain together. A locality should be assigned to them. It should be known as the vakilpura. It would be convenient for the vakils to stay there." Devidas was a vakil on behalf of Sadatulla Khan and the Afghans of Kapada and Karnool. He was a rich man and had elephants for his conveyance. He used to maintain a free kitchen in his camp and feed the poor. The vakils of other chiefs started settling near the camp of Devidas.[1]

Lala Mansaram's recollections offer a vivid example of the rapidly expanding numbers of those serving as diplomatic agents at the courts of eighteenth-century India, as well as of the sharp contrasts between the wealth and prestige of some of them and the straitened circumstances of others. As regional states and smaller political players of all kinds came to terms with the stronger multilateral relationships that developed across the subcontinent in the wake of Mughal decline, a vakil's presence at other courts assumed new importance. Deriving

[1] Madhava Rao, *Eighteenth Century Deccan*, p. 110.

from the Arabic wakāla (one entrusted), the title referred in fact to any person with delegated authority to act on behalf of another.[2] In practice, this could cover many political, juridical, commercial, and administrative functions. For any historian of the eighteenth century, however, it is the "political" vakil that stands out most prominently, sent to other courts to conclude agreements, oversee intelligence sent back home, and negotiate the complex diplomatic protocols of the court to maintain his employer's prestige.

Consequently, we know much about vakils as part of the information and diplomatic order of eighteenth-century India, as well as the apparatus of intelligence gathering and reporting that they usually oversaw. Yet we know rather less about what it actually meant to do the work of political vakils: their social and career aspirations, their understandings of service to individual employers as opposed to service to the state, the portfolio of property and rights they might accumulate, the kinds of influence their position and skills enabled them to wield, and the role of family in their peripatetic lives. Here I explore these questions in the lives of some Marathi-speaking political vakils whose association with the Maratha empire took them to every part of the subcontinent.

Diplomacy as a Portfolio Profession

Like the "new diplomatic history" elsewhere, studies of diplomacy in pre-colonial India now extend well beyond communiqués and treaties to explore diplomacy as a multifaceted dimension of wider power relationships.[3] Christopher Bayly has examined the intelligence-gathering operations of eighteenth-century states, and the apparatus of newswriters, posts, runners, and spies which underpinned vakils' reporting.[4] Michael Fisher has explored the way in which the "residency" system of the East India Company gradually squeezed Indian vakils out of the

[2] Bearman, *Encyclopaedia of Islam*, vol. 11, pp. 57–8.

[3] For an overview, see Hennings and Sowerby, "Practices of Diplomacy", pp. 1–17. For cross–cultural translation in early modern diplomacy, see in particular Subrahmanyam, *Mughals and Franks*, and Guha, "Conviviality and Cosmopolitanism", pp. 287–8.

[4] Bayly, *Empire and Information*, pp. 31–44, 58–66.

flows of information between Indian courts.[5] In an important work, Dominic Vendell has drawn our attention to the language of political ethics that vakils, ministers, and others employed in political negotiations. Vendell notes the emphasis placed on jāb-sāl – the conversational to-and-fro of negotiation – as a means to establish trust, alongside other material ways of affirming friendship in oaths, gifts, and ritual exchanges of religious tokens. Jāb-sāl here constitutes a distinctive form of politics as communicative action, concerned not with abstract notions of sovereignty but rather with the processes through which political alliances or agreements could be shaped and carried forward.[6]

Alongside their work in the inter-state culture of diplomacy, however, political vakils also became deeply involved in many areas of state and military finance. In this era of intense competition for control of agrarian revenues, a key dimension of diplomacy lay in the conduct of agreements about revenue rights. The widespread practice of revenue farming involved political vakils in the supply and disbursement of cash. They ensured that cash gathered in by local collectors was moved on to where it was required, to meet the needs of troops, to pay court officials for a wide range of services, to provide gifts on important diplomatic occasions, and to meet the significant costs of their own establishments. It was also the task of vakils to make the down payments on revenue farms for employers in this lucrative line of business. If merchant and banking families supplied the credit, it was very often vakils who cashed the hundis and physically carried the cash to where it was needed.

These other dimensions of a political vakil's work emerge clearly in studies of regional courts. In Jaipur, vakils stood surety for their masters when they made down payments for revenue farms, paid court officials to procure estates and titles for their masters and to ensure attention for their masters' business, and used cash to pay their own retinues of news-writers and runners. But cash shortages were also a perennial challenge, with salaries unpaid and bankers reluctant to honour their credit.[7] At the Maratha court, formal procedures gov-

[5] Fisher, *Indirect Rule in India*, 47–9, 272–7.

[6] Vendell, "Scribes and the Vocation of Politics".

[7] Sharma, *Vakil Reports Maharajgan*, pp. 31–7. See also Gupta, *Maratha Penetration*, pp. 74–88.

erned vakils' arrival and departure, and the complex mix of salary, court allowances, and one-off rewards in cash, land, or hereditary office through which they were paid.[8] This necessary engagement with local financial as well as political networks meant that vakils often developed their own agents and clients, and portfolios of interests in banking and revenue farming alongside privileged land tenures.[9] Their local embeddedness enabled many of them, quite openly and routinely, to take on work for several employers at a time.[10]

The joint family assumed major importance in managing these extended interests. Many vakil families developed into dynasties, involving several generations and branches of the same family. In these practices, vakil families shared aspects of the culture of "portfolio capitalism" that Bayly and others have identified in the precolonial centuries, when family and mercantile corporations accumulated interests in a wide range of activities, from commerce to revenue farming, office-holding to privileged land tenures.[11] In addition, though, successful vakils had access to subcontinent-wide intelligence networks, expertise in the language of persuasion, and skill in the management of relationships large and small. This unique assemblage of skills, experience, and resources made them one of the most numerous and influential service communities of the eighteenth century, whose importance we have not sufficiently appreciated.

Envoys and Ambassadors in Indo-Persian Scribal Culture

How did the service communities that we identify as the diplomats of eighteenth-century India come to be so deeply engaged in these other roles? In pre-eighteenth-century India, and throughout much of the Islamic world, a range of titles other than "vakil" commonly described envoys of different kinds. Most commonly used were the terms safīr (envoy), rasūl (messenger), and most commonly the term elči, a Turkish word for an ambassador, which also entered Persian as īlchī.[12]

[8] Joshi, "Maratha Ambassadors".

[9] Leonard, "The Hyderabad Political System", pp. 571–3.

[10] Shejwalkar, *Nagpur Affairs*, vol. 1, p. xlvii.

[11] Bayly, *Rulers, Townsmen and Bazaars*, pp. 163–96, and Bayly and Subrahmanyam, "Portfolio Capitalism".

[12] Farooqi, "Diplomacy and Diplomatic Procedure", p. 79; Fisher, *Indirect Rule*

The term elči, from el or il (people, country, or state), with the occupational suffix či, translates literally as one who serves or works for his country.[13] Īlchī seems therefore to denote a person serving one court or state and representing its interests at another.

In Mughal India, an īlchī described both an envoy sent to courts outside India, and those at other Indian courts. Abu al-Fazl's *Akbarnāma* reported that a Portuguese messenger claiming the status of īlchī petitioned Akbar in 1573 to help Christians caught up in the siege of Surat.[14] Ibrahim 'Adilshah of Bijapur sent his īlchī, Shah Khalilullah, to Shah 'Abbas of Iran to offer an alliance against the Mughals.[15] Courts within the subcontinent also exchanged īlchīs: the envoy, Isma'il Mita, sent from the ruler of Bengal Nusrat Shah to Babur in April 1529, was an īlchī.[16]

Perhaps because of their closer links with the Indian Ocean world, the term most commonly used in the Deccan states was hejib, from the Arabic al-ḥājib. Connected with ḥījāb, signifying the curtain screening the monarch from the gaze of courtiers, the term has applied to a variety of roles over its long history, all suggesting connection to a royal court.[17] The Deccan states used the term equally for envoys sent to the Mughal court, to other Indian states, to the European companies, and to courts abroad. Sherwani notes that the Qutb Shahis used three terms: rasūl, or an ad hoc envoy for a particular purpose; Hājib-i Muqīmī, denoting a resident envoy; and Hājib-i Maṣliḥatī, an envoy on a special mission.[18] In practice, however, the term was used loosely. The Nizam Shahi embassy of Chand Bibi to Akbar's son Murad in 1596 was termed a ḥījāb.[19] Following Persian diplomatic usages more closely, the Bijapur court of the 'Adil Shahis termed their ambassadors īlchī, safīr, rasūl, and ḥājib.[20] At the Bijapur court of Shahaji

in India, pp. 47–8; Talbot, *British Ottoman Relations*, 44; Bearman, ed., *Encyclopaedia of Islam*, vol. 8, pp. 811–15.

[13] Bearman, *Encyclopaedia of Islam*, vol. 2, p. 694.

[14] Abu al–Fazl, *Akbarnāmah*, vol. 3, p. 27.

[15] Ahmad, "'Ādilshāhī Diplomatic Missions", p. 146

[16] Dale, *Babur*, p. 189.

[17] Bearman, *Encyclopaedia of Islam*, vol. 3, p. 45.

[18] Sherwani, *History of the Qutḅ Shāhī Dynasty*, p. 514.

[19] Sherwani, *Muḥammad-Qulī Qutuḅ Shāh*, p. 129.

[20] Nayeem, *External Relations of the Bijapur Kingdom*, p. 40.

Bhosle, the poet Jayarama Pindye composed the *Rādhāmādhavavilāsacampū*, which described Shahaji sending a hejib to the Mughal court.[21]

The Maratha court of Shivaji employed the term widely.[22] Its usage suggests that a hejib should be a dignified person, able to oversee the exchange of solemn pledges. The late-seventeenth-century chronicler Sabhasad described how two hejibs, Krishnaji Bhaskar and Gopinath Bokil, the latter otherwise known as Pantaji Pant, were sent to negotiate guarantees of safety before the 1659 meeting between the Mughal general Afzal Khan and Shivaji. As Afzal Khan's hejib, Krishnaji sought assurances for his master. Afzal Khan in turn offered a hastapanjāri, an oath confirmed with a palm print placed on the written document, itself clearly part of the array of bodily and ritual exchanges that Vendell has described. Shivaji's hejib Pantaji Pant stood as guarantor, his solemn oath delivered before witnesses and his status as a holy Brahman serving to reassure Afzal Khan.[23]

Some uses of the term suggest that a hejib's appointment might also extend for a reasonable period. Sabhasad described how Pralhad Pant, son of Niraji Pant and a man of great wisdom, was placed as hejib at the court of Bhaganagar.[24] The Maratha term is ṭhevale (placed), suggesting more than a specific short-term mission. The chronicler Dattaji Vaknis used the same term, describing how, in the wake of Shivaji's raid on the Keladi chief Shivappa Nayak's city of Basnur, Shivaji sent a hejib to restore friendly relations. After the raid, "Uma Pandit was always placed, nehamī ṭhevale, in that location as hejib. From that day, there was friendship with Shivappa Nayak."[25]

From Ilchī and Hejib to Vakil

Alongside the roles of īlchī and hejib went a different kind of agency, that of vakil, associated with authority delegated directly from one person to another. Great ministers of the Bahmani kings such as Mahmud Gawan and his successor Malik Hasan enjoyed the title of

[21] Rajwade, ed., *Rādhāmādhavavilāsacampū*, p. 263.
[22] Mahajan, *Shivaji and His Diplomats*, pp. 4–16.
[23] Hervadkar, *Sabhāsad Bakhar*, pp. 14–16.
[24] Ibid., p. 104.
[25] Vakaskar, *Śrī Śivachhatrapatīnchī 91 Kalamī Bakhar*, no. 65, p. 46.

vakil-us saltānat.[26] The Mughals likewise employed great plenipotentiaries of the kind that Abu al-Fazl described, "the emperor's lieutenant in all matters connected with the realm and the household."[27] Vakils as lesser agents were ubiquitous figures in the houses of the powerful, as in the case of Gobind Das, vakil of Raja Suraj Singh Rathor, described in the memoirs of Jahangir as having murdered the Raja's nephew during a private quarrel, but whose services as a vakil were so valued that he was reluctant to punish him.[28] At a more modest level, Mughal officers maintained their own agents at the imperial court.[29] Lesser lords and men of substance in provincial societies equally needed agents to conduct their business at the local level, in the offices of state officials, army camps, and the houses of merchants and bankers.[30]

Seventeenth-century contemporaries made a clear distinction between these kinds of delegated authority. Sabhasad describes how Raghunath Pant Korde had been serving as hejib at the Mughal court. To prepare the ground for Shivaji's visit in 1666, the Rajput Jaisingh sent his vakil, along with Korde, now serving as Shivaji's vakil.[31] The Jedhe family history also demonstrates a clear sense of the distinction between the roles of hejib and vakil. The entry for May 1672 tells us that Shivaji's hejib Niraji Pant went to Bhaganagar and negotiated an alliance in return for a lakh of gold Hon coins. In November of that year, the peace treaty with the 'Adil Shahi court broke down, and so Babaji Nayak Punde, who had been serving as vakil there, returned home to Shivaji's court.[32]

Envoys between states in eighteenth-century India, however, came everywhere to be understood and titled not as īlchī or hejib but as vakil. How did a term associated with personal agency also come to signify a political vakil's role in representing the interests of states? Christopher Werner's observations about the complex nature of delegated authority in eighteenth-century Iran, with its own multi-layered com-

[26] Anwar, *Mughals and the Deccan*, pp. 2–3.
[27] Abu al-Fazl, *Ā'īn–i Akbarī*, vol. 1, p. 4.
[28] Beveridge, ed., *Memoirs of Jahāngīr*, pp. 291–2.
[29] Fisher, "The Resident in Court Ritual", pp. 425–6.
[30] Calkins, "A Note on Lawyers".
[31] Hervadkar, *Sabhāsad Bakhar*, pp. 55, 61.
[32] Kulkarni, *Jedhe Śakāvalī-Karīṇā*, p. 69.

munities of Persian-trained administrators paralleling those of India, is helpful here. Werner suggests that three overlapping semantic fields were present in the wide application of the title of "vakil" to many different kinds of delegated agency. These were the juridical, with the vakil as a legal agent or proxy; the honorary, in which the vakil represented the ruler or some connected aspect of state power; and the administrative or commercial, in which the vakil conducted business on behalf of his master in many mundane local settings. Despite this breadth of application, the term "vakil" retained its core meaning of an authorised agent or proxy acting on behalf of another person.[33]

What Werner suggests for Iran is helpful in the Indian context. A political vakil could flexibly encompass the roles of īlchī and hejib, but at the same time import them into the familiar world of personal connection, as well as agency in financial transactions, which still lay at the heart of so many eighteenth-century political institutions. This very interdependence of the financial with the political meant that questions of trust, honour, and ethical conduct were more rather than less important. Vendell's conception of the significance of jāb-sāl, the public affirmation of trust, is particularly helpful here. As we will see, however, vakils deeply embedded in these plural roles developed not only concepts of ethical negotiation as practical politics in action, but also a language of the well-being of the state itself.

These multiple roles help us to understand the perplexities of officers of the East India Company when they cast around for an appropriate term for their own envoys to Indian states. As Fisher has shown, they sought the opinion of a local expert on diplomatic practice who told them, "I understand Vakeel, but what is the meaning of Public Minister, I do not know, Vakeel is one thing and Elchei is another."[34] Significantly, one of the few eighteenth-century occasions in which īlchīs continued to be used was when an envoy was sent to a court outside India. When the Mysore ruler Tipu Sultan sent his envoys to the court of Louis XVI in August 1788, the medals struck in their honour celebrated their visit as the īlchīs from Mysore.[35]

[33] Werner, "Ambiguity in Meaning", pp. 317–25.

[34] Fisher, *Indirect Rule*, p. 49.

[35] Lafont, *Essays in Indo–French Relations*, p. 175. I thank Shailendra Bhandare for this reference.

Portuguese diplomatic usages from Goa also reflected these plural roles. The Estado da India issued clear instructions regarding the hierarchy of different diplomatic visitors and the reception to be accorded to each: a sumptuous reception for the embaixador of the Mughal emperor, and a more modest welcome for the enviado of lesser and local courts.[36] But the Portuguese used a further term, "procurador", which shares something of the multivalent meanings of the term "vakil", to denote, broadly, agents deputed to act on their behalf. As we will see, Bahiropant Mehendale, the peshwa's vakil to the British Resident at the Pune court from the mid-1780s, was also appointed as procurador to the Portuguese, responsible for reporting intelligence from Pune to Goa and resolving trade-related disputes between the two courts.[37]

Political Vakils in the Maratha State

Whilst they shared much in common with political vakils elsewhere in India, the Marathi-speaking vakil community also revealed distinctive features. After his accession to the throne in Satara in 1708, the Maratha Raja Shahu revived his grandfather Shivaji's claims to chauth and other levies in the six Mughal provinces of the Deccan. Granted after the visit of the first peshwa Balaji Vishvanath Bhat to Delhi in 1719, the claims brought the Marathas into direct conflict with the emerging Nizam Shahi state. Their political rivalry shaped the politics of central and southern India for the rest of the century, exacerbated by the further right, given under the grant, of Marathi revenue collectors themselves to be stationed in Hyderabad's territories.[38] Chauth claims became a general legal lever as individual Maratha sardars sought to establish domains of their own elsewhere in the subcontinent.[39] The drive to expansion itself, and the legal claims accompanying it, meant that Maratha scribal professionals quickly

[36] Melo, "Respect and Superiority", pp. 146–51.

[37] Sen, *Studies in Indian History*, pp. 71–2.

[38] Nayeem, "The Working of the Chauth and Sardeshmukhi System", pp. 172–5.

[39] For the Mughal grants, see Mawji and Parasnis, *Treaties and Agreements*, nos 1–5; Pawar, "Some Documents", pp. 204–15.

found service as political vakils at the leading edge of Maratha expansion.

These claims, and the growing needs for war finance that they serviced, meant that many vakils were directly involved in negotiations over chauth tribute. They also played a key role in transmitting local intelligence about how far chauth was being successfully collected on the ground by the kamāvīsdārs who followed Maratha raiding parties, taking contracts for revenue collection and transforming military levies into regular civilian taxes.[40] The role of kamāvīsdār was itself a means of upward mobility, offering the chance not only of substantial reward in salary and expenses, but also a more direct connection with the peshwa, since, like political vakils, kamāvīsdārs also worked directly for him.[41] There were other parallels between the roles.[42] Kamāvīsdārs' experience of geographical mobility, collecting local intelligence, negotiating rights to chauth, managing a small team of clerical assistants, and overseeing the transmission of large amounts of cash transferred readily to the role of a political vakil. Both had to raise credit and make loans on behalf of their employers. Political vakils were often remunerated through estates assigned as ijārāh revenue farms, which again drew them close to the operations of revenue collection. Many who started out as kamāvīsdārs went on to become political vakils.

Maratha vakils were also almost exclusively Brahmans, as opposed to the heterogeneous population of political vakils.[43] There were exceptions: the North Indian Kayastha Lala Sevakram and his extended family served in many vakil roles in Satara, Jaipur, and Calcutta.[44] Beniram Pandit and his brother Vishvambhar worked first for the Bhosles of Nagpur, and then as agents of Warren Hastings in Banaras.[45] The great majority of vakils, however, both those employed

[40] Gordon, "Slow Conquest", pp. 16–25; Sen, *Administrative System*, pp. 252–8.

[41] Gordon, "Slow Conquest", pp. 43–4.

[42] Gupta, *The Maratha Penetration*, p. 83.

[43] For this variety, see the names of political vakils posted to the Company in Calcutta, in *Calendar of Persian Correspondence*, vol. 7, pp. 467–8; vol. 8, pp. 649–50; vol. 9, pp. 345–6; vol. 10, pp. 413–15; vol. 11, pp. 413–15.

[44] Disalkar, "Maratha Vakils", pp. 28–9.

[45] *Calendar of Persian Correspondence*, vol. 7, p. 12.

by the peshwas and by the Maratha sardars, were Marathi-speaking Brahmans. Some were family relations of the peshwas, and many others members of the same Chitpavan Brahman caste community, appointed for their administrative skills, their prestige, and their universally recognisable identities as Brahmans.[46]

The documentary sources for this essay reflect this social make-up of those serving as Maratha vakils. As agents in the diplomatic world, their work took place in a multilingual environment, which required familiarity with Persian as the lingua franca of the subcontinent's diplomatic world, with the vernacular language of the local court where they served, as well as with their own Marathi language.[47] As Michael Fisher has shown, the courts of the eighteenth century usually despatched professional news-writers to work alongside political vakils, their reports accompanying and providing contexts for the letters of political vakils themselves. News-writers' letters were usually in Persian, and the Pune court routinely employed Persian-acculturated Kayastha or Khatri families for the role.[48] However, the distinguished Parasnis family of Pune – the hereditary Persian-language secretaries to the Pune court – were Deshastha Brahmans who had acquired their proficiency in Persian during a family member's period of service at the Adil Shahi court in Bijapur.[49] In the later part of the eighteenth century, the peshwas also received Persian news-letters from what seems to have been a commercial syndicated news service operating across a number of North Indian courts, whose news-letters bore the distinctive seal "Khemkaran Mansaram" on them.[50]

For the most part, however, there seems to have been a clear division of labour between on the one hand Maratha vakils who sent back home letters and reports written in Marathi in the Modi cursive script,

[46] For the eighteenth as a distinctively "Brahman century", see Bayly, *Caste, Society and Politics*, pp. 64–96. For pre-colonial Brahman mobility, see O'Hanlon, "Speaking from Siva's Temple", pp. 178–89.

[47] For education in Persian as the language of administration and revenue collection amongst Maratha Brahmans, see Guha, "Serving the Barbarian".

[48] Fisher, "The Office of Akhbār Nawīs", pp. 53–4.

[49] Joshi, *Poona Akhbars*, vol. 1, p. viii; Sarkar, *Delhi Affairs*, p. 2.

[50] Khare, "Notes", p. 135. I am much indebted to Mr Gajanan Mehendale for very kindly sharing this material with me.

and on the other, the Persian scribal secretaries responsible for translating incoming Persian newsletters and diplomatic communications into Marathi, as well as translating the outgoing Marathi responses from the peshwa's and other Maratha courts into appropriately ornate diplomatic Persian. As we will see, there is some evidence, indeed, that even when Maratha Brahman vakils were clearly fluent in Persian, and writing on their own account to Persian-speaking correspondents, they preferred to write in a heavily Persianised Devanagari rather than use the Perso-Arabic script.

The great bulk of Maratha vakils' letters that survive, and that form the basis for this essay, are therefore in Marathi. They follow a common format. They open with greetings to the recipient, confirm the date and place of reception of the letter, and summarise its questions and instructions before launching into the body of the vakil's report. As we will see, the tone of the letters is varied, depending on the relationship between the vakil and his employer. Some letters are deferential in the extreme. Others, from vakils whose families were relatives of the peshwas, or members of Brahman families long in the service of the peshwas, spoke to their employers very much on terms of equality, even upbraiding them periodically for failing to follow advice or neglecting to send the funds essential for a vakil's effective work. In these cases, the Marathi of the letters has a domestic and familial tone to it, written very much in a Sanskritised Brahman idiom, and with very few of the Persian words that occur in so many Marathi administrative documents of this period.[51]

Diplomacy and Finance: Vakilī as a Family Enterprise

While the joint household offered an invaluable resource for many scribal and service families, it offered particular advantages in a political vakil's work.[52] As we will see, vakils clearly learned much of their trade by working alongside their fathers and brothers. Fathers, sons, and

[51] See Guha, "Transitions and Translations".

[52] Chatterjee, *Unfamiliar Relations*, pp. 3–45. For the Maratha household as a corporate enterprise, see Perlin, "Of White Whale and Countrymen", pp. 190–2, and Guha, "The Family Feud".

brothers offered a pool of talent that could be circulated around different courts, contributing to better co-ordination in the reporting of intelligence. Trust between family members was important in managing flows of cash between countryside, court, and army camps. Family connections offered reassurance in the conduct of complex and long-distance political relationships. Families diversified their sources of employment and improved their prospects by moving from kamāvīsdār to vakil work.

Best known of the Maratha vakil families from this era were the Hingnes, originally priests of the peshwas at the shrine town of Nasik. Mahadevbhat Hingne accompanied the first peshwa Balaji Vishvanath on his mission to Delhi in 1719. During the 1720s, he acted as a mobile vakil for the peshwa, moving between Delhi and the Rajput courts. From the 1730s, as links developed between the courts of Jaisingh and the northern Maratha sardars, Mahadev served as the peshwa's vakil at Jaipur. As Jaisingh took an ever larger part in Delhi politics, Mahadev began to spend more time in Delhi, and his eldest son Bapuji became the peshwa's vakil in Jaipur.[53]

By 1744, when he was killed in a brawl between Maratha and Jaipuri troops, Mahadevbhat was both peshwa's vakil at the imperial court and vakil for the new Raja of Jaipur, Ishwarsingh.[54] At this point, Bapuji focused on affairs in Delhi, while his brothers Damodar, Purushottam, and Devarao worked as mobile vakils at other North Indian courts. A deed of grant issued in 1757 by the peshwa Nana Saheb, after a temporary confiscation of the family's offices and estates, reveals an extraordinary array of vakil offices – at the courts of Delhi and Jaipur, with Shuja ud Daula in Awadh, and with the Rohilla and Pathan courts of Ahmad Khan, Sadulla Khan, Dunde Khan, Hafiz Rehmat Khan, and Najib Khan. In an early attempt to channel intelligence through his own vakils, Nana Saheb's grant stipulated that the northern sardars Holkar and Shinde and the Maratha general Visaji Krishna should utilise the services of the Hingnes, and the Hingnes alone, for vakil work in North India.[55]

[53] Khare, *Hingṇe Daftar*, vol. 1, pp. 9–13.

[54] Purandare, *Purandare Daftar*, vol. 1, no. 154.

[55] Kibe, "Some Original Marathi Documents", pp. 1–5.

With the Maratha expedition of 1754 to Delhi under the command of Nana Saheb's less competent younger brother Raghunathrao, we get some sense of the struggle that the next generation of the Hingnes undertook to extract the huge cash subsidies for the Maratha armies promised by Alamgir II's wazir Imad-ul-Mulk. In October 1754, Mahadev's son Bapuji described their role:

> We are constantly pressing the wazir for what he still owes us. But the Emperor has no cash, there is none in the wazir's house, and the soldiers are perishing of hunger. Their blades and daggers lie around in heaps. We are pressing them for money in the midst of all this. There are no ornaments and no cash. The wazir has told us that there are estates near Delhi which have been set aside to feed himself and the emperor, and we should take an assignment on those revenues for the thirteen and a half lakhs we are owed.[56]

After failing to extract cash from the wealthier citizens, Bapu Hingne and the emperor's minister Nagar Mal together attempted to impose a levy on the traders and market people, resulting in closure of the bazaars and major riots. By November, Nagar Mal had taken refuge at the Hingne mansion in Jaisinghpura.[57] So extensive was the Hingnes' portfolio of vakil offices that they delegated their work in Jaipur to another Maratha Brahman family, the Galgalekars, who also combined diplomacy and reporting on tribute collection.[58]

The Kuntes also combined diplomacy with reporting on tribute collection. Serving at the Nizam's court from the late 1720s, they were at the sharp end of Maratha negotiations over chauth in the Nizam's territories. Ganesh Ballal Kunte served as the peshwa's vakil to the Nizam from the late 1720s, reporting from the Nizam's camp the all-too-familiar state of local-level war between forces loyal to the Nizam and Maratha revenue collectors.[59] His younger brother Sadashiv was at the same time keeping him in touch with the latest intelligence from

[56] Sardesai, *Selections from the Peshwa Daftar* (hereafter SPD) vol. 27, no. 90.

[57] Sarkar, *Fall of the Mughal Empire*, vol. 2, pp. 12–17.

[58] Khare, *Hingṇe Daftar*, vol. 1, p. 9, and nos 59, 81, 169; SPD, vol. 2, nos 1, 11, 31; SPD, vol. 27, nos. 106, 107; Shastri, *Zalim Singh*, p. 104.

[59] SPD, vol. 10, no. 59 and letters following.

Aurangabad city.[60] By 1735, Sadashiv was serving as peshwa's vakil in Udaipur, describing the grand diplomatic progress of the peshwa's mother across North India, as well as Bajirao's northern tour the following year to secure written confirmation of his chauth claims.[61] By this time, evidently, Sadashiv had managed to secure a personal jagir, since he slipped in a plea for its exemption amid the rest of his reports.[62] The Hingnes were part of the negotiations, and Sadashiv sent his own advice to Bapu Hingne as to the best means of conducting them.[63] While Sadashiv shuttled between Udaipur and Jaipur, Ganesh Ballal and his son Raghunath Ganesh remained at the Nizam's court, the latter beginning service as vakil in December 1745.[64]

A further area of advantage in the jointness of vakil family enterprise lay in the upwardly mobile path from kamāvīsdār to political vakil. In some cases, such as that of the Gulgules – the Shindes' vakils in Kota – whole families started out as kamāvīsdārs and then moved into roles as political vakils.[65] In other cases, families already successful in vakil service often put out their sons into work as kamāvīsdārs in the hope that they would progress to vakil service. Three generations of the Barve family – Malhar, his son Baburao, and the latter's son Krishnarao – served as vakils to the peshwa, Malhar and Baburao in Delhi and Aurangabad, and Krishnarao at Surat.[66] Having retired from his post as vakil in Delhi, Malhar Barve had acquired lands at Kothur near Nasik, in the Mughal subah of Aurangabad. From this base, he worked through the late 1720s to ensure that Maratha revenue collectors in Nasik had sufficient military backing to see off the rival amils of the Nizam's officer Turkataz Khan.[67] By this time, an entry in the peshwa's diary for October 1728 recorded that Malhar's son, Baburao, had been appointed kamāvīsdār in the Mughal lands in Berar. By May 1729, he

[60] Ibid., nos 39 and 61.

[61] Ibid., nos 128, 134, 142.

[62] Ibid., vol. 30, no. 134.

[63] Ibid., no. 143

[64] Ibid., vol. 25, no. 10; vol. 29, 284.

[65] Sarkar, "A New Source".

[66] SPD, vol. 30, no. 24; vol. 12, no. 32; vol. 15, no. 50; vol. 24, nos 218, 240, 250.

[67] Ibid., vol. 13, no. 25.

had gained his first appointment as a vakil, serving at the Nizam's court in Aurangabad.[68] The year 1737 found him serving as peshwa's vakil in Delhi, received at court and honoured with gifts of an elephant, a horse, ornaments, and robes of honour.[69] He remained there through the invasion of Nadir Shah, impelling his father Malhar to make anxious enquiries about his safety, and received his formal leave to return to the Deccan in April 1740.[70]

Between Personal Service and Service to the State

Running through all of the challenges that political vakils encountered was the tension at the heart of the role, between service to an individual employer and larger obligations to the state. This tension surfaced in a familiar problem for every vakil, that of managing a personal relationship with their employer, often at a long distance, alongside the larger strategic calculations they needed to make as agents of the state in the field. Mahdevbhat Hingne's long relationship with Bajirao I exemplifies this difficulty. As noted above, 1736 was the pivotal year for negotiation of Maratha claims to chauth in North India. Mahadevbhat, along with Rajmal – the dewan of Jaisingh, Rajput ruler of Jaipur – brought down a draft treaty from the emperor to Udaipur, and the Mir Bakshi Nawab Khan Dauran had promised many additional gifts and grants. In January 1736 the terms with Jaisingh were arranged through Mahadevbhat, accompanied by much ceremony.[71]

At this key juncture, it was learned that a body of Bajirao's troops had run amok and captured the fort of Ujjain. On 24 June 1736, Mahadevbhat wrote to Bajirao, describing Khan Dauran's bitter reproaches and withdrawal of the treaty offer. Here we see the language of trust and confidence in negotiations that Vendell has described, now tested and broken when a vakil's employer failed to follow his advice.

[68] Ibid., vol. 12, no. 32.
[69] Ibid., vol. 15, no. 50.
[70] Ibid., vol. 22, no. 145, and vol. 15, no. 76.
[71] Ibid., vol. 14, no. 50.

"It is true that people of the Deccan can be trusted. I have not betrayed your confidence. But if you are going to go behaving like this, what is the point of your presence here? What am I to tell the emperor? You have proved the enemies who speak against you to be right." Thus speaking, the Nawab withdrew all of the promised inām, elephants, horses, jewellery and grants, and recalled the hundīs of two lakhs he had only just instructed Rajmal to issue, and recalled his army and people.

Because of Bajirao's failure to control his troops, Mahadev continued, "the whole mould of our negotiations has been broken." There was only one course of action now, he impressed on Bajirao: "You should withdraw your troops from Ujjain and canton them a few miles away. Get Savai ji to send some influential man and put him in the fort. Write a letter to the Nawab in your own name. Write in that letter that we did not know about this work, it was done by some small man, and we have caught and punished him."

Mahadev further urged an appeal to Mughal vanity: "Write the letter very humbly, and make yourself inferior to them. This is the Moghlai court, and they will be very happy if you write about their greatness." He closed the letter, barely able to contain his exasperation. "Well, go ahead and write whatever letter you want, taking my advice or not. I'm here in the emperor's city, bearing enormous expenses, and with troubles on every side. Write to me quickly. Why on earth did you allow this affair to happen? God only knows."[72]

The corporate interests of the family sometimes ran up against the wider needs of state service, particularly when revenue rights and flows of cash were concerned. Some of the Hingne brothers were notorious for their unprincipled financial dealing, as well as for their long-running personal feud with Antaji Mankeshwar, commander of Maratha forces in Delhi during the 1750s. Damodar Hingne accused Antaji of making false returns of the number of troops on his muster rolls. Antaji in turn complained bitterly that Damodar maligned him to the emperor Alamgir II and to Nana Saheb back in Pune, and alleged Damodar himself took bribes in the course of his work.[73] In the crisis

[72] Khare, *Hingṇe Daftar*, vol. 1, no. 5. I am very grateful to Shailendra Bhandare for his help translating these passages.

[73] SPD, vol. 27, nos 80 and 95.

year of June 1754, as Jats, Gujars, Baluchis, and Rohillas fought for control of Delhi, and Maratha hopes of wealth from the imperial court went up in flames, Nana Saheb admonished Damodar for his failed management of Maratha interests in the city, compared to that of his father Mahadevbhat: "Your father was intelligent, honest and worthy of his post, and because of that it was agreed to make you vakil. For a while you served obediently, and so we looked after you." But these days, every sardar complained about his behaviour. His allegations to the emperor about Antaji had caused great harm to the peshwa's strategy, and he wavered constantly in his political advice, now counselling alliance with one party at court, now another.[74] These complaints culminated in the temporary confiscation of the Hingnes' property in 1757.[75]

The sometimes uncertain nature of delegated authority made itself felt in uses of the formal insignia of a vakil's office, the sanad or deed of grant stamped with the seal of his employer confirming him in his role. Ganesh Ballal's son Raghunath Ganesh, peshwa's vakil to the Nizam in the 1740s, found himself in difficulty in late 1746 as the drought and crop failures of that year began to make themselves felt. Nanasaheb peshwa had been highly displeased to learn that Raghunath had taken liberties with the seals of office. Raghunath had made his own personal seal out of wax and given it out as a dastak (official pass of exemption from transit dues). In November 1746, he wrote in great contrition to explain. There had been a great shortage of grain in Aurangabad. The Nizam's son, Nasir Jang, ordered the city's vakils to issue passes to the grain carriers, as they were allowed to do by local custom, to ensure that supplies were not held up. This placed Raghunath in a quandary, because he did not possess a seal with his own name on it. So, he explained, he had made a seal, but had written only his own name, and the name of the god Sadashiv on it, and not the name of Nana Saheb himself. He concluded with further apology and explanation. "Your servant is certainly guilty. If you give the order, then a seal can be made with your own name on it, and used to issue official passes. If you do not want to do this, then I will plainly tell the

[74] Khare, *Hingṇe Daftar*, vol. 1, nos 91 and 92.
[75] SPD, vol. 2, no. 91.

Nawab that I cannot issue official passes without an order from my lord."[76]

The honour of a vakil in the field was another area in which the sometimes unsettled nature of delegated authority presented challenges. The honour of a vakil was a local and personal matter, yet inextricably bound up with the prestige of his employer, and almost invariably placed under strain by shortages of cash. A protégé of Baburao Barve, Shamji Govind Takle, served as Bajirao I's vakil with the Nizam between the late 1730s and early 1760s.[77] In June 1738, he wrote to Bajirao I's brother Chimaji Appa, reminding him of matters still needing his attention, including Shamji's own financial embarrassments. The issue of Sayyed Jamal Khan's military estate held on a revenue farm had yet to be resolved. He himself was owed money by powerful ministers at court, and he pleaded with Chimaji to send letters to them by fast runner instructing them to pay up. Shamji and his associate Jotipant were responsible for paying the Arab and Siddi mercenary soldiers at the court maintained there by the peshwa. Remittances had fallen behind and the soldiers were becoming belligerent. Nasir Jung and the city's kotwal had been ordered to assist, but refused to act. Shamji begged Chimaji to act speedily: "If you delay my request, then there will be nothing left of my honour. I have tried every trick and device I know, but I am dealing here with absolutely idiotic people."[78] The vakil Raghunath Ganesh was even more explicit about the shame of his financial embarrassments. He wrote to Nana Saheb in April 1747 from his post at the camp of Nasir Jang. The rains were coming, his team was discontented, and his accoutrements were worn out: "Your servant is completely without the proper equipment. The horses of the troopers are not in a good state. The saddles are all worn out. I have a mace-bearer, a pair of runners and two lads to help me, but they are all foreigners. On top of that they are all anxious because the rains are coming and keep asking your servant for permission to leave." Nana Saheb had sent him a draft for 300 rupees, but that was now three months ago. On top of his own expenses, "there are the sundry expenses for Nasir Jang's servants, and on top of that the costs of

[76] Ibid., vol. 25, no. 36.
[77] Ibid., vol. 44, no. 32.
[78] Ibid., vol. 15, no. 70.

the runners and the mace-bearer. Prices are very high in Nasir Jang's army. It would not be fitting for me to ask Nasir Jang for money. I feel very awkward doing that."[79]

On other occasions, vakils abandoned the focus on honour and simply looked to their personal needs. Many hoped to secure a jagir estate as a mark of prestige and a reliable path to security in retirement. Towards the end of his career, Shamji Takle was offered a jagir by Nizam Ali Khan during negotiations with Hyder Ali about a possible alliance against the peshwa Madhavrao I.[80] We saw above that the Udaipur vakil Sadashiv Ballal had secured one for himself. But his nephew Raghunath Ganesh seems to have been less successful. He wrote rather miserably to Nana Saheb in 1748, reminding him of his past promises of a mamledar post on the Konkan coast: "Now, your servant's request is that you look kindly on me and issue orders for the mamledar post to be given to me. Then my family will be established there. We still haven't built a house, and are just eking out our days in a makeshift residence. Your servant is poor, and can't run around any more, because of age and infirmity. That is why I am requesting you."[81] Raghunath's pleas evidently fell on deaf ears. Through 1753 and 1754, he was despatched as vakil to the camp of the French commander Bussy, as part of Nana Saheb's attempts to secure a French alliance.[82]

From these earlier eighteenth-century perspectives, it is possible to see the deep social and financial hinterland of a political vakil's life, which is sometimes obscured by the drama and colour of courtly diplomatic exchange. The expansion of the older and more capacious agential role of vakil to encompass both diplomacy and financial management made the vakils of the eighteenth century much more flexible instruments of the state than their predecessors, the īlchīs and hejibs of earlier centuries. With their extended family networks, their ability to diversify risk across several professions, and their skill in facilitating the business of several employers at once, their presence was as vital to eighteenth-century states as that of merchants, bankers, and revenue contractors.

[79] Ibid., vol. 25, no. 48

[80] Ibid., vol. 37, no. 23.

[81] Ibid., vol. 25, no. 77.

[82] Hatalkar, *Relations Between the French and the Marathas*, pp. 118–20.

Uniquely, though, political vakils were often mobile across subcontinent-wide networks. Their roles as diplomats gave them skills of persuasion that were useful in building their own personal networks and shaping local institutions and relationships around their own interests. At the same time, vakils as well as their employers struggled with the tension between the personal and the state-focused aspects of vakil service, and with the place of the extended family in state service – its independent social and financial imperatives making it sometimes an asset and sometimes a liability.

Mid-Century Transitions

What were the implications for Marathi-speaking vakil communities as the European trading companies expanded their political operations from the middle of the century? As Fisher and others have shown, Indian states tried various means to counter European attempts to control the flow of political information, including developing their own independent networks of vakils. For the Maratha state, this was the trademark of the prominent minister Nana Phadnis (1742–1800), whose grandfather Balaji Bhanu came up from the Konkan with the first peshwa Balaji Vishvanath.[83] Nana Phadnis came to the fore after the Maratha defeat at Panipat in 1761, and rapidly rose to power as leader of the Barbhais, the council of twelve powerful sardars which presided over Maratha affairs after the murder of the young peshwa Narayanrao in 1773. During the 1770s and 1780s, Nana developed an extraordinary network of vakils across the subcontinent. They were moved around as political circumstances and challenges, particularly from the English, demanded.[84]

The other major challenge to Nana's position in the field of intelligence lay in the rise to North Indian dominance of the great sardar and over-mighty subject of the peshwas, Mahadji Shinde (1730–94). First coming to prominence after the Maratha defeat at Panipat in 1761, Mahadji was principally responsible for the defeat of the English in the First Anglo- Maratha War of 1779–83. His military dominance in North

[83] Deodhar, *Nana Phadnis*, pp. 1–3.

[84] Ibid., especially ch. 5.

India enabled him in 1784 to recover the Maratha position in Delhi, when the emperor Shah Alam II conferred on him the title of Vakīl-e Mutlaq, the direct deputy of the emperor, to the great annoyance of Nana Phadnis.[85] As we saw above, the peshwa Nana Saheb had in 1757 been able to decree that Shinde and Holkar should use the Hingnes for all vakil work in North India. It was a measure of the challenge to the Pune court's control over these networks of political vakils that from 1776 Mahadji began to insist on all Maratha communication with the Company flowing through the Resident at his own court in Gwalior.[86]

Maratha vakil families flourished in this new milieu. Some represented the peshwa's interests in Bombay, Madras, and Calcutta, principal among them the Ranchod family in Bombay, the long-serving North Indian Kayastha Lala Sevakram and his extended family in Calcutta, and Janardan Shivram and his brother Nago in 1780s Madras.[87] Janardan's experience offers us a good insight into a vakil's own sense of his career, in a landscape where Indian polities small and large flourished alongside the East India Company as sources of employment as well as of informal advantage. While serving as peshwa's vakil to the Company in Madras, Janardan had been given three villages in inām by the Nayaka chief Venkatappa at Kalahasti, as thanks for Janardan having persuaded Hyder Ali not to plunder his lands. Once secure from Hyder Ali, Venkatappa took his villages back. Clearly fluent in English from his Madras experience, Janardan wrote to the governor of Madras in February 1785, emphasising the personal factotum aspects of a vakil's role: "I am a Vakeel . . . whose Duty is to render Service to those that are desirous and receive from them favors in return." Possession of a jagir or inām lands such as Venkatappa had given him, he explained, was so important to vakils like himself that "they will wait for twelve years to accomplish their Aims." Moreover, he explained to the governor, he was not some fly-by-night vakil but a settled and substantial servant of the peshwa in Madras, whose personal plans depended on recovering the villages: "I am fixt to the

[85] Pandey, *Mahadaji Shinde*, pp. 92–5.

[86] Fisher, *Indirect Rule*, pp. 274–5.

[87] Disalkar, "Maratha Vakils", pp. 27–8.

Office of Vakeel here on behalf of the Mahrattas, and not same as others that remain here to-day liable to be removed the next day. I have therefore rejected the Offer of Money and accepted the village from Colastry Zemindar thinking myself that I shall always have country provisions while I remain at Madras."[88]

Other vakils posted to the Company pursued their own family interests alongside those of the peshwa in other ways. Between 1786 and 1797, Bahiropant Mehendale of the prominent Mehendale political family represented the peshwa with the British Resident Charles Malet in Pune.[89] His younger brother, Bachhaji Raghunath, was at the same time peshwa's vakil to the governor of Madras, William Medows, and was present with Appa Balwant Mehendale at the surrender of Tipu Sultan's sons to Cornwallis in February 1792.[90] Like many others, Bahiropant had early in his career worked as a kamāvīsdār in Surat, when he may have gained the language skills that enabled him to work with the British Resident.[91] As noted above, the Portuguese in Goa also retained Bahiropant's services as procurador at the Pune court, an appointment noted quite matter-of-factly by local Maratha state officials.[92] He worked through Vitthalrao Valavalikar, of the Maratha Brahman Valavalikar vakil family who served the Portuguese in Pune from 1791 to 1808. Bahiropant received various compensations from the Portuguese governor, including fourteen Portuguese gold half dobras as a gift to his new wife.[93] Malet reported him as an exceptionally able and willing channel of communication with the peshwa, although, as he explained to Cherry, Governor General Cornwallis' Persian translator, "the magnitude of Behro Punt's expectations" made the exact form of reward rather difficult.[94] At the end of Malet's tenure as Resident in February 1796, Bahiropant fell victim to the factional fighting in Pune that followed the death of Peshwa Madhavrao II.[95] With his brother

[88] Disalkar, "An English Letter", pp. 236–7.

[89] Sardesai, *Poona Residency Correspondence* (hereafter PRC), vol. 2, no. 2, and other letters in this volume.

[90] Ibid., no. 103; Macdonald, *Memoir*, p. 78.

[91] SPD, vol. 35, no. 132.

[92] Sen, *Studies in Indian History*, p. 128.

[93] Pissurlenkar, *Portuguese–Mahratta Relations*, pp. 238–41.

[94] PRC, vol. 2, no. 155.

[95] Ibid., no. 266.

Bacchaji he was confined and maltreated in Raigad fort in August 1796, and his son Bhaskar turned to Malet for help at this low point in the family's fortunes.[96]

The perspectives emphasised here, of the plural roles and local embeddedness of political vakils, help us to appreciate their individual resilience in the face of European efforts at control. Their ability to deploy family alongside political networks and to transfer skills learned in one role to another, often brought them personal advantage and could sometimes be useful to their employers. But the plural involvements of vakils' lives could also be a disadvantage to their employers, blurring the lines of political loyalty in an age when political advantage lay in tightening them.

Messages from Nana: A Vakil Goes South

Yet the drive to control intelligence was only part of the story for Maratha vakils and their employers as the Company's power expanded. How far did the Company's presence, its consciousness of its dignity and honour as a political player, its legalistic approach to political relationships, and its adroit exploitation of regional rivalries and political factionalism shape the understandings of statecraft and political ethics that Vendell has described?

Let us follow the journey south of Nana Phadnis' vakil Krishnarao Joshi, despatched to Seringapatam in October 1779. His mission was to negotiate terms for a sudden combined attack on the Company by the Nizam Sikander Jah, Mudhoji Bhosle of Nagpur, Hyder Ali, and the Pune court.[97] Travelling with Krishnarao was Hyder's vakil to Pune, Narsinghrao Verulkar, whose brother Anandrao Narsi was then acting as Mahadji Shinde's vakil with Shah Alam I in Delhi.[98] Also travelling were two clerks, Tryambakrao Appaji for Mahadji Shinde, and Govindrao on behalf of Raste, the two sardars who were to stand guarantee for the agreement with Hyder Ali.[99]

[96] Ibid., no. 330.

[97] Kantak, "The Inside Story".

[98] Parasnis, *Itihāsa Sangraha*, vol. 3, May–July 1911; *Aitihāsik Tipne*, pp. 67–9. I thank Sumit Guha for very kindly sharing this material with me.

[99] Rajwade, *Marāṭhyānchyā Ithihāsāchī Sādhane* (hereafter MIS), vol. 19, no. 4.

This journey certainly reveals the closer direction that Nana Phadnis exerted over his vakils' work. A veritable stream of letters followed Krishnarao and his party south. His formal preparations began on 22 October 1779, with the issue of a travel pass to ease his journey.

> To kamāvīsdārs, watchmen and other certain people, village officers, boatmen and guards. The Sarkar has sent Krishnarao Narayan Joshi to Haidar Khan. With him have been sent palanqueens, horses, camels, guards, troopers and bearers. Let there not be any obstruction to his coming and going. At night a watch should be posted for them, and help given them to cross rivers and nullahs.[100]

The vakils were instructed to rendezvous at the Mahuli river confluence to the south, then travel in long marches for maximum speed. Nana repeatedly emphasised that Krishnarao and the two clerks should keep to a common line of argument: "On everything, you should speak with one voice. Once you have arrived, do not in your speech or your behaviour let any differences between you show outwardly."[101] A further stream of anxious letters followed Krishnarao through December into January, demanding news and urging him to make haste. On 20 January 1780, Krishnarao wrote to say that he had arrived in Seringapatam and been given an excellent reception. Two days later, Hyder received them in great state, and negotiations began.

A key obstacle lay in competing claims to the Adoni District in Andhra, which Hyder Ali hoped to secure. Eventually a draft agreement was prepared. But when it came back from Seringapatam to Pune, Hyder was found to have inserted additional clauses in his favour. On 23 February, the commander Hari Ballal sent a query to Krishnarao:

> When the document arrived from Patan, it was as per our agreement. But there was one further item about Adoni. How was it that this new draft was produced? There is a great difference between the first agreement and the present draft. It is very damaging to us. But it is very well known now that we have established a friendship with the Nawab. It would not now be fitting for us to take offence.[102]

[100] Ibid., no. 2.
[101] Ibid., no. 4.
[102] Ibid., no. 66.

On 26 February, Nana sent Krishnarao a further missive on the proper conduct of state policy, where a stronger assertion of the ethical basis of political negotiation for great states is apparent. "The Sarkar's custom is this, that once discussions have happened and a promise been made, it is not right to turn round and make changes to it. In great states, solemn promises and assurances given are the very treasures of the kingdom."[103] There was an additional reason that Hari Ballal adduced as to why the Pune court should not attempt to undo the agreement. It was that friendship with Mysore – and moreover in an alliance against the English – was a new thing for the Marathas. It was no small thing, he said, that the Nawab and the Sarkar should have become friends in order to defeat the English. "Such a friendship and alliance did not happen during the rule of the late peshwa. This union has been brought about in our own time."[104]

The spring passed and the monsoon approached, but despite all Nana's urgings via Krishnarao, Hyder Ali remained in his camp. On 15 May, Nana pressed Krishnarao still more vehemently. "This is a time for speed. Perhaps the Nawab Bahadur will say, the season is over, the rains are coming, so what does it matter? We will go into battle in the rains. Tell him that fighting has already started in Gujarat. Men are coming from Seringapatam by sea to help them. If the Nawab acts to check the English now, help can reach them."

Hyder Ali's troops did eventually move out to engage the English in the Karnatak. Hastings was able to draw the Nizam and Mudhoji Bhosle away from the alliance, and the Treaty of Salbai in 1782 recognised the compromises to be made on both sides.[105] The episode suggests Nana's tight control over his vakils in the field. It also suggests that the process of political negotiation itself, Vendell's jāb-sāl, acted as a focus around which vakils and ministers alike developed more explicit understandings of the marks of a dignified state and what might count as its major achievements amidst the complex political relationships of the subcontinent. Krishnarao was shortly after handsomely rewarded for his services – by the grant of three villages in Sholapur district, worth Rs 10,000 a year.[106]

[103] Ibid., no. 69.
[104] Ibid., no. 132.
[105] Sardesai, *New History*, vol. 2, pp. 94–124.
[106] SPD, vol. 44, no. 5.

Govindrao Kale: A Vakil at the End of Empire

The themes outlined here emerge with particular clarity in the history of Pune's most powerful vakil family in the Deccan. Between the 1760s and the first decade of the nineteenth century, three generations of Kales – Krishnarao, Govindrao, and Govindrao's sons – were peshwa's vakils at the Nizam's court. With its French military force maintained there, Hyderabad remained a key diplomatic arena for Pune. The year 1776 saw a temporary agreement about chauth when Sikander Jah accepted Maratha contentions that the assessment was now a serious underestimate, given the growth in Hyderabad's revenues over the previous half century.[107] By 1781, the agreement had broken down again. During these years of relative stability in Maratha–Nizam relations, many Marathi-speaking military men and scribal communities had entered the Nizam's service, adding to the Marathi revenue collectors already working there and further complicating relations between the two states.[108]

It was not surprising, then, that Krishnarao Kale, a leading political figure in Pune, should have been made Madhavrao peshwa's vakil to the Nizam's court in the 1760s. He had been present with Raghunathrao's army that carried the Maratha flag across the Chenab river into Punjab in 1758, defeating the Durrani forces to take territories around Attock.[109] He remained behind as the peshwa's vakil at the Mughal court, and by 1764 was acting as the peshwa's vakil with the Nizam.[110] Thereafter he combined periodic spells in Hyderabad with a career at the forefront of Maratha politics. He was a member of the council of the Barbhais, and a key liaison between the council and Raghunathrao, thwarted aspirant to the peshwaship.[111] In 1776, he played a major part in the negotiations about a Maratha–French alliance with the French envoy St Lubin.[112] In August 1781, he was once again in Hydera-

[107] Nayeem, "The Working of the Chauth and Sardeshmukhi System", p. 163.
[108] Faruqui, "At Empire's End", pp. 25–8.
[109] Sardesai, *New History*, vol. 2, p. 398.
[110] SPD, vol. 38, no. 140; vol. 20, no. 174.
[111] SPD, vol. 19, no. 72; vol. 36, nos 48–9.
[112] Hatalkar, *French Records*, vol. 2, pp. 51–6.

bad, to renew Maratha chauth claims, armed with copies from the Satara archives of the treaties made under Madhavrao peshwa.[113]

His son Govindrao learned his craft as a political vakil working alongside Krishnarao. Govindrao was with his father in Holkar's camp in Gohud in May 1766, helped to welcome the French envoy St Lubin in July 1776, deputed for his father while Krishnarao was in Hyderabad, and succeeded him as vakil after Krishnarao's death in September 1786.[114] Govindrao possessed a remarkable sense of the long historical trajectory of the Maratha state. Part of this derived from his work alongside his father, with his own substantial North Indian service, and part from the long association with Hyderabad, so central in Maratha political calculations throughout the century. Govindrao also possessed substantial South Indian diplomatic experience. He represented Maratha interests in the negotiations with Tipu Sultan after the fall of Seringapatam in early 1792, and was present, along with Appa Balwant and Bachhaji Mehendale, at Tipu's surrender and the hand-over of his sons as hostages in February 1792.[115]

Govindrao expressed this sense of Maratha history in a lyrical letter to Nana Phadnis shortly afterwards. Written in June 1792, the letter also reflects his skill, gained over long decades in his work as a vakil, in crafting Marathi prose. He had, he wrote, put pen to paper immediately after receiving news of the accord established between Nana and Mahadji Shinde, now just returned with his armies from North India to Pune. The news of the accord had sent a thrill through his whole body. Between the two of them, they had made the land from Attock to the southern sea "the land of the Hindus, and never more of Turakasthan". Begun under Shivaji, this expansive state had been the joint accomplishment of Brahman wisdom in leadership and the martial valour of the Maratha sardars, now returning home in triumph. "Now, because of the Srimant's mighty virtues, and the Patilbava's wisdom and prowess with the sword, all have come home." It was very much

[113] Joshi, *Poona Akhbars*, vol. 1, no. 91.

[114] Apte, *Chandrachūḍ Daftar*, no. 105; Hatalkar, *French Records*, vol. 2, p. 44. For Govindrao's role in Pune, see Joshi, *Poona Akhbars*, vol. 3, nos 168, 179, 194.

[115] Malcolm, *Political History*, vol. 2, Appendix 1, pp. i–xliii; Sardesai, *New History*, vol. 3, p. 191.

a Hindu patriot's view of the state, which had achieved "not just territories and rule, but protection of the Vedas and sastras, the setting up of dharma, the protection of cows and Brahmanas." The gathering to celebrate this wonderful achievement should rightly, he said, have been taking place in the public square of Lahore.[116] Given the apprehensions actually surrounding Mahadji Shinde's return to Pune, and the sensitivities of Brahman and Maratha roles in the state, this was actually a very ingenious diplomat's letter. Like the marks of a dignified polity which emerged out of Nana Phadnis' correspondence with the vakil Krishnarao Joshi, Govindrao's skilful and selective evocation shows how important the conversations of vakils and ministers were for shaping a sense of the Maratha state as arising essentially out of collaborative political relationships developed over its long history.

This sense of the importance of co-operative relations also emerged in Govindrao's negotiations with Hyderabad. The negotiations between 1791 and 1795 swung between acrimony, insult, and protestations of friendship, concluding in a summary defeat of the Nizam's troops at Kharda in March 1795. Throughout, Govindrao's priority seems to have been to deflect Maratha demands, prolong the negotiations, and plead for relations of amity that would benefit both states.

To understand this, we must appreciate Govindrao's remarkable position of accumulated influence in Hyderabad. As Pune's vakil, he had a direct line to Nana Phadnis in Pune, reinforced through his assistant vakil there, Govindrao Pingle. Kale also had two local assistants in Hyderabad, Ethal Pundit and Kunal Pandit, who remained behind with the Nizam when Govindrao himself visited Pune.[117] Writing in January 1794, the Pune Resident Charles Malet, evidently much less tolerant of Govindrao's multiple political involvements, lost no time in educating the incoming Hyderabad Resident James Kirkpatrick about the malign influence of the "two Govindraos". The Nizam's affairs were in their present sorry state because they were "carryd on through Govinrao Kishun, alias Bappo, alias Kalla, this Court's delegate at Hyderabad, whose looseness of conduct has frequently been notorious. His (Govinrow Kishen's) delegate, Govinrow Pingla,

[116] Parasnis, ed., *Itihāsa Sangraha*, vol. 1, pt 3, no. 13, October 1908, pp. 17–18.

[117] PRC, vol. 4, no. 194.

alias Mamma, here acts as far as it meets the views of this Court in concert with Ragotim Rou, the Nazim's own agent here."[118] Kirkpatrick quickly came to the view that, through his "court", Kale's aim ultimately was to "compel His Highness to model his Ministry conformably to his wishes."[119]

Govindrao's private correspondence during the early 1790s also reveals his vakil's involvement in a wide range of agrarian, commercial, and judicial matters. As Pune's representative, his authority in Hyderabad's agrarian affairs derived from Maratha revenue claims and from the practical presence of Maratha kamāvīsdārs and troops on the ground. Kale sent a stream of letters to Pingle, concerning local pleas for relief on revenue demands on account of crop failure, disputes about property between kamāvīsdārs and local people, the issue of passes exempting trade goods from charges, and the troubles of debtors harassed for repayment. In each case, he indicated what letters of instruction Nana was to send in favour of one party or the other.[120]

Govindrao also maintained a voluminous direct correspondence with provincial and district-level officials and holders of jagirdar estates, the great majority of whom were Marathas. He sent instructions on many different matters, from shortfalls in revenue payments, to the levy of payments on villages properly exempt, to the illicit seizure of lands, recompense after theft, and recovery of debt. In most cases, his role seems to have been to chase up orders already given to these Marathi officials, expressing surprise that the officials concerned had not yet acted on them, disappointment at local disorders, and, sometimes, the satisfaction that it would give the Nizam's own high officers to know that a particular dispute had been resolved.[121] This was very much an informal authority, arising as much from the fact that most of those he was writing to were Marathi speakers aware of his influence in Pune, as from his position as a prominent vakil and adviser to the Nizam.

[118] Ibid., no. 54.

[119] Ibid., vol. 2, no. 255.

[120] For Govindrao's correspondence with Pingle, see MIS, vol. 7, pp. 364–499. Letters to other officers in Hyderabad state are in MIS, vol. 2.

[121] These letters, written during 1792 and 1793, are in MIS, vol. 22.

Here, interestingly, Govindrao adjusted his Marathi when addressing Persophone correspondents of rank. He wrote in November 1792 to one Abdul Samad Khan, "honourable friend the Nawab Saheb of exalted fortunes", who was visiting the Hyderabad court, to apologise for the delay in bringing Abdul Samad's business to the attention of the Nizam. Throughout the letter, Govindrao adopted an extremely ornate Persianised style, every other word in the letter a Persian term rather than a Marathi one. Rather than simply choosing to write to this Persian speaker in Persian, however, the basic language and grammar of the letter were Marathi, and the script Devanagari. We can only speculate as to why this might have been. Perhaps Govindrao did not feel sufficiently confident in his own Persian epistolary powers to be able to address a high-ranking visitor whose command of literary Persian was likely to have been superior to his own. Perhaps also, in this particular context, Marathi rather than Persian may have seemed to be the language of power, a reminder of the close political and familial ties that ran direct from Govindrao's establishment at the heart of the Hyderabad court, to the court of the Maratha peshwas in Pune.[122]

Did Govindrao's shielding of the Nizam's state arise from a desire to protect this powerful position? This may be part of the explanation, but not all of it. He was quite capable of lodging vehement protests when the honour of his own master was impugned. The Nizam's minister Mushir ul Mulk harboured a notorious hostility towards Nana Phadnis. As the historian James Grant Duff described it, Mushir ul Mulk was heard in the public space of the Nizam's camp to threaten that Hyderabad would give the Marathas no peace "until they had despatched the Peishwa to Benaras, with a cloth about his loins, and a pot of water in his hand, to mutter incantations on the banks of the Ganges."[123] Undeterred, Nana sent over a detailed statement of revenues owed dating back to 1774, showing debts of some 26 million rupees.[124] "Warm discussions" then took place between Govindrao and Mushir ul Mulk,

[122] MIS, vol. 22, no. 8. I am very grateful to Shailendra Bhandare for his help with reading this letter.

[123] Grant Duff, *History of the Mahrattas*, vol. 3, pp. 75–7.

[124] Fraser, *Our Faithful Ally*, pp. 397–408.

> when at last the former was told, in public durbar, that Nana Furnuwees must himself attend at the court of Hyderabad, in order to afford an explanation of the different items of their intricate claims. The envoy replied, "Nana Furnuwees is much engaged, how can he come?"
>
> "How can he come?", re-echoed Musheer Ool Moolk, "I will soon show how he can be *brought* to the presence."[125]

Mushir ul Mulk then arranged a pantomime of just this event, with men dressed up as Nana Phadnis and other Maratha dignitaries parodying them before the whole court. Deeply insulted, the two Govindraos rose to leave. As a contemporary of the last peshwa later told the story,

> The rest of the company asked why they were leaving, and the pair replied that it was not seemly to sit through this tamasha of their Master. The Nawab called Govindrao over and said, there is no need to go, it is just a tamasha. What, is there a law against it? Govindrao answered him, "This is a royal court, and a mockery of our Lord has been staged here. It gives us no pleasure to sit further."

Issuing their own threats to take the Nizam's minister and grandees to Pune and parade them bodily from door to door, Kale and Pingle made obeisance to the Nizam and returned to Pune.[126] After the prolonged stasis in the negotiations engineered by Govindrao, these insults provided the catalyst for the Maratha attack at Kharda that followed in March 1795.[127]

Even on the eve of battle, however, he demonstrated a remarkable desire to protect the Hyderabad state. Kirkpatrick reported Govindrao having suggested that the two parties should pause, withdraw to the banks of the Godavari where they could wait conveniently, and make another attempt at negotiation.[128] After the defeat, he urged conciliation. When the Nizam's son Ali Jah fled the court in June

[125] Grant Duff, *History of the Mahrattas*, vol. 3, pp. 75–7.

[126] Sane, ed., *Peśvyānchi Bakhar*, pp. 157–9. I thank Shailendra Bhandare for sharing this material with me. For another instance of a court pantomime involving Mahadji Shinde's vakil Anandrao Narsi, see Elliot and Dowson, *The History of India*, vol. 8, pp. 243–4.

[127] Lal, "The Battle of Kharda", pp. 1356–9.

[128] PRC, vol. 2, no. 166.

1795, Govindrao urged Nana to send out troops to bring the rebel to heel. He should "reassure the Nawab and set his mind at rest, that you only have your common well-being at heart. There is no bar to friends being as one heart in their affections. The Nawab's and the Sarkar's prosperity are one and the same. It is the same with their prestige."[129]

He impressed the same message on a deeply suspicious Nizam and his ministers. "Step by step and day by day, our two states should together sweep away the dark grudges between us, and our relations become open and clear, with a comprehensive agreement and treaty that we can keep for good."[130] In a further letter to Nana Phadnis, he returned to the same theme. "The Nawab may understand this, or he may not. But whatever is good for both the Nawab's and the Swami's state, should be done. Even the Nawab will come to understand this. The Swami should give his attention to protecting the Nawab. His state should be preserved."[131]

In this way, Govindrao made clear his sense that states were very much more than their rulers, and that the point of politics was ultimately to preserve states through collaborative relations between them. His position reflected an understanding of the inter-state relationships of the eighteenth century that complemented the culture of jāb-sāl as Vendell has described it. Part of this understanding grew out of the longstanding respect, shared across the legal cultures of the subcontinent, for established precedent in many fields of social practice, particularly those that related to rights of various kinds, and to the long-established structures of political authority from which many rights flowed.[132] This principle was nowhere better enunciated than in the instruction that the Raja Shahu issued to Bajirao I in his dash to Delhi in May 1739. Warning Bajirao against any notion that he might displace the Mughal emperor rather than support his power, the Raja emphasised that "he considers it a higher merit to renovate an old dilapidated edifice than to build a new one."[133]

[129] MIS, vol. 5, no. 50.

[130] Ibid., no. 75.

[131] Ibid., no. 77.

[132] Guha, "The Qazi, the Dharmadhikari and the Judge".

[133] Sardesai, *New History*, vol. 2, pp. 168–9.

The same principle may have shaped Govindrao's own approach to the Hyderabad state. In this, he was again following a longer established Maratha policy. As many historians have observed, for all the long history of hostilities between the Maratha state and the Nizam, the Marathas never set out completely to destroy his state. In part, this may have reflected Maratha regard for Hyderabad's own inheritance of legitimacy from the Mughals, and in part a recognition that, in the contested politics of the Deccan, today's enemy might well be tomorrow's ally.[134] Govindrao's own concern to shield Hyderabad from Pune's demands may also have arisen from his own consciousness of the deep interpenetration of territories, rights, and populations shared between the two states.

Either way, this willingness to live with rivals represented a political ethic fast outliving its currency. Govindrao's personal situation underwent dramatic changes in the months after Kharda, as factional conflict and Hyderabad's failing finances seemed to open up further space for his talents. In July, he reported to Nana that "Everybody here is quarrelling with everyone else. Everyone thinks that I should take over the management of the Nawab's affairs." But, he said, it was a burden few could carry, given dissensions at the court, the huge sums owed to the peshwa, and the refusal of the Nawab to trust anyone.[135]

But his fortunes shifted rapidly after the sudden death of the peshwa Madhavrao in October 1795. Govindrao moved back into Pune and, like the peshwa's vakil Bahiropant Mehendale, was caught up in the turmoil over the succession. Also like Bahiropant, Govindrao now transferred his primary loyalty away from Nana, and to Bajirao II and his party. But the timing of these swings was against Bahiropant, who died in Raigad fort in August 1797 amidst the severities of his detention.[136] With Nana's own brief imprisonment in December 1797, Govindrao himself was elevated to de facto leadership of the Maratha state.[137] In August 1798, Malet's successor in Pune, William Palmer, reported to the newly arrived Governor General Lord Mornington that Govindrao was doing his best to persuade Bajirao against a subsidiary alliance

[134] Kulkarni, *The Marathas*, pp. 132–7.
[135] MIS, vol. 5, no. 77.
[136] PRC, vol. 2, no. 20.
[137] Ibid., vol. 6, no. 135.

with the Company, and had written to Tipu Sultan with offers of a compact.[138] Within months, however, Nana had returned to favour, and Govindrao was himself imprisoned in Satara fort in January 1799. By then, the Nizam's own state had been drawn into a subsidiary alliance with the Company. In July 1800, Palmer reported that Govindrao had been released through the intercession of his sons, now serving as vakils in Hyderabad. But, he warned, "to whatever cause this man owes his liberation, his determined and constant opposition to British interests and influence may be expected."[139] Palmer anticipated rightly. Govindrao was still present in Bajirao's circle in 1817, with other advisers of the old regime pressed back into service in the months of Bajirao's final rebellion and defeat.[140] Grant Duff recorded that on his departure for Scotland in January 1823, Govindrao was still living.[141]

Conclusion

Though greatly amplified by the Maratha presence in Hyderabad and by the failures in authority within the Nizam's state, Govindrao's career nonetheless illustrates the great potential for individual and family advancement that lay in service as a political vakil. Vakils certainly had to negotiate between the competing demands of loyalty to family, obedience to individual employers, and the public performance of their role as representatives of the interests of the state. Those able to do this were uniquely well placed to use their skills in diplomacy, their expertise in the management of personal and political relationships, and their familiarity with the movement of cash and credit, to become exceptionally influential players in eighteenth-century politics. In their dialogues with ministers and others, they also articulated contemporary understandings of the ethical ends of statecraft, as well as its practical means. That they did so as vakils, rather than as īlchī or hejib, was very much a reflection of contemporary conditions, in which the skills of intermediation across different arenas were at such a premium, and the extended Brahman family was such a critical locus of power and resources.

[138] Ibid., no. 134.
[139] Ibid., no. 353.
[140] Sardesai, *New History*, vol. 3, p. 489.
[141] Grant Duff, *History of the Mahrattas*, vol. 3, p. 77.

As Robert Travers has shown, the Company's government took a very different view of the elastic roles of the political vakil. Cornwallis' principal experience of vakils had been in the law courts of Bengal. He felt that they were a poorly qualified group who lacked the legal knowledge needed to represent their employers' interests properly, and whose loyalties were suspect, "often bribed by the opposite party to betray the cause of their constituent." His regulations for fundamental reform of Bengal's judicial system drafted in February 1793 envisaged their replacement by a professional cadre of trained and state-approved "native pleaders" on the model of professional pleaders within the British courts.[142]

Political vakils underwent a second transformation elsewhere in the lower reaches of the colonial bureaucracy. They found a further new role within the "uncovenanted civil service" that supplied the Residents of the princely states. The title of "vakil" disappeared, to be replaced by "munshi", signifying a subordinate Indian clerk and translator to the Resident.[143] In this role, as in the new class of the native pleader, uncovenanted civil servants were increasingly required to pass state-certifying examinations, and were rewarded with individual salaries and pensions rather than with family estates granted in perpetuity.[144] What had been a composite line of work, encompassing many skills and arenas for action, and allowing scope for family as well as individual entrepreneurship, broke apart into distinct and relatively inconspicuous roles at the lower levels of colonial administration.

References

Abu al-Fazl, *Ā'in-i Akbarī*, ed. H. Blochmann, 2 vols (Calcutta: Asiatic Society of Bengal, 1872–1877).

———, *Akbarnāmah*, ed. Maulawi Abd-ur-Rahim, 3 vols (Calcutta: Asiatic Society of Bengal, 1873–1887).

142 Travers, "Indian Petitioning", pp. 118–20. See also Banerjee, "The Vakils in the Early British Judiciary of Bengal", pp. 317–22.

143 For an insightful discussion of this relationship, which offers an interesting contrast with that between political vakils and their employers, see Wilkinson, "Weak Ties in a Tangled Web".

144 Fisher, *Indirect Rule*, pp. 339–42.

Ahmad, N., "Ādilshāhī Diplomatic Missions to the Court of Shāh 'Abbās", *Islamic Culture*, vol. 42, no. 2, April 1969, pp. 143–61.

Andhare, B.R., *Bundelkhand Under the Marathas* (Nagpur: Vishwa Bharati Press, 1984).

Anwar, M.S., *Mughals and the Deccan: Political Relations with the Ahmadnagar Kingdom* (Delhi: B.R. Publications, 2007).

Apte, D.V., ed., *Chandrachūḍ Daftar* (Pune: Aryabhushan Press, 1920).

Banerjee, N., "The Vakils in the Early British Judiciary of Bengal", *Proceedings of the Indian History Congress*, vol. 27 for 1965 (Allahabad: Indian History Congress, 1967), pp. 317–22.

Bayly, C.A., *Rulers, Townsmen and Bazaars: North Indian Society in the Age of Expansion, 1770–1870* (Cambridge: Cambridge University Press, 1988).

———, *Empire and Information: Intelligence Gathering and Social Communication in India, 1780-1870* (Cambridge: Cambridge University Press, 1996).

———, and Sanjay Subrahmanyam, "Portfolio Capitalists and the Political Economy of Early Modern India", in Sanjay Subrahmanyam, ed., *Merchants, Markets and the State in Early Modern India* (Delhi: Oxford University Press, 1990), pp. 242–65.

Bayly, Susan, *Caste, Society and Politics in India from the Eighteenth Century to the Modern Age* (Cambridge: Cambridge University Press, 1999).

Bearman, J., *et al.*, eds, *Encyclopaedia of Islam*, 2nd edn, 12 vols (Leiden: Brill, 1960–2005).

Beveridge, H., ed., *Memoirs of Jahāngīr*, 2 vols (London: Royal Asiatic Society, 1909–14).

Calendar of Persian Correspondence, 11 vols (Calcutta: Superintendent Government Printing, 1911–25).

Calkins, B., "A Note on Lawyers in Muslim India", *Law and Society Review*, vol. 3, no. 2/3, November 1968–February 1969, pp. 403–6.

Chatterjee, Indrani, *Unfamiliar Relations: Family and History in South Asia* (New Brunswick: Rutgers University Press, 2004).

Dale, S.F., *Babur: Timurid Prince and Mughal Emperor, 1483–1530* (Cambridge: Cambridge University Press, 2018).

Deodhar, Y.N., *Nana Phadnis and the External Affairs of the Maratha Empire* (Bombay: Popular Book Depot, 1962).

Dighe, V.G., ed., *Poona Residency Correspondence, vol. 4, Maratha–Nizam Relations 1792–1795* (Bombay: Government Central Press, 1937).

Disalkar, D.B., "An English Letter of Janardan Shivram, the Peshwa's Vakil at Madras, to Macartney, the Governor of Madras", *Journal of Indian History*, vol. 11, nos 1–3, 1932, pp. 234–9.

———, "Maratha Vakils with the British at Bombay, Calcutta and Madras", in V. Rangacharya, *et al.*, eds, *Dr S. Krishnaswami Aiyangar Commemoration Volume* (Madras: Dr S. Krishnaswami Aiyangar Commemoration Committee, 1936), pp. 26–9.

Elliot, H.M., and John Dowson, eds, *The History of India as Told by Its Own Historians*, 8 vols (London: Trübner and Co., 1877).

Farooqi, N.R., "Diplomacy and Diplomatic Procedure Under the Mughals", *The Medieval History Journal*, vol. 7, no. 1, 2004, pp. 59–86.

Faruqui, M.S., "At Empire's End: The Nizam, Hyderabad and Eighteenth Century India", *Modern Asian Studies*, vol. 43, no. 1, 2009, pp. 5–43.

Fisher, M., *Indirect Rule in India: Residents and the Residency System 1764–1858* (Delhi: Oxford University Press, 1991).

———, "The Office of Akhbār-Nawīs: The Transition from Mughal to British Forms", *Modern Asian Studies*, vol. 27, no. 1, 1993, pp. 45–82.

Fraser, H., *Our Faithful Ally, The Nizam* (London: Smith, Elder, and Co., 1865).

Gordon, S., "The Slow Conquest: Administrative Integration of Malwa into the Maratha Empire, 1720–60", *Modern Asian Studies*, vol. 11, no. 1, 1977, pp. 1–40.

Grant Duff, James, *History of the Mahrattas*, 3 vols (London: Longman, Rees, Orme, Brown, and Greene, 1826).

Guha, Sumit, "The Family Feud as Political Resource in Eighteenth Century India", in Indrani Chatterjee, ed., *Unfamiliar Relations: Family and History in South Asia* (New Brunswick: Rutgers University Press, 2004), pp. 73–94.

———, "Transitions and Translations: Regional Power and Vernacular Identity in the Dakhan, 1500–1800", *Comparative Studies of South Asia, Africa and the Middle East*, vol. 24, no. 2, 2004, pp. 23–31.

———, "Serving the Barbarian to Preserve the *Dharma*: The Ideology and Training of a Clerical Elite in Peninsular India, c. 1300–1800", *Indian Economic and Social History Review*, vol. 47, no. 4, 2010, pp. 497–526.

———, "Conviviality and Cosmopolitanism: Recognition and Representation of 'East' and 'West' in Peninsular India c. 1600–1800", in Corinne Lefevre, *et al.*, eds, *Cosmopolitanismes en Asia du Sud, Sources, Itineraires, Langues, (XVIe–XVIIIe siècle)* (Paris: Éditions de l'École des hautes études en sciences sociales, 2015), pp. 275–92.

———, "The Qazi, the Dharmadhikari and the Judge: Political Authority and Legal Diversity in Pre-modern India", in Gijs Kruijtzer and Thomas Ertl, eds, *Law Addressing Diversity: Pre-modern Europe and India in Comparison (13th to 18th Centuries)* (Berlin: de Gruyter, 2017), pp. 97–115.

Gupta, B., *Maratha Penetration Into Rajasthan* (Delhi: Research, 1979).

Hatalkar, V.G., *Relations Between the French and the Marathas (1668–1815)* (Bombay: University of Bombay, 1958).

———, ed., *French Records (Relating to the History of the Marathas)*, 9 vols (Bombay: State Board for Literature and Culture, 1978–1985).

Heravadkar, R.V., *Śiva-Chhatrapatīnche Charitra (Sabhāsad Bakhar)*, (Pune: Vhins Press, 1986).

Joshi, P.M., ed., *Persian Records of Maratha History, vol. 1, Delhi Affairs (1761–1788)*. (*News-Letters from Parasnis Collection*) (Bombay: Director of Archives, Government of Bombay, 1953).

Joshi, R.M., ed., *Poona Akhbars*, 3 vols (Hyderabad: Central Records Office, 1953–6).

Joshi, S.N., "Maratha Ambassadors During the Reign of Peshwa Madhavrao I", *Proceedings of the Indian History Congress*, vol. 14 for 1951 (Calcutta: Indian History Congress, 1953), pp. 285–94.

Kantak, M.R., "The Inside Story of the Anti-British Confederacy of 1779", *Bulletin of the Deccan College Research Institute*, vol. 41, 1982, pp. 89–99.

Khare, G.H., "Notes", *Aitihāsik Fārsi Sāhitya*, vol. 5, pt 2 (Pune: Bharat Itihas Samshodhak Mandal, 1969), pp. 132–9.

———, and S. Athavale, eds, *Hingṇe Daftar*, 3 vols (Pune: Bharat Itihas Samshodhak Mandal, 1945–86).

Kibe, M.V., "Some Original Marathi Documents", *Indian Historical Records Commission, Proceedings of Meetings*, vol. 18, 1942, pp. 1–5.

Kulkarni, A.R, ed., *Jedhe Śakāvalī-Karīnā* (Pune: Diamond Publications, 2007).

Lafont, J.M., *Indika: Essays in Indo-French Relations 1630–1976* (New Delhi: Manohar, 2000).

Lal, K.S., "The Battle of Kharda and Its Significance", *Proceedings of the Indian History Congress*, vol. 3 (Calcutta: Indian History Congress, 1939), pp. 1340–59.

Leonard, K., "The Hyderabad Political System and Its Participants", *Journal of Asian Studies*, vol. 30, no. 3, 1971, pp. 569–82.

Macdonald, A., *Memoir of the Life of the Late Nana Farnavis* (London: Oxford University Press, 1927).

Madhava Rao, Setu, *Eighteenth Century Deccan* (Bombay: Popular Prakashan, 1963).

Mahajan, T.T., *Shivaji and His Diplomats* (New Delhi: Commonwealth Publishers, 1991).

Malcolm, John, *A Political History of India from 1784 to 1823*, 2 vols (London: John Murray, 1826).

Malik, Z., "Chauth-collection in the Subah of Hyderabad 1726–1748", *Indian Economic and Social History Review*, vol. 8, no. 4, 1971, pp. 153–206.

Melo, J.V., "Respect and Superiority: The Ceremonial Rules of Goan Diplomacy and the Survival of the Estado da Índia", *Portuguese Studies*, vol. 28, no. 2, 2012, pp. 143–58.

Nayeem, M.A., *External Relations of the Bijapur Kingdom (AD 1489–1686)* (Hyderabad: Bright Publishers, 1974).

———, "The Working of the *Chauth* and *Sardeshmukhi* System in the Mughal Provinces of the Deccan (AD 1707–1803)", *Indian Economic and Social History Review*, vol. 14, no. 2, 1977, pp. 153–206.

O'Hanlon, Rosalind, "Speaking from Siva's Temple: Brahman Scholar Households and the Brahman 'Ecumene' of Mughal India", *South Asian History and Culture*, vol. 2, no. 2, 2011, pp. 253–77.

Oke, Pramod, *Bālājī Viśvanāth Peśve* (Pune: Continental Press, 2005).

Pagadi, S.M., "Maratha–Nizam Relations: Nizam ul Mulk's Letters", *Annals of the Bhandarkar Oriental Research Institute*, vol. 5, no. 1, 1970, pp. 93–121.

Pandey, R.G., *Mahadji Shinde and the Poona Darbar* (New Delhi: Oriental Publishers and Distributors, 1980).

Parasnis, D.B., ed., *Itihāsa Sangraha*, vols 1 and 3 (Mumbai: Nirnayasagar Press, 1908–11).

Pawar, A.G., "Some Documents Bearing on Imperial Mughal Grants to Raja Shāhu", *Indian Historical Records Commission, Proceedings of Meetings*, vol. 17 (Simla: Government of India Press, 1941), pp. 204–15.

Perlin, F., "Of White Whale and Countrymen in the Eighteenth-Century Maratha Deccan", *The Journal of Peasant Studies*, vol. 5, no. 2, 1977–8, pp. 173–237.

Pissurlenkar, S., *The Portuguese and the Marathas*, ed. and trans. R. Kakodkar (Bombay: Maharashtra State Board for Literature and Culture, 1975).

——, *Portuguese–Mahratta Relations*, trans. T.V. Parvate (Bombay: Maharashtra State Board for Literature and Culture, 1983).

Purandare, K.V., ed., *Purandare Daftar* (Pune: Gaura Press, 2014).

Raj, T. ed., *Chronology of Modern Hyderabad* (Hyderabad: Central Records Office, 1954).
Rajwade, V.K., ed., *Rādhāmādhavavilāsacampū* (Pune: Varada Books, 1989).
———, ed., *Marāṭhyānchyā Itihāsāchī Sādhane* (MIS), 22 vols, www.samagrarajwade.com, Pune, 1898–1926.
Sane, K.N., ed., *Peśvyānchi Bakhar* (Pune: Varada Books, 2019).
Sardesai, G.S., *New History of the Marathas*, 3 vols (New Delhi: Munshiram Manoharlal, 1986).
———, ed., *Selections from the Peshwa Daftar* (SPD), 45 vols (Bombay: Government Central Press, 1930–4).
———, ed., *Poona Residency Correspondence* (PRC)*, vol. 2, Poona Affairs 1786–1797 (Malet's Embassy)* (Bombay: Government Central Press, 1936).
———, ed., *Poona Residency Correspondence, vol. 6, Poona Affairs 1797–1801 (Palmer's Embassy)* (Bombay: Government Central Press, 1939).
Sarkar, Jadunath, "A New Source of Maratha History", *Modern Review*, vol. 77, no. 1, January 1945, pp. 13–15.
Sen, S.N., *The Administrative History of the Marathas* (Calcutta: University of Calcutta, 1925).
———, *Studies in Indian History: Historical Records at Goa* (Calcutta: University of Calcutta, 1930).
Sharma, G.D., ed., *Vakil Reports Maharajgan (AD 1693-1712)* (New Delhi: Radha Krishna, 1987).
Shastri, R.P., *Jhala Zalim Singh (1737–1823)* (Jaipur: Raj Printing Works, 1971).
Shejwalkar, T.S., *Nagpur Affairs*, 2 vols (Pune: Deccan College Monograph Series, 1954–9).
Sherwani, H.K., *History of the Quṭb Shāhī Dynasty* (New Delhi: Munshiram Manoharlal, 1974).
———, *Muḥammad-Qulī Quṭub Shāh, Founder of Haidarabad* (Bombay: Asia Publishing House, 1967).
Sowerby, Tracey A., and Jan Hennings, eds, *Practices of Diplomacy in the Early Modern World c. 1410–1800* (New York: Routledge, 2017).
Subrahmanyam, Sanjay, *Mughals and Franks: Explorations in Connected History* (New Delhi: Oxford University Press, 2005).
Talbot, M., *British–Ottoman Relations 1661–1807: Commerce and Diplomatic Practice in 18th Century Istanbul* (Woodbridge: Boydell and Brewer, 2017).
Travers, R., "Petitioning and Colonial State Formation in Eighteenth Century Bengal", *Modern Asian Studies*, vol. 53, no. 1, 2019, pp. 89–122.

Vad., G.C., V. Mawjee, and D.B. Parasnis, eds, *Selections from the Government Records in the Alienation Office, Poona. Treaties, Agreements and Sanads* (Bombay: P.V. Mawjee, 1914).

Vakaskar, S.V., *Śrī Śivachhatrapatīnchī 91 Kalamī Bakhar* (Pune: Vhins Press, 1962).

Vendell, D., "Scribes and the Vocation of Politics in the Maratha Empire, 1707–1818", Columbia University PhD thesis, 2018.

Werner, C., "Ambiguity in Meaning: The Vakīl in 18th and Early 19th Century Iran", in Charles Melville, ed., *Proceedings of the Third European Conference of Iranian Studies, Part 2: Medieval and Modern Persian Studies* (Wiesbaden: Dr Ludwig Reichert, 1999), pp. 317–25.

Wilkinson, Callie, "Weak Ties in a Tangled Web? Relationships Between the Political Residents of the English East India Company and their Munshis, 1798–1818", *Modern Asian Studies*, vol. 53, no. 5, 2019, pp. 1574–1612.

Wink, A., *Land and Sovereignty in India: Agrarian Society and Politics Under the Eighteenth Century Maratha Svarājya* (Cambridge: Cambridge University Press, 1986).

3

Disciplining the Brahman Household

The Moral Mission of Empire in the Eighteenth-Century Maratha State

Introduction

IN VERY MANY WAYS, the household remains a key but relatively neglected field of discussion for the early modern history of India. As historians in many areas have emphasised, a focus on the household brings into our view a more substantial set of social, political, and material relationships than can be conveyed in the rather abstract term "family".[1] The household in India, as elsewhere in the world, was a site where things were produced as well as consumed, where property was owned within a complex set of relationships, where the division of labour – between men and women, the young and the old – was decided, and where access to resources was negotiated. Pre-eminently in India, with its cultural economy of hereditable occupations, the household was a place where skills of many different kinds – craft, agricultural, intellectual – were passed down between generations. In the sphere of politics, elite households occupied strategic vantage points within the structure of early modern states, and many of their senior personnel exercised important roles in local religious and judicial institutions. The political and cultural relationships between

[1] See in particular Guha, *Beyond Caste*, pp. 117–41; Ghosh, *Sex and the Family*.

institutions of the state, local communities, and elite households thus constituted central parts of the early modern "public sphere". Finally, of course, households were a primary site where social norms and sexual discipline were enforced and contested. Why has this relative neglect persisted in the context of early modern India? There is now an important and innovative body of literature on gender relations and identities for this period, but this does not itself focus on the household as such.[2] It has been explored most extensively at the level of the Mughal patrimonial state, itself a "household" writ large, and of the domestic lives and political relationships conducted amongst the elite women of the Mughal and Rajput royal households.[3] A rather smaller body of work attempts to engage with the household at the level of the locality, exploring both domestic relationships of power and the ways in which local "great households" themselves took leading roles in community institutions and constituted key parts of local states.[4] Nandita Prasad Sahai's work stands out in this setting. It provides a series of unique insights into household structures and gender norms amongst the craft communities of early modern Rajasthan. Her work stands as testimony to what the truly creative historian can do, with relatively sparse and difficult archival sources, to develop our understanding of household and local community histories "from below" in early modern India.[5]

This essay takes as its focus aspects of the household in eighteenth-century Maharashtra. The social history of this period in western India has naturally been strongly shaped by the state of the Maratha peshwas, the Brahman ministers to the Bhosle ruling family, descendants

[2] For an overview, see Chatterjee, "Introduction", in *Unfamiliar Relations*, pp. 3–45.

[3] See in particular Blake, *Shahjahanabad*; Richards, *The Mughal Empire*, pp. 59–78; Faruqi, *Princes of the Mughal Empire*, pp. 66–133; Lal, *Domesticity and Power*; Sreenivasan, *The Many Lives of a Mughal Queen*.

[4] For western India, see Perlin, "Of White Whale and Countrymen", pp. 170–237; Guha, "The Family Feud", pp. 74–94; idem., "Household Size and Household Structure"; Glushkova and Vora, eds, *Home, Family and Kinship*; Singh, "Regulating the Domestic", pp. 69–86. For the scholar-households of Maratha Brahmans, see O'Hanlon, "Speaking From Siva's Temple", pp. 253–77.

[5] Sahai, *Politics of Patronage and Protest*; idem, "The 'Other' Culture", pp. 36–58; idem, "Some Were Larger Than Their Communities", pp. 39–68.

of the great seventeenth-century Maratha warrior leader Shivaji. The peshwas emerged during the eighteenth century as rulers in their own right, and came during the latter part of the eighteenth century to duel with the Afghans and the British East India Company to inherit the waning imperial power of the Mughal throne.[6] As is well known, the social policy of successive peshwa ministers came closely to reflect their Brahmanic values, particularly in the state regulation of the orders of caste, the growing social marginalisation of Dalit communities, and the stricter dharmic norms imposed on women.[7]

Rather than exploring the peshwa state's regulation of the social comportment and household norms of other communities, I have here focused on the disciplining of Brahman households by the Brahman rulers of the Maratha state themselves. For very many reasons, this was a key and contentious issue. The political, military, and financial power that many Brahman families came to enjoy under the leadership of the peshwas had been gained by displacing the Maratha Bhosle family. The death of Raja Shahu in 1749, and the move of the administrative centre of the peshwa's government from Satara to the expanding new city of Pune – with its dominating clusters of Brahman administrators, bankers, scholars and religious specialists – effectively eclipsed the power of the old Maratha rajas.

In this somewhat sensitive situation, many among Pune's new Brahman elites felt that it was particularly important to maintain Brahman solidarity and prestige. Brahman communities should be seen to conduct their mutual relations in a dignified and harmonious way, and to ensure that their social practices were in keeping with the ideal norms of religious law in the dharmasastra. The reality, however, was that social and gender norms varied very widely across western India's many different Brahman subcastes: Chitpavans, Karhades, and Devarukhes from the Konkan littoral; the very large Deshastha community of the Deccan uplands; migrant groupings such as the Shukla Yajurvedis

[6] Gordon, *The Marathas 1600–1800*; Wink, *Land and Sovereignty*; Eaton, *A Social History of the Deccan.*

[7] Guha, "An Indian Penal Regime", pp. 101–26; Kadam, "The Institution of Marriage", pp. 341–70; Wagle, "The Government", pp. 321–60; Fukazawa, "The State and the Caste System", pp. 91–113; Kotani, ed., *Caste System*; Kotani, "Structure of the Caste", pp. 63–85.

who had, after the fourteenth-century fall of the Yadava kingdom, migrated from the Godavari valley to the northern part of the Konkan; and the Saraswats who had moved northwards, after the fall of Goa to the Portuguese, into the southern regions of the Konkan. These Brahman communities, often competitors for local office and the inam lands attached to them, as well as for administrative employment with local states, engaged in frequent public disputes about their relative social rankings and reputations, and periodically suspended relations of commensality and intermarriage.[8] Particularly after the mid-century, successive peshwa governments took it on themselves to try harmonising these relationships by enforcing common social and gender norms, and by encouraging Brahmans to avoid acrimonious social fissions.

As the Marathas extended their power up into Central and North India, moreover, this Brahman drive developed a distinctive, indeed imperial, sense of moral mission. Newly conquered Maratha territories such as Malwa, long a subah (province) of the Mughal empire, were clearly important new sources for Maratha revenue demand, to be administered by the cadres of Brahman accountants and revenue managers who followed in the wake of the Maratha armies.[9] The court of Balaji Bajirao (1721–1761) also expressed great concern for the region's Brahman communities, assuming that they had for centuries lacked proper religious guidance and fallen away from their dharmic duties in their social and family conduct. In a remarkable document produced by the court in 1751, a wide range of norms and injunctions were laid down for correct Brahman conduct in the new provinces. In this document, it was the household – its social and ritual life, the conduct of its women and children, the modes of livelihood on which it depended – that became the key site for the imposition of these more uniform Brahman norms, and for the public display of a restraint and piety in conduct appropriate to the prestige of a Brahman administrative elite. Most interestingly, these norms were not solely "religious" in nature. They seem equally to have been a reflection of social class, of a drive to enforce dignity in bodily comportment, propriety in household arrangements, the right combination of sobriety and luxury in modes of

[8] O'Hanlon and Minkowski, "What Makes People Who They Are?", pp. 381–416; O'Hanlon, "Contested Conjunctures", pp. 765–87.

[9] Gordon, *Marathas, Marauders and State Formation*, pp. 23–63.

consumption, and, above all, the avoidance of practices associated with menial forms of labour. The attempt to enforce these norms also offers us a series of unique insights into the Pune government's own sense of its cultural mission as an expanding imperial state.[10]

Discipline and Brahman Resistance in the Peshwa State

Within the Maratha heartlands of the Deccan and the Konkan, successive peshwa governments sought to bring the social conduct of different Brahman communities into line with dharmic norms. Marriage formed a particular focus for concern. In June 1744, Balaji Bajirao's government issued orders to prevent Shukla Yajurvedi Brahmans from giving their daughters in marriage to their sisters' sons, a South Indian practice into which they had fallen during the centuries of Portuguese rule, and which was argued to be contrary to proper dharmic norms.[11] Great concern was taken to promote the dharmic ideal of marriage as kanyādān (the "gift of a girl"), and to disallow marriages which were alleged to have been forced, or which violated the rules against marriage with a member of the same exogamous gotra or pravara.[12] Peshwa governments found themselves repeatedly having to take action against Brahman communities in the localities who took bride-price at the marriage of their daughters, or who had failed to get them married before the age of eight or nine. In 1798, the court of Bajirao II (1755–1851) sent out letters to state officials across eight different talukas in the Konkan and regions around Pune, instructing them to put a stop to Brahman families exacting bride-price for their daughters, or keeping them unmarried after thc age of nine years.[13]

[10] For parallel attempts to control and discipline women's bodies, but in the context of eighteenth-century Marwar, see Cherian, "Stolen Skin and Children Thrown".

[11] Vad and Parasnis, eds, *Selections*, pt 2, *Ballaji Bajirav Peishwa*, vol. 2, no. 317 of 1744–5, p. 198.

[12] Sardesai, ed., *Selections from the Peshwa Daftar* (hereafter SPD), vol. 43, no. 52 of 16 June 1780; no. 53 of 19 November 1780, pp. 46–9; no. 55 of 13 March 1782, p. 50; no 60, undated, pp. 52–3.

[13] Vad and Joshi, eds, *Selections*, pt 5, *Bajirao II*, no. 241 of 1798–9, pp. 259–60.

The effect seems to have been not just to discourage bride-price, but inflate the price that the families of prospective grooms could demand of a bride's family. Bapu Balavant Dani, a Deshastha Brahman from Saswad outside Pune, wrote a very revealing letter inviting a close relative to the forthcoming marriage of his daughter Bhimabai. He disclosed the date set for the wedding, and related with some satisfaction that the groom found for the girl came from a very prosperous family that enjoyed exclusive rights, in perpetuity, to the office of Kulkarni in four different villages. But the pre-marriage negotiations with the groom's father had apparently contained some surprises:

> We went to meet the gentleman to get to know him better, and we had a talk. He asked for a dowry of two hundred rupees. We replied and said very clearly that we were poor people, and if you take us into your family, there is only the girl and our family's disposition to consider. He asked us, "So what will you give to the bride and the groom?" We replied, "We will give cloth for a turban and a shawl to the groom, and a sari to the bride – that is as much as we can afford." He said, "You come here wanting to arrange the marriage, and so we want to know what benefit in goods there will be for us." So we understood that these days it is not possible to get a groom in a good position, who has forty or fifty khandis of grain and rice coming in every year, inām lands where two hundred mango trees grow, and who draws the wealth of hereditary office in four villages, without a dowry.[14]

With this realisation, Bapu Balavant continued, he had signalled his consent, and the two parties had proceeded to discuss the practicalities of transporting family guests to the wedding. It is not surprising that such families of moderate means should have been taken aback, and perhaps disquieted, at the commercialisation of marriage which appeared to flow from the efforts of successive peshwa governments to enforce the "dharmic" model of kanyādān. The "gift of a girl" clearly entailed many other gifts to be made at the same time.

Concerns such as these were not the only possible source of difficulty facing the peshwa governments as they strove to impose tighter Brahmanic norms on their own caste fellows, and to suppress dissensions

[14] Oturkar, *Peśve-kālīn Sāmājik va Ārthik Patravyavahāra*, no. 146, p. 107. This letter is undated, but is probably of the late eighteenth century. For the high cost of dowries in Brahman families, see also Chapekar, "Chiplūṇkar Yānche Jamākarcha", p. 127, and Chapekar, *Peśvāīchyā Sāvalīt*, pp. 214–15.

between them. Deshastha communities in long-established centres of learning, such as the riverside shrine towns of Paithan, Nasik, and Tryambak, were home to dharmasabha assemblies of learned pandits who had for many centuries brought their expertise to bear on the proper interpretation of dharmasastra.[15] These communities very clearly resented the drive of the peshwa governments to centralise the interpretation, as well as the administration, of justice in religious matters at the peshwa court in Pune. Brahmans in these towns gave their backing to their caste fellows when the latter found themselves the targets of discipline and even attempts to confiscate their property by the Pune court. As described above, the court sought to punish Shukla Yajurvedis of the Konkan for their irregular marriage practices. Taking advantage of their own close links with the Pune court, local Chitpavan Brahmans suggested that the Shukla Yajurvedis were not really Brahmans at all, but inferior ritualists, and appealed to the peshwa to deprive them of their priestly livings. At this assault, Brahman pandits from Tryambak and Nasik came out in support of the Shukla Yajurvedis, forcing the local Chitpavans and their allies in Pune to back down. The Pune government continued its unsuccessful campaign against the Shukla Yajurvedis through into the 1770s, when again its attempt to deprive the community of its ritual offices failed.[16]

On other occasions, it was the Paithan Brahman community that defied the Pune court. For over a decade from the early 1770s, the government of Nana Phadnis struggled to discipline pandits and their relatives from the town. The Paithan dharmasabha had been approached by a Brahman son of the town, Narahari Ranalekar, who had been captured by the Afghans after the great Maratha defeat at Panipat in 1761. Narahari had lived as a Muslim for over a decade, but in 1772 made his way home, where the scholars of the dharmasabha acceded to his request to be given appropriate penance and have his social relationships as a Brahman restored to him. The Pune court disagreed with this verdict, asserting that once out-casted, such a Brahman could never be purified. It put pressure on the dharmasabha to retract the verdict, ordering Narahari's wife to divorce him, imposing severe penances

[15] For these assemblies, see O'Hanlon, "Narratives of Penance and Purification", pp. 65–99.

[16] O'Hanlon, "Contested Conjunctures", pp. 785–6.

[17] Sardesai, SPD, vol. 43, no. 25 of 24 August 1772, p. 25; no. 107, undated,

on some recalcitrant members of the dharmasabha, depriving others of their lands, and threatening to out-caste all those who failed finally to comply. But many members held out until the mid-1780s or longer, having secured the support of authorities in neighbouring states.[17] On other occasions, too, the Pune government strained to control the social conduct of these older regional communities. Only after prolonged negotiation were the Brahmans of Nasik and Tryambak willing, in 1751, to accept Pune directions on the priority to be observed in the reciting of Vedic hymns by Brahmans affiliated to different branches of Vedic learning.[18]

There were other difficulties as well. Precise contemporary evidence is difficult to pin down. However, there seems much to suggest that Brahman communities based in the Deccan not only resented the attempts at centralisation from Pune, but questioned the purity and prestige of the Chitpavan community itself. Peshwa Bajirao I (1700–1740) took as one of his gurus a descendant of the famous sixteenth-century "living god" Morya Gosavi of Chinchvad, who was said to have attempted to raise the status of Chitpavans by declaring them fit to dine with Deshasthas.[19] In his 1820 survey, the Orientalist Walter Hamilton observed that the Deshastha Brahmans of Nasik routinely refused to share food with members of the Chitpavan community, and barred them from access to the steps down to the Godavari river used by local priests.[20]

Writing in the 1870s, the social reformer Gopal Hari Deshmukh described the prejudices that early-eighteenth-century Chitpavan migrants up into the Deccan had encountered in and around Pune. They earned their livings as cooks and attendants and found it difficult to obtain respectable work until mid-century, when Balaji Bajirao brought a large body of Chitpavan boys up to Pune and trained them in the skills of record-keeping.[21] For much of the later part of the century, the

---

p. 92; no. 140 of 1772, p. 111; Vad and Marathe, *Selections*, pt 8, *Sawai Madhavrav Peshwa*, vol. 3, no. 1133 of 1785–6, p. 281, and no. 1136 of 1785–6, p. 282.

[18] Sardesai, SPD, vol. 43, no. 24, p. 24, undated; no. 69 of 1751, p. 62.

[19] Preston, *The Devs of Cincvad*, p. 49; Karve, "Ethnic Affinities of the Chitpavans", p. 133.

[20] Hamilton, *A Geographical, Statistical and Historical Description*, p. 197.

[21] Deshmukh, *Aitihāsik Goṣṭī*, no. 133, p. 77.

peshwa court fought a running battle to suppress puranic manuscript texts, as well as the popular performances through which they were transmitted – which mocked the Chitpavan community for its supposed menial origins.[22]

The Moral Mission of Empire: Maratha Brahmans in Malwa

It was in this context of periodic Brahman intransigence, therefore, that the Pune government of Balaji Bajirao appears to have staged its most ambitious attempts at moral mission. Its focus lay not in the Maratha homelands themselves, but in their territories to the north, particularly in Malwa. As noted above, its ambition lay in the fact that it was directed not so much at discrete areas of social practice such as dharmic marriage, but rather at a comprehensive reformation of every aspect of local Brahman household conduct. The campaign, set out in the remarkable document examined below, reflected a determination to enforce dharmic norms in religious practice. Equally, it reflected a set of status anxieties about the forms of sociability, dress, comportment, and consumption that were evident amongst Malwa's Brahman families, and which were judged quite inappropriate to the proper social dignity and prestige of a Brahman.

There may also have been a further, and imperial, dimension to this reforming campaign and the document in which it was set out. As we shall see, what is remarkable about the document is its tone of absolute authority and abrupt command in setting out the new models of conduct to which Malwa Brahman households were expected to conform. A number of assumptions may have guided the Pune scholars and jurists who drew up the document. It is difficult not to see reflected in it a consciousness of the great, indeed subcontinent-wide authority in matters of dharmasastra that Brahmans from the Maratha country had come to enjoy over the course of the sixteenth and seventeenth centuries, particularly from their base in the city of Banaras, where many Maratha scholar families had made their home and developed a wide reputation for their depth of learning.[23] The early decades of the eigh-

[22] O'Hanlon, "Performance in a World of Paper", pp. 87–126.
[23] O'Hanlon, "Letters Home", pp. 201–40.

teenth century were also a time when Maratha Brahmans fanned out from Banaras to the Rajput courts, their reputations as intellectuals, literary men, teachers, and experts in complex ritual creating considerable demand for their services over a time when Rajput rulers themselves sought to reinvent Hindu royal ceremonial.[24]

As the Marathas extended their political and military horizons northwards to Malwa and beyond to Delhi, therefore, their sense of the meaning and possibilities of a Maratha empire may have been much richer than scholars have conventionally assumed. This is an area yet to receive detailed scholarly exploration, but the sense of moral mission evident here certainly has an imperial, and imperious, tone to it. Its implication was that a Maratha empire under the Pune leadership of Balaji Bajirao had a vital cultural responsibility to fulfil in the benighted regions of Central India that had so long lain under Mughal rule. It offered a revived understanding of the principles of the dharmasastra. It also provided long overdue guidance for Brahman families and households that had not only fallen away from propriety in religious practice but lost their sense of the social dignity and decorum with which all Brahmans should conduct themselves – as befitting their status as the embodiments of religious merit and exemplars of moral accomplishment and social worth.

In addressing the household, moreover, the authors of the document may have had a further set of assumptions in mind. It was to be expected that the household would stand at the centre of any drive to encourage conformity with dharmic norms, since it was the household setting that did most to shape the daily conduct of men and women, and their adherence to the many ritual proprieties incumbent on Brahmans in the most mundane of activities. But the household had a further significance for the intellectual and cultural life of Maratha Brahmans in early modern India. As suggested elsewhere, it was above all within the household that their traditions of scholarship had flourished. It was the household that had long functioned as the site where intellectual resources in books and manuscripts accumulated, expertise in particular fields were sharpened and passed down from fathers to sons, and pupils drawn from across India to live and study within the most prestigious scholars. It was within the household too that marriage

[24] Horstmann, *Visions of Kingship*, pp. 10–35.

relationships were contracted that further consolidated a family's strengths. If the household, the incubator and seedbed of Brahman scholarly accomplishment, was not protected from improper practices and the influence of the ignorant and the plebeian, what hope could there be for the future of Brahman intellectual prestige in the region?[25]

There may have been a further assumption, also imperial in nature, underlying the sense of Maratha Brahman moral mission in Malwa. As described below, the model of conduct held out to the region's Brahman families was undoubtedly very restrictive in nature, and the language used brooked no debate. Yet the model also implied something potentially very attractive. It suggested a potential social association with the new administrative elite of Maratha Brahmans that had consolidated itself in the region during the decade of the 1740s in order to ensure efficient collection of the revenues of this productive province. If older and plebeian customary practices could be set aside, there was the promise, at least, of social and family connections with the new elite, of participation in the religious prestige which Maratha Brahmans commanded, and, possibly, a share in the lucrative new offices that the Maratha administration brought with it.

The *Yādī Dharmasthāpanā*: Reforming Brahman Households

Maratha armies had been carrying out raids into Malwa since the last years of the seventeenth century. However, it was under Bajirao I from 1723 that Maratha armies entered the province to collect their customary demand for chauth or one-quarter of the agrarian revenue due to the state. By 1730, the leading Maratha Sardars – Shinde, Holkar, and Pawar – had all established their headquarters in Central India, and a further decade of warfare saw the consolidation of Maratha strength in the region, and a Mughal agreement in 1741 to cede Malwa itself. The Marathas then set about displacing Malwa's major zamindars and inserting their own local kamāvīsdārs (revenue collectors), many of them Chitpavan Brahmans brought up from the Deccan and Konkan for the purpose. By mid-century, this new provincial administration was

[25] O'Hanlon, "Speaking From Siva's Temple".

largely in place.[26] The kamāvīsdārs were key figures in the new local administration: Gordon records that some fifty new kamāvīsdārs were brought into the system between 1740 and 1755.[27] Aside from revenue collection, they took on responsibility for a wide range of other social and judicial matters.[28]

Perhaps with a clearer sense of local Brahman social practices in the region, in 1751 Balaji Bajirao's court in Pune sent out a yādī or listed items of instruction to kamāvīsdārs in the province, setting out approved and forbidden practices for the region's Brahmans. It was entitled "Yādī dharmasthāpanā śāstrapramāṇa vedapurūṣādnyā-pramāṇa nānā dharma pravrvtta hota nānā sthalī" (Items of instruction to establish dharma according to the sastra and the orders of the Vedas, different dharmas being current in different places).[29] It is not clear who wrote the document, but the timing of its issue may be significant. As noted above, the Maratha state's centre of administration had shifted decisively from Satara to Pune after the death of Raja Shahu in 1749. At this time, the great Pune jurist Ramasastri Prabhune was just emerging as an influential member of the Pune śāstrimaṇḍaḷ, the council of scholars and legislators responsible for administration of justice in the peshwa state. Trained in Banaras himself, Ramasastri had been working in the Pune administration since the late 1730s. He became a member of the śāstrimaṇḍaḷ in 1751, and its chief in 1759, a position he held with great distinction until his death in 1789.[30] We cannot know whether Ramasastri had a direct hand in producing the yādī. However, his background and his ascent give us some sense of the Brahman juridical resources now coming to bear at the Pune court of this period, and perhaps beginning to shape the cultural dimension of the Maratha empire.

A copy of this yādī has survived in the papers of the Dvivedi (or Dube) family, servants of the Pawar ruling lineage in their territories of Dhar in Malwa. A letter from Yashvantrao Pawar (1724 –1761),

[26] Gordon, *Marathas, Marauders and State Formation*, pp. 42–51.

[27] Ibid., p. 43.

[28] Gordon, *The Marathas*, pp. 142–5.

[29] Lele, "The Effects of Maharashtra's Culture", pp. 153–5. I am extremely grateful to Sumit Guha for making a copy of this document available to me.

[30] Athavale, *Rāmasāstrī Prabhune*.

addressed to the kamāvīsdārs of particular parganās (administrative territories) in Dhar, accompanied the yādī:

> In past times there was the rule of the yavana, and so many of the proper customs of the Brahmans fell into disuse. So, with a view to reviving the Vedic practices proper to Brahmans, the pant pradhān [Balaji Bajirao] has given an order to Madhu Bhat Dvivedi of Dhar concerning restoring their customs to that of Vedic Brahmans. He has set out separately in this yādī the customs that Brahmans are to follow. Bringing to mind the rightness of their own dharma, and without making any excuses, he or his agents in the province must see to it that custom is practiced according to this yādī.[31]

In forty-eight separate items, the yādī laid down norms to be followed by all Brahmans, covering every aspect of domestic, ritual and social life.

This document is very revealing in its prescriptions. As might be expected, they were targeted very largely at the conduct of the household. However, the document went well beyond the norms and conduct of family members as they were practiced at home. It focussed on the household in its outward aspects as the public showcase for the dharmic dignity and authority of Brahmans. It set out their proper public relationships with other Brahmans as well as with menial communities whose customs and forms of livelihood Brahmans are urged to abjure. Perhaps most interestingly, the models of behaviour set out in the yādī were not simply religious in content but also reveal a strong class dimension, a drive to purge from these Malwa Brahman communities the rustic styles of life, livelihood, comportment, dress, and popular entertainment that were evidently then their practice. The yādī specifically emphasised that the customary practices of Brahman households then current were to be discontinued, and Brahmans to move to the more refined, dignified, and socially separated norms laid out in the yādī. The heading of the yādī, with its reference to "different dharmas being current in different places", allowed that some local variation in practice was acceptable, and indeed in accordance with the dharmasastra. However, most of the instructions referred to "the

[31] Lele, "The Effects of Maharashtra's Culture", Appendix 2, p. 156.

Brāhmaṇ jāti", "samastha brāhmaṇāhī" (all Brahmans together), or *sakal* "brāhmaṇ jātī" (all of the Brahman caste).

Analysis of the forty-eight different instructions shows that they addressed a number of different areas of social and household practice.[32] In keeping with the wider anxiety of the peshwa court, noted above, to foster solidarity and harmonious relations between Brahman communities, many of the instructions encouraged Brahman families to come together with one another as widely and frequently as possible, even as they were asked to hold themselves apart from other social groups. These instructions pertained to matters of hospitality, feasting, and the sharing of family celebrations (nos 3, 20, 22, 33, 47). In matters of religious instruction, Brahmans were urged to look only to respectable scholars and priests such as themselves, rather than to dubious wandering holy men, bogus yogis, or fake ascetics with matted locks (nos 1, 9, 31, 48).

There was also, as might be expected, a substantial focus on correctness of ritual performance. Brahmans were enjoined to perform all of their daily and periodic rites with the proper Vedic mantras, taking care to maintain their ritual purity, and with appropriate priests in attendance. Here, the instructions extended beyond the performance of rites themselves to cover correctness throughout the highly ritualised modes of daily life seen as appropriate to a Brahman household – in washing, cooking, eating, dressing, conducting social relations with other families, the education of boys, and observing the order of caste (nos 1, 2, 5–10, 15–17, 19–23, 25–8, 31–3, 35–48).

Yet the instructions clearly set out to secure Brahman dignity and prestige through much more than ritual or religious correctness. They set out in remarkable detail appropriate forms of restraint and propriety in bodily comportment, modes of dress and personal ornamentation, sociability and entertainment particularly during marriages, the control of children and the conduct of relations between families. The instructions suggested a vivid picture of the current practices condemned in the instructions: the wearing of rustic or coarsely fashioned bodily ornaments, women's blouses that lacked modesty, the taking of bride-price for women, wedding parties that involved gambling and

[32] See Appendix for a translation of the document.

music, gangs of noisy children and house-to-house visits across the neighbourhood to receive gifts of food (nos 8, 16, 35, 39, 40, 419, 10, 21, 22). Such plebeian practices were to be discontinued, and replaced with new styles of composed and serious behaviour.

Just as important as propriety in social and bodily conduct was the distancing of Brahmans from the world of physical labour. A number of the instructions enjoined Brahmans not to engage in bodily work of different kinds, including spinning and the grinding and pounding of grain. Where bodily labour was undertaken, it was important to do it in ways that maintained bodily decorum. Water pots could be carried, but on the shoulder or hip, not on the head. Particularly to be avoided were ways of carrying burdens associated with menial or plebeian service, such as portering work in which the weight was borne using cords around the forehead (nos 2, 13, 14, 19, 29).

Throughout the yādī, there was a sustained focus on the conduct of Brahman women: in matters of dress, ornamentation, domestic work, marriage both in its social and its emotional aspects, the raising of children, and the norms appropriate to widows (nos 3, 4, 10, 11, 12, 26, 28, 30, 34, 42). Here again, these instructions blended together class concerns, with a drive to get Brahmans to adhere to more stringent norms of dharmic respectability: insisting on a low age of marriage for girls, the ideal of kanyādān at marriage, the model of the deferential pativrata wife at home, and rigid models of bodily and social asceticism for widows.

The last of the orders, it is worth noting, invoked the authority of Kamalakarabhatta, the leading seventeenth-century scholar of the eminent Bhatta family of Maratha Brahman scholars in Banaras. It laid down his *Śūdrākamalākaraḥ* as the guide that Brahmans should follow in their work as priestly officiants for Sudras, emphasising that the latter should receive their rituals in line with this text, and not according to the Vedic rituals to which Brahmans were entitled (no. 48). For the Brahman audiences to which the yādī was addressed, the reference to Kamalakarabhatta further emphasised the prestige of Malwa's new Maratha Brahman elite, with their links to this commanding Banaras authority in the field of learning.[33]

[33] Kamalakarabhatta, *Śūdrākamalākaraḥ*. For this genre of literature, see Benke, "The Śūdrācāraśiromaṇi of Kṛṣṇa Śeṣa".

Conclusion

It is difficult, in our present state of knowledge, to know how far this attempt at an empire of culture amongst Malwa Brahmans met with success. The decade after 1751 absorbed the military energies of Balaji Bajirao himself and of the leading Maratha sardars, as the Marathas themselves became kingmakers in Delhi. In 1761, they suffered their devastating defeat at the hands of the Afghan Ahmad Shah Abdali on the field of Panipat. These were years of persistent financial crises for the Maratha armies in northern India. Their demands for cash to pay their troops are likely to have dominated the lives of the kamāvīsdār revenue collectors in Central India, and may well have pushed many matters of social and household regulation into the background. In addition, Maratha dominance in Dhar and other regions of Malwa always remained uneven, and subject to negotiation with the small armed lineages that continued to exercise a large degree of control over revenue collection on the ground.[34]

Nonetheless, the yādī does convey something of the Pune court's remarkable sense of its imperial mission in its northern territories, and that mission's cultural focus on the household. In it, it is possible to see, more clearly perhaps than in the records of the complex and contested history of Brahman identity at home, what it was that Pune's leading scholars and jurists saw as really making a Brahman, and what it was that threatened to erode and destroy a Brahman's proper place in the world. Being a Brahman, for these arbiters, certainly depended on birth, family, and community belonging, and adherence to ritual norms. But being a Brahman was also shaped by what were essentially class-related questions of social style, bodily comportment, forms of sociability and consumption, and distance from the world of menial labour. "Dharma" for the correctly regulated Brahman household also turned out to be about the kind of bangles and toe-rings its women wore, and how they carried the family water-pot in public. If ritual pollution could threaten a Brahman's public standing, so too could affronts to its bodily dignity and the enjoyment of forms of sociability deemed plebeian in character.

[34] For this period in Maratha politics in North India, and particularly the financial crisis facing Maratha commanders in the field, see Sardesai, *New History*, vol. 2, pp. 419–41.

From the perspective of gender and colonial social relations, too, these developments seem significant. On the whole, scholars have assumed that it was the particular history of colonialism that brought women, the family, and the household to the forefront in the nineteenth-century battles over the moral worth of India's civilisational values. What this research suggests is that, in some social milieux in western India at least, the colonial state inherited frameworks for such debates rather than creating them anew, even if the issues contested were new and distinctively colonial. These elements of continuity should not, in the end, surprise us. For all imperial enterprises with a strong cultural dimension, the household, site of so many relations of power, comes unavoidably centre-stage.

APPENDIX

Yādī dharmasthāpanā śāstrapramāṇa vedapurūṣādnyāpramāṇa nānā dharma pravrvtta hota nānā sthalī.[35]

(Items of instruction to establish dharma according to the sastra and the orders of the Vedas, different dharmas being current in different places.)

1. All of the life stage rituals are to be performed with proper respect to lineage, family, kin subdivision, and other set procedure, with proper bathing and attention to daily ritual obligations. Former usages are to be discontinued.
2. The Brahman caste must not keep spinning wheels in their houses. Women should not spin thread, and should leave off their former customs.
3. Brides should not hang garlands made of almonds and dried dates around their necks which are made by the cobbler. They should make them themselves at home. The Brahman caste should observe [a] fast every eleventh and twelfth day of the

[35] Lele, "The Effects of Maharashtra's Culture", pp. 153–5. The separate items in the list are not individually numbered in this published version of the document. I have numbered them here for ease of reference.

month. They should then offer a pleasing feast to other Brahmans on the thirteenth day.[36]

4. Married women must stick to bangles of glass appropriate for married women, and should not wear bangles of wood or lac.
5. No widow must sit and eat in a row of Brahman wives [when] sitting down to eat.
6. No married woman must sit in a row of widows to eat.
7. If a widow still has a topknot of hair, she may not offer puja to Vishnu. She must give up her topknot and shave her head completely.
8. During Brahman marriages, the husband and wife should not wear slippers when they perform Vedic sacred rites.
9. For the sacred rituals of the wedding ceremony, and for the sixteen saṃskāras, Brahmans must bathe and clothe themselves in newly cleansed pure garments. They must perform the sandhya and brahmayagna rites, make pleasing oblations, then sit down to their meal. They must give up their former practices.
10. The Brahman caste should not allow a delay after a betrothal. The betrothal and marriage should happen at the same time.
11. Married Brahman women should wear the choḷī blouse, and should stop wearing the kāchoḷī blouse.[37]
12. Married Brahman women should wear silver ornaments on their toes. They should throw away the brass ornaments they wear in [the] shape of a scorpion.[38]
13. When Brahmans and women carry water pots, they must carry them on their shoulders or their hips. They should not carry water pots on their heads.
14. The Brahman caste should not do grinding and pounding.
15. The Brahman caste should not give gifts of cooked sweets.

[36] The reference here is to a mochī (cobbler), whose main trade in leather rendered other such articles impure.

[37] The yādī here stipulates a front-fastening blouse, presumably for its greater modesty, than one fastening at the back.

[38] This must be a reference to a style of toe-ring then in vogue amongst women of the region. Silver ornaments are enjoined, rather than brass, probably as representing greater purity and dignity.

16. Only that person who has been invited to a Brahman's house to eat, should go. They should not take a lot of kids with them.
17. No widow should be allowed to sit in a row of Brahmans dining, or in a row of married Brahman women dining.
18. The Brahman caste should not use jivahāḷi.[39]
19. Brahman women who are quarrelsome and use bad words may not wear the wedding necklace. All of their rituals must be done with Vedic mantras.
20. On the occasion of sacred ceremonies, all Brahmans must invite to dinner as many other Brahmans as they can afford.
21. During such feasts, all Brahmans appointed for cooking must first purify themselves very thoroughly. Then they can do all their cooking and serve cooked food of papad, chutney, etc.
22. At all Brahman weddings, both bride and groom should wear garlands of flowers only round their heads. They must not wear garlands made in the homes of cobblers.
23. All Brahman castes should administer rites to the dead as stipulated in the sastra.
24. No woman of a Brahman caste should wear garments of a rose colour.[40]
25. When a Brahman dies, his wife should shave her head on the first or the tenth day. Then only will she be purified.
26. Brahman women should wash themselves fully dressed, and then wash their clothes regularly before putting them on. They should wash the blouse, the sari, and the silk clothing worn for purity.
27. Brahmans must conduct their marriages and other life cycle rituals with proper respect to lineage and Vedic affiliation.

[39] The word jivahāḷi is difficult to translate. It can refer either to particularly sensitive parts of the body, or to those parts of musical instruments, such as the mouthpiece of a horn or the thread of the vina, which create sound. It is possible that the latter meaning applies here, and that what is meant is that Brahmans should not use musical instruments, particularly during prayer, as being a practice more suited to less dignified and popular forms of worship, such as those associated with Sudras and bhakti devotional practice. For this controversy, see Venkatkrishnan, "Ritual, Reflection and Religion", pp. 154–5.

[40] The reference here is guleche vastra, literally "rose-coloured garments". It is not quite clear why such a colour was seen as undesirable.

28. For a Brahman girl who is a widow, as soon as she has had her first menstruation, her head must be shaved, she must take off her ornaments, blouse and sari, and wear a single folded garment only.
29. Married Brahman women must not tie cords around their heads.[41]
30. Married Brahman women must wear golden ornaments on their necks and heads, as much as they can afford. They must not wear silver ornaments on their heads.[42]
31. All Brahmans must take their Vedic mantras from other Brahmans. They should not accept religious instruction or commands from wandering holy men, false yogis, or ascetics with matted locks. Brahmans should avoid such people. Brahmans must receive their instruction from other Brahmans.
32. A Brahman's sacred thread should not be made by the spinning wheel. The thread should be made by hand, and while putting it on, mantras should be said.
33. Brahmans should perform their ablutions, then do puja. The water should not be brought by Sudras.[43]
34. All Brahman women must wear the full sari with a tuck. They must throw out their old waist cloths.[44]
35. Brahmans must not touch each other while eating. Married women must not touch each other.
36. All members of Brahman castes must be married between the ages of seven and ten years old.

[41] The reference here is probably to the use of cords around the head for bearing loads, and has the same implication as no. 13, i.e. that Brahman women should not carry loads on their heads.

[42] While silver ornaments are suitable for wearing on the foot, the more honourable parts of a Brahman's body, the head and neck, require the wearing of gold ornaments. For an account of the differentiated degrees of honour attached to the body, see Carstairs, *The Twice Born*, pp. 77–86.

[43] As Hinduism's lowest recognised varna category, the implication is that water brought by a Sudra would thereby be contaminated.

[44] The implication here is that Brahman women of Dhar were accustomed to wearing a simple waist cloth, lacking the modesty and dignity of thc full sari's tuck at the waist and folds of fabric covering the chest and extending over the shoulder.

37. When a Brahman is to be married, the family should go to the bride's village, set up a pavilion, make offerings to the gods, and perform the marriage ceremony.
38. All Brahmans must get married with the appropriate Brahman rites.
39. Brahman castes must not ask for money for their daughters when marrying them.[45]
40. Brahman castes should not amuse themselves with gambling during weddings.
41. During a Brahman wedding, the bride and groom must not go from house to house taking food. This applies also to Brahman children.
42. When Brahman women cook at home, they must wear appropriate clothing to ensure that they are pure.
43. The person who is cooking in a Brahman household for sacred life cycle rituals must be in a state of fasting. Or give him some small snack only and he should not eat more than that.
44. All Brahman boys must study the Vedas.
45. Any Brahman who does not refrain from bad conduct must be thrown out of [his] caste. He must be given an appropriate penance and so purified.
46. When a Brahman's father dies, a Brahman learned in the Vedas must be called to perform the funeral rites and then only invited to share food.
47. When a Brahman's father has died, all those Brahmans who have been invited to the ceremony must be invited to share food.
48. When a Brahman performs marriages and other rituals at the houses of Sudra menials, they should conduct them according to the procedure set out in the *Śūdrākamalākaraḥ*. They should not conduct them with Vedic rituals.

References

Athavale, Sadashiv, *Rāmaśāstrī Prabhune*, *Charitra va Patre* (Pune: Srividya Press, 1988).

[45] This instruction reflects the concerns about bride-price discussed above.

Benke, Theodore, "The Śūdrācāraśiromaṇi of Kṛṣṇa Śeṣa. A Sixteenth Century Manual of Dharma for Śūdras", University of Pennsylvania PhD thesis, 2010.

Blake, Stephen, *Shahjahanabad: The Sovereign City in Mughal India, 1639–1739* (Cambridge: Cambridge University Press, 1990).

Carstairs, G. Morris, *The Twice Born: A Study of a Community of High Caste Hindus* (London: Hogarth Press, 1970).

Chapekar, N.G., "Chiplūṇkar Yānche Jamākarcha", *Bhārat Itihās Samshodhak Maṇḍaḷ Quarterly*, vol. 4, 1925–6.

———, ed., Peśvāīchyā Sāvalīt (Pune: Bharat Itihas Sanshodhak Mandal, 1937).

Chatterjee, Indrani, ed., *Unfamiliar Relations: Family and History in South Asia* (New Delhi: Permanent Black, 2004).

Cherien, Divya, "Stolen Skin and Children Thrown: Governing Sex and Abortion in Early Modern South Asia", *Modern Asian Studies*, vol. 55, no. 5, 2021, pp. 1461–1509.

Deshmukh, Gopal Hari, *Aitihāsik Goṣṭī* (Mumbai: Nirnayasagar Press, 1892).

Eaton, Richard M., *A Social History of the Deccan, 1300–1761: Eight Indian Lives* (Cambridge: Cambridge University Press, 2005).

Faruqi, Munis, *Princes of the Mughal Empire, 1504–1719* (Cambridge: Cambridge University Press, 2012).

Fukazawa, Hiroshi, "The State and the Caste System (Jati)", in idem, *The Medieval Deccan: Peasants, Social Systems and States* (Delhi: Oxford University Press, 1991), pp. 91–113.

Ghosh, Durba, *Sex and the Family in Colonial India: The Making of Empire* (Cambridge: Cambridge University Press, 2006).

Glushkova, Irina, and Rajendra Vora, eds, *Home, Family and Kinship in Maharashtra* (Delhi: Oxford University Press, 1999).

Gordon, Stewart, *The Marathas 1600–1818* (Cambridge: Cambridge University Press, 1993).

———, *Marathas, Marauders and State Formation in Eighteenth Century India* (Delhi: Oxford University Press, 1994).

Guha, Sumit, "Maharashtra in the Eighteenth Century: An Indian Penal Regime", *Past and Present*, vol. 147, no. 1, May 1995, pp. 101–26.

———, "Household Size and Household Structure in Western India, *c.* 1700–1950: Beginning an Exploration", *Indian Economic and Social History Review*, vol. 35, no. 1, 1998, pp. 23–33.

———, "The Family Feud as a Political Resource in Eighteenth Century

India", in Indrani Chatterjee, ed., *Unfamiliar Relations: Family and History in South Asia* (New Delhi: Permanent Black, 2004), pp. 74–94.

———, *Beyond Caste: Identity and Power in South Asia, Past and Present* (Leiden: Brill, 2013).

Hamilton, Walter, *A Geographical, Statistical and Historical Description of Hindostan*, 2 vols (London: John Murray, 1820).

Horstmann, Monika, *Visions of Kingship in the Twilight of Mughal Rule* (Amsterdam: Royal Netherlands Academy of Arts and Sciences, 2006).

Kadam, V.S., "The Institution of Marriage and Position of Women in Eighteenth Century Maharashtra", *Indian Economic and Social History Review*, vol. 25, no. 3, 1988, pp. 341–70.

Kamalakarabhatta, *Śūdrakamalākaraḥ*, ed. Ganesh Bapuji Malvankar and Vishnu Shastri Bapat (Bombay: Lithographed Text, 1861).

Karve, Irawati, "Ethnic Affinities of the Chitpavans", pt II, *Journal of the University of Bombay (History, Economics and Sociology)*, vol. 2, July 1933, pp. 132–58.

Kotani, Hiroyuki, "Structure of the Caste in Seventeenth-to-Nineteenth Century Western India: The Rural Caste in the Deccan and the Urban Caste in Coastal Gujarat", in idem, ed., *Western India in Historical Transition* (Delhi: Manohar, 2002), pp. 63–85.

———, ed., *Caste System, Untouchability and the Depressed* (Delhi: Manohar, 1997).

Lal, Ruby, *Domesticity and Power in the Early Mughal World* (Cambridge: Cambridge University Press, 2005).

Lele, K.K., "The Effects of Maharashtra's Culture on North India", *Bhārat Itihās Samshodhak Maṇḍaḷ Quarterly*, vol. 6, pt 2, 1926, Appendix 2, pp. 146–56.

O'Hanlon, Rosalind, "Narratives of Penance and Purification in Western India, c. 1650–1850", *Journal of Hindu Studies*, vol. 2, 1, 2009, pp. 48–75.

———, "Letters Home: Banaras Pandits and the Maratha Regions in Early Modern India", *Modern Asian Studies*, vol. 44, no. 2, 2010, pp. 201–40.

———, "Speaking From Siva's Temple: Banaras Scholar Households and the Brahman 'Ecumene' of Mughal India", *South Asian History and Culture*, vol. 2, no. 2, 2011, pp. 253–77.

———, "Performance in a World of Paper: Puranic Histories and Social Communication in Early Modern India", *Past and Present*, vol. 219, no. 1, 2013, pp. 87–126.

———, "Contested Conjunctures: Brahman Communities and 'Early Modernity' in India", *American Historical Review*, vol. 118, no. 3, 2013, pp. 765–87.

———, and Christopher Minkowski, "What Makes People Who They Are? Pandit Networks and the Problem of Livelihoods in Early Modern Western India", *Indian Economic and Social History Review*, vol. 45, no. 3, 2008, pp. 381–416.

Oturkar, R.V., *Peśve-kālīn Sāmājik va Ārthik Patravyavahāra* (Pune: Bharat Itihas Samshodhak Mandal, 1950).

Perlin, Frank, "Of White Whale and Countrymen in the Eighteenth Century Maratha Deccan. Extended Class Relations, Rights and the Problem of Rural Autonomy Under the Old Regime", *The Journal of Peasant Studies*, vol. 5, no. 2, 1977–8, pp. 170–237.

Preston, Lawrence W., *The Devs of Cincvad: A Lineage and the State in Maharashtra* (Cambridge: Cambridge University Press, 1989).

Richards, John, *The Mughal Empire* (Cambridge: Cambridge University Press, 1993).

Sahai, Nandita Prasad, *Politics of Patronage and Protest: The State, Society and Artisans in Early Modern Rajasthan* (New York: Oxford University Press, 2006).

———, "The 'Other' Culture: Craft Societies and Widow Marriage in Early Modern India", *Journal of Women's History*, vol. 19, no. 2, 2007, pp. 36–58.

———, "Some Were Larger Than Their Communities: A Potter's Family, Community and Justice in Early Modern Rajasthan", *Studies in History*, vol. 25, no. 1, 2009, pp. 39–68.

Sardesai, G.S., *New History of the Marathas*, 3 vols (New Delhi: Munshiram Manoharlal, 1986).

———, ed., *Selections from the Peshwa Daftar* (SPD), 45 vols (Bombay: Government Central Press, 1930–4).

Singh, Dilbagh, "Regulating the Domestic: Notes on the Pre-Colonial State and the Family", *Studies in History*, vol.19, no. 1, 2003, pp. 69–86.

Sreenivasan, Ramya, *The Many Lives of a Mughal Queen: Heroic Pasts in India, c. 1500–1900* (Seattle: University of Washington Press, 2007)

Vad, Ganesh Chimnaji, B.P. Joshi, P.V. Mawji, K.B. Marathe, and D.B. Parasnis, eds, *Selections from the Satara Rajas' and the Peshwas' Diaries*, 9 vols (Poona: Deccan Vernacular Education Society, 1905–11).

Venkatkrishnan, Anand, "Ritual, Reflection and Religion: The Devas of Banaras", *Journal of South Asian History and Culture*, vol. 6, no. 1, 2015, pp. 147–71.

Wagle, N.K., "The Government, the Jāti and the Individual: Rights, Discipline and Control in the Puṇe Kotwal Papers, 1766–94", *Contributions to Indian Sociology*, vol. 34, no. 3, 2000, pp. 321–60.

Wink, Andre, *Land and Sovereignty in India. Agrarian Society and Politics under the Eighteenth Century Maratha Svarājya* (Cambridge: Cambridge University Press, 1986).

4

Brahman Lineages Beyond the Mughal Court

Introduction

In Mughal India, as elsewhere in the early modern world, power passed primarily through lineages: family and quasi-family structures through which legitimacy, prestige, property, and intellectual capital were conserved and passed from one generation to the next. The lordly and service lineages within the empire and regional states were dominant political forces. Lineages also offered an important means to secure property at a time when hereditable rights of many kinds were emerging more concretely. States themselves benefitted, since lineages could offer stable relationships that continued from one generation to the next. Quasi-family lineages were important, too, in the gharāṇā households of poets, musicians, and other skilled people. Lineage also stood at the heart of many types of religious culture – in the silsilās of the Sufi orders and the guru–disciple paramparās of Hindu religious culture.[1]

Brahman social organisation in the Mughal world was similarly structured. Lineages of Brahman administrators, religious scholars, and providers of ritual services were an indispensable presence at royal courts and lordly households, and in the hereditary service offices that sustained these roles at the local level. Brahman ascetics were prominent leaders of sectarian orders.[2] A smaller number of Brahman

[1] For an overview, see Chatterjee, ed., *Unfamiliar Relations*.

[2] Flood, ed., *The Blackwell Companion to Hinduism*, pp. 199–287.

lineages acculturated themselves to the world of Indo-Persian service culture.[3] So too did Brahman poets, whose celebrations of divine love were appreciated across North India.[4]

This essay focuses on Brahman scholar lineages, both householders and ascetics. Their organisation took three distinctive forms: relationships between father and son, teacher and pupil, guru and disciple. These relationships often overlapped, forming multiple chains of transmission across many generations.[5] The ancient family system of svādhyāya – a lineage's commitment to the study of a particular Vedic school – reinforced the tradition of conserving scholarly skills within the family. Vedic affiliation was fundamental to Brahman family identity, envisaged as a subcontinent-wide grid charting the primacy of particular schools in particular regions.[6] In the early modern centuries, these divisions were further mapped in complex ways onto North and South, with the assumption that there were ten basic Brahman communities, five gauḍa or northern, and five drāviḍa or southern.[7]

There is much accomplished work on Brahman intellectuals in Mughal India. Their social histories are less well developed, particularly of their lives within one of the prerequisites for intellectual labour – the lineage and its locale in the scholar household.[8] Brahman ascetic households also remain poorly understood. The intellectual work of Dasnāmī ascetics underpinned key transformations in Hindu religious thought, and the ascetics offered forms of social support to the scholar households leading those transformations.[9] There is much about this mutual relationship that we do not yet understand. Together, Brahman scholar householders and Brahman ascetic lineages within the larger Dasnāmī order constituted a formidable social formation by the end of the seventeenth century. Its scholars also stood forward as major cultural interlocutors of the Mughal state.

[3] Kinra, *Writing Self*.
[4] Busch, *Poetry of Kings*.
[5] Minkowski, "Advaita Vedānta", pp.213–16.
[6] Deshpande, "Vedas and Their *Śākhās*", pp. 341–62.
[7] O'Hanlon, "Speaking from Siva's Temple", pp. 257–61.
[8] For this theme in Europe, see Algazi, "At the Study", pp. 17–50.
[9] Minkowski, "Advaita Vedānta", p. 206.

Banaras and Brahman Scholar Lineages

The city of Banaras offered a uniquely favourable locale to the dense network of scholar families and ascetics settled there.[10] Many historians and Indologists have explored the far-reaching intellectual changes that these and other lineages across the subcontinent brought about during the Mughal era. The degree to which this era saw real innovation in Sanskrit intellectual culture has attracted much debate.[11] Less in doubt is the newness of the challenges that scholars faced. The resurgence of bhakti devotionalism, impelled by the social mobility of the Mughal world, raised fundamental issues: with devotion as a path perhaps equal in prestige to knowledge and ritual action, with the status of vernacular languages, with the entitlements of popular classes to dignified ritual, with the forms of worship appropriate to Brahmans themselves.[12] The philosophical and ritual underpinnings of Hindu kingship came under new question as warrior lineages in North and Central India reinvented themselves as royal Rajputs.[13]

In the South, Vijayanagar patronage encouraged a new generation of intellectual supporters of Vedantic dualism, impelling proponents of Advaita Vedanta, many in Banaras, into systematising their own doctrines.[14] This flow of ideas strengthened the intellectual connections between North and South.[15] Developments within the ascetic orders were also important. Mughal India saw the systematisation of the many branches of the Shaivite Dasnāmīs into a single order, driven in part by their wish to secure the advantages enjoyed by the Sufi orders, and in part by patronage for Advaita Shaivism from Vijayanagar and its Nayaka successors.[16] This was also a period of ordering and attempted

[10] O'Hanlon, "Letters Home", pp. 201–5.

[11] See the extended discussion in Pollock, *The Ends of Man*, and for an overview, Patil, "The End of the Ends of Man?" For changing understandings of "newness" as an affective category for early modern philosophy, see Wright, *A Time of Novelty*.

[12] Venkatkrishnan, "Ritual, Reflection and Religion", pp. 147–71.

[13] Horstmann, *Der Zusammenhalt der Welt*.

[14] Stoker, *Polemics and Patronage*; Minkowski, "Advaita Vedānta", pp. 210–13.

[15] Bronner, "North Meets South", pp. 10–31.

[16] Clark, *The Daśanāmī-Saṃnyāsīs*, pp. 228–46.

systematisation for the teaching traditions of the Vaishnavite world, flourishing amid the bhakti resurgence.[17] Scholars within the abstract intellectual disciplines established closer networks among themselves as they also investigated the foundations of their own traditions.[18]

These networks revolved as much around oral and performative spaces as they did around manuscript circulation. We now know more about the world of the scholarly sabha (assembly), and particularly the "Mukti pavilion", the hall in Banaras' temple to Vishvanath where many assemblies were held, and which underpinned the authority of judgments made there.[19] The chance to hear scholars in face-to-face debate was a key part of the "public" life of the Brahman social world. It meant the chance to come face to face with the "glittering eyes" of their supporters, opponents, and often family members lining the halls where such assemblies took place, and to judge their reputations.[20] Social and intellectual relationships were "performed" in assemblies convened to adjudicate important points of law and to congratulate eminent intellectuals. Such assemblies were often structured around ceremonial privileges, as in the rights of agrapūjā (first ritual honours) claimed by the Bhatta family; the title of Bhaṭṭa-bhaṭṭāraka, "a venerable lord", conferred upon the grammarian Narasimha Sesa by the pandits of the Bijapur court; or the entitlement to two such honours (sambhāvanās) that belonged to the Sesa family.[21] These public dimensions of intellectual life bound individual reputations to the prestige of the lineage – prestige vital in attracting pupils and patronage.

Household, Lineage, and the Fortunes of Marriage

The Brahman scholar household was a key mainstay for this intellectual work. Fathers educated their sons alongside sons of other families. Most had teachers in a number of different disciplines, creating

[17] Hawley, *Storm of Songs*, pp. 99–147.

[18] See, for example, Ganeri, *The Lost Age of Reason*, pp. 75–88.

[19] O'Hanlon, "Speaking from Siva's Temple", pp. 264–7.

[20] Venkatkrishnan, "Ritual, Reflection and Religion", p. 153.

[21] Dandekar, *Sanskrit and Maharashtra*, p. 31; Aryavaraguru, "On the Sesas of Benaras", pp. 247–8.

a dense web of social and intellectual connections. Many received initiation from more than one guru during their lives. Gurus could also be teachers, weaving further skeins into this web. Scholars often acknowledged such family, intellectual, and spiritual paternity in their manuscripts. Libraries, the principal working tools of scholars, were usually the accumulated wealth of several generations, the labour of copying important works often the task of young scholars. A further important role of the lineage, both family and intellectual, lay in sending out sons and pupils to establish its traditions in new regions.[22]

Marriage was the bedrock of the scholar household, underpinning the social reproduction of its members and often augmenting its prestige and connections. Scholar lineages often intermarried. The great Bhatta lineage of Banaras produced five generations of active scholars, from Ramesvara who left the family home in Paithan for Banaras in 1522, to his great-great-grandson the scholar-priest Gagabhatta, famous architect of the dharmic consecration in 1673 of Shivaji.[23] The family tree reveals a pattern of intermarriages with the Kale scholar family from Maharashtra. Ganga and her husband Nilakanthabhatta, grandson of Ramesvara, married their daughter, also called Ganga, to the scholar Mahadeva Bharadvaja, of the Kale family. Their son Divakarabhatta authored an extensive digest of dharmasastra, the *Dharmaśāstrasudhānidhi*.[24] The scholar Ramakrishna, grandson of Ramesvara, was married to Uma, whose natal family we do not know. The pair had a daughter as well as three sons, Lakshman, Kamalakara, and Dinakara. This unnamed daughter was married to Mahadeva Kale, son of Ramesvara Kale, and the pair had a son, also called Divakara Kale, a scholar and author of works on dharmasastra.[25] There were other prominent Kales in Banaras at the time, such as the grammarian Nagoji Bhatta (*fl. c.* 1700–1750).[26]

Marriages also involved risk. As described elsewhere, a veritable galaxy of some seventy-seven eminent scholars assembled in 1657 in Banaras' Mukti pavilion to refute rumours that some of their number

[22] O'Hanlon, "Speaking from Siva's Temple", pp. 257–61.

[23] For a family tree, see Kane, *Vyavhāramayūkha*, p. xvi.

[24] Ibid., pp. xiv–xv.

[25] Kane, *History of Dharmaśāstra*, vol. 1, p. 703.

[26] Narayan, *Nāgeśa and the Mahābhāṣya*, pp. 3–8.

had contracted marriages with Brahman lineages of suspect origins. In this milieu, where intellectual reputation and family prestige were bound together, accusations of improper parentage or sexual misconduct could become a polemical instrument employed alongside subtle deployments of reason and logic.[27]

Women and the Emotional Economy of the Scholar Household

Brahman women played a central role in the ritual life of the early modern household.[28] Yet they figure rarely in the writings of Mughal-era Brahman scholars. The Bhatta family history is unusual here. It depicts the role that its author Samkarabhatta believed his grandmother, who is unnamed, played during a key period in the family's life. Having left Paithan to start a school some eighty miles west at the shrine town of Sangamner, Ramesvara was able to entrust the whole running of the household to his devoted wife. She attended his evening discourses on the *Bhāgavata Purāṇa*, when the episode describing Krishna's childhood sparked her desire for a son. After a visit to the family shrine at Kolhapur, and the intercession of a powerful ghost, she conceived. Convinced the boy would grow to be a great scholar, she entreated Ramesvara to take her to Krishnadevaraya's Vijaynagar, where the son in her womb would be surrounded by learning.[29] Happily lodged in the city, she would overhear scholarly discussion in the house from her place in another room. The pair eventually returned home where their son Narayana, who did indeed go on to become the famous scholar and intermediary at Akbar's court, was born in the spring of 1513.[30]

This account plays subtly on themes of piety, power, and womanly duty. The expectations here were not of simple deference. This

[27] O'Hanlon, "Letters Home", pp. 201–40; Minkowski, "I'll Wash Out Your Mouth", p. 123; Bronkhorst, "Bhaṭṭoji Dīkṣita", pp. 12–15.

[28] Leslie, *The Perfect Wife*.

[29] For parallels to this story of unborn sons learning in the womb, see Tokunaga and Smith, eds, *Mahābhārata,* 3.132.8–9, and 7.34.19. I thank Anand Venkatkrishnan for this reference.

[30] Benson, "Śaṃkarabhaṭṭa's Family Chronicle", pp. 105–18.

wife and mother had powerful talents which she directed towards the particular needs of the scholar household. She managed all of its complex demands so her husband could attend to his teaching. She was a woman of strong wishes and knowledge of the world, but her wishes, appropriately, were all for a son. She had powers of subtle perception, but these were focused on her scholar-son soon to be born. She was delighted by learned discussion, but above all for what it promised for her son, and she heard it, appropriately for a woman, from the safe distance of another room.

If this was an ideal, what might we know about the reality of a wife's role in a Brahman scholar household? Elements of this become visible to us when a wife is shown mishandling one of her most important tasks, the management of food and all of its associated implications for substances, spaces, and people in the home. Such a mishap occurred in 1641, in the household of the Brahman Sonprabhu, whose family were the hereditary heads of the important pandit assembly in the shrine town of Nasik. Sonprabhu approached Dinakara, of the Bhatta dynasty referred to above, who was in Nasik at the time. He explained that he and his wife had visited her native village in the Konkan, where they had eaten food in a household that employed a Sudra menial to wash the rice.[31] His wife knew this, but had allowed the pair to eat. Consequently, the Brahmans of Nasik had boycotted them. Dinkara intervened with a judgment that Sonprabhu had sufficiently purified himself, and the boycott was lifted.[32] The incident reveals both the finger-pointing and blame a wife might attract for failing in her elementary duty to ensure that food was untainted, and the degree to which representations of the case circulated in arenas controlled by her husband and his powerful ally from Banaras.

Other family histories offer clues to the emotional economy of the scholar household. Family tradition describes how Vishnu Sesa, probably connected to the Sesa scholar lineage, was impelled to move to Banaras from the family home back in Nanded after developing an intense dislike of his elder brother's wife's scoldings about his study

[31] Sudra women with access to matrilineal property may have commonly served in Brahman households on the south-west coast of India. Derrett, "Kamalakara on Illegitimates", pp. 239–40.

[32] O'Hanlon, "Narratives of Penance and Purification", pp. 48–75.

habits.[33] In other cases, there seems evidence of particular emotional connection between mothers and individual scholar sons. Govinda was the youngest brother of the family biographer Samkarabhatta, and primarily a teacher rather than author of scholarly works. The family history tells us that he had four sons. He taught two of them, as well as groups of students, and died at the young age of forty-eight. He had always helped his mother faithfully since his birth, and died himself soon after her death, the family history suggests, so that he could follow and continue his service to her.[34]

Another trope gives us insights into these spaces of books and learning. The grammarian Nagoji Bhatta gave birth to his own intellectual lineage, gaining him a reputation as a prolific scholar and devoted teacher.[35] As his wife mourned her own childless state, tradition reports that he consoled her with the thought that she should regard his books as her own sons and daughters: "The Śabdenduśekhara is your son; the Mañjuṣā is your daughter / For if these are near, what sort of mental pain can there be?"[36]

Interestingly, the late-seventeenth-century logician of Banaras, Mahadeva Puntambkar, made a similar observation about his books as his family, but a family of the mind. He described two of his treatises, the *Bhavānandīprakāśa* and the *Nyāyakaustubha*, as his sons, while his work the *Sarvopakāriṇī* was his daughter. The mother of these children was his spiritual wife, Buddhi (wisdom).[37]

Also suggestive was the approach of Balambhatta, son of the grammarian Vaidyanatha Payagunde, himself a pupil of Nagoji Bhatta. Sons of scholar lineages sometimes attributed their works to their fathers, fathers to sons, even students to their teachers.[38] But Balambhatta assigned authorship of his legal commentary, the *Lakṣmīvyākhyāna*, to his mother Lakshmidevi, following her child's death. Interestingly, the work offers a particularly favourable interpretation of the rights

[33] Kanole, "Nāṅḍeḍache Śeṣa Gharāṇe", pp. 60–1.

[34] Benson, "Śaṃkarabhaṭṭa's Family Chronicle", p. 114.

[35] Shastri, "Dakshini Pandits", p. 12.

[36] Dandekar, *Sanskrit and Maharashtra*, pp. 19–21. I thank Madhav Deshpande for this reference.

[37] Kaviraj, *Gleanings*, p. 80.

[38] Deshpande, "Disagreement Without Disrespect", pp. 32–49; O'Hanlon, "Speaking from Siva's Temple", pp. 257–8.

to family property of sisters and daughters.[39] Perhaps Balambhatta hoped that Lakshmidevi might gain further solace in seeing her name put forward as author of a work that affirmed the property rights of women.[40]

Lineages of Brahman Ascetics in Banaras

We know much about the transformation of Hindu renouncers in the early modern period, from ascetics whose pitched battles captivated the emperor Akbar, to financiers, protectors of trade, and mercenary soldiers in the unsettled world of the eighteenth century.[41] Prominent orders like the Dasnāmīs enjoyed significant advantages as they formalised themselves into a single order with ten distinct branches. Their military strength provided protection. Their religious prestige often exempted them from customs dues. Their freedom from community ties gave them important roles as witnesses to commercial transactions. Their pilgrimages across the holy places of the subcontinent provided a ready-made trading network.[42] With their quasi-family structure of recruitment, the order also enjoyed the advantages of a family's ability to pass skills and reputation down the generations, and to deploy members to carry its traditions into new regions.[43] However, an ascetic order's capacity for recruitment was not limited by any biological constraints in producing sons, while its property was, in principle, at least, secure from resumption by the state or family demands for partition.[44]

Yet we know rather less about the scholar ascetics of the Dasnāmī order. Most familiar are the later-sixteenth-century figures Madhava Sarasvati and his pupil, Nrsimhasrama; Madhusudana Sarasvati, the distinguished defender of Advaita Vedanta against its southern dualist

[39] Kane, *History of Dharmaśāstra*, vol. 1, p. 459.

[40] For evidence that some women of Brahman households in eighteenth-century southern India were indeed engaged with projects of Sanskrit intellectual production alongside their menfolk, see Gomez, "Sanskrit and the Labour of Gender".

[41] Pinch, *Warrior Ascetics and Indian Empires*, pp. 29–147.

[42] Bayly, *Rulers, Townsmen and Bazaars*, pp. 125–44, 183–6.

[43] Hausner, *Wandering With Sadhus*, pp. 36–58.

[44] Kane, *History of Dharmaśāstra*, vol. 1, pp. 906–12.

critics; Narayanasrama, a pupil of Nrsimhasrama; and the Advaitin scholar Ramatirtha, teacher and guru to a wide circle in Banaras. Also part of this circle, and best known of them, was the poet, diplomat, and sometime Mughal courtier Kavindracaraya Sarasvati, celebrated across India for his defence of the interests of the Hindu pious at the Mughal court of Shah Jahan.[45]

What were these scholars' links to the Dasnāmī order? Three of the ten Dasnāmī lineages – āśrama, sarasvatī, and tīrtha – recruited exclusively from Brahman communities. These were the unarmed monks, known as daṇḍīs from their carrying of a single staff, or śāstradhārīs (holders of scripture), many with knowledge of Sanskrit. Notwithstanding their position as ascetics, they regarded themselves as superior to the other seven lineages, who recruited a more diverse following, and who, after further processes of initiation, could become Nāgās, associated with the "military wing" of the Dasnāmīs and organised into akhāḍā wrestling schools.[46]

The later-seventeenth-century Sanskrit primer *Gīrvāṇapadamañjarī* of Varadaraja offers a satirical depiction of a Banaras maṭha, when one of its ascetics was invited to dine with a Brahman householder.[47] The ascetics were Brahmans from different parts of India, classified into subgroups of the drāviḍa and gauḍa regional divisions referred to above.[48] This description, the wider recruitment of the daṇḍīs, and the long-running debates in texts of the dharmasastra as to whether Brahman ascetics should keep their sacred threads, suggests the persistence of elements of Brahman caste identities well into their lives as ascetics.[49]

Later sources certainly suggest that this was the case. Writing in 1846, H.H. Wilson observed that "the Dandi is distinguished by carrying a small Danda or wand, with several processes or projections from it, and a piece of cloth died [dyed] with red ochre, in which the Brah-

[45] Mahadevan, *Preceptors of Advaita*, pp. 220–32, 254–61; Truschke, "Contested History", pp. 419–52.

[46] Clark, *The Daśanāmī-Saṃnyāsīs*, pp. 39–42.

[47] Shah, ed., *Gīrvāṇapadamañjarī and Gīrvāṇavāṅmañjarī*, pp. 8–9. I thank Anand Venkatkrishnan for his invaluable assistance with these texts.

[48] Shah, *Gīrvāṇapadamañjarī*, p. 1.

[49] Kane, *History of Dharmaśāstra*, vol. 2, pt 2, pp. 963–4.

Image 1: A *daṇḍī*. *Fuqara'-i Hind*. British Library, I.O. Islamic 4777, f. 54. Courtesy of the British Library.

manical cord is supposed to be enshrined, attached to it."[50] The early-nineteenth-century image above, from the Persian *Fuqara'-i Hind*, shows a staff, with ochre-coloured pieces of cloth attached, carried by a young shaven-headed daṇḍī.[51] The missionary and Indologist M.A. Sherring reported that many daṇḍīs in later-nineteenth-century Banaras were learned men, "great readers of the Shâstras, such as the Mîmânsa,

[50] Wilson, *Sketch of the Religious Sects*, pp. 122–3.
[51] *Fuqara'i Hind*. British Library, I.O. Islamic 4744, f.54.

Nyâya, Manjûka, and others, and also of the Purânas. Many Brahmans, even Pandits, or learned Brahmans, come to them for instruction, which they impart freely, without the smallest recompense. All classes of the community pay them the greatest honour, even to worshipping them."[52] Sinha and Saraswati's study of Banaras ascetics in the 1970s reported that the three daṇḍī branches, the āśrama, sarasvatī, and tīrtha, were invariably Brahmans, and classified into gauḍas and drāviḍas.[53]

Would scholars such as Madhava Sarasvati, Nrsimhasrama, Madhusudana Sarasvati, Narayanasrama, Ramatirtha, or Kavindra Sarasvati have identified themselves straightforwardly with the āśrama, sarasvatī, and tīrtha orders?[54] At least one, the prominent seventeenth-century ascetic Brahmendra Sarasvati, had a second initiate name, as Nrsimhasrama, indicating perhaps affiliation with both daṇḍī lineages.[55] Minkowski's pathbreaking work suggests that Advaitin scholar ascetics were indeed connected in this way, their links to the orders bearing their names traceable in long chains of transmission between gurus and disciples.[56] If this was so, we can begin to ask questions about Brahman ascetics' relationship to the maṭhas that helped sustain their intellectual and social lives and shaped their relationships with Brahman scholar households.

Our knowledge about daṇḍī recruitment is patchy. Of Kavindra Sarasvati's recruitment, we know only that he came from a holy place on the Godavari, was initiated at a young age, and migrated to Banaras.[57] Banaras was also the recruiting ground for the ascetic Brahmendra Sarasvati. Born near Pune about 1649 and orphaned by the age of twelve, he subsisted on alms until 1663, when he journeyed to Banaras to search for opportunity, and a guru. He found Jnanendra Sarasvati, a learned ascetic who initiated him and gave him the name of Brahmendra Sarasvati. After fifteen years of wandering, Brahmendra returned to the Maratha country, where he came to prominence in the

[52] Sherring, *Hindu Tribes and Castes*, pp. 258–9.

[53] Sinha and Saraswati, *Ascetics of Kashi*, pp. 66–70, 177–82.

[54] Clark, *The Daśanāmī-Saṃnyāsīs*, p. 226.

[55] Gode, "The Identification of Gosvāmi Nṛsiṁhāśrama", pp. 447–51.

[56] Minkowski, "Advaita Vedānta", pp. 214–15.

[57] Paradkar, "Kavīndrācārya Saraswatī", pp. 378–9.

Maratha empire as political intermediary, spiritual guide, financier, and sponsor of an ambitious shrine to Parashuram near Satara.[58]

Other initiations may have been chosen. Bhanuji, son of the distinguished grammarian Bhattoji Diksita, became the daṇḍī ascetic Ramasrama, whose defence of the Vaishnavite *Bhāgavata Purāṇa* drew the furious ire of Shaivite scholars, helped the text gain mainstream acceptance, and shaped a new genre of polemical writing.[59] What drew Bhanuji to the āśrama daṇḍī order? Perhaps it was a guru offering special intellectual fellowship, and perhaps also prestige, given that the Advaitin ascetic could claim not only to be the highest type of renouncer, but the highest Brahman.[60] It was the names of daṇḍī intellectuals – Madhusudana Sarasvati, Purnendra Sarasvati, and Brahmendra Sarasvati – as well as that of his father, Bhattoji Dīksita, whom Ramasrama invoked as he challenged his opponents' arguments.[61]

What might we know about the social presence of these Brahman ascetic orders? Bernier's memorable description of the "distinguished personage" we now know to be Kavindra is familiar, "a stout, well-made man", met often at the Delhi court or out in the streets, his dress consisting of "a white silk scarf, tied about the waist, and hanging halfway down the leg, and of another tolerably large scarf of red silk, which he wears as a cloak on his shoulders."[62] Kavindra's habitual "red silk scarf" may have been a presentation shawl of the kind with which learned pandits were honoured on public occasions.[63] Its colour may also have gestured to the ochre robe of the Shaivite ascetic, here adapted to reflect Kavindra's own stately persona.

Bernier noticed a larger community of such "respectable" ascetics, marked by their cleanliness and decorum. They enjoyed an entrée to Hindu households not accorded to other ascetics: "they do not beg from shop to shop like many other *Fakires*, but enter freely into the houses of the *Gentiles*, where they meet with a hearty welcome and a hospitable

[58] Parasnis, ed., *Śrī Mahāpuruṣa Brahmendrasvāmī Dhāvaḍaśīkar*, pp. 1–8.

[59] Minkowski, "I'll Wash Out Your Mouth", pp. 117–41.

[60] Olivelle, *Renunciation in Hinduism*, vol. I, p. 35; Nelson, "Madhusudana Sarasvati", pp. 73–89.

[61] Minkowski, "I'll Wash Out Your Mouth", p. 120.

[62] Bernier, *Travels in the Mogul Empire*, p. 341.

[63] I thank Christopher Minkowski for this suggestion.

Image 2: F. Balthazar Solvyns, “Dondys”, 1808–1812.
Courtesy of Cambridge University Library.

reception, their presence being esteemed a blessing to the family.”[64] These “respectable” ascetics may well have been members of the Brahman daṇḍī orders. The illustration here shows the daṇḍī ascetics painted by the Flemish artist Solvyns (1760–1824) during his stay in Calcutta in the 1790s. It depicts two daṇḍī ascetics, a neatly attired man in the foreground, and another walking out of the image on the right. The daṇḍī in the foreground is older than the boyish figure shown in the *Fuqara'-i Hind*. The insignia of his scholarly accomplishments are clearly displayed, in manuscripts set beside on his mat, alongside his shoes and water-pot.[65] Next to his water-pot is his staff, with a small piece of ochre-coloured cloth attached to it.

[64] Bernier, *Travels in the Mogul Empire*, p. 322.

[65] Solvyns, *Les Hindous*, vol. 2, Livraison 2, Place 3.

Brahman Ascetics and Scholar Households

What can we know from these accounts about the social connections, in Banaras and beyond, between the two different kinds of Brahman lineage, householders, and ascetics? Many scholars see their relationship as setting the terms for key identities and hierarchies within Hindu religious cultures.[66] Others have explored the permeable boundaries between asceticism and the world of the household, the complex proprieties around the flow of hospitality, food, alms, and gifts from household to maṭha, the treatment of caste and gender in their different rooms and spaces, and the role of ascetics as spiritual guides in the lives of householders.[67]

Some elements of these mutual relationships are discernible in Mughal India. The daṇḍī orders had intellectual skills, prestige, mobility, and institutional connections across the subcontinent. They attracted gifts from pious and royal patrons, often passed on to the Hindu faithful. Their maṭhas contained important intellectual resources. Their stance above family loyalties gave them wider roles as diplomats and intermediaries. In return, scholar families offered alms, hospitality, new generations of students eager to find gurus and teachers among members of the daṇḍī orders, and sometimes recruits to the orders themselves.

Ascetic Leadership and the World of the Sabha

We have two collections of Sanskrit tributes from this period which thank individuals for their extraordinary services to the Hindu pious. Both are to daṇḍī ascetics. Collected by Krishna Upadhyaya, the mid-seventeenth-century *Kavīndracandrodaya* celebrates with some sixty-six tributes the great services of the daṇḍī ascetic Kavindra.[68] The collection is remarkable for the unusual willingness of Sanskrit

[66] Olivelle, "The Ascetic and the Domestic", pp. 25–42. I thank Sondra Hausner for a discussion of these points.

[67] For a modern example, see Prasad, *Poetics of Conduct*, pp. 191–208.

[68] Sharma and Patkar, *Kavīndracandrodaya*.

literati to acknowledge the presence of the Mughal court, even as they congratulate Kavindra for his generosity and skills of persuasion exercised before the emperor.[69]

It is likely that the addresses were read out in a public ceremony, perhaps before Kavindra himself. Two people were recorded as conveying their praises *in absentia*. The daṇḍī ascetic Padmanabhasrama's good wishes were reported by Visvesvara, father of another admirer, Liladhara. Visvesvara read out Liladhara's own eulogy since, the eulogy reported, Liladhara resided in the city of Prakasa in the South.[70] The fact that several individuals contributed two different addresses indicates two such public ceremonies of felicitation.[71]

Many addresses celebrated Kavindra as a glorious "fixer" with a great network of contacts. Liladhara's address suggested that Padmanabhasrama was actually working in the South as Kavindra's deputy. He asked Kavindra to intervene on behalf of his own holy city of Prakasa.[72] Within his skilful encomium, Mahadevabhatta Patwardhan included a Marathi request for a gift of two hundred silver rupees.[73] Purnananda praised Kavindra for securing large sums of royal cash to give away to pilgrims at Banaras and Prayag.[74]

There are also glimpses into the relations between ascetics and householders. Krishna Upadhyaya's introduction referred to two daṇḍīs, Purnendra and Brahmendra Sarasvati, as leading ascetics of the city.[75] We saw these two above particularly acknowledged in the work of the daṇḍī ascetic Ramasrama. Two of the addresses were from groups rather than individuals. One came from the śiṣṭa or "excellent people" of the city. It referred explicitly to daṇḍīs as one of the many Hindu communities indebted to Kavindra: "He gives great joy to Brahmins, Kshatriyas, Vaishyas, Sudras, ascetics, householders, and those who enjoy the name 'forest-dweller', Daṇḍīs, Avadhūta-ascetics, to all who live in

[69] Truschke, "Contested History", pp. 419–52, and Truschke, *Culture of Encounters*.

[70] Sharma and Patkar, *Kavīndracandrodaya*, 23, vs. 12.

[71] Raghavan, "Kavīndrācārya Sarasvatī", p. 163.

[72] Sharma and Patkar, *Kavīndracandrodaya*, p. 21, vs. 3–4.

[73] Ibid., p. 39, vs. 26

[74] Ibid., p. 16, vs. 4.

[75] Ibid., p. 2, vs. 3.

Kashi, and to the learned and unlearned."[76] This tribute referred to the leading role taken by ascetics in the tributes to Kavindra: "Praised by everybody, led by the group of Brahmendra, Purnendra and Yatindra, the ascetic Kavindra shines forth and looks brilliant with [his]mass of true Dharma."[77] The leadership of Brahmendra in particular was emphasised: "By this man called Kavindra, who has been favoured by Sri Brahmendra Swami, the extraordinary lifting of the tax on Kashi has been accomplished."[78]

The "sanyasis and pandits residing in Kashi" authored the second group tribute.[79] Interestingly, it concluded with skilful lines on the futility and impotence of many ascetics compared with Kavindra himself. Lesser ascetics were like preening birds before the assembly, flapping their wings, their beaks sharp as they took sides in argument:

> Of sharp beaks [tīkṣṇatuṇḍāh] and flaccid staffs [ślakṣṇadaṇḍā],
> full of passion and flapping their wings [rāgiṇaḥ pakṣapātinaḥ]
> Without you, other sanyasis are simply like birds without
> headcrests [viśikhā].[80]

This is a skilful play on words. "Beak" (tuṇḍa) is also a disrespectful term for a mouth. Pakṣapātinaḥ refers both to a bird (pakṣī) and to partisanship in argument. However, their ascetics' staffs (daṇḍa) – and by implication their virile powers – were ślakṣṇa (flaccid). Viśikhā ("without headcrest", which may also mean "without topknot") also implies weakness or impotence.[81] This passage suggests factional division in the city, impelling some to use the public arena of the assembly to express their antagonisms.

The *Nṛsiṃhasarvasvakāvyam* was probably compiled towards the end of the sixteenth century.[82] It felicitated another daṇḍī ascetic,

[76] Ibid., pp. 24–5, vs. 3–4. I thank Gergely Hidas and Csaba Kiss for their kind help with the translation of these Sanskrit addresses.

[77] Ibid., p. 24, vs. 5.

[78] Ibid., p. 25, vs. 7.

[79] Ibid., pp. 31–2, line 14 of main text, and vs 1–2.

[80] Ibid., p. 32, vs. 2.

[81] Accusing ascetics of impotence was a familiar theme. See Olivelle, *The Āśrama System*, p. 237. I thank Anand Venkatkrishnan for a discussion of these points.

[82] Shastri, *A Descriptive Catalogue*, vol. 4, pp. 81–5.

Nrsimhasrama, whose own disciple, Sacchidanandasrama, compiled the addresses. Nrsimhasrama's guru had been Vasudevasrama, and his paramaguru (grand guru) had been Vijnanasrama.[83] Over a hundred names appear, some several times, suggesting multiple occasions of public congratulation. Many are South Indian names, reflecting Nrsimhasrama's subcontinent-wide networks. His Tantric powers blessed the king of Madurai with a son. He intervened to protect Brahmans of the Chola country from state officials. He persuaded Akbar to ban the slaughter of cows, lift taxes on pilgrims, and provide large sums in cash to distribute to pilgrims.[84]

Both praise addresses show a significant reversal of the usual flow of alms and gifts from householders to ascetics. In Mughal India, it is ascetics such as Nrsimhasrama, and Kavindra after him, who pour wealth down upon the grateful Brahman householder. This may reflect the important role suggested above of daṇḍī ascetics as "fixers", able to negotiate across the very different arenas of court, temple, and maṭha to secure support for Brahman householders, and largesse for the Hindu faithful.

What other kinds of leadership did daṇḍī ascetics exercise? An indication emerges from an eighteenth-century story about the bhakti poet Eknath (*c.* 1533–1599).[85] It contained a familiar trope: the ire of learned pandits at devotional poetry written in the vernacular.[86] It described the disciplinary powers of a great Banaras ascetic, when Eknath was found to have composed chapters of the holy *Bhāgavata Purāṇā* in Marathi. Summoned to Banaras for punishment, Eknath arrived meekly at the ascetic's maṭha, where three hundred of his disciples waited to thrash him with their clubs. But reverence overcame them, and they were unable to beat the saintly man. Infuriated, the ascetic challenged Eknath to a public disputation. Eventually, of course, Eknath made a conquest of the ascetic himself, who invited all of the distinguished pandits of the city to a celebration at the maṭha.[87] We cannot know how far this reflects an episode in the life of Eknath himself. The story may,

[83] Ibid., pp. 81–2. This Nrsimhasrama is not identical with his Advaitin contemporary of the same name: Shastri, *A Descriptive Catalogue*, p. 83.

[84] Ibid., pp. 83–5.

[85] Keune, "Eknāth Remembered and Reformed", p. 109.

[86] Eaton, *A Social History of the Deccan*, pp. 134–6.

[87] Abbott, *Eknath*, pp. 173–89.

though, illustrate the consequences that eighteenth-century devotees felt would have followed when the arbiters of dharmic properity in Banaras discovered that a poet had dared to compose parts of the great Bhāgavata in the vernacular.

Social and Educational Interdependencies

There were other relations of mutual support. Scholar householders gained prestige when their pupils became great ascetics.[88] Many ascetics were teachers themselves, offering tuition without recompense when Sherring saw them in the later nineteenth century. The Bhatta family history tells us that Ramesvara Bhatta left Paithan to set up his own school after a local ascetic's teaching deteriorated when he became head of the local maṭha.[89] We have no knowledge of Kavindra's relationship to the city's maṭhas, but Bernier's account suggests that he gave local scholars access to his extensive library.[90]

The daṇḍī orders also lent their authority to the Banaras assemblies. Four daṇḍī ascetics joined the assembly of thirty-four scholars who met in 1631 to review the entitlement of Saraswat Brahmans to receive initiation as renouncers, an entitlement bound up with Brahman identity itself.[91] Daṇḍī ascetics attended the important assembly of 1657 which addressed the sensitive question of some scholar families' marriages. Present were Brahmendra Sarasvati and Purnendra Sarasvati, along with Sacchidananda Sarasvati and Narayanatirtha, accomplished scholar of Mīmāṁsā and one of the teachers of the Advaitin scholar and commentator on the Mahābhārata, Nilakantha Caturdhara.[92] Contemporary accounts show that Nilakantha's son, Govinda, had contracted one of the suspect marriages. Alongside Narayanatirtha appeared also the latter's teacher and fellow tīrtha ascetic, Sivaramatirtha.[93]

[88] Benson, "Śaṃkarabhaṭṭa"s Family Chronicle", p. 12.

[89] Ibid., p. 108.

[90] Bernier, *Travels in the Mogul Empire*, pp. 341–2, and Gode, "Some Evidence", p. 75.

[91] O'Hanlon, "Letters Home", pp. 226–7.

[92] For Narayanatirtha, see Gode, "Date of the Bhāṭṭabhāṣāprakāśikā", pp. 65–71. Minkowski points out that Nilakantha's guru, the householder Lakshmana Pandit, was also present at this meeting, possibly reflecting the important stakes at issue for his disciple. Minkowski, "Nīlakaṇṭha's Teachers and Gurus", p. 44.

[93] For Sivaramatirtha see Gode, "Date of the Bhāṭṭabhāṣāprakāśikā", p. 66.

Ascetics also played an important role as spiritual advisers. The Sanskrit primers discussed above show the visiting ascetic offering moral advice to family members, including a rebuke for the unsuitable marriage of a daughter.[94] Bernier also remarked on the reverence with which women regarded ascetics.[95] We know, too, something about the relationships that women of leading families in Maharashtra cultivated with the ascetic Brahmendra Sarasvati noted above. Their letters reveal a gift economy of blessings, gifts, and money circulating between the women and Brahmendra Sarasvati, which helped secure some of the wider political and financial relationships of the Maratha empire.[96]

Maṭhas and Their Resources

How else might scholar households have benefitted from the resources of Dasnāmī maṭhas? Compared to the great maṭhas of the South, maṭhas in Banaras seem to have been numerous, but relatively small, perhaps reflecting the teaching needs of the city. A census of the city in 1799 recorded 500 maṭhas.[97] In 1817, the missionary William Ward counted some eighty-three maṭhas in the city devoted to teaching, with between ten and thirty students in each.[98] The low visibility of maṭhas in this period may also reflect the gradual merger of precincts of temples and maṭhas recorded by Sinha and Saraswati, who reported that the city's famous Annapurna temple, built within the precincts of a Dasnāmī maṭha, had so expanded that pilgrims forgot they were visiting a maṭha at all.[99]

It is difficult to know how far the wealth of Dasnāmī orders found its way into the networks described here. Scholars have documented the land grants that flowed into the great southern maṭhas from Vijayanagar, and the planting of new maṭhas to extend the field of Advaita

[94] Shah, ed., *Gīrvāṇapadamañjarī and Gīrvāṇavāṅmañjarī*, p. 9 of the Introduction.

[95] Bernier, *Travels in the Mogul Empire*, p. 318.

[96] Parasnis, ed., *Śrī Mahāpuruṣa Brahmendrasvāmī Dhāvaḍaśīkar*, pp. 7–15, 119–32, 245–51, 279–80, 283–5. See also O'Hanlon, 'Intimate Voices of Empire".

[97] Bayly, *Rulers, Townsmen and Bazaars*, p. 126.

[98] Ward, *A View of the History*, vol. 4, pp. 490–3.

[99] Sinha and Saraswati, *Ascetics of Kashi*, p. 171.

influence.[100] The break-up of the Vijayanagar empire left Nayaka states eager to patronise the Advaita maṭhas. The Keladi Nayakas emerged as powerful new sponsors to the Sringeri maṭha. They also directed their patronage into Banaras itself. Three inscriptions of 1655 in Banaras, written in Sanskrit, Kannada, and Persian, recorded their refurbishment of the Kapiladhāra tīrtha tank, part of the sacred fifty-mile "pancha krośī yātra", the pilgrim circuit around the city.[101] However, it is unclear how far other patronage from the South benefitted the households and maṭhas of the city.

This raises the question of Kavindra's own relationship to the Dasnāmī maṭhas. Was he essentially an imperial pensioner who lost Shah Jahan's stipend after Aurangzeb came to power? His efforts to recover it through Bernier's patron, the Mughal courtier Danishmand Khan, suggests its importance.[102] The Bengali scholar Haraprasad Shastri (1853–1931) recorded that Kavindra had lands back in the Maratha country and migrated to Banaras when the Nizam Shahi state of Ahmadnagar fell to the Mughals. His treasurer, Krishna Bhatta, who was also the Krishna Upadhyaya who compiled the *Kavīndracandrodaya*, accompanied him to Banaras.[103] We do not know, therefore, whether Kavindra's famed generosity was supported largely by grants from Shah Jahan's court, or depended on pre-existing landed wealth, or revenues from broader Dasnāmī networks.

It is also worth reflecting on the relationship between the daṇḍī ascetics and the other seven "militant" Dasnāmī branches. The missionary and Orientalist J.N. Farquhar (1861–1929) heard a story from Dasnāmī ascetics in Banaras and Allahabad which has resonated across many generations of scholarship. The ascetics told him that the militant orders were formed at the request of the Advaitin scholar Madhusudhana Sarasvati, who sought Akbar's permission so that scholar ascetics could be protected against armed Muslim orders.[104] In his account

[100] Clark, *The Daśanāmī-Saṃnyāsīs*, pp. 202–14; Stoker, *Polemics and Patronage*, pp. 17–72.

[101] Gai, "Some Problems", p. 21; Sherring, *Benaras*, p. 178.

[102] Bernier, *Travels in the Mogul Empire*, pp. 323–4, 341–2.

[103] Shastri, *A Descriptive Catalogue*, p. 86, and Shastri, "Dakshini Pandits", p. 11.

[104] Farquhar, "The Organization of the Sannyasis", p. 483.

of the "militant" branches of the Dasnāmī order, the historian Jadunath Sarkar also recorded histories that he had heard from some of them. One member of the nirvāṇa akhāḍā recounted that members of his branch had fought the forces of the Sultan in Kashi in the year 1664, and had proved themselves heroes when they "preserved the honour of Vishvanath's seat."[105] This is a reference to the city's famous temple to Vishvanath, often the site of sabha assemblies of the kind described above. We know that this temple was destroyed at Aurangzeb's direction in 1669–70, for reasons that remain unclear.[106]

Did such accounts derive from a later colonial narrative of Hindu–Muslim conflict? The best documented example of armed conflict amongst militant Dasnāmīs involved two sects fighting each other for ceremonial precedence, in the famous incident witnessed by Akbar at Thaneshwar in 1567.[107] In the story attached to Eknath above, it was also to discipline a Hindu that the great Banaras scholar ascetic ordered his clubmen into action. Clark suggests that the Dasnāmīs formalised themselves into ten branches not as a reflection of communal hostilities, but to replicate the structure of the Sufi orders that had benefitted from their clear structure in seeking land grants and other privileges, particularly during the unsettled years after the accession of Aurangzeb.[108]

The military capacities of the non-daṇḍī Dasnāmīs may have been a part of this picture, deployed not to fight "communal" wars, but, perhaps, to protect maṭha, temple, and householder property during periods of civil disorder, as when contending Mughal armies flowed back and forth across North India during the mid-seventeenth-century war of succession. Also, we now know much more about the importance of Banaras' Vishvanath temple, with its "Mukti pavilion", to Brahman scholar householders and Dasnāmī daṇḍī ascetics alike, as the dignified setting for their assemblies and marker of their leadership in matters of religious law. In the light of this, the oral account passed on to Jadunath Sarkar may not represent a later colonial fabrication. Rather, it may be an echo of attempts made to defend what had

[105] Sarkar, *A History of Dasnami Naga Sanyasis*, p. 87.
[106] O'Hanlon, "Speaking From Siva's Temple", pp. 264–7.
[107] Pinch, *Warrior Ascetics*, pp. 30–8.
[108] Clark, *Daśanāmī-Saṃnyāsīs*, pp. 227–46.

become a key marker of Brahman and Dasnāmī authority since its reconstruction under the emperor Akbar, before the order of 1669 to destroy it.

Conclusions

This essay has attempted to explore the Brahman scholar household as the essential setting for the remarkable intellectual achievements of Sanskrit scholars in this period, the site both of their social reproduction, and of the gendered division of labour that made their work possible. It has also presented the Brahman scholar ascetic orders as in some important ways a part of this social formation. It may be that the colonial fascination with the more dramatic forms of ascetic self-mortification has made it more difficult for us to see the quieter and more socially conformist lives of the daṇḍīs, except where we know the most eminent of them as individual Advaitin scholars. However, there is no doubt that these three branches of the Dasnāmī order provided important forms of social and moral support to Brahman scholar households, in addition to the intellectual resources that they brought to key debates of the period. These overlapping forms of lineage not only concentrated scholarly energies, but also provided many of the connections that carried scholars, ideas, and resources across the subcontinent.

From the potent interface between scholar household and ascetic lineage also flowed important political consequences. What made Kavindra such an effective intermediary and interlocutor was very much the degree of prestige he enjoyed among householder communities in Banaras and beyond. The connection did much to add cultural diversity to the Mughal court, and lend depth to its identity as an Indian rather than an Islamic empire. More ominously, it was the accumulated expertise and reputation of the Bhatta lineage that enabled it to promote revived models of dharmic kingship at the court of Shivaji, with far-reaching consequences for Mughal–Maratha relations in the Deccan. Other consequences were less immediately dramatic, but equally significant in the longer term. As Minkowski has suggested, the expansive and systematising work of Advaitin scholar householders and Advaitin ascetics shaped what was to become the mainstream Vedantic Hinduism of the nineteenth century. Perhaps it is a tribute to the enduring folk memory of this relationship that it emerges at the centre of what was to become India's foremost "nationalist" novel in the later nineteenth century, Bankim Chandra Chatterjee's *Ānandamaṭh*, which revolves around the relationship between monks and householders, albeit in very different times and places.[109]

References

Abbott, Justin E., *Eknath. A Translation from the Bhaktalilamrita* (Poona: Scottish Mission Industries Co. Ltd., 1927).

Algazi, Gadi, "At the Study: Notes on the Production of the Scholarly Self", in David Warren Sabean and Malina Stefanovska, eds, *Self and Space in Early Modern European Cultures* (Toronto: University of Toronto Press, 2012), pp. 17–50.

Aryavaraguru, Ranganathasvami, "On the Sesas of Benaras", *Indian Antiquary*, vol. 51, November 1912, pp. 247–8.

Bayly, C.A., *Rulers, Townsmen and Bazaars: North Indian Society in the Age of British Expansion, 1770–1870* (Cambridge: Cambridge University Press, 1988).

Benson, James, "Śaṃkarabhaṭṭa's Family Chronicle: The Gādhivaṃśavarṇana", in Axel Michaels, ed., *The Pandit: Traditional Scholarship in India* (Delhi: Manohar, 2001), pp. 105–18.

Bernier, François, *Travels in the Mogul Empire AD 1656–1668* (London: Humphrey Milford, 1914).

Bronkhorst, Johannes, "Bhaṭṭoji Dīkṣita on Sphoṭa", *Journal of Indian Philosophy*, vol. 33, no. 1, 2005, pp. 3–41.

Bronner, Yigal, "North Meets South: Banaras from the Perspective of Appayya Dīkṣita", *South Asian History and Culture*, vol. 6, no. 1, January 2015, pp. 10–31.

Busch, Allison, *Poetry of Kings: The Classical Hindi Literature of Mughal India* (New York: Oxford University Press, 2011).

Chatterjee, Indrani, ed., *Unfamiliar Relations: Family and History in South Asia* (Delhi: Permanent Black, 2004).

Clark, Matthew, *The Daśanāmī-Saṃnyāsīs* (Leiden: E.J. Brill, 2007).

Dandekar, R.N., *Sanskrit and Maharashtra: A Symposium* (Poona: University of Poona, 1972).

Derrett, J. Duncan M., "Kamalakara on Illegitimates", in idem, ed., *Essays*

[109] Lipner, ed., *Anandamath*.

in Classical and Modern Hindu Law, vol. 3 (Leiden: E.J. Brill, 1977), pp. 230–40.

Deshpande, Madhav M., "Vedas and their Śākhās: Contested Relationships", in François Voegeli, Vincent Eltschinger, and Danielle Feller, eds, *Devadattīyam: Johannes Bronkhhorst Felicitation Volume* (Bern: Peter Lang, 2012), pp. 341–62.

———, "Disagreement Without Disrespect: Transitions in a Lineage from Bhaṭṭoji to Nāgeśa", *South Asian History and Culture*, vol. 6, no. 1, 2015, pp. 32–49.

Eaton, Richard M., *A Social History of the Deccan, 1300–1761: Eight Deccan Lives* (Cambridge: Cambridge University Press, 2005).

Farquhar, J.N., "The Organization of the Sannyasis of the Vedanta", *Journal of the Royal Asiatic Society of Great Britain and Ireland*, July 1925, pp. 479–86.

Flood, Gavin, ed., *The Blackwell Companion to Hinduism* (Oxford: Blackwell Publishing, 2003).

Fuqara'-i Hind, British Library, I.O. Islamic 4744.

Gai, G.S., "Some Problems in the History of the Nayakas of Keladi", in G.S. Dikshit, ed., *Studies in Keladi History* (Bangalore: The Mythic Society, 1981), pp. 17–23.

Ganeri, Jonardon, *The Lost Age of Reason: Philosophy in Early Modern India, 1450–1700* (New York: Oxford University Press, 2011).

Gode, P.K., "Date of the Bhāṭṭabhāṣāprakāśikā and Identification of Its Author with the Guru of Nilakaṇṭha Caturdhara", *The Mīmāṁsā-Prakāśa*, vol. 3, no. 6, 1 June 1938, pp. 65–71.

———, "The Identification of Gosvāmi Nṛsimhāśrama of Dārā Shukoh's Sanskrit Letter with Brahmendra Sarasvatī of the Kavīndracandrodaya", in P.K. Gode, ed., *Studies in Indian Literary History*, vol. 2 (Bombay: Singhi Jain Sastra Sikshapith, 1954), pp. 447–51.

———, "Some Evidence About the Location of the Manuscript Library of Kavīndrācārya Sarasvatī at Benares in AD 1665", in P.K. Gode, ed., *Studies in Indian Cultural History*, vol. 3 (Poona: Bhandarkar Oriental Research Institute, 1969), pp. 71–6.

Gomez, K., "Sanskrit and the Labour of Gender in Early Modern South India", *Modern Asian Studies*, vol. 57, no. 1, 2023, pp. 167–94.

Hausner, Sondra, *Wandering With Sadhus: Ascetics in the Hindu Himalayas* (Bloomington and Indianapolis: Indiana University Press, 2007).

Hawley, John Stratton, *Storm of Songs: India and the Idea of the Bhakti Movement* (Cambridge, MA: Harvard University Press, 2015).

Horstmann, Monica, *Der Zusammenhalt der Welt: Religiöse Herrschaftslegitimation und Religionspolitik Maharaja Savai Jaisings (1700–1743)* (Wiesbaden: Harrassowitz, 2009).

Kane, P.V., *Vyavhāramayūkha of Bhaṭṭa Nīlakaṇṭha* (Poona: Bhandarkar Oriental Research Institute, 1926).

———, *History of Dharmaśāstra*, 5 vols (Poona: Bhandarkar Oriental Research Institute, 1968–77).

Kanole, V.A., "Nāṅḍeḍache Śeṣa Gharāṇe", in Surendranath Sen, ed., *Mahamahopadhyaya Prof. DV Potdar Sixty First Birthday Commemoration Volume* (Poona: Samartha Bharat Press, 1950), pp. 56–73.

Kaviraj, Gopi Natha, *Gleanings From the History and Bibliography of the Nyaya-Vaisesika Literature* (Calcutta: Indian Studies Past and Present, 1961).

Keune, John, "Eknāth Remembered and Reformed: Bhakti, Brahmans and Untouchables in Marathi Historiography", Columbia University PhD thesis, 2011.

Kinra, Rajeev, *Writing Self, Writing Empire: Chandar Bhan Brahman and the Cultural World of the Indo-Persian State Secretary* (Berkeley: University of California Press, 2015).

Leslie, Julia, *The Perfect Wife* (Delhi: Oxford University Press, 1989).

Lipner, Julius, ed., *Anandamath, or The Sacred Brotherhood* (Delhi: Oxford University Press, 2006).

Mahadevan, T.M.P., *Preceptors of Advaita* (Secundarabad: Sri Kanchi Kamakoti Sankara Mandir, 1961).

Minkowski, Christopher, "I'll Wash Out Your Mouth With My Boot: A Guide to Philological Argument in Mughal-era Banaras", in Sheldon Pollock, ed., *Epic and Argument in Sanskrit Literary History: Essays in Honor of Robert P. Goldman* (Delhi: Manohar, 2010).

———, "Advaita Vedānta in Early Modern History", *South Asian History and Culture*, vol. 2, no. 2, April 2011, pp. 205–31.

———, "Nīlakaṇṭha's Teachers and Gurus, Part 1: Lakṣmaṇa Paṇḍita", *Vienna Journal of South Asian Studies*, vol. 55, 2013–15, pp. 33–76.

Narayan, Meenambal, *Nāgeśa and the Mahābhāṣya* (Delhi: Sri Satguru Publishers, 1991).

Nelson, Lance, "Madhusudana Sarasvati on the 'Hidden Meaning' of the Bhagavadgītā: Bhakti for the Advaitin Renunciate", *Journal of South Asian Literature*, vol. 23, no. 2, Summer, Fall 1998, pp. 73–89.

O'Hanlon, Rosalind, "Narratives of Penance and Purification in Western India, c. 1650-1850", *The Journal of Hindu Studies*, vol. 2, no. 1, 2009, pp. 48–75.

———, "Letters Home: Banaras Pandits and the Maratha Regions in Early Modern India", *Modern Asian Studies*, vol. 44, no. 2, March 2010, pp. 201–5.

———, "Speaking from Siva's Temple: Banaras Scholar Households and the Brahman 'Ecumene' of Mughal India", *South Asian History and Culture*, vol. 2, no. 2, April 2011, pp. 253–77.

———, "Intimate Voices of Empire: Women and Letter-Writing in Eighteenth Century India", Cambridge University South Asia Seminar Podcast, https://tinyurl.com/5y27uhjv.

Olivelle, Patrick, *Renunciation in Hinduism: A Medieval Debate* (Leiden: E.J. Brill, 1986).

———, *The Āśrama System: The History and Hermeneutics of a Religious Institution* (New York: Oxford University Press, 1993).

———, "The Ascetic and the Domestic in Brahmanical Religiosity", in Oliver Freiberger, ed., *Critics of Asceticism: Historical Accounts and Comparative Perspectives* (New York: Oxford University Press, 2006), pp. 25–42.

Paradkar, M.D., "Kavīndrācārya Saraswatī, A Native of Mahārāṣṭra", *Journal of the Ganganath Jha Research Institute*, vol. 25, 1969, pp. 378–9.

Parasnis, D.B., ed., *Śrī Mahāpuruṣa Brahmendrasvāmī Dhāvaḍaśīkar, Charitra va Patra Vyavahāra* (Mumbai: Babaji Sakharam and Company, 1900).

Patil, Parimal G., "The End of the Ends of Man?", in Yigal Bronner, Whitney Cox, and Lawrence McCrea, eds, *South Asian Texts in History: Critical Engagements with Sheldon Pollock* (Delhi: Primus Books, 2016), pp. 293–308.

Pinch, William R., *Warrior Ascetics and Indian Empires* (Cambridge: Cambridge University Press, 2006).

Pollock, Sheldon, *The Ends of Man at the End of Premodernity* (Amsterdam: Royal Netherlands Academy of Arts and Sciences, 2005).

Prasad, Leela, *Poetics of Conduct: Oral Narrative and Moral Being in a South Indian Town* (New York: Columbia University Press, 2007).

Raghavan, V., "Kavīndrācārya Sarasvatī", in Bimala Churn Law, ed., *D.R. Bhandarkar Felicitation Volume* (Calcutta: Indian Research Institute, 1940), pp. 159–65.

Sarkar, Jadunath, *A History of Dasnami Naga Sanyasis* (Allahabad: P.A. Mahanirvani, n.d.).

Shah, Umakant Premanand, ed., *Gīrvāṇapadamañjarī and Gīrvāṇavāṅmañjarī* (Baroda: Oriental Institute, 1960).

Sharma, Har Dutt, and M.M. Patkar, eds, *Kavīndracandrodaya* (Poona: Oriental Book Agency, 1939).

Shastri, Haraprasad, *A Descriptive Catalogue of the Sanskrit Manuscripts in the Government Collection Under the Care of the Asiatic Society of Bengal*, 12 vols (Calcutta: Asiatic Society, 1912–66).

Shastri, M.H., "Dakshini Pandits at Benaras", *Indian Antiquary*, vol. 41, January 1912, pp. 7–13.

Sherring, M.A., *Benaras, The Sacred City of the Hindus* (London: Trübner and Co., 1868).

———, *Hindu Tribes and Castes as Represented in Benaras* (London, Trübner and Co., 1872).

Sinha, Surajit, and Baidyanath Saraswati, *Ascetics of Kashi* (Varanasi: N.K. Bose Memorial Fund, 1978).

Solvyns, F. Balthazar, *Les Hindous, par F.B. Solvyns*, 4 vols (Paris: published by the author, 1808–12).

Stoker, Valerie, *Polemics and Patronage in the City of Victory: Vyasatirtha, Hindu Sectarianism and the Sixteenth Century Vijayanagar Court* (Berkeley: University of California Press, 2017).

Tokunaga, M., and John Smith, eds, Bhandarkar Oriental Research Institute Critical Edition of the Mahābhārata, http://sanskritdocuments.org/mirrors/mahabharata/mahabharata-bori.html.

Truschke, Audrey, "Contested History: Brahmanical Memories of Relations with the Mughals", *Journal of the Economic and Social History of the Orient*, vol. 58, no. 4, 2015, pp. 419–52.

———, *Culture of Encounters: Sanskrit at the Mughal Court* (New York: Columbia University Press, 2016).

Venkatkrishnan, Anand, "Ritual, Reflection and Religion: The Devas of Banaras", *South Asian History and Culture*, vol. 6, no. 1, 2015, pp. 147–71.

Ward, William, *A View of the History, Literature and Religion of the Hindoos* (Serampore: Mission Press, 1817–20).

Wilson, H.H., *Sketch of the Religious Sects of the Hindus* (Calcutta: Bishop's College Press, 1846).

Wright, Samuel, *A Time of Novelty: Logic, Emotion and Intellectual Life in Early Modern India, 1500-1700* (New York: Oxford University Press, 2021).

5

Gotmai's Suit

A Brahman Woman of Property in Seventeenth-Century Western India

Gotmai Kale was a widow of a Brahman family based in the taraf (district subdivision) of Chiplun town in the subah (province) of Dabhol in Maharashtra's Konkan littoral. She lived from the middle decades of the seventeenth century through into the early decades of the eighteenth. This was a prosperous region, with trade from the Persian Gulf and Indian Ocean landing at the ports of Dabhol and Cheul, before moving up through the passes of the Western Ghats and into the Deccan. As the last surviving direct descendant of the family, Gotmai found herself drawn into a prolonged struggle to retain control of the family's prestigious hereditary office as district accountants, against distant relatives and outsiders bent on usurping the office and the valuable rights attached to it.[1]

An important question for any scholar interested in the nature of family and lineage in early modern India concerns their nature as complex corporate entities, blending scribal skills, social and marital interdependencies, and material resources, and dependent for their stability above all on the cohesion of their members. For the seventeenth and eighteenth centuries, indeed, it is particularly difficult to gain insights into the mundane and local contexts in which women outside the world of courtly and state elites sought to control their family rights

[1] For a striking parallel example, see Deshpande, *Scripts of Power*, pp. 37–9.

to property and office. Nor do we have very much understanding of women's ability to negotiate the internal family relationships upon which such control often depended in the early modern centuries.

From a range of different intellectual perspectives, this is an important omission. As I have argued elsewhere, Brahman scholarly labour depended overwhelmingly on the resources and cohesion of the Brahman household, with Brahman wives and mothers at its centre. Intellectual prestige was intimately connected with the reputation of the family, both as a provider of teaching for new generations of scholars, and as a vital guarantor of the purity of biological kinship. The largest seventeenth-century gathering of named Brahman scholars that we know of assembled together not in intellectual debate but to assure themselves of the purity of their marriage relationships.[2] In this setting, where intellectual and biological filiation ran through the same skeins of family connection, what forms of agency were open to women?

Women's agency in other kinds of early modern households matters too. As Samira Sheikh, Indrani Chatterjee, and others have observed, our understanding of women's ability to control capital, and their access to the political networks on which such control often depended, is a field still very much under development.[3] How did women of small landholder families, or local office-holders with ancestral lands attached, regard the rights that their families had accumulated? How did they seek to protect them from predatory neighbours or rivals, negotiate with local judicial institutions, handle the documentary culture that accompanied property rights in many parts of India during this period, and invoke the protection of religious authorities or agencies of the state? How far did the family itself, so often the key arena within which women's life chances were determined, also shape their ability to control capital and resources?

Local and apparently obscure as it was, Gotmai's long struggle offers us some sharp insights into many of these questions. She waged her

[2] O'Hanlon, "Letters Home", pp. 229–34.

[3] Sheikh, "Jibhabhu's Rights to Ghee"; Chatterjee, *Forgotten Friends*; Hasan, "Property and Social Relations"; Sreenivasan, "Drudges, Dancing Girls, Concubines"; Bano, "Women and Property"; Guha, "A Locus of Sociopolitical Organisation".

protracted campaign in the intimate surroundings of her home, amid fraught family relationships, in the public space of the local temple, in the neighbourhoods of Chiplun town where she sought refuge in the homes of relatives, and in the office of the provincial governor. Some understanding of the way in which women experienced life at this prosaic interface between family, community institutions, and agencies of the state might have much to tell us about women's scope for independent action in early modern India, their local political competencies, their attitudes to authority, and their ability to protect such access to property rights as they had. It might also illuminate wider social attitudes in this milieu to women themselves, when they sought to become actors beyond the bounds of the domestic sphere. Developing our appreciation of these forms of agency also contributes, of course, to our understanding of their changing history with the coming of colonialism and its new regimes of property right and family law.

Let us look first, then, at this local milieu itself, with its judicial institutions, agencies of the state, bureaucratic culture, and long history of recorded property rights. Unlike Bengal, for example, where most written records of landed rights dated back to, at the earliest, the Mughal period, the Marathi-speaking regions had a much earlier and continuous recorded history of rural settlement, cultivation, and lands gifted by local states in return for service of different kinds. As elsewhere in peninsular India, the village Patil (headman) took a leading role in opening up land for cultivation, and the hereditary cultivator's right of mirās derived from family participation in such early pioneering. Patils were responsible for maintaining cultivation in the village and for overseeing collection of revenue and its regular payment to the state. Rights to offices, such as that of Kulkarni (village accountant), with tax free inām lands attached, could likewise constitute a village mirās. At the supra-village level of the parganạ̄ (a geographical unit of anything between twenty and a hundred villages), the offices of Deshmukh and Deshkulkarni carried responsibility for maintaining cultivation and the flow of revenues, and for local justice and security. The Deshkulkarni, the office of district-level accountant under contention in Gotmai's family, oversaw revenue collection and the framing of accounts for the parganạ̄. Expected to work alongside the Deshmukh, the Deshkulkarni was a state-appointed official remunerated from village revenues and often via land given in inām.

Literacy was essential to both of these offices. As senior state officials, both were expected to attend the periodic assemblies of local officials and holders of hereditary landed rights which were convened whenever these rights were in dispute. The Havaldar was again a state appointment, carrying a wide remit of responsibility for security, military affairs, justice, and revenue collection over several pargaṇās. The administrative division of the subah represented a higher level still. A Subhedar carried the same broad remit as a Havaldar, but over an entire subah, although the size and boundaries of a subah could vary significantly with changes of regime and nomenclature.[4]

This was a setting in which the hereditary property rights of such families were extremely important and tenaciously maintained. Local memory, as well as written records in stone, copper plate, and increasingly from around the fourteenth century on paper, secured these rights and provided evidence that they had been legitimately conferred. This happened either through other mirāsdārs acting collectively, or by the state in return for agreed services. Local judicial assemblies of the caste, or of holders of mirās rights in the locality, with officers of the state present in important cases, could be convened to hear disputes, examine evidence and witnesses, and determine outcomes.[5]

Our source for Gotmai's life and struggle lies in a karina, the kind of lengthy factual statement usually made to a majālis (judicial assembly meeting) to hear a local dispute. We have access only to an early-twentieth-century printed copy of the original Marathi karina, collected in the course of the nationalist historian V.K. Rajwade's tours around western India in search of family papers that otherwise might not survive the colonial state's neglect of private Marathi collections.[6] The form of the document is worth noting. Its opening lines tell us that it was written in the year 1116 of the South Indian regnal year of Shuhur, and the Manmath or 29th year of the Jovian saṃvatsara calendar, which brings us to the CE year of 1715. The long history that it des-

[4] Fukazawa, *The Medieval Deccan*, pp. 1–48, and Deshpande, *Scripts of Power*, pp. 30–47.

[5] For this milieu, see Guha, *History and Collective Memory*, pp. 88–109.

[6] Rajwade, ed., *Marāṭhyānchyā Ithihāsāchī Sādhane*, pp. 52–67. Hereafter MIS karina.

cribes stretches back into the early seventeenth century. It consists of sections of narrative, interspersed with the testimony of the principal disputants in the case, and lists of names of all those who attended the judicial assembly convened to hear the case. Gotmai's active part in the history took place well before 1715. Only two dates emerge in the karina with any certainty. One is the date of its compilation in 1715. It is not quite clear what occasioned its production in that year since, as we shall see, the history that it traced concluded with the period of the Mughal invasions of the Maratha country in the 1690s. It is possible that the Kale family took steps to produce the karina with the return of stability to the region when, in the second decade of the eighteenth century, Shivaji's grandson Shahu consolidated his authority in Satara and appointed his first peshwa, Balaji Vishvanath, in 1713. The document recorded Gotmai as still living at this time, but now an old woman recounting events and a contest that had taken place many decades earlier. The other date we know for certain is 1659. We are able to determine this date because, as we shall see, Gotmai's principal antagonist took the opportunity of the Bijapur general Afzal Khan's entry into the Maratha country to obtain a crucial piece of documentary evidence about the Kale family rights. We know that Afzal Khan set out from Bijapur to take on Shivaji's insurgent Maratha forces in May 1659.[7]

The karina is not in her words, but in those of the scribe responsible for taking down the evidence and collating it into a narrative. However, Gotmai's voice comes through the narrative very clearly. Her account formed one of its major sources, and it contains immediate and striking details of her character, her strategies, her local reputation, and her ultimate success in protecting her family rights. The concluding paragraph of the document, moreover, tells us that "Gotmai related the whole of the present story out of her own mouth."[8]

Before moving on to the narrative, it is worth reflecting on the assembly that the karina recorded as having met earlier to hear the case. Described towards the end of the document, this assembly was very large, reflecting the seriousness with which many local leaders and state officials evidently regarded the dispute.[9] Some 138 individuals were

[7] Mehendele, *Shivaji*, p. 203.
[8] MIS karina, p. 66.
[9] Ibid., pp. 57–60.

named as witnesses, grouped according to their status, place of origin, and profession. There were subah level officials, the Subhedar himself, the Havaldar, then a range of subah-level record-keepers: two daftardars, a majumdar, a chitnavis, and a potnis. Their equivalents from the local administration of Chiplun parganā were also present – some further six officials. There were in addition various groups of Brahmans: astrologers, priests, vaidya medical practitioners, and learned scholar Brahmans from elsewhere resident in Chiplun, amounting to about 28 people. Some 24 shroffs and shetias represented the interests of local bankers and moneylenders. Then there were 13 principal local office-holders of Chiplun itself, the Patil, the Kulkarni, the chaudhari, the potdar, and so on. Representatives from key communities were there too: goldsmiths, oil-makers, and weavers. Some 4 nayakvadis – chiefs amongst the local Dalit Mahar and Berad communities – were present, responsible for village watch and ward. There was a large further group of some 50 named individuals whose titles indicate office or landed rights. Representatives of families who were party to the dispute, some 14 individuals, also attended. This, then, was a huge gathering of local and regional administrative and landed elites, reflecting the importance of the office at stake, and the family issues surrounding it.

Let us turn, then, to the narrative. Its opening is a little difficult to follow because some phrases are missing from the first lines of the printed text. But we manage to learn that the office of Deshkulkarni of Chiplun in the subah of Dabhol had been bestowed on one Hari Krishna. From that time to the date of the karina's writing in 1715, he and his descendants had continuously enjoyed the office. After a short break in the text, we learn that Kalopant, the husband of Gotmai, had been one of these descendants, until he fell victim to a violent murder. Kalo and his wife Gotmai had a son, Antaji Kalo, a boy of great acumen who left Chiplun to work at the Adil Shahi court of Bijapur. This had long been, of course, a well-trodden career path amongst scribal elites in the western Deccan.[10] After his father's murder, the talented son Antaji returned from Bijapur to Chiplun with his family, presumably to take over the Deshkulkarni office. But then he himself died, leaving Gotmai alone with her daughter-in-law, now also a widow.

[10] Eaton, *A Social History*, pp. 144–5.

At this point, Gotmai found herself having to look for a mutālīk, someone to manage the Deshkulkarni office on her behalf. She set about this, the narrative suggests, "chitānarūpa", which means according to her own intelligence and liking – with the implication, perhaps, that she had her own ideas as to the kind of manager she was looking for.[11] There was a male relative who could have done the job, her husband's cousin Balo Vinayak, but he, the karina tells us, "had no education" (vidyā nāhī). So it was settled instead by a local tribunal that Harbaji Datir, the father of Gotmai's now widowed daughter-in-law, should be appointed as mutālīk. Harbaji Datir took on the role of manager and held it for several years.

But then Gotmai and Harbaji Datir fell out. "In order to make a quarrel with him, she began to say that owing to some defect of his daughter, her own son had died, and so she began to slander him and to look for a different mutālīk more to her liking, but without success. Their quarrel became notorious, and people predicted disaster unless it could be calmed."[12]

At this point two new characters came on the scene, Timaji Bhaskar and his brother Gangaji. They had been working as village accountants in the nearby town of Helvak, but then lost their position and came to Chiplun with their families looking for opportunities. Finding a place to stay proved difficult, so they took up residence at the house of Gotmai's paternal uncle, Timaji Deuskar. Once ensconced, and enjoying the good opinion of the local community, they suggested to Gotmai that of the two Bhaskar brothers, Timaji Bhaskar should take on the role of manager. After some days, Gangaji Bhaskar went back to Helvak to carry on the work of village accountant. Timaji Bhaskar had no son to help him, so Gangaji gave him his own son, Hari Trimal, in adoption. Timaji Bhaskar and Hari Trimal secured the agreement of the local panchayat (judicial assembly) that they should do the work. At first they treated Gotmai well, and enjoyed the good opinion of everyone in the district.

Matters then took a darker turn, as Timaji Bhaskar and his adopted nephew evidently decided to exploit their position. "They poisoned

[11] MIS karina, p. 52.
[12] Ibid., pp. 52–3.

their own good fortune. They began to neglect Gotmai, keeping her short of food and clothing, and treating her with contempt. They set out to make themselves masters and proprietors." Wider political circumstances at this time, which this point in the narrative enables us to date to the late 1650s, were in their favour. Assailed by Mughal and Maratha forces alike, the Sultanate state of Bijapur was in a state of near political collapse, its dowager queen Badi Sahiba effectively exercising power on behalf of her young son Ali Adil Shah II (1638–1672) and many of its Irani nobility looking to their own futures. In September 1659, frustrated by Shivaji's raids into Bijapur's territories, the Bijapur court despatched its military commander Afzal Khan to engage Shivaji's forces.

The narrative of the karina referred to this despatch of Afzal Khan, and described the opportunity that his arrival opened up for Timaji Bhaskar. He learned that Afzal Khan's powerful vazir had brought along with him a supply of the Bijapur Sultan's personal ḍaula. These were the pre-prepared blank paper orders, often complete with seals and signatures, that could be filled out with the names of those to be granted offices or estates.[13] Such orders would have been a valuable asset in Afzal Khan's coming campaign. As soon as he heard that Afzal Khan's retinue had a supply of such orders, the karina continued, Timaji Bhaskar made contact with one Kasi Diyanatrao. We know from other sources that Kasi Diyanatrao was another Maratha Brahman in the service of the Bijapur court. He hailed originally from a family of revenue officials near Pune and had survived many contests for revenue rights similar to Timaji Bhaskar's own. His star had risen quickly in Bijapur. He became a member of the royal council of advisers to the sultans Muhammad and Ali Adil Shah II, and confidential adviser to Khawas Khan, one of the leaders of the Dakhani party at the Bijapur court. His services brought him the title of "Diyanatrao", evidently in reference to his piety, and he appears in contemporary records as Kasi Diyanatrao or simply Diyanatrao.[14]

Timaji Bhaskar may well have known him, or known of him, through the networks that connected Brahman families of revenue

[13] For usages of this kind of document, see Moosvi, "Reforming Revenue Administration". I am very grateful to Nandini Chatterjee for this reference.

[14] Khare, "Some Records from a Deshpande Family of Wai", pp. 16–19.

collectors in the western Deccan. The karina described his exploitation of the connection without equivocation: "Timaji got his name inserted onto one of these documents by ingratiating himself with Kasi Diyanatrao, and also by promising to supply 300 boats to Bijapur. By this means, he got Gotmai's name thrown off the document, and without saying anything, returned to Chiplun."[15]

It is likely that Diyanatrao's interest in boats arose in the context of Shivaji's own early experiments in naval warfare at the end of the 1650s. These early experiments were reported, in a letter from the Portuguese governor of Goa in August 1659, as part of the Maratha leader's drive to control Bijapur's territories on the Konkan coast, as well as to strengthen his position against the English and Portuguese factories there.[16]

Evidently, however, Timaji Bhaskar realised that without a properly attested mahzar – the document of right usually confirmed by a local majālis assembly – his own order of appointment meant little, and that any such assembly would have to be packed with influential and supportive witnesses.[17] The karina identified two such witnesses. "It would be important at the very least to obtain the favourable testimony of the respectable merchants, Keshavshet and Gagshet, and when Timaji got a chance he went to ask them."[18] But the two merchants were having none of it. Instead, they went behind Timaji Bhaskar's back, to warn Gotmai. "They told her that Timaji had got his name inserted into one of the Padishah's orders, firmans, and now was looking for witnesses who would help him obtain a confirmatory mahzar issued with his name on it, and that Timaji had visited them to ask them to bear witness in his favour. They asked her, did you have any idea this was going on?"[19]

Gotmai was deeply distressed at this news and confessed that she had known nothing about it. The merchants asked her whether she still had the family's documents of property right in her possession, and she assured them that she had. They urged her to guard the documents

[15] MIS karina, p. 53.

[16] Pissurlenkar, *The Portuguese and the Marathas*, pp. 3–4.

[17] For these judicial forms, see Chatterjee, "Mahzar-namas in the Mughal and British Empires", and Deshpande, *Scripts of Power*, pp. 29–68.

[18] MIS karina, p. 53.

[19] Ibid., pp. 53–4.

carefully and not let anyone else see them. Gotmai took them at their word, but her precautions, the narrative, suggested, were not very sophisticated: "Being a woman, she did not arrange to keep the documents in another place. Instead, she bundled them up and hid them in a pillow that she kept nearby her, so that every day when she rose from her bed, she could press down on the pillow, and check that the documents were still there."[20] Meanwhile, the would-be usurper Timaji Bhaskar decided that, if his quest was to succeed, he would have to search Gotmai's house and get hold of the documents that she possessed confirming the Kale family's rights.

> So he went to see her and appealed to her heart by talking to her of his joys and sorrows. As they talked, he noticed that her hand kept going to the pillow, and guessed that the documents were hidden within it. Eventually, he saw his opportunity. He made up a bundle of documents with his own scrawls on them, thrust them into the pillow, and pulling out her documents, made off with them. In the days that followed, Gotmai felt the pillow to confirm that her documents were still there, and believed that they were safe.[21]

After some days, the karina went on, she began to have her doubts, and so she opened the pillows to look at the documents. But she could not read for herself, and no-one else in the household could read the documents either. So she took them to her father, Krishnaji Deuskar, who examined them. "He became very agitated, and said, they are nothing but scraps of scribble."[22] He stormed off to remonstrate with Timaji Bhaskar, and in a great rage accused him of taking his daughter's family name out of the document. Timaji Bhaskar was at the time still living in the house of Krishnaji Deuskar's brother, Timaji Deuskar. On lcarning of the episode, Timaji Deuskar threw the miscreant Timaji Bhaskar out.

Thwarted thus in his attempt to appropriate the family office, Timaji Bhaskar's relations with Gotmai went from bad to worse. Gotmai strove mightily to have him removed as manager and to have someone else appointed, fearing that her battle might very well end in

[20] Ibid., p. 54.
[21] Idem.
[22] Idem.

her losing her life. But without anyone nearby to take her side, she turned to her maternal nephew, one Krishnaji Somnath, who was then working as an official for the Subhedar of Dabhol, and who used to visit her to ask after her from time to time. "She said to him, you are my son, but misfortune has befallen me, and my trusted mutālīk has turned against me, wiping out my name and pushing his own in instead. But her nephew took little heed of her entreaties."[23] At this point, Gotmai turned to seek refuge in the home of one relative after another, her insistence on the rightness of her cause and her refusal to brook any contradiction leading to frequent quarrels. Rumours and finger-pointing began to follow her, and hostility from every relative in whose home she sought refuge. "They said, she carries a bag of gold around with her, and all she cares about is to protect it. So saying, each made difficulties for her, and threw her out of their homes. Her fate pursued her, and she found no-where to live."[24] Eventually, Gotmai reached a dramatic decision. "I must either flee the country, or drink poison to end my life".[25]

With a fine sense of theatre, however, Gotmai did neither. She took herself to the prominent temple of Parashuram in Chiplun, took up a seat in front of the god, and embarked on a public fast. She impressed the temple priest, Narambhat, who asked her why she had come to the temple. "She said to him, 'I have no place to go, wherever I go those devils in the guise of Brahmans follow me. So I have come here to die near the god.'"[26] The priest's heart melted, the karina went on, and he invited Gotmai to come and stay at his home.

Her public protest caused a wider stir. It brought another local official, Antaji Bavaji, the mazumdar (keeper of revenue accounts) at Chiplun, to enquire into her situation. After hearing her story, he issued a stern rebuke to the would-be usurper Timaji Bhaskar, ordering him to build a separate house for Gotmai, and to keep her well supplied with food and clothing. But the struggle and bitter exchanges between the two continued even worse than before. After some further time, the same Antaji Bavaji, now promoted to be Subhedar of

[23] Idem.

[24] Ibid., p. 55.

[25] Idem.

[26] Idem.

the nearby district of Rajapur, visited Chiplun. He remembered Gotmai's history and enquired after her. The karina described her response in touching detail. We can perhaps again hear Gotmai's own voice as she compares herself to Draupadi, heroine of the Mahabharata, rescued by the god Krishna himself from the malign Kaurava prince Dushashana as he attempted to disrobe her in public.

> She was as happy as if literally her very family god had taken human form and come to meet her. She laid her account before him. He said, "If this goes on, you will be killed, and the office will fall into his hands. So, if you have any relative, bring them, and ask them to take up the office, do not delay." She said, "I am lying helpless at the Swami's feet. Apart from the Swami I have no-one. You yourself are my father and mother, brothers, all my family and relations. I am completely helpless. You came to me just like Sri Krishna came in answer to Draupadi's loud wailing. I have nothing left, please, I beg you to come to my aid.[27]

In the face of this compelling personal drama that Gotmai was able – perhaps very deliberately – to act out, the Subhedar of Rajapur wrote for her a personal letter to Mahadji, the Subhedar of Dabhol, asking him to help her. So she took the letter to Dabhol, where the Subhedar also asked her if she had no relatives. She said that indeed she did – her maternal nephew Krishnaji Somnath, who was then employed in Dabhol, and to whom, as we saw, she had earlier appealed for help. So the Subhedar summoned Krishnaji Somnath, and tried to persuade him to take on the family office. Braving the Subhedar's wrath, Krishnaji refused again and left the place. Then, by a stroke of fate, Vinaji Balal, the young son of Gotmai's unlettered kinsman Balo Vinayak, returned to Chiplun after a long absence. Gotmai was delighted and took him to meet Mahadji, who was relieved at this discovery of a relative. But because Vinaji Balal was also unlettered, he called Krishnaji Somnath back, introduced him to Vinaji Balal, and the two recognised each other as distant relatives. Despite the mediation of Gotmai's uncle Timaji Deuskar, who came from Chiplun, Krishnaji Somnath still declined to take on the position. He suggested instead that his son, Haripant, should take on the office, working alongside the unlettered Vinaji Balal. Documents were prepared to confirm the young Vinaji in the

[27] Idem.

office, and thus Gotmai gave him into the care of Krishnaji Somnath's family.

But there remained the question of the revenues collected while Timaji Bhaskar and his adopted nephew had had control of the Desh-kulkarni office, and of the records maintained during this period. Here again we are reminded of the practical realities of the Brahman scribal household, its deep involvement with local finances, and the key role of family relationships in sustaining these arrangements. By the time the arrangement with Krishnaji Somnath and Vinaji Balal had been made, the karina continued, Timaji Bhaskar himself had passed away, and his brother Gangaji excluded from the business and sent away to Chiplun. Wishing to check on the Deshkulkarni's ṛaṇābandh (the undertaking given to make payments to the state revenues) following its own local collections, Krishnaji Somnath went into the Deshkulkarni's office, met the clerks and other staff, and set about the work. He summoned Gangaji and demanded that he produce the old records and the lists of collections from the province. But Gangaji protested his inability to produce any records, and instead recited his own long tale of woe, which was evidently received with some scepticism.

> He began to weep, and cried, "I used to have these papers, but I kept them in the cowshed. Then one day the cowshed burned down, and they were all destroyed. Not a scrap of them remains". So he started playacting in this way. "My brother Timaji died. My son Hari Trimal has also died. I will soon be dead myself". With this piteous complaining, he fell at their feet and pleaded piteously to be given an honourable discharge from the job.[28]

The implication was that no proper accounts had been rendered for the parganā, which might well explain why Krishnaji Somnath had been so reluctant to take on the job in the first place. When news of this performance reached the shetias, who would likely have had some considerable stake in the correct payment of revenues, they declared that he should not be let off lightly in this way. So Gangaji was taken to the Subhedar Mahadji in Dabhol, who also pressed him for the accounts, but he repeated the same story. He followed it up with a sworn written statement that all the papers he was aware of were destroyed in

[28] Ibid., p. 56.

a fire before his very eyes, and in any case Krishnaji Somnath had no right to press him for information about the profits and losses connected with the office. Evidently unimpressed, Mahadji demanded a payment of the 5000 lārīs said to be outstanding.[29] Various respectable people tried to intercede for Gangaji, but the Subhedar pressed his demand regardless. At this point, Krishnaji Somnath seems to have decided that perhaps Gangaji deserved a second chance in the family, and might be allowed to take on the role of manager of the Deshkulkarni's office so long as he treated Gotmai well. The narrator described his evident contrition. "He began to treat Gotmai not just like a mother, but like a goddess; the cruelties of the past were forgotten, and they lived in amity."[30]

Still, Gotmai was not quite content. Perhaps she felt that only a son of her own could offer security, both for herself and for the family's control of the Deshkulkarni office. "So she went to her nephew Krishnaji, and said, 'You have three sons. May they live as long as the sage Markandeya.' She entreated him earnestly. 'Please, allow me to adopt one of them.'"[31] This posed a puzzle for the local pandits, who looked into the matter and found that as a woman she was not able herself to adopt a son; only a man could adopt in this way. So it was agreed that her kinsman the young Vinaji Balal should adopt one of Krishnaji Somnath's sons, Janardan. We now approach the end of Gotmai's role in this story. Though Vinaji Balal had a son of his own, he wrote a letter before witnesses that he would treat them both as his

[29] The lārīn was a very widely used silver-based currency of Indian Ocean and coastal traders from the Persian littoral to Malabar and Sri Lanka. The lārīns in question here would very likely have been Dabholi lārīns, issued by Ali Adil Shah II of Bijapur for the convenience of his subjects in the Konkan. Husain, "The Silver Larins", pp. 67–8. At that time, Dabholi lārīns were worth a little less than half a rupee, making the debt about Rs 2300, or, given the value of silver, about £160 in the values of the time. This was a very substantial sum: the whole revenue assessment for the important Konkani port town of Cheul in 1679 was just 619 lārīs. It is not surprising, therefore, that the missing cash prompted such consternation. For this and other examples, see Kulkarni, *Maharashtra*, p. 92. I am very grateful to Shailendra Bhandare for his kind help in working out these equivalents.

[30] Ibid., p. 57.

[31] Idem.

own family, and they would all live together in amity, and do the work of the Deshkulkarni office, and enjoy its perquisites from generation to generation. The two sons were put to study so that they could carry out their duties efficiently, and an oath was taken on holy water. Thereafter the work of the office, and relations within the family, were conducted in a very satisfactory way.[32]

This part of the narrative then listed all of the important people, described above, who attended the assembly to hear the case. From the account of the karina, we can deduce that this assembly probably took place in the late 1680s, before the decade of the Mughal invasions in the 1690s. Before this era of warfare, a further challenge to the Kale family's office developed, which Gotmai's maternal nephew Krishnaji Somnath had been forced to contest. The narrative of the karina continued: "After Krishnaji's account was decided to be true, the lawless plundering of the Mughlai occurred, and at that time these two conflicting accounts emerged. Gotmai related the whole of the present story out of her own mouth."[33] Gotmai seems to have taken no part in this later phase, this time her nephew Krishnaji Somnath taking the lead in successfully defending the family's interests. The outcome of this second stage of the judicial narrative drew to a close. Gotmai was still living, and in amity with one of Krishnaji Somnath's sons, Haripant. The narrative then concluded with some reflections on the importance of giving true testimony in any judicial case involving family rights.

Here, then, I think, there is much to interest us in the details of Gotmai's suit, conducted in these mundane but often fiercely competitive lower reaches of state administration. What we see here – the attempt by a manager to appropriate a significant office as his own property, aided by forgery and the manipulation of local justice – was actually quite a familiar situation in these settings. What is remarkable, though, is the degree of traction that the unlettered but determined Gotmai was able to gain in the face of such a challenge. The conflict seems to have been resolved without recourse to formal judicial procedures until the challenge which occasioned the great assembly of the late 1680s, when Krishnaji Somnath defended the family's office. Rather, Gotmai

[32] Idem.

[33] Ibid., p. 66.

conducted her earlier struggle to protect the family's rights through informal social means. She staged a major drama in the local temple, which brought the Subhedar to her aid, and then a further public drama in his office, replete with classical references, as she endeavoured to persuade him to help her by dispensing with the services of her nephew.

She was not herself literate, and, with its stock of male members so depleted, the Kale family had not diversified into scholarly – alongside administrative and revenue management – roles. Nonetheless, it was Gotmai who kept custody of the family's documents of property right, and she knew what to do when she had been the victim of deception. Her lack of literate skills made it impossible for her to exercise the bureaucratic power of the Deshkulkarni in her own right, and in this she was unlike widows who wielded political authority or mercantile influence on the basis of their connections and experience. Yet she was clearly determined to find a manager that she liked, and willing to quarrel with those she saw as unsuitable or disrespectful to her, dragging in the death of her son to strengthen her hand. Ultimately what she wanted, of course, was a male relative to take on the office so that it could be preserved within her family, and she was assertive enough to suggest that she should herself be allowed to adopt one. Her goal was preservation of her family's rights and its name, but to do this she was willing to flout convention, to make herself unpopular, to test the limits of local community tolerance, to take over a temple for the staging of her personal drama, and to put great pressure on state officials.

Her suit also gives us some idea of contemporary attitudes to women and widows such as herself. The scribe's narrative suggests that many people regarded her as a "difficult" woman, quarrelsome by nature and determined to use her deficient woman's judgement in the management of her affairs. She was clearly seen as a soft target by predatory local Brahmans eager to appropriate the family's office. Her nephew was obviously very reluctant to come and work with her, and possibly not just because he may have suspected that the parganā accounts were in disorder, with substantial funds missing. Yet her testimony, told now in what must have been her old age, was certainly regarded as crucial to a correct understanding of the history of the quarrel; and it was presented to an extraordinarily large and distinguished assembly of state officials, local notables, community heads, merchants, and family members.

Although the Kale family itself shared much in common with many Maratha Brahman families of the period, what we have in this karina is the fragment of an archive rather than anything like a larger individual corpus or family history. It is difficult for us to tell how far other women in Gotmai's position might have sought to protect family property and to shape family roles and relations so tenaciously. Such histories may be useful, however, not only to reconstruct something of the household relationships of Maratha Brahman families more widely in this period, but to add to our understanding of the kind of agency that women of such families were able to wield as they negotiated the difficult terrain between household, extended family, local community, and agencies of the state.

References

Bano, Shadab, "Women and Property in Mughal India", *Proceedings of the Indian History Congress*, vol. 68, 2007, pp. 406–15.

Chatterjee, Indrani, *Forgotten Friends: Monks, Marriages, Memories of Northeast India* (Delhi: Oxford University Press, 2013).

Chatterjee, Nandini, "Mahzar-namas in the Mughal and British Empires: The Uses of an Indo-Islamic Legal Form", *Comparative Studies in Society and History*, vol. 58, no. 2, 2016, pp. 379–406.

Deshpande, Prachi, *Scripts of Power: Writing, Language Practices, and Cultural History in Western India* (Ranikhet: Permanent Black, 2023).

Eaton, Richard M., *A Social History of the Deccan: Eight Indian Lives* (Cambridge: Cambridge University Press, 2005).

Fukazawa, Hiroshi, *The Medieval Deccan: Peasants, Social Systems and States* (Delhi: Oxford University Press, 1991).

Guha, Sumit, "A Locus of Sociopolitical Organisation: The Household", in Sumit Guha, *Beyond Caste: Identity and Power in South Asia, Past and Present* (Leiden: Brill, 2013), pp. 117–42.

———, *History and Collective Memory in South Asia, 1200–2000* (Seattle: University of Washington Press, 2019).

Hasan, Farhat, "Property and Social Relations in Mughal India: Litigations and Disputes at the Qazi's Court in Urban Localities", *Journal of the Economic and Social History of the Orient*, vol. 61, nos 5–6, 2018, pp. 851–77.

Husain, M.K., "The Silver Larins", *Journal of the Numismatic Society of India*, vol. 29, pt 2, 1967, pp. 55–72.

Khare, G.H., "Some Records from a Deshpande Family of Wai", in *Proceedings of the Indian Historical Records Commission*, vol. 56, 1979, pp. 16–19.

Kulkarni, A.R., *Maharashtra in the Age of Shivaji* (Poona: Deshmukh and Co., 1969).

Moosvi, Shireen, "Reforming Revenue Administration: Aurangzeb's Farman to Rasikdas, 1665", in idem, *People, Taxation and Trade in Mughal India* (Delhi: Oxford University Press, 2008), pp. 175–86.

O'Hanlon, Rosalind, "Letters Home: Banaras Pandits and the Maratha Regions in Early Modern India", *Modern Asian Studies*, vol. 44, no. 2, 2010, pp. 201–40.

Pissurlenkar, S., *The Portuguese and the Marathas*, ed. and trans. R. Kakodkar (Bombay: Maharashtra State Board for Literature and Culture, 1975).

Rajwade, V.K., ed., *Marāṭhyānchyā Itihāsāchī Sādhane, Dvitīya Sammelan Vṛtta* (1914), pp. 52–67.

Sheikh, Samira, "Jibhabhu's Rights to Ghee: Land Control and Vernacular Capitalism in Gujarat, *c.* 1803–10", *Modern Asian Studies*, vol. 51, no. 2, 2017, pp. 350–74.

Sreenivasan, Ramya, "Drudges, Dancing Girls, Concubines: Female Slaves in Rajput Polity, 1500–1850", in Indrani Chatterjee and Richard M. Eaton, eds, *Slavery and South Asian History* (Bloomington and Indianapolis: Indiana University Press, 2006), pp. 137–61.

6

What Makes People Who They Are?

Pandit Networks and the Problem of Livelihoods in Early Modern Western India

Introduction: A Letter and Its History

IN APRIL 1664 a pandit recorded the proceedings of a remarkable gathering held in the Konkan town of Rajapur in western India.[1] Like many other Konkan ports, Rajapur was built at the head of one of the many rivers that flowed westwards, from the black volcanic mountains of the Sahyadri range, through steep forest-clad valleys and spurs into the Konkan littoral. Here, the rivers turned into broad tidal estuaries and creeks, which were often navigable twenty miles from the sea. Ports like Rajapur were naturally protected from coastal pirates, as well as from raids by the ships of the Siddi rulers of Janjira to the north, while mountain passes through the Sahyadris linked these towns to the interior of the Deccan. Nominally subject to the authority of the Bijapur state, Rajapur and other Konkan ports were important midway points for the coastal trade between western Gujarat and Malabar, and on the sea route from the Persian Gulf and Red Sea to South East Asia. Gujarati cottons, silk, and velvet from nearby Chaul and Thana, and blackwood, teak, and precious stones flowed out through the port; horses from the Red Sea and Persian Gulf ports constituted its main import, in great demand in the Deccan

[1] *Śyenavījātidharmanirṇaya*.

states of Ahmadnagar and Bijapur and their smaller local tributaries. Paramananda Kavindra, commissioned by Shivaji to create an epic from his exploits, described the great wealth and varied trade goods of Rajapur, "long guarded by various tightfisted foreigners . . . where the sea offers up the wealth of sea traders," of precious stones and precious metals, rhinoceros horns and elephant tusks, saffron and sandalwood, quicksilver, beeswax, and saltpetre.[2] Drawn by its importance as an entrepôt, the English East India Company had in 1638 established a large trading factory at Rajapur, as the Dutch had done at the same time at Vengurla in the South, despite the protests of the Portuguese governors of Goa to the Bijapur court. The gathering that the pandit described was an extraordinary one. In format, it was a dharmasabhā, a gathering of local religious experts and officeholders convened to decide a question of ritual rights.[3] That Rajapur was host to such a gathering was no surprise. In common with other towns in western India – Nasik, Wai, Paithan, Sangameshwar – Rajapur had a reputation for the learning of its Brahmans. Records suggest that the office of dharmādhikārī, the head of Rajapur's dharmasabhā, had existed already in 1191.[4]

But this gathering was no ordinary dharmasabhā. It was held at the behest of Shivaji, who had moved his forces into Bijapuri territory in the Konkan early in 1661. Representatives from some of the most distinguished intellectual families of contemporary Banaras had journeyed down to Rajapur especially for the occasion. Intellectuals of these families – Bhattas, Devas, Sesas, Diksitas – had established continent-wide reputations in the sixteenth and seventeenth centuries. Today those intellectuals are best remembered for their transformative work in a range of Sanskrit knowledge systems: from grammar and hermeneutics to the study of the subcontinent's changing social order and the questions of ritual and social entitlement to which those changes gave rise. Also represented at the Rajapur meeting were scholars and officeholders from the Brahman communities that flourished in the shrine towns of the region, and further afield along the Krishna and Godavari rivers. The sastri who presided at the meeting was Gaga-

[2] Laine and Bahulkar, *Epic of Shivaji*, pp. 364–6.

[3] Gune, *Judicial System*, pp. 34–5.

[4] Ibid., p. 110.

bhatta, famous for his role a decade later in consecrating Shivaji with all the rituals of universal dharmic kingship.[5]

The purpose of the assembly convened by Shivaji was to examine the standing of Shenvis, a sub-grouping of the powerful Saraswat Brahmans of Goa and of the Konkan littoral. Shenvis were a mobile and recently very successful people. Some were priests and recipients of pious religious gifts; some combined landholding with petty trade. Some used their scribal skills to work in local administration and revenue management, both for the Portuguese and within the petty states of the Konkan. Shenvis also had a reputation as tutors and educators. Pursuing different livelihoods, they nonetheless claimed to be Brahmans. From what was known of their history, their customary practices, and their mode of daily life, the assembly asked who in fact they were, and where they belonged in the social order. This was not the first time, nor indeed the last that the Shenvis' standing was to come under such scrutiny. Nor, as we shall see, were they the only marginal Brahman group whose history and mode of life raised disturbing questions for scholarly communities in the intellectual centres of western India, and in Banaras itself. In fact, socially heterogeneous Brahman communities raised fundamental issues for contemporary intellectuals, pandits, and social arbiters. What was it that made people who they were? Was it their history, their family, and lineage, their material livelihood, the patterns of their social relationships, or their modes of religious and ritual observance? And given these fluctuating and interrelated determinants, who, could it be agreed, was a Brahman in fact?

Social Orders and Social Change in Early Modern India

As scribal and service specialists, with allied interests in landholding and revenue management, the Konkan's Shenvis personify many of the distinctive skills and energies that we associate with the transformations of India's "early modernity".[6] Many historians have investigated the shared characteristics as well as the regional diversities

[5] Bendrey, *Coronation of Shivaji*; Vajpeyi, "Excavating Identity".

[6] For the "early modern" in India, see in particular Subrahmanyam, "Connected Histories".

of scribal specialists like the Shenvis. Amongst the common features that historians have observed are the mobility with which they offered their scribal and technical skills to regional states, and their engagement with new political ideologies and novel formulations of universal empire which became a prominent feature of political life in the period. Historians have also pointed to important parallels in the practical ability of regionally based service elites to combine forms of scribal power with commercial power, in their exploration of new languages of social classification and new definitions of property right, and in the leading role that they took in developing new literary genres and new modes for the exploration of historicity.[7]

By their nature, the changes that historians have examined in these social processes also had implications for the ways in which contemporaries themselves thought about the different "orders of people" who came within the boundaries of their experience, and the ways in which they tried to make sense of social change. The Konkan littoral was a particularly significant location for the early development of these changes. As the focus of intense political as well as commercial activity from the early sixteenth through the early eighteenth centuries, its societies appear to have been particularly open and fluid, and to have offered many outlets for the skilled and enterprising. Unlike Maharashtra's Deccan uplands, moreover, with their large and relatively homogeneous community of Deshastha or "country" Brahmans, the Konkan was home to many small and competing communities of Brahmans, acutely conscious of their relative standing and prestige. Some of these communities are familiar in later histories: Saraswats, Chitpavans, Devarukhes, and Karhades. Others are less familiar: Javals, Palshes, Padyas, and Kramavants. The presence of so many small Brahman communities, often pursuing diverse livelihoods like the Saraswats, raised the question of who could be considered a Brahman, and what kind of a Brahman, in a particularly acute way.

[7] For the histories of some service groups in this period, see in particular, Alam and Subrahmanyam, "The Making of a Munshi"; Subrahmanyam, "State Formation"; Alam, "Culture and Politics"; Kruijtzer, "Madanna"; Chatterjee, "History as Self-representation"; Guha, "Speaking Historically"; Bayly, *Caste, Society and Politics*, pp. 64–96; Bayly, *Rulers, Townsmen and Bazaars*.

In the process, much wider questions about social being and social identity pressed themselves forward for discussion. Nor were the discussions focused only on Brahmans. The same circles of intellectuals engaged in the interrogation of Kshatriya and Sudra identity, asking whether "real" Kshatriyas could still be recognised in the fallen age of the Kaliyuga, and what it meant to be a Sudra in a more socially mobile world.

At one level, contemporary discussion of these matters was set within long-established parameters of Hindu judicial discourse. Here, both āchāra (inherited and customary) practice, and sastric textual models, determined the dharma of a person or group. The two determinants were understood to be mutually constitutive: the āchāra of good people was in conformity with their dharma as set out in the sastras, while the sastras affirmed that āchāra defined in this way was a prime source for knowing a person's dharma. At the same time, there was inevitably tension between the two, and plenty of room for argument within particular historical settings.[8]

It was within this framework that the Brahmans of the Konkan and Banaras pursued their questions about the nature of social order in the fluid setting of the Konkan, and sought to determine the place of socially mobile or marginal peoples who claimed to be Brahmans within it. At the heart of the discussion was the question of entitlement to a particular and well-defined way of being in the world. Entitlement here lay not only in being considered a Brahman, but also being able to act and to be treated as one. Recognition of this affective way of being depended in turn on a person's meeting a wider raft of conditions: history, lineage, reputation, existing patterns of social relationships and known customary practices, as well as present mode of life. Being a Brahman was also, of course, a matter of bodily substance, and the effects upon it of action in the world.[9]

As Brahman intellectuals of the period deliberated the problem, they added further specifications to what it was that constituted a

[8] For recent discussions of the sources of dharma, see the special issue of the *Journal of Indian Philosophy*, vol. 32, 2004, especially Lariviere, "Dharmaśāstra". See also Davis, "A Realist View of Hindu Law"; Pollock, "The Idea of Śāstra".

[9] For an introduction to the large body of anthropological work on this question, see Bayly, *Caste, Society and Politics*, pp. 1–24.

Brahman, specifications that were very much a reflection of contemporary pressures and circumstances. The difference between Brahmans and others was also the difference between the crude rustic and the refined in culture and deportment, between those who toiled and those whose livelihoods preserved their bodily dignity, between those who had to use their women as economic assets and those whose women were ornaments to their families. As we shall see, such specifications were not developed in formal compendia of dharmasastra alone, but were the subject of intense discussion and scrutiny in other narrative and historical genres, whose illustrative stories circulated among Maharashtrian Brahman communities from the Konkan to Banaras. The stories in turn fed into and provided material for judicial assemblies of the period. The pressures of inter-Brahman competition that the stories reflected seem to have stimulated a more rapid production and circulation of judicial decisions about the relative standing of Brahmans, as well as the development of novel judicial forms. Together, the formal and informal processes began to offer new means by which the Brahman communities of the Konkan could mark out their boundaries and define themselves in relation to others. The reinforced sense of Brahman community history and identity was in turn to open up the sphere of private and domestic life for new forms of scrutiny in this period.

In this essay we explore some of these discussions about Brahmanhood, and some of the institutions and arenas through which they were conducted, for which the networks that linked Banaras with western India and the Konkan littoral were critical. Many of the scholarly families who came to dominate the intellectual life of the city by the middle of the seventeenth century had migrated there from the Marathi-speaking regions over the course of the previous century.[10] The city emerged as a booming intellectual centre, as regionally based royal patrons under the umbrella of Mughal political authority, pious commercial supporters, students seeking instruction, and the pilgrim trade all offered opportunities for the support of scholarly enterprises of different kinds.[11] Leading members of the families based in Banaras also acted as intermediaries in wider arenas of political negotia-

[10] Shastri, "Dakshini Pandits".

[11] Altekar, *History of Banaras*, pp. 31–58.

tion and intellectual exchange. They interceded between the Mughal court and wider constituencies of the Hindu pious, commented on contemporary shifts in religious practice, debated with scholars from other traditions, and advised royal patrons on their responsibilities, most famously, of course in the case of Shivaji and his Banaras-based learned adviser Gagabhatta.[12] The engagements of Banarsi sastris with local affairs in the Konkan may thus illuminate some of the practical settings in which those intellectuals explored the issues of entitlement, belonging, and social order in their works of social theory, and in legal and ritual practice. These debates were, furthermore, a significant intellectual dimension of wider processes of social formation. Within the Konkan, as we shall argue, specifications about what made a Brahman revealed the concerns of the slowly coalescing administrative–political elite that was to emerge from the early eighteenth century to shape the Maratha state, peopling its bureaucratic systems and developing its fiscal institutions. Being able to gain recognition as, and to behave as, a Brahman in these settings was a decisive advantage. It was important for the local hereditary offices and control over revenue that scribal skills could bring, and for access to pious gifts and rights to substantial hereditary lands and livings. Moreover, the requirement for certain kinds of dignity in personal comportment, livelihood, and family conduct, and concord in the conduct of social relations, helped to secure the authority that Brahman men of business were coming to enjoy in the wider world of diplomacy and alliance building. The same qualities also established social distance from lesser and plebeian people, and particularly from competitor scribal communities who were not Brahmans. The Brahman communities of the Konkan carried their skills and advantages with them as they moved into the service of the Maratha state.

History and Community in Parashuram's Country

One text through which Brahman communities reflected on questions of history and identity was the *Sahyādrikhaṇḍa*, whose narratives describe the formation and peopling of the Konkan by the legendary

[12] The intellectual output in Sanskrit of these families, and their own sense that some aspects of their work involved innovation, has attracted much attention.

sage Parashuram.[13] The *Sahyādrikhaṇḍa* is attributed to the *Skandapurāṇa*, one of the eighteen "great" Purāṇas. It comprises a heterogeneous collection of texts, probably written over a very long period, and by many different authors.[14]

The second part (Uttarārdha) of the *Sahyādrikhaṇḍa* offers narrative histories of social formation in the Konkan at two different levels. Its first chapter sets out an all-India classification of Brahmans that is known from earlier sources. It divides them into the pañca gauḍa (five groups of northern Brahmans) – Saraswat, Kanyakubja, Maithila, Gauda, and Utkala; and the pañca drāviḍa (five groups of southern Brahmans) – Gurjara, Maharashtra, Andhra, Karnataka, and Dravida.[15] The later chapters then recount local narratives about the god Parashuram's peopling of the Konkan with its many Brahman communities.[16]

The heroes of the *Sahyādrikhaṇḍa* are very much the Saraswats. The text says that they came from Tirhut in north-eastern India, and so belonged to the five groups of northern Brahmans. They are represented as the best and most virtuous of all of the Brahman communities

---

See Deshpande, "Bhaṭṭoji Dīkṣita's Perceptions"; Bronkhorst, "Bhaṭṭoji Dīkṣita"; Pollock, "New Intellectuals". For the Bhatta family, see Benson, "Śaṃkarabhaṭṭa's Family Chronicle".

[13] The only standard edition is da Cunha, *The Sahyâdri-Khaṇḍa of the Skaṇḍa Purâṇa*. The contentious nature of this Purāṇa's stories of Brahman origin have made the creation of an authoritative edition particularly difficult. As Deshpande points out, the late-nineteenth-century edition of da Cunha was itself a selection from available MSS, and a more recent Maraṭhi translation – Gaitonde, *Sahyādrikhaṇḍa, Skandapurāṇa* – omits some "offensive" passages. Deshpande, "Pañca Gauḍa". References hereafter are to da Cunha's edition.

[14] Deshpande, "Pañca Gauḍa"; and Levitt, "The Sahyādrikhaṇḍa: Some Problems"; and Levitt, "Sahyādrikhaṇḍa: Style and Content".

[15] *Sahyādrikhaṇḍa*, Uttarārdha, Adhyāya 1, "Origins of the Chitpavans", vss 1–20. Quotations here are from da Cunha's edition.

[16] The story goes that after the murder of his father by members of the Haihaya clan, Parashuram slaughtered all India's Kshatriya class of kings and warriors. He expiated his sin by giving the whole of the earth to Brahman sages. Left without anywhere to live himself, he persuaded the sea to give up the lands of the Konkan to him, and peopled this new land with Brahmans to perform the Vedic rites for him.

brought to the Konkan by Parashuram. Many still identifiable villages of the region are named in the account of Parashuram's settling of the Saraswat arrivals. He settled the first and most virtuous in the villages of Kelosi and Kushasthal, the latter the site of one of the four great Saraswat maṭhas (monastic centres) of southern India.[17] The Saraswats were thus the elite of Brahmans in the region, "honoured by the king, attractive, well-behaved, skilled in every rite."[18] These first Saraswats belonged to ten gotras – exogamous family groupings based on descent from a common ancestor – and sixty-six families. The remaining seven gotras and thirty-six families were settled in other identifiable villages of the region: Mathagrama, Varenya, Lotali, Chudamani, Dipavati, and others.[19] The *Sahyādrikhaṇḍa* also describes the gods that Parashuram brought to the region, and whose temples formed part of the landscape of sixteenth-century Goa: Shantadurga, whose temple lay in the village of Kelosi; Mangesha, whose temple lay in Kushasthal; Mhalsa, in Varenya; Nagesha and Mahalaksmi at Bandora.[20] The *Sahyādrikhaṇḍa* also alludes to a pecularity of the Saraswats' diet: "In the Konkan, there are auspicious Brahmans, expert in the Veda, and there are Saraswats, who are reputed to eat fish."[21]

The accounts of Parashuram's creation of other Konkani Brahman communities were much less flattering. He created Chitpavans from low-caste hunters whom he met near a cremation ground on the seashore. He purified them in the pyre (citā) and made them Brahmans, but because of their later sinfulness then cursed them to become the

[17] For a history of this maṭh, see Sarma, *Sārasvata Bhūṣaṇa*, pp. 188–91. The name of the town is given variously as Kushasthala and Kushasthali in the Sanskrit and Maraṭhi sources. In what follows we shall refer to the town as Kushasthal, to distinguish it from another Kushasthali, located in Saurashtra.

[18] *Sahyādrikhaṇḍa*, Uttarārdha, Adhyāya 4, vs. 6.

[19] Ibid., Uttarārdha, Adhyāya 3, "Māhātmya of Goa", vss 16–19; and Adhyāya 4, "Origins of Diverse Brahmans" vss 4–11.

[20] Histories of these temples are given in Sarma, *Sārasvata Bhūṣaṇa*, pp. 96–127. In many cases, the site of these temples shifted following their mid-sixteenth-century destruction by the Portuguese. See Axelrod and Fuerch, "Flight of the Deities"; and Seldekar, *Śrīśāntādurgā*, pp. 40–3.

[21] *Sahyādrikhaṇḍa*, Uttarārdha, Adhyāya 5, "Consideration of Brahmans", vss 13–16.

despised and poor servants of others.[22] Karhades were Brahmans from "Badland" (kārāṣṭra), created from male semen spilled over a heap of the bones of asses (khara). They lost caste for the crime of killing a Brahman, and thereafter made a pact with the goddess Matrika to gain perfection in return for offering a Brahman in sacrifice to her every year.[23] Padya Brahmans were so wicked that they were unfit to study the Vedas, and any ritual in their vicinity was bound to fail.[24]

The *Sahyādrikhaṇḍa* posited a flow of powers, energies, and qualities between peoples and the lands they lived on.[25] Karashtra, between the Vedavati and Koyna rivers, where the Karhade Brahmans lived, was famous as a wicked land, its peoples hard and evil and such poison in its very air as to cause a Brahman's essential virtues to dissipate. Sages and Brahmans expert in the Vedas dwelt in the adjacent land of Karvira. This land was therefore so auspicious that just to see it was to be freed from sin, and its water had powers that could purify even someone who had killed a Brahman.[26] Particularly virtuous was the land of Gomanchala or Goa, its villages peopled by the great Saraswat sages brought there by Parashuram. Powerful gods dwelt there who gave worshippers what they sought and took away obstacles.[27] The very best lands, where the most virtuous Brahmans dwelt, lay in the madhyadeśa, the land between the Narmada and Krishna rivers on the western Deccan plateau.[28]

Success and Its Perils in the Konkan Littoral

The Shenvis were a sub-group of the Saraswat Brahmans of Goa. In the sixteenth and seventeenth centuries, they became a ubiquitous and

[22] Ibid., Adhyāya 1, "Origins of the Chitpavans", vss 39–45.

[23] Ibid., Adhyāya 2, "Origins of the Kārāṣṭras", vss 1–8.

[24] Ibid., vss 18–20.

[25] Humoural understandings of the body and related terrains are discussed in Bayly, *Origins of Indian Nationality*, pp. 13–17.

[26] *Sahyādrikhaṇḍa*, Uttarārdha, Adhyāya 2, "Origins of the Kārāṣṭras", vss 25–32.

[27] Ibid., Adhyāya 4, "Origins of Diverse Brahmans", vss 4–11.

[28] Ibid., Adhyāya 2, pp. 22–4. For discussion of Maharashtra as a landscape charged with qualities, see Feldhaus, "Maharashtra as a Holy Land"; and idem, *Connected Places*.

expansive group in the Konkan.[29] As suggested in the narratives of the *Sahyādrikhaṇḍa*, the most prestigious Saraswat lineages were associated with particular Goan villages, which were the location of lineage deities (kuladevatā). Saraswats had a long tradition of devotion to smārta (Shaivite) masters, who traced their spiritual descent from Gaudapada, held by tradition to have been the guru of Shankaracharya. The ancient maṭha in the village of Kushasthal was a Gaudapada maṭha. At some point before 1500, many families moved their affiliation to the Vaishnava teachings of the religious leader Madhva. For smārtas, the maṭhas in Kushasthal in Goa and Chitrapur in northern Kanara were the most important. The most significant maṭhas for Vaishnavas were at Gokarna in northern Kanara, and Kashimath at Cochin. The heads of the maṭhas were sanyasis, Brahmans who had moved to the fourth, or ascetic stage of life.[30]

Saraswat sectarian affiliation overlapped with patterns of village settlement. Shenvis were smārta Brahmans from the elite Konkani villages of Kushasthal and Keloshi. The term itself is of very long standing: a stone inscription of 1413 in the Goa village of Bandora refers to the gift given to local Brahmans by someone called Mai Shenai for the maintenance of the Saraswat temple of Nagesha in the village.[31] Shenvis were unusual, however, in that their designation did not derive from a place name.[32] Other Saraswat communities did have designations that derived from particular villages in the Konkan: Kudal, Lotali, Bhavale, Sashti, Bardesh, Pedne.[33] Medieval inscriptional evidence shows Brahmans bearing family names from Goa scattered through the Konkan as recipients of religious endowments from pious donors.[34] When the Portuguese consolidated their power in the region

[29] For their early histories, see in particular Sarma, *Sārasvata Bhūṣaṇa*, pp. 62–70; Wagle, "History and Social Organisation", pp. 307–11. For a history of Chitrapur Saraswats, see Conlon, *A Caste in a Changing World.*

[30] Gunjikar, *Sarasvatīmaṇḍal*, pp. 20–4.

[31] See, for example, Valavlikar, "An Eye Copy", pp. 107–8. "Shenai" is a variant spelling of "shenvi".

[32] Later community historians favour the theory that the term originated as a (Persian) honorific title meaning clever or learned (śahāṇā) and was a reference to Shenvis' clerical and scholarly pursuits. Sarma, *Sārasvata Bhūṣaṇa*, pp. 70–1, and Gode, "Antiquity of the Caste Name 'Śenavı'".

[33] Wagle, "History and Social Organisation", pp. 19–20.

[34] Saldanha, "Savantvadi Castes", pp. 500–2.

after 1510, they found Shenvis well established in Goa as holders of superior landed rights of the kind associated with "original" settlement of a village.[35] As such, they enjoyed rights of first worship at temples housing their lineage deities, and control over substantial temple lands. Saraswats were also active as chiefs and administrators in the petty states of the southern Konkan. The Desais of Kudal were of the Kudaldeshkar sub-group of Saraswats.[36] The Desais of Bicholim were Shenvis.[37]

Since they had important temple rights, Shenvis were naturally prominent leaders in the resistance to Portuguese Christianisation. In 1545 Miguel Vaz, Vicar General of the Indies, reported that "a caste of people who call themselves Synaes Brahmans" were leaders of resistance to conversion, and urged that the worst offenders be banished.[38] Many Saraswats left Goa, often carrying their lineage deities with them, and established Saraswat settlements and temples all around the fringes of Portuguese-ruled territories.[39] There was major upheaval after 1564, when the maṭha at Kushasthal was destroyed by the Portuguese. Subsequent heads of the maṭha moved to a new centre in Ratnagiri. In about 1600, the sixty-first guru in the maṭha's succession, Sadananda Sarasvati, moved to Banaras, believing a return to Goa impossible in the near future.[40] Portuguese observers noted the widespread dispersal of Shenvis throughout the Konkan, and that they worked as accomplished scribal specialists and administrators. In 1566, Father Francisco de Souza observed in his *Oriente Conquistado* that "all the Brahmans are known as Xenens which means masters.

[35] Most landed rights in the Maratha regions in this period arose out of local colonisation. Such rights might range from those of a small village headman, to those of elite officers with wider regional responsibilities. See Gordon, *Marathas*, pp. 22–30.

[36] Ajgaonkar, *Kuḍāldedeśkar Samagra Itihās*, pp. 60–8. The Desai was a hereditary state office, responsible for looking after defence, security, and justice in his region.

[37] Sarkar, *Shivaji and His Times*, p. 230.

[38] Wicki, *Documenta Indica*, vol. 1, p. 67.

[39] Wagle, "History and Social Organisation", p. 309; Axelrod and Fuerch, "Flight of the Deities".

[40] Sarma, *Sārasvata Bhūṣaṇa*, p. 187.

In all the lands of Concao, they are the ones who teach the Brahman youths to read, write and count."[41]

Many, though, stayed in Goa and flourished. Following pleas from community members back in the Konkan, the sixty-second guru, Bhavananda Sarasvati, in 1631 adopted a disciple, Sacchidananda Sarasvati, and sent him back to Goa to revive the maṭha. The new maṭha was located at Kavale near Kushasthal, and became once again the focus for smārta worship.[42] In Goa too, with their control over land, capital and local community institutions, Saraswats were well placed to bid for the tax farm concessions – renda – that the Portuguese inherited from the Adil Shahi government. A Shenvi referred to by the Portuguese as Damu Sinay was among the largest investors in the farming of state revenues, having bought the right to collect revenue on cloth.[43] M.N. Pearson has calculated that Shenvis held 44.9 per cent of the total value of all of the renda during the period 1600–1670.[44] Others prospered in other ways. Krishna Shenai served as renter of the customs office, captain of the Indian troops employed by the governors of Goa, and broker for the horse trade. He sailed to Lisbon, where he was presented to the royal family, and knighted on his return to Goa in 1537.[45]

The coming of the Marathas into the Konkan opened up still wider opportunities. Shenvis held all of the higher administrative posts within the Savantwadi state.[46] Pitambar Shenvi was karbhāri (steward) to Lakham Savant, chief of the Savantwadi state, and the envoy that he sent to negotiate with Shivaji during the early 1660s.[47] By 1677, Pitambar was acting as Shivaji's envoy to the Portuguese over the question of Shivaji's demands for levies from recently captured lands.[48] The contemporary Maratha historian Sabhasad referred to Pitambar as a

[41] De Souza, *Oriente Conquistado*, vol. 2, pp. 20–1.

[42] Sarma, *Sārasvata Bhūṣaṇa*, pp. 186–90.

[43] de Souza, *Medieval Goa*, p. 116.

[44] Pearson, *Coastal Western India*, pp. 93–115.

[45] Keni, *Saraswats in Goa*, pp. 52–3; Danvers, *The Portuguese in India*, vol. 1, p. 366.

[46] Saldanha, "Savantvadi Castes", 501.

[47] Khobrekar, *Konkan*, 64.

[48] Khakodkar, *The Portuguese and the Marathas*, pp. 44–7

matsyāhārī brāhmaṇa – a "fish-eating Brahman".[49] Other Saraswats were employed as intermediaries between the Portuguese, the Bijapur state, and the Marathas. Ramoji Shenai Kothari, a Saraswat from Dicholi in Goa, was a much-valued agent of the Portuguese, sent as Portuguese emissary to the Bijapur court in 1659. In 1661, the Portuguese deputed him to negotiate with Lakham Savant, then chafing at his enforced treaty with Shivaji, and he mediated throughout the 1660s between Shivaji and the Portuguese.[50] Shenvis also served the East India Company from an early date. A Narayan Shenvi acted as the East India Company's envoy to Shivaji's court and witnessed his consecration in 1674.[51]

In asking their questions about the Shenvis, therefore, the assembly at Rajapur were not asking about an unknown community. Their questions were rather about where these familiar and recently very successful people, who seemed to move so easily across arenas and livelihoods in the competitive society of the Konkan, actually belonged in the social order. Given the diversity of the Shenvis' roles and livelihoods, we can perhaps understand why other Konkani Brahmans pressed this question. Some Shenvis were priests and recipients of pious donations, while the great majority of Shenvis were scribes, traders, and farmers. Were they, as they claimed, really Brahmans? This was an important question for everyone. It was vital for the Shenvis themselves. Quite apart from questions of authority in their core areas of worship, priestly office, and landed rights, it was vital for their roles as prestigious administrators and envoys. For their fellow Brahmans in the Konkan, the Shenvis' success in so many fields naturally raised competitive resentments, particularly in view of the recent expansion of their numbers in the region.

Two Assemblies: Banaras and Rajapur

The Shenvis' standing had come up some thirty years earlier, in 1631. The occasion was the revival of the Kushasthal maṭha described above. Vitthal, a Shenvi and a resident of Kushasthal, had journeyed

[49] Sen, *Siva Chhatrapati*, p. 96.

[50] Keni, *Sarasvats in Goa*, pp. 52–3; Khakodkar, *The Portuguese and the Marathas*, pp. 8–9.

[51] Bendrey, *Coronation of Shivaji*, pp. 30–1.

up to Banaras to ask for the support of its learned community, whose numbers at that time included Bhavananda Sarasvati, sixty-second guru of the maṭha. Vitthal wanted to be allowed to assume the status of sanyasi (renouncer). That would then entitle him to assume headship of the new maṭha. An assembly of the learned in Banaras met to discuss the question, and issued a sammatipatra ("letter of agreement"), with the signatures of pandits attached to confirm their assent to the judgment it contained.[52] The letter emphasised the assembly's broad representation of different Brahman communities. It was addressed to the Brahmans of the Sahyadri region, who were described in terms of the traditional division of Brahmans into northern and southern groups.

> All of the educated pañca drāviḍas who live in the city of Visvesvara, including the Dravidas, Andhras, Karnatakas, Maharashtras and Gurjaras who come from the seven cities, send greetings to the pañca drāviḍas and pañca gauḍas who live in the region of the Sahyadri mountains of the Deccan. Recently there came to Banaras on pilgrimage a certain Vitthal, son of Shyamraj, from Kushasthal. He made a plea to our whole community that he should be allowed to enter the fourth stage of life.

The learned members of the Dravida community in Banaras had gathered in the Mukti mandapam or "Mukti pavilion" of Banaras' principal temple to Shiva in his form as Visveswara, the Lord of All, and had conducted a thorough investigation. They decided that Vitthal, though a resident of Kushasthal, as a Saraswat Brahman belonged to the five classes of northern Brahmans. However, the assembly evidently found it difficult to grant Vitthal's request without considering the qualifications of the wider Brahman community to which he belonged. There was a sticking point here, the point often mentioned when the status of Saraswats was raised. It was that Saraswats customarily ate fish. However, the assembly did not find this to be an insuperable bar. Those pañca gauḍas in the Konkan who did eat fish were protected by the prescriptions of Parashuram, who had allowed all those who settled in the Konkan to follow their long-established customs. The sastris thus determined that Saraswats were fully Brahmans,

[52] This letter of 1631 is reprinted in Gunjikar, *Sarasvatīmaṇḍal*, Appendix 2, pp. 22–4. See Gune, *Judicial System*, pp. xxii–xxviii, for a classification of judicial documents of this period.

and thereby entitled to all of the sixteen principal saṃskāras (purifying life cycle rituals).

The path was thereby cleared for Vitthal to assume the headship of the maṭh, under the new name of Sacchidanda Sarasvati, his initiatory gurus being the previous head of the maṭha, Bhavananda Sarasvati, and Lakshman of the Bhatta family of Banaras. The assembly instructed him: "Go back now to your own country and, taking up lordship of the maṭha with its carriage, fly whisk, umbrella, and lineage of followers, give out proper guidance, teaching, initiation and so on to members of your own caste." A long list of names was appended to the judgment. These included Bhavananda Sarasvati himself and representatives from the Sesa, Diksita, and Dharmadhikari families. It also included Kamalakarabhatta, uncle of Gagabhatta and an unusually distinguished member of the Banarsi Bhatta family, widely known and read for his broad interests in contemporary societal changes and the challenges these presented to older understandings of the social order. His encyclopaedic *Nirṇayasindhuḥ*, for example, reported details of novel ritual practices that had recently become popular, and offered grounds for disagreement with his grandfather Narayanabhatta on the rights of Sudras to install certain images of deities.[53] His *Śūdrakamalākaraḥ* took up broader questions of the varna order, setting out the ritual rights of Sudras, and suggesting the possible continuing existence of intermediate orders of Kshatriyas and Vaishyas.[54]

Despite this ruling, the Shenvis' standing as Brahmans evidently remained contentious, emerging again some thirty years later at Rajapur. The assembly of 1664, and the nirṇayapatra (letter of decision) pro moted by Gagabhatta, were different. That assembly took place in a Konkan now substantially under the control of Shivaji's emerging Maratha state. For the first time, Banaras came, as it were, to the Maratha country, and in part at the behest of Shivaji himself.

Gagabhatta's letter opened with effusive greetings to the learned Karhade and other Brahman communities of the Konkan. He described the events that led to his writing the letter.

[53] Kane, *History of Dharmaśāstra*, vol. 1, pt 2, p. 935.

[54] Ibid., pp. 930–1. Kamalakarabhatta, *Śūdrakamalākaraḥ*, and idem, *Nirṇayasindhuḥ*.

> You sent me a delegation with a letter of explanation (udantapatra), and made the following representation to me. "Long ago a few people known as 'śeṇavīs', who are designated as Konkaṇas, came here due to the turbulence of the times in (their own) lands and are now residents of Rajapur and Pattana. Some people here have been making vehement objections about them to us, since they are now found here in large numbers. What in fact is their dharma? What is the proper customary mode of life (āchāra) that has come down for them from the past? If you were to write that out and send it to us, then we would be able to guide them along their proper path." The answer that I give to you is as follows.[55]

There followed a praśasti (praise poem) to Shivaji, lauding him as a royal ruler of unparalleled generosity, bravery, and nobility of spirit. Other developments at his court had prompted Shivaji himself to ask the same question about the Shenvis.

> Now on one occasion, while King Shivaji was governing his kingdom, and maintaining it, in its deeds, words and procreation, in the dharma and livelihoods that belong to those of the proper varnas and stages of life, and those also of uncertain origins, he was touring the districts under his control out of a desire to see them. There he saw the Shenvis who live in the Sahyadri and who dress like Brahmans, but make a living from the fields. Bringing various gifts with them, they had assembled with a desire to see the king. Accepting their gifts, he asked the pandits of his court, as well as the dharmādhikārīs of that region, "What is the dharma of these Shenvis, and what is their inherited customary mode of life?"[56]

[55] *Śyenavījātidharmanirṇaya*, 294. This text was preserved in a manuscript kept in the Rajapur Sanskrit Pathashala. The text was reproduced by Rajwade as "Śivakālīn śāśtrī va Paṇdit", in *Bhārata Itihāsa Saṃśodhaka Maṇḍala Vārṣika Itivṛtta*. The colophon of the manuscript gives a date of copying in 1895 and states that it was deposited in the school about a dozen years later. The colophon mentions an exemplar manuscript in the same collection. An earlier closing sentence in the manuscript refers to a scribe of an earlier form of the document called Gopala Gurjara, son of Yajneshvara, and no doubt a descendant of the dharmādhikārīs of Rajapur who are mentioned in the document. It seems likely that it was Gopala who inserted the definition of dharmādhikārīs given in the published text on p. 295, lines 17–28. The text is attributed to Gagabhatta in a number of places, and he is represented as speaking the content of the judgment, but the exact relationship of the extant text as recorded in the manuscript and the original letter dictated by Gagabhatta requires further source material to establish precisely.

[56] Ibid., p. 295.

This, then, was what was at issue with the Shenvis: they appeared to be Brahmans but also made a living as farmers.

The next section of the letter listed the learned Brahmans present at the assembly. This was a stellar gathering that represented most of the families responsible for the intellectual flowering of Banaras over the previous century. Leading the gathering was Gagabhatta himself. Next in the list was Sitikantha Diksita, who may have been a member of the family of the renowned grammarian Bhattoji Diksita (*fl. c.* 1575–1645).[57] Raghunatha Pandita was listed next. He was to go on to become Shivaji's official court pandit. The title of "Panditrao" was conferred on him when he was sent in 1665 to negotiate the treaty of Purandhar with Jaisingh.[58] Then came Shivaji's court poet, Paramananda Kavindra, a close friend of Gagabhatta, who was later commissioned to write an epic poem about Shivaji.[59] Prabhakara Upadhyaya followed in the list. Priest to Shivaji's family in the middle years of the seventeenth century, his adopted son, Balambhatta, was present at Shivaji's consecration in 1674.[60] The "Ananta upādhyāya" listed next was almost certainly Ananta Deva, a member of the prominent Banarasi Deva family of sastris, who were descendants of the seventeenth-century poet Eknath.[61] Mahadeva Sesa represented the Sesa family of grammarians and poets.[62] Next on the list were "the many bright men whose homes are on the Krishna and Godavari rivers, and who were resident in that region."[63] There were members of the Gurjara family, who were the dharmādhikārīs of Rajapur. Also represented was the Purohita family, priests and astrologers to the local raja of Shringarpur, and the Golavalikara Padhye family, who held the office of purohita or family priest to the Brahman communities in that king's domains.

[57] Kane, *History of Dharmaśāstra*, vol. 1, pt 2, p. 966.

[58] Bendrey, *Daṇḍanītiprakaraṇam*, pp. 70–6; and Sen, *Siva Chhatrapati*, pp. 50–1.

[59] Sardesai, *Paramānandakāvya*, p. 49.

[60] Rajopadhyaya, "Śrīśivājī Mahārājanche Kulopadhāyāy", pp. 65–73.

[61] Kane, *History of Dharmaśāstra*, vol. 1, pt 2, pp. 953–63.

[62] Ibid., p. 967. For the Sesa family, see also Aryavaraguru, "On the Sheshas of Benaras".

[63] *Śyenavījātidharmanirṇaya*, p. 295.

Gagabhatta then turned to describe the authoritative texts and commentaries on dharmasastra that had been consulted by the assembly. Prominent among these, and almost certainly the principal sources consulted, were works written either by the sastris present at the meeting, or by earlier members of their Banaras-based families: the *Smrtikaustubha*, the great digest of dharmasastra compiled by Ananta Deva; the *Dinakarodyota*, a compendious work on dharma begun by Gagabhatta's father Dinakara, and completed by Gagabhatta himself; the *Bhagavantabhāskara*, another voluminous and frequently cited treatise by Dinakarabhatta's first cousin, Nilakantha; and the *Govindārṇava*, a compendium of the fifteenth century that was composed by Nrsimha Sesa, who was probably Mahadeva Sesa's ancestor.[64] Having considered the decisions presented in all of these works, Gagabhatta led the assembly in coming to its conclusion, had it written out, and communicated it to the king.[65]

At the heart of these conclusions was the standing of mobile and heterogeneous peoples like the Shenvis. The assembly focused in particular on conditions of emergency, such as famine, when people moved and changed their livelihoods and modes of life. This was central for the Shenvis, as people who had in their history a story of survival during famine. The assembly examined the question of farming and forms of petty trade associated with it. It referred to the Manusmṛti X.92–3 to show the consequences of a Brahman selling agricultural commodities. "He instantly falls (from caste status) if he sells meat, lac, or salt. A Brahman falls to being a Sudra in three days, if he sells milk. But if he sells other, auspicious things, as he wishes, a Brahmin becomes a Vaishya in seven nights." Agricultural operations carried their own implications. The assembly noted among other authorities the words of Parashara:

[64] For the authoritative status of Nilakantha's and other works by the Bhatta family, see Nilakanthabhatta, *Vyavahāra Mayūkha*, pp. v-xxiv, and idem, *History of Dharmaśāstra*, vol. I.2, pp. 937–41. Other works listed by Gagabhatta include older compendia such as Hemadri's *Chaturvargacintāmaṇi*, the *Madanaparijāta* of Visvesvara, the *Smṛticandrikā* of Devanna, and the *Kṛtyakalpataru* of Lakshmidhara. The list also includes all of the canonical smṛti texts, as well as the Purāṇas, and divinatory Saṃhitās.

[65] *Śyenavījātidharmanirṇaya*, pp. 295–6.

> A Brahman who continues to maintain his own dharma, but who wishes to engage in agriculture should, after bathing and doing his morning fire offerings, yoke an able-bodied bull to the plough and after driving (him) for (no more than) half a day, he should bathe the creature. Having split the earth or cut a tree, and thereby having killed worms and insects, the cultivator frees himself from those all those sins by a rite of the threshing floor (khalayajña). When he (the Brahman) has done the ploughing himself, he should offer the five sacrifices with the grain that he has himself harvested, and he should do the dikṣā of other rites.[66]

Harm to draft animals was also a matter for concern. "The controlling and driving of youngling (cattle) is not praised, nor of old ones or weak ones, as the words of Prajapati make clear. 'He should not do violence to the tail of the beasts of burden. He should not put an old one to the yoke, or a worn out one or a diseased one.'" Further authorities were examined that declared the ploughing work of a farmer to be "a form of violence, and dependent on others." The assembly concluded from their examination of sources that the recourse to farming was permissible, but only for a specified period. A Brahman might turn to farming for his livelihood during a period of crisis: but his descendants had then to return to a livelihood fitting for a Brahman within seven generations of the ending of the time of crisis.[67]

There followed a lengthy history of the Shenvis. Gagabhatta did not invoke the histories of the *Sahyādrikhaṇḍa*, perhaps because so many of them favoured the Saraswats so strongly. He referred rather to a tale told by the sage Narada to Ketumali, and attributed to the canonical purāṇic text, the *Padmapurāṇa*.[68] Narada described a period of ancient disorder and famine in the world, arising out of the greed and folly of kings. Many Brahmans perished; many migrated to different places; and all who survived resorted to desperate measures to survive. Some protected their Brahman dharma by limiting themselves to plants or dairy products, grasses, or grain. Others, including the Shenvis,

[66] *Parāśarasmṛti*, vol.2, pp. 4, 6, 10–1.

[67] Ibid., p. 298.

[68] Ibid., pp. 299–300. Note that the passage cited does not appear in the published versions of the (Western recension) of the *Padmapurāṇa*. Like the *Skandapurāṇa*, to which the *Sahyādrikhaṇḍa* is attributed, the *Padmapurāṇa* has a loose structure, and many independently circulating works attribute themselves to it.

resorted to fish, sea creatures, deer, falcons (śyena) and other birds (vī), "and by wild and domestic creatures of different sorts such as wild-cocks, they fostered their own way but abandoned their Brahmanical mode of life."[69] The Shenvis then continued to live as farmers and commercial people long after plenty had returned. Consequently, their status had changed. Since their āchāra or inherited and customary mode of life had been agricultural, they should adopt the rituals appropriate for the third varna, that is, of Vaishyas.[70]

For the Rajapur assembly, then, the issue was not that Shenvis ate fish, but rather the fact that some of them earned their livings as agriculturalists, and had done so over many generations. As presented through the assembly's discussions, the virtues and qualities of a Brahman were particularly mutable and vulnerable in relation to farming. Different agricultural operations and the forms of petty trade that went with them could erode the quality of Brahmanhood, at different speeds. Though not as bad as trade, the cruder operations of agriculture and its associated activities – close and gross contact with animals, pushing a plough through the earth, cutting down trees – jeopardised their Brahmanical status. Perhaps more exposed to the immediacy of local agitation about the status of the Shenvis, the Banaras delegation was now significantly less generous than their predecessors had been, when they considered the status of Saraswats back in Banaras in 1631.

We have no record of a Shenvi response to this decision, but it is hard to see that they could have viewed this judgment as anything other than a slight. It may be significant that this episode finds no mention in later community histories. Why, though, was agricultural work becoming such an issue now, so that the standing of a Brahman community with farmers amongst its members could be challenged in this way? A further implication of this judgment can hardly have escaped the attention of the assembly. Many other Brahman communities in the region had some form of engagement with agriculture or market gardening. Could the judgment be read as applying to them too? Let us turn now to look at some other Brahman communities and their livelihoods in their Konkan setting.

69 Ibid., p. 299.
70 Ibid., p. 300.

Livelihoods and Service in the Konkan Littoral

As we have seen above, Konkani Brahmans found no shortage of lordly patrons willing to give them villages and honours. Many Brahmans were also holders of entitlements to a vṛtti, where a ruler gave in perpetuity the revenues from particular villages to Brahmans who performed specified religious services for the village community.[71] A vṛtti of any size and importance was a prominent public office, carrying entitlement to a variety of privileges and marks of status, such as rights to first worship at temples and precedence in religious processions. The vṛtti of offices such as temple and family officiant, astrologer, and dharmādhikārī were vital sources of livelihood to the families who possessed them, and were inherited from one generation to the next. The copper plate or documentary evidence for their rightful enjoyment was carefully guarded and often reconfirmed with each change of the local political regime.

Brahmans also held local hereditary office as village accountants and served local lords and states as letter-writers, stewards, administrators, revenue managers and political intermediaries. Small-scale agriculture was also important, in the rich alluvial lands at the head of the Konkan's river creeks, where rice fields were often fringed with betelnut groves, plantain, mango, jackfruit, and tamarind orchards. For many Brahman families in the Konkan, a typical combination of occupations would have been market gardening of this kind, supplemented by payments in cash or kind for the performance of religious rituals. This is certainly how Chitpavan family histories describe their livelihoods in the Konkan during this period.[72] Colonial surveys also indicate that substantial numbers of the Konkan's Brahmans continued to be agriculturalists.[73]

Some Brahman families found new opportunities at a different level in the agrarian economy, with the gradual emergence of the

[71] For land grants performed for ritual services, see Kulkarni, *Maharashtra*, pp. 65–6.

[72] Patterson, "Changing Patterns of Occupation"; Limaye, *Limaye Kulavṛttānta*, p. 4. Chitpavans were said to be such skilled farmers that they could turn wasteland into gold: *Bombay Gazetteer*, vol. x, p. 113.

[73] *Bombay Gazetteer*, vol. x, pp. 112–17.

Konkan's own form of superior landed right. The first Bijapur ruler, Yusuf Adil Shah (1459–1511), had appointed one Mustapha Khan to administer the affairs of Dabhol, who installed revenue farmers with the status of village headmen. Many of the appointees were Brahmans and men of capital, and their deeds of title showed that they were granted for the purpose of restoring the prosperity of the villages.[74] From this form of revenue farming evolved the Konkan's distinctive khoṭī system of superior proprietary right, in which revenue farmers' lands were hereditable and transferable.[75] Khoṭs were substantial local figures, responsible for revenue collection and village accounts, and often prominent at meetings of local judicial bodies. They also carried out pioneering work in clearing forests, founding new settlements, digging tanks, and bringing land under cultivation. While many khoṭs were members of leading Maratha families, Brahmans also took on these offices. The Chitpavan ancestors of the nineteenth-century nationalist leader B.G. Tilak had for three centuries been khoṭī landlords in the Ratnagiri village of Chikhalgaon.[76]

Besides local-level opportunities of this kind, historians have observed a longer-term expansion of new kinds of administrative opportunity, first in the service of the Sultanate states of the region, and thereafter in the Maratha states. As Richards, Gordon, Eaton, and others have shown, the states of the Delhi Sultanate leaned heavily on the administrative expertise of local Hindu officials. In particular, Bijapuri rulers took steps to establish the office of Deshakulkarni (accountant) as separate from and an independent check on the power of the Desai.[77] As these hereditary scribal posts took clearer shape over the course of the sixteenth and seventeenth centuries, and became more firmly demarcated from offices carrying local military responsibilities, many of them became the preserve of Brahman families.[78]

[74] Jervis, *Geographical and Statistical Memoir*, pp. 75–6; Rogers, *The Land Revenue of Bombay*, pp. 3–4.

[75] For the history of khoṭī tenure, see in particular Candy, *Selections*; Charlesworth, *Peasants and Imperial Rule*, pp. 31–4. The office of khoṭ was certainly established by 1600: see Potdar and Mujumdar, *Śivacharitra Sāhitya*, vol. 2, p. 340.

[76] Tahmankar, *Lokamanya Tilak*, p. 7.

[77] Fukazawa, "Local Administration", pp. 1–48.

[78] Richards, *Mughal Administration*, pp. 16–18; Gordon, *Marathas*, pp. 49–51; Kruijtzer, "Madanna"; Eaton, *A Social History*, pp. 177–202; Wink, *Land and Sovereignty*, pp. 293–304.

The arrival of the European trading companies and the expansion of Maratha power in the region from the middle of the seventeenth century thus added a further layer of opportunity for the mobile and enterprising, and particularly for those could combine scribal skills with access to cash.

Writing about Maharashtra in 1637, the South Indian Sanskrit poet Venkatadhvari caricatured the importance of service occupations for Maharashtrian Brahmans in his satirical work, the *Viśvaguṇādarśacampū*.[79] "The Brahmans of these parts work as kulkarnīs, do village accounts, farming and trading. They are so much absorbed in these various pursuits that they do not do their bathing and rituals at the proper time. They have given up sacrificing for themselves and others, reading the sacred books for themselves and others, and all of the other sacred rites." Worse, the satirist continued, rather than teaching their boys to study the Vedas, they studied the language of the Yavanas and filled their bellies as servants of Yavana kings. So absorbed were they in the pursuit of state service that they had all but forgotten their traditional learning. If a Maharashtrian Brahman showed that he knew the names of ten books people would acclaim him as a very Vyasa, scribe of the Vedas, while one who could actually quote a Sanskrit verse would be taken for Brihaspati himself, priest to the gods.[80]

The expansion of Maratha power in the Konkan thus represented a further growth of already expanding service opportunities for Brahmans. The increasing importance of service roles suggests a reason for the concerns about farming that appeared in Gagabhatta's judgment on the Shenvis. Farming was physical labour, with its implication of dependency and inferiority. Ploughing itself involved close work with animals, and necessarily killed many small creatures in the soil. The role of humble agriculturalist may have seemed increasingly at odds with the growing prominence of Brahman communities in different administrative, political, and diplomatic fields, in which the dignity of an official combined so effectively with the ritual purity of a Brahman.

By extension, of course, the same judgments might apply to all

[79] Narayana Rao, *et al.*, *Symbols of Substance*, pp. 1–12.

[80] Venkatadhvari, *Viśvaguṇādarśacampū*, vss 133–8, 111–17.

Brahman communities with farmers amongst them. It was the Shenvis, however, who were under scrutiny. Could their position in the social order really stand close examination, when their various occupations were examined? And did these occupations not compromise the standing of the Konkan's other Brahman communities, some of which had gradually transformed themselves into a new kind of service and administrative class?

The Politics of Vṛtti Entitlements

Questions about Brahman standing were also to emerge in another sphere of Konkani social relations, in disputes over the sorts of vṛttis or livings that were described earlier. Conflict over such valuable entitlements was nothing new. It is difficult to know whether it reached a greater intensity in the period under discussion, although the cases explored below certainly suggest that some holders of vṛtti rights felt themselves under particular pressure. What is striking, though, is that questions about the standing of different Konkani Brahman communities affected the terms on which the disputes were fought out, the parties drawn into them, and the strategies that they employed.

We begin here with a dispute between two influential families of Karhade Brahmans that took place during the last decade of the sixteenth century. Representatives of those families were present later, at the Rajapur assembly in 1664. The Purohita family held grants as rājapurohita (ritual officiant to the raja) of Shringarpur and Sangameshwar. The Purohitas fought for many years with the Golavalikara Padhye family over the latter's rights as astrologers and village priests – which, the Padhyes claimed, dated back as far as 1363.[81] In 1600, the Padhyes approached the raja, Kanhoji, to lay out their grievances and to ask for judgment. On 9 October 1600, a local judicial assembly gathered to hear the case, attended by local officials, religious authorities and prominent landholders, including the local khoṭ.

The assembly's judgment, like that of the Rajapur assembly, was conveyed in the form of a letter, in this case from Kanhoji Raja. It too recapitulated every stage of the dispute, often in the reported speech of

[81] Potdar and Mujumdar, *Śivacharitra Sāhitya*, vol. 2, pp. 333–8.

the disputants and witnesses. The judgment thus began in the voice of the principal complainants, the Padhyes. They explained that they had been away from the region, on a great pilgrimage to Banaras. In their absence, three brothers of the local Purohita family had tried to usurp their offices. The Purohita brothers made the ingenious claim that, as priests to the governing family, their rights in fact extended to all of the administrators and state employees of Shringarpur and Sangameshwar. "Having thus violently attacked our honour as priests," the Padhyes complained, "they are not letting us carry on the business which is rightfully ours."[82]

The dispute was not confined to the two families. The local Devarukhe Brahman community used the quarrel to renegotiate their own standing vis-à-vis the Karhade Padhyes. The Padhyes acted for them as priests but refused to share food with them. The Devarukhes seem to have found this increasingly a source of grievance. The Padhyes continued: "Devarukhe people live in the villages of Kolathe, Ambovu, Vada Soneri and Majare Chadivane. We have always acted as their astrologers, priests and dharmādhikārīs. Now they are saying to us 'If you will come and eat with us, then do come and do our work as priests and everything else. But if you won't eat with us, then don't bother coming to our houses at all.'"[83] Assaults on the Padhyes' rights came from other quarters too. Two opportunistic Chitpavan priests, Vaman and Ananta, who lived in a nearby village, had noticed the arrival of some newcomers. Evidently sensing a chance, the two went to the village authorities to suggest that they should act as priests to them. The village authorities had told them that all such rights belonged to the Padhye family. The two then tried a different line of argument: one based on the territorial location of family gods and the rights that this created. The fact was, they said, their family god lived in the newcomers' village. Surely, therefore, they should have some honours and rights there? This prompted discussion in the assembly. What effect did the location of family gods have on the strength of vṛtti claims? The assembly considered the argument, but rejected it. "Someone's family god may be in another village, and there are villages with only one god. But it

[82] Ibid., p. 339.
[83] Idem.

is not lawful for someone from outside to claim connection with the god of the village, and on that basis to try to take over the office of the priest. The vṛtti belongs to the person in that village who has it."[84] The assembly also decided against the Purohita family: they were within their rights to perform ceremonies for the raja's family, but not for all of the families employed in the service of the state. That vṛtti belonged to the Padhyes. However, the family was taking no chances, and continued to guard their rights amid the rapid political changes of the day, obtaining fresh confirmations of their rights in 1636, 1659 and again, on 21 January 1662, from Shivaji himself.[85]

Other contemporary disputes reflect similar elements of proprietorship over territory, competition for vṛtti offices, and for the rights to perform priestly duties. Two families, the Sarjyotishis and the Sapres, fought over a long period for possession of the office of sarjyotishi (head of the local assembly of astrologers) in the southern Konkan region of Phonda. An assembly convened 1667 to consider the matter declared that the Sapres had no entitlement to any vṛtti in the area, and no one should pay them anything. The Karhades and other Brahman communities settled in the area could conduct their own priestly ceremonies for themselves, if they wished. But if they had no officiant of their own caste and employed anyone else, half of his fees had to go to those who held the vṛtti. Over subsequent decades, each family took advantage of changes in local state authority to renew their claims. In a judgment of 1718, the territorial dimension of the dispute became even clearer. The judgment stated that the Karhade Brahmans of Kudal, Phonda, and other towns in south Konkan and Goa possessed no original or mirāsi vṛtti in these areas, and that they were interlopers there, scheming to push the original Brahman residents out and take over their livelihood.[86]

Some later accounts remember this as a time when contemporary social change rendered vṛtti rights particularly vulnerable. A family of astrologers whose rights were resumed by the Peshwa state in 1757, and who fought for their restoration until early in the next century, put their loss down not just to state action, but to the growth of local caste

[84] Ibid., p. 341.
[85] Ibid., pp. 342–7.
[86] Kulkarni, *Maharashtra*, pp. 148–61.

pride. "In the houses of Karhades, there was a Karhade priest; in the houses of Chitpavans, there was a Chitpavan priest. Even the Devarukhes say they have authority for their own dharma and worship. In Kudal, Rajapur and Dabhol, because of the growth of caste pride, from house to house, our vṛtti has been cut away."[87] Thus very extended legal cases could provide a kind of long-running theatre in which the rights of families and communities were debated, as the mobile and the opportunistic sought to exploit the weaknesses in the claims of others to a living: when people were away, when rulers changed, when local quarrels arose that might offer temporary advantage. What these disputes over the course of the seventeenth century suggest is that the drive to establish clearer boundaries and identities for themselves was leading some Brahman communities to take their priestly function "in-house", enabling them to present themselves as self-sufficient communities able to deal with their neighbours on equal terms. In a setting where competition for vṛtti rights was severe, and the principle of territorial affiliation limited opportunities for the expansive and enterprising, such a tactic would certainly have made sense. Such a strategy would also have removed the marker of inferiority that so troubled the Devarukhes, which was that Brahmans from other groups who came in to perform their rituals would leave without touching their food.

Devarukhes in Banaras

The Devarukhes were themselves the subject of recurring assembly discussions and letters of judgment in Banaras, in 1583, 1657, 1683, and then again in a dispute transacted in the Konkan in 1723. We do not know as much about this obscure community as we do about the Shenvis. The early letters of judgment sometimes refer to them as devarukha, just as the disputants in 1600 did, suggesting a connection with the Konkan town of Devarukhe. Sometimes they are referred to as devarṣi, (godly sages), and sometimes as devarāṣṭriya (people of the godly country). As Devarukhes, there is no substantial narrative about them in the *Sahyādrikhaṇḍa*. Devarṣis appear as figures of prestige

[87] Sarma, "Vṛttivijaya", ff. 1–2. The date of composition of the MS is given as 1810.

and learning in some puranic accounts. In others, Devarāṣṭriyas figure amongst lists of peoples with whom it is defiling to eat.[88] As we shall see, the varying names were themselves a reflection of the troubled standing of the community. From 1583, the earliest record of which we are aware, through to the later years of the nineteenth century, Devarukhes fought against the implication of a taint in their history, which led other Konkani Brahmans like the Karhades to refuse to eat with them. We look here at how contemporaries explained this impairment, and the responses to it by pandit communities in the Konkan and in Banaras.

In 1583, one Ganesh Sastri Kozhrekar, resident of Banaras, wrote in Marathi to Krishnaji and Kanhoji Raja at Shringarpur, the latter of whom was to preside over the 1600 dispute described above.[89] The letter contained important news. It concerned two Brahmans, Vitthal Jyotishi and his son Krishna, described in the letter as Devarṣis. The two had decided to train in Banaras as agnihotrīs, Brahmans who took up the ancient Vedic practice of maintaining daily worship of a perpetual, consecrated fire. Having learned their craft, they sought the agreement of Banaras' assembly of Deccani pandits to undertake the practice itself. But there were evidently factions within the assembly, and factions with a history. In the course of its discussion, some Chitpavan Brahmans "of the Chitale party" spoke up. One of them, Janardanabhatta Chitale, told the assembly about a letter in his family's possession. It was an udvārapatra, a "letter of release" which had been written out at his house by a past member of the Chitale family, Anantabhatta. The letter was duly brought and read out. It was a kind of confession. In it, Anantabhatta admitted that he had in the past fomented hatred against the Devarṣis. But he recognised now that this was against the sastras and declared himself willing to see relations between the two communities restored.

Having heard all this, the assembly reaffirmed that Anantabhatta had been correct in writing the udvārapatra. It was contrary to dharmic law to promote such hostility, and Devarukhes had the same ritual

[88] *Sahyādrikhaṇḍa*, Uttarārdha, Adhyāya 20, vs. 26.

[89] Mule, *Devarukhe*, Appendix 3, pp. 90–2. For the provenance of these materials, see O'Hanlon, "Letters Home", pp. 239–40.

entitlements and social standing as other Brahmans. Senior pandits affirmed this decision. "Ganesh Diksita Bhave, head of the Chiplunas, (and) Krishnabhatta Bakhale, head of the Karhades" represented the Konkani communities. Others represented the broad division into northern and southern groups of Brahmans: "Krishnabhatta Sesa, head of the Maharashtras, Gopibhatta, head of the Gurjaras, Vidyanivasa, head of the Gaudas, Raghupati Upadhyaya, head of the Telabhuktas." The first of these, it is worth noting, was the great grammarian, Krishna Sesa, of the Sesa family of pandits noted above. Like others of the Banaras intellectuals of his day, he was the author of an influential work about the rights of Sudras within the contemporary varna order, the *Śūdrācāraśiromaṇi*.[90] Kozhrekar ended his letter by reporting that a copper plate enshrining these orders had been sent from Banaras to the Konkan.

Copper plate or not, the judgment seems not to have resolved the matter. There was a further assembly in Banaras in 1657, again held in the Mukti pavilion of the Visvesvara temple, to consider the question.[91] It is not clear what precipitated it. The assembly's letter of judgment described in Sanskrit the broad regional representation of its Brahman members, "of Maharashtra, Karnataka, the Konkan, the Tailanga region, and of the Dravida and other places." It came to the conclusion that the Devarṣis were appropriate people for other Brahmans to eat with and to marry, and that in fact people who set the standard for what was in accordance with dharma already did so. The judgment carried the names of seventy-two pandits, again representing prominent Maharashtrian families, and including Gagabhatta himself.

Once again, however, this gesture from Banaras did not carry sufficient force down in the Konkan. In 1683, the issue emerged once more. On 7 October that year Hari Diksita, a Devarukhe Brahman, wrote from Banaras to his relative Narayana Diksita back in the Konkan. Hari reported that he had taken Narayana's order to Banaras. "Having arrived in Banaras, the Brahman pandits and Vaidikas who are at odds

[90] Krishna Sesa, *Śūdrācāraśiromaṇi*. For the full lists of pandit names attending the meetings described in this essay, see O'Hanlon, "Letters Home", pp. 223–7, 229–33, 236.

[91] Mule, *Devarukhe*, Appendix 5, pp. 96–8.

with us came to speak to me, along with your son in law, Govinda Diksita Chowdhuri. They said that if we wanted to break the rivalry and the hatred between us, we should give a feast for one or two hundred Brahmans, and that would end the feud."[92] The feast had duly been given, and Hari reported that "all of the Maharashtra Brahmans as listed below came to the feast": 107 names in total were listed. These did not include the names of any members of the prominent pandit families that appeared so frequently in formal letters of judgment.

The implication here was thus still one of a weak position for the Devarukhes. The Devarukhes involved had evidently been men of means, with contacts in Banaras. But the other parties had simply dictated terms, expensive terms, which did not result in the participation of the city's most influential Brahman families. Perhaps not surprisingly, therefore, a further letter of judgment given early in the following century, in 1723, reveals the Devarukhes still in pursuit of recognition. This letter did not come from Banaras, or even from Rajapur, but from the town of Sopare in the Thane district of the northern Konkan.[93] The assembly that issued this letter described itself as "an assembly of the learned, led by upādhyāyas, knowers of jyotiṣa, and dharmādhikārīs" who were "attached through ties of affection" to those to whom they addressed their letter of judgment. Even more than the judgments discussed above, this one contains multiple narratives: it is in effect a story, contained within a petition, in turn recapitulated within a judgment. The document is notable for its selective use of language: it opens with greetings in Sanskrit; the main part of the story is told in Marathi, and the final judgment, with sastric quotations, is again given in Sanskrit.[94]

Like other letters of judgment, this one opens with a salutation to those who had instituted the proceeding, evidently Chitpavans and Karhades, and recapitulated the whole history leading up to it.

> You wrote us a letter and made the following representations. Here in the land of Parashuram, there are Maharashtra and Chitpavan and Karhataka

[92] Ibid., p. 96.

[93] Ibid., Appendix 6, pp. 99–102.

[94] For a discussion of this kind of linguistic heterogeneity in the Maratha country, see Guha, "Transitions and Translations". On the "constative"/"documentary"

> Brahmans, and also some others, Shenvis, Kirvants, and Devarukhes, with entitlement to Vedic rituals. The three castes of Maharashtras, Chitpavanas and Karahatakas all eat together by custom. There are no such relations with the other castes.[95]

The complainants in 1723 go on to tell the following story. Discontented with their situation, the Devarukhes had approached an important Deshastha pandit at the Satara court, Mudgalabhatta. They told him how their present disparagement by other Brahman communities had come about. The other communities of Brahmans used to eat with them, until an event some two hundred years before. A Chitpavan Brahman called Anantabhatta Chitale had been constructing a tank in the Thana District of northern Konkan. In order to procure labour, he stopped passers-by and asked them to dig out a basket of earth. One day a group of Brahmans from Devarukhe came along the road. Anantabhatta duly asked them to help with the digging. But these Brahmans sensed a further implication in his request, given that Ananta bhatta was not himself soiling his hands. The Devarukhes refused. "So he cursed them, and from that time on neither of these castes will come to our houses to eat." This, then, explains the mention of a "letter of release" in the Banaras assembly of 1583. According to the claim of his relative, at some later time Anantabhatta had written an udvārapatra to release the Devrukhes from his curse.

It is not clear whether the pandit Mudgalabhatta knew this part of the history. But he was evidently sympathetic to the Devarukhes' complaint, since he arranged for the ruler of the local Janjira state to bring all of the region's Brahmans together to consider the situation, and to share a meal. The Karhades and Chitpavans resisted, declaring that from time immemorial they had not eaten together with Devrukhes. The Janjira ruler had noticed their discomfiture, and said to them, exasperatedly, "We have sat you down to eat, but you look as though we have served you up hakim's pills to swallow." At this point, Mudgalabhatta also seems to have given up trying to reconcile the parties. Perhaps aware that an approach to the Banaras pandit communities

---

distinction in language choice in inscriptions, see Pollock, "The Sanskrit Cosmopolis".

[95] Mule, *Devarukhe*, Appendix 6, p. 99.

would only elicit further benign assurances that there could be no objection to eating with the Devarukhes, he told the Chitpavans and Karhades that they had two options. They could go to the Maratha court at Satara, or they go back to their own country and "take letters of agreement around from place to place," confirming that they were warranted in their conduct towards the Devarukhes.[96] The Chitpavans and Karhades duly adopted the latter course, and now approached the pandit community at Sopare to issue them with such a letter.

This history was the first part of the document drawn up by the sastris of Sopare. The second part consisted of extracts from dharmasastra texts such as the Manusmṛti, and from the Matsya, Saura, Padma, and Skanda purāṇas. Each of these extracts listed people defiling to Brahmans. The "line-spoilers" ranged from types of northern and southern Brahmans, to "barbarians", forest dwellers, thieves, eunuchs, unbelievers, mad people, and what several of the lists called devarāṣṭriyas (people of the godly country). These, the sastris of Sopare suggested, were in fact the Devarukhes, confirming them as a defiling community with whom other Brahmans should not eat. The central argument of the letter however was based on practice or āchāra, as opposed to textual authority. The assembly in Sopare asserted that in any case local āchāra was a stronger authority than texts were. "Just as there never has been and never will be a lotus that floats in mid-air so there has never been and never will be a sanction from āchāra for taking food with the Devarukhes. Based solely on the evidence of regional practice one can rule out the custom of sitting to eat with them."[97]

Here, then, the Devarukhes engaged in a much more local campaign for acceptance as full Brahmans, perhaps disillusioned with the limited effectiveness of letters of judgment and Brahman feasts staged in Banaras. Chitpavans and Karhades resisted their campaign on the same terms. The Brahman communities thus sought to construct for themselves a new and more local discursive space within which they

[96] Ibid., p. 100.

[97] Ibid., pp. 100–1. Note however that the principle of the "prāmāṇya of āchāra" is invoked based on referring to it in a dharmanibandha, the *Smṛtyarthasāra*. It may be significant that no signatures were attached to the document as the historian Rajwade found it: Rajwade, "Devrūkhe Yanchī Mūlotpatti". These may later have become detached, as Rajwade suggests, or perhaps they were simply never collected: Pimputkar, *Chittalebhaṭṭa Prakaraṇa*, pp. 1–5.

could engage with the implications of the Konkan's shifting social order. There is also a suggestion here of a search for new and more flexible judicial mechanisms, in the pandit Mudgalabhatta's advice to the complainants to equip themselves with a "letter of agreement" defending their position by going about "from place to place" canvassing the opinions of assemblies of the learned.[98]

The accuracy with which the key events and judgments in this history were transmitted is particularly striking. The narrative told in 1724 states that the incident at the tank had happened some two hundred years before, placing the event roughly in the 1520s. It was in 1584 that the assembly at Banaras was told that Anantabhatta Chitale had written a letter releasing the Devarukhes from his curse. Certainly, the event at the tank was close enough in time for the 1584 assembly, gathered to affirm the Devarukhe father and son as agnihotrīs, to know what was being spoken of when the "Chitale party" got up and spoke of a "letter of release". This dating may also explain the resentment of the Devarukhes in 1600, when they used the opportunity of the vṛtti dispute at Shringarpur to try to renegotiate their relations with the Karhades. The *Śatapraśnakalpalatā*, a mixed purana / chronicle composed in 1690, also described the incident at the tank, dating it to 1493 exactly, and explained subsequent Brahman attitudes to the Devarukhes as a consequence of it.[99]

Why, then, were the Devarukhes so disparaged, and what might their position tell us about wider questions of Brahman standing? The dynamics of the incident at the tank are suggestive. Building a tank was exactly the kind of pioneering work expected of the rural role of khoṭ in the Konkan. We know that Chitpavans and other Brahmans held these offices. What may be described here are the attempts of an early holder of superior landed rights to recruit labour to carry out

[98] Attempts to restore relations with the Devarukhes continued through the eighteenth century: see Mule, *Devarukhe*, Appendixes 7 and 8, pp. 102–6. For a further important discussion of this process, see Deshpande, "Localising the Universal Dharma".

[99] Madhava, *Śatapraśnakalpalatā*, ff. 17r–19r. This work is frequently referred to in the debates about caste status in the nineteenth and twentieth century, but the text itself has never been edited or published as a whole.

the work that would have constituted an important part of his task as a landlord.[100] The incident at the tank may further suggest that, just as the reputation of the Shenvis as agriculturalists was used against them in the Rajapur judgment, so in this incident the Devarukhes were perhaps people who might be expected to do agricultural work and who could therefore be commanded to toil in the earth. Some Devarukhes were apparently sensitive to the social implications of such work, and ready to challenge demands from local landholders for their labour. We cannot know with great clarity where contemporary attitudes towards the Devarukhes came from, but the fragmentary evidence that we have suggests that in this period the Devarukhes, like the Shenvis, were beginning to do well. Their members were able to move to Banaras to train as sacrificial priests. They were confident and cohesive enough to threaten the Karhades with deprivation of their rights as ritual officiants, and some were wealthy and well-connected enough by the end of the seventeenth century to lay on a great feast in Banaras. But they may have retained too strong an association with dependent agricultural work for comfort, in a setting where such labour was increasingly seen to be at odds with the proper dignities and prestige of a Brahman.

All of these letters of judgment include indications of their audiences as well as their modes of transmission. The Rajapur letter was directed to Brahmans living in towns and settlements along the Konkan, up into the Sahyadris, and westwards along the Krishna and Godavari rivers. The assemblies of the learned are described as constituting a kind of "panel" consisting of representatives of all of the substantial groupings of "southern" Brahmans. Reference to such a "panel", and to the location of its meeting in the Mukti pavilion of the Visvesvara temple at Banaras, became a standard part of such documents, and a means of conferring authority on them.

While the content of the judgments about particular family rights may only have been of local interest, the minutiae of their carefully reported conversations conveyed the history of the disputes, and the testimonies of the different parties to them, back to their beginning. This form

[100] We are particularly indebted to Madhav Deshpande for conversations that helped to develop this part of the argument.

of narration was another important way of establishing a document's veracity. This construction itself made such documents not only newsworthy: it may also have made them diverting stories to read.

Aftermath: Towards the Peshwa State

The focus here has been the Brahman communities of the Konkan, as emerging service people of the early modern period who reconstituted themselves as a new kind of scribal elite out of their humbler littoral origins. We have explored the narratives through which increasingly bounded communities competed for advantage in this setting, the judicial processes into which their narratives fed, and the localisation of the processes through which contemporaries came to determine who could be said to be a Brahman, and of what kind. As always, lineage and ritual standing mattered, the ability to demonstrate in principle at least that community members could act as priests, and the substantiation of Brahman standing through the sharing of food with other Brahmans. But the right sort of dignified livelihood was also beginning to matter in new ways, as some of the Konkan's Brahmans began to define themselves as a new kind of administrative class, cultivated in habits and unsoiled by menial labour or gross forms of trade.

In the end, of course, it was a matter of social agreement to establish who was a Brahman, an agreement established through an array of procedural, textual, and conversational modes. Formal assemblies might make judgments, which could also be elicited and publicised through the circulation of letters for signature, but the judgments were also discussed and shaped in the vivid histories of the *Sahyādrikhaṇḍa* and allied narratives that circulated among Brahman communities from the Konkan to Banaras.[101]

If this period opened in a new way the question of what it meant to be a Brahman, the learned communities of Banaras and of the Konkan seem in the cases examined here to have given rather different

[101] These narratives and the forms of historicity they seem to contain may have something to contribute to current debates: see Guha, "Speaking Historically"; Eaton, *A Social History*; Deshpande, *Creative Pasts*; Ali, *Invoking the Past*; Narayana Rao, *et al.*, *Textures of Time*; Inden, *et al.*, *Querying the Medieval*.

answers to the question. Perhaps aware of the damage that corrosive public feuding did to the prestige of all of them, Banaras' intellectuals emphasised what Brahmans should share in common, rather than what divided them. They answered the question of who a Brahman was largely, if not exclusively, by reference to textual authorities. For the Konkan's local Brahman communities, different things mattered. Who was a Brahman was to be determined not so much by textual law as by prevailing patterns of customary social relationships. At the same time, however, there seem to have been complex links between these different approaches. The Maharashtrian sastris in Banaras were constantly involved in these very local disputes, and something about their own standing seems to have been at stake in them. The disputes examined above speak, for example, of "parties" (pakṣa) within the Banaras assembly of southern pandits. These were the figures who at the same time contributed so substantially to Sanskrit traditions of learning in this period. Further study of their regional involvements may give us some additional sense of the ways in which their formal and technical concerns can be mapped onto the social changes of the early modern world.

Some of the after-effects of these developments became clear from the 1720s, with the emergence in Pune of a family of Chitpavan Brahmans, the Bhatta family from Danda Rajapuri in the Konkan, as *de facto* leaders of the Maratha state. From then on, Chitpavan Brahmans and others migrated out of the Konkan in large numbers to offer their services to the new state.[102] It was now the Pune government, rather than Banaras, that took the lead in trying to bring about cohesion between the region's Brahman communities. They sought to shift the terms in which Maharashtra's Brahmans were discussed, away from debates about the relative status of different Brahman communities regionally defined and towards a single and monolithic model of ideal Brahman social practice. Individual Brahman identities were not suppressed; what was emphasised was rather their common participation in this ideal. It focused on dignity of comportment and livelihood, but

[102] For these developments, see Gordon, *Marathas*, pp. 91–132; Gokhale, *Poona in the Eighteenth Century*, pp. 106–37; Wink, *Land and Sovereignty*, pp. 67–85; and Desai, *Social Life*, pp. 30–61.

extended much more widely to prohibit the many different rusticities and plebeian customs that the Pune government observed with dismay among their Brahman caste fellows.

This disciplinary and discursive endeavour emerged most clearly in the *Yādī Dharmasthāpanā* (List of orders to establish dharma) issued under Balaji Bajirao in 1751. Written not in Sanskrit but in Marathi, this list laid down a set of fifty-one orders covering every aspect of Brahmanic ritual and social and domestic life.[103] The orders sought to encourage a stronger sense of Brahman community and of separation from other castes, particularly through the sharing of food and the giving and receiving of religious instruction.[104] The orders also had a substantial focus on restraint and dignity in forms of Brahman sociability, dress, and comportment. They urged Brahmans to desist from practices evidently viewed as plebeian in nature, such as listening to jesters' obscene jokes during marriage ceremonies.[105] Many of the orders related to women. No Brahman was to ask for money at a daughter's marriage, to allow a widow's head to stay unshaven, or to permit their women to wear cheap, home-made, or rustic bodily ornaments.[106] The orders also forbade Brahman from any kind of hard physical labour. The same concern for bodily dignity in work extended to Brahman women. When they carried water pots, they should not put them on their heads, but rather carry them at their hips. The last of the orders of 1751 again invoked the authority of the Bhatta family of Banaras, laying down the *Śūdrakamalākaraḥ* of Kamalakarabhatta as the guide that Brahmans should follow in their work as ritual officiants for Sudras.[107]

The Pune court instituted a long struggle through the middle and later years of the eighteenth century to impose these norms on the region's Brahman communities, using the disciplinary and legal powers of state officials.[108] They also drove down the rights of non-Brahman

[103] Bendrey, *Mahārāṣṭretihāsachī Sādhane*, vol. 2, pp. 439–42. For a fuller account, see O'Hanlon, "Disciplining the Brahman Household".

[104] Ibid., order nos 11, 18, 19, 22, 40.

[105] Ibid., nos 9, 10, 21, 22

[106] Ibid., nos 2, 3, 5–8, 15–17, 27–9, 37–8.

[107] Ibid., no. 51.

[108] Kadam, "Institution of Marriage"; Guha, "An Indian Penal Regime".

rivals as scribes.[109] This push seems to have prompted further resistance in the case of the Devarukhes. A gathering to dine was again at the centre of the story. An undated report from a local official of the Pune court reported that a Devarukhe and his wife had come to Pune as guests at the house of a local Brahman. The pair served food to some two hundred of the city's Brahmans. After some days, other Brahmans in the city gathered in protest and lodged a written complaint. Then, perhaps conscious of the pressure coming from the Pune court, they seem to have got cold feet. The official reported that they had come to him in great agitation, saying that they wanted to tear their letter of protest up. With suitable regard for his duties, and perhaps even conscious of the importance of the issue, the official refused. He reported virtuously: "I said to them, you can do whatever you like. I certainly won't give permission to destroy letters."[110]

The endeavours of the Peshwa government were accompanied by a shift in approach to the puranic histories that had so preoccupied Brahmans in the Konkan a century earlier, before the rise of the Chitpavans to political eminence. The early colonial historian James Grant Duff worked closely with officials at the courts of Pune and Satara in writing his history of the Marathas, first published in 1826. During his researches, he noted that officials of the Pune government "carefully suppress or destroy all copies of the *Syhadree Kind*, where their origin is mentioned, and a respectable Bramin of Waee was, a few years ago, disgraced by Bajee Rao for having a copy of it."[111] On the eve of the colonial deluge in western India, such contentious modes of determining who was a Brahman were now, it seemed, closed. A more monolithic image of the Brahman as cultivated administrator and dignified intellectual was now more firmly secured within the judicial and social arenas of the Maratha state, and eventually to be absorbed into the discourses of the colonial state.

[109] Prabhus and Sonars in particular were targets of these punitive measures. See Wagle, "A Dispute"; and Thakare, *Grāmaṇyāchā Sadyanta Itihāsa*, pp. 1–147 and 186–98.

[110] Sardesai, *Selections*, vol. 43, no. 160, pp. 7750–1 (undated). For a further effort made in 1758 to recognise the Devarukhes, see Paṇḍit, *Devarukhyāṃviṣayī Śāstrasaṃata Vicāra*, pp. 53–5.

[111] Grant Duff, *A History of the Mahrattas*, vol. 1, p. 8.

References

Ajgaonkar, G.F., *Kuḍāldedeśkar Samagra Itihās* (Bombay: G.F. Ajgaonkar, 1989).

Alam, Muzaffar, "The Culture and Politics of Persian in Precolonial Hindustan", in Sheldon Pollock, ed., *Literary Cultures in History: Reconstructions from South Asia* (Berkeley and Los Angeles: University of California Press, 2003), pp. 159–71.

———, and Sanjay Subrahmanyam, "The Making of a Munshi", *Comparative Studies of South Asia, Africa and the Middle East*, vol. 24, no. 2, 2004, pp. 61–72.

Ali, Daud, ed., *Invoking the Past: The Uses of History in South Asia* (New Delhi: Oxford University Press, 1999).

Altekar, A.S., *History of Banaras* (Banaras: Culture Publication House, 1937).

Aryavaraguru, Ranganathasvami, "On the Sheshas of Benaras", *Indian Antiquary*, vol. 51, November 1912, pp. 245–53.

Axelrod, Paul, and Michelle A. Fuerch, "Flight of the Deities: Hindu Resistance in Portuguese Goa", *Modern Asian Studies*, vol. 30, no. 2, 1996, pp. 387–421.

———, "Portuguese Orientalism and the Making of the Village Communities of Goa", *Ethnohistory*, vol. 45, no. 3, 1998, pp. 439–76.

Bayly, C.A., *Rulers, Townsmen and Bazaars: North Indian Society in the Age of British Expansion* (Cambridge: Cambridge University Press, 1983).

———, *Origins of Nationality in South Asia: Patriotism and Ethical Government in the Making of Modern India* (Delhi: Oxford University Press, 1998).

Bayly, Susan, *Caste, Society and Politics in India from the Eighteenth Century to the Modern Age* (Cambridge: Cambridge University Press, 1999).

Bendrey, V.S., ed., *Keśava Paṇḍita's Daṇḍanītiprakaraṇam* (Poona: Bharat Itihas Samshodhak Mandal, 1943).

———, *Coronation of Shivaji the Great* (Bombay: P.P.H. Bookstall, 1960).

———, *Mahārāṣṭretihāsachī Sādhane*, 2 vols (Mumbai: Mumbai Marathi Grantha Sangrahalaya, 1966).

Benson, James, "Saṃkārabhaṭṭa's Family Chronicle", in Axel Michaels, ed., *The Pandit: Traditional Scholarship in India*, Delhi: Manohar, 2001), pp. 105–18.

Bombay Gazetteer, vol. X, Ratnagiri and Savantvadi (Bombay: Government Central Press, 1880).

Bronkhorst, Johannes, "Bhaṭṭoji Dīkṣita on Sphoṭa", *Journal of Indian Philosophy*, vol. 33, no. 1, 2005, pp. 3–41.

Candy, E.T., "Selections with Notes, from the Records of Government Regarding the Khoti Tenure", *Selections from the Records of the Bombay Government*, New Series, no. 134 (Bombay: Education Society's Press, 1873).

Charlesworth, Neil, *Peasants and Imperial Rule: Agriculture and Agrarian Society in the Bombay Presidency, 1850–1935* (Cambridge: Cambridge University Press, 1985).

Chatterjee, Kumkum, "History as Self-Representation: The Recasting of a Political Tradition in Late Eighteenth Century Eastern India", *Modern Asian Studies*, vol. 32, no. 4, 1998, pp. 913–48.

Conlon, Frank F., *A Caste in a Changing World: The Chitrapur Saraswat Brahmans 1700–1935* (Berkeley: Center for South and Southeast Asia Studies, 1977).

da Cunha, J. Gerson, ed., *The Sahyâdri-Khaṇḍa of the Skaṇḍa Purâṇa* (Bombay: Nirnayasagar Press, 1877).

Danvers, Frederick Charles, *The Portuguese in India: Being a History of the Rise and Decline of Their Eastern Empire*, 2 vols (London: W.H. Allen, 1894).

Davis, Donald R., "A Realist View of Hindu Law", *Ratio Juris*, vol. 19, no. 3, 2006, pp. 287–313.

de Souza, Francisco, *Oriente conquistado a Jesu Christo pelos padres da companhia de Jesus da Provincia de Goa*, 2 vols (Lisbon: Valentim da Costa des Landes, 1710).

de Souza, Teotonio R., *Medieval Goa: A Socio-Economic History* (New Delhi: Concept Publishing Company, 1979).

Desai, Sudha, *Social Life in Maharashtra Under the Peshwas* (Bombay: Popular Prakashan, 1980).

Deshpande, Madhav M., "Pañca-Gauḍa und pañca-Drāviḍa. Umstrittene Grenzen einer traditionellen Klassifikation", in M. Bergunder and R.P. Das, eds, *"Arier" und "Draviden", Konstruktionen der Vergangenheit als Grundlage fur Selbst-und Fremdwahrnehmungen Sudasiens* (Halle: Verlag der Franckeschen Stiftungen zu Halle, 2002), pp. 57–78.

———, "Bhaṭṭoji Dīkṣita's Perceptions of Intellectual History: Narrative of Fall and Recovery of the Grammatical Authority", Unpublished mss.

———, "Localising thc Universal Dharma: Purāṇas, Nibandhas, and Nirṇayapatras in Medieval Maharashtra", Unpublished mss.

Deshpande, Prachi, *Creative Pasts: Historical Memory and Identity in Western India, 1700–1960* (New York: Columbia University Press, 2007).

Eaton, Richard M., *A Social History of the Deccan, 1300–1761: Eight Indian Lives* (Cambridge: Cambridge University Press, 2005).

Feldhaus, Anne, "Maharashtra as a Holy Land: A Sectarian Tradition", *Bulletin of the School of Oriental and African Studies*, vol. XLIX, pt 1, 1986, pp. 15–31.

———, *Connected Places: Region, Pilgrimage and Geographical Imagination in India* (New York: Palgrave Macmillan, 2003).

Fukazawa, Hiroshi, "The Local Administration of the Adilshahi Sultanate (1484–1686)", in idem, *The Medieval Deccan: Peasants, Social Systems and States* (Delhi: Oxford University Press, 1991), pp. 1–48.

Gaitonde, Gajanan, *The Sahyādrikhaṇḍa of the Skanda Purāṇa* (Bombay: Katyayani Publications, 1971).

Gode, P.K., "Antiquity of the Caste Name 'Śeṇavī'", *Journal of the University of Bombay*, vol. 5, no. 6, 1937, pp. 152–5.

Gokhale, B.G., *Poona in the Eighteenth Century: An Urban History* (Delhi: Oxford University Press, 1988).

Gordon, Stewart, *The Marathas 1600–1818* (Cambridge: Cambridge University Press, 1993).

Grant Duff, James, *History of the Mahrattas*, 3 vols (London: Longman, Orme, Rees, Brown, and Green, 1826).

Guha, Sumit, "Speaking Historically: The Changing Voices of Historical Narration in Western India, 1400–1900", *American Historical Review*, vol. 109, no. 4, 2004, pp. 1084–1103.

———, "Transitions and Translations: Regional Power and Vernacular identity in the Dakhan, *c.* 1500–1800", *Comparative Studies of South Asia, Africa and the Middle East*, vol. 24, no. 2, 2004, pp. 23–31.

———, "An Indian Penal Regime: Maharashtra in the Eighteenth Century", *Past and Present*, vol. 147, 1995, pp. 101–26.

Gune, V.T., *The Judicial System of the Marathas* (Pune: Sangam Press, 1953).

Gunjikar, R.B., *Sarasvatīmaṇḍal* (Bombay: Nirnayasagar Press, 1884).

Inden, R., J. Walters, and D. Ali, *Querying the Medieval: Texts and the History of Practices in South Asia* (New York: Oxford University Press, 2000).

Jervis, T.B., *Geographical and Statistical Memoir of the Konkan* (Calcutta: Baptist Mission Press, 1840).

Kadam, V.S., "The Institution of Marriage and Position of Women in Eighteenth Century Maharashtra", *Indian Economic and Social History Review*, vol. 25, no. 3, 1988, pp. 341–70.

Kakodkar, P.R., ed. and tr., *The Portuguese and the Marathas* (Bombay: State Board for Literature and Culture, 1975).

Kamalakarabhatta, *Śūdrakamalākaraḥ*, ed. Ganesh Bapuji Malvankar and Vishnu Shastri Bapat (Bombay: Lithographed Text, 1861).

———, *Nirṇayasindhuḥ*, ed. Gopal Sastri Nene (Banaras: Chowkhamba Sanskrit Series Office, 1919).

Kane, P.V., ed., *Vyavahāra Mayūkha of Bhaṭṭa Nīlakaṇṭha* (Bombay: Nirnayasagar Press, 1926).

———, *History of Dharmaśāstra*, 5 vols (Poona: Bhandarkar Oriental Research Institute, 1968–77).

Keni, Chandrakant, *Saraswats in Goa and Beyond* (Goa: Murgaon Mutt Sankul Samiti, 1998).

Khobrekar, V.G., *Konkan: From the Earliest Times to AD 1818* (Pune: Snehavardhan Publishing House, 2002).

Krishna Sesa, *Śūdrācāraśiromaṇi*, ed. Narayana Sastri Khiste, 2 vols (Varanasi: Vidya Vilas Press, 1933–6).

Kruijtzer, Gijs, "Madanna, Akkanna, and the Brahmin Revolution: A Study of Mentality, Group Behaviour and Personality in Seventeenth Century India", *Journal of the Economic and Social History of the Orient*, vol. 54, no. 2, 2002, pp. 231–67.

Kulkarni, A.R., *Maharashtra in the Age of Shivaji* (Pune: Deshmukh and Co., 1969).

Laine, James W., and S.S. Bahulkar, *The Epic of Shivaji: Kavindra Paramanand's Śivabhārata* (New Delhi: Sangam Books, 2001).

Lariviere, Richard W., "Dharmaśāstra, Custom, 'Real Law' and Apocryphal Smṛtis", *Journal of Indian Philosophy*, vol. 32, 2004, pp. 611–27.

Levitt, Stephan, "The Sahyādrikhaṇḍa: Some Problems Concerning a Text-Critical Edition of a Purāṇic Text", *Purāṇa*, vol. 9, no. 1, 1977, pp. 8–40.

———, "Sahyādrikhaṇḍa: Style and Content and Indices of Authorship in the Pātityagrāmanirṇaya", *Purāṇa*, vol. 24, no. 1, 1982, pp. 128–45.

Limaye, V.M., *Limaye Kulavṛttānta* (Pune: Maharashtra Press, 1970).

Madhava, *Śatapraśnakalpalatā*, Sanskrit Ms. no 19, P.M. Joshi Collection, Pune: Bhandarkar Oriental Research Institute.

Michaels, Axel, ed., *The Pandit: Traditional Scholarship in India* (Delhi: Manohar, 2001).

Mule, C.Y., *et al.*, eds, *Devarukhe* (Bombay: Devarukh Brahman Mitra Mandal, 1973).

Narayana Rao, Velcheru, David Shulman, and Sanjay Subrahmanyam, *Symbols of Substance: Court and State in Nāyaka Period Tamilnadu* (Delhi: Oxford University Press, 1992).

———, *Textures of Time: Writing History in South India, 1600–1800* (New Delhi: Permanent Black, 2003).

Nilakanthabhatta, *Vyavahāramayūkha*, ed. and trans. P.V. Kane and S.G. Patwardhan (Poona: Aryasamsrkti Press, 1933).

O'Hanlon, Rosalind, "Letters Home: Banaras Pandits and the Maratha Regions in Early Modern India", *Modern Asian Studies*, vol. 44, no. 2, 2010, pp. 201-240.

———, "Disciplining the Brahman Household: The Moral Mission of Empire in the Eighteenth-Century Maratha State", in Kumkum Roy, ed., *Looking Within, Looking Without: Exploring Households in the Subcontinent through Time*" (Delhi: Primus Books, 2015), pp. 367–89.

Pandit, Vishnusastri, *Devarūkhyāviṣayī Śāstrasamat Vichār* (Bombay: Indu Prakash Press, 1874).

Parashara, *Parāśarasmṛti, With the Commentary of Sâyaṇa Mâdhavāchârya*, ed. Vaman Shastri Islampurkar, 2 vols (Bombay: Government Central Book Depot, 1906).

Patterson, Maureen L., "Changing Patterns of Occupation Among Chitpavan Brahmans", *Indian Economic and Social History Review*, vol. 7, no. 3, 1970, pp. 375–96.

Pearson, Michael, *Coastal Western India: Studies from the Portuguese Records* (New Delhi: Concept Publishing Company, 1981).

Pimputkar, R.S., *Citaḷebhaṭṭa Prakaraṇa* (Mumbai: G.S. Joshi, 1926).

Pollock, Sheldon, "The Idea of Śāstra in Traditional India", in A.L. Dallapicola, *et al.*, eds, *Shastric Traditions in Indian Arts*, vol. 1 (Stuttgart: Ergon Verlag, 1989), pp. 17–26.

———, "The Sanskrit Cosmopolis, 300–1300 CE: Transculturation, Vernacularization, and the Question of Ideology", in Jan Houben, ed., *Ideology and Status of Sanskrit: Contributions to the History of the Sanskrit Language* (Leiden: Brill, 1996), pp. 197–247.

———, "New Intellectuals in Seventeenth Century India", *Indian Economic and Social History Review*, vol. 38, no. 1, 2001, pp. 3–31.

Potdar, D.V., and G.N. Mujumdar, eds, *Śivacharitra Sāhitya,* Bhārat Itihās Samśodhak Maṇḍaḷ Svīya Granthamālā, vol. 2, no. 33 (Pune: Bharat Itihas Samshodhak Mandal, 1930), pp. 333–53.

Rajopadhyaya, G.R. "Śrīśivājī Mahārājanche Kulopadhāyāy", in N.C. Kelkar and D.V. Apte, eds, *Śivājī Nibandhāvalī* (Poona: Sri Sivacharitra Karalaya, 1930), pp. 65–76.

Rajwade, V.K., "Devrūkhe Yanchī Mūlotpatti", in M.B. Saha and Girish Mandke, eds, *Itihāsāchārya Vi. Kā Rājāvāḍe Samagra Sāhitya*, vol. 7 (Dhule: Rajwade Samagra Sahitya Mandal, 1998), pp. 186–93.

Richards, J.F., *Mughal Administration in Golconda* (Oxford: Oxford University Press, 1975).

Rogers, A., *The Land Revenue of Bombay: A History of Its Administration, Rise and Progress*, 2 vols (London: W.H. Allen, 1892).

Saldanha, J.A., "Savantvadi Castes and Village Communities", *Journal of the Anthropological Society of Bombay*, vol. 8, no. 7, 1909, pp. 498–519.

Sardesai, G.S., *Selections from the Peshwa Daftar*, 45 vols (Bombay: Government Central Press, 1930–4).

———, ed., *Paramānandakāvya of Kavīndra Paramānanda* (Baroda: Oriental Institute, 1952).

Sarkar, Jadunath, *Shivaji and His Times* (London: Orient Longman, 1973).

Sarma, "Vṛttivijaya", Marathi Ms., British Library Add. Ms., 26502.

Sarma, M.G., *Sārasvata Bhūṣaṇa* (Bombay: Popular Book Depot, 1952).

Seldekar, V.R., *Śrīśāntādurgā Saṃsthāncha Saṃkṣipt Itihās* (Bombay: Tutorial Press, 1912).

Sen, Surendranath, *Extracts and Documents Relating to Maratha History, vol. 1, Siva Chhatrapati* (Calcutta: University of Calcutta, 1920).

Shastri, M.H., "Dakshini Pandits at Benaras", *Indian Antiquary*, vol. 41, January 1912, pp. 7–13.

Subrahmanyam, Sanjay, "Aspects of State Formation in South India and Southeast Asia", *Indian Economic and Social History Review*, vol. 23, no. 4, 1986, pp. 357–77.

———, "Connected Histories: Notes Towards a Reconfiguration of Early Modern Eurasia", *Modern Asian Studies*, vol. 31, no. 3, 1997, pp. 735–62.

Śyenavījātidharmanirṇaya, in V.K. Rajwade, ed., "Śivakālīn śāśtrī va Paṇdit", in *Bhārat Itihās Samshodhak Maṇḍaḷ Varsika Itivṛtta*, sake 1835, BISM Granthamālā, Book 7 (Pune: BISM, 1914), pp. 296–305.

Tahmankar, D.V., *Lokamanya Tilak: Father of Indian Unrest and Maker of Modern India* (London: J. Murray, 1956).

Thakare, K.S., *Grāmaṇyāncha Sādyanta Itihāsa* (Bombay: Tattvavivek Press, 1919).

Vajpeyi, Ananya, "Excavating Identity Through Tradition: Who was Shivaji?", in Satish Saberwal and Supriya Varma, eds, *Traditions in Motion: Religion and Society in History* (Delhi: Oxford University Press, 2005), 240–71.

Valavlikar, Wamanrao R., "An Eye Copy of an Inscription in Devanagari Characters", *Journal of the Bombay Branch of the Royal Asiatic Society*, vol. 23, 1914, pp. 107–8.

Venkatadhvari, *Viśvaguṇādarśacampū of Śrī Venkaṭādhvarī*, ed. Surenda Nath Sastri (Varanasi: Chowkhamba Press, 1963).

Wagle, N.K., "The History and Social Organisation of the Gauda Sarasvata Brahmanas of the West Coast of India", *Journal of Indian History*, vol. 48, no. 1, 1970, pp. 8–25; and idem, vol. 48, no. 2, 1970, pp. 295–333.

———, "A Dispute Between the Pancal Devajna Sonars and the Brahmins of Pune Regarding Social Rank and Ritual Privileges: A Case-Study of the British Administration of *Jati* Laws in Maharashtra, 1822–1825", in N.K. Wagle, ed., *Images of Maharashtra: A Regional Profile of India* (London: Curzon Press, 1980), pp. 129–59.

Wicki, Josef, and John Gomez, eds, *Documenta Indica*, 1540–1549 (Rome: Monumenta Historica Soc. Iesu, 1948).

Wink, Andre, *Land and Sovereignty in India: Agrarian Society and Politics Under the Eighteenth Century Maratha Svarājya* (Cambridge: Cambridge University Press, 1986).

7

The Social Worth of Scribes

Brahmans, Kayasthas, and the Social Order in Early Modern India

Introduction

As a number of historians have remarked, the scribal communities who served the developing states of India's early modern centuries revealed an increasingly self-conscious skilled culture.[1] We have looked less closely at the ways in which these emerging scribal peoples were seen by other people. They were associated with the dignity of literacy, but were essentially servants to masters. They were guardians of access to the powerful, but this naturally made them suspect. Their mobility and command of languages gave them a cosmopolitan prestige, but as a consequence they were frequently seen as outsiders. Often migrating to capitalise on local opportunities for service, skilled communities of scribes were difficult to classify socially. As Derrett observed, Kayasthas, the paradigmatic scribal community of early modern India, "best exemplify the capacity of a caste of indeterminate origin and uncertain position in the hierarchy to turn an aptitude to advantage."[2]

[1] For the culture of scribal communities, see Alam and Subrahmanyam, "Making of a Munshi"; Narayana Rao, Shulman, and Subrahmanyam, *Textures of Time*, pp. 93–139; Chatterjee, "History as Self-Representation", pp. 913–48; Deshpande, *Scripts of Power*, pp. 29–68; Narayana Rao and Subrahmanyam, "Notes on Political Thought"; Kruijtzer, "Madanna, Akanna and the Brahman Revolution"; Guha, "Serving the Barbarian"; Vendell, "The Scribal Household in Flux"; Raman, *Document Raj*.

[2] Derrett, *Religion, Law and the State*, p. 175.

India's Kayastha communities present a complex and interesting challenge to the social historian.[3] Sarkar suggests that the origins of the title, which translates as "that which stays near the body (kāya)", lay in the role of the literate official always at the side of his master.[4] Over a very long period, the term came to refer to a series of regionally based caste communities. We have two main and somewhat contradictory sources for the early history of Kayasthas. First, they appear frequently in the inscriptional record, named sometimes as the scribes who wrote out particular inscriptions, and sometimes as the high-status warriors or cultured pious donors whose generosity the inscriptions celebrated.[5] At both levels, these inscriptions convey a clear consciousness of writing as a pious and prestigious activity.[6] The second source is in the classical literature of negative stereotypes of Kayasthas as corrupt royal officers.[7] By the start of the twelfth century, and probably very much earlier, northern India's Kayasthas were divided into regional lineage groupings. These were to become the subcastes of more recent

[3] For Kayastha histories, see Vendell, "Scribes and the Vocation of Politics", and Vendell, "The Scribal Household in Flux"; Gupta, *The Kayasthas*; Sinha, *Kayasthas*; Kane, "A Note on the Kayasthas", pp. 740–3; Leonard, *Social History of an Indian Caste*.

[4] Sarkar, "Kayastha", pp. 280–4.

[5] See Talbot, *Precolonial India in Practice*, pp. 64–5, for an inscription of 1290 from Andhra describing the virtues of the warrior Kayastha, Ambadeva. This inscription offers an early example of the derivation of the title "Kayastha" from the Sanskrit term kāya, or body.

[6] A late-twelfth-century inscription describes the Kayastha Subhata, of the Vastavya lineage and servants of the Chandela kings of Bundelkhand. Their towns were "purified by the fact that men of the writer caste dwelt in them", and "a resort of the twice-born." The inscription also elaborated on Subhata's splendid Kayastha predecessors, their scribal skills, knowledge of the Vedas, dharmasastras and puranas, and disciplines of nyāya and mīmāṃsa. Kielhorn, "Inscription of the Time of Bhojavarman", p. 336.

[7] This literature emerged as early as the fifth century CE : see Sarkar, "Kayastha", pp. 280–4. However, it seems to have developed with particular force during the twelfth century. For examples from Kashmir, see Baldissera, *The Narmamālā of Kṣemendra*, pp. 39–55. I am grateful to Peter Szanto for this reference. See also Dutt, *Kings of Kāshmīra*, Book 1, pp. 80, 118; Book 2, p. 23. For a South Indian example of the same period, see Krishnamoorthy, *Subhāṣita-Sudhānidhi of Sāyaṇa*, pp. 127–8. I am indebted to Deven Patel for this reference and translation.

Kayastha history.[8] Later, and as a part of the social processes examined here, the same communities came to be identified as "Chitragupta Kayasthas" to distinguish them from the Chandraseniya Kayastha Prabhus, as the largest Kayastha community of western India came to be known.[9]

In cultural terms, western India's Kayastha communities – the subject of this essay – offer a sharp contrast to their counterparts in Bengal and North India. [10] Kayasthas in these regions are familiar to us as part of the official class of the Mughal empire, imbued with its Persian literary culture and ethic of loyalty to Mughal imperial service.[11] Kayasthas in the Maratha regions lived within a very different milieu. Here, the model of the Persianised Kayastha scribe as prestigious servant of the empire was much weaker. As Sumit Guha has shown, the Bahmani kingdom and states of the Deccan Sultanate were dependent on the well-developed scribal skills of a substantial Brahman clerical class.[12] Their authority continued to be rooted in an older Sanskrit literary culture and their role as guardians of dharmasastra. In this context, the prosperity and success of western India's Kayasthas became the focus for a series of key debates. Where did Kayasthas, scribal people with no priestly function, belong in the four-fold varna hierarchy, and what were their ritual entitlements? The question was complicated because many Brahman contemporaries doubted that any pure Kshatriyas or Vaishyas existed in the fallen age of the Kaliyuga.

This was not merely an academic question. We do not know what ritual affirmation Hindu kings in the Maratha country required in the centuries before Shivaji.[13] We do know, however, that Shivaji's bid for the full ritual of royal consecration met with opposition from local

[8] Modern lists describe twelve Kayastha subcastes in North India: Mathura, Bhatnagar, Sakhsena, Srivastava, Kulasresta, Ambasta, Suraj Dhwaja, Karana, Balmika, Asthana, Nigam, and Gour: Prasad and Dusre, *Kayastha Ethnology*, p. 8.

[9] Enthoven, *Tribes and Castes*, vol. 3, pp. 235–47.

[10] Chatterjee, "Scribal Elites".

[11] See Richard, "Comportment Among Imperial Mughal Officers", pp. 269–89, and Bhimsen, *Tarikh-i Dilkasha*.

[12] Guha, "Serving the Barbarian".

[13] For a discussion of royal ritual officiants, see Sanderson, "Religion and the State", pp. 229–300.

Brahmans. His consecration raised the question about varna categories directly. As Pollock has suggested, for some contemporaries consecration alone may not have been sufficient to make a king, for it required a prior upanayana – the investment with the sacred thread that was a privilege of the three twice-born varnas.[14] These considerations made local Brahmans reluctant to support the ceremony. Famously, therefore, it was conducted instead by the eminent Banaras pandit Gagabhatta.[15]

As Madhav Deshpande has noted, these questions had also been raised by the region's communities of Kayasthas. Shivaji's influential Kayastha secretary, Balaji Avaji, helped arrange the consecration and found himself, in consequence, obstructed by local Brahmans when he sought to have his sons invested with the sacred thread. During these years of the late 1660s and early 1670s, the Kshatriya status of the Maratha country's Kayastha communities was at issue as much as that of the Bhosle family.[16]

There was a longer-term history to this dispute. Often migrants who had come into the Maratha regions as servants of the Bahmani kings and the Deccan Sultanate states, Kayasthas were intruders into local societies whose Brahman communities had hitherto commanded more exclusive possession of scribal skills.[17] It was in this context that, from the mid-fifteenth century, periodic but intense conflicts developed between the two groups. At issue was the Kayasthas' right to the dignified public rituals of the twice-born, and in particular to the key saṃskāra (life-cycle rite) of investment with the sacred thread. In defence of these entitlements, and assisted by their own Brahman gurus, Kayasthas worked hard during the following three centuries to consolidate their identities as Kshatriyas, descendants of an ancient line of kings that had flourished before the Kaliyuga, and so entitled to all of the rituals of the twice-born. It was in this context too that Brahmans

[14] Pollock, *Ends of Man*, pp. 69–76.

[15] A detailed account of Shivaji's consecration is in Bendrey, *Coronation of Shivaji the Great*, pp. 1–58.

[16] Deshpande, "Kṣatriyas in the Kali Age?", pp. 1–26.

[17] See Richards, *Mughal Administration*, pp. 16–18; Fukazawa, *Medieval Deccan*, pp. 1–48; Gordon, *Marathas*, pp. 49–51; Kruijtzer, *Xenophobia*, pp. 232–335; Eaton, *Social History*, pp. 177–202; Wink, *Land and Sovereignty*, pp. 293–304.

of the Maratha regions, and their fellow intellectuals in Banaras, developed some of their most important debates about Kshatriyas in the Kaliyuga.

At issue here was also a larger vision of society in the Kaliyuga, which seems to have divided pandit communities in the Maratha localities from some of their compeers in Banaras. For many in the Maratha country, the Kaliyuga presented a landscape only of Brahmans and Sudras. As will be argued, this conception arose from two distinctive features of local politics and society. The first of these lay in the challenge that scribal rivals like the Kayasthas posed to Brahmans as competitors for the same state offices and resources. The refusal to concede that Kshatriyas proper could exist in the Kaliyuga offered an effective way to undermine Kayastha prestige. The second feature lay in the direct relationship of patronage and power between Brahmans and local kings in the Maratha country. This relationship was unmediated by the institution of the temple, as it was in South India, or by the forms of Rajput kingship with their Mughal underpinnings, as it was in the North. The direct relationship between Brahmans and rulers in the Maratha regions made the control of royal ritual entitlements into a key political instrument for Maratha Brahmans in their negotiations with local aspirants for kingly power.

This Brahman determination to maintain a grip on the ritual entitlements of scribal rivals as well as of local kings was very much a reflection of the distinctive Maratha milieu. As we shall see, this was not a position universally shared by Maratha pandit intellectuals in Banaras. Well before the contests over Shivaji's consecration, some were willing to contemplate the possibility of a more diverse social landscape, and to have contemplated it, moreover, in the context of arguments about Kayastha entitlements.

These struggles affected debates about religious law and traditions of thought about political ethics. Narayana Rao and Subrahmanyam have rightly observed that a discourse about nīti (this-worldly political ethics) struggled to establish itself in the Maratha Deccan against conceptions of statecraft rooted in the religious traditions of the dharmasastra.[18] The history explored here offers some explanation of that phenomenon. It was in some part the consequence of this local Brahman

[18] Narayana Rao and Subrahmanyam, "Notes on Political Thought", p. 208.

drive to retain control of ritual rights, and consequently to insist on the primacy of dharmasastra as the normative framework within which politics should be conducted.

This history presents significant difficulties of evidence. Much comes from Kayastha collections of documents made during later episodes of conflict.[19] By the early twentieth century, historical memory within Maharashtra's Kayastha communities was structured around what were represented as a succession of grāmaṇya (caste quarrels with Brahmans), usually nine in number, stretching back to the fifteenth century.[20] Each seems to have galvanised contemporaries into a search for materials about their history and rights. In addition, many of the region's distinctive bakhar (chronicle narratives) were written by Maratha Kayasthas, and promoted the contribution that Kayasthas made to the Maratha state.[21] This has produced a rich seam of material, but one which needs to be treated with great circumspection.

Caste in the Age of Kali

For some decades now, scholars have emphasised the distinctive forms that jati and varna took during the colonial period.[22] Yet early modern social observers too were caught up in arguments about hierarchy and identity in which jati and varna figured strongly. Elsewhere, we have seen something of this debate as it affected Maratha Brahman communities.[23] At the other end of the caste spectrum, it has also been noted

[19] Most important are Gupte, *Ethnographical Notes;* Gupte, *Chāndraseniya Kāyastha Prabhu Grāmaṇya Prakaraṇātīla Pāch Assal Ājnāpatra*; Prasad and Dusre, *The Kayastha Ethnology*; Thakare, *Grāmaṇyāchā Sādyanta Itihāsa*; Gupte, *Rājavāḍyānchī Gagabhaṭṭī*. Also useful is the *Kāyastha Prabhūnchyā Itihāsāchī Sādhane*, published in Pune during the early 1880s by B.A. Gupte of Indore.

[20] For a list of these, which K.T. Gupte provided in 1925 for the encyclopedia of Maharashtra published by the early Marathi ethnographer S.V. Ketkar, see Ketkar, *Mahārāṣṭrīya Dnyānakośa*, vol. 17, p. 244.

[21] For the Marathi bakhar, see Deshpande, *Creative Pasts*, pp. 19–39, and Guha, "Speaking Historically", pp. 1084–1103.

[22] For a summary, see Bayly, *Caste, Society and Politics*, pp. 1–63.

[23] See O'Hanlon and Minkowski, "What Makes People Who They Are?", pp. 381–416; O'Hanlon, "Letters Home", pp. 1–40; Deshpande, "Localising the Universal Dharma".

that the sixteenth and seventeenth centuries saw an intensified discussion of the social worth and ritual entitlements of Sudras.[24]

This concern with different categories of Sudras formed part of another and perhaps more fundamental preoccupation. As is well known, the Kaliyuga as the last and most degenerate of the four ages appeared as a theme in many different literary genres from an early date, often as a framework within which social observers tried to make sense of times that they considered particularly corrupt and debased.[25] For many intellectuals of the early modern period, these were such times. Expansive courts and urban centres made it possible for people to change their modes of life. New livelihoods beckoned to the enterprising, and the wealthy were able to develop new social relationships and marriage partnerships to match. Many rulers were Turks and Yavanas, or local country upstarts, who could not be relied upon to maintain the varnas in orderly separation. This mixing-up of peoples had a further implication for the social order. Had not the sages been correct when they foretold that, with the coming of the Kaliyuga, only Brahmans and Sudras would remain in the world?

The disappearance of intermediate varnas was associated in particular with the story of Parashuram's extirpation of all Kshatriya kings after the murder of his father by the Haihaiya king. Parashuram the warrior Brahman is one of the most familiar figures of epic and puranic literature. However, the older narratives about his exploits in the traditions of the Mahabharata seem to have taken on a new prominence in early modern western India. He was the central figure in Maharashtra's own purana of place, the *Sahyādrikhaṇḍa*. For this purana, the Sahyadri mountain range and the Konkan region were the place where a penitent Parashuram had afterwards made his home.[26]

Linked to this theme, these centuries in western India saw a renewed flourishing of the older Sanskrit literary genre of the *Jātiviveka* (consideration of jatis), familiar in the work of Manu and other authorities on

[24] Vajpeyi, "Dharma and Legal Treatments of Caste", pp. 280–302.

[25] See von Stietencron, "Calculating Religious Decay", pp. 31–49; Yadava, "Accounts of the Kali Age", pp. 31–63.

[26] Karve, "The Paraśurāma Myth", pp. 115–39; Janaki, "Paraśurāma", pp. 52–82. There is only one printed edition of this work: J. Gerson da Cunha, *The Sahyâdri-Khaṇḍa of the Skaṇḍa Purâṇa*.

religious law. *Jātivivevka* texts discussed the heterogeneous communities which seemed to be flourishing in their authors' own times, which, for some pandit commentators at least, seemed to reinforce their sense that no "pure" intermediate varnas survived in the modern age.[27] The genre of the nibandha (compendium), which flourished during these centuries, typically contained a *Jātiviveka* section, along with sections on gifts, penance, life-cycle rituals, death rituals, and other social matters. *Jātiviveka* texts were also written as independent works, appearing in many different parts of India.[28]

An influential text in the Maratha country was the *Jātiviveka* of one Gopinatha.[29] Gopinatha wrote well after 1300, since he alluded to a landscape in which "Turuskas" were well established, "sinful and ruthless foreigners who speak an impossible guttural language, and whose law contains the slaughter of cows."[30] But it was circulating as an authority in 1553, by which time it had been incorporated into the *Paraśurāmapratāpa*, produced for Burham Nizam Shah I of Ahmadnagar (1502–1553) by his protégé Sabajipratapa.[31] Following Manu's classic formula, Gopinatha described the many jatis created when men and women from the four different varnas mixed and produced progeny. Most of the "mixed" jatis listed in Gopinatha's text were classified as Sudras, and as such were entitled to only twelve saṃskāras, as opposed to the full sixteen applicable to the twice-born varnas.

[27] For "mixed" castes in the dharmasastra, see Jha, "*Varṇasaṃkara*", pp. 273–88; Rocher, "Notes on Mixed Castes", pp. 132–46.

[28] The *New Catalogus Catalogorum* (hereafter NCC) lists many works by this name: NCC vol. 7, pp. 234–5. See Nobile, "Jātiviveka", and Kane, *History of Dharmaśāstra*, vol. 1, pp. 548–9, and vol. 2, pt 2, pp. 102–3. For a more detailed exploration of this genre, see also O'Hanlon, "Discourses of Caste".

[29] Gopinatha signed himself "son of Sarngadhara, grandson of Vishvanatha, of the Vasistha gotra, of Pratyandapura", which could possibly be a Sanskritised rendering of Pandharpur. I have here used the only dated text that I have come across to date, Oriental and Indian Office Collections, ms. 1061a, dated sake 1564, or 1642. The NCC lists at least twenty-six different surviving *Jātiviveka* texts ascribed to Gopinatha or Gopinathakavi: NCC vol. 7, p. 234. I am very grateful to Peter Szanto and Nina Mirnig for their translations of this text.

[30] Gopinatha, *Jātiviveka*, f. 124v.

[31] See Gode, "Sābāji Pratāparāja", pp. 156–64, and Sharma, "Paraśurāmapratapa", pp. 1–26.

In addition, where "mixed" jatis belonged in the varna order depended on whether the unions were anuloma or pratiloma, unions in which the father was socially superior to the mother, or vice-versa. The offspring of anuloma unions had an inherent advantage, since they followed the proper order of nature. Pratiloma unions, in which base men bred progeny from women of the higher orders, were always a sign of social degradation. For Gopinatha and many other commentators, pratiloma people were lower even than Sudras, and entitled to only five saṃskāras.[32]

How did Gopinatha's work describe Kayasthas? His portrayal was a departure from earlier classifications. Kulluka's commentary on Manu, one of medieval India's most authoritative texts, described a Kayastha as the son of a twice-born man, born from a mother of the varna immediately below his, and his occupation as attendance on kings and princes.[33] This was a respectable anuloma marriage, as befitting the dignified occupation that went with it. But Gopinatha offered a very different classification.

> A son who is born from a mahisya woman and a vaideha man is called a Kayastha. This is their karma. They earn their living by different kinds of writing, different kinds of calculation and arithmetic. They are even lower than Sudras, so they are permitted only five saṃskāras. By their writing they serve all of the four varnas, and earn their living doing artisan work. They may not wear a shendi like the Brahmans, take the sacred thread, wear red garments or touch the gods.[34]

This was a degraded pratiloma parentage. A mahisya was one born from a woman one varna degree below her twice-born husband. This was the respectable anuloma union that Kulluka's Manu describes. But Gopinatha added a lowly father for his Kayastha: a vaideha is born from a Brahman mother and a Vaishya man, therefore from a degraded pratiloma union. A Kayastha's parentage was therefore also of the

[32] For a discussion of anuloma and pratiloma unions, see Kane, *History of Dharmaśāstra*, vol. 2, pt 1, pp. 51–4.

[33] Jones, ed., *Institutes of Hindu Law*, p. 290. For Kullukabhatta, see Kane, *History of Dharmaśāstra*, vol. 1, pp. 359–63.

[34] Gopinatha, *Jātiviveka*, f. 7v. The lock of hair left on the head of a tonsured Hindu is usually associated with Brahman social practice. For "red garments", see Kane, *History of Dharmaśāstra*, vol. 2, pt 2, pp. 278–80.

degraded pratiloma kind, and Kayasthas lower than Sudras in the social scale, barred from all signs of dignity, entitled only to the five most basic saṃskāras. Gopinatha's text was widely circulated. As we have seen, the courtier Sabajipratapa reproduced it.[35] In the first chapter of his *Śūdrācāraśiromaṇi*, written probably in the late sixteenth century, Krishna Sesa, great grammarian and leader of Banaras's Maratha pandit community, classified Kayasthas simply by borrowing from Gopinatha.[36]

Perhaps we can see in Gopinatha's work something of the hostility that Kayasthas, influential servants of "mlecchas" and "Turuskas", might have evoked among the Brahman commentators who circulated his text. Of course, the allusion may have reminded them that many Brahmans were clerical servants of "mleccha" rulers. Outside the realms of satire and personal quarrels, however, contemporary Brahman commendators did not publicly present such service as an impediment to dharmic propriety very often.[37] But Kayasthas were a different matter, and perhaps here both Gopinatha and his readers might have had in mind the Persianised Kayastha service people of northern and eastern India, as well as their Maratha counterparts. It was difficult to deny that the latter were skilled people in court and countryside. But they were direct competitors for the offices in state service that had become a central part of Maratha Brahman livelihood and ambition. Reference to Kayasthas' degraded origins offered one way to counter their expanding power and prestige.[38]

[35] Sabajipratapa, *Paraśurāmapratāpa-Jātiviveka*, ff. 47–8. In this and many other mss, lines have been inserted at the start of the text, attributed to the *Vāstuśāstra* of Visvambhara. This has caused the *Jātiviveka* of Gopinatha to be described as Visvambhara's work. But this is a misattribution, because the *Jātiviveka* does not appear in the extant mss of Visvambhara's text: Sharma, "Paraśurāmaprātapa", p. 2. Yet the association may not have been an accident. Many passages in the *Jātiviveka* read like regulations for jatis in a bustling urban environment.

[36] Krishna Sesa, *Śūdrācāraśiromaṇi*, pp. 19, 23–4. For Krishna Sesa, see O'Hanlon and Minkowski, "What Makes People Who They Are?", p. 404.

[37] For a satirical reference, see the South Indian poet Venkatadhvari, writing during the 1630s, in his *Viśvaguṇādarśacampū*, vss 133–8, 111–17. The great grammarian Bhattoji Diksita is reputed to have called his rival Panditaraja Jagannatha a "mleccha" for his close associations with the Mughal court of Shah Jahan: Bronkhorst, "Bhaṭṭoji Dīkṣita on Sphoṭa", p. 15.

[38] Gopinatha's text enjoyed a very long afterlife. In the hands of other scribes,

But the following decades were to see an important shift, in the work of Kamalakarabhatta (*fl.* 1610–40), an influential member of Banaras' leading Maratha pandit family, the Bhattas.[39] His *Śūdrakamalākaraḥ* cited the *Jātiviveka* extensively, but included a discussion of Kayasthas that seems quite new in the *Jātiviveka* genre. The first story that Kamalakarabhatta told concerned the figure of Chitragupta, well known in epic and puranic literature as scribe to Yama, judge of the dead, and who sprang from Brahma's body to record the good and bad deeds of people against the time of their death and judgment. Placed next to Yama, Chitragupta enjoyed a foremost position among the gods. Because he came from Brahma's body (kāya), Kamalakarabhatta explained, people called him Kayastha, meaning "dwelling in the body", and "many gotras of his descendants are well known on the earth."[40] This history, which Kamalakarabhatta said was recorded in the *Vāstuśāstra* of Visvambhara, was the origin of India's Chitragupta Kayasthas.

He then turned to describe the history of the Chandraseniya Kayasthas of western India. Kamalakarabhatta offered a history taken, he said, from the *Reṇukāmahātmya* of the *Skandapurāṇa*.[41] As Parashuram rampaged over the earth, the pregnant wife of a king, Chandrasena, sought refuge in the ashram of the sage Dalbhya. Parashuram went to the ashram, where the sage agreed to hand over the woman, but on condition that he could keep her unborn child. To assuage the god's anger, Dalbhya agreed that the child should be educated in the arts of the pen rather than of the warrior, and excluded from the dharma of Kshatriyas (ksātṛadharmāt bahiṣkṛtaḥ). Through Dalbhya's counsel, the child's descendants, the Chandraseniya Kayasthas, became pious people of good conduct.[42] At the end of this passage, Kamalakarabhatta

it developed shorter and longer forms, as well as an outline tabular version. It was reproduced in other influential works of the sixteenth to eighteenth centuries, such as the *Śatapraśnakalpalatā*, of Madhava, ff. 8r – f. 52v. See O'Hanlon, "Discourses of Caste".

[39] For Kamalakarabhatta, see Kane, *History of Dharmaśāstra*, vol. 1, pt 2, pp. 925–37.

[40] Kamalakarabhatta, *Śūdrakamalākaraḥ*, ff. 89v–90r.

[41] The *Reṇukāmahātmya* is usually considered part of the *Sahyādrikhaṇḍa*, and was included in da Cunha's edition: *The Sahyâdri-Khaṇḍa*, pp. 1–144.

[42] Kamalakarabhatta, *Śūdrakamalākaraḥ*, ff. 90r–91v.

reproduced Gopinatha's short description of degraded Kayasthas, but explained that these were a different kind of degraded or "mixed" Kayastha.

But his account left him with another problem: he seemed to be questioning the basic assumption that in the Kaliyuga there were only Brahmans and Sudras left in the world. He ended the *Śūdrakamalākaraḥ*, therefore, with an extended discussion of this very point, in a chapter entitled "Miscellaneous matters" (Saṃkirṇaprakaraṇam). It was true that the Bhagavata and other puranas asserted that no Kshatriyas or Vaishyas remained in the Kaliyuga. But these same authorities also told the story of Meru and Devapi, survivors from earlier races of kings, granted extraordinary long life so they could await the end of the Kaliyuga in the Himalyan retreat of Kalapa, then return to re-establish the varna order on earth. Hence the *Viśnupurāṇa* and *Matsyapurāṇa* conceded that Kshatriyas still existed "in seed form" (bījabhūta). Also, if Kshatriyas and Vaishyas had vanished from the world, how could their continued mingling be said to produce the mixed castes of the present? Kamalakarabhatta thus concluded, indicating that the matter was discussed in his own family, "My father Ramakrishnabhatta says that there still exist in the present age, here and there, Kshatriyas and Vaishyas whose form is concealed and who have fallen away from their own proper observances."[43]

Why might Kamalakarabhatta have made this significant shift? As we shall see, it is possible that these stories were beginning to circulate in new ways in the Deccan, reflecting the slow consolidation of Kayasthas into two distinct and separate jati communities in northern and western India. Broader influences may also have been shaped the position of families like the Bhattas. The high profile at the Mughal court of Rajput rulers as patrons of learning and piety, whose generosity sustained many of the pandit intellectuals of Banaras during the seventeenth century, may have made such families open to the possibility that there were still Kshatriyas, in some form, in the modern age. These were more than just abstract discussions. As Madhav Deshpande has pointed out, Kamalakarabhatta composed a ritual manual for the consecration of kings, anticipating the labours of his nephew

[43] Ibid., ff. 93–4. For a pandit contemporary with a similar view, see Minkowski, "Nilakaṇṭha's Mahābhārata", pp. 3–4.

Gagabhatta half a century later.[44] However, it was in the context of the debates about Kayasthas that many of these discussions were conducted.

Lineages, Ināms, and Gurus: Histories of Kayastha Migrations

Writing in 1925, the civil servant and ethnographer R.E. Enthoven noted two substantial Kayastha groupings in western India. The Chandraseniya Kayastha Prabhus were a community of over 20,000, centred in the Konkan littoral, the western Deccan, and the princely states of the region. Their community traditions, Enthoven noted, asserted that they had migrated into western India after the fall of Yadava Devagiri to Ala al-Din Khalji at the end of the thirteenth century. Pathare Prabhus were a smaller group of some 5000, based mainly in Bombay and the northern Konkan littoral. They also traced their origins to migration, from Kanauj and Rajputana, via Paithan under the Yadavas, and thence to the western Deccan after the fall of Devagiri.[45]

What evidence is there for these migrations? We can learn much from Kayastha family lineages. In the 1720s, Vitthalrao Devaji, the Kayastha Prabhu dewan of Baroda, visited Pune to gather information about Kayastha families. Govind Ramaji and Rango Atmaji Prabhu were revenue officers and village accountants in Kanadkhore district, in the mountainous Maval region west of Pune. Govind Ramaji wrote to him in 1728 with their lineage, "taken from original papers, and heard from the mouths of our fathers and forefathers."[46] During the time of Muhammadshah, their ancestor Kondo Prabhu fled from Hindustan to escape harassment by the mlecchas. He entered the service of Alauddin Hussein, one of the sardars of Muhammadshah who had revolted against him and taken over the Deccan region for themselves.[47]

[44] Deshpande, "Kṣatriyas in the Kali Age?", p. 4.

[45] Enthoven, *Tribes and Castes*, vol. 3, pp. 235–47. The Pathares also described animosities between themselves and local Brahmans, who resented their employment in the service of the Portuguese state. See Moroji, *Śrī Kshatriyavaṃsodgamamālā*, and idem, *A History of the Pattana Prabhus*, pp. 7–11, 48–56, 68–93.

[46] Bendrey, *Mahārāṣṭretihāsāchī Sādhane*, vol. 2, p. 400.

[47] Ibid., p. 401. This "Muhammadshah" was probably Muhammad bin Tughlaq, against whom Alaudin Hussein Bahman Shah revolted in 1347, and went on

For his good service Kondo was given rights, far to the west of the Bahmani capital, in the Mavala hills to the west of Pune. Here, Govind's narrative continued, he was granted the offices of Deshkulkarni (regional revenue officer) and village Kulkarni, along with all their inām rights, for thirty-three villages.[48] He married the daughter of a Kayastha Prabhu officer called Chuil, and they had a son named Visoba. Kondo Prabhu himself lived to be 105. After his death, Visoba took over his father's position. Visoba had a son called Govindrao. At about that time, the narrative continued, "the padishahi came to Delhi, and a new padishah came to sit in Bidar."[49] The new padishah at Bidar called Govindrao into his service and confirmed him in all his offices and lands. Then the emperor Babur at Delhi died, and his son Humayun sat on the throne. Govindrao died at an advanced age at about the time when Humayun was driven out of India by rebels. This would bring Govind's narrative to the early 1540s, when we know that Humayun and his army left North India.

Govindrao left three sons, Timaji, Kondo, and Mahadji Prabhu. The narrative continued: "The padishah was very good. He called Timaji and made over to him the inām of Vinzar village in Kanadakhore district, with letters to confirm it. We have copies of these letters, but the original documents have been eaten by ants."[50] Timaji was succeeded in his office by his son Rudraji. "Then the kingdom of the Khans grew very strong, and there was tumult in the Adilshahi, Kutubshahi, Nizamshahi, and Baridshahi kingdoms. This country of the Mavala was divided between the Adilshahi and Nizamshahi kings." Rudraji had three sons, Baji, Timaji, and Balaji. After Rudraji died, the padishah called

---

to found the Bahmani Sultanate. The Bahmani capital shifted from Gulbarga to Bidar in 1425, and remained its capital until the break-up of the Bahmani Sultanate after 1518.

[48] An undated document from the Shivaji period lists these thirty-three villages of Kanadakhore district as under a Kayastha Prabhu revenue officer. Sardesai, *Selections from the Peshwa Daftar* (hereafter SPD), vol. 45, no. 1, p. 7652.

[49] With the break-up of the Bahmani kingdom after 1518, the Barid Shahi kings established their centre at Bidar.

[50] Bendrey, *Mahārāṣṭretihāsāchī Sādhane*, vol. 2, p. 401. Kanadkhore is one of the twelve Pune Mavalas (narrow river valleys) which run east from the watershed of the Sahyadhri mountain range towards the city of Pune. Raeside, "A Note on the 'Twelve Māvals", p. 393.

Timaji and confirmed his office and ināms. At that time, the Yavanas caused much harassment, and Timaji asked himself why he was serving such an evil kingdom – "but what recourse is there, against someone whose food you have eaten?" Excelling in military skills, Timaji was by this time in the service of Bijapur.[51] He was given charge of the Rairi parganā within which his inām lands were located, "where there are many forts and strongholds."

Govind's narrative continued: The youthful Shivaji, son of Shahaji Bhosle, let it be known that he was looking for supporters to help him capture nearby Torna fort.[52] Baji Pasalkar, Deshmukh of the adjacent Mosekhora, and one of Shivaji's earliest adherents, was sent to invite Timaji to join him. After success in this venture, Timaji entered Shivaji's service, working as karkhanis (commissary) to forts alongside Moro Trimbak Pingle as tipnis (chief accountant). Timaji and his sons Apaji, Rupaji, and Pilaji, continued in Shivaji's service, so distinguishing themselves that "the maharaj gave our father fine inām lands and villages worth five thousand, and letters of congratulation, and we Govind Ramji have these original letters, and copies of them are with Rango Atmaji." This part of Govind's narrative identifies him as the grandson of Timaji. His narrative laid out the achievements of the family up until 1727, concluding with a description of the family's suffering during the tumults of recent times.[53]

Govind appears to provide us here with a remarkably complete history of his family's migrations. There are clearly missing links. There cannot have been only one generation between Kondo's joining Alauddin Bahman Shah in the 1340s, and Govindrao, who died around the time Humayun fled from India in 1540. It is possible that records may have been lost during the great Durga Devi famine of 1396–1407, and subsequent decades of warfare.[54] From the time of Govind, however, the lineage makes sense. Govind died in the early 1540s. His son Timaji

[51] Bendrey, *Mahārāṣṭretihāsāchī Sādhane*, vol. 2, pp. 401–2. Bidar was absorbed by the kingdom of Bijapur in 1619.

[52] Torna fort was built on the mountain spur running between the two river valleys of the Kanada river, where Timaji's inām lands were located, and the Mose river, where Baji Pasalkar, one of Shivaji's earliest adherents, was Deshmukh.

[53] Bendrey, *Mahārāṣṭretihāsāchī Sādhane*, vol. 2, pp. 404–5.

[54] An account of the Durga Devi famine is in Grant Duff, *History of the Mahrattas*, vol. 1, p. 43.

is said to have continued working for the Bidar court, which would take the family history through to the 1580s, placing Timaji's son Rudraji perhaps in the 1610s or 1620s, and Rudraji's son Timaji in the 1640s. This would be consistent with Govind's description of his grandfather Timaji as an established local malik (overseer) in the service of the young Shivaji.

The lineages of Kayastha gurus also offer valuable evidence for these migrations. An undated document said to be from the records of the Khasgivale family – the Kayastha sardars of Baroda – and reproduced in Gupte's early-twentieth-century collection of documents, gives us the lineage of the Takale family of gurus. Almost the last name in the lineage is well known to historians. Abasastri Takale was guru to the Kayastha community in Pune during the 1780s and 1790s.[55] The Takale guru lineage was first constituted, Khasgivale's document records, with three Brahman priests, Vitthalbhatta bin Gangadharbhatta Takale, Narayanbhatta Ganeshbhatta Mahabaleshwarkar, and Krishnabhatta bin Govindbhatta Vateshvarkar.[56] Coming from the town of Amba Jogai, they had moved to Bhopal, where they received patronage from a local ruler with a Deccani minister.[57] While in Bhopal, they came into contact with one Ramnath, a Brahman from the village of Sangi in Maithila, and priest to the local Kayastha community. For reasons not given in the document, the three priests became gurus to this community. Vitthalbhatta Takale himself eventually became a sanyasi, taking the name of Nilakantha. "After this, the Takales wandered as itinerants in two or three places in lower Bhupal. Here is their guru lineage until they came into the Konkan in the sake year of 1542."[58]

[55] Abasastri Takale took a leading role in the major grāmaṇya of 1789–90, when Brahmans from the Konkan village of Pen combined with a faction in Pune to attack Kayastha entitlements. See Wagle, "The Chandraseniya Kayastha Prabhus", pp. 316–21.

[56] The Islamicisation of these Brahman names is not unusual: see, for example, Joshi, "'Ālī Ādil Shāh I of Bījāpūr", for a description of the famous Sesa family of grammarians serving at the Bijapur court.

[57] An important Yadava centre of learning, Amba Jogai had close connections with the Konkan, since the family deity of many Chitpavan Brahmans was Yogesvari of Amba Jogai: Feldhaus, *Connected Places*, pp. 12–13.

[58] Gupte, *Ethnographical Notes*, p. 36.

Sake 1542 (1620 CE) seems to have been an agreed date in histories of the community for this event. Another early-twentieth-century community history gives more incidental detail. "After the Chandraseniya Kayastha Prabhu community had come into the Konkan, Govindbhatta Joshi, Deshastha Brahman, of the kasyap gotra, the descendant of Vitthalbhatta, himself of the Joshi family, which was within the lineage of the Kulaguru, came to the Konkan in sake 1542. From him the Takale lineage flourished in the country of the Deccan."[59]

Khasgivale's document recounts the eleven guru successors to Vitthalbhatta: Vishvanath Joshi Takale, Narayan Joshi, Hari Joshi, Vitthal Joshi, Ganesh Joshi, Nilakantha Joshi, Chintaman Joshi, Kamalakara Joshi, Shivram Joshi, Shridhar Joshi, and Govind Joshi. It was this Govind Joshi Takale who was said to have come into the Konkan littoral in 1620.[60] Eleven generations coming after the three priests were appointed as gurus, and running up to Govind Joshi Takale in 1620, would date the three priests to the later fifteeth century, perhaps, rather than to the early sixteenth. As we shall see, the often-repeated lists of grāmaṇyas in Kayastha community histories actually do give the coming of the three priests from Amba Jogai a definite date. It occurred in 1469, during the first Kayastha–Brahman grāmaṇya, and the guru Nilakantha, who had been Vitthalbhatta Takale before he became a sanyasi, took a leading role in defending the Kayasthas.[61] These two dates seem to be consistent with one another, suggesting that Kayastha tradition may not be too far wrong in dating this first grāmaṇya to the decade of the 1460s.

The Khasgivale lineage then gives the names of the gurus who succeeded this Govind Joshi Takale, running down to Abasastri Takale, active in Pune at the end of the eighteenth century. The evidence for this early period of social history is thus somewhat fragmentary. Nonetheless, lineages of this kind can give us some glimpses of the ways in which Kayastha families might have migrated from North and Central India into the Deccan, finding both livelihoods for themselves and priestly defenders of their ritual entitlements.

59 *Prabhukuladīpikā*, cited in Bendrey, *Daṇḍanītiprakaraṇam*, p. 43.

60 Gupte, *Ethnographical Notes*, p. 36.

61 Ketkar, *Mahārāṣṭrīya Dnyānakośa*, vol. 17, p. 244.

Office and Property: Kayastha Prabhus in Western India

Kayasthas were well placed to exploit the gradual separation between scribal and military skills in the countryside which characterised many emerging states of this period.[62] A further feature in the political culture of the Maratha region favoured them. It early became a principle of sound statecraft to appoint a Brahman and a Kayastha Prabhu to parallel posts, so that each might keep watch on the other. The contemporary account of Shivaji's state by Sabhasad noted this principle. "A Brahman known to the personal staff of the king should be appointed Sabnis [head clerk] and a Prabhu Karkhannis [commissary]. In this manner each officer retained should be dissimilar [in caste] to the other."[63]

Within this institutional context, Kayastha Prabhus were particularly successful in establishing themselves as Deshkulkarnis (regional revenue officers), balanced against their Maratha desai counterparts. Names of those attending judicial assemblies of this period feature many Kayastha Prabhus holding this post.[64] Accounts of village rights in the Mavala hills to the west of Pune reveal Kayasthas as Deshkulkarnis in Nanemaval, Poundamaval, Tamhankhore, Muthekhore, Kanadkhore, and Hardasmaval.[65] The revenue officer of Hardasmaval is well known to historians as Baji Prabhu, who joined Shivaji's forces in 1655, and in 1660 helped Shivaji break out from the siege of Panhala fort. He died holding the mountain pass against the Mughal forces.[66]

Kayasthas often combined the roles of Deshkulkarni with that of Havaldar (district officer). Murar Baji Prabhu was the Deshkulkarni of Mhar and heroic Havaldar of Purandhar fort outside Pune and died

[62] Fukazawa, *Medieval Deccan*, pp. 1–48. I have not here explored the question of Kayasthas' particular skills with the Modi cursive form of Marathi, which was extensively used by scribal specialists in this period. An exceptionally insightful history is Deshpande, *Scripts of Power*. For a suggestion that Modi was invented by Kayasthas, see Gupte, *The Modi Character*.

[63] Sen, ed., Śiva Chhatrapati, pp. 29–30. For a discussion of this strategy of "management by conflict", see Wink, *Land and Sovereignty*, p. 68.

[64] Bendrey, *Mahārāṣṭretihāsāchī Sādhane*, vol. 2, pp. 101–2.

[65] Sardesai, SPD, vol. 45, no. 1, pp. 7645–53.

[66] Grant Duff, *History of the Mahrattas*, vol. 1, p. 133.

holding the fort against Dilir Khan's Mughal forces in 1665.[67] These officials enjoyed judicial powers in addition to their roles as revenue officers. In 1675, one Mahadji Narsa Prabhu, Havaldar and karkun (clerical officer) secretary of Karyati Maval, adjudicated in a dispute within the local Thakar Kulkarni family.[68] In the same year, he appeared in a judicial assembly in a dispute over the rights of a local village headman.[69]

This entrenched position enabled Kayasthas to amass substantial rights and inām lands. A judicial assembly of 25 September 1615 ordered that the revenues and perquisites from the office of Kulkarni of Nagothane village in the northern Konkan be divided between the brothers Gambaji and Harad Prabhu, Sonaji Avaji Prabhu, and Krishnaji Tan Prabhu. The revenues and rights included rights to designated lands, services, rights in kind such as oil and cloth, and rights to precedence on ritual occasions.[70]

Kayasthas were also successful as ministers to local courts. The history of Shivaji's own Kayastha scribe, Balaji Avaji, reveals the opportunities open to skilled writers. The prominent Gholkar family of the Konkan derived their name from Gholavadi village, given them for their service to the Siddhis of Janjira. Ramaji Sriranga of the family was appointed dewan to one Babajikhasa in the Janjira territory. The dewanship was passed down to his son, Hari Ramji, and to his son Avaji Hari. Unfortunately, Babajikhasa died just after Avaji Hari had visited the family god at Jejuri. He was accused of causing the death and made to drink poison. His wife and three sons, including Balaji Avaji, were taken to the Konkan port of Rajapur to be sold as slaves. Fortunately, the wife's brother, Visaji Sankara, was employed as a writer in Rajapur. He helped the family escape and put the boys to work as writers. At about that time, Shivaji's power spread into the region, and his powerful minister Abaji Sonedev was made Subhedar of the new territories.[71]

[67] Ibid., pp. 150–1

[68] Potdar and Muzumdar, "Pune – Honap Deshpāṇḍe Daftar", in Potdar and Muzumdar, *Śiva Charitra Sāhitya*, vol. 2, pp. 146–9.

[69] Ibid., p. 274.

[70] Joshi and Khare, "Nāgoṭhane Kulkarni", in Joshi and Khare, eds, *Śiva Charitra Sāhitya*, vol. 3, pp. 20–1. For Kayastha ritual influence in matters of expiation, see O'Hanlon, "Narratives of Penance and Purification".

[71] Abaji Sonedev was made Subehdar of Shivaji's newly conquered terri-

Abaji recognised the abilities of Balaji Avaji, scion of four generations of a successful scribal family, and took him on in his new revenue administration. Shortly afterwards, he entered the service of Shivaji.[72]

These examples reveal the effectiveness with which Kayasthas had entrenched themselves as revenue officers and holders of landed rights, alongside the region's older Brahman elites. They were evidently sufficiently numerous and prosperous to attract the Kayastha Takale gurus to come down from Hindustan permanently to settle in the Deccan around 1620, "after which the Takale lineage flourished in the country of the Deccan." These, then, were the virtuous clerical people that Kamalakarabhatta described in his early-seventeenth-century review. Is it possible to learn anything more about the earlier histories of their conflicts with local Brahmans?

The Making of a Kayastha Guru

We turn back now to the appointment of the three Brahman priests as gurus to the Kayasthas, which Kayastha histories date to 1469. Another community history, the *Kāyastha Prabhūnchī Bakhar*, offers further information about the three priests. Published in the early 1880s in the short-lived periodical *Kāyastha Prabhūnchyā Itihāsāchī Sādhane*, the bakhar was said to have been written in 1795.[73] It described a conflict in the Konkan involving ancestors of the prominent Gholkar family of Balaji Avaji. After a lengthy account of the Konkan as

---

tories in the Konkan in 1649: Grant Duff, *History of the Mahrattas*, vol. 1, pp. 104–5.

[72] *Kāyastha Prabhūnchyā Itihāsāchī Sādhane*, book 1, no. 1, August 1881, pp. 1–3. Hereafter KPIS. This account was said to have been sent in by Malhar Khanderao Chitnis, a student at Elphinstone College.

[73] This bakhar is a single document, but spread over several issues of the *Kāyastha Prabhūnchyā Itihāsāchī Sādhane*. *Kāyastha Prabhūnchī Bakhar*, in KPIS, book 1, no. 1, ch. 2, August 1881, pp. 1–6; *Kāyastha Prabhūnchī Bakhar*, in KPIS, book 1, no. 2, ch. 2, September 1881, pp. 7–13; *Kāyastha Prabhūnchī Bakhar*, in KPIS, book 1, no. 3, ch. 2, October 1881, pp. 13–18; *Kāyastha Prabhūnchī Bakhar*, in KPIS, book 1, no. 4, ch. 2, November 1881, pp. 19–23, hereafter KPB. In a letter of 1795, believed to have been attached to the narrative, its author, Bachyaji Raghunath, said that he had written it after being asked for information about the history of the Kayasthas, following the recent Brahman attacks on their entitlements.

Parashuram's country, the coming of the Shalivahana era, and then the conquest of Indaprastha (Delhi) by Shyamas, Pathans, Mughals, and other people with unbored ears, the bakhar came to the conflict itself.

> Then some obdurate Brahmans without knowledge of the sastras began to stir up ill-feeling towards the Chandraseniya Kayasthas by alleging that they had no qualifications for any vedic ritual, and so brought difficulties in the way of their ceremonies and observances. Factions opened up from the Savitri river to Mandangad. Then Hari Gholkar, head of the Prabhus, some other Prabhu gentlemen, and the Brahmans came together. They went to the Mughlai amaldar, a yavana official. He said, we are not knowledgeable in the matter of your sastras. The holy place of you Hindus is Banaras. If you go there and get a decision and bring it back, we will proceed.[74]

So the Brahmans and Kayasthas went to Banaras and prayed to the great pandits there, and each of them looked into their own books.

> Then Sripad Guru Govindbhatta who was a great learned man gathered together an assembly of all the pandits in the Manimukta Mandapam. Debates about opinions in the sastras took place, with people saying it is, it is not. With the support of the sastras, all the Brahmans came to understand that the Prabhus were Chandraseniya Kayasthas of Kshatriya lineage, entitled to the three karmas and sixteen saṃskāras and qualifications for vedic mantras.[75]

Then, having examined all of the sastras and puranas, this Govindbhatta wrote his book the *Govindabhaṭṭi* for the Kayasthas. The dispute with the local Brahmans was ended, and the Kayasthas made Govindbhatta their guru, giving him suitable gifts. Govindbhatta then took on three disciples, Mahabaleshvar Karve, Vateshvar Bhatta, and Dinkarbhatta Takale, and himself went off to become a sanyasi. These three disciples became professional itinerant priests and gurus to Kayastha Prabhus everywhere, carrying out their ritual work with the aid of Govindbhatta's book.[76]

[74] KPB, pp. 8–9. For dates and issue numbers, see footnote 73 above.

[75] KPB, p. 9. For the "Mukti mandapam" as the hall in the great Visvesvara temple of Banaras where pandits met to discuss matters of religious law, see O'Hanlon, "Letters Home", pp. 17–20.

[76] KPB, pp. 8–9. Telang drew on this incident described in the KPB as an early

Except that the given name of the first Takale guru differs, these details are consistent with the guru lineage's narrative after the guruship passed to the three priests. The bakhar seems to provide an account of what led up to that event. A conflict over ritual entitlements between Kayasthas and local Brahmans originated in the Konkan. At a Muslim official's suggestion, it was taken for resolution to Banaras. Here, the Kayastha party gained the support of a powerful pandit, Govindbhatta, who produced a ritual guide in support of their claims, and was taken on as their guru. Before himself becoming a sanyasi, Govindbhatta recruited the three priests from Amba Jogai to move around serving the many dispersed communities of Kayasthas in North and Central India, and eleven guru generations later, in 1620, the Takales came down to serve Kayasthas in the Deccan.

Do we know anything more about Govindbhatta, pandit of Banaras and early guru to the Kayasthas? Many Kayastha histories cite his book as one of the founding texts for Kayastha ritual entitlements.[77] It may be that we have a version of this text available to us. The *Kāyasthapaddhati*, by Guru Govind, is an undated Sanskrit mss from the collection of the Bharat Itihas Samshodhak Mandal in Pune.[78] Its author is

---

example of the way in which officials of the Bijapur state referred "Hindu" disputes to Banaras for resolution. Telang, "Gleanings from Maratha Chronicles", in Ranade, *Rise of the Maratha Power*, pp. 126–7.

[77] There is a Sanskrit and Marathi letter to Nana Phadnis, dated Sake 1701 (1779 CE), from "Brahmans bearing such surnames as Bhatta, Dharmadikari, Sesa and residing in the holy place [of Banaras]." This letter describes the authorities that these pandits had consulted in the matter of the ritual entitlements of Kayasthas as "The *Gāgābhatti* and *Kāyasthapradīpa* of Gagabhatta, *Govindabhaṭṭi* of Govind, *Renukāmahātmayā* of the Skandapurāṇa, *Śūdrakamalākaraḥ* of Kamalakarabhatta, and *Jātiviveka*." The letter is reproduced in full in Gupte, *Ethnographical Notes*, Appendix 1. This same list, said to have been provided by Abasastri Takale himself, appears in a sammatipatra ("letter of agreement") attached to the end of the KPB, pp. 21–3.

[78] The *Kāyasthapaddhati* of Guru Govind is an undated 44 folio manuscript in the BISM, mss. 46,326. The authorities cited in this text are all before 1500. I am indebted to Peter Szanto for his excellent translations and insights here and to Alexis Sanderson, who very kindly looked over the text for clues to its dating. It has survived independently of other collections of Kayastha documents. The NCC lists another copy of this ms. in the Asiatic Society of Bengal, IM. 2992, with the

described as śrīparamahaṃsa parivrājakācārya Śrīpādaśiṣya Guru Govind, "Guru Govind who is the disciple of Sripada, of the order of paramahaṃsas, preceptor to the itinerant."[79]

What prescriptions did this Guru Govind make for Kayasthas, and what evidence is there that this text is connected with the events described in the Kayastha bakhar? The text opened with a statement of purpose, that it would address the question of mixed castes. It then proceeded to the lines, said to be from the *Vāstuśāstra* of Visvambhara, with which, as we have seen above, many manuscript copies of the *Jātiviveka* begin. But there was a key addition: Visvakarma was instructed to teach karma and dharma to all castes, but most particularly to the Kayasthas.[80] The text then described the first group of Kayasthas, descended from Chitragupta.[81] The second group Guru Govind termed kṣatrajas, i.e. Kayasthas who come from Kshatriyas. Here, he offered the story of the Kayasthas descended from the king Chandrasena after the rescue of the king's pregnant widow at the sage Dalbhya's ashram.[82]

This Guru Govind therefore looked to the founding story of the Maratha country, Parashuram's slaughter of the Kshatriyas, to find a pedigree for a community of Kayasthas who said they were kṣātrajas, Kayasthas who come from Kshatriyas. This is consistent with the narrative given in the *Kāyastha Prabhūnchi Bakhar* and the guru lineages we have examined: that Kayasthas from the Konkan region who said that they were kṣātrajas, descended from Kshatriyas, went to Banaras to find support for their claim to Kshatriya ritual entitlements, where the Banaras pandit Govindbhatta supported their claims with a paddhati (manual of ritual). If indeed the Guru Govind who authored the text and the Govindbhatta of our Kayastha histories are the same, Guru Govind's narratives for both Chitraguptas and Chandraseniyas would pre-date the very similar origin stories that we saw in the early-seventeenth-

author listed as "Gauda Govindaji." I have not been able to inspect this text. The conclusions offered here are necessarily preliminary.

[79] Guru Govind, *Kāyasthapaddhati*, f. 44r.

[80] Ibid., f. 2r.

[81] Ibid., ff. 5r–5v.

[82] Ibid., ff. 5v–7v. Peter Szanto has kindly allowed me to make use of his translation here.

century work of Kamalakarabhatta, and may have provided the template for them.

However, there was one striking difference between the two. Guru Govind's centrepiece was another narrative altogether, which is quite absent from Kamalakarabhatta's work. This narrative affiliated Kayasthas with Tantric forms of Shaivism. Following on from his account of the Chandraseniya Kayasthas, Guru Govind told another story, part of a "hidden" and "told to no-one" account of the cosmos narrated by Brahma to the sage Narada. It was a goddess, Mahesvari, also called the supreme Shakti, who was first to emerge from the darkness, and with other goddesses created the world of gods and men. At the churning of the ocean, the goddess Padmavati emerged and offered the gods a boon: a clever, skilful, learned man who knew the scripts and languages of all countries, interested in the arts, politics and law, someone whose pen was swift, whose words were skilful, dear to all, who knew all disciplines without having to practice them – in short, a Kayastha. The goddess created such a being from her own body. He was radiant, skilful, all sastras on his mouth, pen and ink in hand, adorned with jewels, a sacred thread on his body, a staff, an antelope skin, and a tilaka. He was peaceful but radiant, intent on reciting the Vedas, on being celibate, and on worshipping Vishnu. He was blessed by Lakshmi and devoted to the Shaiva Agamas, the great revealed scriptures of Shaivite Hinduism. When they saw him, the gods exclaimed "Miracle!" (chitram), and hence he was called Chitragupta.[83]

Guru Govind's account presented what was actually a magnificent hybrid, clearly recalling celebrations of Kayasthas in the early inscriptional record, where, as we have seen, they combined the qualities of scribe and Brahman.[84] This representation was given additional colour and force in Guru Govind's account. Chitragupta was skilled both in languages and penmanship, in the arts, politics, and law. But he was also endowed with quasi-Brahman qualities, accoutred as a Brahman boy about to undergo his upanayana, with sacred thread, staff, antelope skin, and a tilaka on his forehead, and the Vedas and sastras on his lips.[85] He was a being of extraordinary prestige. He was present with

[83] Ibid., ff.7v–10r. I owe the translation here to Peter Szanto.

[84] See fn. 6. above.

[85] For the dress that different authorities prescribe for the upanayana ceremony, see Kane, *History of Dharmaśāstra*, vol. 2, pt 2, pp. 278–82.

Vishnu and Shiva when the ocean of milk was churned, and distributed its treasures. The gods gave him Dakshayani in marriage, daughter of the ancient creator god Daksha, one of Brahma's sons. His son Dharmagupta was given the daughter of Manu, progenitor of mankind. Through his ascetic observances, his other son, Rudragupta, received an apsara as his wife, Svargaga, and from them four sons were born: Mathura, Gauda, Nagara, and Naigama. The goddess revealed their dharma to them, saying "All Kayasthas, who are devoted to their religious obligations, are, [being] my sons, Kaula Shakta Mahesvaras."[86] With these remarks, Guru Govind alluded to four of the major regional jati communities of North Indian Kayasthas and brought in a further set of associations, identifying them as affiliates of one of the major kulas or clans of the divinities within the great sects of Hindu tantrism.[87]

Further elements of hybridity, and further Shaiva connections, emerged as Guru Govind proceeded to list the saṃskāras appropriate to Kayasthas.[88] Twelve, rather than sixteen saṃskāras, supported by puranic rather than Vedic texts, marked Chitragupta's descendants as Sudras. As Alexis Sanderson has pointed out, the most interesting of these was Guru Govind's prescription for what is effectively a kind of upanayana within these twelve saṃskāras. Following Sanderson's analysis, we can see that Guru Govind called it not upanayanam, but upadeśaḥ (teaching). In the fire ritual that preceded the upadeśaḥ proper, the boy performed three ceremonial sippings of water, reciting three mantras as he did so, each addressed to one of the three Tattvas (states of being) set out in the sacred Agama texts of Shaivism: ātmatattvam, vidyātattvam, and śivatattvam. These same mantras were those used by initiated Shaivas in their sipping of water. However, Guru Govind removed the initial OṂ invocation and the initial seed-syllable that marks

[86] Guru Govind, *Kāyasthapaddhati*, f. 10r–12r. Again, I owe the translation here to Peter Szanto.

[87] For a survey of Kaula sects in the wider world of Shaivite religious culture of the first millenium, see Alexis Sanderson, "Śaivism and the Tantric Traditions", in Sutherland, *et al.*, eds, *The World's Religions*, pp. 128–72.

[88] I owe both the detailed translations here, and the analysis of the saṃskāras offered, entirely to the expertise and insight of Alexis Sanderson. Professor Sanderson has been kind enough to allow me to reproduce here both the translations of these parts of the text that he generously made available to me, and his analysis of the Shaivite liturgy.

the Shaiva mantras in their proper form, so that what would have been OṂ HĀṂ ĀTMATTVĀYA SVADHĀ becomes simply ATMATTVĀYA SVADHĀ. This provided a non-Tantric reflex which could be accommodated into the puranic idiom of Guru Govind's work.[89]

The upadeśaḥ itself was not a true upanayana, but drew on Shaiva liturgy to produce something like one. The boy was given a Brahmanical sacred thread and taught a Gayatri mantra. Again, following Sanderson's exposition for this part of the text, it was not the Vedic Gayatri which formed the core of the normal Brahmanical upanayana. It was instead the Shaiva copy of the Vedic Gayatri mantra, known as the Rudragayatri: OṂ TATPURUṢĀYA VIDMAHE MAHĀDEVĀYA DHĪMAHI TAN NO RUDRAH PRACODĀYAT. This was a perfect instrument for Guru Govind's purpose. It offered the basis for a quasi-Vedic upanayana that was not completely out of place within the largely puranic setting of his work. This Gayatri mantra was also quite appropriate for a community of followers of Tantric Shaivism. The Rudragayatri was part of the main Vedic mantra repertoire, but also featured amongst the mantras used by both of the major margas (paths of Shaivite initiates). Following Sanderson's translation, we can see that Guru Govinda says explicitly that this upadeśaḥ takes the place of the upanayana: sthānīyo vratabandhasya upadeśo nirūpyate, "[Now] I shall teach the [ritual] of upadeśaḥ, which [for Kayasthas] takes the place of the vratabandhaḥ [thread ceremony]."[90]

Here, Guru Govind accomplished a complex set of textual manoeuvres. In this text written for western Indian Kayasthas, he drew on the Shaiva Tantric affiliations of North Indian Kayasthas to project the brilliant figure of Chitragupta himself. Such affiliations would not be surprising, given the wide diffusion of these religious cultures during the late classical and early medieval centuries. In fact, we have concrete late-fifteenth-century evidence of the Shaiva Tantric connections of Kayasthas belonging to the same North Indian regional communities as are mentioned in Guru Govind's text. As Gode has pointed out, Kayastha Chamunda, a Kayastha of the Naigama community, son of Kumbha and protégé of king Rajamalla of Mewad (*fl.* 1460–1509),

[89] Alexis Sanderson, personal communication.

[90] Ibid., f. 22: Alexis Sanderson, personal communication.

is well known for his treatises on diseases and their treatment composed during the 1480s and 1490s. But he is also author of the *Varṇanighaṇṭu*, a short vocabulary explaining Tantric terminology, which he wrote in 1482.[91]

It is difficult to know how these Shaiva Tantric elements within Guru Govind's text might have been received by the western Indian Kayasthas who sought his support for their struggles back in the Konkan in the late fifteenth century. Nonetheless, his text offered them a quasi-Vedic upanayana, a firm identification as kṣātrajas, and an account of their origins that located them within the land of Parashuram. Above all, though, it gave them the figure of Chitragupta himself, with whom they were said to share a common dharma: an extraordinary combination of divine resplendence, Brahmanic learning and scribal power.

We do not know details of the early dispute that drove these Konkan Kayasthas to seek help in Banaras. But if we are correct in linking the text examined here with the Guru Govind described in Kayastha histories, the text gives us some sense of the kind of bid for prestige that western Indian Kayasthas of that early period were able to make. The semi-divine figure of the scribe may also help us understand some of the terms in which hostile Brahman pandits sought to represent Kayasthas in their own genres of the *Jātiviveka*, flourishing at this same period. As we have seen above, these particularly specify that Kayasthas should abjure from gestures and accoutrements associated with the twice-born, and Brahmans in particular: wearing a sacred thread and the reddish garments associated with the upanayana ceremonies of the twice-born, tying the hair with a topknot, touching the gods.

Is it possible to say anything more about the relationship between Guru Govind's and Kamalakarabhatta's texts? We know that Kamalakarabhatta's period of literary activity lay between 1610 and 1640.[92] The Takale guru lineage dates Govind Joshi Takale's arrival in the Deccan to 1620. As guru to the Kayasthas, it is likely that copies of Guru Govind's paddhati would have accompanied him. This would have been around the time that Kamalakarabhatta was revising the older *Jātiviveka* traditions about Kayasthas in his *Śūdrakamalākaraḥ*, and

[91] Gode, "Dates of the Works of Kayastha Cāmuṇḍa", pp. 479–86.

[92] Kane, *History of Dharmaśāstra*, vol. 1, pt 2, p. 932.

publicly rethinking older arguments about Kshatriyas in the Kaliyuga. It is possible, although we cannot be certain, that there was a connection between these two events, and that Kamalakarabhatta found in Guru Govind's work the template for his own treatment of Kayasthas. If Kamalakarabhatta was aware of the work, it is also not difficult to understand why he did not also reproduce the extraordinary account of Kayasthas' descent direct from the goddess. Its claims might well have struck him as inflated, if not outrageous.

Kayasthas and the Consecration

It was against this background of a major early-seventeenth-century revision in at least one important pandit intellectual's estimate of the social worth of Kayasthas, and the arrival in the Konkan of the Takale family as gurus to the Kayasthas, that the struggles of the later seventeenth century were fought. It was at this point too that Kayastha entitlement to Kshatriya saṃskāras became bound up with the wider issue of Shivaji's consecration. By the early 1670s, Kayasthas and Balaji Avaji himself had achieved a remarkable degree of influence at the heart of the Maratha court. Preparing his history of the Marathas during the early 1820s, James Grant Duff studied a mass of original Maratha state papers. He observed that "the reader will recognise, in Ballaji Aujee, the person in whose handwriting many of those papers are preserved."[93] Scribes at the court were also entrusted with the all-important task of recording the visitations to Shivaji of Sri Bhavani, tutelary deity to the Bhosle family, and writing down her advice when decisions critical to the Maratha state were to be taken.[94]

It was in this context that Brahman–Kayastha rivalries came to be caught up in the discussions about Shivaji's consecration. As some Brahman factions showed themselves opposed to the consecration, it was natural that the court should turn to Gagabhatta, nephew of Kamalakarabhatta, and already well known at Shivaji's court. In the course of these negotiations, Brahman–Kayastha relations at the Maratha court deteriorated sharply. After the consecration, Balaji Avaji prevailed on Gagabhatta to write a text in support of the Kayasthas, the *Kāyastha-*

[93] Grant Duff, *History of the Mahrattas*, vol. 1, p. 223.

[94] Sen, ed., Śiva Chhatrapati, pp. 50 and 124.

dharmadīpa (Light on the Dharma of Kayasthas), versions of which are still available to us.

The account of the *Kāyastha Prabhūnchi Bakhar* of these events is simple. A faction of local Brahmans questioned the Kayasthas' ritual entitlements as part of their opposition to the consecration. Balaji Avaji had set about arranging the thread ceremony of his sons. "At that time, there was a discussion about a consecration for the Maharaj. With hostility to that in their minds, Moropant Pingale and Balambhatta Chitale brought obstacles up at the ceremony."[95] What is most interesting, though, is the bakhar's account of how Gagabhatta then went about writing his text for the Kayasthas.

> Then in that same year Gagabhatta brought from Varanasi the old document of the *Govindabhaṭṭi*, and looking at the opinion of all the sastras and different books, he got all the Brahmans to accept that it was the opinion of the learned that the Prabhus were Kshatriya Chandraseniya Kayastha pure families, and with authority for karmas, and so he did the sacred thread ceremony of Avajiba and Khanderao Chitnis. This happened in that same year. Then a letter of injunction was sent to all the Brahmans. That the *Gāgābhaṭṭi* book had been written so that in the homes of the Chandraseniya Kayastha Prabhus arrangements for the thread ceremony and marriage should go on as they had before and the proper path of ritual practise established. After some days Shivaji maharaj died.[96]

This suggests that Gagabhatta based his work, the *Kāyasthadharmadīpa*, on the older text of Guru Govinda, which he is described as having brought with him from Banaras. If it is accepted that his uncle Kamalakarabhatta had already drawn on Guru Govinda's work for his own discussion of Kayasthas, Gagabhatta's doing so would follow quite naturally.

[95] KPB, pp. 10–11. Moropant Pingale was Shivaji's minister by the time of the consecration in 1674.

[96] KPB, pp. 11–12. According to the list of grāmaṇya reproduced in Rajwade's *Marāṭhānchya Itihāsāchī Sādhane*, one of the Takale gurus, Ganesh Joshi, who is listed in Khasgivale's lineage, was active in securing this result for the Kayasthas. Rajwade, *Marāṭhānchya Itihāsāchī Sādhane*, vol. 6, no. 444 of 1873, p. 609. Letters said to be the "injunctions" referred to here, dating 23 November 1669 and 18 August 1672, are printed in Thakare, *Grāmaṇyāchā Sādyanta Itihāsa*, pp. 19–21.

But what kind of work did Gagabhatta produce for the Kayasthas, as he adapted "the old document of the Govindabhaṭṭi"?[97] His *Kāyasthadharmadīpa* commenced with a praise poem. He acclaimed Shivaji as an ocean of compassion, destroyer of yavanas, saviour of Brahmans from Aurangzeb, who struck fear into the hearts of the kings of Golconda, Bijapur, and Delhi. Shivaji's father, Shahaji, had emerged as the new embodiment of Kshatriya dharma, and "Kshatriya families, afflicted by the terror of Parashuram, have found shelter beneath Shivaji's royal umbrella."[98]

This was a very a plain statement of his differences with local Brahmans. A new avatar of the Kshatriyas had taken birth in the Kaliyuga: the world as Parashuram had made it had utterly changed. Gagabhatta concluded his poem with praise for the virtuous qualities of Balaji Avaji himself – his wisdom, skill in accomplishing duties, and unremitting labour in the service of the king. All of this must have seemed a very promising reading to the Kayastha audience at Shivaji's court. Not in the distant learned halls of Banaras, but here, in the heart of the Maratha state, the great pandit had affirmed the existence of Kshatriyas in the modern age, opening the way for confirmation of others as Kshatriyas too, albeit Kshatriyas who had laid aside their swords.

But what Gagabhatta seemed to offer with one hand, he appeared partially to withhold with the other. His opening statement of intent said something rather odd: that he had written the work "easily", or, perhaps, "for fun" (līlātahaḥ).[99] The first part of his *Kāyasthadharmadīpa* was a re-working of the *Jātiviveka*.[100] After following something like

[97] I have looked at two versions of this text: *Kāyasthadharmadīpa*, Bhandarkar Oriental Research Institute (hereafter BORI) ms. no. 342 of 1887–91; and Oriental and India Office Collections, Sanskrit ms. 3009m. They are identical, except that the latter includes Gagabhatta's opening praise poem, of twenty-nine verses, to Shivaji, which also describes the text as having been commissioned by Balaji Avaji. I have here used the OIOC text. For a discussion of this praise poem, see Rajwade, "Gāgābhaṭṭa Kṛta Śivarāja Praśasti", in Saha and Mandake, eds, *Itihāsachāraya V.K. Rājavāḍe*, vol. 11, pp. 239–45.

[98] Gagabhatta, *Kāyasthadharmadīpa*, ff. 1v–2v. Peter Szanto has kindly permitted me to use his translations of this text.

[99] Ibid., f. 2v.

[100] Ibid., f. 2v.

Gopinatha's classification, Gagabhatta came to the Kayasthas themselves. They were of three kinds. For "mixed" Kayasthas, Gagabhatta simply reproduced Gopinatha's short and hostile description. But, he said, there were also Chitragupta Kayasthas, and Chandraseniya Kayasthas, and here he followed the broad outlines of Guru Govind's and of Kamalakarabhatta's narrative.[101]

Also, like Kamalakarabhatta, Gagabhatta did not refer explicitly to Guru Govind, or reproduce Guru Govind's celebration of Chitragupta the resplendent scribe. However, Gagabhatta seemed to make knowing references to Guru Govind's text. He included his account of the celestial marriages with which Chitragupta and his sons were favoured, but interspersed his narrative with curious allusions and asides. Chitragupta did indeed marry Dakshayani, but Gagabhatta calls the son not Dharmagupta, but "Vichitragupta" ("strange" or "extraordinary gupta"). This extraordinary Gupta married the daughter of Manu and begot Dharmagupta, who then married "a female gandharva" and begot Rudragupta. As in Guru Govind's text, Rudragupta's sons are Mathura, Gauda, Nagara, and Naigama. But, Gagabhatta added, they are also dubbed Kayastha, Shakta, Kaulika, and Mahesvara.[102] It is difficult, at this distance, to be certain of the exact nuances of Gagabhatta's references to Guru Govind's text here, though the references certainly suggest that the text was known to local audiences. Is it possible that his remarks were a tongue-in-cheek reference to the extravagance of Guru Govind, with its descriptions of the Kayasthas as kaulika Shaktas and sons of the goddess?

Gagabhatta then went on to describe the dharma and saṃskāras of the Chitragupta and Chandraseniya Kayasthas. He affirmed them as virtuous and trustworthy, and, unlike the "mixed" Kayasthas, entitled to up to twelve saṃskāras. However, his conclusion was that while Kayasthas were allowed a kind of upanayana, he emphasised that they had no entitlement themselves to study the Vedas.[103] The elaborate

[101] Ibid., ff. 10v–11r.

[102] Ibid., ff. 10r. There is a scribal error here: "Kaulika" is written here as "Maulika". In the BORI mss, the word given is "Kaulika". Gagabhatta, *Kāyasthadharmadīpa*, BORI ms. f. 12r.

[103] Ibid., ff. 15v. As Madhav Deshpande has pointed out, it is difficult to be certain about Gagabhatta's precise prescriptions because the Kayasthas' opponents

construct of Guru Govind's Shaivite upadeśaḥ did not find its way into Gagabhatta's text.[104]

Although Gagabhatta may not have provided the Kayasthas with the unequivocal support that they looked for, Shivaji's consecration was in other ways a triumph for them. In the same month as the consecration, Shivaji bestowed on Balaji Avaji the permanent office of chitnis (secretary to the court).[105] Shortly after this, Balaji Avaji's name began to appear authorising documents of property right.[106] Sabhasad named him specifically as one of the close supporters who were called around Shivaji's deathbed in 1680.[107] Balaji Avaji himself fell victim to the factional disputes that followed Shivaji's death. His end, like that of his father, was a brutal reminder of the ultimate dependence of powerful scribes on the favour of their masters. He was trampled beneath the feet of an elephant, along with other ministers at court whom Shivaji's son Sambhaji suspected of plotting in favour of his younger brother Rajaram. However, as Balaji Avaji had done after the death of his own father, his son Khando Ballal showed a remarkable ability to recuperate the family fortunes, serving Sambhaji until the latter's execution by the Mughals in 1689, and remaining principal scribe with Rajaram's Maratha court during the years of its siege and exile at Senji.[108]

---

quickly produced their own interpolated versions: Deshpande, "Kṣatriyas in the Kali Age?", pp. 9–10. For an early-twentieth-century Kayastha analysis of these interpolations, see Gupte, *Rājavāḍyānchī Gāgābhaṭṭī*, pp. 6–23.

[104] These may have been the features of Gagabhatta's work that led the Kayastha guru Abasastri Takle to say a century later that Gagabhatta's book had let the Kayasthas down. His reflections are in a series of letters written between 1789 and 1795: *Kāyastha Prabhūnchyā Itihāsāchī Sādhane*, book 1 no. 5, December 1881–January 1882, pp. 6–10. See Wagle, "The Chandraseniya Kayastha Prabhus and the Brahmans", pp. 316–21.

[105] Grant Duff refers to this "original sunnud": *History of the Mahrattas*, vol. 1, p. 223. It is reproduced in Rajwade and Vijapurkar, eds, *Granthamālā: Patre, Yādī, Vagaire*, p. 129, and dated rajyabhiśeka 1, jyeṣṭa vadya pratipada, or two days after Shivaji's consecration on 6 June 1674.

[106] See Deshpande, "Hukerī Paragaṇyāche Deshpānde", *Śiva Chāritra Sāhitya*, vol. 8, pp. 20–3.

[107] Sen, Śiva Chhatrapati, p. 149.

[108] Grant Duff, *History of the Mahrattas*, vol. 1, pp. 263–6.

Conclusions

In the centuries before Shivaji, then, contemporary debates about the existence of Kshatriyas in the Kaliyuga, with all of their implications for the wider architecture of the social order, were shaped in important ways by the position of western India's successful Kayastha communities. Shivaji's consecration posed the same questions, raised many of the same local tensions, and was resolved, in the end, in the same way, through the intervention of pandit intellectuals based in Banaras.

As is well known, the consecration was a key episode in the formation of the Maratha state. It is generally accepted that amongst the Maratha ruler's own purposes was the desire to reinforce his authority among leading Maratha families. But there were other agendas too. We cannot know how much truth there was in Sabhasad's statement that it was Gagabhatta himself who made the case that the Maratha ruler should take to himself the dignity of a throne and royal umbrella, since his vanquished enemies enjoyed these insignia of prestige.[109] The negotiations were evidently complex. But they do signify that some Brahmans in Banaras, familiar with a world in which royal Rajput rulers were important political figures, more exposed to shifts in religious politics at the courts of Shah Jahan and Aurangzeb, and already familiar with the debate in relation to Kayasthas, were by the time of Gagabhatta's generation willing to affirm powerful rulers as royal kings, and to ritualise their status.[110]

Why did the issue seem to be so much more difficult for pandit intellectuals in the Maratha country itself? As suggested at the start of this essay, early modern India may have seen important regional differences in the challenge that emerging new rulers, as well as upwardly mobile scribal people, posed to local Brahman communities. In North

[109] Sen, Śiva Chhatrapati, pp. 113–14.

[110] Ananya Vajpeyi suggests that Brahman attitudes in Banaras were shaped in part by the memory of the old links between Yadava Devagiri and the ancient intellectual centre of Paithan, from whence many Banaras families had migrated after the fall of Devagiri. For these families, Kshatriyas in the modern age were not a threat, but potentially a great asset, and they saw in the figure of Shivaji the possibility of these older links revived. Vajpeyi, "Politics of Complicity", pp. 32–41. However, we do not yet have solid evidence of these associations in the work of the pandits concerned.

India, ruling groups early moved away from the notion of Kshatriya status as the principal mark of rulership, towards a Rajput model which derived from networks of clan membership and forms of participation within regional polities.[111] Recognition of their royalty did not therefore hinge so centrally on Brahman ritual affirmation, a position reinforced during the Mughal period when the Mughal court created its own ritual and visual vocabulary for Rajput lords. Brahmans in Mughal North India were in any case less prominent as elites in state service.

Nor was Kshatriya status bestowed by Brahman priests the primary basis of legitimate kingship in Vijayanagar and its Nayaka successor states in the South. There, legitimate kingship derived rather from the flow of wealth from courts to temples and agraharams. Royal legitimacy came to be vested much more in links with temple deities than with Brahmans, and in the king's status as principal worshipper.[112] Outside the prosperous religious centres of these southern regions, "secular" (niyogi) Brahmans flourished as the basis of its karanam scribal culture, and Kayasthas were much less strongly present as scribal rivals than they were in Central and West India.

The consequences of these various differences emerge with particular clarity at some of the eighteenth-century Rajput courts. At the court of Savai Jaisingh II, the ruler of Jaipur (1688–1743), Kayasthas and Jains, rather than Brahmans, were dominant in the state administration. When the Jaipur state began in the first half of the eighteenth century to experiment with new forms of royal ritual, Savai Jaisingh had therefore to turn to Maratha ritual specialists from Banaras to affirm him as a dharmic king.[113] Peabody has described how representations of royalty at the kingdom of Kota centred only in part on Rajput genealogical descent. As important was the court's association with the Vallabha sect, where the links between ruler and deity were celebrated with lavish public giftings of food. Here, interestingly, Peabody sees

[111] For the "Rajputisation" of Kshatriya status in medieval North India, see Chattopadhyaya, *The Making of Early Medieval India*, pp. 73–86.

[112] For these features of the Vijayanagara and Nayaka states, see Stein, *Vijayanagara*, and Narayana Rao, Shulman, and Subrahmanyam, *Symbols of Substance*.

[113] Horstmann, *Visions of Kingship*, pp. 7–20.

parallels with the direct relationship between deity and ruler characteristic of southern courts, not surprising given that Vallabhacharaya was a South Indian Brahman with a family history of close links to the Vijayanagar court.[114]

In the Maratha regions, however, the position was different. The states of the region rested on the co-operation of substantial Brahman clerical elites still strongly rooted in Sanskritic religious culture. In the absence of the great temple complexes and agraharams of the South, these Brahmans came to depend heavily on local office-holding in regional states. Yet it was precisely here that they came up against competition from Kayasthas, often relative newcomers into the region, as well as – and sometimes better – equipped for these bureaucratic roles. Brahman control over ritual entitlements provided a powerful and durable instrument through which to strike back at these scribal rivals.

The same issue of control extended into Brahman relationships with local rulers. The egalitarian warrior culture of the Maratha country meant that powerful local lords were not "Rajputised". Recognition of legitimate kingship hinged more directly on the relations of patronage and power between rulers and Brahmans. As remarked above, we do not know whether ritual at the courts of Maratha rulers in the centuries before Shivaji required explicit Brahman affirmation of their Kshatriya status. It may be that Brahman ritual recognition of the legitimacy of rulership in earlier centuries took a range of forms. It was in the context of Shivaji's bid for the ritual of royal consecration that the focus narrowed down to the question of Kshatriya status, thus bringing the issue into the field of argument already occupied by Brahman–Kayastha struggles. In this context, it may have made sense for Brahmans defending their positions in the difficult social terrain of the Maratha country to construct a world in which only Brahmans and Sudras survived.

These conflicts cast a long shadow. Their preoccupation with such struggles may have held Maratha Kayasthas back from participating in contemporary debate about political ethics, as their scribal counterparts in other regions of India were able to do. The major text of nīti

[114] Peabody, *Hindu Kingship*, pp. 105–9.

written in the Maratha country during this period, the well-known *Ājnāpatra* of Ramacandrapant Amatya, was by a Brahman.[115] As Narayana Rao and Subrahmanyam have noted, politics and government in the Maratha country continued to be debated primarily as matters of religious law.[116] If Maharashtra's Kayastha communities have left any textual monument to their lives as scribes, it is in the archives of their grāmaṇya with local Brahmans.

Gagabhatta's intervention from Banaras briefly opened up to local Brahmans a window on a more socially diverse world. But this window was to close again just as quickly. As Madhav Deshpande has shown, the Bhatta position was countered by the intellectual tradition of Vaidyanatha Payagunde and his teacher Nagesabhatta of Banaras, representative of a very different Banaras tradition. Their argument that the rules of expiation made it impossible for erstwhile Kshatriyas to remedy their loss of dharma with appropriate penances came to predominate within Pune Brahman circles during the peshwa period.[117] In these circumstances, and following further assaults on their entitlements during the eighteenth century, many Kayasthas migrated again, this time to serve in the Maratha courts of Kolhapur, Satara, Baroda, and Indore.

These developments were to set many of the terms of politics in colonial western India. The old genre of the *Jātiviveka* continued to be powerful in the new setting of colonial discourses about caste. When officials of the East India Company first consulted local pandits about the region's jati communities, it was to the old unreconstructed genre of the *Jātiviveka* that the pandits directed them.[118] It was thus no accident that the earliest work of "non-Brahman" critique in the Maratha country, published in 1861, located itself consciously as a critical voice within the genre of the *Jātiviveka*, as its title, the *Jātibhed Vivekasār* (Essence of the discussion of caste division), made clear.[119] These distinctive colonial forms emerged out of pre-colonial textual genres and histories of social contestation.

[115] See Kulkarni, ed., *Ājnāpatra*.

[116] Narayana Rao and Subrahmanyam, "Notes on Political Thought".

[117] Deshpande, "Kṣatriyas in the Kali Age?", pp. 11–23.

[118] Steele, *Law and Custom*, pp. xi–xii.

[119] Padwal, *Jātibhed Vivekasār*. See O'Hanlon, *Caste, Conflict and Ideology*, pp. 42–5.

The form of these histories is also suggestive from a methodological perspective. Rightly, historians are often reluctant to see very close connections between texts and political strategies, for fear of reducing the meanings of the former to a wholly instrumental expression of the latter. The alternative position is sometimes to see normative Sanskrit texts of the kind studied here as little more than the paper effusions of Brahman intellectuals, scarcely relevant to anyone outside their narrow circles. But what Kayastha histories demonstrate, if nothing else, is the enduring social power of the textualist Brahmanical culture examined in this essay. Flourishing with the great expansion of paper use in many regions of early modern India, this textual culture was a potent force as much in the local world of day-to-day social relationships as it was in the milieu of pandit assemblies and debates, precisely because its malleability made it adaptable to a wide range of local needs and struggles.[120]

The histories of contestation studied here may also be significant from another perspective. It is possible to see prefigured, in the vision of a landscape only of Brahmans and Sudras, the Brahman–non-Brahman conflicts that so profoundly shaped the political culture of the Maratha regions throughout the colonial period and beyond. Of course, South India too was to go on to develop its own forms of non-Brahmanism. However, it is significant that it was also in the dry upland regions of Madras, where Brahmans struggled to find livelihoods in between local communities and state service, that the most radical forms of non-Brahmanism were concentrated.[121] The conceptions of society explored here, with their repudiation of the modern era of the Kali-yuga and its destruction of India's ancient golden age of harmony, order and respect for dharma, pointed to the future in another way too. Here, in the very polarised socio-religious culture to which these these traditions of thought gave rise, we may see some of the paths by which Brahman intellectuals in colonial western India came to articulate the conservative understanding of India's social order which was later to form the basis of Maharashtra's distinctive and influential form of politicised Hinduism.

[120] I am very grateful to Sheldon Pollock for making this point to me. For a study of Brahman pandit households in Banaras as sites of intellectual production, see O'Hanlon, "Speaking from Siva's Temple".

[121] See Baker, *Politics and Social Conflict*.

References

Alam, Muzaffar, and Sanjay Subrahmanyam, "The Making of a Munshi", *Comparative Studies of South Asia, Africa and the Middle East*, vol. 24, no. 2, 2004, pp. 61–72.

Baker, Christopher, *Politics and Social Conflict in South India: The Non-Brahman Movement and Tamil Separatism, 1916–1929* (Cambridge: Cambridge University Press, 1971).

Baldissera, Fabrizia, *The Narmamālā of Kṣemendra: Critical Edition, Study and Translation* (Würzburg: Ergon Verlag, 2005).

Bayly, Susan, *Caste, Society and Politics in India from the Eighteenth Century to the Modern Age* (Cambridge: Cambridge University Press, 1999).

Bendrey, V.S., ed., *Keśava Paṇḍita's Daṇḍanītiprakaraṇam* (Poona: Arya-bhushan Press, 1943).

———, *Coronation of Shivaji the Great* (Bombay: P.P.H. Bookstall, 1960).

———, *Mahārāṣṭretihāsāchī Sādhane*, 2 vols (Bombay: Mumbai Marathi Grantha Sangrahalaya, 1966).

Benson, James, "Saṃkārabhaṭṭa's Family Chronicle", in Axel Michaels, ed., *The Pandit: Traditional Scholarship in India* (Delhi: Manohar), pp. 105–18.

Bhimsen, *Tarikh-i Dilkasha*, ed. V.G. Khobrekar (Bombay: Government of Maharashtra, 1972).

Bronkhorst, Johannes, "Bhaṭṭoji Dīkṣita on Sphoṭa", *Journal of Indian Philosophy*, vol. 33, no. 1, 2005, pp. 3–41.

Chatterjee, Kumkum, "History as Self-Representation: The Recasting of a Political Tradition in Late Eighteenth Century Eastern India", *Modern Asian Studies*, vol. 32, no. 4, 1998, pp. 913–48.

———, "Scribal Elites in Sultanate and Mughal Bengal", *Indian Economic and Social History Review*, vol. 47, no. 4, October–December 2010, pp. 445–72.

Chattopadhyaya, B.D., *The Making of Early Medieval India* (New Delhi: Oxford University Press, 1998).

da Cunha, J. Gerson, *The Sahyâdri-Khaṇḍa of the Skaṇḍa Purâṇa* (Bombay: Thacker, Vining and Co., 1877).

Derrett, J. Duncan M., *Religion, Law and the State in India* (London: Faber and Faber, 1968).

Deshpande, Madhav M., "Localising the Universal Dharma: Purānas, Nibandhas, and Nirṇayapatras in Medieval Maharashtra", unpublished ms.

———, "Kṣatriyas in the Kali Age? Gāgābhaṭṭa and His Opponents", *Indo-Iranian Journal*, vol. 53, no. 2, 2010, pp. 1–26.

Deshpande, Prachi, *Creative Pasts: Historical Memory and Identity in Western India, 1700–1960* (Delhi: Permanent Black, 2007).

———, *Scripts of Power: Writing, Language Practices, and Cultural History in Western India* (New Delhi: Permanent Black, 2023).

Dutt, Jogesh Chander, *Kings of Kāshmīra: Being a Translation of the Sanskrit Work Rājatarangginī of Kahlana Pandita* (Calcutta: Stanhope Press, 1879–98).

Eaton, Richard M., *A Social History of the Deccan, 1300–1761: Eight Indian Lives* (Cambridge: Cambridge University Press, 2005).

Enthoven, R.E., *Tribes and Castes of Bombay*, 3 vols (Bombay: Government Central Press, 1922).

Feldhaus, Anne, *Connected Places: Region, Pilgrimage and Geographical Imagination in India* (New York: Palgrave Macmillan, 2003).

Fukazawa, Hiroshi, *The Medieval Deccan: Peasants, Social Systems and States* (Delhi: Oxford University Press, 1991).

Gagabhatta, *Kāyasthadharmadīpa*, Oriental and India Office Collections, Sanskrit ms. 3009m; and Bhandarkar Oriental Research Institute, Pune, ms. no. 342 of 1887–91.

Gode, P.K., "Sābāji Pratāparāja, A Protégé of Burhān Nizām Shah of Ahmadnagar, and His Works – Between AD 1500 and 1560", *Annals of the Bhandarkar Oriental Research Institute*, vol. 24, pts 3–4, July–October 1943, pp. 156–64.

Gopinatha, *Jātiviveka*, Oriental and India Office Collections, London, Sanskrit mss. nos 1969 and 1061a.

Gordon, Stewart, *The Marathas 1600–1818* (Cambridge: Cambridge University Press, 1993).

Grant Duff, James, *History of the Mahrattas*, 3 vols (London: Longman, Rees, Orme, Brown and Green, 1826).

Guha, Sumit, "Speaking Historically: The Changing Voices of Historical Narration in Western India, 1400–1900", *American Historical Review*, vol. 109, no. 4, 2004, pp. 1084–1103.

———, "Transitions and Translations: Regional Power and Vernacular identity in the Dakhan, *c.* 1500–1800", *Comparative Studies of South Asia, Africa and the Middle East*, vol. 24, no. 2, 2004, pp. 23–31.

———, "Serving the Barbarian to Preserve the Dharma: The Ideology and Training of a Clerical Elite in Peninsular India *c.* 1300–1800", *Indian Economic and Social History Review*, vol. 47, no. 4, October–December 2010, pp. 497–526.

Gune, V.T., *The Judicial System of the Marathas* (Poona: Sangam Press, 1953).

Gupta, Chitrarekha, *The Kayasthas: A Study in the Formation and Early History of a Caste* (Calcutta: K.P. Bagchi and Company, 1996).
Gupte, B.A., *The Modi Character and Its Origin* (Bombay: Education Society Press, 1906).
Gupte, K.T., *Rājavāḍyānchī Gāgābhaṭṭī* (Pune: K.T. Gupte, 1919).
Gupte, T.V., *Ethnographical Notes on the Chandraseniya Kayastha Prabhus* (Poona: Israelite Press 1904).
———, *Chāndrasenīya Kāyastha Prabhu Grāmaṇya Prakaraṇatīla Pāch Assal Ājnāpatre* (Pune: Israelite Press, 1914).
Guru Govind, *Kāyasthapaddhati*, Bharat Itihas Samshodhak Mandal, Pune, ms. no. 46,326, no date.
Horstmann, Monika, *Visions of Kingship in the Twilight of Mughal Rule* (Amsterdam: Royal Netherlands Academy of Arts and Sciences, 2006).
Janaki, Kumari S.S., "Paraśurāma", *Purana*, vol. 8, no. 1, January 1966, pp. 52–82.
Jha, V.N., "Varṇasaṃkara in the Dharmasūtras: Theory and Practice", *Journal of the Economic and Social History of the Orient*, vol. 13, no. 3, 1970, pp. 273–88.
Jones, William, ed., *Institutes of Hindu Law, or, the Ordinances of Menu, According to the Gloss of Culluca* (London: Sewell and Derrett, 1796).
Joshi, P.M., "'Ālī Ādil Shāh I of Bījāpūr (1558–1580 and His Royal Librarian: Two Ruq'as", *Journal of the Bombay Branch of the Royal Asiatic Society*, vols 31–2, 1956–7, pp. 97–107.
Joshi, S.N., "Hukerī Paragaṇyāche Deshpānde', *Śiva Chāritra Sāhitya*, vol. 8 (Pune: Bharat Itihas Samshodhak Mandal, 1942), pp. 15–28.
———, and G.H. Khare, "Nāgoṭhane Kulkarni", in S.N. Joshi and G.H. Khare, eds, *Śiva Charitra Sāhitya*, vol. 3 (Pune: Bharat Itihas Samshodhak Mandal, 1930), pp. 20–37.
Kamalakarabhatta, *Śūdrakamalākaraḥ*, eds Ganesh Bapuji Sastri Malavankar and Vishnu Sastri Bapat (Mumbai: no press given, 1861).
Kane, P.V., "A Note on the Kāyasthas", *New Indian Antiquary*, March 1939, pp. 740–3.
———, *History of Dharmaśāstra*, 5 vols (Poona: Bhandarkar Oriental Research Institute, 1975).
Karve, Irawati, "The Paraśurāma Myth", *Journal of the University of Bombay: History, Economics and Sociology*, vol. 1, pt 1, 1932, pp. 115–39.
Kāyastha Prabhūnchyā Itihāsāchī Sādhane, vol. 1, nos 1–9, August 1881–April 1882.
Ketkar, S.V., *Mahārāṣṭrīya Dnyānakośa*, 23 vols (Poona: Dnyanakosh Press, 1921–9).

Kielhorn, F., "Inscription of the Time of Bhojavarman", *Epigraphia Indica*, vol. 1, no. 38, 1892, pp. 330–8.

Kotani, H., *Western India in Historical Transition: Seventeenth to Early Twentieth Centuries* (New Delhi: Manohar, 2002).

Krishna, Sesa, *Śūdrācāraśiromaṇi*, ed. Narayan Sastri Khiste, 2 vols (Benaras: Saraswati Bhawan Library, 1933–6).

Krishnamoorthy, K., *Subhāṣita-Sudhānidhi of Sāyaṇa* (Dharwar: Karnatak University, 1968).

Kruijtzer, Gijs, *Xenophobia in Seventeenth Century India* (Leiden: Leiden University Press, 2009).

Kulkarni, A.R., ed., *Ājnāpatra* (Pune: Diamond Publications, 2004).

Leonard, Karen Isaksen, *Social History of an Indian Caste: The Kayasths of Hyderabad* (Berkeley: University of California Press, 1978).

Madhav, *Śatapraśnakalpalatā*, Bhandarkar Oriental Research Institute, P.M. Joshi Collection, Sanskrit ms. no 19.

Minkowski, Christopher, "Nilakaṇṭha's Mahābhārata", *Seminar*, vol. 607, April 2010, pp. 1–7.

Moroji, Samarava, *A History of the Pattana Prabhus* (Bombay: Family Printing Press, 1877).

———, Śrī Kshatriyavaṃsodgamamālā (Bombay: Lithograph, 1855).

Narayana Rao, Velcheru, David Shulman, and Sanjay Subrahmanyam, *Symbols of Substance: Court and State in Nayaka Period Tamilnadu* (Delhi: Oxford University Press, 1992).

———, *Textures of Time: Writing History in South India, 1600–1800* (New York: Other Press, 2003).

Narayana Rao, Velcheru, and Sanjay Subrahmanyam, "Notes on Political Thought in Medieval and Early Modern South India", *Modern Asian Studies*, vol. 43, no. 1, January 2009, pp. 175–210.

Nobile, Riccardo, "Notizie sulle sotto-caste Nell' India estratte, pubblicate e tradotte dai codici inediti del Jativiveka", *Atti Della Reale Accademia di Archeologica, Lettere et Belle Arti*, Napoli, Nuova Serie, vol. 1, 1910, pp. 65–94.

O'Hanlon, Rosalind, *Caste, Conflict and Ideology: Mahatma Jotirao Phule and Low Caste Protest in Nineteenth Century Western India* (Cambridge: Cambridge University Press, 1985).

———, "Narratives of Penance and Purification in Western India, *c.* 1650–1850", *The Journal of Hindu Studies*, vol. 2, 2009, pp. 48–75.

———, "Letters Home: Banaras Pandits and the Maratha Regions in Early Modern India", in *Modern Asian Studies*, vol. 44, no. 2, March 2010, pp. 201–40.

———, "Speaking from Siva's Temple: Banaras Scholar Households and the Brahman 'Ecumene' of Early Modern India", *South Asian History and Culture*, vol. 2, no. 2, April 2011, pp. 253–77.

———, and Christopher Minkowski, "What Makes People Who They Are? Pandit Networks and the Problem of Livelihoods in Early Modern Western India", *Indian Economic and Social History Review*, vol. 45, no. 3, 2008, pp. 381–416.

Padwal, Tukaram Tatya, *Jātibhed Vivekasār* (Mumbai: Ganpat Krishnaji's Press, 1861).

Peabody, Norbert, *Hindu Kingship and Polity in Precolonial India* (Cambridge: Cambridge University Press, 2003).

Pollock, Sheldon, "New Intellectuals in Seventeenth Century India", *Indian Economic and Social History Review*, vol. 38, no. 1, 2001, pp. 3–31.

———, *The Ends of Man in the Age of Postmodernity* (Amsterdam: Royal Netherlands Academy of Arts and Sciences, 2005).

Potdar, D.V. and G.N. Muzumdar, "Pune – Honap Deshpāṇḍe Daftar", in D.V. Potdar and G.N. Muzumdar, eds, *Śiva Charitra Sāhitya*, vol. 2 (Pune: Bharat Itihas Samshodhak Mandal, 1930), pp. 113–50.

Prasad, Munshi Kali, and Srivastava Dusre, *The Kayastha Ethnology; Being An Enquiry into the Origin of the Chitraguptavansi and Chandrasenavansi Kayasthas* (Lucknow: American Methodist Mission Press, 1877).

Raeside, Ian, "A Note on the 'Twelve Mavals' of Poona District", *Modern Asian Studies*, vol. 12, no. 3, 1978, 393–417.

Rajwade, V.K., ed., *Marāṭhyānchyā Itihāsāchī Sādhane*, 22 vols, www.samagrarajwade.com, Pune, 1898–1919.

Rajwade, V.K., "Gāgābhaṭṭa Kṛta Śivarāja Praśasti", in M.B. Saha and Girish Mandake, eds, *Itihāsachāraya V.K. Rājavāḍe Samagra Sāhitya*, vol. 11 (Dhule: Rajwade Samagra Sahitya Mandal, 1998), pp. 239–45.

Rajwade, V.K., and V.G. Vijapurkar, eds, *Granthamālā: Patre, Yādī, Vagaire* (Kolhapur: Shri Samarthaprasad Press, 1902).

Raman, Bhavani, *Document Raj: Writing and Scribes in Early Colonial South India* (Chicago: University of Chicago Press, 2012).

Ranade, M.G., *Rise of the Maratha Power* (New Delhi: Government of India, 1974).

Richards, J.F., "Norms of Comportment Among Mughal Imperial Officers", in Barbara Daly Metcalf, ed., *Moral Conduct and Authority. The Place of Adab in South Asian Islam* (Berkeley and Los Angeles: University of California Press, 1984), pp. 255–89.

———, *Mughal Administration in Golconda* (London: Oxford University Press, 1975).

Rocher, Ludo, "Notes on Mixed Castes in Classical India", *Adhyar Library Bulletin*, vols 44–5, 1981, pp. 132–46.

Sabajipratapa, *Paraśurāmapratāpa – Jātiviveka*, Bhandarkar Oriental Research Institute, ms. no. 233 of Visrama (ii).

Saha, M.B., and Girish Mandake, eds, *Itihāsachāraya V.K. Rājavāḍe Samagraha Sāhitya*, 13 vols (Dhule: Rajwade Sanshodhan Mandal, 1995–8).

Sanderson, Alexis, "Śaivism and the Tantric Traditions", in Stewart Sutherland, *et al.*, eds, *The World's Religions* (London: Routledge and Kegan Paul, 1988), pp. 660–704.

———, "Religion and the State: Śaiva Officiants in the Territory of the King's Brahmanical Chaplain", *Indo-Iranian Journal*, vol. 47, nos 3–4, 2004, pp. 229–300.

Sardesai, G.S., ed., *Selections from the Peshwa Daftar*, 45 vols (Bombay: Government Central Press, 1930–4).

Sarkar, N.C., "Kayastha", *Bhāratīya Vidhyā*, vol. 10, 1949, pp. 280–4.

Sarma, H.D., "Paraśurāmapratāpa: Its Authorship, Date and the Authorities Quoted in It", *The Poona Orientalist*, vol. 7, nos 1 and 2, April and July 1942, pp. 1–26.

Sen, Surendranath, ed., *Extracts and Documents Relating to Maratha History, vol. 1: Śiva Chhatrapati* (Calcutta: University of Calcutta, 1920).

Steele, Arthur, *A Summary of the Law and Custom of Hindoo Castes Within the Dekhun Provinces Subject to the Presidency of Bombay* (London: W.H. Allen, 1868).

Stein, Burton, *Vijayanagara* (Cambridge: Cambridge University Press, 2005).

Stietencron, Heinrich von, "Calculating Religious Decay: The Kaliyuga in India", in *Hindu Myth, Hindu History: Religion, Art and Politics* (Delhi: Permanent Black, 2005), pp. 31–40.

Sutherland, Stewart, *et al.*, eds, *The World's Religions* (London: Routledge and Kegan Paul, 1988).

Talbot, Cynthia, *Precolonial India in Practice: Society, Region and Identity in Medieval Andhra* (New York: Oxford University Press, 2001).

Telang, K.P., "Gleanings from Maratha Chronicles", Postscript in M.G. Ranade, *Rise of the Maratha Power* (New Delhi: Government of India, 1974), pp. 117–46.

Thakare, K.S., *Grāmaṇyāchā Sādyanta Itihāsa* (Mumbai: Yashwant Shivaram Raje, 1919).

Vad, G.C., V. Mawjee, and D.B. Parasnis, eds, *Selections from the Government Records in the Alienation Office, Poona. Sanads and Letters* (Bombay: P.V. Mawjee, 1913).

Vajpeyi, Ananya, "Politics of Complicity, Poetics of Contempt: A History of the Sudra in Maharashtra, 1650–1950 CE", University of Chicago PhD thesis, 2004.

———, "Excavating Identity through Tradition: Who was Shivaji?" in Satish Saberwal and Supriya Varma, eds, *Traditions in Motion: Religion and Society in History* (New Delhi: Oxford University Press, 2005), pp. 240–71.

———, "Dharma and Legal Treatments of Caste", in Timothy Lubin, Donald R. Davis, and Jayanth Krishnan, eds, *Hinduism and Law, An Introduction* (Cambridge: Cambridge University Press, 2010), pp. 280–302.

Vendell, Dominic, "Scribes and the Vocation of Politics in the Maratha Empire, 1708–1818", Columbia University PhD thesis, 2018.

———, "The Scribal Household in Flux: Pathways of Kayastha Service in Western India", *Indian Economic and Social History Review*, vol. 57, no. 4, 2020, pp. 384–451.

Wagle, N.K., "A Dispute Between the Pancal Devajna Sonars and the Brahmans of Pune Regarding Social Rank and Ritual Privileges: A Case-Study of the British Administration of *Jati* Laws in Maharashtra, 1822–1825", in idem, ed., *Images of Maharashtra. A Regional Profile of India* (London: Curzon, 1980), pp. 129–59.

———, "The Chandraseniya Kayastha Prabhus and the Brahmans: Ritual, Law and Politics in Pune, 1789–90", in G.D. Sontheimer and P.K. Aithal, eds, *Indology and Law: Studies in Honour of Professor J. Duncan M. Derrett* (Wiesbaden: Franz Steiner Verlag, 1982), pp. 303–29.

Washbrook, David, *The Emergence of Provincial Politics in Madras Presidency* (Cambridge: Cambridge University Press, 1976).

Wink, Andre, *Land and Sovereignty in India: Agrarian Society and Politics Under the Eighteenth Century Maratha Svarājya* (Cambridge: Cambridge University Press, 1986).

Yadava, B.N.S., "The Accounts of the Kali Age and the Social Transition from Antiquity to the Middle Ages", *The Indian Historical Review*, vol. 5, nos 1–2, July 1978–January 1979, pp. 31–63.

8

Discourses of Caste Over the Longue Durée

Gopinatha and Social Classification in India, *c.* 1400–1900

Introduction

ON 18 OCTOBER 1779, an assembly of learned Brahmans in Banaras despatched a lengthy Sanskrit letter of judgment to the Maratha court in Pune. The court's powerful minister Nana Phadnis had sought their guidance in the vexed matter of the ritual entitlements of Kayastha scribes. Were they a menial caste of mixed origins, mere scribbling servants of others, or trusted supports to rulers, of royal descent themselves? It was a fraught time in Pune, as Nana Phadnis strove to hold together a Maratha alliance against the advancing power of the East India Company. The Kayasthas too were in difficulty, recovering from the incrimination of leading Kayasthas in the murder of the young peshwa Madhavarao I, in 1772, and the community's association with the ambitious pretender Raghunathrao, who was by 1779 working in alliance with the Company to seat himself on the throne in Pune.[1]

The assembly pointedly emphasised its authority. The letter began: "Many salutations from Brahmans bearing surnames such as Bhatta, Dharmadhikara and Sesa, and residing in the holy city." Yet its tone was pained. "Since great men insist, it is necessary to meet their objections and

[1] Sardesai, *New History of the Marathas*, vol. 3, pp. 25–33.

satisfy them by sacred authorities." The assembly had consulted many: "[T]he *Gāgābhaṭṭī* of Gagabhatta, *Kāyasthapradīpa*, *Govindabhaṭṭī* of Govindbhatta, *Reṇukāmāhātmya* of the *Skandapurāṇa*, the *Śūdrakamalākaraḥ* of Kamalakarabhatta, and the *Jātiviveka*." These authorities indicated that there were three sorts of Kayasthas: those descended from the divine scribe Chitragupta; those descended from king Chandrasena, whose royal lineage had been preserved from the wrath of the god Parashuram by their having taken up livelihoods as scribes; and "Kayasthas of mixed blood." It followed that descendants of royal Kshatriyas continued to exist in the world, and in the Chandraseniya Kayastha community under discussion. Nor was it true that the Kayasthas, descended from king Chandrasena's son and a Brahman woman, were degraded by this transgressive pratiloma marriage of an inferior man with a superior woman. History furnished many examples of virtuous princes marrying the daughters of the gods. "Why then look to the origin?" the pandits asked. "Whose pedigree is without a flaw in it?"[2]

Such questions about descent and identity were a key element in what we call "caste". Recent research has illuminated the ways in which such assemblies of scholars adjudicated them.[3] Prestige and ritual entitlement were only one aspect of the "caste" affiliation that they considered. Another was the right to practice particular professions. Like the Kayasthas, "Rathakara" communities had a contested history. Those claiming this rank included diverse artisan and service people, from prestigious builders of temples and sculptors of figures of the gods to goldsmiths, gem-workers, engravers, painters, blacksmiths, and simple carpenters. Questions about entitlement to practice the most prestigious and lucrative of these professions provoked frequent contests in medieval and early modern India. Who exactly was a Rathakara, and what were their proper callings? Indeed, were Rathakaras really, as some asserted, born from the five mouths of the divine Visvakarman, architect to the gods, or were they in fact menial workers in handicrafts?[4] Questions about "caste" identity affected many key questions

[2] Gupte, *Ethnographical Notes*, Appendix 1, pp. 1–7. See also Wagle, "The Cāndrasenīya Kayastha Prabhus".

[3] Davis, "Recovering the Indigenous Legal Traditions"; O'Hanlon and Minkowski, "What Makes People Who They Are?"

[4] Derrett, "Two Inscriptions"; Aiyer, "Largest Provincial Organisations". For inscriptions, see Shastri, "Annual Report", and Rice, "Shikarpur Taluq", pp. 82–3.

of social standing and entitlement, including property rights, marriage, inheritance, and punishments for crime.[5]

This essay explores these themes through the work of Gopinatha, a scholar of the Maratha country.[6] He was a traditional Smarta Brahman, from a Shaivite scholar family in which Kashmiri Shaivite influences were strong. In Sanderson's terms, Gopinatha seems not to have been an initiate into a particular Shaivite sect, but rather to have worshipped Shiva within a broad framework of Vedic ritual and Smarta attachment to the principles of varnasramadharma (the orders of castes and life-stages).[7] As noted above, the Banaras pandit assembly consulted his work, the *Jātiviveka* (Discernment of Jatis). He wrote it sometime between the middle of the fourteenth century and the later fifteenth.[8] He offered it as a defence of varnasramadharma against the degenerated social condition of varnasamkara (confusion of varnas), a state to be expected in the fallen age of the Kaliyuga, and portending great harm to dharma in the world.

In an era when most Sanskrit digests no longer furnished detailed information about jatis, Gopinatha's *Jātiviveka* provided a comprehensive guide to the "mixed castes". He explained: "This book of *Jātiviveka* was expounded by the wise Gopisvara in the world, extracting [the subject] from a great corpus of texts, including Manu and other smrtis and sastras."[9] The work listed the parentage, proper occupation, and ritual entitlements of some eighty-five local jati communities. Gopinatha entered spiritedly into social controversies, such as the worth of people he called "Vaishnavas", and the ritual standing of

[5] Davis, *Spirit of Hindu Law*, pp. 144–65.

[6] For caste in early India, see Sharma, *Sudras in Ancient India*; Chattopadhyaya, *A Social History*; Parasher-Sen, *Subordinate and Marginal Groups*; Thapar, *Early India*, pp. 260–2, 462–6; Talbot, "A Revised View".

[7] Sanderson, "Śaivism and the Tantric Traditions".

[8] Gopinatha, *Jātiviveka*. Hereafter JV. Partly (and unreliably) published manuscript, British Library Sanskrit manuscript no. 1969. There is no scribe's name or date on this copy. Eggeling estimates that it dates from about 1700: see idem, *Catalogue of Sanskrit Manuscripts*, vol. 1, p. 518. Nobile, "Notizie", offers a partial translation, drawing on two versions of this text in the British Library: BL Sanskrit manuscript no. 1969 and no. 1061a. Nobile cites these as BL Sanskrit manuscript nos. 1638 and 1639. Eggeling lists both call marks for these two manuscripts.

[9] JV, f. 27r.

Kayasthas and Rathakaras. Whilst he worked within the caste categories of Manu and Yajnavalkya, his treatise provided greater detail, a larger range of caste communities, many Marathi equivalents for Sanskrit caste names, and explanations for local peculiarities of practice.

There were also tensions in his work. It made reference to the court and its service people, yet the world he described was one in which royal Kshatriyas seemed curiously absent. The "mixed castes" he detailed encompassed every service community imaginable, rural as well as urban, the world therefore consisting effectively of many small units generated by the intermixture of the varnas. By implication, at least, this meant a social order consisting really only of two varnas. There were Brahmans like himself, and a great mass of mixed people. Their motley parentages required them to be placed, with the assistance of manuals like the *Jātiviveka*, somewhere on the edges of the Sudra fold, or outside the varnas altogether. While his work looked back to a time when royal power had been an active principle in the world of castes and other corporate communities, that link seemed to have weakened in his present. Gopinatha's treatise raises important questions about the way in which conservative Brahmans viewed the decline of Hindu royal power in western India, and the consequent weakening of older forms of royal support for the preservation of the orders of caste and life stages.

Although Gopinatha developed his treatise within familiar models, he seemed nonetheless to have hit upon a remarkably useful formula. Many later intellectuals and social observers borrowed from his treatise, following his assumption about the pervasiveness of "mixed" people in their own contemporary world. In their work, the ever more minute study of such communities, and the generative logic of varna mixing presumed to underlie their proliferation, came to be normalised as an independent field of scholarly expertise. Assemblies like that described above used the *Jātiviveka* to inform their deliberations, sometimes in routine professional, ritual, and juridical disputes, sometimes in debating the great questions of their age. These included the forms of ritual life proper to Sudras, and the ritual status to be accorded to people exercising the power of kings. By the early nineteenth century, East India Company officials gave "the *Jātiviveka*" a central place in their counsels, to the consternation of those who feared its classifications as an instrument of conservative Brahman ideology.

Classification and the Idea of Varnasamkara

According to the *Mānavadharmśāstra* ("Laws of Manu"), compiled early in the first millennium CE, the "confusion of varnas" came about when good people lost rank by neglecting ritual obligations, when children were born of illegitimate relationships, but above all when people married outside their own varna.[10] While people should marry within their own varna, it was acceptable for a woman of a lower varna to marry upwards, in line with the approved hypergamous principle of anuloma ("following the direction of the hair"). Women should always marry social equals or superiors, never inferiors, for in marriage a woman assumed the identity of her husband, like a river uniting with the sea.[11] The four varnas yielded six permutations of anuloma marriage, and six of pratiloma (disapproved unions "against the hair"), in which men of lesser rank produced progeny from superior women. These twelve "primary" mixed castes in turn created further, indeed infinite possibilities for mixing. In these contexts, Manu used the terms "varna" and "jati" in interchangeable and rather general ways to denote birth, parentage, rank, and social status.[12]

Manu enumerated some forty categories so created, devoting particular attention to pratiloma unions and listing them in rank order as follows:

Kshatriya man and Brahman woman = Suta, overseer of horses and chariots.
Vaishya man and Brahman woman = Magadha, trader.
Vaishya man and Kshatriya woman = Vaideha, guardians of the harem.
Sudra man and Vaishya woman = Ayogava, mason.
Sudra man and Kshatriya woman = Kshatra, hunter.
Sudra man and Brahman woman = Chandala, outcaste from the village.[13]

Further mixings produced even more debased people. Some were progeny of parents with particularly impure professions. Some were

[10] Olivelle, ed. and trans., *Law Code of Manu*, ch. 10, vs. 24.
[11] Ibid., ch. 9, vs. 22.
[12] Kane, *History of Dharmaśāstra*, vol. 2, pt 1, pp. 54–5.
[13] Olivelle, ed. and trans., *Law Code of Manu*, ch. 10, vss. 11–12.

vratyas, offspring of Kshatriya parents who had lapsed from their observances. Some – Yavanas, Sakas, Pahlavas, Dravidas – were classed as dasyu enemies, not belonging to any of the four varnas that sprang from the sacrificed body of the Primal Man. Critically, Manu emphasised that even if these original parentages were obscure, a community's origins, virtuous or debased, could nonetheless be back-read from its observable circumstances in the present. "These castes, arising from intermixture and described above according to their fathers and mothers – whether they conceal their caste or are open about it – should be recognised by their respective activities."[14] Subsequent major commentators – Yajnavalkya, Medhathiti, Vijnanesvara, and many puranic texts – followed Manu's basic mode of classification.[15]

Many historians have emphasised that this remarkable obsession with social categorisation arose as a Brahman fiction, associated with the early expansions of northern Brahmans into peninsular India. So constructed, the varna order offered a set of rules capable of generating an infinite number of more and less disapproved categories. Through them, many new demographic groups – incomers into India, migrants and the upwardly mobile, tribal people, people from new regions, sects and cults dissenting from the principle of varnasramadharma – could be assigned a place within the dominant varna system. At the same time, the classification offered great flexibility. Through the principle that past parentages could be inferred from present practice, approved people could always be supplied with "good" parentages to distinguish them from lesser jati communities within the same occupational field.

Yet this ideology was not a "fiction" in a trivial sense. In it, what had become a core principle of dharma – that men of superior rank be given greater access to women of equal and lesser status than allowed to men of inferior rank – helped shape what Tambiah has called "the general Indian aspiration for maintaining and increasing status and honour through the institution of marriage."[16] Hypergamous marriage during these centuries lay at the centre of Hindu society in many parts

[14] Ibid., ch. 10, vs. 40.

[15] On varnasamkara, see Jha, "Varṇasaṃkara"; Rocher, "Notes on Mixed Castes"; Tambiah, "From Varna to Caste"; Brinkhaus, *Die Altindischen Mischkastensysteme*.

[16] Tambiah, "From Varna to Caste", p. 223.

of India, a focal point of its structure and closely integrated with caste. The value placed on women marrying upwards reinforced other relationships of power and dependency, between chief and vassal, landlord and tenant, master and servant. In addressing questions of parentage, marriage and descent, therefore, Gopinatha addressed key institutions of Hindu social organisation.

Contexts: From the Yadava Kingdom to the Deccan Sultanate States

When Gopinatha wrote his treatise, the Yadava kingdom would have been a fairly recent memory. From their capital at Devagiri, the Yadavas commanded a thriving kingdom that included present-day Maharashtra, northern Karnataka, and parts of Madhya Pradesh. They patronised a range of religious cultures. Dhere has described their important role in creating a Vaishnavite and Vedic religious culture around the worship of the folk god Vitthal at Pandharpur.[17] The Yadava kings also demonstrated strong public commitment to the values of varnasramadharma. The copper plates recording the Yadava king Ramachandra's gift in 1310 CE, of tax-free lands to his powerful Brahman minister Purushottam, praised the latter for "having shown by his brilliant command separate courses of conduct for the castes and orders of life, even as a cloud shows different paths by its lightning."[18] Ramachandra's minister, the great scholar Hemadri, composed his famous *Chaturvargacintāmaṇi*, an encyclopaedia of the ritual observances necessary for adherence to the orders of varna.[19] His work became widely influential: the Reddi king Vema boasted of having made every religious gift it prescribed.[20]

The traditions of the heterodox Mahanubhava sect suggest the wide social diffusion of these values in the Yadava kingdom. When local Brahmans discovered that people of their village worshipped an untouchable Chamar as a saint after he shared a betelnut with the Mahanubhava leader Chakradhar, they complained his behaviour would pollute the whole village. A learned Brahman consulted his religious

[17] Dhere, *Rise of a Folk God*, pp. 220–70.

[18] Mirashi, "Purshottampuri Plates", pp. 213–14, 222, 224.

[19] Hemadri, *Chaturvargacintāmaṇi*; Verma, *Yadavas*, pp. 262–3.

[20] Hultsch, "Vanapalli Plates", p. 64.

manuals and prescribed burial in a limestone pit as the appropriate punishment.[21] The eminent pandit assembly of Paithan famously tried Chakradhar for his association with the destitute women attracted into his movement. He mildly acknowledged the assembly's authority, addressing it as "the leading people of the eighteen great communities of subjects" before his punishment. As the villagers drove one of his followers out of town, they called after him, "Rob him of his wife. He has not accepted our community rule (samaya). Throw him out, throw him out of our Maharashtra."[22]

These references point to the culture of the samaya (mutual compact) within which jati communities were located. Both rural and urban citizenry organised themselves into corporate bodies of different kinds – regional and local assemblies, guilds, clans, castes, professional communities, and religious and sectarian bodies. They policed themselves, with the support of royal officials contributed to the life of the temple and the community, and took part in important court occasions. They played an active part in the life of the state and were "supports" to the king because through their own virtuous adherence to their proper customs and occupations they increased dharma in the world. The term samaya referred both to the caste or other corporate group itself, and to the social compact that bound its members to observe its conventions and collective agreements.[23]

Contemporary descriptions of these corporate bodies convey their bustling urban setting and their active role in the life of the state. Northern Karnataka was home to the famous merchant association of the Ayyavole 500, led by the Banajiga community of long-distance traders, traditionally said to be head of the eighteen castes or professions of Karnataka.[24] Thc idea that there were eighteen service communities gained wide currency, although "eighteen" in this setting also conveyed

[21] Sontheimer, "God, Dharma and Society", pp. 321–2.

[22] Ibid., p. 322.

[23] For samaya, see Inden, *Imagining India*, pp. 225–6; Davis, "Intermediate Realms of Law", pp. 94–8, 107–10; Aiyer, "Largest Provincial Organisations", vol. 45, no. 1 (July 1954) and no. 2 (October 1954); Dikshit, *Local Self Government*.

[24] Abraham, *Two Medieval Merchant Guilds*.

the idea of the totality of such groups in a particular context.[25] Lists of the "eighteen" mention Brahman priests and astrologers, scribes, accountants, bards, goldsmiths, masons, tailors, oil pressers, barbers, potters, blacksmiths, braziers, washermen, carpenters, betel-leaf growers, flower sellers, garland makers, basket makers, and leather workers. Many accounts referred to the assembled communities as the eighteen praja ("subjects") of the state, or as its eighteen prakrti (active elements), presenting them as partners in gifting and making regulations alongside village heads and local lords.[26] Early in the second millennium CE the term samaya gained wider currency for service communities and their social compacts. Thus a Kannada inscription in the town of Shikarpur from *c.* 1200 records gifts made for the repair of the temple in which "the eighteen samayas (hadinentu sameyavu) are agents for this work of merit."[27] Sometimes the term "jati" was also used, although, as Talbot has noted, it was a general term for a kind, category, or sort and did not specifically denote a subcaste.[28]

In 1345 Devagiri passed into Bahmani hands. Much about the Bahmani court – its Timurid style, its sharp rivalries between Deccanis and Iranian "westerners" – has been well documented.[29] There were important continuities with the Yadava period. The Sultanate form of polity distinguished between the religious and political domains of life, making it possible for Brahmans seeking patronage to offer praise poems to Muslim rulers.[30] The state still depended on local military estate holders, and Brahman scribal and judicial expertise.[31] Emerging in the 1490s out of the ruins of the Bahmani kingdom, the Ahmadnagar state continued to employ high-level Hindu ministers and

[25] Sircar, *Indian Epigraphical Glossary*, pp. 31–2; Dirks, *The Hollow Crown*, p. 140; Talbot, "A Revised View", p. 22; pp. 72–3.

[26] Dikshit, *Local Self Government*, pp. 70–1, 77–8, 143; Inden, *Imagining India*, p. 225.

[27] Rice, "Shikarpur Taluq", nos. 227, 232, and 133.

[28] Talbot, "A Revised View", p. 22.

[29] Sherwani, *Bahmanis*; Eaton, *A Social History of the Deccan*, pp. 59–77.

[30] Eaton, *A Social History of the Deccan*, p. 193; Chattopadhyaya, *The Making of Early Medieval India*, p. 197.

[31] Sherwani, *Bahmanis*; Shyam, *Kingdom of Ahmadnagar*; Gordon, *Marathas*, pp. 17–18.

military officers. The Brahman Dalapati served Ahmad Nizam Shah I (*fl.* 1470–1509) as chief minister and record keeper, and commissioned in his honour an extensive digest of dharmasastra, the *Nṛsiṃhaprasāda.*[32] His successor Burhan Nizam Shah I (1502–1553) promoted Brahman servants such as the officer Sambhaji Chitnis, rewarded with the title of Pratap Rai. Sambhaji, who styled himself "Sabajipratapa" in his text, also offered his patron a massive digest of dharmasastra, the *Paraśurāmapratāpa.*[33] This dates his text to the period of Burhan Nizam Shah's reign, 1510–53.

Gopinatha's work provides insights into the concerns of conservative Brahman scholars perhaps less integrated into the syncretic culture of the Sultanate court. Embedded in the *Upodghātakāṇḍa*, or "Introductory part" of the *Paraśurāmapratāpa* – a large work of some sixteen different parts – was the first version of Gopinatha's treatise to which some approximate date can be assigned.[34] The *Paraśurāmapratāpa* opened with praise of Burhan Nizam Shah and his city, "the lively Ahammadpura, famous by virtues, where kings live in highest delight and affluence." It described the immediate forebears of Sabajipratapa, and his guru, Sri Kurma, "well versed in all the sastras in the field of legal procedures and engaged in serving the noble ones," who had actually arranged the work.[35] After further general remarks over some forty-four folios – on the nature of dharma, the four varnas, the six karmas, the four stages of life, the duties of women – the compiler of the *Paraśurāmapratāpa* incorporated the *Jātiviveka*, consisting of some twenty additional folios, to complete this part of his text. He introduced it as Gopinatha's work: "Following Gopinatha's doctrine, the determination of jatis is taught [as] Gopinatha is the capable com-

[32] Dalapati, *Nṛsiṃhaprasāda*; Gode, "Identification of Dalpat Rai"; Kane, *History of Dharmaśāstra*, vol. 1, pp. 406–10. This work lists a *Jātiviveka* as an authority consulted, but it is not clear whether this was Gopinatha's treatise: *Nṛsiṃhaprasāda Saṃskārasāra*, p. 7.

[33] Sabajipratapa, *Paraśurāmapratāpa, Upodghātakāṇḍa*, f. 44r. Another Brahman scholar receiving patronage at Ahmadnagar was Ramesvara Bhatta, founder of the great Bhatta lineage of scholars in Banaras. Benson, "Saṃkarabhaṭṭa's Family Chronicle", pp. 108–9. We thank Jon Keune for this reference.

[34] Gode, "Sābāji Pratāparāja"; Sharma, "Paraśurāmapratāpa".

[35] Sabajipratapa, *Parśurāmapratāpa*, *Upodghātakāṇḍa* f. 2v, and f. 44r.

piler of songs, literature, medical science, poetry, agamas, sastras, and arts."[36]

The *Jātiviveka*: Early History of the Text

We know therefore that Gopinatha compiled his *Jātiviveka* before 1553, the year of Burhan Nizam Shah's death. That the text was in existence by the 1460s is suggested in the *Kāyasthapaddhati* of Guru Govind, a defence of the ritual entitlements of Kayasthas written in Banaras during that decade. As O'Hanlon has suggested elsewhere, this is almost certainly the text cited in the 1779 Banaras assembly as the "*Govindabhaṭṭī* of Govindbhatta".[37] Guru Govind referred to "the *Jātiviveka*" as an authority and, as we shall see, quoted verses on the origins of Kayasthas that can be traced back to Gopinatha's text. There are no direct clues to a *terminus post quem*, but it seems clear that Gopinatha wrote it after the fall of the Yadavas, since he referred to "Turks" as a disagreeable and coercive local presence.

This essay draws on three versions of Gopinatha's text. The first is that inserted into the *Paraśurāmapratāpa*. The second is the British Library manuscript 1969 referred to above. This British Library copy probably represents the earlier form of the text. It begins with obeisances to Shiva and a lengthy account of Gopinatha's lineage. The *Paraśurāmapratāpa* omitted these preliminaries, introducing the work as Gopinatha's, going straight into the main body of his text, and returning in its final colophon to Burhan Nizam Shah and his servant Sabajipratapa. The final colophon of British Library manuscript 1969 returned to Gopinatha and his labours in collecting his materials. There are other small differences between the two texts. In some places, the *Paraśurāmapratāpa* offered clarifications of Gopinatha's text, and in others sought to shift its tone slightly with quotations from other authorities. It seems likely that the arranger of the *Paraśurāmapratāpa* inserted Gopinatha's text, without its preliminaries, after the main part of the *Upodghātakāṇḍa*, inflated it with additional smrti

[36] Ibid., f. 44v.

[37] Guru Govind, *Kāyasthapaddhati*, f. 12v. For Guru Govind's text, see O'Hanlon, "The Social Worth of Scribes", pp. 578–84.

quotations, and replaced Gopinatha's final colophon with one referring to Burhan Nizam Shah and his servant Sabajipratapa. The third version of Gopinatha's text examined here is British Library manuscript 1061a. The scribe was one Mhalgi Kanhabhatta, and the scribal date 20 October 1642.[38]

"The Discernment of Jatis": Gopinatha and His Text

Gopinatha wrote in slokas, dividing his treatise into three chapters. He declared his Shaivite affiliations in his opening obeisances to the five faces of Shiva and to Shakti in her three forms of will, knowledge, and action.[39] He invoked four generations of his illustrious forebears, Brahmans of the Vasistha gotra. Narayana and his son Samaraja lived in the town of Pratyanda, where the family gained the title of Bhatta for their learning.[40] Samaraja had four sons, Vishvanath, Mahadeva, Bhanu, and Lakshmidhara. Vishvanath's son was Sarangadhar, talented in all the arts. From him was born Gopinathakavi, "Gopinatha the poet" himself, who now presented the "virtuous and crystal-clear" treatise on jatis.[41] He explained:

> This book of *Jātiviveka* was expounded by the wise Gopisvara in the world, extracting [the subject] from a great corpus of texts including Manu and other smrtis and sastras, just as the Sun absorbs the juices of the ground and rains down the water in the rainy season to favour the people, the one always to be respected, the one conferring riches.

His wisdom, Gopinatha pointed out, came in a concentrated form, like nectar, "for if art is too extensive, it should be condensed."[42] He emphasised the significance of his subject at the outset. Only by distinguishing between the jatis could people – and Gopinatha clearly envisaged an audience of Brahmans like himself – hope to understand

[38] Kanhabhatta, *Jātiviveka*.

[39] JV, f. 1v.; Flood, "The Saiva Traditions".

[40] JV, f. 1v. "Pratyanda" is probably a Sanskritisation of Paranda, a town of cultural and military importance some 150 km south-east of Ahmadnagar. Haig, "History of the Nizām Shāhī Kings", pp. 106 and 167.

[41] JV, f. 2r.

[42] JV, ff. 2r–2v.

the three great fields of Hindu law: achara (proper conduct), vyavahara (legal procedure), and prayaschitta (penance and retribution).[43] "The twice born will be worthy of the truth concerning proper conduct, legal procedures and especially penance and retribution, when they have got to know the *Jātiviveka*."[44] He indicated the complexity of the task. There were six kinds of anuloma mixed jatis and six pratiloma. "These twelve mixed ones are mixed [again] with the four varnas." Gopinatha explained: "The forty-eight classes make up sixty with the twelve [previous ones]."[45] At this point, as if to clarify the wider context for these communities, Sri Kurma, compiler of the *Paraśurāmapratāpa*, interjected a sentence of his own: "The sixty well-connected classes are called 'praja'."[46] As described above, this usage was common in the Yadava period and after. Sri Kurma may well have been suggesting this connection, and, as we shall see, Gopinatha drew the same link.

The further possible combinations arising from these categories, Gopinatha explained, were limitless. "Classes and subclasses of them arise in the Kali Era and they become innumerable. Who could count them?"[47] Following Manu and Yajnavalkya, he described the main approved and disapproved pairings as we saw them above.[48] He closed his first chapter with further information about his father. "Here ends the first chapter, named 'The Elucidation of Mixed Jatis', in Gopinatha the poet's work. He was [the son of] Sarangadhara Acharya, the teacher of the entire true [Shaiva] tradition, the king of editors, who possessed ahambhava."[49] Gopinatha here identified his father as an adherent of Kashmiri Shaivism who had attained ahambhava, or pure consciousness of the self's identity with Shiva, characteristic of the highest Shaiva adept.[50]

43 Olivelle, "Dharmaśāstra", p. 45.

44 JV, f. 2v.

45 JV, f. 3r. Whereas the manuscript gives "twice-eight" this number seems to be forty-eight elsewhere and logically should be forty-eight.

46 Sabajipratapa, *Parśurāmapratāpa*, *Upodghātakāṇḍa*, ff. 44v–45r.

47 JV, ff. 2v–3r. The calculation here is that the twelve mixed castes, mixed in turn with the four varnas, produced a total of sixty different possible pairings.

48 JV, ff. 3r–4r.

49 JV, f. 4v.

50 Dyczkowski, *Doctrine of Vibration*, pp. 133–4.

From here, Gopinatha described many other mixed categories. He began with "mixed" priestly people and other skilled classes: the Bhojaka and Devalaka temple priests, the Murdhavasiktaka or royal officer, the Suta or manager of elephants and horses, the Ambhastha or physician, the Mahishya or astrologer, the Magadha or panegyrist.[51] Then he listed some eighty-five lesser service people: the Rathakara or craftsman, the Parasava or goldsmith, the Abhira or cowherd, the warrior, different classes of bards, the barber, the prize fighter, the Kayastha scribe, the parasol bearer, the royal palanquin bearer, the jailer, the potter, the coppersmith, the harem guard, the courtesan, the hunter, the garland maker, the cook, the bell-ringer, the musician, the dresser of hair, the carrier of messages, the offspring of Shaiva ascetics, the guard, the itinerant performer, the dancer, the maker of arrows, the betel seller, the masseur, inferior kinds of cook and cowherd, the herder of goats, the royal bed guard, the keeper of the king's dogs, the mason, the tailor, the coiner, the blacksmith, the washerman, the oil seller, and so on, right down to catchers of snakes and rats, butchers, executioners, scavengers, and assistants at the cremation ground. "Jati" was the term he used for "mixed" people, whom he termed as in "misrajati" or "samkirna jati", and in the title of his treatise itself, the *Jātiviveka*. Like his predecessors, however, he also applied the term to particular mixed groups, such as the "Magadha jati", and to varna categories, as in the "Sudra jati" and the "Vaishya jati".[52]

For each, he provided parentages, a profession, and some indication of ritual status. Alongside the Sanskrit, he often gave the "vernacular" equivalent (loke), or "used in the vernacular language" (lokabhashya). He began with various kinds of degraded priest. The Devalaka or temple priest, a category familiar from Manu's classification, came from a respectable parentage – a Brahman father and a Magadhi mother – but his work as a priest for hire degraded him. "He worships Vishnu images, marked with a conch. He lives off money generated by worship. He is not to be accepted into the line of those who dine together."[53]

[51] JV, ff. 5r–6r.
[52] JV, ff. 5r–5v, 8r.
[53] JV, f. 5r.

The Devalaka was known in popular speech, loke, as a Vaduva.[54] The Ugra warrior came from a Kshatriya father and a Sudra mother, an anuloma union, was cruel by nature, and skilled in military arts. His dharma was Sudra, and he was also known as a Rayutara.[55] A coppersmith or Tamrakuttaka was the progeny of a Kshatriya father and a Parasavi mother, herself born from a Kshatriya father and a Sudra mother, making this a respectable anuloma union. The coppersmith made copper vessels, was called a Kinasha in the sastras, but was known in popular usage as a Tambata.[56] A Sutradhara (performer) entertained in the king's court with the four kinds of gesture given in Bharata's *Nāṭyaśāstra*, but used the language of the country, deshbhasha.[57] Many professions appeared under recognisable Marathi names: the Sali weaver, Teli oil seller, Govari cowherd, Kolhati performer, Koli fisherman. Some suggested Hindusthani and Persian influences: a worker in leather was a Mochi, and a palanquin bearer a Kahara.[58]

For the most marginal, Gopinatha still provided parentage and profession. The Ahitundika snake charmer, whose Marathi name was Garudi, was born from a Nishada or hunter father and a Vaidehi mother, both parents the product of pratiloma unions. "With respect to dharma, he is similar to the seven Antyajas. He puts many big, venomous snakes in baskets. He plays with them for a living."[59] The Domba assistant at the cremation ground came of a Chandala father and a Nishada mother. "He lives in cremation grounds, provides protection [. . .] and helps Sati women, selling wood for cremation."[60] Having described some eighty-five mixed jatis, Gopinatha ended his second chapter. "The anuloma and pratiloma mixed jatis have been explained clearly by the wise Gopinatha, from Brahmans to Chandalas, as well as their dharmas and activities and how they make a living."[61] At this point in his text, the arranger

[54] JV, f. 5r. A Badava is a hereditary priest serving in the great temple to Vitthal at Pandharpur. Molesworth, *Dictionary*, p. 363.

[55] JV, f. 7r.

[56] JV, f. 10r.

[57] JV, f. 19v.

[58] JV, f. 21r, 9r.

[59] JV, f. 23r.

[60] JV, f. 24v.

[61] JV, f. 25v.

of the *Paraśurāmapratāpa* inserted an additional sentence: "After many rebirths they will be freed because of the disappearance of their karmas. The Vedanta teaches us: liberation comes only from knowledge."[62] His intention may have been to moderate Gopinatha's Shaivite tone with a reminder of the broader theology of the Vedanta.

Gopinatha's final chapter moved to the larger framework of samaya and praja. He used the term samuha, a collection or assemblage, rather than samaya, but he seems to have intended the same meaning.[63] "Now the famous category of communities (samuha) is to be expounded properly." He explained that when the twelve mixed groups were themselves mixed with the main varnas, "they become sixty in number. They are called praja."[64] He then offered lists of service communities within this number, beginning with what he called "the eighteen samuha".[65] They were made up of workers with gems, copper, pots, gold, iron and wood, tailors, weavers, dyers, basket makers, collectors of tolls, sack makers, salt makers, sellers of gold scraps, coin makers, outcastes and those whose actions had made them outcastes. To these he added the seven "Antyaja" communities, five "middle ones" amongst the degraded communities, five who were equivalent to Yajnavalkya's five great sinners, the six middle-ranked communities among the eighteen samuha, and the six superior. He further added lists of the nine types of "mixing" to be avoided: sharing a bed, a seat, a queue, dishes, cooked food, a sacrifice, recitation, a womb, or a common meal.[66] He referred to the Gita and the Mahabharata on the virtues of following one's own dharma, and to the Yogavasistha further emphasising the importance of knowledge: "The great medicine for the sickness of samsara is thought. Thinking will sharpen your mind and you will see the highest abode."[67]

[62] Sabajipratapa, *Paraśurāmapratāpa, Upodghātakāṇḍa*, f. 55r.

[63] See Davis, "Intermediate Realms of Law", p. 102; Desai, *Corpus of Inscriptions*, pp. 29–30, 49; *Corpus Inscriptionum Indicarum*, p. 614. Sometimes a town assembly was described as a samuha: Dikshit, *Local Self Government*, p. 145.

[64] JV, f. 25v.

[65] JV, f. 25v.

[66] JV, ff. 25v–26r.

[67] JV, f. 27r. This suggests the influence of Kashmiri Shaivite understandings of the key role of reason in the attainment of liberation. Dyczkowski, *Doctrine of Vibration*, pp. 168–70.

A New Discourse of Caste

As he unfolded his themes, Gopinatha evoked the older orders of samuha and praja associated with a royal court. Many professions he described were courtly: royal palanquin bearer, royal parasol bearer, harem guard, courtesan, musician, hairdresser, masseur, actor, dancer, royal bed guard. He described royal arrangements. The Jhalla (royal prize-fighter) trained the royal princes in the use of weapons and missiles.[68] The Vaideha (harem guard) provided excellent protection for kings.[69] Itinerant bards praised kings and Brahmans.[70] The king enjoyed his courtesans, learned in the sixty-four arts of the Kamasastra and the eight pleasures of the *Ratirahasya*.[71] The Mandalaka kept the royal dogs for hunting and fighting.[72]

Yet the world Gopinatha described was nonetheless curiously bereft of royalty itself. When he spelled out entitlements to saṃskāra (life-cycle rites), he mentioned "dvijas" (members of the twice-born) with sixteen, Sudras with twelve, and the "mixed jatis" with just five.[73] Under this last category, however, he included the great majority of the eighty-five or so different artisan and service communities whose "mixed" origins he described. The intermediate varna categories of Kshatriya and Vaishya certainly appeared in his work, but more as theoretical progenitors of the mixed communities he observed than people who might still be found in the world in their pure form. His determination that Kayastha scribes and Rathakara craftsmen, both with a long history of claiming twice-born status, should be classed as "mixed" jatis pointed in the same direction. The Kayastha was the progeny of a degraded pratiloma union between a respectable Mahishya woman and an inferior Vaideha man. His servile duties indicated a debased parentage. "[The Kayastha] performs service for all of the four varnas through his writing of scripts."[74] His work also lay in counting, algebra, and arithmetic. "The Kayastha's livelihood

[68] JV, f. 7v.
[69] JV, f. 10r.
[70] JV, f. 8r.
[71] JV, ff. 10v–11r.
[72] JV, f. 11v.
[73] JV, f. 8r.
[74] JV, f. 8v.

depends mainly on these activities. He is lower in rank than those of the Sudra jati, and is entitled only to five saṃskāras."[75]

Gopinatha gave the conventional parentage for a Rathakara – an approved anuloma combination of a Mahishya father and a Karanī mother – but declared that the Rathakara "has no sacred thread, and not even Sudra dharma. He earns his living by handicrafts, using the sastras on handicrafts."[76] He might well have a respectable parentage, but his profession placed him among the pettiest of craft workers. As we have seen, even Rayutara warriors, descended from Kshatriya fathers and Sudra mothers, were themselves to be classed only as Sudras. Gopinatha's was a world, therefore, in which there were few people of worth, apart from Brahmans. There were only Sudras, or other mixed people of more menial status still, whose uncertain identity posed a threat to dharma in the world.

Gopinatha also demonstrated marked hostility to bhakti religion, ascribing menial parentages to "Vaishnavas". The Pushpashekhara community of professional bards were the debased pratiloma offspring of a Katadhana father, a lowly bard or singer, and a Brahman mother. "In the vernacular," Gopinatha asserted, "they call such a person a Vaishnava." Such "Vaishnavas" were lower than Sudras. "They follow a popular custom, and they are not of the Sudra dharma."[77] The Mandalaka community, royal dog-keepers, had fathers from the same fallen bardic community, and Karmachandala as mothers, women out-casted by their own bad actions.[78] Towards the end of his text, Gopinatha made plain his real objections to "Vaishnavas". They deluded themselves that repeating the name of God was the summit of virtue and a substitute for following their own prescribed place in the social order. Citing the *Viṣṇupurāṇa*, he asserted: "Those who abandon their karma and just recite 'Krishna, Krishna!' are sinners in the eyes of Hari. The birth of Hari is for the sake of Dharma. If you follow your varna, ashrama, and the prescribed conduct, you actually worship Vishnu, the Highest Man. There is no other way to satiate Him."[79]

[75] JV, f. 8r.
[76] JV, f. 6r.
[77] JV, f. 7r.
[78] JV, f. 16v.
[79] JV, f. 27r.

Gopinatha wrote briefly, but vehemently, about the "Turuṣka" rulers of the Deccan. He classified them as a jati of menial parentage, illegitimate progeny of a Sairamdhra father, a masseur and body servant, and a Meda mother, a woman from a forest tribe. The further detail that he gave suggested that they were an immediate and disagreeable presence, but one offering possible temptations. "[Even] a Chandala is better than him. He is merciless and cruel. In the west, there is Mleccha land. They kill cows. One should not speak the Mleccha language at any rate. He earns his living by cruelty."[80]

How might we understand Gopinatha's apparently contradictory sense of the presence of royal power in the world? It is present in the courtly professions he describes, and in the domestic needs and enjoyments of kings set out in his text. Yet it seems absent in his sense that the social world he observed was an irredeemably mixed one. It is difficult to know how far the absence of Kshatriyas in particular reflected his sense of an evacuation of the royal power of Kshatriya kings from the Maratha regions in his own times.[81] Gopinatha did not say this explicitly. It was certainly an older question, predating his lifetime, as to whether the sages were correct in predicting that, in the fallen era of the Kaliyuga, the confusion of varnas would be such that only Brahmans and a great mass of Sudras and other social inferiors would remain in the world.[82] Yet in its vision of a social world populated very largely by Brahmans like himself, and a great mass of Sudras and fallen "mixed" jatis, Gopinatha's treatise seemed to make this connection. Perhaps the best way to make sense of his position is to see him both looking backwards, and forwards. He looked back to a world in which the royal court stood as the natural centre of the city and its constituent communities. But he also seems to anticipate a future in which the labours of scholars like himself, in assembling and tabulating information on the proliferating jati communities of the age, would take on a greater importance in preserving the integrity of dharma in the world.

[80] JV, f. 24r.

[81] For another suggestion that the fall of the Yadavas influenced later generations of Maratha Brahman scholars in this way, see Vajpeyi, "Politics of Complicity".

[82] Vaidya, *History*, vol. 2, pp. 312–17; von Stietencron, "Calculating Religious Decay".

The *Jātiviveka*: Circulation of a Serviceable Text

At least one scholar, the Banaras Kayastha champion Guru Govind, had engaged with Gopinatha's treatise by the 1460s. As we have also seen, sometime between 1510 and 1553 the compiler of the *Paraśurāmapratāpa* incorporated it wholesale into his digest. Other scholars rewrote Gopinatha's text in "expanded" and "abbreviated" versions, or borrowed large parts of it for their own commentaries. Under its own and other names, major intellectuals in Banaras quoted it in their discussions of Sudras, of indeterminate communities such as Kayasthas and Rathakaras, and of the ritual dignities proper to kings. By the time of its assimilation into colonial discourses on "caste", the *Jātiviveka* had emerged as a major authority.

Sometime in the later sixteenth century, one Ramachandra Bapat wrote a *Bṛhajjātiviveka* ("Expanded Jātiviveka"). He gave his treatise, of twenty-eight folios, the same tripartite division as Gopinatha's work. He commenced with Gopinatha's introductory matter, including his name and family details.[83] The second chapter reproduced many of Gopinatha's classifications, although not in the same order, and included further Marathi equivalents. In the third chapter he dropped Gopinatha's references to samuha and praja. He inserted instead a description of the royal city, with the fort at its centre, and its residential districts patterned according to the distinctions between anuloma and pratiloma jatis. "There should be streets and crossways full of goods and the best merchant should live in the crossways. The other ones, appointed by him, should live in the streets. The anuloma jatis should live left of the fort. The pratiloma jatis should live south of the fort. Those lower than the anuloma jatis, the best of the pratiloma jatis, should live west of the fort."[84]

Bapat then offered further practical examples of anuloma and pratiloma mixings in the case of particular jatis: "Now the mixture of mixed varnas is shown by the lower-higher distinction. The low ones are pratiloma, the high ones are anuloma."[85] For Nishadas, he explained:

[83] Bapat, *Bṛhajjātiviveka*, f. 1v. We thank the Asiatic Society, Mumbai, for their kind permission to consult this manuscript.

[84] Ibid., f. 26r.

[85] Idem.

> For a Nishada father [Brahman+Sudri], there is one for anuloma mixing [Sudra wife], three for pratiloma [Vaishya, Kshatriya, Brahman]. For a Mahishya [Kshatriya+Vaishya], there are two for anuloma mixing [Vaishya and Sudra wife], two for pratiloma [Kshatriya and Brahman wife]. One anuloma for an Ugra [Kshatriya+Sudri], three pratiloma. For a Karana one anuloma, three pratiloma. This is how the twenty-four are born from the aforementioned six.[86]

Here, then, Bapat sought explicitly to replace the older order of samuha and praja with anuloma and pratiloma groupings, but to maintain their connection with the royal city. He also added comments reinforcing some of Gopinatha's hostility to Vaishnavas. In the last lines of his text, he declared: "Dance, music, singing and sporting a burnt-mark etc, are for Sudras, never for the twice-born."[87]

We know that Bapat had access to Gopinatha's own work, since he reproduced Gopinatha's family history, and referred to points of jati distinction that Gopinatha had demonstrated.[88] However, it is likely that he also had access to the version of the *Jātiviveka* in the *Paraśurāmapratāpa*. His work contained passages from that text which did not appear in Gopinatha's earlier treatise, including a lengthy extract from the *Śivadharmottara* on the practices of Shaiva ascetics.[89] This suggests that Bapat was writing after 1553, the *terminus ante quem* for the *Paraśurāmapratāpa*. A further work of "commentary" suggests that the *Bṛhajjātiviveka* was in existence by 1577. Madhava, author of the *Śatapraśnakalpalatā* (Wishing Tree of 100 Questions), and evidently a devotee of the South Indian philosopher Madhva, introduced his text:

> Salutations to Sri Bindhu Madhva. I revere my guru named Madhva, and I write this good book named *Śatapraśnakalpalatā*. I write in the year 1499 after the birth of Shalivahana, following the ancient style of sentences. I will tell one hundred stories, having carefully looked at what

[86] Ibid., ff. 27r–27v.

[87] Ibid., f. 28v. *Taptamudrās* are sectarian marks branded on the body by worshippers of Vishnu and particularly associated with Madhva sectarian practice in this period. See Entwistle, "Vaiṣṇava Tilakas", pp. 19–22, and Fisher, "Public Philology".

[88] Bapat, *Bṛhajjātiviveka*, ff. 6r, 13r.

[89] Ibid., ff. 22v–24r; Sabajipratapa, *Paraśurāmapratāpa*, ff. 50r–50v.

the authors of the smrtis have said, and at what venerable people think is suitable.[90]

Madhava's "hundred questions" was an enormous text of some 165 folios, part caste purana and part sectarian polemic. He added scurrilous origin stories and parentages for western India's various "mixed" Brahman communities, which he said were "from the *Jātiviveka*".[91] He did not mention Gopinatha by name, simply referring to "the *Jātiviveka*" as a work of authority. He did, however, refer to the *Paraśurāmapratāpa*, explaining that the Parashuram who made the Konkan lands was different from the writer of the book *Paraśurāmapratāpa*.[92] He also made plain his debt to the *Bṛhajjātiviveka*. The second part of the *Śataprasnakalpalatā* began: "In the first chapter, the *Jātiviveka* was taught in a condensed manner. [The author] explains the very same [work, i.e. the *Jātiviveka*] in this chapter in the manner of the commentary given in the *Bṛhajjātiviveka*."[93] This second chapter then reproduced much of Gopinatha's second chapter, but in prose form, with Marathi equivalents for almost every jati, and some additional commentary. It concluded with a tabulated list of contents, which followed Gopinatha's text exactly. The third part continued with its theme of origins. Here, then, Gopinatha's work served Madhava very well, supplying the core around which to build his "one hundred questions".

Probably pre-dating these processes of transmission, Gopinatha's text began to circulate as part of another text entirely, the *Vāstuśāstra* of one Visvambhara. This placed it within the Sanskrit vastusastra genre of city and residential design.[94] The connections are difficult to trace. A conventional vastusastra text of one Visvambhara once existed. The Yadava minister Hemadri quoted from the *Viśvaṃbhara Vāstuśāstra* in a passage of his *Chaturvargacintāmaṇi* describing pavilions.[95] Gopinatha himself quoted at one point from an authority he

[90] Madhava, *Śatapraśṇakalpalatā*, f. 1v. Sake 1499 suggests a date of 1577 CE: O'Hanlon, "Performance in a World of Paper", p. 114.

[91] Madhava, *Śatapraśṇakalpalatā*, ff. 9v–11v.

[92] Ibid., f. 10v.

[93] Ibid., f. 56r.

[94] Sachdev and Tillotson, *Building Jaipur*, pp. 11–31.

[95] Hemadri, *Chaturvargacintāmaṇi*, vol. I, *Dānakhaṇḍa*, pp. 123–4.

called "Viśvaṃbhara", on the skills of the Sairamdhra (hairdresser/masseur).[96] The late-fifteenth-century defender of Kayastha rights Guru Govind referred to above quoted nine verses from the *Viśvaṃbhara Vāstuśāstra* in the preface to his *Kāyasthapaddhati*. He described how Brahma created the four varnas, and instructed Visvakarman, the divine architect, to build cities and palaces for them, and to teach the principles of karma and dharma to all castes, but particularly to Kayasthas.[97] In its portion dealing not with caste, but with life-cycle rituals, the *Paraśurāmapratāpa* also referred to what it called the *Viśvaṃbhara Śāstra*, but only as quoted by Hemadri.[98] Madhava above also referred to "Visvambhara", but his reference reproduced the passage in Gopinatha.[99] "Visvambhara" was therefore a familiar name to scholars of western India, but latterly seemed to have been passed around through its quotation in other texts. No copy of an "original" vastusastra text of Visvambhara appears to have survived.

However, a number of extant works do describe themselves as the *Vāstuśāstra* of Visvambhara. All of these so far located are in actuality Gopinatha's *Jātiviveka*, but simply prefaced with the nine verses from the *Viśvaṃbhara Vāstuśāstra* with which the *Kāyasthapaddhati* of Guru Govind began. Examining three such manuscripts in the Bhandarkar Oriental Research Institute in Pune, the scholar of the *Paraśurāmapratāpa*, H.D. Sharma, concluded that "in these Mss of *Jātiviveka*, a quotation from the *Viśvaṃbharavāstuśāstra* has been inserted in the beginning by some late hand."[100] In his catalogue of manuscripts in the Ulwar library, Peterson referred to a *Jātiviveka* by Gopinatha, concluding that "The tract is part of a *Viśvaṃbharavāstuśāstra*, which is

[96] JV, f. 13r.

[97] Guru Govind, *Kāyasthapaddhati,* ff. 1v–2r.

[98] Sharma, "*Paraśurāmapratāpa*", p. 22.

[99] Madhava, *Śatapraśṇakalpalatā*, ff. 68v–69r.

[100] Sharma, "*Paraśurāmapratāpa*", p. 2. The BORI manuscripts to which Sharma refers are no. 46 of A 1883–4, no. 185 of 1886–92, and no. 361 of 1895. We have examined no. 361 of 1895, *Jātiviveka*, from *Vāstuśāstra of Viśvaṃbhara*. The text following the Viśvākarman/Brahma opening is Gopinatha's, from the opening lines of the JV, including the Shaiva invocation and details of his family, but omitting the last smṛti citations and the colophon at the end of Gopinatha's third chapter. No scribal name or date is given.

quoted by Hemadri and Kamalakara."[101] It has not been possible to examine this text, but extracts from it indicate that it is also Gopinatha's text with the short discourse between Brahma and Visvakarman at the start.[102] There is a further "*Vāstuśāstra of Viśvaṃbhara*" in the National Archives in Nepal which follows this broad structure, although shorn of the opening matter about Gopinatha's family.[103]

Details in Guru Govind's later-fifteenth-century *Kāyasthapaddhati* suggest that Gopinatha's treatise was already in circulation as part of the *Viśvaṃbhara Vāstuśāstra* by that time. Guru Govind evidently knew of Gopinatha's text, and wished to engage with its conclusions. He cited its passage about Kayasthas as a menial pratiloma community, attributing it to "the *Jātiviveka*".[104] However, he asserted, these Kayasthas were quite different from the high-born Kshatriya Kayasthas, descendants of royalty, who were the subject of his own treatise.[105] But he seems to have known Gopinatha's text as part of the *Viśvaṃbhara Vāstuśāstra*, since he prefaced his treatise with the same nine verses that we meet elsewhere prefacing Gopinatha's work in its guise as the *Viśvaṃbhara Vāstuśāstra*, and Guru Govind attributed the verses to this latter text. It is likely, therefore, that he borrowed these verses from Gopinatha's work already circulating under the authorial name of "Visvambhara", and used the verses to open his own treatise on the different groupings of anuloma and pratiloma Kayasthas.

Why might scholars have "re-branded" Gopinatha's treatise? The most likely explanation is that they wished to add to its weight by asso-

[101] Peterson, *Catalogue*, no. 1323, 58.

[102] Peterson, *Second Report*, no. 46, pp. 116–17.

[103] *Vāstuśāstra of Viśvaṃbhara*, ff. 1v–2v. Péter Szántó kindly made a copy of this manuscript available to us. Under "*Viśvaṃbharavāstuśāstra*", Aufrecht cites only the references in Hemadri, Kamalakarabhatta, and the Peterson catalogue. Aufrecht, *Catalogus*, p. 585. Mitra's listing of vastusastra texts cites the same references: Mitra, *Contribution*, p. 209. There is also a *Viśvaṃbharavāstuśāstra* listed, under *Silpaśāstraprakaraṇa,* "the science of construction", in the library catalogue of the great mid-seventeenth century Banaras scholar Kavindracarya. We do not know whether this was Gopinatha's text. Sastry, *Kavīndrācāryasūcipatram*, no. 2148, p. 33.

[104] Guru Govind, *Kāyasthapaddhati*, ff. 12v–13r; the same passage is at JV, f. 8r.

[105] Guru Govind, *Kāyasthapaddhati*, ff. 5v–7v.

ciating it with an ancient authority, drawing attention away from, and sometimes erasing altogether the merely human fact of Gopinatha's authorship. But why a work within this genre? Most works of vastusastra prescribed a location for different professions and varnas within towns and cities.[106] Gopinatha himself made connections with the life of a royal city. The author of the *Bṛhajjātiviveka* appreciated this association, enhancing Gopinatha's text with descriptions of the place of anuloma and pratiloma jatis within the city. It would have been quite plausible, therefore, to present Gopinatha's text as part of a larger and more venerable work of vastusastra earlier in circulation in western India, enhancing its authority and connecting it with a wider field of learning. In addition, the genre offered the link with Visvakarman, divine architect and great artificer to the gods. As indicated above, many craft communities laid claim to Visvakarman as a powerful validating figure for their professional skills and dharmic prestige. Connecting Gopinatha's text with Visvakarman gave it additional significance for those interested in the "real" identity of such communities.[107]

Gopinatha in Banaras

Like Guru Govind, the major Banaras intellectuals who borrowed from Gopinatha during the sixteenth and seventeenth centuries modified his implied doubts about the survival of Kshatriyas in the world, and his severe approach to "mixed" communities. As Benke has argued, many scholars in this period sought to identify a legitimate ritual life for the increasingly prosperous and powerful Sudras of their own time, who might otherwise find themselves drawn further towards the culture of bhakti.[108] Pre-eminent amongst them were Krishna Sesa, leader of Maratha Brahmans in Banaras in the closing decades of the

[106] Acharya, ed. and trans., *Architecture of Manasara*, pp. 74–7; Sachdev and Tillotson, *Building Jaipur*, p. 16.

[107] It is also possible that Gopinatha simply copied his entire text from the earlier *Viśvaṃbhara Vāstuśāstra*. However, this seems unlikely. Gopinatha's text is more detailed and focused on the principles of "mixing" than usually seen in a vastusastra work. There is also a consistency in the "Viśvaṃbhara" texts containing Gopinatha's work, suggesting a successful "re-branding".

[108] Benke, "Śūdrācāraśiromaṇi".

sixteenth century, and Kamalakarabhatta, most famous of the celebrated Maharashtrian Bhatta dynasty of Banaras scholars, who flourished during the early and middle decades of the seventeenth century. They were major scions of the Sesa and Bhatta pandit lineages whose later members added lustre to the Banaras pandit assembly of 1779 described above. Their treatises on the dharma of Sudras emerged as particularly authoritative texts.[109]

Writing probably in the 1580s or 1590s, Krishna Sesa relied heavily on Gopinatha's treatise. He explained that his patron, the king Pilaji, had commissioned him to write his *Śūdrācāraśiromaṇi* (The Gem Treatise of Good Sudra Conduct), out of his concern at the confusion and mixing of dharmas. It was an easy but complete guide to the dharmas of each of the four varnas, written for the benefit of Sudras.[110] Without mentioning Gopinatha, he cited "the *Jātiviveka*" and "*Viśvaṃbhara*" extensively in his first chapter, describing the anuloma and pratiloma castes. The descriptions are either identical with, or closely resemble Gopinatha's.[111] However, Krishna Sesa turned Gopinatha's information to his own purposes. As Benke has argued, "good" Sudras for Krishna Sesa included all well-conducted householders who followed the dharma proper to their caste and obediently served the twice-born in their proper professions.[112] This opened a "good" Sudra dharma to a wider range of middling service communities than Gopinatha had been willing to admit. Krishna Sesa drew on Gopinatha's text for the profession and parentage of such communities, but withheld his strictures on their exclusion from Sudra dharma.[113] He reproduced Gopinatha's text on the low entitlements of Kayasthas almost word for word, but classified the contentious community of Rathakara craftsmen more positively, citing Yajnavalkya and Vijnanesvara's *Mitākṣarā* to the effect that the community were twice-born and entitled to wear the sacred thread.[114] He also left out Gopinatha's slights against "Vaishnavas".

[109] Krishna Sesa, *Śūdrācāraśiromaṇi*; Kamalakarabhatta, *Śūdrakamalākaraḥ*.
[110] Benke, *Śūdrācāraśiromaṇi*, p. 85.
[111] Krishna Sesa, *Śūdrācāraśiromaṇi*, pt 1, pp. 19–24.
[112] Benke, *Śūdrācāraśiromaṇi*, p. 247.
[113] Krishna Sesa, *Śūdrācāraśiromaṇi*, pt 1, pp. 19–24.
[114] Ibid., pp. 22–3.

Kamalakarabhatta, famous son of the Banaras Bhatta family, also detailed an appropriate ritual life for Sudras in his *Śūdrakamalākaraḥ*. Again without mentioning Gopinatha's name, he referred frequently to "the *Jātiviveka*" and "the *Viśvaṃbharaśāstra*". While Krishna Sesa elaborated the rules for anuloma and pratiloma "mixed jatis" at the start of his treatise, Kamalakarabhatta did so in his final chapter, entitled *Jātinirṇayaprakaraṇa* (The Determination of Jatis).[115] Many of his citations reproduced the information in Gopinatha on the occupation and parentage of each jati community, either word for word, or very closely.[116] Like Krishna Sesa, Kamalakarabhatta preferred to leave open the relation to Sudra dharma of many middling professions. He followed Krishna Sesa in omitting the attacks on "Vaishnavas", and in his positive classification of Rathakaras.[117]

Kamalakarabhatta made a further very significant change. He asserted that some authorities were correct in their belief that Kshatriyas and Vaishyas could still be found in the contemporary world, albeit in concealed and partly fallen forms. Having run counter to the spirit of Gopinatha's text, he then deployed its very flexibility to open the door to a higher status for Kayasthas. He reproduced Gopinatha's description of degraded pratiloma Kayasthas, but explained that they were different from the respectable high-born Kayasthas, descended from King Chandrasena, who were analogous to Kshatriyas and entitled to a non-Vedic sacred thread ceremony.[118]

Kamalakarabhatta's text was to be widely influential, not only in Banaras and the Maratha country, but in northern India. When the Maratha government at Pune sought to promote new dharmic norms in its recently conquered lands in Malwa in the 1730s, Malwa Brahmans were instructed to follow the *Śūdrakamalākaraḥ* in their work as ritual officiants for Sudras.[119] The text appeared in 1754 amongst the impor-

[115] Kamalakarabhatta, *Śūdrakamalākaraḥ*, p. 75. Some versions of the text omit these headings; for one that includes this heading, see Javaji, ed., *Śūdrakamalākaraḥ*, p. 238.

[116] Kamalakarabhatta, *Śūdrakamalākaraḥ*, pp. 82–9.

[117] Ibid., p. 82.

[118] Ibid., pp. 89–90.

[119] O'Hanlon and Minkowski, "What Makes People Who They Are?", pp. 410–11.

tant manuscript texts listed in the household accounts of the Maratha court at Pune along with the prices charged for its copying.[120] As seen above it also appears, alongside the work of Guru Govind and "the *Jātiviveka*", as one of the works consulted by the Banaras pandit assembly convened in 1779 to determine the entitlements of Kayasthas.

Neither of these major scholars mentioned Gopinatha by name. Yet it is clear that a version of his treatise carrying his name was still in independent circulation at the time that Kamalakarabhatta was writing. This is evident from the copy, referred to above, completed in 1642 by the scribe Mhalgi Kanhabhatta. With a few changes, this was Gopinatha's text. After a brief invocation to Ganesh, it started halfway through Gopinatha's family history with the reference to his father Sarangdhara.[121] Kanhabhatta also omitted some of Gopinatha's supplementary smrti quotations. He followed the example of Krishna Sesa and Kamalakarabhatta in excluding the material most obviously hostile to "Vaishnavas", although he did not follow them in the flexibility offered to Kayasthas, simply repeating Gopinatha's own text.[122] Compared to Gopinatha's earlier work, in which Sanskrit and many Marathi jati names were given side by side, Kanhabhatta shifted markedly towards purely Marathi terms to describe the different jatis.

Gopinatha's work found a further new role during the turbulent decade of the 1670s, when Gagabhatta, nephew of Kamalakarabhatta, arranged the consecration, as a Kshatriya and a dharmic king, of Shivaji. Leading Kayasthas at Shivaji's court pressed Gagabhatta for recognition of their own claims to twice-born status and investiture with the sacred thread.[123] Drawing on Kamalakarabhatta's more accommodating approach, Gagabhatta wrote for them the *Kāyasthācāradīpikā* (Light on the Proper Conduct of Kayasthas).[124] Gagabhatta deployed Gopinatha's text in the opening section, entitled *Jātivivekanirūpaṇa* (The Examination of Jātiviveka). Citing the "Vāstuśāstra of Viśvaṃbhara", Gagabhatta described the six anuloma and six pratiloma born in terms that followed Gopinatha's text very closely.[125] His main discus-

[120] Sardesai, *Selections*, vol. 22, p. 94.
[121] Kanhabhatta, *Jātiviveka*, f. 1v.
[122] Ibid., ff. 7v–8v.
[123] O'Hanlon, "The Social Worth of Scribes".
[124] Gagabhatta, *Kāyasthācāradīpikā.*
[125] Ibid., ff. 4r–4v.

sion of the mixed jatis also borrowed heavily from Gopinatha, and he included many Marathi jati names, although his ordering of jatis was different.[126] This discussion gave Gagabhatta the framework for his treatment of Kayasthas in the remainder of his text. He did the same in his prescriptions for Sudra ritual, the *Śūdra[dharma]uddyota* (Illumination of [the Dharma of] Sudras), prefacing the text with what he called a *Śūdradharma-Jātivivekanirūpaṇa* (The Examination of the Discernment of Jatis in the Dharma of Sudras).[127] As we have seen, scholars continued to find Gopinatha's text useful into the eighteenth century. The questions it raised, particularly the standing of Kshatriya kings in the Kaliyuga, continued to generate new controversy. This was particularly so at the Rajput courts, where rulers sought to develop more consciously dharmic models of Hindu kingship.[128]

The *Jātiviveka* and Colonial Caste

Gopinatha's text continued to exercise influence in the nineteenth century, shaping both social reform debates and the emerging politics of non-Brahmanism. In the mid-1820s, the East India Company assumed responsibility for the administration of Hindu law. Many caste communities sought to test the new arrangements but found themselves struggling against the early-nineteenth-century inheritors of the conservative tradition outlined above, led by Nilakanthasastri Thatthe.[129] They discovered that some Bombay government officials regarded the *Jātiviveka* as a source of impeccable authority. Arthur Steele, charged with compiling an accurate account of the "law and custom" of Hindu communities in the Company's new Deccan provinces for use in the Bombay courts, cited "the Jatiwiwek, the Brohud Jatiwiwek, Jatdurpun, Madhwu Kulpuntu and Perseram Prutap" as works particularly recommended for their account of caste classification.[130] When the

[126] Ibid., ff. 5v–6r; 7r–10r.

[127] Gagabhatta, *Śūdra[dharma]uddyota*, ff. 3v–22r.

[128] Deshpande, "Kṣatriyas in the Kali Age?", pp. 16–21; Horstmann, *Der Zusammenhalt der Welt*.

[129] Wagle, "Ritual and Change"; Deshpande, "Kṣatriyas in the Kali Age?", pp. 11–16. For Thatthe's nineteenth century significance, and the caste disputes described below, see the Introduction to this collection of essays.

[130] Steele, *A Summary of the Law and Custom*, pp. xi–xii.

Sonar community of goldsmiths petitioned the Bombay government in defence of their rights, as high-born Rathakaras, to Vedic ritual, the *Jātiviveka* was one of the works cited by H.H. Wilson, Secretary to the Committee of Public Instruction, and William Chaplin, Commissioner of the Deccan, against their case.[131] The earliest work of "non-Brahman" critique in the Maratha country, published in 1861, identified itself consciously as a voice of opposition within the genre of the *Jātiviveka*, as its title, the *Jātibhed Vivekasār* (Essence of the Discernment of Distinctions between Jatis) made clear.[132]

Champions of the rights of artisans and scribal people continued to inveigh against the tradition of the *Jātiviveka* through the 1870s. Writing in 1877, Samarava Moroji Nayaka of the Bombay Pathare Prabhu scribal community described the *Jātiviveka*, the *Bṛhajjātiviveka*, the *Paraśurāmapratāpa*, and the *Śatapraśnakalpalatā* as books that gave no proper account of his community "for the reason that they are written by the sastris and not by the sages of ancient times."[133] In the same year, the *Jātiviveka* entered the literature of later colonial anthropology through the work of John Wilson, who described "the Jati-Viveka, the Brahajjati-Viveka, the Madhava-Kalpalita, and the Parashurama Pratapa" as "works of authority among the Maratha Brahmans."[134] As late as 1919, the Kayastha writer and non-Brahman activist K.T. Gupte railed against the *Jātiviveka* as a text that "determined everyone other than Brahmans to be inferior and Sudras. In its opinion, goldsmiths, carpenters, weavers, gardeners, braziers and coppersmiths are all inferior and Sudras."[135]

Conclusions

Gopinatha's treatise came to occupy a pivotal place in the changing history of caste in medieval and early modern India. What gave his text its striking sway and longevity was its suggestion that the "discern-

[131] Wagle, "A Dispute", p. 138.

[132] Padwal, *Jātibhed Vivekasār*. For a recent analysis, see Jaywant, "Reshaping the Figure of the Shudra".

[133] Nayaka, *A History*, p. 30.

[134] Wilson, *Indian Caste*, vol. 1, p. 64.

[135] Gupte, *Rājavāḍyānchī Gāgābhaṭṭi*, p. 42.

ment of jatis" really meant the discernment of mixed jatis, in a world very largely made up of such people, in which the active ordering principle of Hindu royal power had weakened or disappeared. It now fell more to scholars, Gopinatha's text suggested, to defend the integrity of dharma in the world. They could best do so by ensuring adherence to the proper order of castes and stages of life. His manual, with its attempt to develop older models of caste categorisation into something like a vernacular sociology, offered them the knowledge and "discernment" needed to do this: to assign each community its place within the orders of jati and varna, and make accurate decisions about their ritual lives, their professions, their customs and practices. Gopinatha's work formed part of the longer-term process by which the "discernment of jatis" emerged as a more elaborated and independent field of scholarly expertise. It provided the base from which many other scholars developed their own renderings and addressed the pressing political and religious questions of their own times.

Sharp internal disagreements marked this "new discourse of caste". On the legitimate ritual life of Sudras, and the existence of Kshatriya kings in the fallen world of the Kaliyuga, Gopinatha's position differed from the view that was to emerge amongst scholars in Banaras some two centuries after his lifetime. His work nonetheless seems to have provided part of the template, and much of the practical information that these and other scholars used. Such questions went on to become central to caste politics in western India during the three centuries that followed, from the struggles over the consecration of Shivaji to the emergence of the non-Brahman movement.[136]

Gopinatha's presentation of jatis as ranked communities defined by parentage and shorn of their older constitutive role in relation to the state finds echoes elsewhere in the subcontinent. It seems to have much in common with the process that Ronald Inden has observed in medieval Bengal. As the links between corporate groups and the state weakened within the new Sultanate milieu, occupational groups slowly became the ranked jatis that we have come to know as "caste", separated from the state and free standing as a principle of social organisation. "Caste", in its modern form, emerging in the thirteenth

[136] Deshpande, "Kṣatriyas in the Kali Age?".

and fourteenth centuries, was in some part at least, the consequence of the local collapse of Hindu kingship.[137] This part of Inden's argument has attracted scholarly criticism.[138] However, the question he raises is an important one, and this essay lends support to his findings. Given the close connections observed between state formation and caste in India's early history, it would be surprising if the weakening of Hindu kingship in many parts of India after 1300 was without consequences in this area.

These are large questions. However, mapping the long processes of transmission through which Gopinatha's treatise came down into the colonial world may provide some clues. It adds to the evidence that caste was not a changeless system until the colonial "reinvention" about which so many scholars have written.[139] Rather, the colonial state inherited an order of varna and jati marked by acute and still developing tensions, whose consequences continued to reverberate through many areas of nineteenth- and twentieth-century society.

References

Abraham, Meera, *Two Medieval Merchant Guilds of South India* (New Delhi: Manohar, 1988).

Acharya, Prasanna Kumar, ed. and tr., *Architecture of Mānasāra* (London and New York: Oxford University Press, 1933).

Aiyer, K.V. Subrahmanya, "Largest Provincial Organisations in Ancient India", *Quarterly Journal of the Mythic Society*, vol. 45, no. 1, July 1954, pp. 28–47; vol. 45, no. 2, October 1954, pp. 71–98; vol. 45, no. 4, April 1955, pp. 271–86; vol. 46, no. 1, July 1955, pp. 8–19.

Aufrecht, Theodor, *Catalogus Catalogorum. An Alphabetical Register of Sanskrit Works and Authors*, 3 vols (Leipzig: German Oriental Society, 1891).

Bapat, Ramachandra, *Bṛhajjātiviveka*, Sanskrit manuscript no. 685 of Bhau Daji Collection, Asiatic Society, Mumbai.

Bayly, Susan, *Caste, Society and Politics in India from the Eighteenth Century to the Modern Age* (Cambridge: Cambridge University Press, 1999).

[137] Inden, *Imagining India*, pp. 217–28; Inden, *Marriage and Rank*, pp. 73–82.

[138] Jaiswal, *Caste*, p. 19.

[139] Bayly, *Caste, Society and Politics*; Dirks, *Castes of Mind*; Guha, *Beyond Caste*; Cherien, *Merchants of Virtue*.

Benke, Theodore, "The *Sūdrācāraśiromaṇi* of Kṛṣṇa Seṣa. A 16th. Manual of Dharma for Sudras", University of Pennsylvania PhD thesis, 2010.

Benson, James, "Saṃkarabhaṭṭa's Family Chronicle: The Gādhivaṃśavarnana", in Axel Michaels, ed., *The Pandit: Traditional Scholarship in India* (Delhi: Manohar, 2001), pp. 105–18.

Brinkhaus, Horst, *Die Altindischen Mischkastensysteme* (Wiesbaden: Franz Steiner Verlag GmbH, 1978).

Chattopadhyaya, Brajadulal, *A Social History of Early India* (New Delhi: Pearson Longman, 2009).

———, *The Making of Early Medieval India* (Delhi: Oxford University Press, 2012).

Cherien, Divya, *Merchants of Virtue: Hindus, Muslims and Untouchables in Eighteenth Century South Asia* (Berkeley: University of California Press, 2023).

Corpus Inscriptionum Indicarum: Inscriptions of the Kalachuri-Chedi Era, vol. 4, pt 2 (Ootacamund: Government Epigraphist for India, 1998).

Dalapati, *Nṛsiṃhaprasāda Saṃskārasāra of Srīdalapatimahārāja*, ed. Acharya Sri Ramagovinda Sukla (Varanasi: Sampuranand Sanskrit University, 1985).

Davis, Donald R., "Recovering the Indigenous Legal Traditions of India: Classical Hindu Law in Practice in Late Medieval Kerala", *Journal of Indian Philosophy*, vol. 27, no. 3, 1999, pp. 159–213.

———, "Intermediate Realms of Law: Corporate Groups and Rulers in Medieval India", *Journal of the Economic and Social History of the Orient*, vol. 48, no. 1, 2005, pp. 92–117.

———, *The Spirit of Hindu Law* (Cambridge: Cambridge University Press, 2010).

Derrett, J. Duncan M., "Two Inscriptions Concerning the Status of Kammālas and the Application of Dharmaśāstra", in J. Duncan M. Derrett, ed., *Essays in Classical and Modern Hindu Law* (Leiden: E.J. Brill, 1976), vol. 1, pp. 86–110.

Desai, P.B., *A Corpus of Inscriptions in the Kannada Districts of Hyderabad State* (Hyderabad: Government of Andhra Pradesh, 1958).

Deshpande, Madhav, "Kṣatriyas in the Kali Age? Gāgābhaṭṭa and His Opponents", *Indo-Iranian Journal*, vol. 53, no. 2, 2010, pp. 1–26.

Dhere, R.C., *The Rise of a Folk God: Viṭṭhal of Pandharpur*, trans. Anne Feldhaus (New Delhi: Permanent Black, 2012).

Dikshit, G.S., *Local Self Government in Mediaeval Karnataka* (Dharwar: Karnatak University, 1964).

Dirks, Nicholas, *The Hollow Crown: Ethnohistory of an Indian Kingdom* (Cambridge: Cambridge University Press, 1987).

———, *Castes of Mind: Colonialism and the Making of Modern India* (Princeton: Princeton University Press, 2001).

Dyczkowski, Mark S.G., *The Doctrine of Vibration: An Analysis of the Doctrines and Practices of Kashmiri Saivism* (Albany: State University of New York Press, 1987).

Eaton, Richard M., *A Social History of the Deccan 1300–1761: Eight Indian Lives* (Cambridge: Cambridge University Press, 2005).

Eggeling, Julius, *Catalogue of the Sanskrit Manuscripts in the Library of the India Office* (London: Secretary of State for India in Council, 1887).

Entwistle, A.W., "Vaiṣṇava Tilakas: Sectarian Marks Worn by Worshippers of Viṣṇu", *International Association of the Vrindaban Research Institute Bulletin*, vol. xi–xii, December 1981–June 1982, pp. 11–12.

Fisher, Elaine, "Public Philology: Text Criticism and the Sectarianisation of Hinduism in Early Modern South India", *South Asian History and Culture*, vol. 6, no. 1, 2015, pp. 50–69.

Flood, Gavin, "The Saiva Traditions", in Gavin Flood, ed., *The Blackwell Companion to Hinduism* (Oxford: Blackwell Publishing, 2003), pp. 200–28.

Gagabhatta, *Kāyasthācāradīpikā*, Unpublished manuscript, British Library, Sanskrit manuscript no. 3009m.

———, *Śūdra[dharma]uddyota*, Unpublished manuscript, British Library, Sanskrit manuscript no. 2800.

Gode, P.K., "Identification of Dalpat Rai Mentioned in Burhan-i-Masir with Dalapatiraja the Author of the Dharmasastra work called the Nrsimhaprasad", *Proceedings of the Indian History Congress*, vol. 2, 1938, pp. 313–18.

———, "Sābāji Pratāparāja, A Protégé of Burhān Nizām Shah of Ahmadnagar, and His Works – Between AD 1500 and 1560", *Annals of the Bhandarkar Oriental Research Institute*, vol. 24, nos 3–4, July–October 1943, pp. 156–64.

Gopinatha, *Jātiviveka*, Unpublished manuscript, British Library, Sanskrit manuscripts nos 1969 and 1061a.

Gordon, Stewart, *The Marathas*, 1600–1818 (Cambridge: Cambridge University Press, 1993).

Guha, Sumit, *Beyond Caste. Identity and Power in South Asia, Past and Present* (Leiden: Brill, 2013).

Gupte, K.T., *Rājavāḍyānchī Gāgābhaṭṭī* (Pune: Indu Prakash Press, 1919).

Gupte, T.V., *Ethnographical Notes on the Chandraseniya Kayastha Prabhus* (Poona: Israelite Press, 1904).

Guru Govind, *Kāyasthapaddhati*, Unpublished Manuscript, Bharat Itihas Samsodhak Mandal, Pune, Sanskrit manuscript no. 46,326.

Haig, Lt Col. T.W., "The History of the Nizām Shāhī Kings of Aḥmadnagar", *The Indian Antiquary*, April 1920, pp. 66–75; May 1920, pp. 84–91; June 1920, pp. 102–8; July 1920, pp. 123–8; September 1920, pp. 157–67; October 1920, pp. 177–88; November 1920, pp. 197–204; December 1920, pp. 217–24.

Hemadri, *Chaturvargacintāmaṇi*, ed. B.C. Siromani, *et al.*, 6 vols (Calcutta: Biblioteca Indica, 1873–1911).

Horstmann, Monika, *Der Zusammenhalt der Welt: Religiöse Herrschaftslegitimation und Religionspolitik Maharaja Savai Jaisings (1700–1743)* (Wiesbaden: Harrassowitz, 2009).

Hultzsch, E., "Vanapalli Plates of Anna-Vema – Saka Samvat 1300", *Epigraphia Indica*, vol. III, no. 10, 1894–5, pp. 59–66.

Inden, Ronald, *Marriage and Rank in Bengali Culture: A History of Caste and Clan in Middle Period Bengal* (Berkeley: University of California Press, 1976).

———, *Imagining India* (Oxford: Blackwell Publishers, 1992).

Jaiswal, Suvira, *Caste: Origin, Function and Dimensions of Change* (New Delhi: Manohar, 2000).

Jātiviveka from *Vāstuśāstra of Viśvaṃbhara*, No author given, Unpublished manuscript, Bhandarkar Oriental Research Institute, Pune, Sanskrit manuscript no. 361 of 1891–5.

Javaji, Pandurang, ed., *Śūdrakamalākaraḥ* (Mumbai: Nirnayasagar Press, 1928).

Jaywant, Ketaki, "Reshaping the Figure of the Shudra: Tukaram Padwal's *Jatibhed Viveksar* (Reflections on the Institution of Caste)", *Modern Asian Studies*, vol. 57, no. 2, 2022, pp. 380–408.

Jha, V.N., "Varṇasaṃkara in the Dharma Sūtras", *Journal of the Economic and Social History of the Orient*, vol. 13, no. 3, November 1970, pp. 273–88.

Kamalakarabhatta, *Śūdrakamalākaraḥ,* ed. Ganesh Bapuji Sastri Malvankar and Vishnu Sastri Bapat (Mumbai: No press given, 1861).

Kane, P.V., *History of Dharmaśāstra*, 5 vols (Poona: Bhandarkar Oriental Research Institute, 1968–77).

Kanhabhatta, Mhalgi, *Jātiviveka*, Unpublished manuscript, British Library, Sanskrit manuscript no. 1061a.

Krishna Sesa, *Śūdrācaraśiromaṇi*, ed. Pandit Narayana Sastri Khiste (Banaras: Vidya Vilas Press, 1933).

Madhava, *Śatapraśnakalpalatā*, Unpublished manuscript, Bhandarkar Oriental Research Institute, Pune, P.M. Joshi Collection, Sanskrit manuscript no. 19.

Mirashi, V.V., "Purshottampuri Plates of Ramachandra: Saka 1232", *Epigraphia Indica*, vol. XXV, no. 24, 1939–40, pp. 145–50.

Mitra, Haridas, *Contribution to a Bibliography of Indian Art and Aesthetics* (Calcutta: Visvabharati Research Publications Committee, 1980).

Molesworth, J.T., *A Dictionary, Marāṭhi and English* (Bombay: Education Society's Press, 1857).

Nayaka, Samarav Moroji, *A History of the Pattana Prabhus* (Bombay: Family Printing Press, 1877).

Nobile, Riccardo, "Notizie Sulle Sotto-caste Nell' India", *Atti D.R. Accademia di Archeologica, Lettre et Belle Arti*, Nuova Serie, vol. 1, Naples, 1910.

O'Hanlon, Rosalind, "The Social Worth of Scribes: Brahmans, Kayasthas and the Social Order in Early Modern India", *Indian Economic and Social History Review*, vol. 47, no. 4, 2010, pp. 563–96.

———, "Performance in a World of Paper: Puranic Histories and Social Communication in Early Modern India", *Past and Present*, vol. 219, May 2013, pp. 87–126.

———, and Christopher Minkowski, "What Makes People Who They Are? Pandit Networks and the Problem of Livelihoods in Early Modern Western India", *Indian Economic and Social History Review*, vol. 45, no. 3, 2008, pp. 381–416.

Olivelle, Patrick, ed. and tr., *The Law Code of Manu* (Oxford: Oxford University Press, 2004).

———, "Dharmaśāstra: A Textual History", in Timothy Lubin, Donald R. Davis, and Jayanth Krishnan, eds, *Hinduism and Law: An Introduction* (Cambridge: Cambridge University Press, 2010), pp. 28–57.

Padwal, Tukaram Tatya, *Jātibhed Vivekasār* (Bombay: Ganpat Krishnaji's Press, 1861).

Parasher-Sen, Aloka, *Subordinate and Marginal Groups in Early India* (New Delhi: Oxford University Press, 2004).

Peterson, Peter, *A Second Report of Operations in Search of Sanskrit Manuscripts in the Bombay Circle, April 1883–March 1884* (Bombay: Society's Library, 1884).

———, *Catalogue of the Sanskrit Manuscripts in the Library of His Highness the Maharaja of Ulwar* (Bombay: No publisher given, 1892).

Rice, Benjamin Lewis, "Shikarpur Taluq", *Epigraphia Carnatica*, vol. 7: *Inscriptions in the Shimoga District*, pt 1 (Bangalore: Mysore Government Central Press, 1902).

Rocher, Ludo, "Notes on Mixed Castes in Classical India", *The Adhyar Library Bulletin*, vol. 44–5, 1980–1, pp. 134–46.

Sabajipratapa, *Paraśurāmapratāpa. Jātiviveka, with Upodghātakāṇḍa*, Unpublished manuscript, Bhandarkar Oriental Research Institute, Pune, Sanskrit manuscript no. 233 of Viśrāma Collection ii.

Sachdev, Vibhuti, and Giles Tillotson, *Building Jaipur: The Making of an Indian City* (London: Reaktion Books, 2002).

Sanderson, Alexis, "Śaivism and the Tantric Traditions", in Stewart Sutherland, *et al.*, eds, *The World's Religions* (London: Routledge and Kegan Paul, 1988), pp. 660–704.

Sardesai, G.S, *New History of the Marathas*, 3 vols (Bombay: Phoenix Publications, 1968).

———, ed., *Selections from the Peshwa Daftar*, 45 vols (Bombay: Government Central Press, 1930–4).

Sastry, R. Ananta Krishna, ed., *Kavīndrācāryasūcipatram. Kavindracharya List* (Baroda: Baroda Government, 1921).

Sharma, Har Dutt, "Paraśurāmapratāpa: Its Authorship and the Authorities Quoted in it", *The Poona Orientalist*, vol. 7, nos 1–2, April and July 1942, pp. 13–26.

Sharma, Ram Sharan, *Sudras in Ancient India* (Delhi: Motilal Banarsidass, 1980).

Shastri, Krishna, *Annual Report on Epigraphy for 1909* (Madras: Government of Madras, 1909).

Sherwani, Haroon Khan, *The Bahmanis of the Deccan* (New Delhi: Munshiram Manoharlal, 1985).

Shyam, Radhey, *The Kingdom of Ahmadnagar* (Delhi: Motilal Banarsidass, 1966).

Sircar, D.C., *Indian Epigraphical Glossary* (Delhi: Motilal Banarsidass, 1966).

Sontheimer, Gunther-Dietz, "God, Dharma and Society in the Yādava Kingdom of Devagirī According to the Līḷācaritra of Cakradhar", in Gunther-Dietz Sontheimer and Paramesvara Arthal, eds, *Indology and Law: Studies in Honour of J. Duncan M. Derrett* (Wiesbaden: Franz Steiner Verlag, 1982), pp. 321–58.

Steele, Arthur, *A Summary of the Law and Custom of Hindoo Castes within the Dekhun Provinces Subject to the Presidency of Bombay* (Bombay: Courier Press, 1827).

Talbot, Cynthia, "A Revised View of 'Traditional' India: Caste, Status and Social Mobility in Medieval Andhra", *South Asia: Journal of South Asian Studies*, vol. 15, no. 1, 1992, pp. 17–52.

Tambiah, S.J., "From Varna to Caste through Mixed Unions", in Jack Goody, ed., *The Character of Kinship* (Cambridge: Cambridge University Press, 1973), pp. 191–229.

Thapar, Romila, *Early India: From the Origins to AD 1300* (London: Penguin Press, 2002).

Vaidya, C.V., *History of Medieval Hindu India*, 3 vols (New Delhi: Cosmo Publications, 1979).

Vajpeyi, Ananya, "Politics of Complicity, Poetics of Contempt. A History of the Sudra in Maharashtra, 1650–1950 CE", University of Chicago, PhD thesis, 2004.

Vāstuśāstra of Viśvaṃbhara, Unpublished manuscript, Bhandarkar Oriental Research Institute, Pune, manuscript no. 361 of 1891–5.

Vāstuśāstra of Viśvaṃbhara, Unpublished manuscript, Nepalese German Manuscript Cataloguing Project, manuscript no. B352/15.

Verma, Onkar Prasad, *The Yadavas and Their Times* (Nagpur: Vidharba Samshodhan Mandal, 1970.)

von Stietencron, Heinrich, "Calculating Religious Decay: The Kaliyuga in India", in Heinrich von Stietencron, *Hindu Myth, Hindu History: Religion, Art and Politics* (Delhi: Permanent Black, 2005), pp. 31–49.

Wagle, Narendra, "A Dispute Between the Pancal Devajna Sonars and the Brahmins of Pune Regarding Social Rank and Ritual Privileges: A Case-Study of the British Administration of *Jati* Laws in Maharashtra, 1822–1825", in N.K. Wagle, ed., *Images of Maharashtra* (Curzon Press: London, 1980), pp. 129–59.

———, "The Cāndrasenīya Kayastha Prabhus and the Brahmans: Ritual, Law and Politics in Pune: 1789–80", in Gunther-Dietz Sontheimer and Paramesvara Arthal, eds, *Indology and Law: Studies in Honour of J. Duncan M. Derrett* (Wiesbaden: Franz Steiner Verlag, 1982), pp. 303–28.

———, "Ritual and Change in Early Nineteenth Century Society in Maharashtra: Vedokta Disputes in Baroda, Pune and Satara, 1824–1838", in Milton Israel and N.K. Wagle, eds, *Religion and Society in Maharashtra* (Toronto: University of Toronto, 1987), pp. 145–81.

Wilson, John, *Indian Caste*, 2 vols (Bombay: Times of India Office, 1877).

9

Performance in a World of Paper

Puranic Histories and Social Communication in Early Modern India

Introduction

A KEY ELEMENT OF "early modernity", as historians commonly describe the era of transformations in the world's history from the fifteenth to the eighteenth centuries, lies in the widespread adoption of paper as a medium for communication, and the new technologies of print.[1] These technologies had, of course, their origins in Asia. In China and Japan, where paper had been in existence early in the first millennium, the revolution in communication took place through new methods for printing, including woodblock and moveable type. Paper manufacture and use spread slowly through the Islamic world during the last centuries of the first millennium, reaching Europe during the tenth century via Islamic Spain, and spreading through southern Europe to reach Germany by the end of the fourteenth century.

Yet it was in Europe where these developments were most clearly bound up with rapid, indeed sometimes explosive societal change. Expanding paper use and the printing press quickened the spread of Renaissance culture across Europe. The printing press provided a key early means through which the ideas of the Reformation reached broader audiences. Paper records transformed state practices, as the bureaucracies of Europe's states worked to raise their revenues, expand

[1] For a recent overview, see Pollock, ed., *Forms of Knowledge*, pp. 2–5.

their judiciaries, and enlarge their armies. The many different communicative possibilities of print lay at the heart of other profound societal changes, from the emergence of new traditions of political radicalism to shifts in household consumption and leisure.

As historians have observed, however, paper and print did not displace older modes of oral communication, but rather stimulated and facilitated them. Thus Kevin Sharpe has explored the ways in which new images of royal power across a variety of visual, print, and performance media stimulated the popular discussion of monarchy in sixteenth-century England.[2] Andrew Pettegree has demonstrated the interplay between Reformation printed tracts, woodcuts, and images, and a powerful oral sphere of performance, popular songs, preaching, and discussion.[3] The greater availability of printed texts of all kinds opened up the fast-moving social changes of the early modern centuries to the scrutiny of regional and local audiences.[4] Many scholars have identified these expanding realms and networks of communication as early forms of the modern "public sphere".[5]

Historians have looked for these changes in the world beyond Europe too. Debates about early forms of a "public sphere" in Ming and Qing China have focused on the academies that prepared candidates for the civil service examinations. These were forums for public discourse where intellectuals could critique the "corrupt officials" who threatened the ethical norms of Confucian scholar gentry.[6] Beyond the world of the academies, operas and dramas depicted the challenges that new forms of social mobility presented to traditional status relationships, and helped create a sixteenth-century boom in commercial publishing.[7] Rapid urbanisation as Japanese warlords sought to curb the

[2] Sharpe, *Selling the Tudor Monarchy*.

[3] Pettegree, *Reformation and the Culture of Persuasion*. See also the pathbreaking work of Scribner, *For the Sake of Simple Folk*.

[4] For an overview of recent literature in the English context, see Baker and McGruer, *Readers, Audiences and Coteries*.

[5] Habermas, *The Structural Transformation*. For examples of recent engagements with this theme, see Lake and Pincus, eds, *The Politics of the Public Sphere*; Yachnin and Wilson, eds, *Making Publics*; Warner, *The Letters of the Republic*.

[6] Bin Wong, "Great Expectations"; Wakeman, "Boundaries of the Public Sphere".

[7] Chow, *Publishing, Culture and Power*; Brokaw and Chow, eds, *Printing and Book Culture*; Mei, *The Novel and Theatrical Imagination*.

military power of the samurai class was the context in which Japan's publishing industry entered its seventeenth-century boom. For new communities of city people, fiction, kabuki drama, and puppet theatres provided opportunities not only for satire and social critique, but for the development of ideas about political ethics and proto-nationalist sentiment towards the Japanese state.[8]

Yet not all "paper revolutions" were followed by the coming of print. The great bureaucratic states of the Ottoman empire, Safavid Iran, and Mughal India rested on a massive expansion in paper use. Reinforced by generous royal patronage, universities, sectarian institutions, and communities of scholars and literati supported an increasingly interconnected manuscript culture. But until the late eighteenth century, print found no central role in the operations of the state or the worlds of learning and culture.[9] This phenomenon of "paper without print" has drawn the attention of many historians. Some have explored the reasons for the "failure" of some early modern states and societies to adopt print, when its use elsewhere was familiar.[10] Others have looked at the nature of social communication that could be achieved by an expansive manuscript culture, to ask whether anything like a "public sphere" could have emerged without print's capacity to expand and depersonalise communication and to make knowledge of different kinds available without the personal mediation of masters and teachers.[11] These are key questions for current debates about the nature of "modernity" and the ways in which what some historians have called "multiple modernities" may have begun to emerge simultaneously in different parts of the world during the early modern centuries.[12]

For India, Christopher Bayly has examined what he has called the "ecumene" of pre- and early colonial India. This was a shared quasi-

[8] Berry, *Japan in Print*; Bernstein, Gordon and Nakai, eds, *Public Sphere, Private Lives*.

[9] Bloom, *Paper Before Print*; Atiyeh, ed., *The Book in the Islamic World*; Messick, *The Calligraphic State*; Robinson, "Technology and Religious Change".

[10] Bayly, *Empire and Information*, p. 200.

[11] Warner, *Letters of the Republic*. For the Islamic world, see Rahimi, *The Theater-State*; for India, Bayly, *Empire and Information*, pp. 180–211; Green, "The Uses of Books"; and Ogborn, *Indian Ink*, pp. 1–26.

[12] Narayana Rao, Shulman, and Subrahmanyam, *Textures of Time*; Kaviraj, "An Outline"; Bhargava, "Are There Alternative Modernities?".

public space for discussion within which state servants, scholars, urban gentry, and religious leaders felt able to hold government to account and to offer a critique of the social costs and consequences of Mughal decline and the expanding power of the East India Company.[13] The present essay also focuses on India, but in relation to an indigenous discursive sphere concerned with social relationships and identities amongst early modern India's leading Hindu scribal people. Brahmans worked as accomplished administrators, priests, and ritual specialists. They were highly mobile, their skills in increasing demand as royal courts looked to develop more prestigious forms of ritual and to build up their revenue administrations to supply the growing needs of their armies. Susan Bayly has seen in these developments the making of a "Brahman raj", as Brahman statecraft and scribal expertise made them indispensable to the rulers of India's regional states.[14]

This success created its own tensions. Sanskrit intellectuals flourished during these centuries, and many consciously reformulated their relationship to their own traditions.[15] There were struggles between theological and sectarian groupings, and the beginnings of an intellectual attempt to define the pluralist perspective of Advaita Vedanta as a kind of "big tent" Hinduism.[16] There were other questions too. Brahman scholars developed the theological and ritual framework for new ideologies of Hindu kingship, yet many Brahmans were also servants of the "yavana", of Mughal and Muslim courts.[17] With the aid of a flourishing manuscript culture, India's Hindu devotional movements advanced ever more penetrating critiques of Hindu caste itself, and of Brahman priestly elites. Brahman social mores – their caste history, their modes of life and livelihood, their ritual correctness, the conduct of their women – were opened up to intense social scrutiny.

This scrutiny came in part from external observers, but the sharpest critiques often came from other Brahmans. Many were acutely competitive, jealous of their reputations for ritual purity, priestly skill,

[13] Bayly, *Empire and Information*, pp. 180–211.

[14] Bayly, *Caste, Society and Politics*, pp. 64–96. See also Wink, *Land and Sovereignty*, pp. 66–85.

[15] Pollock, "New Intellectuals".

[16] Minkowski, "Advaita Vedānta".

[17] Guha, "Serving the Barbarian".

scholarly distinction, and administrative expertise. But Brahmans also struggled to develop new kinds of solidarity. These centuries saw the development of an India-wide classification of Brahman identities within which every "genuine" Brahman community was ostensibly located. During these centuries, India's regional states were developing deeper political and cultural roots, and supplementing the cosmopolitan languages of Persian and Sanskrit with greater use of the regional vernaculars in state administration.[18] The geography of major vernacular languages provided Brahmans with the basis for their India-wide classification, which distinguished between the five gauḍa groups of the North and five drāviḍa groups of the South.[19] To build their solidarities, Brahman scholars also sought to define the ritual privileges of a "full" Brahman. They debated what livelihoods were appropriate to the true dignity of a Brahman. They struggled to reconcile these ideal unities with the divergences of custom evident between regional Brahman communities. It was important to do so because the "portability" of a Brahman identity was a key asset, enabling Brahmans to compete for patronage and employment right across the cities and courts of the subcontinent, and thereby to build up very effective all-India connections.

Brahman judicial assemblies in India's major shrine towns and pilgrimage centres were key to these connections.[20] They adjudicated Brahman disputes and promoted the new solidarities with the circulation of nirṇayapatra, a form of "public" letter of judgment. Literary genres were also important. Men of letters debated Brahman identity through Sanskrit kāvya narrative poetry. Brahman history and identity were prominent themes in the puranas, Hindu India's ubiquitous performance genre. Some came to be so popular for their exposés of Brahman histories that eighteenth-century states attempted to destroy the bodies of manuscript material that contained them. These were not simply narrow "caste" disputes. A new type of all-India discursive activity emerged during this period, concerning Brahman status, history,

[18] Pollock, *The Language of the Gods*, pp. 330–437.

[19] For an extended discussion of this social geography, see O'Hanlon, "Speaking from Siva's Temple", pp. 261–4.

[20] Kane, *History of Dharmaśāstra*, vol. 2, pt 2, pp. 965–73. For assemblies in the Maratha regions, see Gune, *The Judicial System*, pp. 26–39.

and ritual privilege. An early modern "reinvention" of caste seems to have taken place during these centuries, well before the "colonial" invention of caste, which has attracted so much scholarly attention.[21]

These developments offer a fascinating counterpoint to regions of the early modern world in which the development of print followed on closely from the "paper revolution". In India, too, the readier availability of paper texts of all kinds gave additional vitality to oral networks. Paper, and the purana in particular, made it easier for texts and the stories they contained to circulate across different communicative arenas, opening them up to new audiences dispersed across the subcontinent, who possessed a clear awareness of their shared interest in these critical social questions.

Focusing on the Brahman communities of the Marathi-speaking regions of western India, the present essay examines the way in which manuscripts, particularly puranic manuscripts, circulated in this discursive world. It examines the social networks through which texts travelled and were discussed, news and gossip passed on, and the content of performances argued over. It concludes with a discussion of the way in which western India's Maratha state attempted to regulate and police these early "publics" because of the threat they seemed to pose to its Brahman elites.

The Making of a Paper World

When paper first entered India towards the end of the first millennium, it entered a world in which documents were recorded on palm-leaf, birch-bark, cloth, baked clay, cloth, copper plate, and stone.[22] Imported paper found ready markets, but it was not until the coming of the Delhi Sultanate in the thirteenth century that an indigenous paper-making industry established itself.[23] Local centres of production emerged, as the new state developed a paper-based bureaucracy and flourishing court culture to which the epistolary arts were central. Some grades of paper were carefully reused. Writing in 1358, the Delhi historian Ziauddin Barani recorded the fate of books that failed to sell:

[21] See, for example, Dirks, *Castes of Mind.*

[22] Gode, "Migration of Paper"; Rahman, "Paper Technology".

[23] Soteriou, *Gift of the Conquerors.*

"Histories written by persons of no standing and account become old in bookshops; they are then given back to the paper merchants and the paper is washed white."[24] Lesser grades of paper had petty commercial applications: Barani also recorded that sweet-sellers in Delhi's bazaars used paper wrappings.[25] Banaras silk merchants used a coarse grade of paper to wrap their wares.[26]

Paper did not immediately displace older materials. It was vulnerable to insects, damp, and fire in a way that stone and copper plate were not, and it had less potential for public display. The Kavale family, priests to the Yadavas of Devgiri in Central India, migrated west to the Maratha regions after the fall of the city to Alauddin Khilji in 1294 CE. They were confirmed in their new lands with a Persian paper document of property right. But the local raja also ordered that villages whose revenues were gifted to the family should have a stone placed at each corner of their boundaries, "and this deed of charity should be engraved on them."[27] When the family's rights were challenged in 1416, the paper document of right was produced for inspection, but the inscription on the boundary stones was also read out before assembled state officials and village notables.[28]

By the late sixteenth century, paper had come to underpin every important aspect of state activity in the Mughal empire. As Mughal governments began to demand payment of land revenues in cash, it was on paper that records of village payments were kept.[29] Paper made possible the operations of merchant and banking houses and the increasingly sophisticated credit networks which came to underpin the imperial fiscal system.[30] Paper was key to the operations of the Mughal royal chancellery and office of accounts.[31] Paper was the medium for the

[24] Habib and Begum, *The Political Theory of the Delhi Sultanate*, p. 122.

[25] Barani, *Fatāwā-i Jahāndārī*, cited in Habib, *Medieval India*, p. 70.

[26] Rahman, "Paper Technology", p. 264.

[27] Puntambekar, *Uttar Konkanātīl*, pp. 1–11. I thank Madhav Deshpande for generously making this material available and Muzaffar Alam for assistance with the Persian language used in the document.

[28] Puntambekar, *Uttar Konkanātīl*, pp. 21–30.

[29] Abul Faz'l, *A'in-i Akbari*, vol. 2, pp. 43–7. For a superb local study, see Perlin, *The Invisible City*, pp. 40–2.

[30] For an overview, see Subrahmanyam and Bayly, "Portfolio Capitalists".

[31] See Abu al-Fazl, *Ā'in-i Akbarī*, vol. 1, pp. 259–63.

court's important epistolary culture, and for its painters, calligraphers, poets, and scholars. The Mughal imperial library was a library of paper.[32] India's regional states likewise came to depend on paper for their key operations during these centuries.[33]

The coming of paper created new media and new arenas for the discussion of Brahman identity. It greatly expanded access to manuscript texts. As John Seyller has observer, books were actually much the most affordable of luxury items in Mughal India.[34] Individual scholars were able to accumulate significant libraries. In March 1651 in Pune, the Maratha scholar Narayanabhatta Arade composed a digest of correct ritual practices. But he apologised for its shortcomings for, he explained, he had not been able to consult the library at his Banaras residence.[35] Collections like these supported both scholarly and teaching activity within the household.[36]

The coming of paper also led to the creation of new literary genres. Since the middle of the first millennium CE, learned commentaries had dominated the field of Hindu textual law. In the twelfth century, commentaries lost their pre-eminence to the new form of the nibandha (digest), a compilation of extracts from older works handily gathered together in a single authoritative volume.[37] As Pollock and others have suggested, the production of digests seems to follow the southwards advance of the Delhi Sultanate. This impelled Brahman scholars to create authoritative texts of Sanskrit religious law, both to affirm its identity in the face of an advancing "other", and for use when Hindu litigants approached courts under Islamic jurisdiction.[38]

The digests were also taken up as a key resource by Brahman judicial assemblies. In an age of social mobility, where questions of ritual entitlement might involve Brahmans from different regions, digests offered comprehensive information covering many contingencies. The

[32] For an introduction to the arts at the Mughal court, see Asher and Talbot, *India Before Europe*, pp. 186–224.

[33] For state bureaucratisation in western India, see Guha, "Speaking Historically", and Eaton, *A Social History*, pp. 145–50.

[34] Seyller, "The Inspection and Valuation of Manuscripts", p. 278.

[35] Katre, "Nārāyaṇabhaṭṭa Ārḍe", p. 86.

[36] O'Hanlon, "Speaking from Siva's Temple", pp. 258–9.

[37] Olivelle, "Dharmaśāstra", pp. 52–6.

[38] Pollock, "Deep Orientalism", p. 106.

assemblies' judgments frequently described the learned works they had at hand to guide them.[39] Paper facilitated another aspect of their workings. In earlier centuries, judgments were recorded on stone or copper plate. Paper judgments could be more easily produced and widely circulated, enabling wider Brahman audiences to share in the deliberations and weigh up the conclusions of the assembly concerned. In addition, judgments began to carry the individual signatures of scholars present, which was an innovation very much associated with paper. Many of the scholars would have been known, by reputation at least, to the Brahman audiences reading them, further strengthening the sense of a shared discursive arena.

Performance and Social Uncertainty in Early Modern India

The coming of paper affected the purana as an arena for discussion of Brahman history in a different way. Supposedly first narrated by the great sage Vyasa, puranas were essentially "authorless" texts, a blending of stories about the gods, royal genealogies, sectarian narratives, caste histories, and social commentary.[40] Puranas varied enormously in their degree of textual unity. Some, like the *Bhāgavata Purāṇā*, devoted to the life and worship of the god Krishna, bear some of the hallmarks of single authorship.[41] At the other end of the spectrum the *Skandapurāṇa* is an enormous corpus of texts, which had a single textual "original" but has been added to over a millennium or more by many further undated compositions declaring themselves to be "part of the *Skandapurāṇa*". This makes it difficult to distinguish the original "core" of the purana from its many later accretions.[42] In the corpus of Sanskrit manuscript texts that survive in libraries and archives in India and elsewhere, portions of puranas are often more numerous than copies of the "whole", where we can determine with any accuracy what that "whole" might have been.[43]

[39] O'Hanlon and Minkowski, "What Makes People Who They Are?", p. 395.

[40] Rocher, *The Purāṇas*.

[41] Ibid., pp. 144–51.

[42] Bakker, ed., *Origin and Growth*.

[43] See Rocher, *The Purāṇas*, pp. 67–80, and Rocher, "Reflections", for a discussion of these difficulties.

Puranas were not only, or even mainly, written texts. They were certainly expected to have a Sanskrit textual form with a recognisable core. Many revealed a clear textual consciousness, alluding to the merit derived from the text's presence in the house or copying and giving it away as a virtuous act.[44] But the greatest spiritual benefit lay in listening to the purana performed by a specialist puranika.[45] He based his performance on his Sanskrit text, its visible presence a guarantee of the performance's authority. But much of it was extemporised in the vernacular, and given fresh colour and an individual twist with allusions to local matters. The puranika's exposition was usually constructed as a dialogue between the sage Vyasa and his interlocutor, in which the sage tells a familiar story, and is then pressed to regale his audience with something new and diverting.

Rather than discrete manuscript texts, therefore, puranas may be best thought of as linked discursive fields within which many different social, political, or religious concerns could find expression. Some offered a literary vehicle for royal genealogies.[46] Some expressed the ambitions of competing castes or sects. Pious Brahmans used puranas to incorporate folk religion into a wider Sanskritic culture.[47] All of these characteristics made puranas compelling sites for the discussion of pressing local issues.[48]

The coming of paper amplified this role. It is likely that puranic texts became more widely available over the centuries, both as older texts were copied, and new ones written and performed under the patronage of aspirant rulers and caste or sectarian leaders. Puranas also found an expanded social and judicial role. As noted above, these were centuries when skilled scribes, artisans, military people, and priestly specialists moved frequently to find new patronage and employment. Refurbished histories were an important means of establishing mobile communities in new places as people of dignity, attractive marriage

[44] Brown, "Purāṇa", pp. 76–8.

[45] Bonazzoli, "Remarks on the Nature of the Purāṇas".

[46] Thapar, "Society and Historical Consciousness", and Thapar, *History and Beyond.*

[47] Chakrabarty, *Religious Process*; Narayana Rao, "Purāṇa as Brahmanic Ideology"; Sathaye, *Crossing the Lines of Caste.*

[48] Chatterjee, *The Cultures of History.*

partners and worthy of the offices they sought. Such mobility equally created tensions, since ambitious new arrivals might threaten existing rights.

Puranas therefore became effective platforms for the histories of the mobile and the identities of the settled. With their popularity, their theatrical qualities, and the local information they contained, puranas could confirm these histories, but could also undermine them. An apparently respectable community might be hiding disreputable secrets. A local lord might be the usurper of lands that the gods had intended for Brahmans. Mountains, rivers, and other features of the local landscape might themselves be the dwelling places of the gods, with great consequences for the human communities who lived there. Control over the production of puranic stories was therefore a vital means of securing rights and identities in early modern India, for rulers as much as for their humbler subjects. Through the genre of the purana, with its linking of Sanskrit and vernacular languages, text and oral performance, local histories and all-India gods, India's "paper revolution" helped to create an arena within which the discursive contests of Brahman elites were at the same time opened to a wider popular scrutiny and critique.

A further development lent puranas new significance. The changing textual forms of Hindu jurisprudence drew them into a new relationship with Hindu religious law. In their search for comprehensiveness, as well as for topicality, authors of digests began to include passages from puranas, and Brahman judicial assemblies began to invoke them as evidence.[49] The world of the purana and that of textual law came closer in other ways too. A by-product of the assimilation of puranas into works of religious law was to create a sharpened consciousness amongst the authors of digests that textual transmission itself might be problematic, that it might be necessary to distinguish between "authentic" and "fabricated" puranic texts.[50] This is a consciousness usually associated with the world of clearly authored texts and print culture, but it was clearly a concern in India's flourishing manuscript world.

[49] Olivelle, "Dharmaśāstra"; Derrett, "The Purāṇas".

[50] McCrea, "Hindu Jurisprudence", pp. 135–6. Madhva, the great thirteenth-century founder of the Dvaita or dualist school of Vedantic thought, particularly attracted later accusations that his puranic sources were fabricated.

In "God's Country": Parashuram as Brahman Patron

As described elsewhere, Western India's Konkan littoral was home to many small and often very competitive communities of Brahmans: Shenvis or Saraswats, Chitpavans, Devarukhes, Karhades, Javalas, Palshes, Padyas, and Kramavants.[51] They were small farmers, holders of landed rights, priests, and astrologers. Many pursued mundane avocations as village accountants, revenue collectors, and administrators in the service of local states, or as traders in the profitable routes between the coast and the uplands of Central India. Some prospered as they migrated to serve rulers elsewhere in India, or attracted the patronage of pious merchants, while others struggled on as petty village priests or small farmers. Different histories of migration, varying sectarian allegiances, and disagreements over which communities could claim the status of full ṣaṭkarmī Brahmans, fuelled the competition between them. These were vital questions. Someone who was not a ṣaṭkarmī, with authority to perform the full six Vedic karmas associated with study, sacrifice, and gifting, could not properly receive royal grants of land, discharge the offices of priest or astrologer, or find patrons for their learning.[52] Doubts cast on ritual standing affected patterns of intermarriage and commensality, and might carry the risk of further splits between already small communities. Impeccable Brahman religious standing carried considerable advantages in administrative employment, where rulers and great households sought prestigious servants to conduct their affairs. Threats to reputation or ritual authority had implications that went much further than the immediate domain of religious practice itself.

As Brahman communities wrestled with these questions, many of the stories they told about themselves focused on the god Parashuram, "Rama with the axe", warrior Brahman, and sixth of the ten incarnations of the god Vishnu. Parashuram featured frequently in Hindu India's great epics and puranas. He was tutor in the military arts to

[51] O'Hanlon and Minkowski, "What Makes People Who They are?", pp. 383–7.

[52] For a fuller description, see O'Hanlon, "Letters Home", pp. 224–5, and the Introduction to the present work.

leading figures in the Mahabharata, slayer of corrupt kings during an ancient age of warfare, and a penitent atop Mount Mahendra who forced the gods of the western ocean to surrender up land, on which he settled deserving Brahmans to perform his sacrifices.[53]

Many regional cultures engaged with these all-India themes.[54] Parashuram had a particular association with the long coastal littoral of western India, where the story of his recovery of land from the ocean gained verisimilitude in the local geology, which demonstrated many features of an ancient sea bed.[55] The region itself was often described as paraśurāma kṣetra (the sacred land of Parashuram).[56] Many puranic texts and histories of sacred places in Karnataka, Kerala, and the Tamil country focused on these and other episodes in Parashuram's life.[57] For the Maratha regions it was the *Sahyādrikhaṇḍa*, supposedly part of the great *Skandapurāṇa*, where these stories were told.[58] In them, Mount Mahendra, where Parashuram retired to perform his penances, was none other than the Sahyadri range above the Konkan coast, and its lands were those that he reclaimed from the sea and settled with Brahmans.

The *Sahyādrikhaṇḍa* was not, therefore, a "discrete" text. Its stories were variations on common themes in Hinduism's great epics and puranas, and many smaller texts claimed affiliation with it, making it part of a wider discursive field within which Brahman communities argued out their histories and competing identities. As a text, it was in existence by the end of the thirteenth century. Fragments are quoted in what has come down to us as one of the very early digests discussed

[53] For key themes in the remarkable all-India mythology of Parashuram, see Collins, *The Other Rāma*. For an interpretation of Parashuram's prominence in Brahman religious cultures of early modern India, see Bayly, *Caste, Society and Politics*, pp. 76–7. For similar associations between gods, landscapes, and puranic accounts of Brahman identity, see Sathaye, *Crossing the Lines of Caste*, pp. 140–74.

[54] Donaldson, "The Cult of Paraśurāma".

[55] Karve, "The Paraśurāma Myth".

[56] Kumari, "Paraśurāma", p. 62.

[57] Ibid., pp. 73–4; Karve, "The Paraśurāma Myth"; Saletore, *Ancient Karnataka*, 9–38; Menon, *History of Kerala*, vol. 1, pp. 17–76, and Gail, *Parasurama*.

[58] Rocher, *Purāṇas*, pp. 235–6; Gail, *Parasurama*, pp. 200–6; Rao, "The Historical Tradition"; Rao, "Reconstructing the Social History"; and Axelrod and Fuerch, "Flight of the Deities".

above, the *Chaturvargacintāmaṇi* of Hemadri, mid-thirteenth-century minister to the Yadava kings of Devgiri.[59] The core of the purana consisted of thirty chapters containing two sets of narratives, one almost certainly written later than the other. The earlier stories concerned Brahman village settlements fallen from virtue through sexual misdemeanours, degrading menial work, or neglect of ritual obligations.[60] These were probably written before or around the end of the first millennium, since they described Brahmans simply by their village of origin and their gotra (exogamous patrilineal descent group). The second set identified Brahmans by vernacular language region, a practice that gradually became common during the thirteenth and fourteenth centuries, and emerged thereafter as the basis for the tenfold regional classification of the subcontinent's Brahman communities, referred to above.

It was in this second set of stories in the *Sahyādrikhaṇḍa*, narrated as a dialogue between the god Shiva and his son, the great war-god Skanda, that the debates about Brahman identity and social worth were played out. While Shiva set out the differences between the gauḍa Brahman communities of the North and the drāviḍas of the South, he also emphasised to his son that differences in local custom were quite compatible with a shared pan-Indian Brahman culture of ritual privilege. Far from constituting a shortcoming, regional variations were an integral part of this culture. It was right for every Brahman community to follow its own customs, and sinful to follow those of another.[61]

The Shenvis were emphatically the heroes of the *Sahyādrikhaṇḍa*. The purana described them with their more dignified title of "Saraswat", thereby identifying them as one of the five "northern" or gauḍa Brahman communities. Shiva described how the god Parashuram brought them to the Konkan from Tirhut in north-east India. Powerful deities

[59] Siromani, *et al.*, eds, *Chaturvargacintāmaṇi*, vol. 1, pp. 718–19; vol. 3, p. 306.

[60] See Levitt, "The Patityagrāmanirṇaya", and Levitt, "Sahyādrikhaṇḍa".

[61] See footnote 19 above. All of these stories were gathered together and published in an attempt at a critical edition by the Saraswat scholar J. Gerson da Cunha, in his *The Sahyâdri-Khaṇḍa*. Da Cunha recorded that he collated fourteen different manuscripts of the purana, obtained from Cochin, Junnar in northern Maharashtra, Bombay, Karnataka, Goa, and Banaras: pp. 25–6. For a critique, see Levitt, "The Sahyādrikhaṇḍa". References that follow are to da Cunha's edition.

accompanied them, whose temples actually formed part of the landscape of sixteenth-century Goa: Shantadurga, Mangesh, Mhalsa, Nagesh, and Mahalakshmi.[62] Parashuram settled the earliest arrivals, "honoured by the king, attractive, well-behaved, skilled in every rite" in the Konkani villages of Kelosi and Kusasthal.[63]

Shiva then described the origins of the Saraswats' rivals, the Chitpavans. They also owed their place in the lands of the Konkan to Parashuram, but theirs was a history of menial beginnings and a fall from grace. They were once common fishermen. Having created his lands, Parashuram wondered how to people it with Brahmans.

> In the morning going for a bathe he met some people at the chita (burning ground) on the sea shore. "What is your jati, and what is your dharma, and where do you live?", he asked. The people replied, "Our jati is Kaivartaki. We live on the shore of the sea and are skilled as fishermen." So Parashuram purified them in the funeral pyre and gave them Brahmanhood. Because they were purified (pāvana) in a chita (pyre), so they are called Chitpavanas.[64]

By Parashuram's grace, these Brahmans were made wise and fair-skinned, with beautiful light-coloured eyes. But the one-time fishermen then became arrogant. On his departure, Parashuram assured his protégés that if in distress he would always come to their aid. In their pride, they decided to test the god, summoning him by means of a trick. Parashuram came, but seeing through the pretence cursed them, telling them that in future they would live in poverty in a barren land, jealous of each other's learning, in servitude to kings and disgraced by taking money for their daughters at marriage.[65]

Shiva's account of the Karhade Brahmans was even less flattering. Skanda asked him, "Tell me the story of the origins of the Brahmans of Karashtra." Shiva told him that there was a famously wicked land of

[62] *Sahyādrikhaṇḍa*, Uttarārdha, Adhyāya 3, "Gomāncalakṣetra-māhātmya", vss. 19–27.

[63] *Sahyādrikhaṇḍa*, Uttarārdha, Adhyāya 4, "Vividhabrāhmaṇotpattiḥ", vss. 4–11.

[64] *Sahyādrikhaṇḍa*, Uttarārdha, Adhyāya 1, "Citapāvanbrāhmaṇotpattiḥ", vss. 30–7.

[65] Ibid., vss. 38–45.

this name. "All who live there are hard, evil people who do bad things. The Brahmans are called karashtras, born in transgression, fallen due to their commission of vice. Their birth, those wicked ones, came about when semen was spilled on a heap of asses' bones."[66] There is a play on words here. "Karashtra" translates literally as "evil country", and included is a further play on words, "khara asthi", "bones of asses". In addition, Shiva said, these fallen Brahmans regularly made offerings to Matrika, a wicked local goddess whose worship caused immediate loss of caste. Even the air there was poisonous and polluting.[67] Shiva then told many other stories about smaller Brahman communities in the region, the customs peculiar to them, and the incidents of their histories.

These stories expressed the Brahman social tensions outlined above. There is the appeal to the all-India classification, and the assertion that regional differences of custom do not detract from, but are rather proper to the cohesive Brahman identity expressed in the classification as a whole. Within it, every community respected both its own individual history and that of others – particularly if it had been determined by the god Parashuram. At another level, the purana was a paean to the excellence of the Shenvis at the expense of their local rivals, the Chitpavans and Karhades. It affirms the Shenvis' links to the sacred places of the Konkan, the temples of their family deities, and the villages within which the god Parashuram had settled them. Its narratives described the flow of energies and qualities – good and evil – between people and the lands they lived on, and the moral identification of particular communities with specific places and lands.

Purana and Local Knowledge in the Dharmasabha

Let us look now at the way in which some of these puranic stories were told within Brahman judicial assemblies, where they had begun to be treated as part of religious law. There were such assemblies in market and shrine towns throughout India. However, particularly con-

[66] *Sahyādrikhaṇḍa*, Uttarārdha, Adhyāya 2, "Kārāṣṭrabrāhmaṇotpattiḥ", vss. 2–6.

[67] Ibid., vss. 6–9.

tentious issues were referred to the most authoritative of them, which met in the sacred city of Banaras. The assembly's gathering place was the Mukti mandapam, the "pavilion of liberation" in Banaras' great temple to Shiva, which had been rebuilt and gloriously refurbished in the 1580s with Mughal assent.[68]

In the spring of 1630, the Banaras assembly considered a complaint from Brahmans in Bombay. Brahmans from the two most powerful Shenvi settlements in Goa at the time, Kusasthal and Sasashti, had been performing rituals for which they had no authority. After discussion, the assembly returned their judgment, addressed as follows: "To the Deshastha, Chitapavana, Karnata, Gurjara and others living in Mumbapuri, Dadambhatta of the Bhatta family, and others from Kasi [Banaras] send their homage and greetings."

> You posed an objection that in your country the members of the Kushasthal and Sasashti families are performing the six karmas. But it is impossible to say that they are ineligible for the actions, since it is seen in the Deccan uplands that they are admitted to the status of ascetics, and everywhere they are seen performing the Srauta and Grhya Vedic rituals such as the Agnihotra. This much is heard from the mouths of the learned. And what is more, Kamalakarabhatta has established the greatness of the fourth stage of life [that of sanyasi, or ascetic] for these castes. They are part of the gauḍa category of Brahmins, and to be honoured within their own caste. And everyone has seen that document.[69]

The author of the judgment, Dadambhatta, was a member of the prestigious Bhatta pandit dynasty of Banaras, leaders of the powerful Maratha Brahman community that had gradually consolidated itself in the city since the start of the sixteenth century.[70] He based his judgment on two considerations. One was that it was "impossible" to deny that Shenvis from the two villages were entitled to these rights, because "everywhere they are seen" to be exercising them in the normal course of their lives: visibly cooking, eating, performing rituals with other Brahmans who clearly accepted them as social equals, and

[68] See O'Hanlon, "Letters Home".

[69] Apte, "Sārasvatāche Brāhmaṇatva", pp. 2–3. I thank Chris Minkowski for his translation of this tcxt.

[70] For the Bhatta family, see Kane, ed., *Vyavahāramayūkha*, pp. v–xvi.

being formally admitted as ascetics, a status usually reserved for Brahmans alone.[71]

The second consideration was that Kamalakarabhatta himself – one of the best known and most influential members of the Bhatta dynasty – had affirmed their right to become ascetics, and identified them as "part of the gauḍa category of Brahmans."[72] Almost in the same breath, Dadambhatta appealed to the common knowledge of his Brahman audiences, familiar with the same paper text: "everyone has seen that document." Status and entitlement were to be known in part by reference to textual authorities, but also by what their neighbours and caste-fellows reliably knew about them. The circulation and wide diffusion of paper documents like these contributed to this stock of common knowledge. What was "heard from the mouths of the learned" also fed into it.[73]

The deliberations of this Brahman assembly thus brought together the contents of a well-known text by a leading Banaras scholar, and the common store of information that Brahman communities possessed about their neighbours' habits of sociability and ritual practice. This textual and local knowledge moved along the conduits of news, discussion, gossip, and social observation which linked Brahmans in Banaras with those in western India. The texts had their status and influence very much in the context of these circuits of oral exchange, where their evidence was weighed and the appeals that they made were judged in the light of local information.

The following year saw a further development, which suggests what was at stake in the Shenvis' ritual assertions. In 1631, one Vitthal, a resident of Kusasthal, journeyed up to Banaras to ask its pandit communities for help. The Hindu residents of Kusasthal wished to revive its great Advaita monastery, destroyed by the Portuguese in 1564. Its spiritual heads had left the town for Banaras, where Bhavananda Saraswati, sixty-second guru, was then living.[74] Vitthal now wanted himself to take up the headship of the revived monastery. But heads of

[71] Kane, *History of Dharmaśāstra*, vol. 2, pt 2, pp. 962–4.

[72] Dadambhatta's reference suggests that Kamalakarabhaṯṯa had written a text focused on the Shenvis, but I have not been able to identify it.

[73] For the relationship between textual law and social practice, see Davis, *The Spirit of Hindu Law,* pp. 144–65.

[74] Sarma, *Sārasvat Bhūṣaṇ*, p. 87.

monasteries were almost always Brahman ascetics. Unless the full Brahman identity of Shenvis was accepted, Vitthal could not be admitted into the life of an ascetic, and could not take up the headship of the monastery.

The assembly met again, its judgment specified – very much to emphasise its authority – in the sacred "pavilion of liberation". The pandits' judgment described the extensive enquiries they had made. "Who were these residents of Kusasthal, what are their relations, what is their origin, what is their varna, their dharma, their karma?"[75] Opponents of the Shenvis had pointed to the fact that these Brahmans customarily ate fish. To defend the Shenvis, the assembly invoked the god Parashuram, the stories of the *Sahyādrikhaṇḍa*, and the principle that Brahman difference at this level was legitimate. In fact, the assembled scholars argued, Parashuram permitted all of the Brahmans he settled in the Konkan to continue the practices brought with them from other countries, including the eating of fish, and the practice in no way detracted from their prestige as Brahmans. The path was thus cleared for Vitthal to become an ascetic, under the new name of Sacchidanda Sarasvati, one of his initiatory gurus being the previous head of the monastery, Bhavananda Sarasvati. A long list of signatures of leading Brahman scholars from Banaras, including that of Kamalakarabhatta himself, was appended to the judgment before it was circulated.[76]

Narratives from a puranic text thus featured in the learned discussions of a judicial assembly, whose written judgments about the moral worth of a particular Brahman community then moved out along the circuits of news and information that linked Brahmans in Banaras with the scattered communities of western India. Expanding paper use helped create these new audiences able so readily to see key works of religious law for themselves, to familiarise themselves with the India-wide classifications of Brahman identity that they proposed, and to inspect the signed judgments of the assemblies as they were circulated.[77]

[75] Gunjikar, *Sarasvatīmaṇḍal*, Appendix 2, pp. 22–3.

[76] Ibid., p. 23. For a further discussion of Saraswat rights and identity at an assembly held in 1664, see O'Hanlon and Minkowski, "What Makes People Who They Are?", pp. 393–8.

[77] For the bureaucratisation of these assemblies, see O'Hanlon, "Narratives of Penance and Purification".

Proof in the Pavilion of Liberation

Shenvis were not the only contributors to such narratives. The *Vāḍeś-varodaya-kāvyam* celebrated the temple to Vadeshvara, family deity of many Chitpavan Brahmans, in the Konkan town of Guhagar.[78] Though a work of kāvya (Sanskrit narrative poetry), it has many of the characteristics of a mahātmyā or puranic celebration of a holy place, and draws on the stories that we have seen above in the *Sahyādrikhaṇḍa*. The work was completed in the third or fourth decade of the seventeenth century by one Vishvanath Pitre. The name identifies him as a Karhade Brahman, although his account of this temple town of the Chitpavans was quite a sympathetic one.[79] Having recounted the many sacred spots created by Parashuram in his new land, Vishvanath described how the god had brought sixty particularly holy Brahman families from Central India and invited them to colonise his new lands. The Brahmans were known as Chitpavan, because they purified the heart (*chitta*) of Parashuram.[80]

Perhaps with a touch of schadenfreude, however, Vishvanath also included an allusion to the Chitpavans' fall from grace. All had gone well until the coming of the age of corruption associated with the goddess Kali, when some Chitpavan lads fell under her malign influence. They decided to test Parashuram's promise, summoning him with the help of a fake corpse. The god soon saw through the pretence, but senior members of the community pleaded on behalf of the youthful sinners. Thus mollified, Parashuram agreed to continue to protect the Chitpavans in secret (*guha*), thus giving the town of Guhagar its name.[81]

Vishvanath gave his stories additional moral force by connecting them with the world of Brahman scholarly learning and religious law. Many stories concerned the mountains of the Sahyadri range. Brahma, Vishnu, and Shiva were present there in the form of three great peaks, standing at the confluence of the Savitri and Gayatri rivers with the sea.

[78] Paradkar, *Viśvanāthakṛta Śrivāḍeśvarodayakāvyam*. See also Pusalkar, "Vāḍeśvarodaya-Kāvya", pt 1, pp. 66–78.

[79] Gode, "Origin and Antiquity", p. 25.

[80] Paradkar, *Viśvanāthakṛta Śrivāḍeśvarodayakāvyam*, p. 51.

[81] Ibid., pp. 69–77.

These gods in the forms of mountains were actually made of gold, although in the Kali age they appeared as mere earth to human eyes. This fact had been established, Vishvanath asserted, in the sacred pavilion of liberation at Banaras. The audience there had been listening to a puranika discoursing on the mountains, and some had disbelieved him when he said that they were made of gold.

Vishvanath then described in knowing detail the debate that ensued. Was śabdaprāmaṇya (the authority of the scriptures) greater than that of pratyakṣaprāmaṇya (the authority of evidence that could be seen)? Or was it the case that in fact the authority of puranic histories such as they just heard weakened with the lapse of time? The pandits despatched one of their number to find out. When he arrived on the mountainside, he picked up a handful of soil and found it to be ordinary earth. He carried it back to Banaras to show the outcome of his investigations. But – Vishvanath's storyteller clearly had a good feel for the dramatic pause – as soon as the lump of earth was brought within the city boundaries, it changed to pure gold. After seeing it, the doubters were restored in their confidence in the truths of the eternal Vedas. Perhaps the Konkani audience for Vishvanath's story was also comfortably reassured that even the learned scholars of Banaras discoursing in their sacred pavilion, had acknowledged the presence of the gods in the mountains of the Sahyadri range.[82]

Vishvanath's poem included a description of the foundation of Guhagar town by one Sridhara, a learned Brahman of great yogic powers, who gained permission from the king to found a town on the sands near the Chitpavan temple to Vadeshvara. The king agreed to exempt the town from future taxes. Trees, tanks, wells, and cattle sheds were built. Lands were gifted for the support of temples and the pious Brahmans that now settled in the town. Its privileges were recorded on a copper plate with royal seals, so that they could be remembered in perpetuity.[83] Here, we see very concretely the implications of Brahman identity for landed rights and special status in relationships with the local state.

How might Vishvanath's work have been performed? The history

[82] Ibid., pp. 108–19.
[83] Ibid., pp. 120–33.

of the neighbouring village of Murud also represented it as having been founded by a charismatic Brahman pioneer. The history detailed the ritual year observed in the village, and the occasions – particularly the nine nights of Navaratra devoted to worshipping the goddess – when the population of the village congregated in the evening to hear puranas and kathā stories.[84] Such festivities in Guhagar may have furnished an occasion for the reading of poems like Vishvanath's, although the work may also have been valued by Chitpavans whose lives had taken them far from the Konkan coast.

Secrets and Lies in the Land of Parashuram

The vitality of the *Sahyādrikhaṇḍa* as an arena for competing Brahman histories is also clear from the proliferation of connected puranic stories from this period. Told as a conversation between Agastya and Kauleya, the *Varijākṣacaritra* concerned the god Varijaksha, "Lotus-eyed one", born within a Saraswat Brahman family.[85] The text was written from a Saraswat perspective, and Karhade Brahmans were one of its targets. Gender was a key theme, some of its stories describing in prurient detail the moral defects of Karhade women. Other stories offered a furious critique of the adherents of Madhva, heretics who advocated dualistic theories of the world – not surprising, given that many Karhades were themselves Madhvas.[86]

One of the stories connected the text squarely to Vitthal's revival of the Saraswat monastery in 1631. It described Varijaksha's sponsorship of a grand twelve-year-long sacrifice on the Konkan sea shore, the gods and sages who came, the puranas recited, the prestigious ascetics present. Kauleya asks who came, and Agastya replied:

> The embodiment of Maheshvar, the Gaud Saraswat Shri
> Bhavananda Sarasvati came to the sacrifice
> Born from his lotus hand, an ocean of knowledge about truth,

[84] Mandlik, "Preliminary Observations", pp. 1–48.

[85] *Varijākṣacharitra*. It describes itself as the uttarakāṇḍa of the *Prajñānacumudachandrikā* of the *Brahmāṇḍapurāṇa*. I thank Peter Szanto for his translation of this text. For the date and authorship of this text, see Bhandarkar, "Reports on the Search for Sanskrit Manuscripts" in *Collected Works of Sir R.G. Bhandarkar*, vol. 2, pp. 134–6.

[86] Ibid., p. 135.

Sacchidananda Saraswati the great ascetic came to the sacrifice
Born from his lotus hand, the great lord of ascetics Shivananda
Sarasvati also came to the sacrifice
Born from his lotus hand, an ocean full of knowledge,
Ramananda Sarasvati also came to the sacrifice.[87]

According to Saraswat community histories, these great ascetics and the further dozen or so names that followed were the successive heads of the great Saraswat Advaita monastery at Goa.[88] Vitthal himself appeared here, under his new name of Sacchidananda, below that of his initiatory guru, Bhavananda. Given that the list of gurus started with Bhavananda, it seems most likely that the great cosmic sacrifice described here was held in connection with the re-founding of the monastery. This makes the attack on the Karhade Madhvas the more understandable: a purana celebrating the revival of a great monist Advaita monastery was an eminently suitable place to attack the dualist Madhva affiliations of the Saraswats' rivals, the Karhades.

This great event provided the backdrop for an extremely insulting story which Agastya tells about the Karhades. A group of them came to sit in the sacrificial enclosure, but the divine artificer Vishvamitra drove them away. Varijaksha asked Vishvamitra who they were: "[W]hat is their origin in past times, in which land? I desire to hear all this from you, great sage!"[89]

So Vishvamitra told the story of the Karhades' "real" origins. There had been a young Brahman prostitute infatuated with a handsome Saraswat boy. In the fever of her desire, she climbed into his bed one night. The boy awoke, but he was a celibate, in full control of his senses, and a master of all the Vedas. Furious at her mere touch, he gave her a good beating with his slipper. Thus thwarted, the girl went to an outhouse of untouchables, where she calmed her desires with animal bones (karasthi). She conceived, and a son was born to her, but despised by everyone she moved to a distant land where she passed herself off as a virtuous widow. The Brahmans of that place were deceived. Her

[87] *Varijākṣacharitra*, ff. 88r–88v.

[88] Sarma, *Sārasvat Bhūṣaṇ*, pp. 186–7. Dates of the guru lineage make it likely that this version of the purana was written in the 1840s, probably as an updating of earlier versions of the text.

[89] *Varijākṣacharitra*, f. 91r.

son was admitted to all the Vedic rituals of a true Brahman, married a local girl of good family, and their sons married in their turn. After some time, they returned as respectable Brahmans to the Konkan. It was from these impostors, Vishvamitra said, that the Karhades were descended. "They have gained their brahminship thus, through deception. Hence these travelling Karhatakas are not Brahmins. They do not have the right to study the Vedas; their studies to become priests are in vain."[90]

Another narrative that played with these themes of Brahman origins was the Sanskrit *Śatapraśnakalpalatā* (Wishing creeper of a hundred stories), told by one Madhava.[91] This was not a purana, but a "composite" text of the kind that Sumit Guha has described, combining puranic stories with caste histories and genealogies of other kinds.[92] Madhava gave his text a date, and identified himself as its author. His "hundred stories" were an extended rumination on the origins of things, from Brahman communities to the great sects of Hindu tradition, schools of philosophy, Mughal emperors, lands and rivers, features of the body and different kinds of plants and foods. He announced himself as an adherent of the dualist school of Madhva in his opening words: "Saluting my guru Śri Bindumādhava, I write this good book called the *Śatapraśnakalpalatā*. I write it in the year 1499 of the Śālivāhana era, following the ancient style. Having looked carefully at what the authors of the smṛtīs have said, and what the learned have written down as suitable to be followed, I now tell these hundred stories."[93] Madhava offered a defence of the Karhades. They had had difficulties in their past, when a wicked Brahman impostor had insinu-

[90] Ibid., f. 92r.

[91] Madhava, *Śatapraśnakalpalatā*. This text is difficult to date. In the BORI ms. used here, Madhava gives the date of his writing as 1499 of the Śalivāhana era, or 1577 CE. But printed portions of the text circulating in the nineteenth century have him writing at 1690 CE: see Pandit, *Devarukhyāviṣayī Śāstrasamat Vichāra*, 20. A pointer to the earlier date is that the text appears in the library catalogue of the mid-seventeenth century Banaras scholar Kavindracaraya: Sastry, *Kavindracharya List*, p. 21.

[92] Guha, "Speaking Historically", pp. 1084–1103.

[93] Madhava, *Śatapraśnakalpalatā*, f.1v. I thank Jim Benson and Chris Minkowski for assistance with translations of this text.

ated himself into their midst. Realising their mistake, they performed penance in the proper manner. Their name simply came from the town Karhad on the Krishna river where they had gone to live. All were eventually purified by their worship of the goddess Durga.[94]

It is possible that this pro-Madhva author was sympathetic to the Karhades known for their Madhva affiliations, and possible that he was himself a Karhade. He did not offer a competing account of Saraswat origins. He suggested something less direct, but even more interesting: a distinction between "true" puranas and others that were ancient falsehoods. This reflects something of the emerging consciousness, noted above, that in an expanding manuscript culture, when puranas were being treated increasingly as a source of religious law, it was necessary to distinguish between "authentic" and "fabricated" puranic texts. The *Sahyādrikhaṇḍa* itself, the great epic of Saraswat virtue, Madhava asserted to be a concoction of this kind. He brought this adroitly into his discussion of the origins of the Chitpavans. Chitpavans were actually descended, he said, from Brahman families living on the coast who "by chance and a stroke of fate were abducted by barbarians, who lived in the middle of the ocean."[95] They mixed so promiscuously with their captors that they began to resemble them and utterly lost their caste purity. All this happened long before the coming of Parashuram, to whom the fallen Brahmans subsequently went for purification. "Since they had their minds (chitta), purified by Parashuram, they came to be called chittapāvanas." But their purification was in fact a sham. For, Madhava explained, alluding to the Chitpavans' reputation for the degraded practice of taking bride-wealth for their daughters, "they sell their daughters, because they have no control over their senses."[96] This, not the stories told in the *Sahyādrikhaṇḍa,* was the real truth. But in this present age, Madhava said, "in order to deceive everyone they promulgate a story in the worlds which they say is ancient."[97]

[94] Ibid., ff. 8r–9v.

[95] Ibid., f. 9v

[96] Ibid., f. 10v. For Chitpavan Brahmans taking bride-wealth, see Vad and Joshi, *Selections*, vol. v, Bajirav II, pp. 259 and 266.

[97] Ibid., f. 11r. Perhaps Madhava made these accusations of textual fabrication as a way of hitting back at the same charge commonly levelled at his "guru" Madhva. See footnote 50 above.

Here, then, we get some sense of the wider world of performance, public allegation, and sometimes denunciation within which paper texts like these were circulated. As Brahmans listened to these puranic stories about themselves and their neighbours, the same persistent themes emerged. Local knowledge and memory could confirm the identities of respectable neighbours, and their rightful place in the all-India classification. But even the most reputable might conceal within their histories an underlying world of fabrication and deceit. At the same time, Madhava placed his story within more than just a local frame, connecting the origins of the Chitpavans with a history of kidnapping and miscegenation by barbarian pirates on the Indian ocean, and the community's eventual purification by one of Hinduism's great gods.

Tellings in the Magistrate's Tent

The audiences for discussions about Brahman identity and moral worth thus ran along the circuits of news and information linking intellectuals in Banaras with the Brahman communities of western India, and the great monastic centres of the South. Puranic performances of many different kinds found an eager audience among Brahmans. Sometimes, puranikas performed for elite households alone. Raghunathrao, younger brother of the Maratha peshwa Balaji Bajirao, wrote in 1756 to his trusted man Vishnuram, and advised him: "Unless you listen to the puranas, your mind will not become clear. Appoint a puranika without fail, and listen to him for one part of the day. Be sure to listen to the *Revamāhātmaya* or the *Revakhaṇḍa*. If you can't find a puranika, then you must read them yourself, and take in as much as you can."[98]

Particularly skilled puranikas were in high demand. In 1762, Gopikabai, widow of Balaji Bajirao, sent from Poona to the southern town of Sawantwadi to procure the services of one Bapubhat Jambhekar Pauranik.[99] Individuals took pains to build up their collections of puranic texts. Balaji Bajirao wrote to his military servant Naro Shankar in the holy city of Nasik, pressing him to search for a copy of the important Vaishnava *Brahmavaivarta Purāṇa*, set in the ancient province

[98] Bhave, *Peśvekālīn Mahārāṣṭra,* pp. 82–3.
[99] Sardesai, *Selections*, vol. 32, no. 115.

of Bengal, and describing the creation of the universe, the feats of gods and goddesses and the birth and life of Krishna.[100] In 1747–8, the *Sahyādrikhaṇḍa* featured among a long list of puranas, digests and other Sanskrit works obtained for the Pune court from the Rajput ruler Jagat Singh at Udaipur.[101] Often the books were borrowed to be copied, sometimes a portion of the manuscript at a time. In 1750, Balaji Bajirao's servant Antaji Narayan borrowed a copy of the *Padma Purāṇa*, devoted to the life of Rama, so that his scribe Amanapant could copy it out for him.[102]

Puranic performances drew popular audiences too. Rocher has described an itinerant Gujarati puranika, turning up in the evening in a village square, announcing his arrival with rapid beating on a small hand drum. With most of the village gathered, he would start to play. His performance was based on a text, but with much extemporised fresh local detail added. It continued well into the night, pausing only for the puranika to ask what pious villager would offer him food and accommodation for the days of his stay.[103] Puranas were not just enjoyed in the setting of village or urban life. The camps of pre-colonial Indian armies provided many opportunities for entertainers of different kinds, including puranikas.[104] There seems to have been a lively exchange of the Sanskrit texts, so that performers in the camps could vary their repertoires. During the campaign against Haidar Ali of Mysore in the 1770s, the Maratha general Gopalrao Patwardhan of Miraj had with him the text of the *Gaṇeśa Purāṇa* – perhaps a useful asset in a military camp since the god Ganesh enjoyed a reputation for the removal of difficulties. The Maratha commander Naro Shankar wrote to him: "You sent the first portion of the *Gaṇeśa Purāṇa* to me with Brahmagiri, and it has arrived. Now please send the latter portion. I will listen to it and then send it back to you."[105] In his description of life in the camp of the Maratha sardar Daulatrao Shinde, campaigning in Rajasthan during 1809, Colonial Thomas Duer Broughton described

[100] Sardesai, *Selections*, vol. 18, no. 79.
[101] Vad and Joshi, *Selections*, pt 3, vol. 2, p. 199.
[102] Bhave, *Peśvekālīn Mahārāṣṭra*, pp. 82–3.
[103] Rocher, "Reflections", p. 73.
[104] Bayly, *Empire and Information*, pp. 43 4.
[105] Bhave, *Peśvekālīn Mahārāṣṭra,* p. 85.

the many itinerant bards that entertained the soldiery.[106] These performers are likely to have been drawn from humbler origins, often working across a number of performance genres in the Marathi vernacular in order to make a living.[107]

But how far would the popular audiences for these major puranas have also come to listen to the performances about Brahman moral worth described above? Fortunately, we have a detailed account of the performance of episodes from the *Sahyādrikhaṇḍa* from the middle of the nineteenth century, which may offer some clues. Arthur Crawford was an assistant magistrate in the Konkan between 1859 and 1862. He went regularly to hear Raghoba Mahadevrao, a famous Chitpavan performer. He described Raghoba: "He was nearly 60 years of age; he possessed such a collection of ancient Sanskrit slokas and tattered manuscripts as would be worth their weight in gold to the Royal Asiatic Library." Amongst Raghoba's collection, which he carried wrapped up in a cloth bundle, were three little books containing individual stories from the *Sahyādrikhaṇḍa*. Crawford persuaded him to come to his tent every evening and recite some of the verses to him so that he could write them down.[108]

Raghoba's first performance, as retold by Crawford, is a wonderfully colourful description of Parashuram and his brother Lakshman's journey to the Konkan to visit Samudra the sea-god, to persuade him to withdraw his waters.

> It was the beginning of the Mrig-sal, (constellation of Mriga) the Indian summer at the end of May; the black clouds, rain charged, of the south west monsoon, rolled up every night from the sea, only to be dispersed by the fierce red morning sun. The heat was so suffocating during the day that all nature seemed to wither away; only the cicada's chirrup, and the fever-bird's maddening reiterated cry was heard, or the hoopoo's metallic taptaping. All nature was asleep at noon. Sri Parasuram and his disciple brother slept heavily. They had just made one march from Nasik (250 miles) and only twice slaked their thirst, from the river at Wai, and at Helwak, a village on the junction of the Koyna and Krishna river.[109]

[106] Broughton, *Letters*, pp. 70, 130–2, 194.

[107] Bhave, *Peśvekālīn Mahārāṣṭra*, p. 90. For performers, see Novetzke, *Religion and Public Memory*, pp. 90–8.

[108] Crawford, *Legends of the Konkan*, pp. 1–2.

[109] Ibid., p. 7.

Raghoba's performance consisted of reading the Sanskrit verses "in nasal sing-song with many gestures of hands, and much wagging of his pious poll." Crawford's account makes it clear that Raghoba did read the Sanskrit verses from his battered text. But much of the narrative consisted of lively conversation between Parashuram and his brother, as they talked to the langur monkeys in the forest who offered to show them a short cut to Chiplun, encountered a huge python in the jungle near Karhad, then arrived at the sea shore to find the sea god lashing the cliffs with great waves in his anger at being disturbed. Crawford's quotations suggest that Raghoba extemporised these elements of his narrative in Marathi, even with some Hindi words thrown in. "'Bulla Bulla! Mera Bhai' grunts Luxman. 'Kahi zhalè?' 'Ishwarás máhit' ejaculates Máhá-Indra."[110]

The second and third books described the origins of Chitpavans. Here, Raghoba seemed to set out deliberately to pique his listener's interest in the kinds of story he carried in his bundle, and could tell if he chose. In the second book, Parashuram came to visit his new country, but was at a loss to find people to live there. The sea god derisively threw up onto the shore the corpses of some drowned Arab sailors. Parashuram took them, and raised them from the dead, and so the Chitpavans were created. But, Raghoba said, these were malicious inventions, concocted by the Chitpavans' enemies: "My lord must not credit the Shenvi slanders, of course, they are all lies."[111]

His third book, he said, contained the "true" history of the Chitpavans. Parashuram and Lakshman learned that the people of the Konkan were sorely in need of priests, for the local Deshastha Brahmans treated them with contempt. So Lakshman collected the dried sea foam, and from it sprang a band of handsome young men with fair complexions and grey green eyes. Thus came into being the Chitpavans. For their upkeep, Parashuram gifted local seven meadows and seven tanks, and assured them that they would never die, unlike their other Brahman neighbours.[112]

Even here, though, Raghoba's story contained elements of humour and relish in the humbling of proud people. The Chitpavans prospered and began to get above themselves. One day, a party of them

[110] Ibid., p. 12.
[111] Ibid., p. 25.
[112] Ibid., pp. 25–9.

wondered whether Parashuram was really as good as his word. Raghoba evidently entered into his Chitpavan characters with great gusto. "'Tis all very well my brethren! True that none of us have yet died like these Deshast Brahmins above the Ghauts; or these impure Shudras round us," (here he spat vigorously on the ground). "But what security have we after all that we shall never die, eh?" So they tested Parashuram by carrying a mock bier up to his shrine on the Mahendra mountain. They rang the bell to summon the god, "Arè Narrayen Ból! Narrayen!" and, standing in the darkness of the shrine, insolently demanded an explanation. Raghoba's telling reached its dramatic climax.

> Suddenly, a terrific flash of lightening reveals the deity to the terror-stricken conspirators, and a voice thunders: "Treacherous and accursed race! The cup of your iniquities is filled to overflowing (apale páp bharile gèle! Ye ask a sign! Take it from the bier! So shall ye all die in future!" Behold, the shammer was as dead as any Deshasth. "The story is quite true, Saheb," said the old bard. "There is the Banyan tree out there by the tank; *there* are the seven 'Mullas' and 'Tullas' still so registered in the Revenue Register of the Town, and Chitâwan Brâhmins die, Vishnoo be praised! Like other people!"[113]

Again here, Raghoba rendered the speech of his characters in Marathi. This may have enabled him to get much more effectively into the roles of his characters, as well as making the story accessible to audiences unable to follow the Sanskrit verses. His telling ended with a wonderful embedding of the story in the local landscape of fields, tanks, and the town's paper revenue records.

Is it possible to draw any conclusions from Raghoba's performance as to how far audiences for performers like him extended beyond the Brahman communities whose stories he told? Although on this occasion he was performing for Crawford alone, his humour and gusto do suggest a larger audience. There are also internal clues. Much of his account was spoken in the Marathi vernacular, not just in Sanskrit. He spat theatrically on the ground, a gesture which might have repelled purity-conscious Brahmans. His acting out of the contemptuous Chitpavan reference to "these impure Shudras round us", immediately before the Chitpavans' downfall, seemed calculated to

[113] Ibid., pp. 25–30.

appeal to a gleeful audience of just those plebeian Sudras, members of Hinduism's lowly fourth varna to which local peasant farmers, artisans, and labourers would have belonged. If Raghoba's performance was anything to go by, therefore, a wider "public" did hear and participate in these discussions about Brahman moral worth. In this case they were able to connect the trees and tanks of their own village to an ebullient tale of Brahman come-uppance at the hands of the great god Parashuram.

Censorship Between Performance and Paper

There is further evidence from the later eighteenth century of these wider "publics". By then, there were new reasons to enjoy malicious performances about Chitpavans. As the political elite of the peshwa regime based in Pune, they were an obvious target of jealousy not only from other Brahmans, but from all those who resented the way in which, from the middle of the eighteenth century, this regime had drawn power away from the Maratha kings at their courts in Satara and Kolhapur.

These courts emerged as patrons of performers of songs and stories about the misdeeds of Chitpavans, written now in Marathi vernacular. At the Satara court in 1820, one Anand wrote a narrative poem entitled *Chitpāvan Bhāgyodya Dīpikā* (Light on the Rise to Good Fortune of the Chitpavans). He described the menial origins of the Chitpavans, "Brahmans who belonged to one of the two groups of five, gauḍas and drāviḍas."[114] The corpses from which Parashuram made them were not just dead fishermen, but dead "barbarian" fishermen. The poem then followed the Chitpavans' history through the Muslim conquest of India, the Maratha ruler Shivaji's struggle against the Mughal emperor Aurangzeb, and then the Chitpavans' eventual and disastrous usurpation of the powers of the Maratha kings.

It was in this context that the last peshwa, Bajirao II, launched a systematic attempt to censor these performances.[115] Agents were sent

[114] Sastri, *Sadbodhachintāmaṇī,* p. 282. For a further discussion of this composition, see the Introduction to the present work.

[115] For a discussion of the "security" concerns of eighteenth-century states, see Bayly, *Empire and Information*, p. 200.

out with the Maratha armies, whose function was to find and destroy the manuscripts on which subversive puranic stories about the Chitpavans were based. Colonel Mark Wilks served in Madras during between 1782 and 1808. He reported these episodes of manuscript destruction amongst the soldiery of the Maratha armies amongst who, as we saw above, puranic performances formed a staple of entertainment. Chitpavan Brahmans, Wilks said,

> compose a large portion of the ruling characters in the Mahratta state; and in their various predatory incursions into other countries are stated to seek with avidity for the copies of a work containing the history of their origin, for the purpose of destroying it; and the eastern Brahmins affirm that the orders for this purpose given to their illiterate troops have produced a large and indiscriminate destruction of manuscripts.[116]

The peshwa's court also targeted individual Brahmans who had such texts in their possession. In his *History of the Mahrattas*, first published in 1826, James Grant noted that state officials "carefully suppress or destroy all copies of the Syadree Kind, where their origin is mentioned, and a respectable Bramin of Wai was, a few years ago, disgraced by Bajee Rao for having a copy of it."[117]

Crawford the Konkan magistrate reported a similar story, perhaps told to him by his informant Raghoba. The peshwa "was so enraged that he ordered all the copies to be called in and burnt by Mhângs, decreeing that any person thereafter found to possess a copy should be hanged; a sentence which was actually suffered subsequently by one Deshast Brâhmin."[118] The reference to the burning of a puranic text by a Mang untouchable is remarkable in a religious culture which usually viewed such texts as sacred things which, if they had to be disposed of, were immersed in water rather than being cast out as rubbish.[119] It is difficult to know how successful these attempts at censorship were. There is some evidence that the *Sahyādrikhaṇḍa* had become more difficult to obtain in the last decades of the eighteenth century. In 1787, parties to a dispute over ritual entitlements in Bombay needed to con-

[116] Wilks, *Historical Sketches*, vol. 1, pp. 157–8.

[117] Grant Duff, *History of the Mahrattas*, vol. 1, p. 8.

[118] Crawford, *Legends of the Konkan*, p. ii.

[119] Minkowski, "Sanskrit Scientific Libraries", p. 88.

sult the work, but had to send to the library of the great Shringeri monastery in Karnataka to obtain the relevant pages.[120]

Consciousness of these stories survived into the colonial setting at many levels. The categories of gauḍa and drāviḍa found a central place in colonial classifications of India's Brahman communities.[121] Critiques of Brahman caste pride and political usurpation came to form an important basis for the "non-Brahman" movements of the nineteenth century.[122] As non-Brahman intellectuals struggled to understand an emerging colonial social order in which the scribal skills of Brahmans seemed to carry such advantage, they continued to engage with the puranic narratives examined above, but with a crucial difference. The god Parashuram now appeared as the leader of an ancient wave of Brahman invasion and settlement which deprived India's "indigenous" Sudra orders of their land and ancient identities. These discourses and the puranic texts on which they were based in turn shaped colonial Orientalist studies of an "Aryan invasion" of the Indian subcontinent that was supposed to have taken place in the remote past.[123]

The debates also continued within the new sphere of vernacular print, with publication in 1878 of da Cunha's edition of the *Sahyādrikhaṇḍa.* The historian of Maharashtra's Brahman communities, R.B. Gunjikar, was evidently familiar with the stories of Chitpavan origins, and the eighteenth-century efforts to destroy the texts that contained them. "People say that this story is in the *Sahyādrikhaṇḍa*. But even that impure book called the *Sahyādrikhaṇḍa*, which is now available in Mumbai, does not mention that story. Who knows, perhaps the story is in some handwritten little book somewhere. People say that the peshwa went to great lengths to get hold of copies of the *Sahyādrikhaṇḍa* so that he could burn them." So, Gunjikar concluded, "this story must have been in the original book, but because that book was destroyed and scattered, perhaps it must have disappeared." But the

[120] Nayak, *A History of the Pattana Prabhus*, p. 86.

[121] Deva, *Śabda-Kalpadrumah*, p. 370; Prinsep, "Census", pp. 491–3; Steele, *The Law and Custom*, pp. 79–80; Thurston, *Castes and Tribes*, vol. 1, pp. 268–9; Russell and Hira Lal, *Tribes and Castes*, vol. 2, p. 357.

[122] Pandian, *Brahmin and Non-Brahmin*; O'Hanlon, *Caste, Conflict and Ideology*.

[123] Trautmann, *Aryans and British India*; Ballantyne, *Orientalism and Race*.

attempt to obliterate the text had been a mistake, "because now people wonder whether perhaps there really was some blemish in their origins, otherwise why would they have tried to destroy the book?"[124] For this commentator of the late nineteenth century, the printed book was but a flawed guide to the prolific and fluid world of pre-colonial manuscript culture, whose social themes continued to compel interest and speculation into his own times.

Conclusion

Early modern India thus offers important and arresting insights into the communicative potentialities of an expanding manuscript culture during the age of the "paper revolution". For Brahman communities themselves, the accelerated circulation of manuscript texts of all kinds at once offered new means to pursue local rivalries, but also to limit and contain them within an all-India discursive sphere that promoted a classificatory ideal of social cohesion. Brahman identity in this setting was "transportable" because it could now be mapped across the subcontinent, along the lines of regional vernacular languages. Brahmans could build their India-wide networks of patronage, family migration, and scholarly exchange with reference to a common framework, in which diversity itself could be understood as an aspect of Brahman unity. Corrosive local rivalries could threaten this ideal. However, India's "paper revolution" also provided the means to contain them. Digests offered comprehensive works of reference to guide assemblies of learned scholars in their role as arbiters, and enabled them to circulate paper judgments to alleviate local enmities.

Far from being local caste quarrels about bodily purity, the developments examined here represent an attempt to forge new all-India solidarities and social mechanisms to protect them when they were under threat. These solidarities and the accompanying assets of ritual prestige and bureaucratic skill were to become powerful shaping forces in British India: in the information order of the colonial state,

[124] Gunjikar, *Sarasvatīmaṇḍal*, p. 142–3. For further discussion of Gunjikar's engagement with these themes, see the Introduction to the present work. The stories continued to appear in Brahman caste histories of the early twentieth century: see Limaye, *Limaye Kulavṛttānta*, pp. 2–8.

its administrative character and the ideological struggles that emerged as Indians themselves sought to redefine their histories and identities in the colonial setting. In the light of this evidence, it may be worth re-examining the colonial history of caste, as well as of aspects of "Orientalist knowledge", for rather older antecedents than some scholarship has allowed.[125]

Puranic literatures also opened up these histories to wider and popular scrutiny. The interplay between what was read, told, and performed gained additional dynamism through the spread itself of paper use. If anything, a manuscript culture, and particularly the fluid and "authorless" genre of the purana itself, opened greater opportunities to writer-performers like Raghoba, making it possible for them to improvise their material to pique their audiences' interest, flatter their self-esteem or amuse them with scurrilous tales about their social superiors. This manuscript world helped to shape a popular subculture of critique of the pretensions of scribal elites, which grew more pointed as scribal people and Brahmans in particular developed influential positions for themselves in the states and economies of early modern India. This subculture retained its vitality in the colonial setting, helping to shape the "non-Brahman" ideologies that dominated politics in western and southern India.[126]

In what sense, if any, can we regard these Indian spheres of debate and discussion as forms of an early modern "public"? What has been examined here constitutes only a small part of the puranic and puranic-styled narratives that circulated amongst the different Hindu audiences of this period, where one might look for further evidence of subcontinent-wide networks and a regionally based inter-caste ecumene of listeners. Other genres, such as the literatures associated with early modern India's flourishing devotional movements, also brought local audiences into contact with subcontinent-wide perspectives and local audiences.[127]

[125] See, for example, Cohn, *Colonialism and Its Forms of Knowledge*.

[126] From this perspective, it may be worth re-examining arguments about the essential "modernity" of non-Brahman politics. See Bayly, *Caste, Society and Politics*, pp. 239–44.

[127] I am very grateful to John Keune for emphasising this point to me: personal communication, 22 June 2012.

But the evidence explored here indicates the communicative potential that puranas and their allied texts possessed in this period. At once recognised as sources of religious law appropriate for learned assemblies, and the basis for highly enjoyable popular performances, puranas offered a shared discursive space that transcended the locality and connected audiences across the subcontinent. This space was open to humbler audiences as well as to elites, for the telling of social histories, real and imaginary, and the weighing of community reputations far and near. The concerns discussed there certainly had a "public" dimension to them, which became very much more explicit when they re-emerged in the context of colonial politics and its new cultures of print. Given their ritual prestige and their growing mundane power as elite administrators in the states of early modern India, the history and moral worth of different Brahman communities were seen very much as a matter of legitimate common scrutiny. Brahman commentators themselves shared this scrutiny, sometimes with great seriousness, sometimes in knowing and humorous ways. But so too did lesser folk, such as the common Maratha soldiery who listened to puranic performances, and found in their stories a robust repertoire of social information with which to challenge, and sometimes ridicule their Brahman superiors.

References

Abu al-Fazl, *Ā'in-i Akbarī*, trans. H.S. Jarrett, 3 vols (Calcutta: Asiatic Society of Bengal, 1891).

Apte, D.V., "Sārasvatāche Brāhmaṇatva", *Bhārat Itihās Samshodhak Maṇḍaḷ Quarterly*, vol. 15, no. 4, 1935, pp. 2–3.

Asher, Catherine B., and Cynthia Talbot, *India Before Europe* (Cambridge: Cambridge University Press, 2006).

Atiyeh, George N., ed., *The Book in the Islamic World. The Written Word and Communication in the Middle East* (Albany: State University of New York Press, 1995).

Axelrod, Paul, and Michelle A. Fuerch, "Flight of the Deities: Hindu Resistance in Portuguese Goa", *Modern Asian Studies*, vol. 30, no. 2, 1996, pp. 387–421.

Baker, Geoff, and Ann McGruer, *Readers, Audiences and Coteries in Early Modern England* (Newcastle: Cambridge Scholars Publishing, 2006).

Bakker, Hans T., ed., *Origin and Growth of the Purāṇic Text Corpus, with Special Reference to the Skanda Purāṇa* (Delhi: Motilal Banarsidass, 2004).

Ballantyne, Tony, *Orientalism and Race: Aryanism in the British Empire* (Basingstoke: Palgrave, 2002).

Bayly, Christopher, *Empire and Information. Intelligence Gathering and Social Communication in India* (Cambridge: Cambridge University Press, 1996).

Bayly, Susan, *Caste, Society and Politics in India from the Eighteenth Century to the Modern Age* (Cambridge: Cambridge University Press, 1999).

Bernstein, Gail, Andrew Gordon, and Kate Nakai, eds, *Public Sphere, Private Lives in Modern Japan, 1600–1950* (Cambridge MA: Harvard University Press, 2005).

Berry, Mary, *Japan in Print: Information and Nation in the Early Modern Period* (Los Angeles: University of California Press, 2006).

Bhandarkar, R.G., *Collected Works of Sir R.G. Bhandarkar*, 4 vols (Poona: Bhandarkar Oriental Research Institute, 1927–33).

Bhargava, Rajeev, "Are there Alternative Modernities?", in Karan Singh and N.N. Vorah, eds, *Culture, Democracy and Development in South Asia* (Delhi: Shipra Publications, 2001), pp. 9–26.

Bhave, V.K., *Peśvekālīn Mahārāṣṭra* (Pune: Varada Press, 1998).

Bloom, Jonathan M., *Paper Before Print: The History and Impact of Paper in the Islamic World* (New Haven CT: Yale University Press, 2001).

Bonazzoli, Giorgio, "Remarks on the Nature of the Purāṇas", *Purāṇa*, vol. 25, no. 1, 1983, pp. 77–113.

Brokaw, Cynthia A., and Kai-wing Chow, eds, *Printing and Book Culture in Late Imperial China* (Berkeley: University of California Press, 2005).

Broughton, Thomas Duer, *Letters Written in a Mahratta Camp During the Year 1809* (Westminster: Archibald Constable and Company, 1892).

Brown, C. Mackenzie, "Purāṇa as Scripture: From Sound to Image of the Holy Word in the Hindu Tradition", *History of Religions*, vol. 26, no. 1, 1986, pp. 68–86.

Chakrabarty, Kunal, *Religious Process: The Purāṇas and the Making of a Regional Tradition* (New Delhi: Oxford University Press, 2001).

Chatterjee, Kumkum, *The Cultures of History in Early Modern India: Persianisation and Mughal Culture in Bengal* (New Delhi: Oxford University Press, 2009).

Chow, Kai-Wing, *Publishing, Culture and Power in Early Modern China* (Redwood City: Stanford University Press, 2004).

Cohn, Bernard S., *Colonialism and Its Forms of Knowledge: The British in India* (Princeton: Princeton University Press, 1996).

Collins, Brian, *The Other Rāma: Matricide and Genocide in the Mythology of Paraśurāma* (New York: SUNY Press, 2020).

Crawford, Arthur, *Legends of the Konkan* (Allahabad: Pioneer Press, 1909).

da Cunha, J. Gerson, *Sahyâdri-Khaṇḍa of the Skaṇḍa Purâṇa* (Bombay: Thacker, Vining and Co., 1877).

Davis, Donald R., *The Spirit of Hindu Law* (Cambridge: Cambridge University Press, 2010).

Derrett, J. Duncan M., "The Purāṇas in Vyavahāra Portions of Medieval Smṛiti Works", *Purāṇa*, vol. 5, no. 1, 1963, pp. 11–30.

Deva, Radha Kanta, *Śabda-Kalpadrumah*, 3 vols (Varanasi: Vidya Vilas Press, 1961).

Dirks, Nicholas B., *Castes of Mind: Colonialism and the Making of Modern India* (Princeton: Princeton University Press, 2001).

Donaldson, Thomas Eugene, "The Cult of Paraśurāma and Its Popularity in Orissa", in R.T. Vyas, ed., *Studies in Jain Art and Iconography* (Vadodara: Oriental Institute, 1995), pp. 159–92.

Eaton, Richard M., *A Social History of the Deccan, 1300–1761: Eight Indian Lives* (Cambridge: Cambridge University Press, 2005).

Gail, Adalbert, *Parasurama: Brahmane und Krieger* (Wiesbaden: Harrassowitz, 1977).

Gode, P.K., "Migration of Paper from China to India, AD 105–1500", in *Studies in Indian Cultural History*, vol. 3, ed. P.K. Gode (Poona: Bhandarkar Oriental Research Institute, 1969), pp. 1–12.

———, "The Origin and Antiquity of the Caste-Name of the Karahāṭaka or Karhāḍa Brahmins", in P.K. Gode, ed., *Studies in Indian Cultural History*, vol. 3 (Poona: Bhandarkar Oriental Research Institute, 1969), pp. 1–36.

Grant Duff, James, *History of the Mahrattas*, 3 vols (London: Longman, Rees, Orme, Brown and Green, 1826).

Green, Nile, "The Uses of Books in a Late Mughal *Takiyya*: Persianate Knowledge Between Person and Paper", *Modern Asian Studies*, vol. 44, no. 2, 2010, pp. 241–66.

Guha, Sumit, "Speaking Historically: The Changing Voices of Historical Narration in Western India, 1400–1900", *American Historical Review*, vol. 109, no. 4, 2004, pp. 1084–1103.

———, "Serving the Barbarian to Preserve the Dharma: The Ideology and Training of a Clerical Elite in Peninsular India", *Indian Economic and Social History Review*, vol. 47, no. 4, 2010, pp. 497–526.

Gune, V.T., *The Judicial System of the Marathas* (Poona: Sangam Press, 1953).

Gunjikar, R.B., *Sarasvatīmaṇḍal* (Bombay: Nirnayasagar Press, 1884).

Habermas, Jurgen, *The Structural Transformation of the Public Sphere*, ed. and trans. T. Burger and F. Lawrence (Cambridge MA: MIT Press, 1989).

Habib, Mohammad, and Afsar Begum, *The Political Theory of the Delhi Sultanate, Including a Translation of Ziauddin Barani's Fatawa-i Jahandari, circa AD 1358–9* (Delhi: Aakar Books, 2020).

Kane, P.V., ed., *Vyavahāramayūkha of Bhaṭṭa Nilakaṇṭha* (Bombay: Nirnayasagar Press, 1926).

———, *History of Dharmaśāstra*, 5 vols (Poona: Bhandarkar Oriental Research Institute, 1975).

Karve, Irawati, "The Paraśurāma Myth", *Journal of the University of Bombay: History, Economics and Sociology*, vol. 1, pt 1, 1932, pp. 115–39.

Katre, S.L., "Nārāyaṇabhaṭṭa Ārḍe, His Works and Date", *Bhāratīya Vidya*, March–April 1945, pp. 74–86.

Kaviraj, Sudipta, "An Outline of a Revisionist Theory of Modernity", *European Journal of Sociology*, vol. 46, no. 3, 2005, pp. 497–526.

Kumari, Janaki S.S., "Paraśurāma", *Purāṇa*, vol. 8, no. 1, 1966, pp. 52–82.

Lake, Peter, and Steven Pincus, eds, *The Politics of the Public Sphere in Early Modern England* (Manchester: Manchester University Press, 2008).

Limaye, V.M., *Limaye Kulavṛttānta* (Pune: Maharashtra Printing Press, 1970).

Levitt, Stephan, "The Patityagrāmanirṇaya: A Purāṇic History of Degraded Brahman Villages", University of Pennsylvania PhD thesis, 1974.

———, "The Sahyādrikhaṇḍa: Some Problems Concerning a Text-Critical Edition of a Purāṇic Text", *Purāṇa*, vol. 9, no. 1, 1977, pp. 8–40.

———, "Sahyādrikhaṇḍa: Style and Content and Indices of Authorship in the Pātityagrāmanirṇaya", *Purāṇa*, vol. 24, no. 1, 1982, pp. 128–45.

Madhava, *Śatapraśnakalpalatā*, Bhandarkar Oriental Research Institute, P.M. Joshi Collection, Sanskrit ms. no 19.

Mandlik, V.N., "Preliminary Observations on a Document giving an Account of the Establishment of a New Village named Murūḍa, in Southern Konkaṇa", *Journal of the Bombay Branch of the Royal Asiatic Society*, vol. 8, 1865, pp. 1–48.

McCrea, Lawrence, "Hindu Jurisprudence and Scriptural Hermeneutics", in Timothy Lubin, Donald R. Davis, and Jayanth K. Krishnan, eds,

Hinduism and Law: An Introduction (Cambridge: Cambridge University Press, 2010), pp. 123–36.
Mei, Chun, *The Novel and Theatrical Imagination in Early Modern China* (Leiden: Brill, 2011).
Messick, Brinkley, *The Calligraphic State: Textual Domination and History in a Muslim Society* (Berkeley: University of California Press, 1993).
Menon, K.P. Padmanabha, *History of Kerala*, 4 vols (Ernakulam: Cochin Government Press, 1924).
Minkowski, Christopher, "Advaita Vedānta in Early Modern History", *South Asian History and Culture*, vol. 2, no. 2, April 2011, pp. 205–31.
———, "Sanskrit Scientific Libraries and Their Uses: Examples and Problems of the Early Modern Period", in Florence Bretelle-Establet, ed., *Looking at It from Asia: The Processes that Shaped the Sources of History of Science* (Springer: Paris 2010), pp. 81–114.
Narayana Rao, Velcheru, "Purāṇa as Brahmanic Ideology", in Wendy Doniger, ed., *Purāṇa Perennis: Reciprocity in Hindu and Jaina Texts* (Albany: State University of New York Press, 1993), pp. 85–182.
———, David Shulman, and Sanjay Subrahmanyam, *Textures of Time. Writing History in South India 1600–1800* (New Delhi: Other Press, 2001).
Nayak, Shamrao Moroji, *A History of the Pattana Prabhus* (Bombay: No press given, 1877).
Novetzke, Christian, *Religion and Public Memory* (New York: Columbia University Press, 2008).
Ogborn, Miles, *Indian Ink: Script and Print in the Making of the English East India Company* (Chicago: University of Chicago Press, 2007).
O'Hanlon, Rosalind, *Caste, Conflict and Ideology: Mahatma Jotirao Phule and Low Caste Protest in Nineteenth Century Western India* (Cambridge: Cambridge University Press, 1985).
———, "Narratives of Penance and Purification in Western India, *c.* 1650–1850", *The Journal of Hindu Studies*, vol. 2, 2009, pp. 48–75.
———, "Letters Home: Banaras Pandits and the Maratha Regions in Early Modern India", *Modern Asian Studies*, vol. 44, no. 2, 2010, pp. 201–40.
———, "Speaking from Siva's Temple: Banaras Scholar Households and the Brahman 'Ecumene' of Mughal India", *South Asian History and Culture*, vol. 2, no. 2, April 2011, pp. 253–77.
———, and Christopher Minkowski, "What Makes People Who They Are? Pandit Networks and the Problem of Livelihoods in Early Modern Western India", *Indian Economic and Social History Review*, vol. 45, no. 3, 2008, pp. 381–416.

Olivelle, Patrick, "Dharmaśāstra: A Textual History", in Timothy Lubin, Donald R. Davis, and Jayanth K. Krishnan, eds, *Hinduism and Law: An Introduction* (Cambridge: Cambridge University Press, 2010), pp. 28–57.

Pandian, M.S.S., *Brahmin and Non-Brahmin: Genealogies of the Tamil Present* (New Delhi: Permanent Black, 2007).

Pandit, Vishnu Parashuram Sastri, *Devarukhyāviṣayī Śāstrasamat Vicāra* (Mumbai: Indu Prakash Press, 1874).

Paradkar, M.D., *Viśvanāthakṛta Śrivāḍeśvarodayakāvyam* (Mumbai: Raghunath Hari Apte, 1981).

Perlin, Frank, *The Invisible City: Monetary, Administrative and Popular Infrastructures in Asia and Europe, 1500–1900* (Aldershot: Variorum, 1993).

Pettegree, Andrew, *Reformation and the Culture of Persuasion* (Cambridge: Cambridge University Press, 2005).

Pollock, Sheldon, "Deep Orientalism: Notes on Sanskrit and Power Beyond the Raj", in Carol A. Breckenridge and Peter van der Veer, eds, *Orientalism and the Postcolonial Predicament* (Philadelphia: University of Pennsylvania Press, 1993), pp. 76–133.

———, "New Intellectuals in Seventeenth Century India", *Indian Economic and Social History Review*, vol. 38, no. 1, 2001, pp. 3–31.

———, *The Language of the Gods in the World of Men: Sanskrit, Culture and Power in Premodern India* (Berkeley and Los Angeles: University of California Press, 2007).

———, ed., *Forms of Knowledge in Early Modern Asia: Explorations in the Intellectual History of India and Tibet, 1500–1800* (Durham: Duke University Press, 2011).

Prinsep, James, "Census of the Population of the City of Banaras", *Asiatic Researches*, vol. XVII, 1832, pp. 470–98.

Puntambekar, Narayan Vitthal Vaidya Purandare, *Uttar Konkanātīl Prācīn Gangātīrastha Śuklayajurvedīya Brāhmaṇ* (1884; reprinted Bombay: Aksharadhan Publishers, 2007).

Pusalkar, A.D., "Vāḍeśvarodaya-Kāvya of Viśvanātha", *Journal of the Bombay Branch of the Royal Asiatic Society*, vol. 27, pt 1, 1951, pp. 66–78.

Rahimi, Babak, *The Theater-State and the Formation of the Early Modern Public Sphere in Iran: Studies on Safavid Muharram Ritual 1590–1641* (Leiden: Brill, 2011).

Rahman, A., "Paper Technology in India", in idem, ed., *History of Indian Science, Technology and Culture A.D 1000–1800* (New Delhi: Oxford University Press, 1999), pp. 261–73.

Rao, Nagendra E., "The Historical Tradition of South Kanara and the Brahmanical Groups", *Indica*, vol. 35, no. 1, 1998, pp. 1–12.

———, "Reconstructing the Social History of South Kanara: A Study of the Sahyadri Khanda", *Indica*, vol. 36, no. 2, 1999, pp. 81–8.

Robinson, Francis, "Technology and Religious Change: Islam and the Impact of Print", *Modern Asian Studies*, vol. 27, no. 1, 1993, pp. 229–51.

Rocher, Ludo, "Reflections on One Hundred and Fifty Years of Purāṇa Studies", *Purāṇa*, vol. 25, 1, 1983, pp. 64–76.

———, *The Purāṇas* (Wiesbaden: Harrassowitz, 1986).

Russell, R.V., and Rai Bahadur Hira Lal, *Tribes and Castes of the Central Provinces*, 4 vols (London: Macmillan and Co., 1916).

Saletore, B.A., *Ancient Karnataka* (Poona: Oriental Book Agency, 1936).

Sardesai, G.S., *Selections from the Peshwa Daftar*, 45 vols (Bombay: Government Central Press, 1930–4).

Sarma, M.G.S., *Sārasvat Bhūṣhaṇ* (Bombay: Popular Book Depot, 1950).

Sastri, Lalji Vaijanath, *Sadbodhachintāmaṇī* (Bombay: Arya Prakash Press, 1875).

Sastry, R. Ananta Krishna, *Kavindracharya List* (Baroda: Central Library, 1921).

Sathaye, Adeesh A., *Crossing the Lines of Caste: Viśvāmitra and the Construction of Brahmin Power in Hindu Mythology* (New York: Oxford University Press, 2015).

Scribner, Robert W., *For the Sake of Simple Folk: Popular Propaganda for the German Reformation* (Cambridge: Cambridge University Press, 1981).

Seyller, John, "The Inspection and Valuation of Manuscripts in the Imperial Mughal library", *Artibus Asiae*, vol. 57, nos 3–4, 1997, pp. 243–9.

Sharpe, Kevin, *Selling the Tudor Monarchy: Authority and Image in Sixteenth Century England* (New Haven: Yale University Press, 2009).

Siromani, B.C., *et al.*, eds, *Chaturvargacintāmaṇi by Hemādri*, 7 vols (Calcutta: Asiatic Society of Bengal, 1873–1911).

Soteriou, Alexandra, *Gift of the Conquerors: Hand Papermaking in India* (Ahmedabad: Grantha Corporation, 1999).

Steele, Arthur, *The Law and Custom of Hindoo Castes Within the Dekhun Provinces Subject to the Presidency of Bombay* (London: W.H. Allen, 1868).

Subrahmanyam, Sanjay, and C.A. Bayly, "Portfolio Capitalists and the Political Economy of Early Modern India", in Sanjay Subrahmanyam, ed., *Merchants, Markets and the State in Early Modern India* (Delhi, Oxford University Press, 1996), pp. 242–63.

Thapar, Romila, "Society and Historical Consciousness: The Itihāsa Purāṇa Tradition", in Sabhyasachi Bhattacharya and Romila Thapar, eds, *Situating Indian History* (Delhi: Oxford University Press, 1986), pp. 353–83.

———, *History and Beyond* (Delhi: Oxford University Press, 2000).

Thurston, E., *Castes and Tribes of Southern India*, 7 vols (Madras: Government Press, 1909).

Trautmann, Thomas R., *Aryans and British India* (Berkeley: University of California Press, 1997).

Vad, Ganesh Chimnaji, B.P. Joshi, P.V. Mawji, and D.B. Parasnis, eds, *Selections from the Satara Rajas' and the Peshwas' Diaries*, 9 vols (Poona: Deccan Vernacular Education Society, 1905–11).

Varijākṣacharitra, Bhandarkar Oriental Research Institute, Pune, ms. no. 467 of 1883–4.

Wakeman, Frederic, "Boundaries of the Public Sphere in Ming and Qing China", *Daedalus*, vol. 127, no. 3, 1998, pp. 167–89.

Warner, Michael, *The Letters of the Republic: Publication and the Public Sphere in Eighteenth-Century America* (Cambridge MA: Harvard University Press, 1990).

Wilks, Mark, *Historical Sketches of the South of India*, 3 vols (London: Longman, Hurst, Rees, Orme and Brown, 1810–17).

Wink, Andre, *Land and Sovereignty in India: Agrarian Society and Politics under the Eighteenth Century Maratha Svarajya* (Cambridge: Cambridge University Press, 1986).

Wong, R. Bin, "Great Expectations: The "Public Sphere" and the Search for Modern Times in Chinese History", *Chugokushi gakku* (Studies in Chinese History), vol. 3, 1993, pp. 7–50.

Yachnin, Paul, and Bronwen Wilson, eds, *Making Publics in Early Modern Europe: People, Things, Forms of Knowledge* (New York: Routledge, 2009).

10

In the Presence of Witnesses

Petitioning and Judicial "Publics" in Western India, *c.* 1600–1820

Introduction

INDIAN OBSERVERS OF THE East India Company's emerging political order in the late eighteenth century were, as is well known, struck by the inaccessibility of its officials to their Indian subjects. Both Indo-Muslim traditions of akhlāq, and Sanskrit-influenced norms for nīti (political ethics), emphasised the duties of rulers, or those they deputised, to be vigilant in their watch over the condition of their subjects, to listen to their concerns, and offer them regular opportunities to present their pleas for justice.[1] As the Company's Bengal government struggled to develop effective judicial systems, its own servants became sharply aware of the difficulty of balancing accessibility with the disorder that might overwhelm its courts unless petitioners could be channelled into a formal judicial system.[2] By the 1820s in western India, and certainly in the mind of the first governor of Bombay Mountstuart Elphinstone, Bengal's judicial system had become a byword for paralysis, with its delays, ill-informed or inert judges, and the endless layers of intermediaries interposed between petitioners and

[1] Chatterjee, "History as Self–Representation", p. 937; Alam, *The Languages of Political Islam*, p. 58; Narayana Rao, Shulman, and Subrahmanyam, "A New Imperial Idiom", p. 90.

[2] See in particular Wilson, *The Domination of Strangers*, and Travers, *Ideology and Empire*.

magistrates. He contrasted it with the situation in western India. "Here, every man above the rank of a Hircarrah sits down before us, and did before the Paishwa; even a common Ryot, if he had to stay any time, would sit down on the ground." With their deep local knowledge and familiar principles of procedure, traditional "panchayat" assemblies in particular "retained in a great degree the confidence of the people."[3] He urged that the panchayat be retained as a local part of the Bombay government's own judicial system.[4]

Elphinstone's characterisation of the panchayat as the region's "traditional" judicial forum was not quite accurate. It was in fact only from the 1720s that the panchayat came to occupy centre stage in the judicial institutions of the Maratha state. It appeared alongside older corporate bodies, operating under the sponsorship of leading local gentry, urban heads of guilds, and caste and village headmen. These older bodies were the gota ("family" or "community"), the dharmasabhā (assembly of pandits) knowledgeable in matters of religious law, and the majālis, an often more substantial assembly bringing representatives of many local communities together with officials of the state.

These bodies constituted a remarkable landscape for the submission of petitions and the hearing of suits. Here, all justice started with a petition. Depending on their rank, their resources and the significance of their suit, petitioners of the sixteenth and seventeenth centuries addressed themselves to a range of different sources of justice – the royal courts of the Deccan Sultanate states, state officials in the localities empowered to hear suits, lordly patrons, and community tribunals of different kinds. Many petitioners were individuals, but often represented extended families, caste communities, village brotherhoods, and local religious corporations. Their suits were usually local in nature, concerning disputed rights to property or office and its perquisites, and were heard initially before local communities of stake-holders, knowledgeable people, and local state officials. Many petitioners also pursued

[3] Elphinstone, *Report on The Territories*, pp. 59 and 95—101.

[4] For Elphinstone's approach, see most recently Jaffe, *Ironies of Colonial Governance.* There is also a substantial older literature on Maratha judicial institutions and their early colonial inheritors. See Sen, *The Administrative History of the Marathas*; Franks, *Panchayets under the Peshwas*; Gune, *The Judicial System*; Ballhatchet, *Social Policy*; Choksey, ed., *Twilight of the Maratha Raj.*

their causes far beyond the locality, seeking redress across political networks that ran to regional and sometimes subcontinental levels.

The petitions also contained a powerful ethical and political dimension. Part of this consisted in a fierce rhetoric of community, brotherhood, and personal witness in the defence of local rights. There were ethical concerns too with proper procedure in paper record-keeping and the verification of documents. Petitioners, tribunals, and state authorities alike demonstrated an intense preoccupation with the documentary evidence needed to support claims, and a set of clearly understood routines for their authentication. It is worth emphasising here that this petitionary culture was not the monopoly of Brahman and other literate elites. The examples explored here include Brahmans certainly, but also Sonar goldsmiths, Maratha village headmen, the gathered village servants and cultivators of a single village, shepherds, and Mahar Dalit communities.

From the early eighteenth century, the new form of the panchayat came to supersede the older tribunals of gota, dharmasabhā, and majālis. A small panel of appointed members or panchas heard the proceedings, and local corporate bodies had no right to attend. The proceedings often focused more heavily on testimony submitted to the panchayat in writing by witnesses who did not always attend in person. The written judgment of the panchayat gained its authority through endorsement by the state, rather than by the assembled will and witness of local corporate bodies. However, the very flows of documents came to connect petitioners, their audiences, and state officials in new ways, expanding a world of discussion and circulation of news now linked as much by the written as by the spoken word.

The petitions studied here differ from the collective "public" petitions addressed to local or royal authority that we know about in early modern Europe. Petitioning in Europe developed within new forms of the public sphere, in which communication was facilitated by print and public social action of every kind was shaped by the emerging institutions of "civil society".[5] The later eighteenth century in particular saw the growth of newly assertive forms of popular political engagement, in which collective groups of petitioners and other

[5] See in particular Zaret, *Origins of Democratic Culture*.

associations strove to influence established political authority.[6] In recent years, the diversity of petitioning practices in Europe has also become apparent, and with it, understandings of what "civil society" constituted in different settings. Petitions from individuals as much as from associations constituted an important part of the public sphere, and the unlettered as well as the literate sought to engage the state and their social superiors with their suits.[7]

As scholars have increasingly come to appreciate that forms of "modernity" emerged in many locales across early modern Eurasia, exploration of "publics" of different kinds in early modern contexts outside Europe has also flourished in recent years. This array of institutions and arenas between the state and the private sphere does not conform to the older "civil society" model with which the European public sphere has been associated, although, as indicated above, that model has itself become more open and flexible.[8] Following this scholarship on Eurasian "early modernities", I suggest that the early modern Indian petitionary culture outlined above also reveals elements of a recognisable "public".[9] The arenas within which petitions were heard and disputes arbitrated – heterogeneous assemblies of local notables, peasant brotherhoods, extended families, groups of office-holders, and state officials – constituted a space between the official and the local community and familial. Assembly hearings themselves were important public occasions in which witnesses and locally knowledgeable people of every social rank spoke about what they knew and helped to lay down what became a form of common memory. The heavier emphasis on written testimony with the panchayat extended this public. The flow of such documents linked local arenas and

[6] van Voss, "Petitions in Social History", pp. 1—10; Bailey, *Popular Influence on Public Policy*.

[7] See, for example, Beales, "Joseph II, Petitions and the Public Sphere", pp. 249—68; Würgler, "Voices from Among the 'Silent Masses'", pp. 11—34; da Costa, "Identity, Authority and the Moral Worlds of Indigenous Petitions", 669—98.

[8] See in particular Bayly, *Empire and Information*; Eisenstadt and Schluchter, eds, "Early Modernities"; Hoexter, Eisenstadt, and Levtzion, eds, *The Public Sphere in Muslim Societies*.

[9] For this argument in other contexts, see O'Hanlon, "Speaking from Siva's Temple", pp. 253—77.

provided petitioners, their audiences, and state officials with a focus for discussion away from the site of the panchayat itself.

The petitionary culture explored here offers other perspectives also. What emerges is certainly something like the picture that Lauren Benton offers in her study of the judicial pluralities of early modern empires.[10] The elaborate documentary culture revealed here also complicates the now familiar supposition that the coming of colonialism entailed a "documentary culture" of a wholly new kind.[11] Acute concern with correctness in judicial procedure, propriety in the verification of evidence, and the ever-present danger of forged documents marked state and community institutions alike in pre-colonial western India. Lastly, the emergence of the panchayat suggests that it was not only the East Indian Company that struggled, often unsuccessfully, to narrow the channels through which suits, petitions, and complaints reached its courts and judges. So too did the Maratha state over the same decades, responding to some of the same pressures, and subject to many of the same frustrations.

Local Rights and Corporate Bodies in Early Modern Western India

The institutions of gota, dharmasabhā, and majālis were part of western India's pre-Mughal history of local corporate institutions.[12] Unlike Bengal, where most written records of landed rights dated back to the Mughal period at the earliest, the Marathi-speaking regions had a much earlier and continuous recorded history of rural settlement, cultivation, and lands gifted by local states in return for service of different kinds. As elsewhere in peninsular India, the village headman – Patil or Mokadam – took a leading role in opening up land for cultivation, and the hereditary cultivator's right of mirās or vatan derived from family participation in such early pioneering. Rights to the offices of the Kulkarni (accountant), and the Joshi (priest), could likewise

[10] Benton, *Law and Colonial Cultures*.

[11] See, for example, Cohn, *Colonialism and Its Forms of Knowledge*; Smith, *Rule by Records*; Ogborn, *Indian Ink*; Raman, *Document Raj*.

[12] See Gune, *Judicial System*, pp. 7—37; Kulkarni, *Maharashtra*; Perlin, "Of White Whale and Countrymen", pp. 172–237; Guha, "Speaking Historically", pp. 1084–1103.

constitute a village mirās. At the interface between these communities and the local state lay the key office of Deshmukh ("mouth of the country"). The Deshmukh was himself usually also a Patil. He had in addition responsibility for maintaining cultivation and the flow of state revenues, and for oversight of local justice and security. These responsibilities carried considerable rewards in land, services and rewards in kind, which were often dispersed through the many villages over which the Deshmukh had charge.[13]

The fourteenth-century consolidation of the Bahmani Sultanate in western India, and its successor in the states of the Deccan Sultanate incorporated rather than replaced the layer of conservative Brahman accountants and administrators who had served the earlier Yadava kingdom. With literate skills, religious prestige, and access to cash, these long-settled Brahman families accumulated many kinds of connected rights. Their presence also contributed to the region's well-developed culture of written records for rights, in stone, copper plate and, with increasing frequency from the thirteenth century, on paper.[14]

These rights were granted and defended within different corporate bodies. The oldest, dating back to the first millennium, was the gota, from the Sanskrit gotra, or exogamous kin group. Looked on as a brotherhood or family unit, a gota was the collective body of all those who held the same kinds of local proprietary rights. These might be holders of permanent mirās rights, either in land or in hereditary village service offices. Gotas were not just local village bodies: there were also gotas of the qasbā or town, and of the parganā, the largest administrative unit. Members of the same caste community also constituted a gota. Gotas met to hear complaints and disputes, inspected documents, interviewed witnesses, and determined fair outcomes. The gota had a close relationship with the state, often taking its decisions to state authorities for enforcement. This early corporate form was taken up into the bureaucracy of the Bahmani kingdom and then the Deccan Sultanate states, and persisted through into the eighteenth century.[15]

When property rights of any kind were at issue, however, state officials – the local Havaldar, Qazi, and Amin – were present, while

[13] Gordon, *The Marathas*, pp. 26–34.

[14] For paper use in western India, see Perlin, "State Formation Re-Considered", pp. 453–5; O'Hanlon, "Performance in a World of Paper", pp. 87–126.

[15] Gune, *Judicial System*, pp. 51–63.

rulers themselves might demand to hear the most important cases. Such assemblies or majālis included members of the relevant gota, together with state officials, Muslim clerics, Brahman scholars and priests, Deshmukhs, village headmen, and holders of local mirās rights. The meetings might vary in size from a dozen to several hundred people in attendance. They were held in public, often at a local fort or district headquarters, and conducted in Marathi. They called witnesses at all social levels, and from all sides in a dispute, and inspected documents, their content, and their seals. Where the property in question was substantial, the majālis might be attended by many dozens, sometimes hundreds of people, many of them village Patils and Kulkarnis holding mirās rights from many villages around, who wished to ensure that the rights of people like themselves were respected, and the majālis conducted its proceedings in the proper manner. Disputes were not the only occasion for the holding of a majālis. Uncontested sales or transfers of property were held before a majālis, and a mahzar document issued to confirm them. Requests for the issuing of new documents of right often required the authority of a majālis. At the end of the proceedings, unsatisfied parties could ask to have their case heard by a majālis in a different place, or one with wider regional representation where there might be less risk of bias in favour of one of the parties. Both in the case of the gota and of the majālis, dissatisfied complainants could also offer proof in the form of divine revelation through an ordeal, and thus offer dramatic bodily demonstration of their truthfulness.

They could also petition for a hearing at a dharmasabhā, which was a tribunal of learned pandits under the authority of a dharmādhikārī, a hereditary office commanding substantial local influence and perquisites. Religious questions actually covered a wide range of possible disputes, since many proprietary rights flowed from particular religious claims. Like the gota, the dharmasabhā often worked hand in hand with the majālis, operating as a court of appeal for discontented suitors as well as the first forum for hearing matters of religious dispute.[16] Suitors therefore had many avenues through which to seek re-

[16] O'Hanlon, "Narratives of Penance and Purification", pp. 48–75; and Kotani, *Western India*, pp. 222–38.

dress, and, as we shall see, one arena often served as a court of appeal for another within this system.

Elaborate bureaucratic routines marked these arenas. A wide range of Persian, Arabic, Sanskrit, and Marathi terms described their operations, reflecting the prominent role of Muslim state officials in the judicial and revenue affairs of the Maratha countryside.[17] A respectful request for intervention (vinanti karṇe), or a representation (vidhit karṇe), marked the start of the process. Petitioners made their request to one of the range of people with the authority to institute an enquiry: the Havaldar responsible for hearing complaints at the level of the parganā or district headquarters, the officers of the local taraf or administrative subdivision, or to headman of the village. These might then instigate a mansubī (investigation or arbitration). Parties were asked to submit a written statement (takrīr or karina). If any of the parties decided that they wished their case heard before a majālis from a different place, they would have to submit a thalpatra. A government messenger might take a talabrokhā (written summons) sent to witnesses, sākṣīmozā, or shāhidī. The messenger would expect to levy a fee (masālā) for his services. Parties to a dispute would have to submit a muchalkā to the majālis – a written bond of agreement under penalty to abide by its decision. To do so, they might need a zāmīn – a bondsman – able to put up surety in the case. The taking of evidence would include purśīs (the interrogation of witnesses), and perhaps sadi (a written or oral statement given in evidence). The majālis would note the contents – majamūn or mazkūr – of documents submitted to it, and might decide that they were authentic (bajinnas) or false (layini). The majālis would issue a mahzar to the successful party, but state officials might also confirm this with a jayapatra, a letter confirming the successful outcome, registered in the state records. The successful litigant would pay a sum of money (harkī) to the majālis to signify his pleasure. The vanquished party had to issue a yejitpatra – a statement in writing admitting his failure.[18]

Ordeals of different kinds also had their own intricate procedures

[17] Guha, "Bad Language and Good Language", pp. 49–68, and Guha, "Transitions and Translations", pp. 23–31.

[18] Gune, *Judicial System*, pp. xxii–xxviii.

and terminology. They were usually conducted publicly before the local temple to Shiva. A day or two in advance of the ordeal, the hands of the plaintiff were washed and inspected, and bandages applied with seals. A bhālpatra ("forehead letter") recording the purpose of the ordeal was placed on his forehead. He then walked over seven concentric circles drawn in front of the temple, with the defending party walking behind him – sāvali karṇe ("making a shadow"). The plaintiff then recited the purpose of the ordeal written on the bhālpatra. His hands were freed, and in front of the assembly he plunged them into a pot of boiling oil and ghee to recover a piece of metal, a ravā, from it. His hands were then bandaged under seal again for two days, then opened before the majālis. Unmarked hands signified truthfulness, marked hands pointed to falsehood and guilt.[19]

The business of the dharmasabhā was likewise conducted through a series of well understood bureaucratic procedures. Applicants wishing to be exculpated from some wrongdoing started with a petition, known as a dośapatra. Taken down by the scribe to the assembly, it confessed transgressions and asked for suitable penance at an appropriately sacred place. Once the penance had been performed, the dharmasabhā of that place issued a śuddhipatra ("letter of purification"), which the suitor carried back home, and with it sought readmission to the village or caste community. The caste gota often issued a gotapata patra to confirm his social rehabilitation.[20]

Witness to Rights in the Mahzar

The key outcome of a successful petition, therefore, was a paper mahzar, correctly recorded and attested by the members of the majālis assembly.[21] In form, a mahzar was written by a scribe on pieces of

[19] Ibid., pp. 93–4.

[20] O'Hanlon, "Narratives of Penance and Purification", pp. 55–6.

[21] For an extended reflection on the mahzar in the broader context of Indo-Islamic law in Mughal and British India, see Chatterjee, "Mahzar-namas in the Mughal and British Empires", pp. 379–406. On these documentary cultures, see Deshpande, *Scripts of Power*, pp. 41–53, and also the extensive digital resource at Chatterjee, "Lawforms", https://humanities–research.exeter.ac.uk/lawforms/index.html, accessed 29 August 2023.

handmade paper, 6 to 8 inches wide, glued together to form a roll that might extend to several feet, depending on the length of the various testimonies to be incorporated and the numbers of witnesses whose names were to be added. Each join was stamped on the rear side with seals to guard against later fraudulent alterations. At the end it was signed or marked by those in attendance, although the process of taking signatures sometimes continued several days after the meeting.[22] While state officials would retain a copy for the state records, the mahzar itself was given to the party whose rights it thereby confirmed. Thus constituted, it was a complex social artefact of great value, a tangible embodiment of the common rights of all who had witnessed and signed it with mark or signature. It was usually stored in a sealed bamboo tube or stone pot, to guard against house fires and damage from insects or water.[23]

Mahzars followed a standard form. They stated the date and place of the majālis, and the names of the state officials in attendance. There followed the names of the principals present, their place of origin, their office, and sometimes their age, as evidence of their worth as witnesses. The main text was usually presented as an address to the petitioner: that he had come to the Huzoor, and made the following representation. The next part of the narrative reproduced what the petitioner had said, which might include histories of earlier cases and judgments relevant to the case in hand. The testimony of different witnesses followed, sometimes in great detail, sometimes very briefly. The mahzar concluded with the consensus reached and the judgment given. A protracted dispute might generate a mahzar judgment containing many histories within its narrative, covering several generations and lengths of paper roll.

Although state officials were present, the authority of the majālis derived from its character as an assembly of local holders of rights and people with local experience and knowledge. The term mahzar itself comes from the Arabic huzoor ("present"). The personal testimony of knowledgeable witnesses, questioning of parties to the case, and direct inspection of documents were central to its proceedings. There

[22] Gune, *Judicial System*, p. 207.

[23] Ibid., p. 80.

was another close link with local holders of rights. They were entitled to attend the majālis and put seal, sign, or signature to the mahzar recording its decisions. Holders of different kinds of rights had their own signs which might be used instead of a signature: the village headman put his mark as a plough, the potter as a wheel, the carpenter a chisel, the merchant a pair of balances, and so on.[24] These practices reflected the fact that a mahzar was given not by state officials or by royal authority, but by the assembled community of rights-holders attending the majālis itself, and signifying their assent.

What can we say about the language of the petitions, and the mahzars within which they were incorporated? As seen above, they drew on an amalgam of Persian, Arabic, Sanskrit, and Marathi terms, their authors careful to use the correct Persian terms wherever rights were bound up with revenue arrangements. The language reflected the fact that petitioners did not always see themselves as humbly approaching a remote state authority. Certainly, a petitioner might submit a deferential arjī, the Persian term for a humble request, as when certain cultivators of Saswad near Pune made a plea to the chief revenue officer for abatement of their revenues due on account of failed rains and widespread dearth.[25] Sometimes petitioners used the equivalent Marathi term vinanti karṇe, to make a respectful request. More often, however, the Marathi term used was the more neutral vidhit karṇe. It meant simply that a suit was put forward or represented, and its matter-of-fact tone may have reflected the view of the petitioners that they were appealing to a corporate body of their own social equals, at least in the kinds of rights that they held.

Petitions also emphasised the continuity of rights possessed piḍī dar piḍī (from generation to generation), or lekarāche lekarī (from children to their children). Rights were described in direct rather than impersonal terms: they were not "held" or "enjoyed", but rather "eaten" (khāṇe). Some standard phrases stressed comprehensiveness of attendance at the majālis: samasta deśaka (all of the headmen of the villages), samasta gota (the whole gota), samasta bāp-bhau va mirāsdār kunbi (all brothers of the same father and mirāsdār cultivators), samasta

[24] Idem.

[25] Oturkar, *Peśve-kālīn Sāmājik va Ārthik Patravyavahār*, nos 12 and 13, p. 7.

peṭha (the whole town), samākul pāṇḍhrī va bārābalute (the whole village community and the village officers). A strong ethical and ideological dimension thus marked the language of these corporate bodies. They emphasised the principle that legitimate rights should be enjoyed continuously down the generations of families who held them. Prominence was given to mirās-bhau, the brotherhood of those who possessed the same hereditary village rights. Above all, the language used affirmed the inclusiveness of these corporate bodies, and the unanimity of their sentiment and action.

Testimony, Rhetoric and Record: The Majālis as a Public Space

Through their linked social networks and arenas for meeting and hearing suits, the majālis, gota, and dharmasabhā together contained a significant public dimension. This appears at three different levels. First, through their recognised procedures for receiving "representations", assembling all of the key local parties in a single place, hearing direct personal testimony, sometimes witnessing ordeals, and affirming consent through the many individuals who signed or marked the mahzar, the majālis and other bodies created an occasion which remained in collective memory.

Let us look, for example, at a majālis which met on 1 September 1636 to hear the petition of the Brahman Padhye family. The family claimed the offices of dharmādhikārī and priest to some seventy-five villages in the Konkan province of Sangamesvara. These were key offices, their legitimate possession a matter of deep local interest. They had been the subject of a long-running dispute, dating back to 1600 or earlier, with another local family of priests, the Purohits.[26] In 1636, the challenges to their offices seem to have been revived by another priestly family, the Joshis, who may have been connected to the earlier case. Perhaps because of this background, the Padhyes approached the state officials at Muzaffarabad directly with their petition. The majālis to hear it was held before some thirty-six people, including the Havaldar, Qazi, other

[26] See O'Hanlon and Minkowski, "What Makes People Who They Are?", pp. 400–2.

Muslim officials, Deshmukhs, Patils, Kulkarnis, Shroffs, and a significant number of nayakavadi – Mahars or other menial village servants acting as district revenue sepoys.[27] After listing those in attendance, the mahzar began its narrative with the Padhe's "representation".

> We have possessed the mirāsī rights to dharmādhikārī and joshi from generation to generation. But then Krishna Joshi of Sangamesvara went to the Huzoor, gave false information, and made a complaint about our mirās. They produced a document of grant from Humayun. But we are ancient mirāsdārs from the time of the Hindu kings, and we have copper plates from that time at our house to show our possession, and can bring it before you to confirm this. [28]

The Padhyes duly produced their copper plates. The assembly decided that the copper plates confirmed their continuing rights, and dismissed the Joshi family's case. "The mirās of dharmādhikārī and joshi belongs to them, and they have enjoyed it from one generation to the next. According to the copper plate, the mirās belongs to the Upadhyes, and Krishna Joshi has no possession in it. This is the mahzar, just as it is signed, at the fort of Rajgad."[29]

Perhaps as a consequence of these challenges, the Padhyes were careful over subsequent decades to confirm their rights. In 1659 they asked for replacement papers for those destroyed in a house fire. In 1662, with the extension of Shivaji's control over the Konkan, they requested fresh documents, and did so again in 1709 at the accession of the Raja Shahu II.[30] The same dispute was to emerge, and the same documents demanded, in a particularly dramatic form, a century later. The documents – bearing the marks or signatures of key witnesses present – had a public life beyond the moment of the judgment they recorded, their production required in later hearings, at other places, where the information they contained bore on the matters in hand.

In most cases, however, the gota and majālis worked together to investigate the truth of competing claims and the histories on which they

[27] Potdar and Muzumdar, "Golavalīkar-Pādhye", pp. 342–6.

[28] Ibid., p. 344.

[29] Idem.

[30] Ibid., pp. 345–7.

were based. The Dhangar shepherd communities of the Maharashtra's Konkan littoral did not possess the privileges of priestly office enjoyed by Brahman Padhye and Purohit families above. Nonetheless, senior state officials convened a majālis to hear an important dispute within the community. In 1697, brothers of the Gotara and Savalakar families put forward competing claims to seniority in headship of the village of Peth Dhangar in Maharashtra's Konkan littoral, and the accompanying honours and perquisites. The narrative of the whole case, stretching back more than two generations, was contained in the final mahzar of the majālis assembled at the nearby town of Chiplun. The Gotara brothers had made a complaint to the local Havaldar, who asked the local gota to take initial statements from the two parties. The Gotaras stated that a moneylender had forced their father to move away from their Konkan village to live up in the Deccan, and in their absence the Savalakar family had moved in to usurp their historic rights. The Savalakars countered by listing six generations of their forebears who had enjoyed rights of seniority in the village. They asserted that the Gotaras were in fact relative newcomers to the village, notwithstanding their attempts to institute cases against them from their new home up in the Deccan. "We have been here from the very first, and carry on in the same way. But now Bakoji and Manaji Gotara have raised this case against us, and gone around to several places asking for investigations against us."[31]

The gota heard these statements, and testimony from a number of local people, "and brought old men before it as witnesses."[32] Most of these, whose names and ages are given in the document, testified that the Gotaras were unknown in the village. However, the strongest testimony for the Savalakars was provided by the local Brahman priests. They brought with them their letters of right to tax-free lands granted to them in 1740–1 by the peshwa Nana Saheb, following his visit to a local shrine. There, listed as leading witnesses, were members of the Savalakar family. The gota concluded that this proved beyond doubt that they were the senior family at the time. "The father of the Savalakars issued the grant of lands to the priests of that place. His name,

[31] V.S. Bendrey, ed., *Mahārāṣṭretihāsāchī Sādhane*, vol. 2, no. 210, p. 243.
[32] Idem.

Sirsoji, is on the letter. Whoever took part in issuing such a letter could not have done so without seniority."[33]

As a last throw, the Gotara brothers asked for the case to be decided by the ordeal of ravā described above. Bakoji Gotara offered to undergo it. When the gota met on 25 April 1697, many local leaders and officials gathered to witness the dramatic moment when his hands were unwrapped, including the Subhedar, the Havaldar, the heads of the Brahman dharmasabhā and other senior officers, as well as "the people, soldiers, village heads and gentlemen of the district."[34] On inspection, Bakoji's hands were found to be burned. The Gotaras lost their case, and the Savalakars were confirmed in their rights. The mahzar to that effect was issued by a majālis held three weeks later, on 16 May 1697 at Chiplun. It was attended by some seventy-five named witnesses, including senior state officials, village heads, Brahmans of the local dharmasabhā, the local non-Brahman priests, senior merchants, hereditary artisans, and menial village servants.[35] The judgment was thus addressed to widely dispersed communities of caste, village brotherhood, extended family, and office-holders of different kinds, all with an interest in the decision.

Ethics of Brotherhood, Ethics of Procedure

The second way in which the petitions and the meetings where they were considered constituted a kind of public occasion lay in their frequent invocation of the ethic of brotherhood. Petitions frequently referred to mirāsī brotherhood (mirāsī-bhau), along with the brotherhood of those born of the same father (bāp-bhau). Part of this ethic lay in a rhetoric of mutual solidarity and support for one another's rights, and a concern that the nature of rights and the means by which rights were created should be properly understood. Part of the ethic also lay in mutual respect for the proper documentary procedures through which oral testimony was translated into tangible judgments, complete with seals and signatures. These dimensions of the majālis meant

[33] Ibid., p. 244.
[34] Ibid., p. 245.
[35] Ibid., pp. 240–2.

that such assemblies were never just about individual outcomes. Rather, they affirmed general principles about rights and procedures, of interest to all who held similar entitlements.

This rhetoric appeared not only in cases of disputed property, but in documents of sale, which also required the imprimatur of a majālis to confirm their authenticity. In 1670, the mirāsdārs of Tadali village in Junnar province decided to sell the mirās offices of village accountant and priest. This was not in any sense a petition. It was rather a public declaration by village rights-holders of their collective purpose in a matter of key importance to them, which required comprehensive public witness and affirmation. They gathered in a majālis and described their proceedings in a mahzar mirāsī patra. The document opened: "On Friday the eighth day of the light half of Mārgeśvara in the sake year of 1592. The hāzīr majālis of Tadali village, Takali, in taraf Rajangaon, pargana Junnar. In the temple of Śri, in the absence of the Huzoor." The document then named some twenty-five individuals from different villages in attendance – Patils, Kulkarnis, priests and village servants. In a few cases their ages were listed, perhaps as an indication of their depth of local knowledge: two men, one a Chamar, gave their ages as eighty. But the gathering seems to have been much larger, the list indicating ". . . and the whole village" next to some of the village names. On this important occasion absences were listed too: it was recorded that "Rayaji Adhau Mokadam was not present."

The mahzar was addressed to the purchasers of the office, Nilo Sondev and Abaji Sondev.

> Sivaji bin Jait Patil and Manaji bin Vevoji Bhose Mokadam, of Tadale village, Takali, taraf Rajangaon, pargana Junnar, and all brothers who share the same father [bāp-bhau], the twelve village servants, the mirāsdārs kunbis, write this document of mirās. Kumaji was our mirāsdārs Kulkarni and Joshi. But his lineage died out. So we villagers appointed a deputy who carried on the work of the Kulkarni. We village people ourselves calculated the auspicious times for marriages. Then we all came together and decided that we would sell the Kulkarni and Joshi offices and make you our brother in mirās. So we came to you in Rayri. Of our own will, we sell to you the Kulkarni and Joshi offices of Tadali village and the house that goes with them, and we give the mirās to you. May you and your children's children enjoy it [lit. "eat it"] in happiness. With the seal of the

> Deshmukh and the signature of the Deshpande, we make you our brother in mirās [mirās-bhau]. If any mirāsdārs comes in the way of your possession of these offices, we the headmen, the twelve village servants, all we brothers who share the same father, and the mirāsdārs kunbis will prevent them. You will be free from interference.

We see here very much the invocation of "the whole community" as seller of the rights and guarantor of their future security. The mahzar then listed the land, gardens, and goods in kind attached to the offices, and stipulated the price of the sale at 150 hons. It concluded: "May you and your descendants eat these in happiness, and if we turn out to be false, then may the goddess bring down destruction on us." There was no state official at this meeting, as its opening explicitly mentioned: the document, with its narrative, its witnesses, signatures, and seals, and perhaps the all-seeing eye of the goddess, were the guarantees.[36]

The office of priest and its perquisites in kind often occasioned dispute. Brothers of priestly families frequently disagreed about the practical division of proceeds from a shared office. Priestly rights usually took in the entitlement to perform domestic rituals for all Hindus within a village, whether their priestly services were wanted or not. A family's attempt to engage the services of a new priest often signalled an attempt to improve its caste standing and the ritual dignities it might claim. Sonar goldsmiths belonged to the wider community of early modern India's elite artisan castes – prestigious builders of temples and sculptors of figures of the gods to goldsmiths, gem-workers, engravers, painters – with a history of asserting twice-born and sometimes Brahman status for themselves.[37] A series of letters and petitions in Nasik in the 1640s suggest that western India's Sonars were developing their own such claims. A leading member of the community, Jakhoji Sonar, had evidently engaged the services of his own priest, one Shivabhat Kshemakalyani. This brought him into conflict with the powerful dharmādhikārī family of the town, who claimed the rights to all such services. In May 1646, the dharmādhikārīs protested to local state officials that Shivabhat had carried out the ceremonies and

[36] Joshi and Khare, "Bāvadekar Amātya", pp. 37–41.

[37] See O'Hanlon, Hidas, and Kiss, "Discourses of Caste over the Longue Durée", pp. 102–29.

endeavoured to collect the perquisites on the grounds that the family employed him to do so.

A majālis was convened, with the Qazi and the Amin, as well as the Deshmukh, the Deshpande, the Patil, merchants, and shetias. The assembly heard that Shivabhat had disregarded an earlier judgment given against him, and in his resentment had come to blows with one of the dharmādhikārī brothers. The assembly's judgment cut through the argument about what it was that created priestly rights. "Sonars, or other Hindus, may have their own maintained people in their households. But the fact of being maintained does not create one single right." The judgment notwithstanding, Sonars continued to try choose their own priests. In 1649 the Nasik dharmādhikārīs approached local state officials to complain that another Sonar family was endeavouring to place marriage ceremonies in the hands of its own employed priest.[38]

This rhetoric of brotherhood was still alive and flourishing in the middle of the eighteenth century. In 1746, two mirāsī families in the village of Saswad near Pune quarrelled over the honours on public occasions that were associated with the offices of Kulkarni and Joshi. Brothers of the Brahman Panse family complained to their fellow villagers that their fathers had observed the proper order of seniority quite harmoniously. Just recently, however, there had been disagreement and litigation. "We do not know the meaning of this. You and we are brothers in our rights, and we should behave in the same way that our fathers did."[39]

The Majālis and Regional Networks

The third sense in which the proceedings of these assemblies incorporated a public dimension lay in the sheer numbers recorded to have attended many of them, and the range of different locations at which petitioners might ask for their cases to be considered. Perlin notes that there may have been a peak in the frequency of large majālis meetings in the Deccan. Regional assemblies with many dozens, and in some cases hundreds in attendance, seem to have met most often during the troubled middle and later decades of the seventeenth century as Shivaji fought

[38] Ibid., no. 299, pp. 300–1.

[39] Oturkar, *Peśve-kālīn Sāmājik va Ārthik Patravyavahār*, no. 49, p. 36.

to carve out his own domain. In 1649, for example, 77 named people or individuals identified by their role attended the majālis at which the powerful Jedhe Deshmukh family divided their rights beween their five sons.[40] In 1652, 72 people assembled to resolve arguments over shares in the Kulkarni office of Khanapur and surrounding villages.[41] In 1675, 238 people met to resolve a dispute over the Patil's office in Pali village of Karad province.[42] In 1688, 185 people attended a meeting about the Deshkulkarni and Kulkarni offices of Wai province.[43] In 1725, 80 people attended a meeting about transfer of ownership of the Patil's office in villages of the Maval region.[44] Large assemblies to confirm rights were to be expected as prolonged warfare eroded the power of established families, created opportunities for ambitious new leaders, or simply resulted in the destruction of documents which families then strove to replace. But Perlin suggests that these may also have been occasions when family heads could concert their alliances as political circumstances shifted, calculate their fortunes under different leaders, affirm old loyalties or seek out new allies.[45]

It is difficult to know how far this might have been the case at a large majālis held at Saswad near Pune in May 1657. It met to hear a dispute over the honours and perquisites that came with the headship of the local Mahar caste community. The gathering does, though, demonstrate how a single case could be contested in dramatic fashion through a number of different forums, drawing in a wide range of personnel who constituted a local public for the case. That the rights of Dalit Mahars were given such attention should not surprise us, since the role was an important one in village life, and the perquisites substantial. The Mahar brothers Nagnak bin Kernak and Tukanak bin Dadnak Ranbise claimed exclusive ancestral rights to the hooves and heads of dead cattle, the wheat cakes placed in the fire of the Holi festival, the dress of honour due to the Mahar caste headman, the office of naik (guard) at the local police station, and the right to play music before the houses of the

[40] Gune, *Judicial System*, p. 176.
[41] Joshi and Khare, "Khānāpūr – Kūlkarṇī", pp. 218–21.
[42] Gune, *Judicial System*, pp. 196–8.
[43] Ibid., pp. 205–7.
[44] Ibid., pp. 227–8.
[45] Perlin, "State Formation Re-Considered", pp. 453–5.

village on festival occasions. Their opponent, Mahadnak Sabala, claimed that his own ancestors had always enjoyed a share in those honours and perquisites.

The mahzar judgement in the case described the dispute. It went first to the Mahar caste gota, which was unable to reach a resolution. A majālis then heard the case and reprimanded the two parties for their quarrelsomeness. Unsatisfied, Mahadnak took his suit to the great Maratha military commander Netaji Palkar then commanding the nearby Purandhar fort. Netaji summoned the two brothers to Purandhar and kept them there for a month while the claims were investigated. Confined in the fort, the parties agreed to an ordeal. Mahadnak not only proposed to take the ravā ordeal, but offered to pay a fine of 150 tankas if he failed it. His opponents affirmed that they were willing to subject themselves in the same way: "Nagnak bin Kernak and Tukanak bin Dadnak said they agreed to Mahadnak's offer. All of them were willing to take the ravā ordeal."[46] An instruction from the fort then went back to the village, ordering the ordeal to take place, "because without the ordeal, there can be no decision in the case."[47] No sooner had the state officials issued the instruction than the two brothers retracted, offering instead to take the role of defendant in the ritual, following Mahadnak in "making a shadow" as he walked over the circles drawn before the temple before taking up the ravā in his hands. This was agreed, and a large majālis of some fifty-four individually named witnesses gathered to watch the unwrapping of Mahadnak's hands, after the drama of failed negotiations and last-minute changes of planned ordeal. They included the heads of all of the village's artisan and service castes, leading merchants and money-lenders, as well as provincial-level state officials.[48]

It was not only their size and positioning within a wider social network that enabled the majālis to serve as a kind of public arena. Unsatisfied petitioners could submit a thalpatra, asking to be heard before the majālis of another place. Even more striking in the range of locations

[46] Purandare and Apte, "Hāzīr Majālas Karyāt Sasavad", pp. 60–4. For Dalit castes in this period, see also Kotani, *Western India*, pp. 115–35.

[47] Ibid., p. 63.

[48] Ibid., pp. 61–2.

it brought together is the 1611 case from the Marathi-speaking regions of Bijapur state that has been described by Richard Eaton. The family of a village headman in Satara district quarrelled with the servants of a Sufi shrine in the village over entitlements to shrine offerings. There were murders on both sides, the headman was killed, and his office passed to his son. Eventually, a local Muslim merchant petitioned the region's deputy governor at the district headquarters in Karad, to whom he was related by marriage. He asked him to take action against the headman's family. The deputy governor did so, fining the son heavily and transferring the office to the merchant. The son eventually died, and his son took up the cause. He made a direct approach to the Bijapur court, asking for the headship to be returned to his family. After further manoeuvring on both sides, the case was referred to a majālis back in Karad, which ruled that the headship should indeed be returned. At this, however, the Muslim merchant complained of local bias, and asked that the case be heard this time by a dharmasabhā assembly of religious scholars, and not in Karad, but in Paithan, some 200 miles distant, where the assembly enjoyed an ancient reputation for its experience and fairness. This was agreed, but his petition here was no more successful. As a last throw, the merchant's family challenged their opponents to an ordeal. Interestingly, the pandits in this case felt that there was no need to seek divine forms of proof. They replied: "When there are witnesses and documents in the case, why should we hand out an ordeal?"[49]

For seventeenth-century petitioners, therefore, the majālis, gota, and dharmasabhā offered well-understood local public spaces with their own carefully guarded procedures. In them, local knowledge and oral testimony came together with a highly developed documentary culture. The narratives of the mahzar at once offered histories of the particular rights in question, affirmed general principles as to the basis of rights, and articulated an idealised ethic of solidarity binding together those who held them. Yet in no sense did the majālis offer an exclusive route to justice, or one insulated from wider sets of social relations. Petitioners

[49] The original document is printed in Rajwade, ed., *Marāṭhyānchyā Ithihāsāchī Sādhane*, vol. 15, no. 6, pp. 13–16. There is a partial translation in Smith and Derrett, "Hindu Judicial Administration", pp. 417–23. Eaton's discussion is in Eaton, *A Social History of the Deccan,* pp. 145–50.

could apply to a plurality of authorities. Relations outside the majālis could be mobilised to try to affect its proceedings, or inducements offered to key officials in the hope of evading the scrutiny of gota members and holders of mirās rights. These features sometimes made it difficult for petitioners to gain finality in their suits. On the other hand, a degree of inconclusiveness may have made for better local social cohesion, avoiding the permanent alienation of dissatisfied parties who might still hope for redress in later generations.

Towards the Panchayat: Justice as a Procedure of State

As elsewhere in the subcontinent, the growth of stronger regional successor states from the late seventeenth century slowly cut into these local autonomies. In western India, this process began from mid-century, with Shivaji's drive to restrict the administrative and tax-related powers of regional and village headmen, and to reward loyal servants with cash grants rather than permanent alienations of land.[50] Maratha defeats at the hands of Mughal forces after Shivaji's death, and the twenty years of Maratha civil war that followed reversed these efforts at state-building. However, the emergence from 1714 of the ambitious Bhat family from the Konkan as ministers to the Maratha kings at their Satara court inaugurated a new drive to take closer control over the administrative and revenue-gathering structures of a Maratha state now with major North Indian military ambitions. It was in this context that we see, from the early decades of the eighteenth century, a move towards the smaller body of the "panchayat" ("council of five"), composed usually of between three and fifteen members or panchas, convened ad hoc for each case.[51]

In some respects, the panchayat continued the older practices of the

[50] Kulkarni, *Maharashtra*, pp. 30–2; Gordon, *The Marathas*, pp. 85–7; Heravadkar, ed., *Shiva Chhatrapatīnche Charitra: Sabhāsad Bakhar*, pp. 21–38.

[51] The term "panchayat" itself seems to have had a long tradition of use in the subcontinent as one of a number of older Sanskrit-based generic terms – pāñca-maṇḍaḷī, śreṇi, gaṇ, kulāni – used to describe tribunals of different kinds: Kane, *History of Dharmaśāstra*, vol. 3, pp. 280–1. See also the suggestion of Sen, *Administrative System of the Marathas*, pp. 565–7.

majālis. Suitors still approached state officials or senior men of the village or caste to ask for the arbitration of a panchayat. Its mechanisms for summoning witnesses and examining testimony continued the practice of the majālis. Like the mahzar, its document of decree contained the original petition, the evidence given by witnesses, a listing of documents presented, and the eventual judgment. Like the majālis, panchayats met in a wide range of venues. Those that went before the most senior judges in Pune assembled in a variety of central venues. Some of their business was conducted in the halls of the peshwa's palace at Shanvarwada, some in or near local temples, and some in the homes of senior judges themselves.[52] Panchayats held in the localities met under the direction and at the convenience of the senior community leaders appointed to conduct them.

However, there were also very significant differences which bore critically on the panchayat's potential as the focus for a local public. The panel of panchas was made up of the petitioners' nominees on each side, usually friends or knowledgeable community seniors. Members of the wider gota and local mirāsdārs had no automatic right to attend. Where the petitioners could not agree on the membership, local state officials selected the panchas and were themselves an essential part of the proceedings. The panchayat received much more of its evidence in the form of written testimony, often sent by witnesses from a considerable distance. In his own early account of the panchayat, Elphinstone noted that "accounts and other written evidence were called for after examination of the parties, and likewise oral evidence when written failed; but a great preference was given to the evidence of written documents." As we shall see, much of the investigative work of the panchayat was done by correspondence, and witnesses questioned on the statements they had submitted, or on statements submitted by others not present.

What was missing here was the majālis' broad community attend-

[52] See, for example, the panchayat held in 1779–80 to resolve the disputed adoption case of the important Chaskar banking family. The proceedings, from scrutiny of the evidence to examination of witnesses, were conducted in a variety of different venues in the peshwa's palace, including the temple to Sri Omkaresvara and the judge's own residence. See Rajwade, ed., *Marāṭhyānchya Itihāsāchī Sādhane*, vol. 11, no. 1, pp. 11–20.

ance, as of right, by local caste and community heads, and local people who themselves held rights of the kind under discussion, including the entitlement to assent to, with individual sign or signature, the verdict of the assembly. Without this broader attendance in person, the proceedings of the panchayat developed a different quality, with a more business-like judicial focus on the succession of documents and witnesses brought before it. As we shall see below, its document of judgment reflected this difference. It still contained the same essential elements as the mahzar. However, the mahzar's character as the record of a drama, in which witnesses and audience were all present at the same occasion, was subtly weakened. The judgment of the panchayat was presented rather as a seamless narrative of witnesses questioned and documents scrutinised.

The material documentary form of this judgment also differed. The panchayat's detailed written record, taken down by village officers, was termed a sārāṁśa ("essence of the judgement"). Its accuracy was certified by the recording village officers, not by the authority of the individual panchas who were not usually named in the sārāṁśa. Like the mahzar, a copy of the sārāṁśa was retained in the district revenue office or, in important cases, in the archives of the Pune court. However, it was only when the sārāṁśa was recast as an official decree, a nivāḍapatra ("letter of decision"), with royal seal and endorsements of the state officials responsible for levying fees and fines, that it became an instrument of executive authority. The nivāḍapatra was thus essentially the sārāṁśa, but now issued as a document of state. The deliberations of gathered mirāsdārs and heads of villages standing in witness to a local decision no longer gave it its authority, but rather these forms of state affirmation.[53]

A variety of pressures shaped the move towards the panchayat. The form of the majālis itself seems to have declined in prestige. The signatories to a "letter of purpose" (nischayapatra), written in June 1726, observed something of this process. The letter concerned affairs within the Pathane Prabhu community in the important port towns of Cheul and Revdanda to the south of Bombay. The letter seems to have been more of a signed appeal about affairs within the com-

[53] Gune, *Judicial System*, pp. 49–50, 83–6.

munity, intended for circulation rather than part of a formal judicial procedure. The signatories lamented the decline in recent years of mutual respect within the community, and particularly the attitude of its younger members to established legal procedures. "They have no regard any more for senior people in the community. Even the prestige of the majālis has disappeared."[54] It is possible that this perception of declining importance may have been connected with the diminishing status under Maratha rule of the Qazi and other Muslim state officials who had earlier supervised the majālis, and now found their role contracting to one of supervision of the religious and judicial needs of local Muslim communities only.[55] The creation from the early eighteenth century of new cadres of Brahman regional heads and revenue collectors vested with judicial responsibilities and accountable directly to Shahu's powerful peshwa ministers may also have drawn authority away from the majālis.[56] There is also evidence of a new consciousness of the authority of panchas themselves, both as defenders of correct judicial procedure, but also, in some cases, as usurpers of older rights whose authority was uncertain.

Changing priorities at the centre may also have contributed to the panchayat's eclipse of the majālis. Its multiple sites for appeal and sometimes indefinitely deferred conclusions may have become increasingly uncongenial to the Maratha state, given its need for reliable revenue streams and a stable regime of property rights. In addition, some outside the peshwa state's elite circle of banking and military families did not wholly accept either its displacement of the Maratha royal family, or the peshwa's own family as impeccable Brahmans.[57] The death of the Maratha Raja Shahu II in 1749, and the transfer of effective power from Satara to the peshwa's court at Pune, was therefore accompanied by fresh attempts to bring judicial processes more directly under the control of what eventually emerged at the "huzoor panchayat" ("pan-

[54] *Bhārat Itihās Samshodhak Maṇḍaḷ Quarterly*, vol. 28, nos 3–4, January–April 1948, no. 31, pp. 32–4. I thank Amol Bankar for sharing this material with me.

[55] Gune, *Judicial System*, p. 24.

[56] For these changes in Maratha administration, see Kulkarni, *The Marathas*, pp. 146–8; Gordon, *The Marathas*, pp. 139–43.

[57] See the observations in Hamilton, *A Geographical, Statistical and Historical Description of Hindostan*, p. 197.

chayat of the state"). It was based at the Pune court, with a standing staff of scribes and record keepers to assist in its work. However, the shift was to be a slow and partial one, the panchayat emerging within the framework of and alongside the older bodies.

The Panchayat and Its "Publics"

What, then, can the documentary form and narratives of the panchayat tell us about its effect on the public dimensions of petitioning identified above? The panchayat convened in June 1723 to hear a case relating to the important Gijare family of Brahmans offers some insights. It is worth looking at this case in some detail to get a sense of the tenor of its proceedings. The nivāḍapatra represented these as an unbroken narrative stream, as the panchas examined one submitted document after another, with brief reported intermissions for the questioning of witnesses.

Two branches of the family were involved. Sadashivbhat Gijare complained that Narayanbhat and Gopalbhat Gijare had denied him his rightful enjoyment of the perquisites attached to the role of priests to the astrologer and accountant families serving across five villages in the district of Karad. The case was complex because there were many Gijare brothers, and branches of the family scattered across towns and villages of the district. The business of the panchayat opened with presentation of the written statements of each party. Sadashiv affirmed that he, Narayan, and Gopal shared a common ancestor in Ramesvara, to whom the rights in question had originally belonged. From Ramesvara's three sons had descended the present three branches of the family, who currently lived in Wai, Karad, and Dushere, respectively. Sadashiv himself belonged to the Wai branch of the family, and claimed that this link entitled him to a portion of the rights in question. However, his forebears had given the original documents of right to other family members for safekeeping during a visit to Banaras, and now the documents could not be traced. In their own written statement, Narayan and Gopal, who belonged to the Karad branch of the family, asked Sadashiv to produce evidence to support his claim.[58]

The panchas then questioned both parties in person, and also

[58] Rajwade, ed., *Marāṭhyānchyā Itihāsāchī Sādhane*, vol. 21, no. 111, pp. 117–36.

asked Sadashiv to produce copies of the papers, and witnesses to his claims. A further written statement from Sadashiv followed, stating that copies of the papers had been given to two relatives, Moresvara and Pilambha, now deceased. The panchayat asked Babdev, the son of Moresvara, to submit a katba – a sworn written statement – which formed the next item examined by the panchas. The statement confirmed that his late father did have papers, "but I do not have copies of those papers, or of papers from his hands."[59] The panchayat then questioned Narayan and Gopal about their claims, and specified the papers from that side of the family they wished to examine. Further statements from witnesses in favour of Sadashiv arrived, but the witnesses themselves did not appear. The panchas asked for and received additional written statements from descendants of other sons of Ramesvara, the original ancestor. One statement contained a family tree showing the three sons of Ramesvara and their descendants, and affirmed that Sadashiv did not share this ancestry. Another descendant, Vishvanath, reported that he had gone to Wai to consult his grandmother, Kashibai, about the family tree, but she had known only that there were branches of the family in Wai, Karad, and Mahuli, but "the infirmity of age" made it difficult to confirm the connection between them.[60]

Further written testimony followed from different branches of the family, some of whom were called in for questioning. Sadashiv's relatives supplied written evidence, one affirming that he had seen family papers that looked like astrologers' charts, rolled up in a bundle, another that he thought he saw his late father's handwriting on some papers, but did not see them close up enough to read what they said. The narrative of the nivāḍapatra continued. "Questioned, one said, 'I do not know anything at all. The handwriting is not ours, and I do not remember anything.' The second gave witness that 'Papers were given, but I do not know what they were, because I did not see them'."[61] Asked for his written testimony, the revenue officer of the region sent the panchas further documents relevant to the case, but suggested that a meeting of the caste gota be called to determine the question of descent. The parties to the case duly submitted written confirmation that they were content with the place nominated for the gota. The nivāḍapa-

59 Ibid., pp. 122–3.
60 Ibid., pp. 127–8.
61 Ibid., pp. 128–9.

tra gave no details of the gota's proceedings, but reproduced the family tree that its members agreed to be correct. This showed the relation between the Karad, Wai, and Dushere branches of the family descended from Ramesvara, to which Sadashiv's line was not connected. In further questioning, the panchas declared that it was doubtful that Sadashiv's witnesses could really have recognised copies of the lost documents from a distance, and again ordered him to supply documentary proofs of his claims.

On his failing to do so, the nivāḍapatra narrated the verdict of the panchas. They declared Sadashiv's claims to be unfounded. The real descendants of Ramesvara had denied that he was any brother of theirs. Such papers as he had produced were forgeries. The witnesses he had produced "said in front of you, that they did not know anything."[62] The panchas ordered him therefore to produce a letter acknowledging his defeat. The nivāḍapatra recorded that Sadashiv had promised to come back that evening to write the letter.

However, Sadashiv clearly had one last throw. The nivāḍapatra's narrative continued. Instead of coming back to write his letter, Sadashiv had journeyed instead to see the senior judge at the Satara court, and persuaded him to ask the panchas to transfer the case to a different venue for a further hearing. Their reply reflected their sense of their independence of the state, and their commitment to proper judicial process:

> We are not officials of the dewan. He has not taken proper statements from the parties or agreements to abide by the verdict. We ourselves do not have any vested interest in the case. We asked both parties to the dispute whether they would accept the verdict in this place of our meeting, or whether they wanted the dispute heard in a different place. Both parties told the panchayat very sincerely that they accepted the place appointed, and gave us a written undertaking that they would abide by the verdict given here.

Sadashiv's last throw having failed, the panchas once more returned their verdict in favour of the brothers Narayan and Gopal. The nivāḍapatra was issued back at the Satara court, in the presence of some twenty-six district, town, and village level officers. Interest-

[62] Ibid., p. 135.

ingly, this meeting validating the proceedings of the panchayat referred to itself as a a majālis, perhaps reflecting still something of the prestige of that body.[63]

What kind of a public can we see gathered round the panchayat in this example? With its greater reliance on written evidence, succession of witnesses, and detachment from local communities of rights-holders, the panchayat lost something of the majālis' capacity to affirm a collective oral memory through a single meeting. The Brahman caste gota remained an active presence in this institutional landscape, convened when the panchas found themselves unable to ascertain the relationships between widely dispersed branches of the family. Yet its role was advisory, a guide to the panchayat rather than a source of authority in its own right. The nivāḍapatra, while valuable for the judgment it conveyed and its marks of royal approval, was no longer a material expression of the consent of local communities of rights-holders, a tangible fragment of the public they represented. With its audience restricted to a panel of panchas questioning a succession of witnesses, the panchayat also did not seem to prompt witnesses into general rhetoric about the moral norms of brotherhood. If any were so prompted, fewer people heard them, and their remarks did not appear in the smooth narrative flow of the nivāḍapatra. The nivāḍapatra did contain an affirmation of the moral standing of the panchayat, but it lay in the declaration of the panchas themselves, in which they constituted themselves very much as the principal defenders of community rights and proper procedure.

If these elements of a local and face-to-face public were weakened, however, the very documentary emphasis of the panchayat drew local communities into a wider network of communication composed of flows of documents. Documents themselves emerged out of meetings and conversations as witnesses constructed their testimony. State officials, witnesses, and widely dispersed family members were linked as they sought to reconstruct local histories, speculated about the role of different parties in the case, and heard news about the panchayat's proceedings. Indeed, the sheer proliferation of written evidence called for seems itself surprising, given that the complainant Sadashiv appears to have had a relatively weak case. Echoing the older practice

[63] Ibid., p. 117.

of the majālis, it may be that the very exhaustiveness of such enquiries was intended to help reconcile unsuccessful litigants to their defeat.

Other cases from these decades illustrate a similar blending of old and new forms. In October 1733, Keroji and Mankoji, representing two branches of a Maratha Patil family with shares in the headship of Sirsophal village near Satara, sought a hearing. At issue was the relative seniority of three brothers of the family from which the disputants were descended, and the associated rights and perquisites. The Satara court ordered an investigation. The gota of the village took the leading role, examined the family trees, ordered the two parties to wash themselves in the water of the temple well and then state truthfully which brother was senior. Mankoji failed to follow the instructions, saying that his claims dated back to shares established early in the life of the village, and before the lifetimes of any witness still living. Pressed for the ancient mahzar that would substantiate his claim, he produced papers which were then formally scrutinised by a majālis, but one led by senior men who were referred to as panchas. Led by the panchas, the majālis determined that the seals and signatures on the document were falsified or absent. It lacked the proper Persian signature and seal of the Muslim state official of the time, and the names of the witnesses were incorrectly recorded.

Interestingly, both the panchas and Mankoji seem to have been sensitive to the more narrowly based authority of the assembly. Recording that Mankoji's document was forged, the panchas pointed out to Mankoji that the pānḍhari – the "whole village community" – had also given witness that Mankoji's family was the junior descendant. Mankoji himself then seems to have challenged the authority of the panchas. "At this, Mankoji said, 'So you will follow what these five people say?' The panchas said to him, 'The pānḍhari and the brothers have enough weight between them. Keroji's house is senior, and Mankoji's is junior'.". The narrative of the case, contained in the final judgment, described how the panchas had made their report to the Satara court, and a vatanpatra – a document of right to the village office – duly issued in favour of Keroji.[64]

Even as the new form of the panchayat became routinised in local

[64] Gune, *Judicial System*, Appendix B I, no. 13, pp. 288–91.

practice, other pressures worked against the attempt to focus judicial decisions on a smaller group of community leaders. The spread of Maratha power into central and northern India meant more, not fewer, authorities to whom discontented litigants could turn. Greater dependence on documentary testimony meant increased risk of forgery. The nivāḍapatra of a panchayat held in June 1765, four years after the Marathas' disastrous defeat at the battle of Panipat outside Delhi, recorded a dispute between the Brahman Garge and Mule families. With its references to "bundles" of accompanying documentary evidence, it reveals the extent to which this particular panchayat depended on written evidence sent in to it. At the same time, the channels through which written information about these and other Maratha rights now flowed spanned the subcontinent, connecting powerful families, state officials, and local village communities. When influence across long-distance networks counted, elite families such as these naturally enjoyed an advantage.

The nivāḍapatra recorded that brothers of the Brahman Mule family had come to the Pune court and complained that the Garge family were attempting to usurp their rights as priests and dharmādhikārīs in the village of Tasgaon outside Pune. Sadashivrao Bhau, nephew of the peshwa, had heard the case and decided in favour of the Mules. But the Garges disregarded the verdict, gave out false information about the judgement, and forcibly assumed control of the Mules' offices. So, the nivāḍapatra continued, voiced in the narrative of the Mules:

> We went to see the Bhausaheb in Hindustan. We told him that Garge had given out false information about the judgment he had earlier given (bundle 2) and seized our property. So the Bhausaheb gave us a letter for Nana Saheb peshwa, saying that in the judgement given, Garge had put forward a false case. He gave us a written affirmation that the Mules should be allowed to resume their property, and we came back to Pune. Then Nana Saheb peshwa died. But the Swami saw the letters and issued instructions to the revenue officers and the villagers that Garge had been found false and should be made to release the property, and the Mules allowed to resume their rights. So then Garge approached Mahadji Shinde and made a complaint to him, and also demanded a fee of 200 rupees from the village Patil (bundle 3). The villagers said that the Mules would have to pay this fee. Then Garge took us before Mahadji Shinde, and demanded

> with menaces that we should give him our letters from the Sarkar. Then an order from the Sarkar went to Shinde's dewan to say that Garge had no case, and the fee the Mules had paid should be returned to them.[65]

At this point, the Mule's narrative continued, Garge resorted to another tactic. "He wrote out a document admitting his defeat. He said, 'I will make a copy of the papers and give it to you.' Then he took our papers to make copies of them, but instead of returning them, he tore them all up."[66] The Mules pointed out another difficulty: "In his impudence, Garge would not write a letter admitting defeat. An order can be issued to him, but it is not possible to punish a Brahman."[67] Eventually, as in the Gijare case, the panchas retreated to the older methods of taking witness evidence. Officials summoned the villagers and asked them, under oath, who their hereditary priest really was. The villagers testified that the office belonged to the Mule family, and wrote out a document to confirm the fact. With this confirmed, the nivāḍapatra concluded with a brief declaration in favour of the Mule family.[68]

The complex history of the Padhye family referred to above further reveals the publics that now gathered around the panchayat, connected by documentary flows as well as by reported news, here of sensational events connected with the panchayat's proceedings. With the coming of the peshwa government, the Joshis once more raised their challenge to the Padhyes' rights, but now, perhaps, with greater hope, since they were family relations of the peshwas. We have two accounts of what happened: one in a nivāḍapatra that was the outcome of a panchayat of 1763, and another in a later Padhye family history. According to the lengthy narrative of the nivāḍapatra, the peshwa Madhavrao Ballal convened a panchayat at the Pune court itself. The panchayat asked the Padhye family for documentary evidence of their claim. Disputing the panchayat's competence, the family head Kashi Padhye refused to attend or to produce their documents, asserting "You have no capacity to give a just judgment in this matter."

The panchayat met anyway. Fourteen people, a combination of

[65] Ibid., p. 313.

[66] Idem.

[67] Idem.

[68] Idem.

state officials and holders of mirās rights, attested in favour of the Joshis, who seem to have had two star witnesses. One was a goldsmith, Ramshet Sonar, who described how Kashi Padhye had taken him to his home back in the Konkan.

> He told me he wanted me to engrave a copper plate. I said to him, 'I am a poor man, I can't do something like that.' Padhye said, 'Don't be afraid. Our copper plate is very old, and it has worn out. I just want to make a new copy.' So saying, he brought a new copper plate three hands long and one hand span wide and gave it to me. Then, in a private place, he would write four or five lines neatly in ink on the copper plate, and I would engrave it. After 10 or 15 days, three letters in all had been written and engraved in this way.

Seals were added by the goldsmith, and he was rewarded for his work with gifts of cloth. Another witness, Bal Joshi, testified that "Kashi Padhye asked me if I would calculate what day of the week did the third day of the dark half of Vaishakh month fall on in the sake year of 106. I did the calculation, and told him. This was about 20 years ago." The panchayat decided that Kashi Padhye had forged his documents. The Joshis were entered in the Pune records rightful owners.[69]

But the family history presents a further narrative which demonstrates the flow of reported news that accompanied the movement of documents. After Kashi Padhye's refusal to appear, state officials arrived at the Padhye home in the Konkan. They found a servant, Govind, and demanded the family's copper plate and paper documents. Govind protested that he did not know where they were. He had heard that some were destroyed during local warfare on the coast some years before, and others sent back to Pune. The peshwa's men took him out into the forest and beat him, then imprisoned him in nearby Torna fort. News of his maltreatment reached the Padhye brothers in Pune. At this point, the peshwa was in camp on his way to Aurangabad. The brothers pursued him and staged a fast at the door to his tent. The peshwa released the servant, but still demanded the documents. The brothers retorted "You have already committed violence at our house in pursuit of these documents. If we bring them to the court, you will seize them

[69] Rajwade, "Pādhye va Joshi Assal Nivādapatra – sake 1688".

from us."[70] The peshwa disregarded their complaints and went ahead with the panchayat that transferred the Padhye's rights to the Joshi family. The end was dramatic. The elder brother Anant went back to the Konkan and set fire to the family home. He brought some of the ashes back with him to Pune, where he accosted the peshwa one day riding in his palanquin. He threw the ashes into the palanquin with the words "You have brought ruin on our house, and in the same way will your whole lineage be destroyed."[71] As a renunciate from his new base in the shrine town of Pandharpur, Anant and his successors remained persistent opponents of the peshwa's family, drawing a wide local following and finding support from the powerful Shinde family.

By the 1790s, the form of the panchayat had become very much the centrepiece in the judicial administration of the Maratha state. Its position emerges clearly in a Marathi report, written sometime after 1795, contained in the judicial records of the Pune court. There is no indication as to the author. However, the report offered a remarkable survey of the Maratha judicial apparatus between 1774 and 1795. These were years when the Brahman statesman Nana Phadnis led the administration, and its chief officer of justice was the formidable Ramsastri Prabhune.[72] The report described the authority vested in officials at different levels of regional administration empowered to hear petitions about mirās rights and to issue decrees with official seals. It laid out procedures for receiving suits, summoning the parties, receiving testimony, scrutinising documents, issuing judgments, handing down punishments of different kinds, keeping records, and maintaining a staff of knowledgeable officials. It described the central role of the Pune panchayat in these processes:

> Sometimes a senior judge of the court would himself sit in on hearings. Once all enquiries were completed, and written agreements to abide by the decision were taken from all the parties, the panchas and the senior judge would sit. Once the parties had given all the testimony they wished, the panchas would come to a determination they considered just, and they

[70] Pangarkar, *Moropant*, p. 109.

[71] Ibid., p. 110.

[72] For Ramsastri's period as chief law officer at the Pune court, see Athavale, *Rām Śāstrī Prabhuṇe*.

would issue their sārāṁśa. The judge did not sit alone to dispense justice.[73]

This Marathi report proved remarkably influential. By 1819, Elphinstone had assumed the governorship of Bombay. One of the subordinates commissioned to gather information about Maratha judicial institutions was N.J. Lumsden, who submitted his report, "Some account of the manner in which justice was administered in the Poona State during the ascendancy of Nana Furnavees", on 24 January 1819.[74] Comparison between the two texts reveals that Lumsden based his account very largely on the Marathi document, which may itself have been written in answer to Lumsden's enquiries. Lumsden's account provided much of the basis for Elphinstone's own description of the panchayat's working within the territories of the peshwa.[75]

As Jaffe has demonstrated, Lumsden was one of a group of collectors and political agents whom Elphinstone tasked with gathering information on the workings of the panchayat in the Maratha country.[76] These officers consulted three different pandits with experience of the panchayat. They were named in the officers' reports as Raggopunt Tuttee, Ramesshur, and Nucca Ram Pandit, and provided a range of different answers to Elphinstone's questions.[77] Like the author of the Marathi report that Lumsden used, these pandits also emphasised the central role that the Pune state and its officials took in the workings of the panchayat, but also the difficulties the officials sometimes encountered in controlling its deliberations. Asked how members of the panchayat were selected, "Raggopunt" explained that they were selected by government, but "liable to be challenged by the parties." In cases of disputes over debt, "Ramesshur" described how frustrated creditors had

73 Sardesai, ed., *Selections from the Peshwa Daftar*, vol. 45, no. 48, pp. 134–41.

74 Lumsden, "Report on the Judicial Administration of the Peshwas", pp. 372–84.

75 Elphinstone, *Report on the Territories*, pp. 76–88.

76 Jaffe, *Ironies of Colonial Governance*, pp. 21–47.

77 'Notes, Memorandum and Relative Letters regarding the Powers of Patails and Punchayets', Mountstuart Elphinstone Papers, India Office Records, ms. Eur. F. 88/408, ff. 86r–100r.

sometimes to take the law into their own hands when panchayats were "too stubborn to be guided" in their proceedings.[78]

Some of the limitations in the more centralised form of the panchayat may even have been reflected in popular usage of the term. The young linguist and army officer James Molesworth, who began in 1818 to compile one of the first Marathi dictionaries, gave its conventional meaning as an assembly of arbitration. However, he also provided some of its popular usages. A panchayat was the assembly of arbitrators or the deliberations of such an assembly, but was used freely to denote "a state of exigency or of bewilderment or of difficulty in general"; "Blabbing abroad or making to be publicly talked about"; "Vain or needless discussing or objecting".[79]

Conclusion

It seems clear, then, that petitionary cultures in pre-colonial India have much to offer social and political history. Here, the deep penetration of paper use and allied bureaucratic conventions created a set of linked small publics. They developed in the space between the official and the familial, and gathered around the corporate bodies described in this essay. The petitioners who came before them shared a deep concern with rights, a rhetoric about the brotherhood of rights-holders, acute sensitivity to the importance of procedure, and sharp awareness of the field of social relations through which all avenues to justice ran. The eighteenth-century emergence of the panchayat weakened the broad community base of these corporate bodies and made the authority of their judgments contingent on ratification by the state. However, the panchayat did not snuff out these local publics. Rather, its greater focus on written testimony connected them to the wider social networks through which such documents flowed as they were constructed for judicial use, their contents shared as reported news between families, fellow villagers, other witnesses, and state officials. Reflecting the greatly expanded horizons of the peshwa state, such social networks could extend well beyond its boundaries, to

[78] Ibid., f. 86r and ff. 99r–99v.

[79] Molesworth, *A Dictionary, Marāṭhi and English*, p. 482.

Maratha domains in the north and Maratha armies as they campaigned there.

In the state of our current knowledge, it is difficult to know how far the changing shape of petitionary "publics" identified here occurred in other polities across the subcontinent. The Maratha country was certainly not alone in developing the rich ecology of local corporate institutions and judicial procedures described here.[80] However, further research is needed to ascertain how far their petitionary cultures reveal elements of a recognisable "public". Particular exigencies of the peshwa state may have shaped the panchayat and its "publics". As the peshwa government sought to concentrate authority on the Pune court and its cadres of administrative servants, the panchayat may have seemed a natural development. At the same time, the emergence of alternative sources of Maratha power in central and northern India lengthened the lines of communication along which judicial documents flowed, and expanded the "publics" that could gather around a particular petition.

In the early-nineteenth-century systems that Elphinstone observed, the panchayat was still very much a part of the broader judicial structure, although petitioners with influence and resources could still find multiple arenas and sources of authority to which they could appeal. In his prescriptions for the future, he argued that

> Our principal instrument must continue to be the Punchayet, and that must continue to be exempt from all new forms, interference and regulation on our part. Such forms would throw over this well-known institution that mystery which enables litigious people to employ Courts of Justice as engines of intimidation against their neighbours, and which renders necessary a class of lawyers, who among the Natives are the great fomenters of disputes.[81]

He was successful in this argument for retention of the panchayat as the most local level of justice in the new administrative order of the Bombay government. The Elphinstone Code of 1827 created a three-tiered judicial system, composed of a Sadar Adalat, a Zillah Adalat,

[80] See, for example, Davis, "Intermediate Realms of Law", pp. 92–117; Roy, *Company of Kinsmen*, pp. 45–73; Sahai, *Politics of Patronage and Protest*, pp. 89–123.

[81] Elphinstone, *Report on the Territories*, pp. 99–100.

and "Native Commissioners of Justice" to oversee what Elphinstone hoped would be a continuing panchayat system of an informal kind. However, this attempt at preservation proved difficult to implement. As James Jaffe has shown, officials within Elphinstone's government sought to reform and regulate the operation of the panchayat system throughout during the 1820s, limiting its remit to small and local civil disputes, introducing penalties for delay, and routinising its proceedings to make them more "efficient". As a consequence, fewer and fewer litigants chose to take their disputes to a panchayat, preferring instead to take them to British courts with their greater emphasis on the summary enforcement of decisions.[82] As the peshwas themselves had found, the creation of higher levels of authority in a formal court judiciary meant that authority leaked away from these local structures, in offering to dissatisfied petitioners alternative and higher levels of appeal.

By mid-century, the form of the panchayat had so dwindled in its significance that the Indian Law Commission, reporting in 1856 on the future development of colonial India's judiciary, declared that outside the three Presidency towns, India had in effect no functioning civil law at all, beyond the "special laws of their own" that Hindus and Muslims respectively were deemed to possess.[83] The spaces for petition opened up in the newly codified judicial landscape of the 1860s had their own new protocols, and in them success relied not so much on the ability to appeal to local solidarities, and more on the mastery of the technical language of colonial law. The panchayat itself, meanwhile, also acquired its own new future. Successive generations of colonial sociologists and nationalist intellectuals, from Henry Maine to Gandhi, reimagined and appropriated it to their own visions of India's ancient traditions of local self-government.[84]

References

Alam, Muzaffar, *The Languages of Political Islam in India* (Delhi: Permanent Black, 2004).

[82] Jaffe, *Ironies of Colonial Governance*, pp. 74–6.

[83] *Parliamentary Papers, Second Report of Her Majesty's Commissioners*, vol. 25, no. 2036, p. 7.

[84] Jaffe, *Ironies of Colonial Governance*, pp. 209–91.

Athavale, Sadashiv, *Rām Śāstrī Prabhuṇe, Charitra va Patre* (Pune: Shrividya Press, 1988).

Bailey, Raymond C., *Popular Influence on Public Policy: Petitioning in Eighteenth Century Virginia* (Westport, Connecticut: Greenwood Press, 1979).

Ballhatchet, K.A., *Social Policy and Social Change in Western India, 1817–1830* (London: Oxford University Press, 1958).

Bayly, C.A., *Empire and Information. Intelligence Gathering and Social Communication in India, 1780–1870* (Cambridge: Cambridge University Press, 1996).

Beales, Derek, "Joseph II, Petitions and the Public Sphere", in Hamish Scott and Brendan Simms, eds, *Cultures of Power in Europe During the Long Eighteenth Century* (Cambridge: Cambridge University Press, 2007), pp. 249–68.

Bendrey, V.S., ed., *Mahārāṣṭretihāsachī Sādhane*, 2 vols (Pune: Mumbai Marathi Grantha Sangrahalaya, 1966).

Benton, Lauren, *Law and Colonial Cultures: Legal Regimes in World History, 1400–1900* (New York and Cambridge: Cambridge University Press, 2002).

Bhārat Itihās Samshodhak Maṇḍaḷ Quarterly, vol. 28, nos 3–4 (Pune: Bharat Itihas Samshodhak Mandal, January–April 1948).

Chatterjee, Kumkum, "History as Self-Representation: The Recasting of a Political Tradition in Late Eighteenth Century Eastern India", *Modern Asian Studies*, vol. 32, no. 4, 1998, pp. 913–48.

Chatterjee, Nandini, "Mahzar-namas in the Mughal and British Empires: The Uses of an Indo-Islamic Legal Form", *Comparative Studies in Society and History*, vol. 58, no. 2, 2016, pp. 379–406.

———, "Lawforms: Digitised Legal Documents from the Early Modern Persianate World", available at https://humanities-research.exeter.ac.uk/lawforms/index.html, accessed 29 August 2023.

Choksey, R.D., ed., *Twilight of the Maratha Raj 1818* (Poona: Sakal Printing Press, 1976).

Cohn, Bernard, *Colonialism and Its Forms of Knowledge: The British in India* (Princeton, NJ: Princeton University Press, 1996).

da Costa, Ravi, "Identity, Authority and the Moral Worlds of Indigenous Petitions", *Comparative Studies in Society and History*, vol. 46, no. 3, 2006, pp. 669–98.

Davis, Donald, "Intermediate Realms of Law: Corporate Groups and Rulers in Medieval India", *Journal of the Economic and Social History of the Orient*, vol. 48, no. 1, 2005, pp. 92–117.

Deshpande, Prachi, *Scripts of Power: Writing, Language Practices, and Cultural History in Western India* (New Delhi: Permanent Black, 2023).

Eaton, Richard M., *A Social History of the Deccan, 1300–1761: Eight Indian Lives* (Cambridge: Cambridge University Press, 2005).

Eisenstadt, Shmuel M., and Wolfgang Schluchter, eds, "Early Modernities", *Daedalus*, vol. 127, no. 3, 1998.

Elphinstone, Mountstuart, *Report On The Territories Conquered From The Paishwa* (Calcutta: Government Gazette Press, 1821).

———, Papers, India Office Records, ms. Eur. F. 88/408.

Franks, H. George, *Panchayets Under the Peshwas* (Poona: Poona Star Press, 1930).

Gordon, Stewart, *The Marathas 1600–1818* (Cambridge: Cambridge University Press, 1993).

Guha, Sumit, "Speaking Historically: The Changing Voices of Historical Narration in Western India", *American Historical Review*, vol. 109, no. 4, 2004, pp. 1084–1103.

———, "Transitions and Translations: Regional Power and Vernacular Identity in the Dakhan, 1500–1800", *Comparative Studies of South Asia, Africa and the Middle East*, vol. 24, no. 2, 2004, pp. 23–31.

———, "Bad Language and Good Language: Lexical Awareness in the Cultural Politics of Peninsular India, *c.* 1300–1800", in Sheldon Pollock, ed., *Forms of Knowledge in Early Modern Asia* (Durham and London: Duke University Press, 2011), pp. 49–68.

Gune, V.T., *The Judicial System of the Marathas* (Poona: Deccan College Research Institute, 1953).

Hamilton, Walter, *A Geographical, Statistical and Historical Description of Hindostan* (John Murray: London, 1820).

Heravadkar, R.V., ed., *Śiva Chhatrapatīnche Charitra: Sabhāsad Bakhar* (Pune: Vhins Press, 2002).

Hoexter, Miriam, Shmuel N. Eisenstadt, and Nehemia Levtzion, eds, *The Public Sphere in Muslim Societies* (Albany: State University of New York Press, 2002).

Jaffe, James, *Ironies of Colonial Governance. Law, Custom and Justice in Colonial India* (Cambridge: Cambridge University Press, 2015).

Joshi, S.N., and G.H. Khare, "Bāvadekar Amātya", in S.N. Joshi and G.H. Khare, eds, *Shiva Charitra Sāhitya*, vol. 3 (Pune: Bharat Itihas Samshodhak Mandal, 1930), pp. 37–50.

——, "Khānāpūr – Kūlkarṇī", in S.N. Joshi and G.H. Khare, eds, *Shiva Charitra Sāhitya*, vol. 3 (Pune: Bharat Itihas Samshodhak Mandal, 1930), pp. 218–21.

Kane, P.V., *History of Dharmaśāstra*, 5 vols (Poona: Bhandarkar Oriental Research Institute, 1968–77).

Kotani, Hiroyuki, *Western India in Historical Transition* (New Delhi: Manohar, 2002).

Kulkarni, A.R., *Maharashtra in the Age of Shivaji* (Poona: Deshmukh and Co., 1969).

———, *The Marathas* (Pune: Diamond Publications 2008).

Lumsden, N.J., "Report on the Judicial Administration of the Peshwas", 24 January 1819, Deccan Commissioner's Daftar, vol. 95, in V.T. Gune, *Judicial System of the Marathas* (Poona: Deccan College Research Institute, 1953), pp. 372–84.

Molesworth, J.T., *A Dictionary, Marāṭhi and English* (Bombay: Education Society's Press, 1857).

Narayana Rao, Velcheru, David Shulman, and Sanjay Subrahmanyam, "A New Imperial Idiom in the Sixteenth Century: Krishnadevaraya and his Political Theory of Vijayanagara", in Sheldon Pollock, ed., *Forms of Knowledge in Early Modern Asia* (Durham and London: Duke University Press, 2011), pp. 69–114.

Ogborn, Miles, *Indian Ink: Script and Print in the Making of the English East India Company* (Chicago: University of Chicago Press, 2007).

O'Hanlon, Rosalind, "Narratives of Penance and Purification in Western India, *c.* 1650–1850", *Journal of Hindu Studies*, vol. 2, 2009, pp. 48–75.

———, "Speaking from Siva's Temple: Banaras Scholar Households and the Brahman 'Ecumene' of Mughal India", *South Asian History and Culture*, vol. 2, no. 2, 2011, pp. 253–77.

———, "Performance in a World of Paper: Puranic Histories and Social Communication in Early Modern India", *Past and Present*, vol. 219, May 2013, pp. 87–126.

———, Gergely Hidas, and Csaba Kiss, "Discourses of Caste over the Longue Durée: Gopinatha and Social Classification in India, *ca.* 1400–1900", *South Asian History and Culture*, vol. 6, no. 1, January 2015, pp. 102–29.

———, and Christopher Minkowski, "What Makes People Who They Are? Pandit Networks and the Problem of Livelihoods in Early Modern Western India", *Indian Economic and Social History Review*, vol. 45, no. 3, July–September 2008, pp. 381–416.

Oturkar, R.V., *Peśve-kālīn Sāmājik va Ārthik Patravyavahār* (Pune: Bharat Itihas Samshodhak Mandal, 1950).

Pangarkar, L.R., *Moropant: Charitra āṇi Kāvyavivechana* (Mumbai: Hindu Agency Booksellers and Publishers, 1908).

Parliamentary Papers: Second Report of Her Majesty's Commissioners Appointed to Consider the Reform of the Judicial Establishments, Judicial Procedure and Laws of India (London: Her Majesty's Stationery Office, 1856).

Perlin, Frank, "Of White Whale and Countrymen in the Eighteenth-Century Maratha Deccan: Extended Class Relations, Rights and the Problem of Rural Autonomy in the Eighteenth -Century Maratha Deccan", *Journal of Peasant Studies*, vol. 5, no. 2, 1978, pp. 172–237.

———, "State Formation Re-considered", *Modern Asian Studies*, vol. 19, no. 3, 1985, pp. 415–80.

Potdar, D.V., and G.N. Muzumdar, "Golavalīkar-Pādhye", in D.V. Potdar and G.N. Muzumdar, eds, *Shiva Charitra Sāhitya*, vol. 2 (Pune: Bharat Itihas Samshodhak Mandal, 1930), pp. 333–54.

Purandare, K.V., and B.D. Apte, "Hāzīr Majālas Karyāt Sasavad", in K.V. Purandare and B.D. Apte, eds, *Shiva Charitra Sāhitya*, vol. 7 (Pune: Bharat Itihas Samshodhak Mandal, 1938), pp. 60–4.

Rajwade, V.K., "Pādhye va Joshi Assal Nivādapatra – sake 1688", in M.B. Saha and G. Mandake, eds, *Itihāsācharya V. K. Rājavāḍe Samagra Sāhitya*, vol. 11, no. 55, pp. 442–8.

———, ed., *Marāṭhyānchya Itihāsāchī Sādhane*, 22 vols (Pune: Bharat Itihas Samshodhak Mandal, 1898–1926), also available at www.samagrarajwade.com.

Raman, Bhavani, *Document Raj: Writing and Scribes in Early Colonial India* (Chicago and London: University of Chicago Press, 2012).

Roy, Tirthankar, *Company of Kinsmen: Enterprise and Community in South Asian History, 1700–1940* (New Delhi: Oxford University Press, 2010).

Saha, M.B., and G. Mandake, eds, *Itihāsāchārya Vi. Kā. Rājavāḍe Samagra Sāhitya*, 13 vols (Dhule: Rajwade Samshodhan Mandal, 1995–8).

Sahai, Nandita Prasad, *Politics of Patronage and Protest: The State, Society and Artisans in Early Modern Rajasthan* (New Delhi: Oxford University Press, 2006).

Sardesai, G.S., ed., *Selections from the Peshwa Daftar*, 45 vols (Bombay: Government Central Press, 1930–4).

Sen, Surendranath, *The Administrative History of the Marathas* (Calcutta: University of Calcutta Press, 1925).

Smith, Graham, and J. Duncan M. Derrett, "Hindu Judicial Administration in Pre-British Times and Its Lessons for today", *Journal of the American Oriental Society*, vol. 95, no. 3, 1975, pp. 417–23.

Smith, Richard Saumarez, *Rule by Records: Land Registration and Village Custom in Early British Panjab* (Delhi: Oxford University Press, 1996).

Travers, Robert, *Ideology and Empire in Eighteenth Century India: The British in Bengal, 1757–93* (Cambridge: Cambridge University Press, 2008).

van Voss, Lex Heerma, "Petitions in Social History", *International Review of Social History*, vol. 46, 2001, pp. 1–10.

Wilson, Jon E., *The Domination of Strangers: Modern Governance in Eastern India, 1780–1835* (Basingstoke: Palgrave Macmillan, 2008).

Würgler, Andreas, "'Voices from Among the "Silent Masses': Humble Petitions and Social Conflicts in Early Modern Central Europe", *International Review of Social History*, vol. 46, 2001, pp. 11–34.

Zaret, David, *Origins of Democratic Culture: Printing, Petitions, and the Public Sphere in Early-Modern England* (Princeton, N.J: Princeton University Press, 1999).

Index

Names or terms that occur only as passing references have not been included.

Abu al-Fazl 112, 114
Advaita Vedanta 75, 177; Advaitin scholar ascetics 183–4, 186–7, 193–4; "big tent" Hinduism and 97, 197, 352
Ahmadnagar, Nizam Shahi court 274, 319–20
Akbar, emperor 67, 70, 74, 112, 180, 183, 192, 195–7
Ambedkar, Dr Babasaheb 4
Anand 5–16, 379
Arade family 74, 77–8, 88
Aryan invasions, theory of 32–6, 43–4, 381; *see also* Caste
Aurangzeb, emperor 196, 299

Bahmani kingdom 69, 113, 269–70, 280n, 319, 397
Bairy, R. 2
bakhar chronicles, *see* Sabhasad; Kayasthas
Bakker, Hans T. 71n
Banaras
  Bharatendu Harischandra in 26–7
  Brahman ecumene and 68, 74–5, 83
  Brahman migration to 70–4
  Dasnāmī scholar ascetics in 183–97
  Kāśīkhaṇḍa and 71–2, 89–92, 96
  Kavindracaraya Sarasvati in 184, 186–7; Hindu patron 189–91; *Kavīndracandrodaya* 189–9; library of 93; Mughal court and 74–5; source of wealth 195
  Maratha Brahman learning in 74–83, 177–8; move to Maratha courts and 95–7; "southern" learning and 84–5; Sudra ritual and 335–8
  Mughal court and 68, 70, 226–7
  Visvesvara temple and 71, 89–96, 178, 196–7, 235; Mukti mandapam and 71, 91–5, 178, 196, 235, 250, 255
  See also Brahman power
Bapat, Vishnu Bapuji 36–7
Bayly, C.A. 68, 74, 109, 111, 351
Bayly, Susan 9, 352
Bendrey, V.S. 21–2
Benke, Theodore 76, 335–6
Benson, James 84n
Bernier, François 187–8
Bhāgavata Purāṇa 180, 187, 192
Bhagwat, Rajaramsastri 33–4, 43
bhakti, Bharatendu Harischandra and 26; "Brahman double" and 3–4; conservative hostility to 335–6; Eknath and 192; Prarthana Samaj and 33–4; *see also* Brahman power
Bhalekar, Krishnarao 47–8
Bhandare, Shailendra 216n
Bhandarkar, R.G. 33
Bharadvaja scholar family 72, 76, 179
Bhatta scholar lineage (in chronological order)
  Ramesvarabhatta, *f.* of Narayanabhatta, founder of lineage 180–1
  Narayanabhatta, *f.* of Ramakrishnabhatta, rebuilding of Banaras Visvesvara temple and 89; *Tristhalīsetuḥ* guide of 91–2
  Ramakrishnabhatta, *f.* of Dinkarabhatta, caste in the Kaliyuga and 78
  Samkarabhatta, *s.* of Narayanabhatta, Bhatta family history of 81–2;

intermarriage with Kale lineage and 179
Nilakanthabhatta, *s.* of Samkarabhatta, intermarriage with Bharadvaja lineage and 76; nineteenth-century influence of 97; views on scholar family property of 79–80
Dinkarabhatta, *f.* of Gagabhatta, Konkan caste dispute and 181; works on dharma of 239
Gagabhatta, Kayasthas at Shivaji's consecration and 294–9, 338–9; Rajapur assembly and 222–3, 236–40; story of family extinction and 10, 49
Kamalakarabhatta, *s.* of Dinkarabhatta, nineteenth-century influence of 35–7; *Nirṇayasindhuḥ* of 80, 236; Rajapur assembly and 236; *Śūdrakamalākaraḥ* of 164, 258, 277–8, 293–4

Bhavalkar, Keshav Shivram 29, 31
Bhave, Vinoba 51
Bijapur, Adil Shahi court 73, 112, 207–8, 210–11, 222, 234, 243
Botre, S. 52
Brahman identity, caricatures of 26–7, 244; instability of 3; nineteenth-century contests about 32, 38–45, 50–3; popular performance about 11–12, 15–16, 359, 369–72, 374–9, 383–4; social fissions within 221–66, 353–4; struggle to build solidarity and 44, 152, 163, 353; sub-caste, class, and regional differences within 6–8, 68–70, 152–4; *see also* Brahman subcastes
Brahman power
Anglophone education and 24–5
assemblies, Banaras and 88–95, 235–6, 248–51, 364–7; dharmādhikārī office and 222, 236–8, 251, 403–4, 408–9; dharmasabha form of 156–7, 222–3, 236–41; felicitation ceremonies and 189–93; letters issued by 40, 235–6, 353; performance in 178; *see also* paper use
bhakti critiques of 3, 26, 33–4, 69, 177–8, 192–3, 328
Brahman reformism and 28–34, 50–1
caste adjudication and 6–7, 9–12; in *Jātiviveka* 311–39; local influence of 303, 337–9; nineteenth century and 18–23, 36–7, 339–40; Sudra ritual and 10–11, 236, 277–8, 336
intellectual standing and 5–6, 67–8, 177–8, 352–4; new Sanskrit textual genres and 356–7, 359
libraries and 74, 78–9, 179, 356
mobility and 24–8; portable identities and 2, 353, 382; social geographies and 85–9, 184, 228, 235
non-Brahmans and 5, 16–17, 31, 34–6, 45, 302–3, 340–1, 383; non-Brahman elites and 18, 23, 49–51; Vishnusastri Chiplunkar and 46–9; *see also* Bhalekar, Krishnarao, Padwal, Tukaram Tatya, Phule Jotirao
office-holding and 242–5; privileged landed rights and 205–6, 245–8
royal power and 96, 327–9, 341–2; royal ritual and 269–71, 296, 299–301
scholar household and 6; education in 74–83, 159–60; emotional economy of 181–3; food discipline in 181; marriage strategies of 18, 76–7, 155, 179–80, 193; relations with daṇḍī ascetics and 75, 189, 193–4, 231; *see also* Bhatta scholar lineage; libraries
śiṣṭa, idea of 69–70, 85, 94, 190
social prestige and 3, 5, 162–5, 225–7; bodily comportment and 164, 239–41, 244, 252
vakils in Maratha diplomacy and 108–43
See also Banaras; Caste; Maratha empire; Peshwai
Brahman subcastes
Banaras scholar view of 8, 93
histories of 7–8, 224–5, 360; Chitpavan 9, 15–16, 19, 36–9, 48, 52, 157–8,

160, 242–3, 257–9; Deshastha 118, 152, 155–7, 224, 377; Devarukhe/ Devarsi 43–4, 93–5, 248–55, 259; Karhade 74, 94, 230, 245–8; Shenvi Saraswat 38–45, 93–4, 223–4, 230–41; Shukla Yajurvedi 153–4, 156
rivalries between 38–45, 93–5, 228–30, 234–41, 248–56
Sahyādrikhaṇḍa and 11, 15, 34–5, 41–3, 48, 86, 227–31, 259, 360–4, 367–8, 370, 373, 375–9, 381–2
Śatapraśnakalpalatā and 11, 41, 254, 331–2, 340, 372–3
Vāḍeśvarodaya–kāvyam and 368–70
Varijākṣacaritra and 370–2
See also Brahman identity
Brahman women, bodily norms for, 164–70; Brahmendra Sarasvati and 194; scholar household and 180–3; widowhood and 38, 43–4, 164, 203, 218
See also Gotmai Kale
Brahmendra Sarasvati, daṇḍī ascetic 186–7, 190–1, 193; *see also* Narsimhasrama
Brahmendra Sarasvati, guru and financier 186–7
Bronkhorst, Johannes 77n, 276n

Carstairs, G. Morris 169n
Caste
Aryan theory and 32–6, 43–4, 381
colonial state and 14–23, 28–54, 339–42
"culturalization" of 2, 53
discourses of 315–17; varnasamkara mixing and disapproved categories and 313, 315–17, 323–6
hypergamy and 7–8, 275–6, 315–17
Kaliyuga and 272–9, 303; *see also* Deshpande, Madhav
kingship and 5n, consecration of Shivaji and 269–71, 294–6; Gopinatha and 327, 329–31, 341–2; Hindu 42, 341–2; Maratha 49, 197, 301; Rajput 177, 271, 300–1; South India and 300
Kshatriya varna and 9–11, 34–5, 50, 225, 296, 301
regional differences and 271, 299–303
ṣaṭkarmī/trikarmī status and 4, 39, 360
status pressures, Chitpavan Brahmans and 157–8, 373, 377–81; Devrukhe Brahmans and 43–4, 93–4, 248–55, 259; Shenvi Saraswat Brahmans and 38–44, 93–4, 230–42, 362–3, 365–7; Tukaram Tatya Padwal and 34–5
Sudra varna, demeaning modern classification of 5, 34–8, 47–9; Gagabhatta and 339; *Jātiviveka* texts and 273–6, 327–9, 335; *Sūdrakamalākaraḥ* and 10–11, 23, 164, 170, 236, 277–8, 293–4, 337; *Śūdrācāraśiromaṇi* and 11, 250, 276, 336
Vedokta protests and 9–10, 16–21, 49–50
vernacular sociology of 338, 341
See also Brahman power; Kayastha
Caturdhara, Nilakantha 72, 77, 84; son Govind of 193, 251; *see also* Minkowski, Christopher
Chaskar banking family 414n
Chatterjee, Bankim Chandra, *Ānandamaṭh* of 198
Chatterjee, Indrani 204
Chatterjee, Nandini 400n
Chickerur, Shraddha 52n
Chiplunkar, Annasaheb 29
Chiplunkar, Krishnasastri 46, 48
Chiplunkar, Vishnusastri 45–50
Chitnis scribal lineage, *see* Kayastha
Chitragupta 290–1, 293, 297
Clark, Matthew 196
Collins, Brian 11
Cox, Whitney 85
Crawford, Arthur 376–9
da Cunha, J. Gerson 42, 381

dakṣiṇā 19, 22, 28–32

Dalits, colonial educational policy and 36; Jotirao Phule and 31; judicial assemblies and 208, 394, 404; Pune court and 4, 152; rights of 410–11
Dasnāmīs 177, 183–95; armed orders of, and Sufism 195–7; daṇḍī ascetics of 184–5, 190, 197; *see also* maṭhas
Davis, Donald R. 76n, 366n
Derrett, J. Duncan M. 68, 267
Deshpande, Madhav 20, 33, 69, 81, 87, 228n, 270, 278, 302
Deshpande, Prachi 13, 203n, 284n
Deshpande, Satish 2
Deva scholar family 72, 76, 95–6, 238–9; *see also* Venkatkrishnan, Anand
Devgiri, *see* Yadava kingdom
dharmādhikārī office 222, 238, 242
dharmasabhā assembly 222, 235–41, 249–52, 393–4, 400
Diksita, Bhattoji 77, 81, 238; son Ramasrama and 187
Dīn Bandhu, *see* Bhalekar, Krishnarao
diplomacy, Deccan states and 112–13; Indo-Persian scribal culture and 111–16; Mughal India and 112, 114; new diplomatic history and 109–10; *see also* Maratha empire
Divekar, Mahadevsastri 50–1
Dongare, Mahadev Ganesh, *Śrīsiddāntavijayagrantha* of 10n, 19n
Dvijarājodaya, *see* Dhiresvara Misra

early modernity 70, 97, 223–4, 383, 395
East India Company 115, 143, 222, 234, 302, 392–3
Eaton, Richard 243, 412
ecumene, *see* public sphere
Eknath 192–3, 238
Elphinstone, Mountstuart 18, 392–3, 426, 428–9
Enthoven, R.E. 279

Fisher, Elaine M. 75n
Fisher, Michael 109–10, 115, 12
French diplomacy 127, 134–5
Fuller, C.J., and H. Narasimhan 2

Gandhi, M.K. 50–1, 53, 429
Godse, Vishnu Bhatt 27–8
Gomez, K. 183n
Gopinatha 274–6, 311–42
Gordon, Stewart 161, 232n, 243
gota assemblies 393–4, 397–8
Govindabhatta/Guru Govinda, *Kāyasthapaddhati* of 287–98, 312, 334–5
grāmaṇya disputes, *see* Kayasthas
Grant, James 12–15, 138–9, 259, 294, 380
Guha, Sumit 6n, 83n, 84n, 118n, 296, 372
Gulāmgirī, *see* Phule, Jotirao
Gunjikar, Ramchandra Bhikaji, *Sarasvatīmaṇḍal* of 42–3, 381–2
Gupte, K.T. 272n, 340
Gupte, T.V. 272n, 288n
Gurevitch, Eric 7n

Harischandra, Bharatendu 26–7
Hawley, John Stratton 84n
Hedgewar, Keshav Baliram 51
hejib 112–14
Hemadri 86n, 317, 332–4, 361–2
Hindu dharma 30; conservative Chitpavan approach to 39; defence of dakṣiṇā and 31; individual āchāra and 225; widow remarriage and 38, 44
Hindu nationalism 4, 26–7, 50–1; non-Brahman articulations of 50
Hindu religious law 68, 96; colonial state and 339–40; nibandha genre and 356; puranas and 359
Hyderabad, Nizam Shahi court, negotiations with peshwa state and 134–42; vakil arrangements in 108
hypergamy, *see* Caste

ilchi 111–15
impotence, ascetics and 191
Inden, Ronald 341–2

Jade family 74, 78
Jaffrelot, Christophe 4, 51
Jambhekar, Balsastri 24–5
Jātibhed Vivekasār, *see* Padwal, Tukaram Tatya

Jātiviveka texts 273–6; Marathi terms in 314, 338; vernacular sociology and 341; *see also* Gopinatha
Jaipur, royal ritual in 300; vakils at court of 110, 117, 120
Jaisingh, Raja of Amber 91, 114, 120, 123, 238
Jaywant, Ketaki 34–5
Joshi, Krishnarao 131–4
Joshi, Laxmansastri 50

Kale, Gotmai 203–19
Kale, Govindrao 135–42
Kale scholar family 179
Kaliyuga, *see* Caste
Kamalakarabhatta, *see* Bhatta scholar lineage
Kanavinde, Bhavani Vishvanath 39–45
Kanyakubja Brahmans 84–5
karīnā 206–19
Kāśīkhaṇḍa 71–2, 89–92, 96
Kavindracaraya Sarasvati, *see* Banaras
Kāyasthapaddhati, *see* Govindabhatta/ Guru Govinda
Kayasthas
- early modern image of 267–8
- in western India 269–72
- Chandraseniya Prabhu
  - bakhar chronicles of 12–15, 272, 286–90, 295
  - Brahman gurus of 286–94
  - Brahman scribal rivals and 12–23, 270–2, 275–8, 286–303
  - Chitnis scribal lineage of 12–17, 285–6, 294–5, 298
  - grāmaṇya historical memory of 272, 283, 302
  - migrations of 279–83
  - property rights and offices of 284–6
- Chitragupta 269, 277, 297
- Pathare 279, 340
- *See also* Caste; Vendell, Dominic

Kolhapur, Ramesvarabhatta in 180; Vedokta controversy in 49–50
Konkan 92, 216n, 221–34, 242–7, 376–9; *see also* Gotmai Kale
khoṭī rights 243, 245
Kidambi, Prashant 40n
Kshatriya, *see* Caste
kulavṛttānta 52–4
Kulkarni, A.R. 12–13, 16n
Kunte, Ganesh Ballal 121–2, 125
Kunte, Raghunath Ganesh 126–7

libraries, nineteenth century 23, 29, 37, 376; Kavindracaraya and 78, 193, 372n, 334; Mughal imperial 356; *see also* Brahman power
Lokahitawadi 28–32

Madhava Sarasvati 183
Madhava, *Śatapraśnakalpalatā* of 11, 41, 254, 331–2, 340, 372–3
Madhusudhana Sarasvati 187, 195
Madhva 81, 231, 331, 359n, 370–3
majālis 206–8, 393; mahzars and 400–3; panchayats and 413–17; regional networks of 409–13; *see also* Peshwai
Malvankar, Ganesh Bapuji 23, 38–41, 44; *Śūdrakamalākaraḥ* of 36–8
manuscripts, circulation of 78–9, 177–8, 330–9, 351–2, 354; *see also* paper use
Manusmṛti 36, 239, 253; *Jātiviveka* and 273–5, 315–16, 324
Maratha Chhatrapatis, consecration of 10, 13, 49, 269–71, 294–6, 299; Pratapsinh I of Satara 12–15; Sambhaji 21–2, 298; Shahu of Kolhapur 49; Shahu I of Satara 13; Shahu II of Satara 10, 13; Shivaji 4, 10, 49, 113–14, 222–3, 236–8, 269–70, 281
Maratha empire
- diplomacy in 110, 115, 133, 140; residency system in 109–10; vakils in 109–11, 116–43; *see also* Vendell, Dominic
- judicial administration in 206–8, 245–6, 396–400; mahzars in 400–3; majālis assemblies in 403–6; mirāsdārs as brothers in 406–9; panchayats in 413–25; property

rights in 205–6, 394, 396–400; transition to colonial state in 426–9; witnesses in 403–6
Persian language secretaries in 118–19
revenue administration in 205–6, 242–3, 396–7; chauth in 116–17, 121–3, 134–5, 160; kamāvīsdārs in 117, 120, 122, 130, 132, 137, 160–2
statecraft in 31–3, 140–2, 284; Govindrao Kale and 134–42
See also Brahman power; Peshwai
maṭhas 75, 78; Advaitin 195; Dasnāmīs and resources of 194–7; Eknath and 192; Kavindracaraya and 195; libraries of 78; Saraswat 231–6, 234–6; satirical depiction of 184, 186–7
McCrea, Lawrence 359n
Mehendale, Bahiropant 130–1
Michell, George 89, 96n
Minkowski, Christopher 97, 186, 193n, 197
Misra, Dhiresvara, *Dvijarājodaya* of 84–5
Mughal empire, Brahman ecumene and 68, 74, 97, 350–1; Brahman opportunities in 67–70, 175–6; decay of, and Brahman scholars 96–8; diplomacy in 112, 114, 116, 121–5; models of kingship and 9, 278, 299–300; paper use in 355–7; Visvesvara temple and 89, 365; *see also* Banaras
Mukti mandapam, *see* Banaras
Mysore state, Hyder Ali of 131–3; Tipu Sultan of 115, 135

Nagoji Bhatta (Nagesabhatta) 179, 182, 302
Narayana Rao, Velcheru 271, 302
Narayanasrama, pupil of Narsimhasrama 184
Naregal, Veena 4n, 25n, 29n, 31
Narsimhasrama, Advaitin daṇḍī scholar 183; as Brahmendra Sarasvati 186
Narsimhasrama, daṇḍī ascetic of South India 192
Natrajan, Balmurli 2
Natu, Balajipant 13–15, 18, 20, 22
Newbigin, Eleanor 80n
Nibandhamālā, *see* Chiplunkar, Vishnusastri
nirṇayapatra 236, 353
Nirṇayasindhuḥ, *see* Bhatta scholar lineage
non–Brahmans, *see* Caste
Novetzke, Christian 3–4, 376n

Olivelle, Patrick 191n
ordeals 399–400, 411

Padhye family, of Golavali 238, 245–7, 403–4, 423–5
Padwal, Tukaram Tatya, *Jātibhed Vivekasār* of 34–6, 38, 41, 47, 132
Paithan 72, 82, 156, 179–80, 193, 299n, 317–18
panchayats 393–4
Pandian, M.S.S. 2
Pandit, Vishnusastri 33, 43–4
paper use, Brahman power and 303, 352–4, 366–7, 382–3; early modern world and 349–51; India and 354–7, 354–7; puranic circulation and 357–9, 383–4; *see also* manuscripts
Parabhūjātinirṇaya 21
Parāśarasmṛti 240–1
Parashuram 9, 11, 187, 213, 227–30, 235, 251, 273, 277, 289, 296; western India's Brahman communities and 360–4
Parasnis family 118
Paraśurāmapratāpa, *see* Sabajipratapa
Patil, Urmila 39–40
Patwardhan, Chintamanrao 18–22
Payagunde, Vaidyanath 182, 302; son Balambhatta of 182
Pendse, Krishnaji Vinayak 53
performance, court pantomime in 139; Gotmai and 213–14; *see also* Brahman power
Perlin, Frank 409–10
Peshwai, Bhat family peshwas of 15, 159, 161–2, 311, 379–80;

Brahman social norms and 152–4; censorship in 79–82; Chitpavan dominance in 157–8; conflicts with Kayasthas in 302; conflicts with regional Brahman assemblies in 156–7; development of centralised panchayat in 413–27; discipline of Malwa Brahmans in 158–64, 258–9; dowry costs in 155; empire as a Hindu mission in 135–6; Nana Phadnis in 128, 131–4, 136, 311, 425–6; Ramsastri Prabhune in 161, 425; suppression of bride-price in 154–5; vakils and 122–43; *see also* Brahman power; Maratha empire
petitions 392–6
Phadke, Narayan Sitaram 52
Phule, Jotirao 29, 31; *Gulāmgirī* of 46–8
Pitre, Vishvanatha, *Vāḍeśvarodaya-kāvyam* of, *see* Brahman subcastes
Pollock, Sheldon 9, 270
Portuguese 112–13, 116, 130, 211, 222–3, 231–4
Pradnya Pathshala 50–1
Prarthana Samaj 33, 39
print, vernacular 38–45; early modern spread of 349–51
public sphere 75, 88, 383; Brahman ecumene and 68, 74, 97, 350–1; and panchayats 417–21; *see also* Banaras
Puntambkar, Mahadev 182
puranas 11; copying texts of 374; discursive fields of 357–60, 366–7; oral performance of 374–9; *see also* paper use
Purnendra Sarasvati 187
Purohita family 245–7

Raghoba 376–9
Rajput courts, dharmic kingship in 339
Rajwade, V.K. 50, 206, 237n, 253n, 295n, 412n, 414n, 424n
Ramasrama 187
Ramatirtha 183
Ramdas 79
Ranade, M.G. 33, 38, 45
Rashtriya Swayamsevak Sangh 51
Rathakaras 312–13, 327–8; and Sonars 340
Reṇukāmahātmya 277, 312
Richards, John 243

Sabajipratapa, *Paraśurāmapratāpa* of 274, 320–2
Sabhasad, Krishnaji Anant 113–14, 233, 284, 298–9
Sahyādrikhaṇḍa, *see* Brahman subcastes
Sahyadris 11, 92, 94, 235, 255, 368–9; *see also Sahyādrikhaṇḍa*
samaya 318–19, 326
sammatipatra 40, 253, 288n; newspapers and 40–1
saṃskāra 10, 270, 274–5, 291, 294, 297
Sanderson, Alexis 288n, 291–2, 313
Sanskrit knowledge systems 222
Sārasvata Bhūṣaṇa, *see* Sarma, M.G.
Sarasvatīmanḍal, *see* Gunjikar, Ramchandra Bhikaji
Sarkar, Jadunath 196
Sarma, M.G. 229n; *Sārasvata Bhūṣaṇa* of 229n, 231n
Sarvajanik Sabha 45
Sarwate, Rahul 29n, 50–2
Śatapraśnakalpalatā, of Madhava, *see* Brahman subcastes
Satara court, Kayastha rights at 12–18, 21; judicial assemblies at 419, 421; peshwa move from 152, 416
Sathaye, Adheesh 7n, 361n
Sathe, Morsastri 22, 31, 49
ṣaṭkarmī/trikarmī status, *see* Caste
Savarkar, V.D. 4, 50
Sen, S.N. 413n
Sesa, Krishna, *see* Sesa scholar lineage
Sesa scholar lineage 72–4, 76–7, 81; grammarian Narasimha of 73, 76; Krishna Sesa, *s.* of Narasimha, at Mukti mandapam assembly 250; *Sūdrācāraśiromaṇi* of 276, 335–7
Shaivism, Dasnāmī orders in 177; Gopinatha and 313, 331–3, 326; Kashmiri 313, 323; 177; Tantric forms of 290–4

Shaligram, Tryambaksastri 22, 37
Shankaracharya, of Shankeshwar 19–21
Shankarsheth, Jagannath 19
Sheikh, Samira 204
Sherring, M.A. 185
Shinde, Mahadji 128–9, 131
Shiva, in Banaras 70–1, 91
Shivram, Janardan 129–30
Shrotri, Malhar 18–19
Shukla Yajurvedis 154, 156
Sivaramatirtha 193n
Skandapurāṇa 228, 277, 357, 361
Smith, Travis LaMar 71–2n
Solvyns, F. Balthazar 188
Sonar 19, 340
Śrīsiddāntavijayagrantha, *see* Dongare, Mahadev Ganesh
Steele, Arthur 339
Sturman, Rachel 24, 32
Subrahmanyam, Sanjay 109n, 271, 302
Subramanian, Ajantha 2
Sudra, *see* Caste
Śūdrācāraśiromaṇi, *see* Sesa scholar lineage
Śūdrakamalākaraḥ, *see* Bhatta scholar lineage
Śyenavījātidharmanirṇaya 237–9

Takale, Kayastha guru lineage of 282–3, 286, 293
Takle, Shamji Govind 126
Talbot, Cynthia 268n, 319–20
Tavernier, Jean-Baptiste 89–91
Thatthe, Narayansastri 18, 22, 31
Thatthe, Nilakanthasastri 18–23, 31, 37, 45–6, 49
Tilak, Lokamanya 45, 49–50, 243
Tucker, Richard 2

upanayana 10–11, 291–2, 297

Vāḍeśvarodaya-kāvyam, of Vishvanath Pitre, *see* Brahman subcastes
Vaishnavism, conservative Brahman hostility to 328, 331; and Shenvi Saraswats 231
Vajpeyi, Ananya 299n, 329n
vakils and vakil families 119–20; Barve 122–3; Galgalekar 121; Gulgule 122; Hingne 120–5; Joshi 131–3; Kale 134–42; Kunte 121–2, 125–7; Mehendale 116, 130–1, 135–41; Pingle 136–9; Ranchod 129; Shivram 129–30; Takle 126–7; Valavalikar 130; Verulkar 131
Varijākṣacaritra, *see* Brahman subcastes
Vāstuśāstra of Visvambhara 277, 289, 332–4
Vedic schools 176
Vedokta, *see* Caste
Vendell, Dominic 13n, 26, 46n, 110, 113, 115, 131, 133, 140, 267–8n
Venkatadhvari 244
Venkatkrishnan, Anand 168n
Vijayanagar 82, 84n, 177, 194–5, 300–1
Visvesvara temple *see* Banaras
vṛtti 242, 245–8

Wagle, Bal Mangesh 38–9
Werner, Christopher 114–15
Wilkinson, Callie 143n
Wilson, H.H. 184
Wilson, John 36, 340
Women, agency of 204–5; Brahmanendra Sarasvati and 194; daṇḍī ascetics and 194; hypergamy and 315; local rights of 204; *see also* Brahman power; Gotmai Kale
Wright, Samuel 177n

Yadava kingdom 317–19, 355, 362